Growing Pains

TIMOTHY J. COLTON
and
JERRY F. HOUGH
Editors

Growing Pains

Russian Democracy and the
Election of 1993

BROOKINGS INSTITUTION PRESS
Washington, D.C.

Copyright © 1998 by
THE BROOKINGS INSTITUTION
1775 Massachusetts Avenue, N.W.
Washington, D.C. 20036

Library of Congress Cataloging-in-Publication data:

Growing pains : Russian democracy and the election of 1993 / Timothy
J. Colton and Jerry F. Hough, editors.
    p.   cm.
Includes bibliographical references and index.
ISBN 0-8157-1522-6 (cloth). –ISBN 0-8157-1521-8 (pbk.)
    1. Presidents—Russia (Federation)—Election—1993. 2. Russia
(Federation)—Politics and government—1991– . 3. Democracy—
Russia (Federation) I. Colton, Timothy J., 1947– . II. Hough, Jerry
F., 1935– .
JN6699.A5G76 1998   97-45314
324.947'086—dc21   CIP

9 8 7 6 5 4 3 2 1

The paper used in this publication meets the minimum requirements of
the American Standard for Informational Science—Permanence of
Paper for Printed Library Materials, ANSI Z39.48-1984

Typeset in Times Roman

Composition by AlphaWebTech
Mechanicsville, Maryland

Printed by R. R. Donnelley and Sons
Harrisonburg, Virginia

THE BROOKINGS INSTITUTION

The Brookings Institution is an independent organization devoted to nonpartisan research, education, and publication in economics, government, foreign policy, and the social sciences generally. Its principal purposes are to aid in the development of sound public policies and to promote public understanding of issues of national importance.

The Institution was founded on December 8, 1927, to merge the activities of the Institute for Government Research, founded in 1916, the Institute of Economics, founded in 1922, and the Robert Brookings Graduate School of Economics and Government, founded in 1924.

The Board of Trustees is responsible for the general administration of the Institution, while the immediate direction of the policies, program, and staff is vested in the President, assisted by an advisory committee of the officers and staff. The by-laws of the Institution state: "It is the function of the Trustees to make possible the conduct of scientific research, and publication, under the most favorable conditions, and to safeguard the independence of the research staff in pursuit of their studies and in the publication of the result of such studies. It is not a part of their function to determine, control, or influence the conduct of particular investigations or the conclusions reached."

The President bears final responsibility for the decision to publish a manuscript as a Brookings book. In reaching his judgment on competence, accuracy, and objectivity of each study, the President is advised by the director of the appropriate research program and weighs the views of a panel of expert outside readers who report to him in confidence on the quality of the work. Publication of a work signifies that it is deemed a competent treatment worthy of public consideration but does not imply endorsement of conclusions or recommendations.

The Institution maintains its position of neutrality on issues of public policy in order to safeguard the intellectual freedom of the staff. Hence interpretations or conclusions in Brookings publications should be understood to be solely those of the authors and should not be attributed to the Institution, to its trustees, officers, or other staff members, or to the organizations that support its research.

Foreword

WHEN THE SOVIET REGIME broke down in 1991, many citizens of the successor countries, along with many foreign observers and well-wishers, believed that a smooth "transition" was in the works and that democratic states with well-functioning market economies would be the more or less inevitable and early result. The years since then have constituted a fascinating and often bitter education in the difficulties involved in the transformation of communist systems of rule. It is one thing to destroy the institutions of an outmoded regime; it is quite another to forge effective new institutions and the norms that underpin them.

Nowhere has this been more apparent than in the Russian Federation. The economic reforms unleashed by Boris Yeltsin in 1992 have made undeniable progress, but they have also brought about a drastic drop in national output and the impoverishment of millions of people. In the political sphere, competitive elections have been held and political parties have proliferated, but the post-Soviet state is ineffectual and frequently rudderless. There are no guarantees about the stability of present arrangements once President Boris Yeltsin leaves the scene.

The election of December 12, 1993, was a watershed in the evolution of the new state. It was the first national election to be fought in Russia on a multiparty basis since before World War I. It occurred after a constitutional conflict between president and parliament spun out of control and erupted in violence in Moscow, treating the world to the bizarre spectacle of an elected president's ordering army tanks to shell the headquarters of an elected parliament. Confident of victory in the campaign, the Yeltsin administration escalated its ambitions, folding a constitutional referendum into the parliamentary election. It achieved at best a mixed result, as the Russian people narrowly ratified the president's draft constitution but voted resoundingly against his favored party, Russia's Choice.

Timothy Colton and Jerry Hough organized a major research project in 1993 to track and analyze the election. They used survey methods to tap public opinions and preferences. They and their colleagues also used qualitative techniques to study the campaigns of the major parties, the mass media, and the course of the struggle in ten regions of the federation. *Growing Pains* reports on this multifaceted research and goes a long way toward explaining the uneasy political and institutional outcome with which Russia and the world still live a half decade later. It makes clear that the Russian experience continues to challenge the West to modify and extend its theories of social and political change and to develop responsible foreign policies in the light of those theories.

The survey and other field work in Russia was generously funded by the Carnegie Corporation of New York and the John D. and Catherine T. MacArthur Foundation. National Science Foundation grants SBR-94-12051 and SBR-94-02548 assisted with the national opinion surveys and with cleaning and weighting of the data. The editors greatly appreciate this support. They are also grateful to the Brookings Institution for a grant enabling them to carry out a Moscow briefing workshop in November 1993 for Russian sociologists participating in the survey work. John Steinbruner of Brookings took a personal interest in the project from beginning to end. Susan Blanchard shepherded the manuscript through the review process. The book was edited by Deborah Hardin and Deborah Styles; Bridget Butkevich, Julien Hartley, and Andrew Solomon verified its factual content; Patti Isaacs prepared the maps (with research assistance from Elsa Ransom at the Davis Center for Russian Studies at Harvard University); and Sherri Smith compiled the index.

The views expressed in the book are those of the authors and editors and should not be attributed to the organizations whose assistance is acknowledged above or to the trustees, officers, or other staff members of the Brookings Institution.

MICHAEL H. ARMACOST
President

July 1998
Washington, D.C.

Preface

THE PROJECT THAT PRODUCED *Growing Pains* grew out of conversations between the two editors in the winter of 1992–93 about the growing air of crisis and confrontation in Russian politics and the likelihood of its leading soon to a national election that would settle matters. We decided to organize a collective project, involving a substantial number of other scholars whose skills differed from ours, and to bring out the results in a collective volume as soon as possible after the election.

The record shows that some of our expectations were better grounded than others. The first post-Soviet national election was indeed held in Russia by the end of 1993. It was a defining moment. We did assemble a team of smart and dedicated researchers to study the phenomenon. And we did come up with interesting findings. In one respect only were we gravely disappointed—in the timing of the appearance of the published results. The delay owes a lot to small snags and coordination problems that often bedevil a joint research endeavor. It is also the product, though, of a complexity in the research task that we did not fully appreciate when we embarked upon it. We are immensely grateful to our coauthors for their perseverance in seeing the project through to its conclusion. We hope they are as proud as we are of the result.

A number of the chapters in the book refer to data from a national survey and regional surveys of Russian citizens. Let us be clear on the instruments. Using a network of sociologists in provincial universities, Jerry Hough supervised the conduct of a preelection survey of registered voters in fifty-three of the regions of Russia. Sampling was done by the cluster method. He made some use of these data in this book, and some is being used in other studies. Timothy Colton was responsible for a two-wave panel survey of 3,905 eligible voters from across Russia. Ninety-three primary sampling units were drawn randomly from a list of districts and urban communities, with probability of selection proportional to population size in the 1989 Soviet census. The ninety-three primary sampling units were located in sixty-seven of Russia's regions, from Arkhangel'sk in the northwest to Primor'e in the southeast. Seven substitutions of primary sampling units had to be accepted, mostly in Siberia and the Far East and mostly because of climatic considerations and geographic accessibility. Interviewers selected respondents by stepping at equal intervals through voters' lists. Substitution of respondents was allowed after three attempts to interview. Field managers submitted only completed questionnaires from individuals who had been interviewed twice—once between mid-November and election day and again in the several weeks after the election. Checks on sampling and interviewing were done within the budget's resources, with an average of one-tenth of all interviews verified after the fact by a separate researcher.

The national sample data, given the shortcomings in the sampling process, overrepresented certain groups in the population, in particular urban dwellers, women, older persons, and the better educated. Accordingly, the sample was poststratified to accord with a crosstabulation of the 1989 national population by urban/rural location (dichotomized), sex, age group (eighteen to thirty-nine, forty to fifty-nine, sixty and over), and educational level (less than secondary, secondary or vocational, higher). Similar weights from regional census data were applied to the survey data from the six regions in which preelection surveys were done and were subsequently made available to chapter authors, namely, Moscow, St. Petersburg, Kursk, Saratov, Tatarstan, and Bashkortostan.

Sergei Tumanov of Moscow State University and Mikhail Guboglo of the Institute of Ethnology and Anthropology of the Russian Academy of Sciences managed the survey work on our behalf—Tumanov in the oblasts and krais inhabited mainly by Russians, Guboglo in the minority republics. They bore up under countless strains, often with more grace than their American colleagues. Susan G. Lehmann participated actively in designing and carrying out the surveys and was a co-investigator on the two NSF grants. She carried out the weighting of the regional survey data, assisted by Deborah Hordan. Josephine Andrews did the key work on sample frame for the national survey. Michael Swafford advised sagely on sampling. He and Polina Kozyreva worked with Tumanov and Guboglo in organizing the Moscow workshop and preparing training tapes for interviewers.

All the chapter authors did yeoman work under arduous field conditions, improvising as events demanded. Besides toiling in Russia, they took part in a preelection workshop and a postelection conference at Harvard University. We are especially thankful to Yitzhak Brudny and Michael McFaul for scouting out data needed by other members of the project and sharing it with them.

At Harvard's Davis Center for Russian Studies (the Russian Research Center until 1996), Judith Mehrmann assisted ably in administering travel and other practical aspects of the project, and Christine Porto superintended finances and reporting requirements. Todd Weinberg arranged scholars' travel and accommodation in the Russian regions.

Contents

SVALBARD
(Norway)

FRANZ JOSEF
LAND

North
Sea

NORWAY

DENMARK

SWEDEN

GERMANY

Murmansk

Barents
Sea

Kara Sea

FINLAND

Baltic Sea

Kaliningrad

RUS.

EST.

POLAND

LAT.

LITH.

St. Petersburg

BELARUS

UKRAINE

Moscow

MOLDOVA

Kursk

Nizhnii Novgorod

TATARSTAN

SVERDLOVSK
OBLAST

Black
Sea

Saratov

BASHKORTOSTAN

Kemerovo

TURKEY

GEORGIA

ARMENIA

SYRIA

AZERBAIJAN

KAZAKHSTAN

Aral Sea

Lake
Balkhash

IRAQ

Caspian
Sea

IRAN

TURKMENISTAN

UZBEKISTAN

CHINA

KYRGYZSTAN

CHAPTER ONE

Introduction

The 1993 Election and the New Russian Politics

Timothy J. Colton

RUSSIA HAS thrown off the Communist dictatorship, but it has yet to recast itself as a well-rounded democracy. The post-Soviet Russian Federation is at best a protodemocratic mélange, mixing ingredients of representative government with generous portions of bossism, corruption, and anarchy.

This book presents a multidimensional study of a watershed in the evolution of that mixed polity. In that bottom-up selection of major officeholders is a criterion—some would say the irreducible criterion—of the presence of democracy, a contested election is a revealing occurrence in any society moving away from authoritarianism. The ballot of December 12, 1993, has the distinction of being the first general election in the new Russian state and the first to be waged on partisan lines in Russia since World War I. The leaders who instigated it, moreover, conceived of it architectonically, as an *engineered founding election,* molded if not monopolized from the top down, the results of which would set the country's path for years to come.

The 1993 election was a benchmark episode, as hindsight verifies, the junction between what has been dubbed the "First Russian Republic" that supplanted the dying Soviet regime in 1991[1] and what we might label a "Second Republic," whose underpinnings were to be upheld by Boris

Yeltsin's reelection as president in mid-1996. The national politics of a sovereign Russia had hitherto been characterized by institutional confusion, billowing conflict between the executive and legislative branches, and the emergence of Moscow-based opposition parties long on rhetoric but short on organizational capacity. The election of December 1993 reshaped the scene dramatically, but in contradictory ways not always in keeping with the intentions of its orchestrators. On the one hand, the freewheeling campaign encouraged political parties to proliferate and to cultivate popular followings through the mass media and other channels. On the other hand, the only party wholeheartedly behind the government's reform program and political tactics, Russia's Choice, reaped far fewer votes than forecast. At the same time an improvised referendum accompanying the election ratified a lopsided presidentialist constitution— foretelling the executive supremacy that has left Russia's welter of parties and the federal parliament where they sit largely disconnected from state decisionmaking.

The co-organizers of this study hatched the project in the early summer of 1993, in anticipation of an air-clearing parliamentary election by year's end, although we had no way of knowing its timing, the violent circumstances in which it would eventually be called, or its exact stakes and rules. As the drama unfolded that autumn, we used multiple approaches and techniques to probe it, all the while holding participants in the research to a common agenda of inquiry. We did extensive survey research, as outlined in the preface, to permit quantitative analysis of the election's mass aspect. For qualitative analysis and the behavior of elites, we recruited and relied on fifteen specialists who, with our support, immersed themselves directly in the campaign. Three of them monitored the parties' national campaigns, two the news media, and one the city of Moscow. Not wishing to repeat the error of overlooking the Russian provinces—a mistake endemic among politicians as well as scholars[2]—we sent nine scholars to regions outside of Moscow: St. Petersburg, the nation's second city; Kursk, in the Central Black Earth zone; Nizhnii Novgorod, in the Volga-Vyatka area; Saratov, downstream on the Volga; Sverdlovsk, in the Ural Mountains that seam Europe and Asia; the Kuzbass (Kemerovo), in western Siberia; Primor'e, on the Pacific shore; and the two most populous minority homelands, Bashkortostan and Tatarstan.

The ultimate objective of *Growing Pains: Russian Democracy and the Election of 1993* is to tease out the implications of the election for fundamental tendencies in contemporary Russian politics. To have a basis for doing so, we must put its outcomes on the record and account for them. And to lay the groundwork for that, it is necessary first to describe the framing of the electoral struggle, the roles of the movers and shakers, and the campaign's flavor and texture.

Elections and the Russian Transition

Scholars have explained the onset of democracy in sundry ways. One time-honored paradigm singles out civic ideas and cultural compatibility with democratic values. Another correlates democratization with underlying social variables, especially those (such as urbanization, educational attainment, and economic prosperity) that change as part and parcel of modernization. Recently, many analysts have hinged their explanations on elite conduct and elite-mass linkages, chiefly during the historical moment when authoritarian controls slip and a replacement regime is crafted.

In cultural and societal models of regime change, elections, seen as emblematic more of arrival at the destination (democracy) than of the voyage toward it, hold no great fascination. In elite-centered interpretations, though, elections loom large. As Samuel P. Huntington puts it, elections "are not only the life of democracy; they are also the death of dictatorship."[3]

Contemporary theorists of democratizing transitions ascribe three functions to elections. Giuseppe Di Palma emphasizes signaling. A democracy-bound leadership must communicate its commitment to an expeditious reform timetable, and in that mode, "The most significant signal . . . is very likely the calling of free elections." Huntington highlights the "stunning election." His standard democratizing sequence is ignited by a liberalizing strongman who rashly embraces an election as a way to buttress his legitimacy, only to be routed at the polls or to discredit himself by indulging in electoral fraud.[4]

Guillermo O'Donnell and Philippe Schmitter, in their oft-cited work on Latin America and southern Europe, have a third take that is germane to this volume. They identify the *founding election* as a turning point in democratization. Sparked usually by old-regime softliners in partnership with temperate oppositionists, the founding election turns spontaneously into a bridge to a new politics. Beyond trumping the hardliners, it confirms the ethic of popular rule, occasions an outpouring of "civic enthusiasm," and lets political parties come out of the closet and connect with social constituencies, commonly with a "freezing effect upon subsequent political developments."[5]

The first two parts of this triad fit latter-day Russia well. Multicandidate elections were the ultimate signal that Mikhail Gorbachev was sincere about reform, and they had truly stunning effects, starting with the ballot for the USSR Congress of People's Deputies in 1989. The local and republic elections of 1990 gave Westernizing democrats the strength to make Yeltsin, the apparatchik from the Urals who had split with Gorbachev in 1987, chair of the Russian parliament. Yeltsin then overwhelmed five rivals in a presidential vote on June 12, 1991. The string of elections had cascading consequences for the authority of the old regime and of key political players. Without these elections, Yeltsin could not have stared down the reactionary putsch of August 1991.

Yet, when it came to erecting a postauthoritarian edifice—integrating a new system rather than disintegrating the old—O'Donnell and Schmitter's founding election arguably would have made the greatest contribution. Here Russian experience was at odds with comparative expectations. Formally sanctioned political parties, posited to be the principal beneficiaries of a founding election and the perpetuators of its alignment of forces, were legalized in Russia only after the 1990 voting and barely figured in the next year's presidential election. Yeltsin gained the presidency on a personalistic and populist platform, as most voters, in the words of his lieutenant, Gennadii Burbulis, "did not go for a thought-out program of reforms but for a savior."[6] In the post-coup euphoria several months later, Yeltsin rejected advice to seek a fresh parliamentary election, which any alliance led by him would in all likelihood have carried hands down. As of the demise of the Soviet Union, then, Russia's protoplasmic democracy had still not had its founding election.

Setting the Stage

The overdue postcommunist election was triggered by a deep constitutional crisis, which in turn was rooted in the murky inheritance of Soviet communism. Governmental organs set up to do the bidding of the hegemonic party, and riddled with inconsistencies, were thrust almost overnight to political center stage. A conundrum in all ex-Leninist states, institutional indeterminacy was crippling in Russia because its state machinery had been more or less a legal fiction within the USSR. Yeltsin's response even before June 1991 was to demand that the executive wing of Russia's government be shored up, justifying this at the outset as a means to realize

Russian statehood and fend off the still intact Soviet center. The Russian Congress of People's Deputies delegated extraordinary decree-issuing powers to him that November, just before the liquidation of the USSR, but it balked at prolonging them in December 1992.

Yeltsin's priority his first year in office was not politics but a price-freeing shock therapy for the economy propounded by Yegor Gaidar, the youthful economist whom he made deputy prime minister and minister of finance. As Yeltsin saw it, these "painful measures," accompanied by an inflationary spiral and a slump in output, "required calm," not more political "upheavals." He later conceded that his choice had its drawbacks. Besides making government reorganization hostage "to perpetual compromises and political games," it left Gaidar's reforms "hanging in midair" for lack of backup.[7] Despite the dilution of shock therapy and Gaidar's replacement in December 1992 by a veteran of the Soviet industrial bureaucracy, Viktor Chernomyrdin, executive-legislative friction intensified, reaching a fever pitch at the intermittent convocations of the congress.

The notion of slicing through the Gordian knot by bidding for a popular mandate cropped up with growing frequency. After months of wrangling, punctuated by threats of presidential special rule and impeachment by the congress, Yeltsin and Ruslan Khasbulatov, the parliamentary speaker, sponsored a four-question referendum on April 25, 1993. It went largely Yeltsin's way, as 59 percent expressed confidence in him, 53 percent approved of his economic policies, and 67 percent favored preterm (dosrochnyye) legislative elections, with a shade fewer than 50 percent wanting an early presidential election.[8] Because of technical requirements in Russia's statute on referendums and Yeltsin's retracted threats to take it as carte blanche to foist a presidentialist constitution, the poll was not binding. The referendum, in short, "left hazy the locus of political power in Russia."[9]

Taking the offensive, Yeltsin in June 1993 appointed a constitutional convention to complete the work of composing a new basic law for Russia that a commission answerable to the legislature had been debating since 1990. The convention handed him an acceptable text July 12, at which time Khasbulatov scheduled a deputies' congress for November 17, 1993, which presumably would have scuttled the draft. Yeltsin hinted cryptically that a general election to settle matters once and for all should occur that autumn.

We still do not know exactly when he decided to act or if his constitutional posturing was a mere smokescreen. Yeltsin reminisces in a memoir that he resolved on a lightning strike in "early September," telling his most trusted aide, Viktor Ilyushin, to enlist a "crack team of professionals" to ink the requisite decrees. Prime Minister Chernomyrdin cosigned the still secret main directive "with a bold flourish" on September 13.[10]

At 8:00 P.M. on Tuesday, September 21, Yeltsin informed Russians in a somber pretaped television address that he had unilaterally prorogued the legislature, ordered an election for the lower house of a bicameral "Federal Assembly" on December 11 and 12 (streamlined ten days later to Sunday, December 12), and enacted interim governing arrangements pending adoption of a democratic constitution by the parliament. Presidential Decree No. 1400, "On Step-by-Step Constitutional Reform in Russia," was splashed over the front pages of the newspapers the next morning. To preempt any boycott, documents released September 24 fixed a quorum of 25 percent of the electorate (all nonincarcerated citizens aged eighteen or older), not the 50 percent required in late-Soviet elections.

Yeltsin maintains in his memoir that he suffered mental torture over the coup, even though the Brezhnev-era constitution he overturned was "bad law." Pricks of conscience aside, the gambit had grave risks by the most cold-blooded Machiavellian calculus. The deputies' congress, as Yeltsin foresaw, briskly convened, passed an act of impeachment investing his estranged vice president, Aleksandr Rutskoi, as "president," and appointed rebel ministers of a shadow government. Several hundred deputies barricaded themselves in the Moscow White House, the parliamentary palace from which Yeltsin himself had rallied the antiputsch forces in 1991. Nor was dissent confined to this predictable quarter. By Yeltsin's account, his own chief of staff, Sergei Filatov, denounced the scheme on September 21, and Yeltsin had to browbeat Defense Minister Pavel Grachev into commanding his troops and tanks to take action when the showdown turned ugly two weeks later. Throughout, Yeltsin says plaintively, "The people in the Kremlin—me among them—feared ending up in the role of the August [1991] coup plotters."[11]

Talks over a face-saving pact, incorporating both parliamentary and presidential elections, came tantalizingly close to fruition. Yeltsin told 150 regional leaders on September 18 that he was not averse to standing again before the voters.[12] On September 24, two days after lowering the boom on the congress, he handed down a decree calling a presidential election for June 12, 1994. Over the next nine days brokers bruited an accord pegged to simultaneous campaigns for parliament and president early in 1994, keeping the constitution on the back burner until after that. Valerii Zor'kin, the chief justice of the Russian Constitutional Court, reported afterward that on the morning of October 3 Chernomyrdin told him by telephone that Yeltsin, Rutskoi, and Khasbulatov were coming to a consensus.[13]

Any prospect of agreement slipped away that afternoon when an armed anti-Yeltsin mob, egged on by deputies and paramilitary squads, ran amok in downtown Moscow, bursting into the Ostankino television tower and the headquarters of Mayor Yurii Luzhkov. On October 4 Russian Army and Interior Ministry commandos bombarded and stormed the parliamentary palace (the Russian White House) and led off Rutskoi, Khasbulatov, and other holdouts in handcuffs. The official body count from thirty hours of mini civil war was 170. When the smoke had cleared, Yeltsin, in another televised homily on October 6, remarked that the tragedy of the "uprising" made parliamentary renewal more inescapable than ever and reiterated that the election would take place on schedule.

An Engineered Founding Election

For Yeltsin, private, programmatic, and institutional considerations converged on the expediency of an armageddon election. Personal antagonism toward his parliamentary opponents was reinforced by a gut feeling that they stood between him and unimpeded pursuit of nation-saving reforms. Constitutionally, Yeltsin wanted Russia made over into a presidential republic, with parliament essentially a mannerly check on a potent, activist executive reporting to him alone. A first item of business for the revamped legislature would be to enact the long-awaited basic law without which the legislature's existence would be meaningless.

The master conception, then, was of the election as a pivotal, system-anchoring event—an act of "stabilization," as the president and his men said again and again.[14] At a stroke, it would consolidate Yeltsin's power and reputation, his stalled drive to remake society, executive dominance, and political support networks reaching down to the grassroots.

It is not an inordinate stretch to say that the Yeltsin leadership meant to preside over a founding election with a difference—an engineered founding election.[15] Unlike the archetype initiated by a coalition of liberalizing autocrats and social groups, this election was the concoction of the vanguard faction of a government verbally committed to universal democratic principles, moving without partners from below and at times resorting unapologetically to force. Those in the driver's seat were determined to leave as little as possible to chance and to guide though not blatantly dictate the electoral process. The goals they hoped to achieve, nonetheless, were not dissimilar to those promoted in the textbook founding election—an outburst of civic enthusiasm, development of parties, and a "freezing" of government and politics in a broadly democratic mold.

Needless to say, Yeltsin's numerous detractors reacted to the démarche with fury. *Pravda,* the mouthpiece of the Communist Party of the Russian Federation (KPRF), intoned after September 21 that he was outdoing Joseph Stalin and Augusto Pinochet in amassing power. "The puppet 'duma'" to be chosen in December, it continued, would be "the sort of 'parliament' the cannibal Bokassa had"—a caustic reference to Eddine Ahmed Bokassa, the despotic president and later emperor of the Central African Republic in the 1960s and 1970s. Even many long-standing admirers expressed profound reservations. Yeltsin's "radical democratism" and retrograde tactics, wrote one columnist in a liberal daily in October, share "much more with Bolshevism than with democracy."[16]

Neither friendly nor unfriendly critics had far to look for evidence that the presidential circle was exploiting the circumstances of the traumatic ouster of parliament, often through ostensibly temporary abridgments of freedoms of movement, expression, and association (see Chronology of Main Election Events, 1993).[17]

Citing the state of emergency in Moscow, one ministry suspended *Pravda* and a dozen other antigovernment newspapers and censored articles slighting the president and the army. Another sealed the offices and froze the bank accounts of associations accused of complicity in the Moscow disturbances. Proscribed were not only inciters of mayhem, like the Russian Communist Workers' party (RKRP) and the Russian Officers' Union, but the National Salvation Front, an umbrella for antigovernment factions, the oppositionist but not criminal KPRF, and Rutskoi's People's Party of Free Russia. Twenty-one politicians, including Rutskoi and Khasbulatov, who each sat out the election campaign in Moscow's Lefortovo prison, were barred from standing for individual seats in the Duma. The Ministry of Security and the federal procuracy, both taken over by Yeltsin's people, busily pitched in, and the zeal of the Moscow police extended to interrogating and deporting thousands of unregistered residents, many of them members of dark-skinned ethnic minorities.

The escalation of Yeltsin's ambition and high-handedness in the electoral sphere furnished further grounds for alarm. So frenzied was the pace, and so frequent the changes in arrangements, that the overall impression in

Chronology of Main Election Events, 1993

September 21	President Yeltsin dissolves parliament, calls State Duma election for December 11–12, establishes governing organs for "transitional period"
September 24	Nikolai Ryabov appointed chair of Central Electoral Commission (CEC); Yeltsin decrees presidential election for June 12, 1994
October 1	Yeltsin promulgates revised election rules for Duma
October 3	Street violence in Moscow; local state of emergency declared
October 4	Government troops attack and capture parliament building; Ministry of Information suspends thirteen newspapers
October 6	Yeltsin confirms Duma election for December 12, proposes simultaneous local and regional elections; Ministry of Justice bans three political parties and thirteen other opposition groups
October 9	Yeltsin disbands lower-level soviets, orders elections of new regional councils for December 1993 to June 1994
October 11	Yeltsin decrees popular election of Federation Council December 12
October 15	Yeltsin sets constitutional referendum for December 12
October 18	Moscow state of emergency lifted
October 19	Yeltsin bars individuals indicted for Moscow violence from running in election; Ministry of Justice applies to twenty-one persons
October 26	Yeltsin decree on restructuring of local government
October 27	Yeltsin decree on land reform
October 29	Yeltsin decree on "informational guarantees" for election campaign
November 6	Yeltsin announces he will serve full presidential term to June 1996
November 10	Draft constitution published; CEC certifies thirteen parties eligible for State Duma election
November 20	CEC completes registration of individual candidates for Duma and Federation Council
November 22	Unpaid television broadcasts by parties open
December 8–9	Televised debates among party leaders
December 12	Election day

the early days was of an election being pushed to a predetermined conclusion. The time available for the direct participants to mobilize their forces and bid for support compared unfavorably with the last parliamentary election of the Soviet epoch, held in the spring of 1990.

The only election authorized in Decree No. 1400 had been for the State Duma, the lower house of the central parliament. Stung by hostile resolutions coming out of local and regional councils, Yeltsin on October 9 shut down most of the lower-level "soviets" and prescribed election of diminished provincial assemblies over several months beginning in December.[18] Another regal edict included the upper house, the Federation Council, in the parliamentary vote. Yet another and crucial change lifted *constitutional* ratification from the jurisdiction of the Federal Assembly and directed that an updated draft, vetted by Yeltsin, be put to a referendum concurrent with the Federal Assembly election on December 12. As he threw more issues into the electoral pot, Yeltsin took his own job out, reneging on the September pledge of a presidential election in mid-1994. A government press organ went so far as to print a letter purportedly signed by 1,600 persons asserting that his showing in the referendum of April 1993 entitled him to serve without the nuisance of reelection until April 25, 1998.[19]

As if this were not enough, the fine print in the announced procedures of the core election to the State Duma was repeatedly rewritten. On October 1, for example, the presidential pronouncement that finalized the Duma electoral formula was fine-tuned to hike the total of seats from 400 to 450 and those elected by party list from 130 to 225. The constitutional draft overrode the October 1 rescript by halving the term of the first Duma to two years (a nasty surprise to those who thought they had volunteered for four) and giving cabinet ministers and other civil servants the right to serve. Another eleventh-hour rewrite, on November 6, eliminated a clause voiding the election in any territorial district in which the votes cast for the option "against all candidates" exceeded those for the top finisher.

Overseeing the campaign was a twenty-one-member Central Electoral Commission (CEC) impaneled by Yeltsin, which on more than one occasion gave proof of less than perfect impartiality and competence. It was chaired by a defector from Khasbulatov's coterie, Nikolai Ryabov, who boasted of his express telephone line to the president and did not hide his admiration for Yeltsin's constitutional project. The CEC accredited the national parties running for the Duma on November 10, in the nick of time for ballot papers to be run off. Because of the dragged-out registration of individual candidates, official gazettes printed full listings of Federation Council and State Duma nominees, shot through with inaccuracies, only on November 27 and 30.

Adding to the air of arbitrariness was the triumphalist entry of a status quo party into the electoral ring: the Russia's Choice movement. Chartered only in June 1993 and headed by Gaidar—who was returned to the cabinet as a first deputy premier September 17—it was one of the first groups registered by the CEC. Crowning the candidates' list picked at a nominating convention extravagantly covered by state television were Gaidar, five colleagues on the Council of Ministers, and Sergei Filatov.[20] Christening it the "party of power" *(partiya vlasti),* a tag that stuck, pundits spoke of its victory as a foregone conclusion. One speculated that it would bag 50 percent or more of the State Duma seats and that the majority that would fall to it and the other reformist parties "may . . . be overwhelming." Another said that 65 percent of the total votes could be within the reach of Russia's Choice alone. Still another apostrophized that for practical purposes, "we may already call it the governing [party]."[21]

The Limits of Engineering

The advance celebration of victory turned out to be premature and in large part misplaced. The verdict of the Russian people on December 12 was to lock in Yeltsin's presidentialist constitution—the most enduring result, maybe, of the three-month battle. But in the strictly electoral realm it offered little comfort to the would-be party of power or its Kremlin patron.

In sizing up the chain of events, we cannot lose sight of the administration's arrogance, hubris, and propensity for fudging the rules. But neither can we overlook that nothing like the result that ensued would have been conceivable had the direst suspicions about a stage-managed election been borne out—this in the country whose Communist rulers once pioneered the totalitarian pseudoelection. In the final analysis, Yeltsin—impelled by some blend of moral inhibitions, self-interest, and responsiveness to complaint—ceded significant latitude to public opinion and to political entrepreneurs to define the outcome. What came to pass, its flaws notwithstanding, was a competitive election. There were severe limits to the degree to which it was and could be engineered.

The most egregious of the political restraints imposed during the October confrontation did turn out to be temporary. The police and army terminated the Moscow state of emergency on October 18, and censorship and self-censorship ended at roughly the same juncture. *Pravda* and the bulk of the other enjoined periodicals were back on the newsstands by the first week of November. Several truculent organizations remained suspended for the rest of 1993; this is not surprising, what with their role in the recent mutiny.

The electoral procedures divulged September 21—as distinct from the manner of their invention—were never terribly draconian. Any political party or movement duly registered with the Ministry of Justice, or any "bloc" of such bodies or of other licit organizations, could take part, provided it presented the signatures of 200,000 citizens vouching for it by forty-five days before December 12. A legislative committee chaired by a respected professor of international relations, Viktor Sheinis, had already worked out provisos along these lines; they were agreeable to most factions, although the size of the signatures quota remained a sore point.[22] The revised regulations of October 1 actually lowered the hurdle to 100,000 signatures. Three of Russia's forty-odd political parties were among the organizations outlawed October 4. The prohibition on the KPRF, the least militant and the only one to have a sizable following, was revoked in late October. At the urging of its leader, Gennadii Zyuganov, the Communists dove into the electoral fray and were granted registration.

Yeltsin stoutly maintained that the ambit of choice in the election was unprecedented. "The spectrum of political positions taken by the participants in [the campaign] is unaccustomedly wide," he stated on November 2. "I don't think there has been a thing like it here since the elections to the Constituent Assembly in 1917," before that body's suppression by Lenin weeks after the Bolshevik Revolution.[23] Yeltsin had a point: this was indeed the first parliamentary campaign in which parties and near-parties nominated candidates and slates and stumped freely for them. Although not all parties that wanted to got in on the competition (as will be discussed), those that did embodied every major point of view in Russian politics. The blacklist of twenty-one individuals came to about 0.5 percent of the horde of candidates; other figures who had been on the losing side in October 1993 or August 1991 (or both) dotted the candidates' rolls.[24]

Even had Yeltsin been inclined toward a blanket crackdown on dissent or a crass rigging of the election, he would have had a hard time ignoring certain external restraints. An iron-fist policy would have alienated the Western alliance and the International Monetary Fund. It would have been no less devastating to his strained relations with Russia's intellectual and mass media elite, which backed him during his climb to power and was still intimately interconnected with his corps of advisers and ministers. Liberal writers hotly protested the newspaper closings and censors' scissors (less so the bans on associations and parties), revisiting themes of the human rights campaigns against the Soviet Politburo.[25] Yeltsin's October 29 decree on "information guarantees" in the campaign allowed a modicum of equity in media coverage, and Yevgenii Bragin, the head of the state-owned Ostankino network, who had brazenly signed onto the Russia's Choice slate, quit it in November. Hoots of derision greeted a ham-handed attempt by Yeltsin subordinates to gag negative comments about the draft constitution; the CEC, showing unwonted independence, upheld the critics on December 2.

Also staying the hand of hawks in the administration on some issues, at least, was the demonstrable political pluralism within its ranks. Longstanding differences on how to handle the deputies' congress reverberated in muted form in September–October 1993, and fissures within Russia's Choice and within the Council of Ministers over political and economic questions were quite visible throughout the autumn. As nominations and election propaganda began in earnest, it turned out that far from everyone was eager to jump on the bandwagon of the party of power. Premier Chernomyrdin conspicuously abstained, grumbling about "multipartism [mnogopartiinost'] in the government" and telling his ministers to campaign only "outside of working hours."[26] Six cabinet members bore the Russia's Choice banner for the State Duma, but five, including two deputy prime ministers, stood for other parties, as did several presidential advisers.[27]

Magnifying the effects of incipient multipartism and principled discord were the haste and amateurish staff work behind the definitive decrees and instructions on the election. Contrary to Yeltsin's image of a "crack team" in charge, Yurii Baturin, his aide for legal affairs, said of the measures executed September 21 that "various parts of this packet were prepared in various places and by various people, who did not know in detail what others were doing."[28]

Most jarring to the image of governmental single-mindedness is the enigmatic performance of the engineer-in-chief of the election. Whatever he may have anticipated when he launched it, a psychological change seemed to come over Yeltsin in mid-autumn. Holding aloof from the grind of the campaigning, he limited his comments to the constitutional referendum, which was undoubtedly his preoccupation, and to defense of the probity of the election. To the consternation of Gaidar, whose relations with him would never be the same again,[29] Yeltsin did not endorse Russia's Choice.

Rules

Let us now look more closely at the rules of the election game. Yeltsin's seminal decrees underwrote a two-track competition for seats in a single legislative body, the State Duma. Their authors, without much interference on his part, patterned the rules loosely on the dual formula for the election of the Bundestag, postwar Germany's lower house. With the tumble of events, an already complicated election transmogrified into a war on four fronts—over the two halves of the Duma, the Federation Council, and the constitution—and in some areas over local issues as well.[30] The emphasis in this book will be on the linked subelections for the Federal Assembly, especially the Duma.

The amended regulation of October 1 bisected the State Duma. Half the mandates were to be awarded by proportional representation (PR) vote in an all-encompassing "federation-wide electoral district." Proportional representation, Viktor Sheinis and his colleagues were convinced, would be conducive to the formation of a multiparty system.[31] Parties and near-parties—"electoral associations" *(izbiratel'nyye ob"edineniya)* generically—would first assemble lists of up to 270 nominees. Criteria for inclusion were lax as the nominees had only to consent to being listed and to meet the age requirement for deputies (twenty-one); they did not need to be members of the given group and could withdraw at will. To get a spot on the national ballot, an aspiring party was obliged to deposit at the CEC 100,000 proper signatures of eligible voters, with home addresses and passport serial numbers appended; no more than 15 percent could come from any one province.

The PR ballot slip would reproduce the names of the CEC-registered electoral associations (in alphabetical order) and of the three senior candidates on each ticket. Parties also had the option of designating "regional groups" of candidates in some or all regions. The top three candidates in any region would get their names on the PR ballot along with the party's three leading national candidates—making for a bewildering profusion of ballot forms. After December 12, the 225 all-federal seats were to be divvied up in arithmetical proportion to the valid votes received, subject to a 5 percent threshold for winnowing out fringe parties. A qualifying party's candidates would be seated in descending order of their placement on national and regional lists.[32]

The second half of the State Duma was to be elected in 225 "single-member territorial districts" *(odnomandatnyye izbiratel'nyye okruga).* The

CEC drew their boundaries to weight votes equally, with discrepancies to accommodate the smaller federal units.[33] Candidates (again free to withdraw at any time) could either be independents nominated by "groups of voters," which first had to sign up 1 percent of the district's electors or run for a political party or bloc accredited in the PR subelection, which was absolved of the signatures requirement. The ballot in any case would bear only the name of the candidate and a few biographical snippets, omitting any partisan affiliation.[34] Individuals on national party lists could stand for election in one local district. A minimum of two nominees and a 25 percent turnout were required for the vote to go forward. An unqualified plurality (first-past-the-post) rule determined the winner, so that someone could prevail with far fewer than half the votes cast, especially in a crowded field.

Regulation of campaign activity by the CEC and other state agencies was light. Its principal components were the following:

—Parties and candidates had to pay their bills through "election fund" accounts opened in Russian banks. Persons could donate up to 20 times the minimum monthly wage to a candidate and 30 times that to an electoral association; for businesses and other organizations, the limits were 200 and 20,000 multiples of the minimum wage. Financial reports were to be filed with CEC auditors within sixty days of the election.

—Publicity materials were immune to previous censorship but could not be anonymous and could not advocate revolution or secession from the federation.

—Publicly owned mass media outlets were to provide equal access to all election contenders. Individual candidates had the right to a minimum of one appearance each on state television or radio. Parties got one hour of prime time on all central television and radio stations in the final three weeks of the campaign.

—Data from public opinion polls could not be disseminated in the last ten days of the campaign.

Yeltsin at first did not intend a popular election for the upper house of parliament, the Federation Council. He had labored all summer to institute a presidential advisory panel going by that very name—seating the head administrator and chair of the soviet of each region—and spoke before its inaugural meeting September 18. Under the state blueprint he promulgated days later, the council was simply to be converted after December 12 into a part-time legislative chamber. Its membership was to continue to consist ex officio of the senior pair of officials from each of the eighty-nine "subjects of the federation." Federal-regional interlock had been recommended by the Constitutional Convention, impressed by the comity produced by somewhat similar arrangements in postwar Germany. It was also patently useful to Yeltsin, who had appropriated the right to hire and fire all provincial governors ("heads of administration") in 1991 and clearly expected them and the chief legislators to go along with him during the fall campaign.[35]

These assumptions were foiled by the resolve of a good many local officials not to knuckle under to Yeltsin's coup.[36] The flurry of challenges led him to a hurried decision to force elections to restyled regional legislatures—and perforce to rampant uncertainty about one half of the membership of his Federation Council. After several weeks of conflicting signals, Yeltsin decreed on October 11 that the Federation Council, also, would be publicly elected for its maiden term.[37]

Federation Council districts were coterminous with the eighty-nine regions: twenty-one *republics* and eleven other ethnically defined units of lower status; six sprawling provinces known as *krais*; forty-nine more homogeneously Russian *oblasts*; and the two "cities of federal stature," Moscow and St. Petersburg. Each elected two members (from three or more candidates, to ensure competition) and citizens cast two votes. Nomination instrumentalities differed subtly from those for the State Duma. Again, either nonpartisans or partisans could run, but each had to collect the signatures of 2 percent of the electorate (or 25,000 persons, whichever was less), not 1 percent; the requirement was not waived for parties.[38] All other campaign procedures mirrored those for the Duma.

The final matter to be dealt with December 12 was the constitution. The enabling decree termed the consultation with the populace a "vote" *(golosovaniye)*, not a referendum. This word trick sidestepped the Russian referendum law of 1990, which stipulated that 50 percent of the entire electorate must lodge votes in favor for a referendum proposition to pass.[39] Under Yeltsin's edict of October 15, the draft constitution would be adopted if 50 percent of the electorate voted—double the proportion required in the parliamentary election—and if a majority of participants, not of the electorate, indicated approval. The question was straightforward: "Do you support the adoption of the new constitution of Russia?"

Players

The players varied widely from one dimension of the election to another. In the high-profile PR subelection for the State Duma, thirty-five associations pulled out the stops to submit slates and signatures by the November 6 deadline.[40] Twenty-one managed to accomplish the feat. The CEC in a two-day hearing disallowed eight applicants for irregularities in the signatures and companion documentation.

Several of the disqualified organizations accused the police and government agents of harassing their signature drives and the CEC of political bias. Their margin for error on signatures was slender, as they came to the CEC with an average of 107,000 names, not much more than the mandated 100,000. The thirteen parties that passed muster averaged 172,000 signatures each, the Agrarian party alone garnering 500,000. Coincidentally or not, four of the eight rejected—the Russian People's Union, the Constitutional Democratic party, the National Republican party, and the Russian Christian Democratic party—were of nationalist persuasion, rabidly anti-Yeltsin. Two others, the Transformation Bloc and the Party of Consolidation, were middle of the road. The remaining two, the Association of Independent Professionals and New Russia, were proreform; New Russia, once out of the election, urged its adherents to vote Russia's Choice.[41]

Table 1-1 presents summary information on the thirteen that made it to the starting gate, crudely sorted into five ideological groupings. Russia's Choice, the only party we classify as radical reformist, was unreservedly for Yeltsin's policies to date and led by the person most identified with them, Gaidar. The three groupings that we refer to as moderate reformist, although in general harmony with the post-1991 line, distanced themselves from it on particular points. The platforms of the six centrist entrants, the largest cluster, were remoter still from government policy but did not go so far as to reject altogether the post-1991 trajectory. The three remaining parties—labeled as nationalist and socialist here and often called the "hard opposition" elsewhere—not only lashed out at Yeltsin and his allies but found fault with the preceding perestroika era. Led by Vladimir Zhirinovskii, the misnamed Liberal-Democratic Party of Russia (LDPR)—which to the astonishment of most prognosticators led the polls December 12—railed at the government from a nationalist standpoint. The KPRF and the Agrarians did so in the vocabulary of state socialism. The five-part taxonomy we adopt is, to repeat, an imprecise one, but it does allow us to make some general points about party types.[42]

The party contenders can be distinguished on the organizational as well as the ideological plane. None in its present form was old, but the KPRF, formally founded only in February 1993, more or less picked up where the

Table 1-1. Party Lists in the Elections

Organization	Date founded	Size of list[a]	Regional sublists	Top candidate on slate	Position on constitution
Radical reformist					
Russia's Choice	June 1993	212	Yes	Yegor Gaidar (first vice premier)	For
Moderate reformist					
Yabloko (Yavlinskii-Boldyrev-Lukin Bloc)		172	Yes	Grigorii Yavlinskii (economist)	Against
PRES (Party of Russian Unity and Accord)	October 1993	193	Yes	Sergei Shakhrai (vice premier)	For
RDDR (Russian Movement for Democratic Reform)	February 1992[b]	153	No	Anatolii Sobchak (mayor of St. Petersburg)	For
Centrist					
Women of Russia	October 1993	36	No	Alevtina Fedulova (chair of women's union)	None
DPR (Democratic Party of Russia)	May 1990	167	No	Nikolai Travkin (party leader)	Against
Civic Union for Stability, Justice, and Progress	October 1993[c]	184	Yes	Arkadii Vol'skii (president of Russian Union of Industrialists and Entrepreneurs)	Against

Party	Date	No.[a]		Leader	Vote
Future of Russia–New Names	October 1993	95	Yes	Vyacheslav Lashchevskii (secretary of Russian Union of Youth)	None
KEDR (Constructive Ecological Movement of Russia)	March 1993	44	No	Lyubov Lymar' (chair of Association of Soldiers' Mothers)	For
Dignity and Compassion	October 1993	58	No	Konstantin Frolov (vice president of Academy of Sciences)	None
Nationalist					
LDPR (Liberal Democratic Party of Russia)	March 1990[d]	147	No	Vladimir Zhirinovskii (party chair)	For
Socialist					
KPRF (Communist Party of the Russian Federation)	February 1993	151	No	Gennadii Zyuganov (party chair)	Against
Agrarian Party of Russia	February 1993	145	Yes	Mikhail Lapshin (party chair)	Against

a. These are the figures given in the initial public listing by the CEC, in *Rossiiskaya gazeta*, November 12, 1993, pp. 3–12. About forty candidates were cut from the lists by December 12, but the breakdown by party was never publicly divulged.
b. The RDDR evolved out of a USSR-level Movement for Democratic Reform established in July 1991.
c. This organization was a reconstructed version of the original Civic Union, a political alliance formed in June 1992.
d. An antecedent club was created as early as 1989. The LDPR registered as a Russian political party in December 1992.

defunct Communist Party of the Soviet Union (CPSU) left off, and the LDPR and the Democratic Party of Russia (DPR) had been fixtures since noncommunist parties were first admitted in 1990. Nine of the thirteen came into being in 1993, six of them after September 21.

The thirteen party lists subsumed 1,757 names.[43] This was 135 per slate, although it varied from the 200-plus posted by Russia's Choice to the 36 for Women of Russia. Only six parties availed themselves of the option to compile regional sublists. The slates also had very different occupational, generational, and gender makeups.

The subgame within the territorial districts—local arenas composed of approximately 475,000 registered voters each—was far less tightly structured than the PR contest. The CEC logged in 1,578 individual candidates, or 7.0 for each of the 224 participating districts (the separatist Chechnya republic prevented the election from being held there). A few names were added on appeal, but late withdrawals lowered the total to 1,519, or 6.8 per district, on election day.[44] Slightly more than half were independents nominated by the signature-collection route; 46 percent were partisan nominees (see table 1-2). The party effort again varied widely, from the 105 district candidates delegated by Russia's Choice to the 6 by Women of Russia.

Commentators on the election have not always appreciated that there was huge overlap between the party rosters in the districts and on the na-

Table 1-2. *Party Participation in Nominations in the Single-Member Districts*

Party	Total candidates	Districts contested[a]	Candidates also on national list	Candidates also on a regional sublist
Russia's Choice	105	103	99	94
Yabloko	85	84	84	82
PRES	62	61	60	57
RDDR	59	57	55	0
Women of Russia	6	6	6	0
DPR	57	56	54	0
Civic Union	72	70	70	68
Future of Russia	33	33	33	30
KEDR	22	22	21	0
Dignity and Compassion	15	15	15	0
LDPR	59	59	58	0
KPRF	55	55	54	0
Agrarian	67	67	62	55
All parties	697	202	671	386

a. Although regulations prescribed only one party nominee per district, some duplication was tolerated.

tional lists. *Ninety-six percent* of the district candidates nominated by electoral associations were cross-listed on their Russia-wide lists for the Duma.
For the six parties that formed regional sublists within the national PR list,
96 percent of their nominees in single-member districts were also cross-
listed on a local sublist within the national master list, almost always for the
province in which they were running.[45]

The improvised run for the Federation Council was less competitive than
the State Duma subelections and more distant from national concerns. The
parties refrained from nominating candidates, dissuaded by the signatures
requirement, the greater importance attached to the Duma, and the manic
schedule dictated by Yeltsin's eleventh-hour decision on public election.
Four hundred and eighty-nine individuals were nominated for the upper
house.[46] This comes to a mean of 5.6 for each of the 88 participating regions, or 1.2 less than in the State Duma districts; because each region sent
two deputies to the Federation Council, the ratio of nominees to seats available was 2.8 to 1.

The competition for votes was most understructured of all in the corollary constitutional referendum. Yeltsin made several declarations on the
draft from the presidential pulpit, trumpeting it as the only antidote to insta-
bility and civil war. But he abdicated most of the selling job to a government committee chaired by First Deputy Prime Minister Vladimir Shumeiko, who doubled as information minister and concentrated on
squelching criticism of the constitution rather than touting its virtues. No
countercommittee existed for opponents. Russia's Choice and four other
parties supported the constitution, five parties were adamantly against it,
and three were neutral (see table 1-1).

Results

According to the sketchy statistics proffered by the CEC, 54.8 percent of
Russia's 106 million eligible voters turned out to polling stations December
12. In the annex to the parliamentary election so dear to Yeltsin, 58.4 percent of them are said to have voted "yes" in the constitutional referendum
(majorities in seven republics and ten oblasts voted "no"). Thirteen days
later, the "Yeltsin constitution" went into force.

History will likely remember the election primarily for its headline-
grabbing element: the PR vote for the State Duma. As table 1-3 reminds us,
the obstreperous LDPR swept to the front of the pack with nearly 23 per-

Table 1-3. *Election Results for the State Duma*

Party or party grouping	Percentage of party-list votes	Deputies elected on list	Percentage of district votes[a]	Deputies elected in districts
Party				
LDPR	22.9	59	3.6	5
Russia's Choice	15.5	40	8.3	25
KPRF	12.4	32	4.1	9
Women of Russia	8.1	21	0.7	2
Agrarian	7.9	21	6.4	16
Yabloko	7.9	20	4.2	7
PRES	6.8	18	3.2	3
DPR	5.5	14	2.5	1
RDDR	4.1	0	2.5	5
Civic Union	1.9	0	3.6	6
Future of Russia	1.3	0	0.9	1
KEDR	0.8	0	0.7	0
Dignity and Compassion	0.7	0	1.0	3
Against all parties	4.3	n.a.	n.a.	n.a.
Party grouping				
Radical reformist	15.5	40	8.3	25
Moderate reformist	18.8	38	9.9	15
Centrist	18.3	35	9.4	13
Nationalist	22.9	59	3.6	5
Socialist	20.3	53	10.5	25
Independent candidates	n.a.	n.a.	58.3	136

n.a. = not applicable.
a. Excludes votes cast against all candidates, which were not given in the election returns.

cent of the popular vote, and the two socialistic parties picked up another 20 percent. Russia's Choice was held to under 16 percent and the three moderate reformist parties to under 19 percent. Centrist slates harvested a little more than 18 percent of the votes, almost half of that going to the Women of Russia movement. Slightly more than 4 percent of the electors opted to vote against all the parties. When the dust had settled, eight of the thirteen blocs made it over the 5 percent barrier.

These returns raise intriguing questions. For what reasons did Yeltsin get his way on the constitution, the one bright spot for him in the returns? Why did the vaunted behavioral engineers behind the election not match their narrow constitutional victory with a triumph in the State Duma that would enact laws under the same constitution? If a disappointing electoral showing did not "found" the kind of state-society relationship the radical democrats wanted, did some other kind of lasting political alignment take shape in December 1993?

In the partisan core of the election, what factors bore on citizens' choices? How engaged were they with the campaign? Did voting decisions grow out of likes or dislikes of the parties or out of assessments of leadership qualities and style? Were demographic traits and social structure associated with political preference? Did citizens take guidance from strong opinions of their own on national issues? In what way did they learn about the issues and the parties?

In the district segment of the State Duma subelection, Russians cast 58 percent of their votes for nonpartisan candidates, who made up 62 percent of the 219 deputies elected.[47] It is hard to see how the process could have obeyed the same logic as the PR subelection, in that the communication channels and interpersonal networks involved were, on the surface of it, quite different. Furthermore, for those deputies elected in the districts who were nominees of the national parties, table 1-4 betrays a curious lack of congruence with the PR results. How can it be, for example, that the LDPR, a powerhouse in the party-list campaign, fizzled at the district level, whereas Russia's Choice and the Agrarians fared relatively well?

One hundred and seventy-one candidates were elected to the Federation Council.[48] No party-related table would summarize the returns there, for the parties did not get their feet wet in this subelection. "The results," as one scholar remarks, "are difficult to fit into the pattern of bloc politics."[49] That being so, what other factors were at work? A glance at the council benches suggests an overrepresentation of regional administrative elites and a rather more reformist hue than the State Duma, something confirmed by the election of Vladimir Shumeiko as its chair in January 1994.[50] What systemic or individual-level factors might account for one house of parliament acquiring a different political coloration from the other?

An aspect of the results that attracted a fair amount of attention is the question of irregularities in the counting of the votes. To be most charitable about it, the CEC, overburdened by ill-considered reorganizations—mainly the elimination of analogous commissions within administrative districts and towns—was less than efficient in tallying the votes. It gave different totals for registered voters in December 1993 and February 1994, and both were inexplicably lower than the number registered for the referendum of April 1993.[51] It *never* published candidate-by-candidate returns for either the single-member Duma districts or the Federation Council, limiting itself to the votes lodged for winning candidates.

In February 1994 the magazine editor Kronid Lyubarskii alleged that not only inaccuracy but fraud, perpetrated locally and winked at by the CEC,

Table 1-4. A Thumbnail Sketch of the Ten Regions in the Study

Region	Capital	Distance from Moscow (km)	Population[a]	Area (sq. km.)	Urbanization (percent)[a]	Employees in defense industry (percent)[b]	Major civilian industries	Top three ethnic groups (percent)[a]
City of Moscow	Moscow	—	8,967,232	1,050	100.0	24	Automotive, light, consumer and food	Russian (89.7), Ukrainian (2.9), Jewish (2.0)
City of St. Petersburg	St. Petersburg	651	5,023,506	639	100.0	34	Electrotechnical, machinery, consumer and food	Russian (89.1), Ukrainian (3.0), Jewish (2.1)
Nizhnii Novgorod oblast	Nizhnii Novgorod	606	3,714,322	74,800	77.3	32	Automotive, chemical and petrochemical, pulp and paper	Russian (94.6), Tatar (1.6), Mordvinian (1.0)
Sverdlovsk oblast	Yekaterinburg	1,667	4,716,768	194,800	87.0	33	Machinery, metallurgy, chemical	Russian (88.7), Tatar (3.9), Ukrainian (1.7)
Saratov oblast	Saratov	858	2,686,483	100,200	74.4	32	Machinery, chemical and petrochemical, food	Russian (85.6), Ukrainian (3.8), Kazakh (2.7)

Kursk oblast	Kursk	536	1,339,414	57.9	14	Machinery, mining, chemical and petrochemical	Russian (96.9), Ukrainian (1.7), Belorus (0.3)
Kemerovo oblast	Kemerovo	3,482	3,176,335	87.4	11	Machinery, chemical, mining and metallurgy	Russian (90.5), Ukrainian (2.1), Tatar (2.0)
Primorskii krai	Vladivostok	9,302	2,258,322	77.5	16	Fish processing, machinery, forestry	Russian (86.9), Ukrainian (8.2), Belorus (1.0)
Tatarstan republic	Kazan	797	3,637,809	73.0	30	Automotive, chemical and petrochemical, oil	Tatar (48.5), Russian (43.3), Chuvash (3.7)
Bashkortostan republic	Ufa	1,519	3,943,113	63.8	29	Oil, chemical and petrochemical, machinery	Russian (39.3), Tatar (28.4), Bashkir (21.9)

a. Taken from the 1989 Soviet census.
b. Calculated from residuals in unpublished Soviet data for 1985 and given in Brenda Horrigan, "How Many People Worked in the Soviet Defense Industry?" *RFE/RL Research Report*, vol. 1 (August 21, 1992), pp. 36–37.

had corrupted the vote counting.[52] When the daily press picked up his attack, Yeltsin assigned a panel headed by the former Russia's Choice delegate to the CEC, a natural scientist named Aleksandr Sobyanin, to investigate. Their seventy-page report made a raft of sensational charges, notably that regional "working groups" tallying the precinct returns had inflated turnout by 7 or 8 percent to ensure passage of the constitution, thrown up to 6 million votes from Russia's Choice to opposition groups (above all the LDPR), and helped elect governors to the Federation Council by marking up ballot papers and deliberately miscounting votes.[53]

Sobyanin's indictment rests on inference from aggregate election and referendum data. The techniques employed, in the words of two methodologically skilled analysts (one Russian, one American) who checked them later, "are ill-equipped for detecting [fraud], for measuring its magnitude, or, given the quality of the data available, for distinguishing between the null hypothesis that there was fraud . . . and the hypothesis that there was no fraud."[54] Regrettably, the physical evidence that would allow a close check of Sobyanin's charges is unavailable. Ryabov indignantly rejected them and Yeltsin quickly dropped the issue.

If nothing else, the CEC's statistical bungling shows the inadequacy of protections against abuse. It is quite believable that some participation totals would have been padded and some ballots tampered with, especially for the Federation Council.[55] It is not particularly believable that there would have been wholesale shenanigans without a smoking gun falling into the hands of muckrakers in the news media. Nor is it apparent how scattered bureaucrats could have distorted the returns time after time to privilege Yeltsin's constitution but short-change the "party of power" or shunt votes to the LDPR, for which few had the slightest affinity. Unless and until more damning information sees the light, the announced results are the best known approximation of the factual distribution.

The Plan of This Book

Growing Pains: Russian Democracy and the Election of 1993 examines the election from different angles that illuminate different aspects of the phenomenon. The first half of the book, panoramic in scope, pulls out threads that run through the election in its entirety. In chapter 2, coeditor Jerry F. Hough reviews the election results and relates them to the institutional landscape and rules. I delve into the heart of the election, the vote for the party lists, in chapter 3. Quarrying national-sample survey data, I tie partisan preference to social structure and issue opinions.

The next three chapters cover the national campaigns of the chief contenders in the election, detailing how they were formulated and managed and offering interpretations of their successes and failures. Michael McFaul (chapter 4) draws a bead on Russia's Choice, the putative juggernaut that fell short of expectations. Daniel Treisman (chapter 5) treats the rather amorphous set of parties, moderate reformist and centrist, arrayed between Russia's Choice and the hard opposition. Evelyn Davidheiser (chapter 6) analyzes the nationalist and socialist foes of the government.

The next three chapters cover the mass communications media, the predominant channel through which the electorate was educated about the election. Laura Roselle Helvey (chapter 7) and Joel M. Ostrow (chapter 8) discuss television and the printed press, posing parallel questions about media content, quality, and autonomy. In a companion chapter (chapter 9), I use survey data to clarify citizens' exposure and response to media messages.

My chapter (chapter 10) on public opinion and the constitutional referendum rounds out the first part of the book. The constitution, although not the focal point of our project, may in retrospect be the most lasting legacy of the turmoil analyzed in this book. Subsequent happenings, including Yeltsin's style of rule, the peaceful staging of a second State Duma election in December 1995, and his election to a second term as president in June 1996, underline its importance.

The second half of the book complements the national-scale chapters by spotlighting the elections in discrete regions of Russia. A member of the research team visited each locality in November–December 1993, interviewed participants, and gathered election statistics, often more precise than those emitted by the CEC. In some but not all places, preelection mass surveys were done to which the scholar had access later.

The regions were selected with an eye to capturing basic elements of the geographic, social, and economic diversity of the Russian Federation. The map preceding this chapter will help the reader locate the regions; table 1-4 lays out some rudimentary facts and figures.

The regions range from Moscow, whose outermost suburbs are a half-hour by taxi from Red Square, to Primorskii krai, whose capital, Vladivostok, is a one-week train ride away. Moscow is the most populous unit and Kursk oblast the least; Sverdlovsk oblast is the most extensive in area, St. Petersburg the least. Moscow and St. Petersburg are 100 percent urbanized, whereas 40 percent of the denizens of Kursk oblast, at the rural extreme, live in villages. Before the manufacturing depression brought on by the Yeltsin-Gaidar reforms, the military-industrial complex employed 30 percent or more of the workforce in half of the regions, led by St. Petersburg, while encompassing less than 20 percent of employment in three of them.[56] Civilian industry assumes markedly different profiles in various regions. All the regions have considerable internal diversity in economic specialization. In ethnic terms, Russians predominate in nine regions, including one (Bashkortostan) in which another nationality (the Bashkirs) is the "titular" group; the Tatars are the most populous nationality in Tatarstan and outnumber the Bashkirs in Bashkortostan. The Russians' proportion goes from fewer than 40 percent (in Bashkortostan) to almost 97 percent (in Kursk oblast), and eight minority groups occupy second or third place within the regions' populations.

The ten regions evince political variation, too. Votes for Yeltsin in the 1991 presidential election and the referendum of April 1993 are a handy barometer (see table 1-5). Five regions were above the national mean in support for Yeltsin in June 1991 and five were below; in April 1993, six were above the average and four below it. Both times, the most pro-Yeltsin of the selected regions (and of all regions in Russia) was Sverdlovsk oblast, his home province, followed by cosmopolitan Moscow. Table 1-5 lists a convenient indicator for each region of the degree of reformism displayed by deputies elected from the area in 1990, at the start of the parliamentary term truncated by Yeltsin in 1993. "Sobyanin scores," compiled on the basis of

Table 1-5. *Some Earlier Political Indicators for the Ten Regions*

Region	Voted for Yeltsin for president, June 1991 (percent)	Voted confidence in Yeltsin, April 1993 (percent)	Average Sobyanin score for deputies, First Congress, 1990[a]
City of Moscow	75.1	76.4	92
City of St. Petersburg	70.1	73.8	84
Nizhnii Novgorod oblast	72.2	65.2	–2
Sverdlovsk oblast	86.4	85.9	18
Saratov oblast	57.5	52.8	–25
Kursk oblast	56.7	42.9	–65
Kemerovo oblast	40.6	53.9	44
Primorskii krai	64.0	65.9	35
Tatarstan republic	48.5	68.5	20
Bashkortostan republic	50.1	40.7	4
Russia as a whole	59.7	59.9	7

roll-call votes by Aleksandr Sobyanin and his associates, range from -100 for the least radical legislator to +100 for the most radical.[57] By this yardstick, Moscow and St. Petersburg parliamentarians were far and away the most radically inclined of our ten regions, with Kursk and Saratov oblasts bringing up the rear.

Our sample regions exhibited pronouncedly different political sentiments in December 1993. Most striking was the spectrum manifested in the party-list vote (see table 1-6). In Moscow, Russia's Choice won 35 percent of the votes and together with the moderate reformists surpassed 60 percent. In Bashkortostan, Russia's Choice was held to 9 percent of the vote, and in three regions (Kursk, Bashkortostan, and Saratov) the proreform parties combined could not clear 30 percent. The LDPR led the pack in five of our regions, Russia's Choice in four, and the Agrarian party in one, Bashkortostan. Other indicators also show a wide range (see table 1-7). The turnout to vote was a mere 13 percent in Tatarstan, whose president boycotted the ballot, but at the high end was 63 percent in Kursk oblast. Support for the constitution ran the gamut from 80 percent in Sverdlovsk oblast to scarcely more than half that in Bashkortostan. Sobyanin scores for the two-year terms of deputies elected in single-member districts evince a vast spread, from an average rating of +57 in the State Duma for legislators selected in Moscow to −87 for their counterparts from Kursk oblast.

Table 1-6. *Votes for Groups of Parties in Party-List Vote in the Ten Regions*[a]

Percent

Region	Radical reformist	Moderate reformist	Centrist	Nationalist	Socialist
City of Moscow	34.7	25.8	14.2	12.8	12.5
City of St. Petersburg	27.0	34.0	12.4	18.0	8.6
Nizhnii Novgorod oblast	14.0	22.2	23.2	19.9	20.7
Sverdlovsk oblast	25.2	27.4	20.0	17.7	9.8
Saratov oblast	12.3	16.8	21.4	26.6	22.9
Kursk oblast	10.6	11.5	12.9	33.5	31.5
Kemerovo oblast	13.7	19.0	22.6	29.4	15.2
Primorskii krai	14.1	22.4	28.9	23.3	11.3
Tatarstan republic	22.4	24.7	19.4	22.0	11.5
Bashkortostan republic	8.5	19.5	19.6	12.6	39.8
Russia as a whole	16.2	19.5	19.1	23.9	21.3

a. Excludes votes cast against all parties, which were not broken down by region in the election returns.

Table 1-7. *Some Other Election Indicators for the Ten Regions*

Region	Turned out to vote (percent)	Voted for constitution (percent)	Average Sobyanin score for deputies, 1993–95[a]
City of Moscow	50.6	69.9	57
City of St. Petersburg	51.7	71.6	42
Nizhnii Novgorod oblast	50.4	57.5	59
Sverdlovsk oblast	47.5	79.8	−1
Saratov oblast	57.1	51.1	−32
Kursk oblast	63.0	44.8	−87
Kemerovo oblast	51.1	62.3	−35
Primorskii krai	49.8	71.4	49
Tatarstan republic	13.4	74.8	−9
Bashkortostan republic	60.8	42.0	−65
Russia as a whole	54.3	58.4	−13

Each regional chapter leads off with a synopsis of the social and political background of the region. The author then carries out the threefold tasks set for the book: describing the campaign process, identifying determinants of the outcomes, and generalizing from the election to the new Russian politics. Recognizing the heterogeneity of the regions, we gave our researchers the green light to "go with the story" and give prominence to those features posing the most practical and theoretical interest on the given turf.

Thus the nub of Judith S. Kullberg's essay on Moscow (chapter 11) is the fierce infighting between the capital city chapters of the big political parties. Yitzhak M. Brudny (chapter 12) is taken with the robustness of the liberal tradition in St. Petersburg. Robert G. Moser, for Sverdlovsk oblast (chapter 13), and Nigel Gould-Davies, for Nizhnii Novgorod (chapter 14), deal with heretofore liberal preserves in which economic setbacks and the reformists' disorganization made life miserable for Russia's Choice. Regina Smyth's paper on Saratov oblast (chapter 15) and Neil J. Melvin's on Kursk (chapter 16) depict regions that have been conservative throughout the democratizing period and where the firmest trend would seem to be toward revival of the old nomenklatura. The crux of the election in the Kuzbass, Stephen Crowley asserts (chapter 17), was the complex social politics of a region in which blue-collar rage at the CPSU was once pervasive but populist local leaders now hold sway. In Primor'e, Katherine G. Burns shows (chapter 18), the election testified to the depth of anti-Moscow feeling and the appearance of a business-linked regional political machine. In Bashkortostan and Tatarstan, Henry E. Hale (chapter 19) and Pauline Jones Luong (chapter 20) find nationality issues to have pervaded the campaign, gaining expression in complicated interethnic alliances in Bashkortostan and in a defiant, elite-led resistance to the election itself in Tatarstan.

In the conclusion (chapter 21), Jerry F. Hough recaps the book's findings and ponders some lessons for the future of Russia's protodemocracy and for Western policy toward it.

Notes

1. Dwight Semler, "The End of the First Russian Republic," *East European Constitutional Review,* vols. 2/3 (Fall 1993/Winter 1994), pp. 107–14.

2. The neglect of post-Soviet politics and government in the provinces is beginning to be remedied. See, for example, Theodore H. Friedgut and Jeffrey W. Hahn, eds., *Local Power and Post-Soviet Politics* (Armonk, N.Y.: Sharpe, 1994); Peter Kirkow, "Regional Politics and Market Reform in Russia: The Case of the Altai," *Europe-Asia Studies,* vol. 46 (November 1994), pp. 1163–88; Gavin Helf, "All the Russias: Center, Core, and Periphery in Soviet and Post-Soviet Russia" (Ph.D. dissertation, University of California at Berkeley, 1994); Peter Kirkow, "Regional Warlordism in Russia: The Case of Primorskii Krai," *Europe-Asia Studies,* vol. 47 (September 1995), pp. 923–48; Jane E. Prokop, "Industrial Policy and Marketization in Russia's Regions, 1990-1994" (Ph.D. dissertation, Harvard University, 1996); and Kathryn Stoner-Weiss, *Local Heroes: The Political Economy of Governmental Performance in Provincial Russia* (Princeton University Press, 1997).

3. Samuel P. Huntington, *The Third Wave: Democratization in the Late Twentieth Century* (University of Oklahoma Press, 1991), p. 174.

4. Giuseppe Di Palma, *To Craft Democracies: An Essay on Democratic Transitions* (University of California Press, 1990), p. 80; Huntington, *Third Wave,* pp. 174–91.

5. Guillermo O'Donnell and Philippe C. Schmitter, *Transitions from Authoritarian Rule: Tentative Conclusions about Uncertain Democracies* (Johns Hopkins University Press, 1986), pp. 61–62.

6. *Izvestiya,* October 26, 1991, p. 2.

7. Boris Yeltsin, *The Struggle for Russia,* trans. Catherine A. Fitzpatrick (New York: Times Books, 1994), p. 127.

8. Foreshadowing the parliamentary election later that year, the method of tallying the votes, and especially the proportions of the whole, was controversial in April 1993. Invalid ballots were counted in the denominator of the referendum results. Thus, although about 1.6 million more voted in favor of an early presidential election than voted against it, the record showed fewer than 50 percent of the official vote total (including invalid ballots) appoving a presidential election. *Rossiiskaya gazeta,* May 6, 1993, p. 1.

9. Wendy Slater, "No Victors in the Russian Referendum," *RFE/RL Research Report,* vol. 2, no. 21 (May 21, 1993), p. 19.

10. Quotations from Yeltsin, *Struggle for Russia,* pp. 242, 248.

11. Ibid., pp. 242, 251, 276–79, 281.

12. Reliably reported in *Segodnya,* September 21, 1993, p. 1.

13. Interview in *Nezavisimaya gazeta,* November 12, 1993, p. 1.

14. After making an unconvincing claim that he feared the rise of "a new Russian Stalin" if the quarrel with the legislature were not resolved, Yeltsin in his memoir restates the case for parliamentary dissolution and the election in these terms: "I. . . chose my option for stabilization." Yeltsin, *Struggle for Russia,* p. 248.

15. Although I make somewhat different links with the comparative literature, my reading of Yeltsin's intentions is broadly similar to Michael Urban's. In an insightful review published soon after the election, Urban called it an exercise in "democracy by design" comparable to attempts under Gorbachev to draw up electoral procedures that would "ensure an outcome favorable to the designers themselves." The resulting institutions, he said, tend to be "fragile entities, not resolving conflict but extending it." Michael Urban, "December 1993 as a Replication of Late-Soviet Electoral Practices," *Post-Soviet Affairs,* vol. 10 (April–June 1994), p. 128.

16. Sergei Kara-Murza in *Pravda,* September 29, 1993, p. 2, and Sergei Chesko in *Nezavisimaya gazeta,* October 10, 1993, p. 5. It is interesting to note that even the Communist press cited liberal values in its critique of Yeltsin. In a broadside in *Pravda,* November 4, 1993, pp. 1–2, Yurii Glukhov invoked the memory of Andrei Sakharov, the late dissident persecuted by the Soviets.

17. Most of the decisions referred to in the table and text can be found in the government-published newspapers *Rossiiskiye vesti* and *Rossiiskaya gazeta,* but some were unearthed only by journalists writing for nonstate papers.

18. The decrees were not binding on the twenty-one ethnic republics within Russia. They were given only a "recommendation" to hold elections. Most in fact did so.

19. See *Rossiiskiye vesti,* November 9, 1993, p. 1.

20. The other ministers on the Russia's Choice ticket were Anatolii Chubais and Boris Fedorov (deputy premiers), Andrei Kozyrev (foreign affairs), Ella Pamfilova (social security), and Yevgenii Sidorov (culture).

21. Anatolii Antonov in *Rossiiskiye vesti,* October 19, 1993, p. 1; Dmitrii Kuznets in *Segodnya,* October 26, 1993, p. 3; Yevgenii Krasnikov in *Nezavisimaya gazeta,* October 19, 1993, p. 3.

22. There was a range of opinion about the rules, but Sheinis's draft seems to have been at its midpoint. Sheinis ran for the State Duma for the "Yabloko" slate, not Russia's Choice.

23. *Rossiiskiye vesti,* November 3, 1993, p. 1. Yeltsin spoke before the CEC winnowed the parties in the running to thirteen. Following that step, Ryabov reiterated his point, proclaiming that in the election "there is present the entire spectrum of political forces, speaking from diverse positions, standing on various platforms—propresidential and progovernmental, centrist, representing both soft and hard opposition." *Izvestiya,* November 11, 1993, p. 1.

24. The CEC refused to accept papers filed by Ruslan Khasbulatov, Il'ya Konstantinov, the head of the National Salvation Front, and Stanislav Terekhov of the

Union of Officers. Prominent among the hard-liners who did stand were Anatolii Luk'yanov, the former speaker of the Soviet parliament (a candidate for the KPRF), and Vasilii Starodubtsev (a candidate for the Agrarian party), an agricultural organizer who was indicted along with Luk'yanov for his role in the failed coup of August 1991.

25. "One of the most obvious indications of a change of attitude among the intelligentsia is the growing number of periodicals that have suddenly become critical of Yeltsin and his supporters." Even newspapers loyal to Yeltsin "are now publishing much more critical material than ever before." Julia Wishnevsky, "Liberal Opposition Emerging in Russia?" *RFE/RL Research Report,* vol. 2, no. 44 (November 5, 1993), p. 6.

26. *Segodnya,* November 4, 1993, p. 2.

27. Deputy premiers Sergei Shakhrai and Aleksandr Shokhin, Justice minister Yurii Kalmykov, Labor minister Gennadii Melik'yan, and Sergei Stankevich, Yeltsin's counselor for political affairs, ran for the Party of Russian Unity and Accord. Aleksandr Zaveryukha, the deputy premier for agriculture, was a candidate for the Agrarian party, and Yekaterina Lakhova, Yeltin's adviser on women's issues, was the second-ranked nominee of Women of Russia.

28. Baturin in *Izvestiya,* September 25, 1993, p. 3.

29. Gaidar was to leave the Council of Ministers soon after his party's poor showing in the election and to break with Yeltsin completely when the president intervened militarily in Chechnya in late 1994. He fought the 1995 parliamentary election as a spokesperson for the "democratic opposition" to the government, but in 1996 reluctantly endorsed Yeltsin for reelection as the only candidate who could defeat a KPRF-led coalition.

30. For example, Moscow and Moscow province elected municipal councils on December 12, and Bashkortostan chose a republic president.

31. There is abundant comparative evidence that PR systems have this effect. See Arend Lijphart, *Democracies: Patterns of Majoritarian and Consensus Government in Twenty-One Countries* (Yale University Press, 1984), chap. 9.

32. Any candidate on the list of a party that cleared 5 percent and who won election in a single-member district was automatically seated from the district. Among candidates on party lists only, precedence went to nominees registered on the party's national PR list but without a regional listing. The party was to allocate any remaining places to regionally registered candidates in proportion to the share of the popular vote received by the party in the respective regions. Spoiled ballots and votes cast against all parties were excluded from these prolix calculations.

33. Malapportionment within the Duma made no constitutional sense once it was decided to have the Federation Council popularly elected as well. The largest number of votes cast in a single-member district (the 565,682 in district 3, in Bashkortostan) exceeded by more than 100 to 1 the smallest number of votes (the 5,378 cast in district 224, in the northerly Evenk autonomous district).

34. Urban ("December 1993," p. 138), citing an interview source, claims that this was accomplished by an unpublished CEC regulation. No such order would have been necessary. Articles 24(2) and 35(3) of the regulation promulgated Octo-

ber 1 stated that the ballot slip was to contain the full name, date of birth, occupation, and place of residence of each candidate.

35. "Obviously, the authors of the text [of Decree No. 1400] had in mind that the prospect of donning a senator's toga would incline the leaders of the regions to the presidential side." *Segodnya,* October 12, 1993, p. 1.

36. Eighty-three of eighty-nine regional legislatures passed resolutions condemning Yeltsin's actions in September. Vladimir Gel'man, "Novaya mestnaya politika," in *Ocherki rossiiskoi politiki (issledovaniya i nablyudeniya 1993–1994 gg.).* (Moscow: Institut Gumanitarno-politicheskikh issledovanii, 1994), p. 73. On September 25 Yeltsin dismissed the heads of administration of the Bryansk and Novosibirsk regions for their outspoken opposition.

37. Only three days before the decree, Sergei Filatov said Russia might have a unicameral parliament for an interim period. From October 11 to late in the month, the government and CEC counted on the Federation Council being elected for a four-year term, although Ryabov said this might be "corrected" to two years or even modified by rotation. The draft constitution specified a two-year first term, the same as the State Duma.

38. The decree on the Federation Council also stated that a regionally based political movement or organization could nominate candidates, whereas for the State Duma it had to be a centrally registered organization.

39. This point is well explained in Richard Sakwa, "The Russian Elections of December 1993," *Europe-Asia Studies,* vol. 47 (March 1995), pp. 197, 222.

40. The Russian press gave conflicting figures for associations and signatures. I use those in *Izvestiya,* November 9, 1993, p. 2.

41. Ryabov stated after handing down the CEC decision that the two centrist groups and three of the nationalist blocs did not collect the necessary number of signatures, and the names submitted by the fourth nationalist party, the Russian People's Union, were regionally imbalanced and had also been improperly solicited among ethnic Russians in Estonia and Moldova. New Russia and the Association of Independent Professionals, Ryabov added, withdrew their petitions when grilled by the CEC. *Rossiiskaya gazeta,* November 12, 1993, p. 2.

42. One can readily discern substantial differences in program and gradations in antigovernment animus within all the four opposition groupings. Among the moderate reformists, for instance, Yabloko, which campaigned against adoption of the draft constitution, was much more anti-Yeltsin than PRES, whose slate contained four cabinet ministers. The centrist parties all had personalities of their own. In the hard opposition, the LDPR engaged in intemperate antigovernment rhetoric, yet also endorsed the constitution. The KPRF, the stronger of the two socialist parties, had been banned in October and seriously considered boycotting the election once reinstated. The Agrarians, by contrast, had kept a low profile during the October crisis and occupied several seats in the Council of Ministers—which they were content to retain throughout a campaign in which their party attacked the government's economic line and advised rejection of the draft constitution.

43. Total in the initial listing in mid-November (see table 1-1). Subsequently, the CEC removed a number of individuals from the party lists, at the candidates' and the parties' request, but the public notices given were incomplete. On the eve

of the election, Ryabov said there were 1,717 candidates on the party lists, or an average of 132 per party. The official communique on election results stated that 1,713 remained on December 12. *Rossiiskaya gazeta,* December 11, 1993, p. 1, and "Figures for Party Support, Duma Seats Released," *Interfax,* December 25, 1993, in Foreign Broadcast Information Service Daily Report, Central Eurasia, December 27, 1993, p. 1.

44. The official CEC compendium in *Rossiiskaya gazeta,* November 30, contained the 1,578 names. Ryabov said at the close of the campaign (ibid., December 11, 1993, p. 1) that the up-to-date figure was 1,586, a sum used by Western and Russian analysts. I arrived at 1,519 by searching line by line through an unpublished final listing by the CEC, acquired through the good offices of Michael McFaul: "Rezul'taty golosovaniya na vyborakh v Gosudarstvennuyu Dumu po odnomandatnym izbiratel'nym okrugam" (Moscow: Tsentral'naya izbiratel'naya komissiya Rossiiskoi Federatsii, n.d.). All references in this chapter to candidates and votes in the single-member districts are based on this document. Not included in the 1,519 is the one candidate registered in District 25, in Tatarstan, where the election was abrogated for lack of the required two candidates.

45. Inexplicably, 10 of the 386 persons in this category ran in single-member districts not located in the region for which they were listed in the nominating party's master list.

46. Again, there are incongruities in the reported figures. The 489 is for the original list reported in the official media November 27. Ryabov said later that the number of candidates had risen to 494 (*Rossiiskaya gazeta,* December 11, 1993, p. 1).

47. Table 1-3 draws on the CEC's in-house "Rezul'taty golosovaniya." Other scholars, relying on summary statements by officials, have given slightly different and inaccurate totals. As mentioned previously, the election was aborted in Chechnya. In Tatarstan, in addition to the district where only one candidate was nominated, the results were invalid in four districts because participation fell below the 25 percent quorum.

48. Apart from Chechnya, low turnout forced a repeat election in Tatarstan and a shortage of candidates did the same in Chelyabinsk oblast. In the Yamal-Nenets autonomous district, the CEC declared only one candidate elected.

49. Sakwa, "Russian Elections," p. 211.

50. The speaker of the State Duma, Ivan Rybkin, ran as an Agrarian and was a kingpin of the Communists of Russia faction in the Congress of People's Deputies.

51. This and other anomalies are carefully reviewed in Sakwa, "Russian Elections," pp. 218–20.

52. Kronid Lyubarskii, "Falsifikatsiya," *Novoe vremya,* no. 7 (1994), pp. 4–11, and "Falsifikatsiya-2," *Novoye vremya,* no. 9 (1994), pp. 10–13.

53. A. A. Sobyanin and others, "Vybory i referendum 12 dekabrya 1993 g. v Rossii: Politicheskiye itogi, perspektivy, dostovernost' rezul'tatov" (Moscow and Arkhangel'skoye, processed, 1994); copy obtained directly from Sobyanin. See also the fuller presentation in A. A. Sobyanin and V. G. Sukhovol'skii, *Demokratiya, ogranichennaya fal'sifikatsiyami: Vybory i referendumy v Rossii v 1991-1993 gg.* (Moscow: Proyektnaya gruppa po pravam cheloveka, 1995).

54. Mikhail Filippov and Peter C. Ordeshook, "Fraud or Fiction: Who Stole What in Russia's December 1993 Elections," Division of Humanities and Social Sciences, California Institute of Technology, *Social Science Working Paper 963* (April 1996), p. 2.

55. As Sobyanin stressed in an interview in June 1994, voters were issued a single Federation Council ballot on which they were to mark two names. For voters who chose one name, it would have been easy for outsiders to check off a second box.

56. The 24 percent for Moscow understates the significance of the military-industrial complex there. It hosted as much as three-quarters of all of the USSR's defense-related research and development, which is mostly counted as scientific employment.   .

57. Sobyanin computed his scores by identifying the "most significant" roll-call votes in the Congress of People's Deputies, calculating the percentage of votes on which the deputy voted with the "reformist" position, and subtracting the percentage of votes for the "conservative" position. There is a subjective element to the scores, but they are a useful rough measure of reformism in the legislative setting. For a clear statement of his method, see Alexander Sobyanin, "Political Cleavages among the Russian Deputies," in Thomas F. Remington, ed., *Parliaments in Transition: The New Legislative Politics in the Former USSR and Eastern Europe* (Boulder, Colo.: Westview, 1994), pp. 192–93. Remington correctly compares the device to the ratings of U.S. congressional representatives compiled by interest groups such as Americans for Democratic Action. All actual Sobyanin scores used in the present volume are taken from Michael McFaul and Nikolai Petrov, eds., *Politicheskii al'manakh Rossii 1995* (Moscow: Moscow Carnegie Center, 1995), which is a gold mine of information about post-Soviet Russian politics.

CHAPTER TWO

Institutional Rules and Party Formation

Jerry F. Hough

ONE OF THE most active subfields in political science in recent years has been the study of the relationship of electoral rules and party system. Building on Maurice Duverger's 1954 *Political Parties*, a number of scholars have attempted to refine his analysis by examining an ever-widening number of cases. They have used highly sophisticated statistical methods to try to define the relationship more definitively.[1] The deputies' working group that played the crucial role in drafting the electoral law in Russia was made up of a number of academics who were quite familiar with this literature.

Originally the Supreme Soviet Committee for the Work of Soviets drafted an electoral law that provided for the election of all deputies in single-member districts without a runoff (the so-called Balala draft), but a deputies' working group within the Constitutional Commission produced a rival draft that became the base of the actual electoral law. The members of this group, headed by Viktor Sheinis and including other academics, were convinced that strong parties were vital for a well-functioning democracy in Russia.[2]

The Sheinis group favored for the State Duma a variant of the German electoral law. Half the deputies of the Duma would be chosen by party list through proportional representation of parties that received more than 3 percent of the vote and with half chosen in single-member districts without a runoff. The drafters knew that the party-list election would by definition force the formation of parties, and they knew that the 3 percent rule and the lack of runoffs in the single-member districts created strong incentives for an amalgamation of parties, especially given the connections they built between the two elections.[3]

It eventually was decided to raise the minimum cutoff for party representation to 5 percent. This should have increased the incentive for party amalgamation, but little occurred in 1993. Thirteen parties qualified for the ballot, and several others likely would have qualified if they had not been barred. The nomination of candidates in the districts was haphazard, and there were 6.8 candidates per district despite the lack of a runoff. It was easy to think that the lack of strategic planning on the part of the candidates and parties resulted simply from the extraordinarily brief time between the proclamation of the electoral law, the closing of nominations, and the election itself. Yet in 1995, with essentially the same rules in place for the election of the Duma and two years for the political actors to prepare, the number of parties that qualified for the ballot rose from thirteen to forty-three, and the number of candidates in the districts rose to 12.1.

The development of a stable party system requires a period of learning, especially when the new rules are instituted from above. In Japan, to take an extreme example, there were more than 363 parties in the first election to the Diet in 1946, and the leading party (the Liberals) had but 30 percent of the seats.[4] But in Japan the number of parties steadily fell. In 1949, the Democrats received 44 percent of the vote and 57 percent of the seats, and in 1955 the two leading socialist and two leading conservative parties merged.[5] In the first West German election in 1949, thirteen parties ran, and ten received more than 1 percent of the vote. The CDU/CSU coalition won only 31.0 percent. In 1953 only six parties won seats, only four in 1957, and only three in 1961.[6]

When, however, the second election, under the same set of rules, produces an even more "irrational" result than the first, as in Russia, it is important to reflect on the surprising outcome. When political actors in a nonrevolutionary situation have time to calculate their strategy, they may or may not make the most rational decision, but they are not likely to make a clearly irrational one. Surely Russian politicians were responding in 1993 to incentives beyond those imbedded in the electoral system.

In speaking of an engineered founding election, Timothy Colton points in the right direction. At one level every founding election—certainly any change in a electoral system—is engineered, but the question is who is doing the engineering and for what purpose. The literature on Latin America tends to treat the engineers as representatives of the major elite social groups, whereas the literature on electoral systems tends to focus on the country's major political leaders of different persuasions. In either case, the negotiated result is more or less likely to represent the existing balance of social and political forces in a country.

But sometimes the engineering is done to ensure that the outcome does not accurately reflect the existing balance of social and political forces. The English kings supported overrepresentation of the so-called rotten boroughs in proroyalist southern England. Tsar Nikolai II introduced an electoral system for the Imperial Duma that was meant to deny fair representation to workers and peasants. When the first Duma was too radical, he modified the electoral system to produce a more pliable legislature.[7] After World War II, the conservative and moderate elites of France, Germany, Japan, Austria, and Italy, with the encouragement or even dictation of the United States, introduced electoral systems designed to bar or underrepresent undesired political forces.[8] The Algerian army in 1992 called off one election out of fear that Islamic fundamentalists would win, launched a five-year repression of the fundamentalists in which 60,000 people died, and then introduced an electoral law that outlawed fundamentalist parties.

The phrase "engineered founding election" properly refers to electoral systems introduced to produce an unrepresentative result. In the words of Michael Urban, "Rather than an accord among rivals that signals a common commitment to the rules of the political game, competitive elections in the late Soviet period [and 1993] were conducted within frameworks drafted and imposed by only *one* of the contending parties."[9] The engineering is designed to distort an equitable representation of existing social forces rather than facilitate it. Urban documents how Russia's Choice was formed as a "party of power" from within the administrative structure and took over the final drafting of the institutional rules.[10]

Those in a position to engineer election rules are also in a position to institute other incentives and restraints. If we are to understand the impact of Douglass North's "institutions" (rules, laws, incentive systems), we must go beyond an examination of the formal logic of the electoral system and look at the whole system of incentives and restraints to which political actors respond.[11] This point is crucial in understanding both the evolution of Russia and the relationship of institutions and political life.

Factions and Parties

Most Western countries created national legislatures before they developed mass political parties. The franchise was severely limited at first, and there often was little correspondence between the size of the population in a territory and the number of representatives it was granted. In these circumstances the counterparts to political parties arose more to organize business within the legislature than to contest elections. In his classic 1902 study, Moisei Ostrogorski noted that for a long time parties had no distinguishing life of their own except in parliament.[12] They had little contact with the broad population, and subsequent scholars have called them factions, cliques, parliamentary groups, groups of notables, or the like. The difference in terminology is partly a matter of scholarly taste and partly a reflection of differences from country to country.

For example, in England as late as 1761, Lewis Namier notes, not a single member of parliament was elected because of his party. Rather, the parliament member assumed a party label once in parliament—or was given one by political opponents. In the eighteenth century, there was "no trace of a two-party system, or at all of party in the modern sense; the group which in 1760 went by the name of Tories a generation later is referred to simply as 'independent country gentlemen,' the name of Tory being practically in abeyance."[13]

The United States had the broadest franchise of any country at the end of the eighteenth century, and hence its party system was best developed. Meaningful parties that competed for votes had arisen in some of the colonies, and they continued to function as such on the state level. Nevertheless, there had been no national legislature before 1775, and the members of the Continental Congress during the Articles of Confederation were not chosen in competitive elections that stimulated party formation. The chief specialist on political parties during the era of the Articles of Confederation was able to write a 400-page book on the subject without mentioning any parties except those on the state level.[14]

The two principal authors of *The Federalist Papers* were Alexander Hamilton and James Madison. Madison was the first Speaker of the House of Representatives, and his friend Thomas Jefferson had been secretary of state in Washington's cabinet (where Hamilton served as secretary of treasury). From 1789 to 1793, the supporters of Hamilton and those of Jefferson and Madison began taking opposing positions within the Congress. In 1793, as they looked forward to Washington's retirement and to the struggle to succeed him, they chose foreign policy (the orientation toward England and France) as the symbolic emotional issue on which to differentiate themselves into formal parties (the Federalists and Republicans) instead of a domestic issue. This suggested that they were thinking of a mass audience. In the process, the parties became more cohesive within the Congress.[15]

Nevertheless, senators and sometimes presidential electors were selected by the state legislatures, and presidential candidates were nominated by a congressional caucus until 1824.[16] The Federalists disappeared after 1812, and the selection of James Monroe of Virginia as president in 1816 and John Quincy Adams of Massachusetts as secretary of state (at that time the post of the heir apparent) meant that the country was largely functioning as a nonparty system until the late 1820s.

As Duverger argues, true parties classically were formed when the suffrage was extended. The parliamentary groups were transformed into parties as their leaders responded to the need for mass support in a broad electorate:

> The more the right to vote is extended and multiplied, the more necessary it becomes to organize the electors by means of committees capable of making the candidates known and of canalizing the votes in their direction. The rise of parties is thus bound up with the rise of parliamentary groups and electoral committees. . . . The general mechanism of this genesis is simple. First there is the creation of parliamentary groups, then the appearance of electoral committees, and finally the establishment of a permanent connection between these two elements.[17]

In the United States, male suffrage was increased substantially in the 1810s and again in the 1820s, when the election of the president was democratized.[18] Martin Van Buren created a real party to help elect Andrew Jackson in 1828, and conservatives soon followed with the Whig party. Political scientists called the party system that arose "the second-party system," but in a real sense it was the first system.[19]

The same pattern was found in other countries. Modern parties began developing in England after the Reform Act of 1832.[20] The Japanese legislature after 1890 featured an intense struggle between two major groups of legislators, but they began to develop grassroots organizations only in the 1920s and the 1930s, as universal suffrage was introduced in 1925. The process was cut short by a military coup.[21] In Germany a social democratic party did not arise within the Prussian legislature, with its very limited suffrage, but was created when Bismarck introduced mass male suffrage in the German Reichstag.[22]

Once universal suffrage was established, however, it was natural for new parties to be created from outside the parliament by trade unions, churches, philosophical societies (or intellectuals), secret societies, and in a few cases businesses and banks. "Creation outside parliament becomes the rule and creation within parliament becomes the exception," Duverger observes, with the formation of social democratic parties by the trade unions the classic example. Nevertheless, Duverger warns,

> Exception must be made of countries new to democracy, that is to say, countries where political assemblies and universal suffrage have scarcely begun to function properly: Here the development of parties conforms to the [parliamentary creation pattern]. This does not contradict the preceding affirmation—on the contrary it emphasizes its truth by showing that the electoral and parliamentary creation of parties corresponds to a certain phase of democratic evolution, that of the progressive establishment of universal suffrage. . . . In other words, the first type described corresponds to the creation of political parties in a country where no system of organized parties yet exists. As soon as such a system is at work, the second type of creation becomes the more usual.[23]

In the classic pattern in Asia and Africa, a dominant single party was formed that included all elements of those in the anticolonial movement. (In essence this is a formal version of the pattern of the early United States.) Because all of the leaders of the dominant party came out of the legislature, it was natural for the leaders of any new parties to come out of it as well. However, the literature of party formation in Asia and Africa in the 1960s emphasized the personalistic character of parties, and the literature twenty-five years later was similar in its conclusions: "It is perhaps misleading to say that every party needs a leader when often the leader precedes the party. . . . Even if they emerge independently, Third World political parties very frequently come to be dominated by a single leader who in turn tends to determine who is to be recruited into the 'high command.'"[24]

Factions in the Russian Congress of People's Deputies

As in so many of the democracies that predated it, meaningful political parties developed in Russia after the formation of the legislature rather than before it. Activists formed what they called "parties" from 1989 on, but the vast majority were little more than a collection of friends.[25] The editors of one set of booklets about "parties, associations, unions, and clubs" in 1991 counted 457 of them in the introduction; at the end of the volume the editors added 107 more that had been founded or formed by the time the volume was put together.[26] Another guide devoted to more serious political parties and organizations discovered "only" 207 of them.[27]

But the sheer number of parties attested to their unimportance. By far the best sense of these parties is conveyed in the interviews with their leaders and the accompanying analysis in Michael McFaul and Sergei Markov's *The Troubled Birth of Russian Democracy: Parties, Personalities, and Programs*, published in 1993.[28] This book is even more valuable in retrospect because it deals with a carefully selected group of parties and movements "that were the most prominent in Russian politics in 1991." The book published interviews with fifteen of the party leaders and included the names of another thirty-two leaders whose interviews were excluded for space considerations. The politicians were, in fact, well chosen. Vladimir Zhirinovskii was one of them, but his party was the only one of the twelve to be on the Duma ballot two years later and one of two to be on the forty-three-party ballot four years later. Only five of the forty-seven interviewees were elected to the Duma in December 1993. The interviews give an excellent sense of the reasons that the parties were unsuccessful—the personal rivalries and suspicion, the lack of a collective sense, the neglect of (or even scorn for) organizational work.

The election to the USSR Congress of People's Deputies took place in 1989, when the formation of competing parties or factions within the Communist party was still prohibited. The Communist party did not officially nominate candidates, but in the first round the nomination process remained under the control of the party in most areas through district registration committees. In the city of Moscow, however, Boris Yeltsin succeeded in being nominated in the large national territorial district embracing all of Moscow.[29]

A radical Interregional Group of some 200 deputies led by Andrei Sakharov and Yeltsin had been grudgingly tolerated in the USSR Congress, but neither formal parties nor factions were permitted to form until the end of 1990—after they had formed in the Russian Congress. The Interregional Group served as a vocal opposition, but it never tried to form a real party in the country. It did not even nominate or support candidates for the 1990 Russian election.[30]

The district committee control was largely ended in the election to the Russian Congress of People's Deputies in March 1990, and the nomination process was relatively open. The number of candidates per district in Russia rose from 1.9 in 1989 to 6.3 in 1990. However, the constitutional prohibition against competing parties was ended only after nominations to the Russian Congress closed and the Communist party again did not nominate candidates.[31]

Loose groupings did, however, form during the 1990 campaign. The two most prominent were the Russian Patriotic Bloc, composed of right-wing nationalists; and Democratic Russia, in conjunction with Election-90, which supported the establishment of democracy and a market economy.[32] They informally called themselves the "patriots" and the "democrats."[33] The Patriotic Bloc had no success, but Democratic Russia was said by February 20 to be supporting more than 5,000 candidates for the Russian Congress and local soviets.[34] "Support" really meant candidates who generally associated themselves with the movement.

The rules in effect for the 1990 Russian congressional election required majority support for victory in the first round. If only one or two candidates had been nominated and no one received a majority, then the election would have had to be held again, with new nominations. (This was the source of so many spectacular defeats of candidates who ran unopposed in the 1989 USSR congressional election.) If three or more candidates were running, then a runoff was held, with only a plurality required in the second stage. The defeats of 1989 surely helped persuade the leaders to permit a freer nomination process in the 1990 Russian Congress, and the nomination of candidates was usually quite personalistic. The requirement of a runoff meant that like-minded candidates often could run in the first round and use it as a kind of primary.

Runoffs were required in 913 districts,[35] and informal, temporary parties or at least groupings tended to form in the period before the second round to support the more congenial of the two runoff candidates. The informal groups associated with Democratic Russia played a more important role at this stage, and after the election, a group of these deputies met at the invitation of Mikhail Bocharov, a close associate of Yeltsin, to form a Democratic Russia "association of deputies" to prepare for the forthcoming Congress.

In reality, Democratic Russia was a classic legislative embryonic party whose primary purpose was to elect Yeltsin as chair of the Supreme Soviet and to enact its radical program. Two hundred deputies attended its opening meeting, but Bocharov claimed that 370 deputies supported the association.[36] When the first organizational meeting of deputies was held on March 30, again only 215 deputies appeared,[37] but Bocharov proved to be right about the size of Democratic Russia's consistent voting support at the first Congress.

Instead of denouncing Democratic Russia as an improper faction, the conservatives formed another large group, Communists of Russia, which was said to embrace 355 deputies. Communists of Russia was misnamed, because nearly 90 percent of all deputies were members of the Communist party at the time of the election, including three-quarters of the 400 most radical deputies supporting Democratic Russia.[38] In practice, Communists of Russia included the more conservative deputies, but these were both the relative conservatives who still supported Gorbachev in 1990 and the hard-core conservatives who opposed him.

The rules on procedure proposed before the opening of the First Congress of the Russian Congress officially sanctioned organized political groups. Any group of fifty deputies could form a "faction" (*fraktsiya*) and register it formally, and each deputy could join up to five factions. Two weeks after it opened, the Congress had thirty-two such factions, of a territorial, occupational, or ideological type.

The Russian Congress of People's Deputies comprised more than 1,000 deputies, and the struggle of deputies to gain access to the microphone resulted in utter chaos. A sequence of steps ensued that provides a casebook example of the reasons factions or parties are needed to organize the work of a legislature. When speakers were chosen on the basis of when they submitted their requests to speak, hundreds submitted requests before the debate really began. When regions were allowed to propose speakers, the number of regions was excessive, and their top officials selected themselves and gave speeches about their regions unrelated to the issues. Only the issue-oriented factions proved an effective mechanism to serve the function of organizing debate. The Congress leadership began giving the leaders of those factions a key role in selecting congressional speakers and representatives to ad hoc "reconciliation commissions" formed to resolve conflicts at the Congress.

Giving each faction the right to nominate speakers and to be represented on the reconciliation commissions did, however, have at least one undesired consequence. Deputies could belong to five factions, so factions proliferated. At the Fourth Congress in May 1991, Deputy Gennadii Sayenko charged that this is precisely what had happened. He accused both Communists of Russia and Democratic Russia of spinning off satellite groups in order to multiply their membership on the reconciliation commissions. The number of group members, he reported, exceeded the number of deputies. Saenko proposed that the Congress distinguish between deputy groups and factions, that only the latter be allowed on the reconciliation committees, and that each deputy be permitted to join only one faction.[39] This proposal was accepted and put into place. Several occupational groups (the industrialists, agrarians, and the military) transformed themselves into issue groups, and the occupational and territorial factions essentially disappeared.

The voting in the first four Congresses suggested that a two-party system—or perhaps a three-party system—might be forming. Although the organizers of Democratic Russia and Communists of Russia both proclaimed that their groups were not parties, they essentially functioned as legislative parties. They nominated candidates, they mobilized deputies into common voting behavior, and they took the lead in organizing the agenda. In early 1991 a cochair of the Communists of Russia could still insist that the thirty-two different groups in parliament were really on two sides of a barricade.[40] A sophisticated factor analysis by Western scholars found a similar bipolarization in this period.[41] It was easy to believe that Democratic Russia and the Communists of Russia would evolve into two large umbrella parties.

The deputies in the middle were contemptuously called the "bog" by those on either side, but their roll-call voting on a series of issues gave the impression of consistency. It was also easy to imagine the "bog" deputies forming a third, centrist party. Indeed, many enlisted in a broad centrist coalition known as Civic Union that was formed in June 1992.

Yet when the role of factions was institutionalized within the legislative process of the Congress during its last two years, the "party system" that emerged consistently contained thirteen to fourteen factions. As table 2-1 indicates, the pattern of their membership was suspicious. Except for the Agrarian Union, the number of deputies in each faction was close to fifty. In addition, the average ideological rating scores of the factions did not spread evenly over the spectrum but were bunched into five, or probably four, groups that seemed like natural parties. Using a scale in which 1 was an extreme radical and 8 an extreme conservative, we find that three radical factions (Agreement for Progress, Democratic Russia, Radical Democrats) had an almost identical average score of about 1.35, five (Left Center, Motherland, Workers' Union, Change, Free Russia) had a score of about 3 (moderate radical), two (Russia and Industrial Union) about 5.2 (center-right), two (Agrarian Union and Sovereignty and Equality) at about 5.8 (moderate conservative), and two (Fatherland and Communists of Russia) were quite conservative with scores of near 7. Indeed, the center-right and moderate conservative factions should probably be combined in terms of ideological ratings.

This is clearly a case in which the rules of the legislature had a decisive impact on the structure of the factions. The rules continued to put the minimum size of a faction at fifty, and the factions both controlled access to the

Table 2-1. *Size of Membership and Average Ideological Rating, Russian Congress of People's Deputies, June 1993*

Name of faction	Number of members	Rating score
Agreement for Progress	54	1.33
Democratic Russia	47	1.36
Radical Democrats	47	1.36
Left Center	61	2.72
Motherland	52	3.10
Workers' Union	49	3.10
Change	52	3.12
Free Russia	53	3.19
Industrial Union	54	5.17
Russia	53	5.26
Sovereignty and Equality	46	5.70
Agrarian Union	128	5.84
Fatherland	49	6.82
Communists of Russia	66	7.17

Source: The membership in the factions was calculated from the computerized Supreme Soviet directory of Congress deputies. The rating score was computed from the roll-call rating calculated by Aleksandr Sobyanin for deputies at the First Congress. Ratings represent: 1, extreme radical; 2, radical; 3, moderate radical; 4, left center; 5, right center; 6, moderate conservative; 7, conservative; and 8, extreme conservative.

floor and were represented equally in the "reconciliation" commissions in which the key work of the Congress took place. The Agrarian Union deputies were disproportionately farm managers with little interest in politics and low attendance in Congress, but in other cases deputies rearranged themselves to give their point of view or their interests maximum access to congressional politics.

Whatever the reasons—and the fact that factions arose only in response to legislative rules must have been one of them—the factions had little meaningful connection with party-like bodies at other territorial levels. Even the Communist party made no effort to develop ties between its parliamentary groups and the party organs at various levels. The founding Congress of the Russian Communist party began just as the first Congress of People's Deputies ended, but the leaders of Communists of Russia were not elected to the party Central Committee. There seemed to be little interaction between, for example, the Central Committee secretary for agrarian policy and the relatively conservative Agrarian Union faction in the Congress. There was little contact between the Communist faction in the USSR Congress and the Communists of Russia in the Russian Congress.

As a consequence, the factions did not develop name recognition among a broad public. The nationwide sample of 3,800 respondents reported by Colton was supplemented by random preelection surveys of 1,000 respondents in thirty-four regions (oblasts and krais) and sixteen former autonomous republics.[42] Interviewers were instructed to do one-third of the interviews each week of the three-week survey and to keep the mixture of urban and rural respondents more or less even each week. This provided an average of 1,700 respondents for each day of the campaign and the possibility of doing a day-by-day study of the campaign on a detailed level. The amalgamated data set from the thirty-four oblasts was not a scientific random sample, but the biases within it tended to cancel out, and in practice the marginal results on each question were usually only a few percentage points different from the random sample.[43]

Table 2-2 provides an analysis from this broader data set, and it shows how many respondents claimed to know of the various parties both at the beginning and the end of the campaign. Zhirinovskii and his Liberal Democrats had been known since his run for the presidency in 1991, and the name recognition for the new party, Russia's Choice, testifies to the power of television. However, Civic Union and the Agrarian parties were based on two of the most prominent legislative groups and were continually discussed in the central newspapers in 1992 and 1993. Their existence clearly had not registered on the broader population even a week into the campaign. It seems laughable that only slightly more than 60 percent of respondents could say they had heard of the Communist party and that fewer than half had an opinion about it, but, in fact, there were several Communist parties and a Communists of Russia faction in the Congress. It was the strategy of Russia's Choice and its allies to lump all Communists together and ascribe the views of the most extreme to Zyuganov's Russian Communist party. Even a moderately well-informed citizen might confess to confusion in 1993, and one would guess that the lack of real knowledge was even greater than table 2-2 indicates.

The 1993 Electoral Law and the Logic of Party Formation

The Sheinis deputy group was sympathetic to the argument that the electoral law should discriminate against small, extremist parties and that a party system with a few broad parties was most conducive to political stability. Historically this viewpoint has led to support for elections of legislators in single-member districts without a runoff (the so-called first-past-the-post system). The major alternative to this system—proportional representation—almost invariably produces a multiparty system, and district

Table 2-2. *Survey of Familiarity with Political Parties in the Russian Election, November 18–20, 1993–December 7–11, 1993*
Percent

| | November 18–20 | | December 7–11 | | |
| | Know party | Opinion on it | Know party | Opinion on it | Final party vote |
Name of party					
KEDR–Ecology	27.0	16.2	42.7	27.8	0.76
Future of Russia	29.4	17.6	46.3	27.4	1.25
Dignity and Compassion	32.6	21.8	42.3	26.2	0.70
Women of Russia	46.5	34.6	64.5	50.3	8.13
Civic Union	43.4	28.1	57.3	37.4	1.93
Agrarian	46.7	32.1	58.0	41.0	8.00
Yabloko	56.6	41.0	68.5	50.4	7.86
RDDR–Sobchak	59.4	46.1	70.3	52.0	4.08
Communists	61.2	47.2	70.3	55.0	12.40
PRES–Shakhrai	62.1	43.6	72.0	53.2	6.73
Democratic party	62.6	44.3	73.3	54.4	5.52
Liberal Democrat	73.2	60.3	81.8	68.4	22.92
Russia's Choice	74.4	60.5	83.2	68.8	15.51

Source: National election survey.
Note: N = 33,869.

elections with a runoff also create no incentive for parties to coalesce before the second round.

By contrast, if legislators are elected in single-member districts by plurality vote, then either side of the spectrum can usually win by coalescing to support a single candidate if the other side is represented by a number of candidates. The logical outcome is for each side to coalesce and a two-party system to emerge. If a third party were to be formed, those who voted for it would generally reduce the vote of the major party closest to their views and allow the perceived worst alternative to win. Proponents of single-member districts argued that the requirements of building a coalition before the election demand moderation and skills of cooperation that would contribute to stability after the election.[44]

The argument that single-member districts with plurality elections always lead to two-party systems was not airtight. There is no inherent reason why the two parties in one district have to be the same as the two parties in another district; this in fact has happened often in Canada.[45] In practice, there were a number of embarrassing exceptions—for example, the long survival of the Liberal party (now the Liberal-Democratic party) in Great Britain.[46] And even in the United States, a third party obtained at least 5 percent of the popular vote in six of the presidential elections in the twentieth century, and another third party carried four states in another election.

The worst deviations from theory have occurred in the early stages of democratization. Two political parties dominated the American political system from the early 1830s to the early 1850s, but this scarcely ensured political stability. The major historian of the early Democratic party, Roy Nichols, characterized "the disorganized state of American politics at that particular time" in the early 1850s as a key factor in the mistakes that led to Civil War:

> Politics, it can be seen, were thus in such confusion that a maximum number of politicos were disturbed and disoriented by it. An unusual number were uncertain of their proper roles and were confusedly groping for new alignments which would insure some greater security and more certain prospect of victory. Under such circumstances, any legislation which offered opportunity for political controversy and advantage would be seized upon. For this purpose the Nebraska question was ideal.[47]

Nichols saw the phenomenon as part of a broader pattern that covered an entire century: "In the United States in the 19th century there were such periods of disintegration and reintegration in politics every twenty years or thereabouts just as there were financial panics."

It would scarcely be reassuring to Russians to be told that single-member districts might produce a stable party system after some decades—even a century—of turmoil. In the short run, the drafters of the Russian electoral law were afraid that an electoral system with districts alone, whether with a plurality or a majority required for victory, would simply lead to the personalistic nominations and elections found in 1990 and a new legislature that had no more than factions:

> Elections should produce a parliament with political factions which will not be clubs of deputies with similar interests and inclinations, as at the present, but organized representation of politically organized social forces which rest on support outside parliament. The proponents of the district system say that we still don't have nationwide political parties which deserve the name. But until we conduct elections at least partially on a party basis, parties will not appear.[48]

In the months before the dissolution of the Congress, the major political forces in Moscow moved toward agreement on a modification of the German electoral system in which half of the deputies would be elected by proportional representation from party lists and half in districts. The use of proportional representation based on party lists would, by definition, require parties to be formed, and a rule giving representation only to parties that received a minimum of 5 percent of the vote would, it was believed, discourage small parties. The members of the working group understood that party formation was a gradual process, but they attempted to encourage partial amalgamation by including among acceptable electoral units not only parties and political units but also blocs.

The formation of alliances before the election was further encouraged by the abolition of the runoff in the single-member district. In 1990 an average of 7.3 candidates had been nominated in each district, but this meant only that the first round of the election served as a kind of primary among the candidates. The two weeks between the first and the second round gave the political forces of the region the opportunity to gather around the person in the runoff closer to their own points of view. If seven candidates ran in a district election without a runoff, the winner theoretically might win with fewer than 20 percent of the vote and often might win with fewer than 30 percent. In fact, with an average of 6.8 candidates in each Duma district in 1993, the average winner received 29 percent of the vote. If parties with similar views split the vote on their part of the political spectrum in the district, they risked giving the opposition an unearned victory.

There were two major differences between the Russian electoral law and the West German system that seemingly strengthened the incentives for large parties to form. First, in Germany, separate party lists were formed in each *Land* (province), and hence the election in form at least was regional in character. It was feared that this rule in Russia would produce regional nationalist parties in the non-Russian areas of Russia. In Russia, the party list could be nationwide and, as Colton points out, this was the case in seven out of thirteen cases. Even in the party with the most regionalized list, Russia's Choice, nineteen of the leaders were on the national list and thus guaranteed of election if the party received as much as 9 percent of the vote.

Second, seats that a German party earns in districts are subtracted from the those received on the party-list vote in a region, and hence the German system is close to pure proportional representation. As Max Kaase puts, the opportunity to elect local representatives does little more than reduce the usual impersonality of the party-list voting and create the opportunity for more "personalized proportional representation."[49]

In Russia, by contrast, deputies elected in the districts were added to those elected by party list. More important, a party's candidates could be placed simultaneously on its party list and nominated in the districts. A person who was high enough on a party list to be elected by proportional representation and who also won in a district received the latter mandate. The next lowest person on the party list was moved up and declared elected. Thus Vladimir Zhirinovskii naturally headed the party list of the Liberal Democratic party, but he was also elected in the Shchelkovo district of Moscow oblast and hence is not on the list of LDPR deputies elected by proportional representation. This normally would have meant that the person originally number sixty on the party list was included in the fifty-nine deputies elected, but because he too was elected in a district, number sixty-one on the list automatically became a deputy. This rule created a powerful reason for a party to nominate all the strong candidates on its list as candidates in the districts as well. This in turn created powerful incentives to form local branches that could nominate and support candidates.

There were a number of reasons that this system was introduced. As already noted, the academics feared that the experience in the 1989 and 1990 elections would make *them* the founding elections in legitimating nonparty elections with personalistic nominations and campaigning—a reasonable fear, as the 1993 and 1995 Duma elections were to show. Academics wanted to ensure the creation of parties, but they believed the argument in the traditional Western literature that proportional representation leads to a multiplicity of parties and a fragmentation of the political system.

Those in power found the proposal of the academics congenial for their own reason. Yeltsin, like Charles de Gaulle before him, wanted to rule above parties and was suspicious of them. His closest adviser, Gennadii Burbulis, frequently proposed that he create a presidential party, but Yeltsin always resisted. In an interview, Burbulis said that Yeltsin feared a party would limit him, that it would commit him to a policy position and limit his freedom of action.

However, Yeltsin was not particularly interested in the character of the party system within the Duma. What mattered to him was that the Duma have little power vis-à-vis the president and that the most prominent opposition within it be illegitimate. The ideal outcome for him was that which actually occurred—a victory for a political party that raised the specter of a new Hitler abroad but whose members were quite corrupt and willing to be bought off to support the new constitution and the government on key measures. It is not yet clear if this was fortuitous for Yeltsin or whether he had a hand in the granting of television time and the mysterious financing for Vladimir Zhirinovskii and the Liberal Democrats (to be discussed in chapter 6) and that he hoped it would end up as it did. I assume the latter, because Yeltsin has always been extremely focused in the struggle for power and has had unparalleled political instincts. However, I have seen no evidence to support this assumption.

But whatever Yeltsin was thinking about the Duma, he clearly favored another feature of the German electoral system: the selection of the second house of the legislature by the regional governments. In Germany, the members of the Bundesrat, like the U.S. Senate before1913 (Seventeenth Amendment to the U.S. Constitution) are elected by the regional legislature (in reality by the cabinet elected by the regional legislature).

The 1993 constitution gave the Federation Council exclusive control over most key issues for the president—confirmation of decrees on martial law or state of emergency, establishment of the date for presidential elections, impeachment, confirmation of members of the constitutional court, and selection and removal of the procurator general. If the president controlled the Federation Council, he had enormous power. Because a presidential veto could be overridden only by a two-thirds vote of both houses and because the president had broad power to issue decrees in case of legislative deadlock, presidential control over one-third of the Federation Council deputies would allow him to block almost any legislative action.[50]

For anyone familiar with the old communist system, such a Federation Council would be very much like the plenary session of the Central Committee of the Communist party. In what Robert Daniels called the "circular flow of power,"[51] the general secretary was elected and removable by the Central Committee. The Central Committee was elected at the party congress, whose delegates were selected in regional conferences under the control of the regional party secretaries. Because the general secretary had the key role in selecting and removing regional party secretaries, the latter not surprisingly became the base of support of the general secretary, even if (like regional secretaries in 1981 such as Mikhail Gorbachev, Yeltsin, and Eduard Shevardnadze) they disapproved of his policy. The Yeltsin forces must have hoped that the heads of administration would serve a similar role, and Yeltsin persistently opposed the election of local governors. Even when they began to be elected, the regions were denied any independent taxing ability, and hence their governors remained dependent on the central government.

If the chief executives in the regions (*glava administratsii,* or head of administration) continued to be appointed from above rather than elected, they would be especially vulnerable to presidential power and Yeltsin would have a total veto on any legislative action that required approval of the Federation Council. If Yeltsin approved an electoral system for the State Duma that seemed modeled on the German system, it would be easier for him to insist on the German model for the upper house as well.

Leading politicians in Russia also found the modified German system congenial. The leaders of the legislature, as well as the nonlegislative Moscow political leaders, were afraid that they would not win a district election, especially because a decline in the number of districts from 900 to 225 meant that their old district would be amalgamated with others and the advantage of incumbency would be reduced. With 225 Duma seats to be distributed by proportional representation, any party that reached the required 5 percent minimum vote would receive at least eleven seats in the Duma. Political leaders who could place themselves among the top eleven spots on the party list could guarantee themselves a seat in the parliament. The drafters privately acknowledged that one major purpose of enacting the German system was to protect "the most valuable members" of the parties from electoral defeat in the districts.

By contrast, regional political leaders who might be placed low on party lists by their Moscow leaders were reassured that they would have a good chance in district elections—or at least that the winner would be responsive to local influences. Indeed, the fact that a person on a party list could also run in a district gave an important politician two shots to be elected. Thus the deputy mayor (deputy premier) of Moscow, Aleksandr R. Braginskii, was number six on the list of the failed Russian Movement for Democratic Reform (RDDR) but was still elected in a Moscow district.

When the nomination and election process became extremely hurried after the dissolution of the Congress, many in the working group proposed returning to the run-off system for the 1993 election in order to ensure voters a meaningful choice. However, the final drafting of the election decree was taken over by the government, and it retained the original rule. The government analysts apparently were quite convinced that Russia's Choice would receive between a quarter and a third of the votes and thought that this would give it a plurality in the first round. They thought it might have more difficulty in a runoff when opposition voters could coalesce around an opposition candidate.

The Party System in Place

Political parties did, of course, form to run in the election. The election results demonstrated that the leading politicians were justified in their fears that they would not survive an electoral system based on districts alone. Of the 112 persons high enough on the Agrarian, Communist, and LDPR party lists to be elected under pure proportional representation, fifty-seven also ran as candidates in the single-member districts. Only seven of them won.

The dynamics of an election with districts alone would have been different, all the more so because districts would have been half the size and more homogeneous in character. However, an extremely high percentage of the persons elected to the Duma through the party lists—surely between 175 and 200 of them—would not have been elected deputies without the new system.[52]

Nevertheless, as Colton's analysis in chapter 1 shows, the other expected results of the electoral system largely failed to materialize. First, instead of merging into larger parties and blocs before the election, thirty-five parties made a serious effort to gain enough signatures to be placed on the ballot,[53] and many parties were formed on the eve of the election. A number of others would have made the attempt if they and their leaders had not been outlawed because of their participation in the October bloodshed in the crisis at the White House. Twenty-one parties came close enough to meeting the requirements to claim to have succeeded, and the electoral commission certified thirteen of them.

Second, the pattern of party formation suggested by Duverger failed to develop. Instead of legislative factions' reaching out to form local branches of a mass party, the legislative factions listed in table 2-1 largely disappeared, as did the earlier factions that had formed in the Congress in 1990. Only three of the fourteen factions formed the base of a 1993 party, even if Civic Union—a coalition of centrist factions—is considered a faction. Even this figure is an exaggeration, because the Communist party of Russia was largely unconnected with the Communists of Russia faction. Out of the first fifty persons on the Communist party list, only six had been Congress deputies. The Agrarian party seemed closest to the Agrarian Union faction, but only nine of its twenty-one deputies elected by party list were former deputies.

The lack of correspondence between Congress factions and the parties in the 1993 election was not a simple matter of names being changed. The 225 deputies elected by party lists included only 35 former Russian deputies, and 40 percent of them had moved into the executive by the summer of 1993. Most of the parties that were successful were associated with prominent politicians outside the legislature who had become well known through television, frequently as a result of their high office in the executive.

Third, the party nomination process in the districts had little relationship to expectations and can only be described as chaotic. Colton reports (see chapter 1) that 96 percent of the candidates who ran with party endorsement in the districts were also on the party list of that party. The reverse, however, was not the case. At the beginning of the campaign, even Russia's Choice endorsed a candidate in only 47 percent of the districts, Yabloko in 33 percent, Civic Union and Agrarian party in 31 percent, Party of Unity and Accord (PRES) in 30 percent, the Democratic party in 27 percent, the Liberal Democrats in 26 percent, and the RDDR and the Communists in 25 percent. The newer parties had far fewer candidates in the districts.

Of course, to a large extent, the failure of the Russian experience in 1993 to correspond to Duverger's predictions or to the expectations of the legislative working group can be explained by the unexpected timing of the election and the small amount of time in which parties had to be formed and organized. Parties could form blocs on the national level easily enough, but there was not enough time for the blocs to agree beyond this and nominate a single candidate in the districts. Without the latter, parties should have formed as if it were a system with straight proportional representation. There was little incentive other than the 5 percent minimum to encourage amalgamation of parties. Those who formed RDDR, the party of the older democrats, miscalculated their chances to reach the minimum, but otherwise Russia's Choice was wrong to complain about the creation of PRES and Yabloko. They increased the democratic vote rather than decreased it.

Although a shortage of time can explain the 1993 election, it cannot explain the behavior of the parties in the Duma or party formation in the 1995 election. Rules were established in the Duma to ensure that party factions had a more important role than in the Supreme Soviet. Factions had played a crucial role in the Congress, but they had been relatively unimportant in the Supreme Soviet. The crucial body in the Supreme Soviet had been the Presidium, which was composed primarily of the committee chairs. In the Duma, by contrast, the factional leaders were given a vote in the leading organ of the legislature, the Council of the Duma, and the committee chair attended without a vote.

Any party that won 5 percent of the national vote could form a faction, and so could any group of thirty-five deputies. The legislative rules were more powerful than the electoral rules for the 1995 election in shaping faction formation. At the beginning of the Duma, before the thirty-five minimum was established, eleven factions formed: Russia's Choice (seventy-five), the radical 12th of December (twenty-five), PRES (thirty),

Table 2-3. *Turnover of Party-List Deputies to the Second Duma (1995)*
Who Served in the First Duma (1993)

Party or faction	Deputies elected in 1995	1995 deputies elected to 1993 Duma	1995 deputies elected in by-elections, 1993–95
Communist	99	16	3
Liberal Democratic	50	26	0
Our Home Is Russia	45	4	0
Yabloko	31	13	2

Source: Author's calculations based on *A Directory of Members of the Russian Parliament, January 1996* (London: BBC Monitoring, 1996).

Yabloko (twenty-seven), Women (twenty-three), Democratic (fifteen), the moderate conservative New Regional Policy (sixty-six), the nationalist Russia's Path (fifteen), Agrarian (fifty-five), Communists (forty-five), and Liberal Democrats (sixty-four).

The 1995 Duma election was a shock for any who took electoral rules seriously. Instead of thirteen parties on the ballot in 1993, there were forty-three in 1995. Not one of the new factions in the Duma became the base for a new party, and with the exception of the Communists and the Green party KEDR (which rose from .8 of 1 percent to 1.4 percent), every 1993 party suffered a major decline in 1995, many of them a catastrophic decline (Agrarian party from 7.9 percent to 3.8 percent; the Liberal Democratic party from 22.9 percent to 11.2 percent; PRES from 6.8 percent to .4 of 1 percent; Russia's Choice from 15.5 percent to 3.9 percent; Women of Russia from 8.1 percent to 4.6 percent; Yabloko from 7.9 percent to 6.9 percent).

An examination of the names of the deputies elected in 1995 shows virtually as much turnover as between the Congress and the First Duma. This was only in part a result of the failure of some of the old parties to receive 5 percent of the vote, for the successful parties had relatively few candidates at the top of their list, especially if the Liberal Democrats are excluded. (See table 2-3 for a breakdown of turnovers during this period.)

The District Elections

All deputies of the Russian Congress had been elected as part-time legislators, but a quarter of them were to work full time as Supreme Soviet deputies. Gorbachev originally had thought of Supreme Soviet work as temporary one-year service, but the experience of the USSR Congress had shown this to be unrealistic. Forty percent of the original USSR Supreme Soviet deputies wanted to leave that body by January 1991,[54] and many part-time deputies had no desire to leave their job for a year to serve in Congress. Moreover, if the Supreme Soviet was to be a competent legislature, it was precisely the deputies who were interested in legislative work and had gained experience in it who should *not* be rotated out.

The Russian Constitution Commission took cognizance of the problem by speaking simply of "rotation" without specifying any required number of terms. In practice, anyone who wanted to be a full-time, paid legislator soon was allowed to do so in committee work if not as a Supreme Soviet deputy with voting rights. According to the Supreme Soviet computer directory of Congress deputies, 34 percent of the original Congress deputies were working full time in the legislature in June 1992, and 36 percent in June 1993.

It is not surprising that those who remained part-time deputies in the summer of 1993 were unlikely to seek election to a full-time Duma, but many full-time legislators shared the same doubts. In the spring of 1991, when Colton surveyed 307 deputies who were either Supreme Soviet deputies or active participants in committee work, he found that a large number even of these "professional" legislators did not see themselves in these terms. Only 21 percent said that they intended to run in the next election, 29 percent denied such an intention, and 47 percent said they would decide later.[55]

In fact, only 80 of the 869 former deputies from Congress territorial districts ran in June 1993. In addition, two deputies elected in June 1990 who had left the Congress and twenty-one former deputies from the 168 national-territorial districts also ran as candidates in Duma single-member districts. Some of them ran against each other, and only 71 of the 219 districts had at least one deputy from a territorial district among its candidates; another 15 had a former deputy from a national-territorial district.[56]

As a consequence, the Duma deputies elected from single-member districts were certain to include many new faces, but it was still a surprise to find only 36 deputies from the Russian Congress among the 219 new Duma deputies elected in the districts.

As already indicated, the electoral law created powerful incentives for parties to nominate their strongest candidates in the district and the parties to form alliances to reduce the number of candidates in the district elections. Except for a few strategic withdrawals in the last days of the cam-

Table 2-4. *Attitudes toward Reform among Deputies Elected on Party Lists and in Districts*

Percent

	Proreform	Generally proreform	Antireform	Strongly antireform
Deputies elected by party list	28.1	7.7	10.4	53.8
Deputies elected in districts	34.4	14.2	15.1	36.2

Source: Calculated from "Golosovaniia deputatov Gosudarstvennoi Dumy, 11 ianvaria–11 fevralia 1944 goda," pp. 4–9.

paign, neither of these expectations were met. An average of 7.2 percent of the candidates were nominated in each district, and this fell to 6.8 candidates by the time of the election. Nearly 55 percent of these candidates ran as independents (that is, officially were nominated by "groups of eligible voters"). The independents provided 62 percent of the deputies elected.

Zhirinovskii's Liberal Democrats received fifty-nine seats in the Duma on the basis of its vote in the party-list portion of the election and only five seats in the districts, and the radicals seem to have done better in the districts. These facts led to considerable criticism of the electoral system that had been introduced and to the argument that an all-district system would have produced a more representative legislature or at least one more supportive of the Yeltsin position.

The deputy ratings produced by Aleksandr Sobyanin and his colleagues suggest that the scores of deputies elected in the districts were on average less conservative than the deputies elected by party list. On an index in which 0 was the most conservative score and 200 the most radical, the deputies elected on the party list averaged 92.8 and those in the districts 102.0 in their voting in the first month of the Duma.[57]

Using undefined criteria, Sobyanin divided the deputies into four groups: *proreform* (150 to 200 on the index), *generally proreform* (100 to 149), *antireform* (50 to 99), and *strongly antireform* (0 to 49). Using this scale, 139 deputies can be classified as proreform, 49 as generally proreform, 56 as antireform, and 200 as strongly antireform—that is, 188 on the reform side and 256 conservatives. As table 2-4 shows, those elected by party list included an especially large number of the strongly antireform deputies.

Indeed, it was often argued that the democratic forces would have elected even more deputies in the districts had not multiple democratic candidates split the vote. The case most often cited was District 210 in St. Petersburg, where a conservative television personality, Aleksandr Nevzorov, won with 28.6 percent of the vote and a democrat came in second with 27.1 percent, with three other democratic candidates cutting into his vote. It is easy to find other such examples—for example, in Saratov where a Liberal Democrat won when two other reform candidates split the vote.

We should, however, be cautious with our judgments. When Yeltsin banned a number of extreme conservative parties, he removed a number of parties that would have received less than 5 percent of the vote and would have had their vote redistributed across the spectrum. As a result, there were only three parties, all fairly well known, on the conservative side of the spectrum, and all the parties with less than 5 percent of the vote were on the reform or centrist part of the spectrum. The conservatives therefore received 43 percent of the votes cast for a party but were allocated 50 percent of the seats. If they had only received 43 percent of the seats, the results shown in table 2-4 would be far less striking.

Without the party-list section of the election, the number of single-member districts would not have been 225 but probably 450. To be sure, if Moscow leaders had to rely on districts to be elected, they undoubtedly would have acted more strategically in the districts. Nevertheless, incumbents would have had more of an advantage in smaller districts, and there would have been more rural and small-town districts. When the number of deputies elected in the district was reduced from two-thirds to one-half of the total deputies in October, Sheinis claimed that this was an effort to avoid the excess influence of local bosses and help reform parties.[58]

If the election had been limited to districts, the Liberal Democrats, whose candidates other than Zhirinovskii were quite unknown, clearly would have done much worse in an all-district election, and the Agrarians and Communists would have done better. But with the population in a mood to make a protest vote, the absence of the outlet of the party list would not likely have prevented it from expressing its frustration in some other way. Zhirinovskii proved highly supportive of Yeltsin and the government on key issues.

It would also be a mistake to assume automatically that the democrats received disproportionately too few seats in the Duma because of splits within their ranks. The average winner in the country received only 29.0 percent of the valid votes cast, a figure that dropped to 22.3 percent in Moscow and 19.0 percent in St. Petersburg. The absence of a runoff and the per-

Table 2-5. *Number of 1993 Deputies Elected in Districts Who Were Reelected to the Duma in 1995*

1993 faction	Total 1993 deputies elected in districts	Total reelected in 1995 overall	Total reelected in districts
12 of December	22	6	6
Agrarian	16	11	11
Communist	10	10	10
Democratic	1	0	0
Liberal Democratic	5	4	0
New Regional Policy	65	14	14
PRES	4	4	4
Russian Path	14	8	8
Russia's Choice	34	11	11
Women's	2	0	0
Yabloko	7	4	1
No faction	11	1	1

Source: Author's calculations based on *A Directory of Members*.

sonalistic nature of the campaign introduced a random element into the election results. Other democrats also undoubtedly lost because multiple candidates split their vote. In chapter 19, Henry Hale reports that a district in Bashkortostan containing the capital plus 18 percent rural population elected a conservative collective farm chair with 29.8 percent of the vote because six candidates split the city vote and because the chair was a Tatar who picked up some Tatar votes in the city.

Yet in many other districts a democrat won because the conservative vote was split among a number of candidates. For example, in Nizhnii Novgorod oblast, Nigel Gould-Davies (see chapter 14) credits the support of the governor, Boris Nemtsov, in electing two liberal candidates in conservative districts, but, as he notes, Nemtsov's help would not have mattered if conservative candidates had not split the vote. The three liberal incumbents lost in 1995. Similarly, a Russia's Choice candidate won in District 115 in Murmansk oblast with 29,494 votes against a Communist with 28,346 votes. Agrarian and Civic Union candidates received more than 51,000 votes, and two other democratic candidates received 29,700. In Stavropol District 56, a moderate democrat won with 38,093 votes when six conservative candidates split 141,000 votes. (The eighth candidate, nominated by Russia's Choice, received 23,656 votes.)

We need to be careful even in the well-known cases. Aleksandr Nevzorov clearly had a sense that his election in a St. Petersburg district containing the university was a fluke, and in 1995 he decided to run in the more conservative Pskov region, where he won fairly easily. But those who talk about the inappropriateness of Nevzorov's victory in St. Petersburg fail to mention that 22.5 percent in the district voted against all candidates and that the turnout was 47.2 percent, one of the lowest in the country.[59] Obviously the problem was not that three popular democratic candidates were splitting the vote, and it is not absolutely clear that one of them alone could have defeated a popular journalist such as Nevzorov in a two-candidate race.

Overall, the impact of chance factors on the Duma as a whole should not be exaggerated. Those looking at the forest from afar would reach a somewhat different conclusion than those walking among trees. For all the chaos of the single-member-district elections, the districts based on smaller cities and containing large numbers of rural voters elected on the average more conservative deputies than those based on the larger cities, just as they had in the past. In districts in which the largest city had a population of 100,000 or fewer, 46 percent of the deputies were conservatives and 19 percent radicals, and in those in which the largest city had between 100,000 and 500,000 people, 42 percent were conservatives and 29 percent radicals. Those based on a city with between 500,000 and 2,000,000 people elected 29 percent conservatives and 44 percent radicals, and Moscow and St. Petersburg elected 9 percent conservatives and 78 percent radicals. Clearly the purely chance effect of candidate popularity and campaign skill would have produced a different outcome.

"Against All": A Test of Party Theory

In the previous section, we noted that in Nevrozov's election 22.5 percent of the voters cast a ballot against all candidates. The formal "against all" option was an innovation in the 1993 election. In the past—both in one-party Soviet elections and the competitive elections of 1989 and 1990—the voters had not voted *for* a candidate, as is done in the United States, but had done so indirectly through crossing out the names of the undesired candidate or candidates. When a majority of voters crossed out the name of a candidate, he or she was defeated even if the only candidate on the ballot. In 1993, the method of voting was changed, and the voters had to make a positive mark to vote for a candidate. However, in order not to deprive the voters of an earlier right, the regime included an extra line on the ballot: "against all."

Hence the analysis of both Russia and comparative voting behavior has a new indicator to examine, and it has particular interest because the Russian voter had to vote in four separate elections at the same time—ratification of the constitution, the Duma party-list vote, the Duma single-member district election, and the Federation Council two-member district election. The constitution ballot was marked in the old way (crossing out as a sign of disapproval), while the candidate elections were marked in the new manner.

The change in the way ballots were marked clearly led to confusion, for the election was featured by a large number not only of votes "against all" but of invalid ballots—ballots that were spoiled in some manner. The Central Electoral Commission did not report the collective number of invalid ballots, but they can be calculated from the individual regional data given and were 2.4 percent of the ballots cast for the constitution and 7.3 percent in the Duma single-member districts. It is likely that the difference reflected voter confusion over the different methods of voting, but it is also probable that an effort was made not to count a vote for the constitution invalid.

The "against all" vote is much more difficult to analyze—indeed, impossible from the official record, for the election was reported incompletely. In the party-list election, the Central Electoral Commission did report the number of valid ballots cast and the total number of votes for each party individually. If the latter are added together and the total subtracted from the number of valid ballots, the result presumably is the number of votes against all parties—4.1 percent of the valid ballots.[60]

The number of votes received by each of the candidates in the Duma or Federation Council district elections was never reported; therefore, neither was the number of votes against all candidates, even indirectly. The Central Electoral Commission published only the name of the winner in the Duma district election and the two winners in the Federation Council district election, together with the total number of votes that the winner or winners received.

The regional press in nearly 70 percent of the oblasts and former autonomous republics did report the votes received by all the local candidates, and the number of "against all" votes can be calculated with some reliability by subtracting the total number of candidate votes from the number of valid ballots. The average "against all" votes in these 101 districts turned out to be 16.7 percent.[61]

Unfortunately, full election reports usually were not published in the local press of the largest cities. This included many of the most democratic cities, including Moscow, St. Petersburg, Yekaterinburg, and Nizhnii Novgorod. They also often were not available in many of the ethnic "subjects of the federation."

It always seemed highly probable that the failure of the regime to report full election returns from the larger cities indicated that an even more embarrassing number voted against all candidates in them. So it turned out to be. The Center RF–Politika published a number of results from all districts, including the votes cast against-all candidates. The average figure for the country as a whole was 16.8 percent. However, it was 16.7 in districts in the ethnic Russian republics and krais and 14.1 in districts in the ethnically based oblasts, but 19.7 percent for St. Petersburg and 20.4 percent for Moscow.[62] (It was also 19.5 in the two districts in Yeltsin's home town of Yekaterinburg.) In districts whose winners were labeled conservative by Sobyanin, 15.3 percent of the voters voted against all, but in districts with proreform or generally proreform winners, this figure rose to 17.9 percent.

The late decision by the regime to change the rule requiring the district winner to defeat "against all" proved to be farsighted. "Against all" actually won in thirty-two districts. These included six of the fifteen districts in Moscow, five of the ten in Moscow oblast, three of the eight in St. Petersburg, one of the two in Leningrad oblast, both in Novosibirsk city, and one of the two in Yekaterinburg. In seven of these districts, the Russia's Choice candidate won eleven, the Yabloko candidates won three, and a PRES candidate won one.

There were two other interesting results in district elections held at the same time. The Federation Council elections, as Colton indicates in chapter 1, normally featured several prominent candidates, usually including the equivalent of the regional governor. The Center RF–Politika also reported results for these elections, and the average "against all" vote in these elections was 11.9 percent.[63] At the same time, local elections were held in some areas, including for deputies of the Moscow city soviet. The "against all" vote was reported to have exceeded 25 percent in many of the districts and to have "won" in twenty-nine of the thirty-one districts of the capital.[64]

Clearly some of the "against all" votes were cast as a protest against the Yeltsin regime or the character of the election being held. However, the Federation Council elections featured the most established of the local candidates, and the "against-all" vote in these was relatively low. Moscow, St. Petersburg, and Yekaterinburg have always been supportive of Yeltsin and his policies. Moscow provided the greatest support in the country for Russia's Choice at 34 percent and St. Petersburg the second greatest, but they each had 20 percent "against all." There was no reason to punish candidates to the Moscow city soviet for sins of the central government.

The 4 percent of the electorate who voted against all parties probably were a thoroughly disenchanted group, but the larger figures in the other elections surely were a protest against the need to make an uninformed decision in a particular election itself. Everyone knew something about some of the parties on the party-list ballot, and nearly all felt they had some party for which they could vote. At a minimum, they knew that a vote for the Liberal Democrats or the Communists was a far more hurtful protest against Russia's Choice than "against all."

The Federation Council election featured some better known candidates, and the fact that the election was regionwide meant it was better covered by the local media. However, the number of candidates in the Duma district elections was quite large, party identification meant little, and the candidates had neither the time nor the money to get their messages across. The problem was particularly great in cities such as Moscow and St. Petersburg where local television and newspapers could give little attention to fifteen separate races. In addition, information about the candidates in the Moscow city council election was completely lost in the information about the national election.

The number of candidates is clearly not the only crucial variable. In the 1995 Duma election, the number of candidates rose to an average of 11.9 from the 6.8 of 1993, but the "against all" vote in the district elections declined to 10.0 percent. There continued to be a general relationship between size of city, number of candidates, and votes "against all": the districts in which the largest city was under 1,000,000 had 10.8 candidates and 9.4 percent vote "against all," and Moscow and St. Petersburg had 16.7 candidates and 12.5 percent "against all."[65] The key difference between 1993 and 1995 was that candidates had two years to prepare for the election instead of two months, and the population had more chance to learn something about at least some of the candidates. But again, the largest cities with centralized media created the greatest difficulty for citizens to learn about candidates elected out of ward-like districts, and it was those voters who expressed the greatest frustration.

In short, the various district elections strongly confirmed a key proposition in party theory—the need for meaningful parties to give signals to voters who otherwise do not have sufficient information to make a decision.

The connection between the new national parties and the local candidates was so tenuous that even when local candidates had a party identification or support, the party could not serve its traditional information function. The low turnout in an election that was a referendum on the shelling of the Congress building (allegedly 54.8 percent as against 69 percent in the 1990 election and 64 percent in the April 1993 referendum) was one sign of voter frustration;[66] the easy vehicle of protest in the district elections for those who did come to polls to vote on the constitution and a party in the party list was even more dramatic.

Conclusion

Rational-actor analysis can demonstrate the logic of particular electoral systems. Statistical data can demonstrate the extent to which the developments in a particular country correspond to predictions of that analysis in a particular election. However, it is clear from the data presented in this chapter that the Russian elections of 1993 and 1995 confirm few of the central propositions of electoral-system analysis.

Thus proportional representation did result in multiple parties, but the 5 percent minimum requirement did little to restrain the number of such parties. Indeed, the number of parties on the ballot rose from thirteen in 1993 to forty-three in 1995. With only four parties achieving the 5 percent minimum in 1995, however, one would certainly expect some consolidation in the 1999 Duma election, assuming that the election rules are not changed in response to considerable pressure, that the election is held as scheduled, and that it is not dominated by a presidential party, presumably of a new president.

The abolition of the runoff of single-member districts similarly has not led to a decrease in the number of candidates per district but rather to an increase from 6.3 in 1990 to 6.8 in 1993 to 11.9 in 1995. The combination of proportional representation and districts, which should have increased the pressure to limit the number of parties to a relatively few, actually led to an increase in a greater number of parties being represented in the Duma than would have been produced by proportional representation alone. The reason was that some candidates high on the lists of parties that failed to reach the minimum succeeded in winning a seat in the districts. They generally did not retain their party identity in the 1993–95 Duma, but this was not true in 1995 when twenty-two parties won at least one seat, usually including one of their top leaders.[67]

Finally, mass parties are formed for the purpose of mobilizing greater voter turnout, and they generally have this impact. This certainly did not occur in 1993, and it is somewhat of a surprise. The dissolution of the Congress and the shelling of the parliament building (the White House) were certainly dramatic. Four separate elections—party, district, Federation Council, and constitution—were being held. A party-list election seemingly gave the electorate the chance to express a clear opinion about the fall of the former regime and about the results of two years of economic reform.

Some of the reasons for and implications of these results have already been suggested in this chapter. However, hypotheses and explanations, although rational-choice theorists do not like to admit it, generally come from experience and observation rather than from theory, and anthropological work needs to accompany survey work and rational-actor analysis. The articles by the younger scholars in this book are precisely such anthropological work. Once the evidence of this anthropological work has been examined, it will be possible (and appropriate) to assess the broader implications of the 1993 Russian election and the growing pains of Russian democracy.

Notes

1 Classic studies are Maurice Duverger, *Political Parties: Their Organization and Activity in the Modern State* (London: Methuen, 1954); Douglas Rae, *The Political Consequences of Electoral Laws*, rev. ed. (Yale University Press, 1971); Rein Taagepera and Matthew Soberg Shugart, *Seats and Votes: The Effects and Determinants of Electoral Systems* (Yale University Press, 1989); and Arend Lijphart, *Electoral Systems and Party Systems: a Study of Twenty-Seven Democracies, 1945–1990* (Oxford University Press, 1994). Of course, sophisticated statistical methods can lead to controversy as well as definitive clarification. See Alberto Penades, "A Critique of Lijphart's 'Electoral Systems and Party Systems,'" and Lijphart's answer, "The Difficult Science of Electoral Systems: A Commentary on the Critique by Alberto Penades," both in *Electoral Studies*, vol. 16, no. 1 (March 1997), pp. 59–72.

2. Olga Bychkova, "Partiinye spiski v redaktsii Viktora Sheinisa," *Moskovskiye novosti*, June 20–25, 1993, p. 9. Before 1985, Sheinis had been a scholar studying southern Europe and Latin America. See Jerry F. Hough, *The Struggle for the Third World* (Brookings, 1986), pp. 63, 64, 96, 102, and 140.

3. See B. A. Strashun and V. L. Sheinis, "Politicheskaya situatsiya v Rossii i novyy izbiratel'nyy zakon," *Polis*, no. 3 (1993), p. 68, for the 3 percent limit pro-

posal. The group also favored lowering the minimum turnout required for a valid election from 50 percent to 25 percent. Six Congress seats were never filled because turnout never reached the 50 percent level, even after several repeat elections. It was more difficult to arouse sufficient interest in by-elections, and in July 1993, seats were vacant in thirty districts. The lowering of the turnout requirement did solve the problem. With the exception of five districts in Tatarstan where the president actively discouraged voting and one district in Chechnya where no candidates were nominated and the election was not held, the turnout always met the minimum 25 percent turnout threshold. If the old rule had remained in place, the elections would have been invalid in thirty-nine districts, even excluding Tatarstan.

4. Masumi Junnosuke, *Postwar Politics in Japan, 1945–1955* (Berkeley: Institute of East Asian Studies, University of California, 1985), p. 96.

5. Ibid., p. 178; and Masumi Junnosuke, "The 1995 System: Origin and Transformation," in Kataoka Tetsuya, ed., *Creating Single-Party Democracy: Japan's Postwar Political System* (Stanford, Calif.: Hoover Institution Press, 1992), pp. 34–54.

6. Tony Burkett, *Parties and Elections in West Germany: The Search for Stability* (London: C. Hurst, 1975), p. 89; Stephen L. Fisher, *The Minor Parties of the Federal Republic of Germany: Toward a Comparative Theory of Minor Parties* (The Hague: Martinus Nijhoff, 1974), pp. 45–50.

7. Students of contemporary Russia should give much more attention to Geoffrey A. Hosking, *The Russian Constitutional Experiment and Duma, 1907–1914* (Cambridge: Cambridge University Press, 1973) and Terence Emmons, *The Formation of Political Parties and the First National Elections in Russia* (Harvard University Press, 1983). Indeed, as Thomas H. Rigby reminds us, previous tsars had experimented with consultative or representative bodies—the *Boiarskaia Duma* (Boyars' Council) and the *Zemskii Sobor* (Assembly of the Land), the latter of which had an interesting role in the first half of the nineteenth century. T. H. Rigby, "Yeltsin's Presidency and the Evolution of Representative and Responsible Government in Russia," in John Lowenhardt, ed., *Cutting the Gordian Knot: Responsible Government and Elections in Russia, Slavic Research Center Occasional Paper No. 49* (Sapporo, Japan: Slavic Research Center, Hokkaido University, 1994), pp. 6–9.

8. For the U.S. cancellation of the 1946 Japanese election and the purge of prospective candidates that "went beyond even the wildest expectations" and affected 83 percent of the incumbent representatives, see Masumi, *Postwar Politics in Japan*, pp. 92–95. For the argument that the British willingness to license (permit) state (*Land*) parties a year before the Americans had a major role in the rise of Konrad Adenauer in West Germany, see R. E. M. Irving, *The Christian Democratic Parties of Western Europe* (London: George Allen & Unwyn, 1979), p. 117. For the preference given by the Allies to three parties in Austria, see Louise Powelson, "The Political Parties of Austria, 1945–1951" (Ph.D. dissertation, Yale University, 1953), pp. 80–82.

9. Michael Urban, "December 1993 as a Replication of Late-Soviet Electoral Practices," *Post-Soviet Affairs*, vol. 10, no. 2 (April–June 1994), p. 128.

10. Ibid., pp. 129–32, 136–39.

11. Douglas North, *Institutions, Institutional Charge, and Economic Perform-ance* (Cambridge University Press, 1990).

12. Moisei Ya. Ostrogorski, *Democracy and the Organization of Political Par-ties: Vol. I—England*, edited and abridged by Seymour Martin Lipset (Garden City, N.Y.: Anchor Books, 1964), pp. 70 and 196.

13. Lewis B. Namier, *Monarchy and the Party System* (Oxford: Clarendon Press, 1952), pp. 4, 26.

14. Jackson Turner Main, *Political Parties before the Constitution* (University of North Carolina Press, 1973).

15. For a good discussion of the key role of the Jay Treaty, see Joseph Charles, *The Origins of the American Party System: Three Essays* (Williamsburg, Va.: In-stitute of Early American History and Culture, 1956). For the evolution in party co-hesion in the Congress, see John F. Hoadley, *Origins of American Political Par-ties, 1789–1803* (University Press of Kentucky, 1986).

16. See Richard P. McCormick, *The Presidential Game: The Origins of Ameri-can Presidential Politics* (New York: Oxford, 1982); and James W. Ceasar, *Presi-dential Selection: Theory and Development* (Princeton University Press, 1979).

17. Duverger, *Political Parties*, p. xxiv.

18. The classic description of the expansion of the electoral system was Chilton Williamson, *American Suffrage: From Property to Democracy, 1760–1860* (Princeton University Press, 1960). Turnout rose from 55.4 percent in the 1832 presidential election to 57.8 percent in 1836 to 80.2 percent in the famous "Tippan-canoe and Tyler Too" election of 1840. For turnout figures, see *Historical Statis-tics of the United States: Colonial Times to 1970*, part 2 (U.S. Department of Com-merce and Bureau of the Census, 1975), p. 1072. For the vigorous party campaign of 1840, see Robert Gray Gunderson, *The Log-Cabin Campaign* (University Press of Kentucky, 1957).

19. Richard P. McCormick, *The Second American Party System: Party Forma-tion in the Jacksonian Era* (University of North Carolina Press, 1966). John Her-bert Aldrich, *Why Parties?* (University of Chicago Press, 1995).

20. Ostrogorski, *Democracy and the Organization of Political Parties: Vol. I—England*, p. 72.

21. J. A. A. Stockwin, "Japan: The Leader-Follower Relationship in Politics," in Alan Ware, ed., *Political Parties: Electoral Change and Structural Response* (New York: Basil Blackwell, 1987), pp. 100–01. The classic detailed history of this period is Robert A. Scalapino, *Democracy and the Party Movement in Prewar Ja-pan: The Failure of the First Attempt* (University of California Press, 1953).

22. Charles Seymour and Donald Paige Frary, *How the World Votes: The Story of Democratic Development in Elections*, vol. 2 (Springfield, Mass.: C. A. Nichols Company, 1918), pp. 16–40.

23. Duverger, *Political Parties*, p. xxxi, xxxvi–vii.

24. Vicky Randall, ed., *Political Parties in the Third World* (London: Sage Pub-lications, 1988), p. 175.

25. B. I. Koval', *Rossiya Segodnya: Politicheskii portret v dokumentakh, 1985–1991* (Moscow: Mezhdunarodnye otnoshenii, 1991), pp. 3–7. Vera Tolz,

"The USSR's Emerging Multiparty System," *Washington Papers 148* (New York: Praeger, 1990).

26. V. N. Berezovskii, N. I. Krotov, and V. V. Chervyakov, *Rossiya: Partii, assotsiatsii, soiuzi, kluby Spravochnik,* vol. 1, part 1 (Moscow: Rau-Press, 1991), pp. 3 and 336–37.

27. Vladimir Pribylovskii, *A Guide to New Russian Political Parties and Organizations* (Moscow: Panorama, May 1992), pp. i–viii.

28. Michael McFaul and Sergei Markov, *The Troubled Birth of Russian Democracy: Parties, Personalities, and Programs* (Stanford, Calif: Hoover Institution Press, 1993), p. xi.

29. If no candidate in a one-candidate or two-candidate race received a majority of the votes, the rules required a new election, but a runoff was permitted if there were three or more candidates. In forty-six districts, a new election was required, and in many areas the Communist party threw up its hands and allowed a free nomination process and a large number of candidates to ensure a runoff. See Central Electoral Commission, "Soobshcheniye Tsentral'noi izbratel'noi komissii ob itogakh vyborov narodnykh deputatov SSSR v 1989 godu." *Izvestiya,* no. 95 (April 5, 1989), p. 1. For a full discussion of the 1989 and 1990 elections, see Jerry F. Hough, *Democratization and Revolution in the USSR, 1985–1991* (Brookings, 1997).

30. Seven of the top seventeen persons on the RDDR list were radical deputies in the USSR Congress, and, in a sense, it was the Interregional Group revived.

31. There still was to be no Russian Communist party until June 1990, but the organizational bureau of that party could have nominated candidates if it had chosen to do so.

32. For a well-documented discussion of the groups and political organizations that formed in the process of the Russian campaign, see Brendan Kiernan, *The End of Soviet Politics: Elections, Legislatures, and the Demise of the Communist Party* (Boulder, Colo.: Westview Press, 1993), pp. 161–71.

33. "Kogo predpochet Rossiya?" *Sovetskaya Kul'tura,* February 10, 1990, p. 3.

34. "A. Uglanov interviews N. Travkin, a member of the People's Deputies of the USSR and of Democratic Russia," *Argumenty i fakty,* no. 8 (February 24/March 2, 1990), p. 8.

35. G. Alimov, "Vperedi-vtoroi turi i portornye vybory," *Izvestiya,* March 14, 1990, p. 7.

36. Lev Aksenov, "'Democratic Russia' Bloc Formed," (Moscow: TASS International Service), April 1, 1990, as found in FBIS-SOV-90-063, April 2, 1990, pp. 104–05.

37. Yu. Velyayev, S. Karkhanin, S. Skorokhodov, "My vse v otvete za Rossiyu," *Sovetskaya Rossiya,* May 10, 1990, p. 2.

38. In the early summer thirty-nine deputies left the Communist party, reducing the percentage of Communists among all deputies to 86 percent and among the 400 most radical to 66 percent.

39. *Chetvertyi (Vneocherednoi) s"yezd narodnykh deputatov RSFSR, 21–25 maya 1991, Stenografischeskiy otchet,* tom 1 (Moscow: Izdaniye Verkhovnogo Soveta RSFSR, 1991), pp. 200–01.

40. *Vtoroi (Vneocherednoi) s''yezd narodnykh deputator RSFSR, 27 noy-abrya–15 dekabrya 1990 goda*, tom 1 (Moscow: Izdatel'stvo "respublika," 1992), p. 212.

41. Thomas F. Remington and others, "Transitional Institutions and Parliamentary Alignments in Russia, 1990–1993," in Thomas F. Remington, ed., *Parliaments in Transition: The New Legislative Politics in the Former USSR and Eastern Europe* (Boulder, Colo.: Westview Press, 1994), pp. 167–70.

42. The national and oblast preelection questionnaires were identical, with Timothy Colton having prime responsibility for the election questions, Jerry Hough for those on economic and political reform, and Susan Goodrich Lehmann for the sixty-question demographic and sociological section. A number of ethnic identity, language, and nationality policy questions were added to the questionnaires in the republics, many coming from another project in which Hough and Lehmann collaborated with David Laitin and Mikhail Guboglo. The postelection national questionnaire was written solely by Colton; he took responsibility for the national survey data set, and the 51,000-respondent oblast and republic data set was the responsibility of Hough and Lehmann. A number of works have been produced out of this data set. A preliminary reporting of results and methodology on attitudes toward economic reform and democracy out of the 33,869-respondent oblast data set is found in Jerry F. Hough, "The Russian Election of 1993: Public Attitudes toward Economic Reform and Democratization," *Post-Soviet Affairs*, vol. 10, no. 1 (January–March 1994), pp. 1–37. The republican data set is used in Mikhail Guboglo, *Razvivaiushchiiasia elektorat Rossii: Ethnopoliticheskii rakurs* (Moscow: Rossiiskaya akademiya nauk, Tsentr po izucheniyu mezhnatsionalnykh otnoshenii), vol. 1. For an article from this data set on language use, see Jerry F. Hough, "Sociology, the State, and Language Politics," *Post-Soviet Affairs,* vol. 12, no. 2 (April–June 1996), pp. 95–117, and for differences in religious attitudes in the five Muslim republics of Bashkortostan, Chechnya, Dagestan, Kabardino-Balkaria, and Tatarstan, see Susan Goodrich Lehmann, "Islam and Ethnicity in the Republics of Russia," *Post-Soviet Affairs*, vol. 13, no. 1 (January–March 1997), pp. 78–103.

43. The republics were not included, for the large number of small rural republics produced an excessive underrepresentation of the large urban areas in a 51,000-respondent data set.

44. The classic statement about the effects of party systems is Duverger, *Political Parties*. For a collection of short articles presenting the case for single-member districts and proportional representation, see Arend Lijphart and Bernard Grofman, eds., *Choosing an Electoral System: Issues and Alternatives* (New York: Praeger, 1984), pp. 15–69. Subsequent articles discuss a series of variations in electoral systems.

45. In 1997, five parties received at least twenty seats, but the Reform party was based in the West, the Bloc Quebecois in Quebec, and the Progressive Conservatives largely in the Atlantic provinces. Anthony DePalma, "Canadian Leader Keeps Majority but Loses Strength," *New York Times*, June 4, 1997, p. A3. Howard Schneider, "Canadian Voters Create a Political Patchwork," *Washington Post*, June 4, 1997, p. A26.

46. The 1997 British election was described as a massive landslide for the Labour party, and in practical terms it was. Yet, Labour received less than half the vote: 43.1 percent in contrast to 30.6 percent for the Conservative party, 16.7 percent for the Liberal-Democrats, and 9.6 percent for 8 smaller parties. Warren Hoge, "Out of an Office One Day, Out of a Home the Next," *New York Times*, May 3, 1997, p. 7.

47. Roy F. Nichols, "The Kansas-Nebraska Act: A Century of Historiography," in Joel H. Silbey, ed., *National Development and Sectional Crisis, 1815–1860* (Random House, 1970), pp. 204–05.

48. Strashun and Sheinis, "Politicheskaya situatsiya v Rossii i novyi izbiratel'nyy zakon," p. 66.

49. Max Kaase, "Personalized Proportional Representation: The 'Mode' of the West German Electoral System," in Lijphart and Grofman, *Choosing an Electoral System*, pp. 155–64.

50. The only important independent power of the Duma is to confirm the chair of the government (prime minister) and to pass a vote of no confidence in the government, in both cases by a majority vote. If the president does not agree, the government rules for three months, at which time the process is repeated. If the president does not agree a third time, the Duma is dissolved and new elections held. A Duma majority convinced that it would fare well in an election against an unpopular president and prime minister could force an election. The old government rules until a new one is chosen, and the process could obviously be repeated. Presumably, however, a president in full control of the Federation Council and determined to fight the Duma to the end would be more inclined to declare a state of emergency.

51. Robert V. Daniels, "Soviet Politics since Khrushchev," in John W. Strong, ed., *The Soviet Union under Brezhnev and Kosygin* (New York: Van Nostrand-Reinhold, 1971), p. 20, and Hough, *Democratization and Revolution in the USSR*, pp. 80–86.

52. It might be argued that voters engaged in strategic voting, assuming that a person on the list would be elected without a district election. However, it is unlikely that most voters knew who was on the list, and, in practice, the well-known ministers highest on party lists were the most likely to win—reportedly because of both name recognition and voter calculation that a powerful representative of the district would be useful in obtaining appropriations. Moreover, as has been seen, victory in a district did not deprive a party of a seat, for a person lower on its list moved up to fill its quota.

53. As Colton indicates, statistics in Russian sources are not always consistent on such cases, and I have accepted his figures.

54. See Hough, *Democratization and Revolution in the USSR*, pp. 336–37.

55. Timothy J. Colton, "Professional Engagement and Role Definition among Post-Soviet Legislators," in Remington, *Parliaments in Transition*, pp. 56 and 61.

56. In all, twenty districts had a former deputy from a national-territorial district among its candidates, but five ran in districts in which a former deputy from a territorial district was also running and two ran in one district against each other.

57. The index score for each deputy is given in "Golosovaniia deputatov Gosudarstvennoi Dumy, 11 ianvaria–11 fevralia 1994" (Moscow: Informatsionno-analiticheskaya grupa, 1994), pp. 4–9. Actually the Sobyanin index extends from +100 to -100, but we have simply added 100 to each score to make all index scores positive. We have calculated the average scores for deputies elected on party lists and in districts. Sobyanin's summary scores for deputy voting behavior for the entire two years of the Duma correlate with his score for the first month by 0.91. The latter scores are found in Michael McFaul and Nikolai Petrov, eds., *Politicheskii al'manakh Rossii 1995* (Moscow: Carnegie Endowment for International Peace, 1995), pp. 718–31.

58. Quoted in Jonathan Steele, "New Electoral Rules Aim to Drum up Support," *Guardian*, October 8, 1993, p. 12.

59. Vladimir Varov and Dmitri Yurev, eds., *Revansh—Nedoperevyvorot: Versiya tsentra "RF-politika"* (Moscow: Literatura i politika, 1994), p. 272.

60. *Biulleten' Tsentral'noi izbratel'noi komissii Rossiiskoi Federatsii*, vol. 12, no. 1 (1994), p. 67.

61. The data from the local press were collected in Moscow libraries by Violetta Pavlovna Rumyantseva.

62. Varov and Yurev, *Revansh*, pp. 220–51.

63. Ibid., pp. 302–48.

64. Tat'yana Shumilinia, "Zanimatel'naya arifmetika dlya gorodskai dumy," *Pravda,* January 4, 1994, p. 2.

65. For the 1995 election results, see Evgenii P. Ishchenko, Yurii Ya. Mikheyev, and Valerii V. Fadeyev, *Gosudarstvennaya Duma Federal'nogo Sobraniya Rossiiskoi Federatsii vtorogo sozyva: Spravochnik* (Moscow: Ves' mir, 1996).

66. For the statistics on election returns from 1989 to 1995, see McFaul and Petrov, *Politicheskii al'manakh Rossii*, pp. 649–79. Of the various charges of fraud in the vote counting in the 1993 election, those about voting on the constitution and about turnout were the most creditable, but not definitive.

67. The Agrarian party, with twenty seats, and Nikolai Ryzhkov's People Power faction, with nine seats, actually became major factions in the 1995 Duma when independents and some Communists joined them. *A Directory of Members of the Russian Parliament, January 1996* (London: BBC Monitoring, 1996).

CHAPTER THREE

Determinants of the Party Vote

Timothy J. Colton

THE MACROCHOICE embodied in any competitive election sums up a myriad of microchoices made by individual citizens. The microchoices that pose the greatest analytical interest in Russia in 1993 are those concerning the *electoral associations,* the newly minted parties and near-parties that battled it out over the 50 percent of the State Duma seats allotted by proportional representation. Data from our two-part nationwide survey of the electorate let my colleagues and me delve into the main determinants of the party-list vote through statistical analysis. To frame the discussion, I borrow propositions from the voluminous literature on electoral decision-making in other political systems.

Voters and Parties

In established democracies, it is customary to begin the examination of a general election with an inquiry into the distribution within the population of psychological identification with the parties. Enduring affiliations with political parties, in many countries passed from one generation to the next by childhood socialization, have often been found to be the strongest single predictor of voting decisions.[1]

In the protodemocratic setting of Russia's inaugural multiparty election, entrenched partisan identification cannot be seriously entertained as the engine of citizen behavior. The rock-bottom reality is that none of the thirteen parties registered—the oldest dating back to 1990 and nine of them founded in the year 1993—had been on the scene long enough or with sufficient organizational presence to spawn stable loyalties. Because any survey question about habitual partisanship would have mystified the survey participants, none was written into either the preelection or the postelection interview.

This is not to say that the citizens quizzed came across as uninformed or unopinionated. It would be more accurate to speak of selective familiarity with the embryonic parties than of wholesale political illiteracy (see table 3-1). Notice in the table that participant voters, those who came to the polls December 12, were more savvy across the board than abstainers. Notice also that passive knowledge, as evoked by questions about parties or leaders read out by the interviewer, outpaced the active knowledge tapped by eliciting a name or an exacting fact about them. The typical respondent, who on the eve of the election spontaneously recalled only about four of thirteen parties, could tender an assessment of five or six when the parties were enumerated in the postelection interview. Likewise, although correctly naming the parties headed by about three of seven party leaders, the typical respondent recognized and evaluated on a "feeling thermometer" five leaders out of eight recited.[2]

Previous awareness and approval undoubtedly had some repercussions on electoral choices. Individuals who cast their votes for a given party were markedly more likely than adherents of other parties or nonvoters to have revealed acquaintance with it in interviews and to have appraised it favorably (see table 3-2). It is hard to see how it could have been otherwise.

Yet this information imparts nothing about when or by what means orientations toward the contending parties took shape. Oblique evidence suggests that in 1993 most impressions of the parties were shallow and tentative and bore little resemblance to long-term identification in its usual connotation. Our Russian informants reported in their debriefing after December 12 extraordinary delays in deciding how to vote—the diametric op-

Table 3-1. *Public Knowledge of Political Parties and Leaders*

	Voters	Abstainers	All respondents[a]
Parties recalled (of thirteen)	4.2	2.6	4.9
Parties recognized and evaluated (of thirteen)	5.4	3.7	4.9
Leaders recognized and evaluated (of eight)	5.2	4.0	4.9
Leaders matched with party (of seven)	3.5	2.2	3.1

a. Excludes small number of respondents (about 1 percent of sample) who could not remember or would not say whether they voted.

Table 3-2. *Recognition and Evaluation of Parties by Voting Choice*

Measure	Vote for given party	Vote for another party[a]	Abstained	All respondents[b]
Recognized party in preelection interview (percent)				
LDPR	75	69	50	63
Russia's Choice	74	65	48	60
KPRF	72	52	34	47
Women of Russia	60	42	33	40
Agrarian	63	31	17	27
Yabloko	72	42	28	39
PRES	70	51	34	45
DPR	78	52	34	46
RDDR	72	49	33	44
Civic Union	48	30	17	25
Future of Russia	32	19	12	17
KEDR	77	21	14	19
Dignity and Compassion	47	22	14	19
Mean evaluation of party (scale 0–3) among those who recognized party				
LDPR	2.3	0.9	1.1	1.2
Russia's Choice	2.2	1.0	1.2	1.3
KPRF	2.6	1.0	0.9	1.1
Women of Russia	2.8	2.4	2.3	2.4
Agrarian	2.7	2.0	1.9	2.0
Yabloko	2.7	2.0	1.9	2.0
PRES	2.4	1.7	1.7	1.7
DPR	2.4	1.8	1.8	1.9
RDDR	2.2	1.5	1.5	1.5
Civic Union	2.7	1.7	1.5	1.7
Future of Russia	3.0	1.9	1.7	1.8
KEDR	2.9	2.2	2.1	2.1
Dignity and Compassion	2.6	2.1	2.0	2.1

a. Includes respondents who voted against all parties.
b. Excludes respondents who could not remember or would not say whether they voted.

posite of how reflexive partisans would act. Fifty-two percent remembered making up their minds as late as the dying days of the campaign or on the very day of the election (see table 3-3); slightly more than 20 percent had done so earlier than one month before the election.[3]

To be sure, the most politically engaged, who came to closure relatively early, contrasted with the politically apathetic, who if they voted at all were much more apt to decide at the last instant.[4] There was also variety by party supported. One in three Communist Party of the Russian Federation (KPRF) voters and better than one in four Russia's Choice voters said they had finalized their decisions longer than one month prior to December 12.[5] At the foot-dragging extreme, none of the eventual voters for the splinter

Table 3-3. *Voter-Recalled Timing of Decision about Party List*[a]

Percent

Party	More than one month before election	One month before election	Two weeks before election	Final days of campaign	Election Day
LDPR	16	12	18	44	11
Russia's Choice	27	14	13	36	10
KPRF	34	14	9	33	10
Women of Russia	5	12	18	46	20
Agrarian	9	14	24	38	14
Yabloko	20	13	19	39	10
PRES	9	19	18	44	10
DPR	7	12	27	41	13
RDDR	21	12	6	52	9
Civic Union	14	18	23	32	13
Future of Russia	0	10	42	43	6
KEDR	0	17	25	43	15
Dignity and Compassion	5	17	32	37	9
All parties	18	14	17	40	12

a. Excludes respondents who voted against all parties, who all reported having made decisions in the final days of the campaign or on election day.

Future of Russia and Constructive Ecological Movement of Russia (KEDR) groups and only 5 percent of Women of Russia voters said the same.

Volatility accompanied this procrastination. A startling 40 percent of voters who disclosed a party-list preference before the election told us afterward that they had voted inconsistently with it (see table 3-4). Intracampaign turnover was several times higher than turnover *between* elections in consolidated democracies.[6]

The picture of irresolution and drift is moderated by the lower incidence of switching among citizens who were confident about their choice or were interviewed late in the campaign (leaving them fewer days to flip flop). Again, there were divergences between parties, with the biggest parties having the most luck keeping their sympathizers in the fold; projected KPRF voters were the least apt to switch, followed by Russia's Choice and the Liberal Democratic Party of Russia (LDPR). And when voters did stray, it was more often than not to parties whose programs had a family similarity to the one they started with (see table 3-5). In all of our five groupings of parties, and especially at the radical reformist and socialist poles, waverers normally stuck with their original group[7] or defected to an ideologically proximate one. Sixty percent of the voters surveyed stood pat

Table 3-4. *Consistency of Party-List Vote with Voters' Intentions*[a]
Percent

Voters	Vote December 12 same as intention in preelection interview
All voters	60
By date of interview	
Before November 27	54
November 28–December 4	60
After December 4	63
By degree of certainty of voting intention	
Some uncertainty	53
Certain	64
By party for which respondent intended to vote	
LDPR	71
Russia's Choice	72
KPRF	76
Women of Russia	65
Agrarian	51
Yabloko	52
PRES	54
DPR	37
RDDR	47
Civic Union	35
Future of Russia	23
KEDR	23
Dignity and Compassion	23

a. Excludes respondents who did not give a voting intention or who voted against all parties.

with the party they first meant to vote for; 6 percent opted for a cognate party in the same grouping; 16 percent migrated to one in a neighboring column of table 3-5; and 18 percent in all executed a more drastic switch of two or more columns.

These qualifications are not enough to blunt the thrust of the argument. The parties were insubstantial arrivistes in Russia's engineered founding election. Most citizens had no emotional allegiance to any, put off settling which to endorse until the eleventh hour, and had an almost even chance of amending their opening preference by election day. Abiding party sentiment is not the key to deciphering the election.

Social Structure

Another way of conceiving of electoral choice draws inspiration from political sociology instead of social psychology. Voting decisions in this reading "are basically seen as reflecting broadly based and long-standing

Table 3-5. *Consistency of Party-List Vote between Groupings*[a]

Percentages

	Intended vote				
Actual vote	Radical reformist	Moderate reformist	Centrist	Nationalist	Socialist
Radical reformist	72	15	14	3	4
Moderate reformist	9	60	11	9	4
Centrist	9	10	56	8	7
Nationalist	5	11	9	71	11
Socialist	5	4	10	8	74

a. Excludes respondents who voted against all parties.

social and economic divisions within society, and the cleavage structure is thought of in terms of social groups and of the loyalties of members to their social groups."[8] In the most oft-quoted exegesis of the paradigm, Seymour Martin Lipset and Stein Rokkan, illustrating from Western Europe after World War II, depicted mass politics as breaking down along objective, bedrock cleavages engendered spontaneously by the global process of modernization (and concomitants such as industrialization, urbanization, secularization, and administrative rationalization) and by the peculiar sequence in which social change unfolded in the country setting. Lipset and Rokkan detailed four pervasive conflicts that social factors transcribed onto the party system: between center and periphery and between church and state (both of them products of what they termed the national revolution), and between town and country and between capital and labor (throw-offs of the industrial revolution).[9]

In principle, this second mode of analysis should be fruitful in Russia. Granted, its social morphology differs mightily from the Western archetype, and the chaotic breakdown of socialist authoritarianism has muddied group identities and solidarities.[10] This having been said, post-Soviet Russia assuredly exhibits some universalistic lines of social differentiation—between urban and rural sectors, between the old and the young, between the genders, and among ethnic groups, to cite a few—which have the potential of being put into play in the political game. As for others, in particular, socioeconomic cleavages, it is an empirical question of how much of the preexisting fabric remains and how quickly new forms are supplanting it.

So far as the Duma campaign of 1993 goes, it cannot be overlooked that most of the parties openly courted specific social constituencies. Three went so far as to construe themselves as agents of exclusive groups: Women of Russia (women), the Agrarians (peasants and rural folk), and Future of Russia (youth). Several of the more inclusive parties featured blatant appeals to target groups in their campaigns: the LDPR (ethnic Russians), Russia's Choice (business entrepreneurs and intellectuals), the KPRF (pensioners), Yabloko (the "technical intelligentsia"), and the Party of Russian Unity and Accord (PRES; residents of the non-Russian republics). Beyond this, any party could have made inroads with discrete social groups accidentally or casually without knowingly courting them.

The individual-level survey data, which record both personal traits and the voting decision, offer invaluable insight on the social correlates of partisan support. Let us hypothesize, with the aid of the data, that eleven sociological variables *may* have had an impact on party preference in 1993. Eight—urbanization, occupation, income, change in economic well-being, education, ethnicity, religion, and region—are versions of the sources of cleavage sketched by Lipset and Rokkan and stem in sundry ways from the industrializing and nation-building dynamics of modernization. Two— gender and age—are ascriptive characteristics not emphasized by Lipset and Rokkan. The eleventh attribute—past membership in the CPSU, the Communist Party of the Soviet Union—is an artifact of Soviet and Soviet-bloc history.

Urbanization

We could not fail to ask about the rural-urban continuum, a discriminating factor in the political life of dozens of countries. Did voters in Russia's least modernized communities, its far-flung villages, differ in their partisan tastes from urban voters, and was there a gradation among the urbanites? I use a straightforward measure of community size (population in the 1989 census) to set up this question.

Occupation

No less obvious would be a query about the person's place in the world of work and wages. Western-regarding typologies that posit a divide between working class and middle class, or between labor and capital, jar with socialist and early postsocialist realities. For Russia in 1993, where private ownership of economic assets began to revive only months before the election, property-centered definitions offer little purchase. The most expedient starting point is a rudimentary distinction between manual workers and nonmanual employees.[11]

Income

Russians in our sample were asked their personal and family incomes for the month of October 1993. Because refusal to answer this delicate question was more widespread for individual than for household incomes (26 percent as opposed to 12 percent), and because family earnings is probably a superior marker of welfare, I used the household measure, grouped by quintile, as the income indicator.

Living Standard

A corollary indicator is the response to a question about changes in the family unit's standard of living over the preceding twelve months. Thirty-five percent of respondents agreed that it had worsened a lot and 24 percent reported that it had deteriorated a little; only 16 percent saw an improvement.[12]

Education

Social scientists trying to situate an individual in the status hierarchy will often use educational attainment as a supplement to occupation and income, and sometimes as a substitute. Formal education may also be understood as a generator of knowledge and cognitive sophistication. A stock finding in comparative research is that persons with more advanced educations incline toward more liberal and cosmopolitan currents in politics. To see whether this was so in the State Duma election, I bifurcated respondents into those with a higher, college-level education and those without.

Ethnicity

Although not as heterogeneous as the Soviet Union, the Russian Federation is a multinational country whose Russian majority amounts to about 82 percent of the population and dozens of minorities, many quite small in demographic mass, make up the remainder. Ideally, we wanted to know not only whether Russians and non-Russians voted differently but also whether there were differences in the give-and-take between the twenty-one national republics, where the indigenous, titular group enjoys legal privileges for promotion of its culture and language, and the oblasts and krais, where Great Russians are demographically predominant and no ethnic group is politically advantaged. Accordingly, the ethnicity indicator employed is a categorical variable with two values for oblasts and krais (for Russians and non-Russians) and three for the republics (for the titular nationality, non-Russian minorities, and Russians).

Religious Affiliation

Organized religion, primarily the Russian Orthodox Church, was a pillar of precommunist society. Despite the efforts of the Soviet authorities to inculcate atheism, Orthodoxy weathered communism and its implosion better than just about any traditional institution. Forty-five percent of those in our sample said they were believers, of whom most (36 percent) professed Orthodoxy and 10 percent practiced the rites of the faith. For the voting analysis, a three-way variable was constructed, with values for observant Orthodox, nonobservant Orthodox, and non-Orthodox.[13]

Region

As has been noted time and again since the late 1980s, the results of Russian elections and referendums are geographically imbalanced. Areas such as Moscow and its environs, the northern provinces of European Russia, and the Urals have turned out in force for radical candidates and causes; others, such as the breadbasket provinces between Moscow and the Caucasus Mountains and the southern fringe of Siberia, have leaned against reform. As can be seen from the entries for the eleven census regions[14] in table 3-6, spatial asymmetry was again evident in the party-list voting in December 1993. Russia's Choice, for one, did markedly better in northern parts of European Russia than in the south; for its harshest antagonists, the nationalist and socialist oppositions, the reverse was true. Until 1993 most analysts, disposing of only aggregate data, could not discern whether region or regional subculture per se was the root cause or if an area's politics stemmed from other characteristics of the population, such as level of urbanization or ethnic composition.[15] Individual-level data culled for a large national sample should allow discrimination between regional and other social effects in

the 1993 election. Even at that, though, the statistical task is daunting unless the number of regions for which we test for a spatial effect is kept to a
minimum. I have thus bracketed the eleven census regions into five macroregions, which I label the Center, the European North, the European
South, the Urals, and the East. Their boundaries, and totals of party-list
votes in each, may be found in table 3-6.

Gender

We would expect Women of Russia, led by women and vaguely feminist
in its platform, to have received the lion's share of its 8 percent of the popular vote from women. But just how wide was the gender gap in 1993, and
did the other parties suffer an equal hemorrhage of female votes? Gender,
needless to say, codes as a binary variable.

Age

Political scientists in the West have devoted much effort since the 1970s
to exploring value and behavioral disparities between human generations.
They have documented several different generational phenomena: a life-
cycle effect, inducing young persons to deviate from their elders but move
closer to conformity with their parents as they mature; a cohort effect, im-
printed indelibly on an age group in its formative years; and a period effect
that touches all age groups that live through a historical experience. One
can reliably distinguish among these only by studying public opinion longi-
tudinally, along a series of time points, and not by a snapshot such as in this
project.[16] But elementary age data from 1993 suffice for us to make out in
preliminary fashion whether significant cross-generational variation on
partisan political issues existed at all in early post-Soviet Russia.

Soviet Power Structure

The final personal characteristic whose potency should be gauged describes location in the apparatus of power of the defunct USSR. The badge
of entry into the Soviet establishment was enrollment in the CPSU. The
same card from "the party" that hedged an individual's freedom also bestowed information and opened career doors. Have such pragmatic involvements, not to mention the beliefs and corporate ethos that went with
them, left any political residue? Erstwhile CPSU members cannot be

Table 3-6. *Party-List Election Results by Macroregion and Census Region*[a]

Percent of popular vote

Region	Radical reformist	Moderate reformist	Centrist	Nationalist	Socialist
Center	19.4	18.9	18.1	23.8	19.7
Central Industrial	21.3	19.3	22.2	23.7	18.4
Volga-Vyatka	11.8	17.3	21.5	24.2	25.1
European North	21.0	24.2	17.5	25.1	12.2
Northern	20.7	19.8	21.8	24.7	13.3
Northwestern[b]	21.2	26.7	15.3	25.3	11.6
European South	11.2	17.2	17.4	26.0	28.2
Central Black Earth	11.0	12.8	15.5	33.3	27.3
Volga	13.3	17.6	19.3	24.9	24.9
North Caucasus	9.7	19.3	16.8	22.8	31.4
Urals	18.4	21.4	21.1	17.6	21.5
East	14.4	19.8	22.7	24.7	18.4
West Siberian	14.5	18.5	21.3	25.0	20.6
East Siberian	14.1	20.8	22.2	25.4	17.5
Far East	14.4	21.3	25.9	23.4	14.9
All regions	16.2	19.5	19.1	23.9	21.3

a. Excludes votes cast against all parties.
b. Includes Kaliningrad oblast, which officially does not belong to any census region.

clones, because most of those in the successor elite, from Boris Yeltsin on down, are ex-Communists. But we may properly wonder if they are biased on average, if not in each and every case, toward any post-Soviet parties and political groupings, the KPRF included. Nearly all respondents in our preelection survey, when asked whether they had belonged to the CPSU before its liquidation in 1991, gave an answer. The response has been rendered as a binary variable.[17]

Mathematical Model

These, then, are the social-structural variables and the indicators that operationalize them. To marshal them on the subject of this chapter, it is necessary to introduce them into a mathematical model that will ascertain their statistical relationship to the voting decision.

The tool routinely used in the social sciences to investigate such effects is regression analysis, which estimates the effects of a plurality of independent or explanatory variables on a common dependent variable, exerting control throughout over the collateral influence of the other variables. A sticking point is that the outcomes considered in this chapter are dichotomous—the decision to vote for a party can have only two values, yes or no—and dichotomous dependent variables violate the statistical premises of linear or ordinary least-squares regression, the usual regression method. I resort, therefore, to logistic regression, a related technique that requires some effort to interpret but finesses the limitations of ordinary least-squares.[18] For parsimony's sake, I concentrate on the eight parties that cleared the 5 percent threshold for seating in the State Duma, garnering altogether 87 percent of the tallied votes, and the five party groupings (two of which coincide with single parties).

Table 3-7 lays out the logistic regression coefficients for our core social characteristics, plotted as independent variables against the vote for each of the parties and party groupings as dependent variables. Six of the eleven independent variables—for occupation, education, ethnicity, macroregion, gender, and CPSU membership—are rendered as binary or multivalue categorical variables. The model supplies coefficients for the number of measurement categories minus one, reserving one value as a foil for the others (and assigning it a coefficient of 0). The remaining five independent variables—for community size, household income, change in economic circumstances, religion, and age—are continuous or interval variables. In order to expedite comparison of coefficients, they have been rescaled to run from 0 to 1, the same limits as for the categorical variables.

Technically, the logistic regression coefficients represent the proportional change in the log odds of the voting outcome occurring that is associated with a one-unit change in the independent variable. Positively signed coefficients denote a stimulating effect, negatively signed coefficients a depressing effect. To illustrate, the first entry in the second column of table 3-7 signifies that, for a voter whose chances of selecting Russia's Choice on the party list were otherwise 50-50, the log odds of his doing so leapt by a factor of 1.12 if he lived in the largest community in our sample (Moscow) as compared to the smallest village in the sample. To restate with a different statistic, not divulged in the table, the probability of that citizen voting Russia's Choice would rise from 50 percent to 75 percent by virtue of his big-city location.

Table 3-7 conveys forcefully that social structure did have multiple linkages with partisan preferences in 1993. Each of the Duma-bound parties and of the party groupings struck a chord with some audience or other.

The party whose voting base was shaped by the most sociodemographic factors (nine out of eleven) was the top-finishing LDPR. All other things being equal, villagers and small town dwellers, blue-collar workers, the poorly educated, ethnic Russians in the oblasts and krais, the Orthodox devout, provincials from the European South, the young, males, and persons who had been outside the CPSU under Soviet rule leaned more than other citizens toward the LDPR. For the third-finishing KPRF, the illiberalism and fierce hostility to the government that it shared with the LDPR make it all the more striking that its subelectorate was so disparate at the grassroots. Support for the KPRF, unlike the LDPR, was not correlated with urbanization, education, or gender but was highly correlated with self-assessed decline in economic welfare. Geographically, KPRF strengths were quite different from the LDPR's, and for all other social factors the two parties betrayed opposing effects, with the KPRF evincing popularity among nonworkers, non-Russians in the republics, the irreligious, older voters, and former card holders in the CPSU. The KPRF's fellow socialists, the Agrarians, displayed an astronomically high negative coefficient for urbanization, some rapport with the titular groups in republics, and a geographic weakness in most macroregions except the Center.

The turnout for Russia's Choice also had a palpable sociological profile. The "party of power" was moored in urban centers, in the better-educated stratum, in regions outside the European South, and among voters who felt relatively well off financially. In ethnic terms, it did well among non-Russians living in the oblasts and krais but poorly with non-Russians in the republics, especially with the titular peoples.

As a group, the moderate reformist parties had more amorphous followings. Yabloko, besides resembling Russia's Choice on points of community size and educational background, scored best with secular voters and in the European North. PRES, the only party other than Russia's Choice to charm economic achievers, also did well among all ethnic categories in the national republics. Women of Russia, the biggest of the centrist parties, hauled in votes mostly from women and the Orthodox,[19] and support for the smaller Democratic Party of Russia (DPR) was skewed toward persons with more formal education, the economically aggrieved, and men and away from former members of the CPSU and from two analogous minority camps: non-Russians resident in the oblasts and krais and Russians in the republics.

The incipient social politics woven through the election was not fueled by all social divisions in equal proportion. Socioeconomic distinctions, as

Table 3-7. Effects of Social Characteristics on Party Vote (Logistic Regression Coefficients)

Social characteristic	Radical reformist	Moderate reformist			Women of Russia	Centrist		Nationalist		Socialist	
	Russia's Choice	Yabloko	PRES	All		DPR	All	LDPR	KPRF	Agrarian	All
Community size[a]	1.12*	.97*	-.46	.48	-.67	.17	-.77*	-1.19*	-.36	-18.79*	-1.31*
Manual worker	-.03	.04	-.25	-.20	.27	-.15	.06	.24*	-.39**	.18	-.15
Family income[a]	.01	.27	.36	.38**	.68	.07	.10	-.02	-.09	-.46	-.30
Improved living standard[a]	.84*	.09	.62**	.45**	.15	-.84**	-.23	-.21	-1.69*	-.16	-1.14*
Higher education	.33*	.69*	-.26	.28	-.01	.68**	.15	-.75*	-.24	-.04	-.24
Ethnicity[b]											
Titular in republic	-1.02*	-.22	1.18*	.06	-.37	-.22	-.45	-1.44*	.98*	.82*	1.22*
Nontitular in republic	-.60	.04	.88**	.48*	-.07	-.92	-.48	-.39	1.47*	.18	1.19*
Russian in republic	-.20	-.20	.84**	.38**	-.39	-1.74**	-.43**	.08	.41	.10	.40
Non-Russian in oblast	.51*	.18	.13	.17	.15	-1.85**	-.04	-.09	-.68	-.69	-.72**
Orthodox[a]	.13	-.39*	-.03	-.26*	.30*	-.17	.12	.21**	-.27**	-.18	-.26**
Macroregion[c]											
European North	.15	1.00*	-.88**	.48*	-.10	-.98**	-.19	.34	-.71**	-1.04*	-.96*

European South	-.43*	-.03	.42	.17	.13	-.29	.02	.30*	.32	-.64*	-.10
Urals	.22	.21	.44	.38**	.50**	-.33	.19	.15	-1.06*	-.82*	-1.13*
East	-.09	.24	-.11	.06	.51**	-.30	.21	.10	-.46**	-.03	-.33
Woman	.05	.20	.42**	.24**	1.44*	-.46**	.70*	-.96*	-.01	-.26	-.12
Age[a]	-.28	-.32	.23	-.07	.17	-.92	-.09	-.59**	2.29*	.63	1.80*
Former CPSU	.00	-.24	-.01	-.20	-.01	-.67**	.38	-.70*	1.04*	.31	.90**
Constant	-1.86*	-2.57*	-3.03*	-1.72*	-3.53*	-3.03*	-2.09*	-.92*	-2.44*	-2.26*	-1.57*
Model improvement[d]	5.7	5.6	5.5	3.1	8.4	5.9	3.18	8.5	13.5	13.6	11.8
Cases correctly predicted[d]	78.4	91.3	93.9	83.0	89.0	95.6	1.6	79.9	89.9	93.1	83.8
Reduction of errors[d]	2.7	1.1	None	None	0.9	3.4	0.5	None	1.0	2.8	0.6

*p <.01
**p <.05
a. Variable rescaled to range 0 to 1.
b. Omitted category is ethnic Russians in oblasts.
c. Omitted category is Center macroregion.
d. Percent.

reckoned by occupation, economic welfare, or education, told on the votes of six of the eight largest parties—all except Women of Russia and the Agrarians—and of all of the party groupings in the aggregate except the centrists. But they had to share the stage with other, cross-cutting social variables. In fact, it was region that had the most associations with party choice (eight), and ethnicity was not far behind (six). Urbanization generated four associations: As we would have anticipated from the comparative literature, the liberal Russia's Choice and Yabloko led the vote cavalcade in the big cities and nationalists and socialists prevailed in the countryside and smaller towns. Effects for religion and gender were in evidence for four parties each and for CPSU membership for three.

The mobilization of social groups in 1993 was partly the outgrowth of hard-nosed, calculating leadership. Vladimir Zhirinovskii's "patriotic" populism found the greatest resonance among working-class Russians, the subgroup he cultivated the most fervently, and sparked the foreseeable backlash among white-collar employees and the titular nationalities in the republics. By the same token, Russia's Choice reaped electoral rewards among the economically successful from its commitment to accelerate the marketization process, and it and to a lesser extent Yabloko and the DPR helped make the case with voters of superior social status by recruiting professors and arts figures onto their party lists. The KPRF, the party most dead-set against market reforms and most solicitous of groups disadvantaged by them, fared well among persons who had been hurt by reform and among citizens of pension age. Women of Russia and the Agrarian party got some of the women's and peasants' votes for which they beat the drums. And PRES made headway on its plan to woo the republics in the name of "national reconciliation."

Other times, the connection with social structure may have owed more to happenstance and to the inadvertent consequences of leaders' and campaign managers' decisions than to purposive strategy. The chauvinistic Zhirinovskii made few references on the stump to Orthodoxy, but the LDPR probably profited from a nostalgic coupling in some believers' minds of the faith and the national heritage. Although the LDPR did not set out to alienate women, female voters shunned it on December 12, in large part, I would surmise, as a result of unease at Zhirinovskii's swaggering masculinity and the violent undercurrents in his rhetoric. In the same vein, Russia's Choice did not choose at the outset to make itself anathema with non-Russians; its devotion to President Yeltsin, with his hard line on republic rights, seems to have had this consequence.[20] The KPRF's electoral exploits in the republics were likely triggered less by its 1993 manifestos than by the recollection that the forerunner CPSU in its day kept the lid on ethnic enmities and sponsored affirmative action for minorities. On the down side, the party's historical baggage dissuaded youthful voters at the same time as it comforted the elderly.

In sum, the case for a social nexus in the election is respectable and cannot be overlooked. Nonetheless, it should not be overstated, either. As can be seen in the "model improvement" row toward the bottom of table 3-7, societal variables make but modest additions to the goodness of fit between observed values (actual votes cast) and the probabilities predicted by the consecutive regression equations.[21] Model improvement runs from about 6 percent for Russia's Choice, Yabloko, and PRES to about 14 percent for the KPRF and the Agrarians. It is no higher than that because, when all is said and done, the social groups themselves fell so far short of electoral unanimity in 1993. Even when the regression coefficients signal a big effect on propensity to vote for one or another party, that effect was *in no case* potent enough to tilt an absolute majority of a demarcated social category into that party's camp. The most sizable positive coefficient in table 3-7, for instance, links past membership in the CPSU with a vote for the KPRF, but only 21 percent of the ex-CPSU members in our sample who voted on December 12 marked their ballots for the KPRF. The parameter for women and support of Women of Russia was also extremely high, yet a mere 17 percent of the women interviewed chose Women of Russia. Various aspects of social structure did influence voting decisions, but they did so by providing pockets and crannies of support, not by forming hard-and-fast cleavages. The election did not come close to partitioning the electorate into tidy social blocs.[22]

Issue Voting

The third stylized approach to electoral behavior emerged in the advanced democracies in the 1970s as a critique of models hinged on party identification and social structure. Conventional theories, revisionists studying Western Europe argued, were too static to handle developments such as television campaigning, voters' increasing skill and independent-mindedness, the blurring of class boundaries, and the eruption of movements of popular protest and direct political action. As party systems were destabilized and "dealigned," voters were not as encumbered by conformity to party or secondary social group and warmed more to lifestyle and value questions. Scholars detected a parallel drift toward "policy voting" or "voting the issues" in the United States.[23]

It would be futile to look for a literal reenactment of this trend in post-Soviet Russia: its people have barely been initiated into democracy and have had neither perennial party loyalties nor a sturdy social cleavage-based political alignment to supersede. To dismiss issue voting outright, though, would be to toss out the baby with the bath water. Issue effects in any country are complementary to party identification and social variables, not black-and-white alternatives to them. Party affiliation does not spring up in a motivational vacuum; parties gather and expand their followings when initial rapport over some public choice evolves into a psychological bond that can be perpetuated over time. By the same token, a sociological characteristic must be mediated by an attitude or mental state for it to color voting behavior.

It makes sense then, and is a good benchmark for the future, to ask to what extent beliefs and opinions impinged on voting in the 1993 election. We obtained some leverage by inviting our respondents in the postelection survey wave to articulate in their own words up to five of "the most important problems . . . Russia has faced in recent times," and then to say which they felt to be the most pressing. A generic coding scheme was drawn up after the fact. More than 70 percent of our voters (see table 3-8) put their finger on some kind of economic issue as the nation's most burning problem, and seven of the ten specific problems most often brought up were economic. Law and order, the nationality question, social problems, and politics and the constitution followed, with foreign policy bringing up a distant rear.[24]

Appreciation of a problem's urgency, of course, should not be confused with having a shared standpoint on what to do about it. Ivanov and Petrov might agree that the Russian economy is in dire straits and still disagree bitterly over whether the government should remedy it by fast-forwarding marketization, muddling through, or reinstating central planning. To flush out respondents' issue preferences, as distinct from issue salience, we administered a battery of several dozen policy-related questions, ranging from the somewhat abstract to the highly tangible. The largest subset touched on economic crisis and reform, aptly so for a campaign whose agenda was dominated by economics. Because screening of the question responses showed many of them to be interrelated, some but not all can be integrated into scales that will serve as efficient predictors in subsequent analysis.[25]

Table 3-8. *Responses about the Most Important Problem Facing the Country*[a]

Problem	Percent
Type of problem	
Economic	71
Law, order, and morals	9
Nationality	8
Social	6
Political and constitutional	6
Foreign policy	0.4
Ten most frequently mentioned problems	
Economic crisis in general	27
Inflation	19
Decline in standard of living	8
Crime	6
Unemployment	6
Dissolution of the USSR	4
Fall in economic output	4
Weak and unstable government	2
Ethnic conflict	2
Privatization	2

a. Omits the 17 percent of respondents who were not able to give a response.

Five measures may be taken as approximations of normative attitudes toward compelling national issues at the time of the election.

State Control of the Economy

One issue cluster had to do with state ownership and control of economic assets, against which Yeltsin's reform administration had made a concerted assault since the collapse of the USSR. Opinion on the reform course and underlying issues covered a wide spectrum in late 1993, from bristling hostility to marketization to enthusiastic acceptance. I represent it by a scale combining the responses to eight question items on economic transition and the suitability of Western models for Russia.[26]

Welfarism

A second bundle of issues was about what Russians call "social protection," welfare-state commitments that shelter vulnerable individuals and groups from the vagaries of economic change. The center of gravity of public opinion in this realm was perceptibly more conservative than on questions of state control. The index built conjoins questions about a government guarantee of full employment and limitations on food prices, income inequality, and imports of foreign-manufactured goods.[27]

The Soviet Legacy

Regrettably, we did not ask incisive survey questions about law, order, and morals, the problem area that proved to rank second to economic and socioeconomic policy among the worries of the populace. But we can provide an imperfect proxy in a scale averaging affect toward three heads of the defunct Soviet regime: Vladimir Lenin, Joseph Stalin, and Leonid Brezhnev. Among other things, this index will tap some of the implicit conceptions of right, wrong, and human rights that played during the 1993 campaign around concrete issues such as crime and corruption.[28]

Presidential Power

Dissension over how Russia was to be governed, most sensationally the clash between President Yeltsin and the Congress of People's Deputies, precipitated the destruction of the "First Russian Republic" and the election of 1993. In studying the election, it proved impossible to derive a composite scale blending popular attitudes toward all constitutional and institutional issues. I pegged the voting analysis to a survey question about the most vexed institutional controversy, over the prerogatives of president and parliament. (See chapter 10 for more on public opinion and the constitution.)

Rating of Yeltsin

It is fitting to incorporate the voter's performance evaluation of the man who has towered over Russian politics in the 1990s. A four-way question about how much the respondent "approve[s] of the activity of B. N. Yeltsin in the post of president of Russia" furnishes a handy yardstick of political outlook. Its predictive power can then be compared with measures of opinion on more particularized issues.

As is evident from the correlations in table 3-9, attitudes toward state economic control, welfarism, Soviet leaders, presidentialism, and Yeltsin's reign overlapped, although they certainly did not coincide.[29] The more pro-

Table 3-9. *Correlation Matrix (Pearson's r) for Five Opinion Variables*

	Welfarism	Soviet leaders	Presidentialism	Yeltsin approval
State control	.54*	.42*	-.23*	-.40*
Welfarism		.36*	-.16*	-.24*
Soviet leaders			-.15*	-.22*
Presidentialism				.31*

* $p <.01$ (two-tailed test)

market a citizen in economics, the greater the chances he or she would advocate individual over state responsibility in social policy, think poorly of the Soviet dictators, support a presidential regime, and admire Yeltsin's record.

With the groundwork done, we can rerun the regression analysis of party-list voting, this time trying out policy-related opinions, not social structure, as explanations for voting behavior. For ease of comprehension and comparability, the five attitudinal variables have been bounded at 0 and 1, the same limits as the sociological variables.

Table 3-10 sets forth logistic regression coefficients that estimate the impact of opinions on the party-list vote, following the same methodology used in table 3-7. The parameters demonstrate strong evidence of opinion effects, though anything but uniformly so. All five variables prejudiced the likelihood of voting for or against at least one of the parties, and all parties and groupings of parties were subject to the influence of at least opinion.

The configuration varied markedly by issue domain. Esteem of Yeltsin and of the Soviet leaders were both statistically predictive of partisan preference for five among the eight parties. But the three indicators most intimately tied to the State Duma campaign—state control of the economy, welfarism, and presidential power—guided electoral choice for but two parties apiece.

The party whose support was most responsive to opinions was the KPRF. Holding high the banner of traditional socialist values, it exerted a hold on voters of the same stripe—unflinchingly pro-state control, pro-welfarism, pro-Soviet, antipresidential, and anti-Yeltsin. The mindset of the backers of Russia's Choice was almost a mirror image of the KPRF's, because they were promarket, antiwelfarist (this association was not significant at the usual statistical threshold),[30] anti-Soviet, propresidential, and pro-Yeltsin. To rephrase the coefficients for one of the five opinion indicators, the state control index, all other things being equal, having the maximum preference for state management of the economy would have lifted

Table 3-10. Effects of Opinions on Party-List Vote (Logistic Regression Coefficients)

Opinion	Radical reformist	Moderate reformist			Centrist			Nationalist		Socialist	
	Russia's Choice	Yabloko	PRES	All	Women of Russia	DPR	All	LDPR	KPRF	Agarian	All
State control of economy scale	-1.20*	-.72	-.67	-1.00*	.60	-.78	.35	-.56	2.57*	.69	2.02*
Welfarism scale	-.49	-.68	.19	-.18	1.16*	-.22	.66**	.05	1.04**	.86	.92**
Soviet leaders scale	-1.42*	-2.02*	.48	-1.07*	-.02	-.96**	-.46	1.51*	2.38*	.60	1.81*
Presidentialism	.62*	-.10	.10	.10	-.13	-.50	-.35**	-.01	-.77*	-.09	-.54*
Yeltsin approval	1.81*	-.32	.67**	.17	.33	.21	.38	-1.19*	-1.56*	-1.09*	-1.47*
Model improvement[a]	14.3	4.9	1.0	3.0	1.2	1.6	0.7	4.3	19.3	4.2	15.7
Cases correctly predicted[a]	79.5	91.2	93.9	83.0	88.9	95.6	81.7	80.0	89.8	92.9	82.7
Reduction of errors[a]	7.7	None	None	None	0.4	None	None	None	None	None	None

*p <.01
**p <.05
a. Percent.

the probability of a citizen voting for the KPRF by about 43 percent as compared to a minimum score and would have lessened the probability of voting for Russia's Choice by 27 percent. For both KPRF and Russia's Choice, the opinion variables do a better job of accounting for voting propensity than the social-structural variables, as reckoned by model improvement.

When we look beyond the KPRF and Russia's Choice, the party subelectorates lag well behind in terms of attitudinal coherence. For the other six parties, opinion is inferior to social characteristics as a predictor of the vote. If opinions alone are used to forecast partisan choice, on only two of the five commanding dimensions—evaluations of Soviet leaders and of Yeltsin—could they be related to the likelihood of voting for the LDPR. On both scores, the inclinations of LDPR voters were conservative, although markedly less so than for the KPRF. For the remaining five parties, a statistically significant correlation appears for but one issue cluster per party: approval of the president for PRES (pro-Yeltsin) and the Agrarians (anti-Yeltsin), the Soviet leaders for Yabloko, and the social safety net for Women of Russia.[31]

It is entirely legitimate to explore issue opinions independently of social infrastructure, because they have integrity and causal worth in their own right. But it would be artificial to put the two species of explanation in sealed compartments. Social structure affects attitudes in Russia, as anywhere in the world, and inasmuch as it tells on political behavior it does so through psychological intermediaries. The five macro-issues we have extracted from the 1993 election relate in orderly ways to social indicators (see table 3-11). Crossed with our sociological variables, the five opinion scores are correlated with them in some degree in more than 80 percent of the dyads. For the most part, city dwellers, white-collar workers, people with higher and improving living standards, the better educated, ethnic Russians, nonbelievers, nonsoutherners, males, the young, and persons who never joined the CPSU hewed to more reform-friendly positions on the issues in 1993.

An instructive exercise is to repeat the logistic regression, using as explanatory variables in this rendition both attitudes *and* the sociological variables. Were social traits to be highly determinative of attitudes, and were those attitudes to be highly determinative of voting conduct, the magnitude and statistical significance of the coefficients for the social variables would drop in the merged regression; their impact on partisan preference would be suppressed by the more proximate opinion measures. Alternatively, a combined regression equation might spotlight social variables that bore a rela-

Table 3-11. *Associations between Opinions and Social Characteristics (Pearson's* r*)*

Social characteristic	State control	Welfarism	Soviet leaders	Presidenti-alism	Yeltsin approval
Community size	−.11*	−.07*	−.12*	.04*	.12*
Manual worker	.19*	.17*	.16*	−.02	−.06*
Family income	−.25*	−.24*	−.20*	.06*	.10*
Improved living standard	−.33*	−.28*	−.16*	.12*	.22*
Higher education	−.18*	−.20*	−.16*	−.03	.04**
Ethnicity					
Titular in republic	.09*	.04**	.09*	−.04*	−.08*
Non-titular in republic	.00	.03**	.07*	−.06*	−.00
Russian in republic	−.02	.02	−.00	−.01	−.03
Non-Russian in oblast	−.02	−.01	−.02	.02	.02
Orthodox	.11*	.11*	.07*	.04*	.04*
Macroregion					
European North	−.06*	−.07*	−.07*	.05*	.05*
European South	.14*	.12*	.20*	−.07*	−.12*
Urals	−.07*	−.01	−.10*	.01	.05*
East	−.08*	−.09*	−.11*	.02	.01
Woman	.11*	.16*	.05*	.00	−.01
Age	.37*	.32*	.26*	−.07*	−.02
Former CPSU	.03	.00	.02	−.09*	−.01

*p <.01 (two-tailed test)
**p <.05 (two-tailed test)

tionship to the voting outcome over and above any effect realized through the attitudinal indicators at hand.

As expected, the opinion coefficients survive in the simultaneous regression (see table 3-12) and in most cases are diminished only slightly by the introduction of the social indicators.[32] Regressing the vote on the attitudinal and social variables together reduces the number of statistically significant coefficients in the social category, although the preponderance of them remain significant correlates of some voting choices.[33] Notably robust are the relationships involving community size, ethnic identity, some macroregions, age, and erstwhile membership in the CPSU. For all parties, it should be stressed, the joint regression produces greater model improvement than an equation using either social factors or opinions in isolation.

Before leaving voter opinions behind, it pays to take yet another cut at the link with electoral choice. Fixing voters' attitudes toward the issue agenda is one thing; learning how they relate their policy opinions to the political parties (issue proximity, as it is called in the voting literature) is another. On the latter score, we put a series of questions to respondents in the postelection interview about the fit between their beliefs and the programs of the parties. For four prominent public issues, we asked them to volunteer up to three parties whose "positions are closest to your point of view" and up to three parties with positions "especially remote from your point of view" on the problem. On three of the issues—the transition to a market economy, social protection, and presidential versus parliamentary government—we already possess refined measures of the voter's personal preferences.[34] The extra information enables us to check separately for the relevance of citizen-party distance to voting decisions.

These survey questions were demanding, because they forced respondents to calibrate their own ideas with judgments about where a slew of parties, most of them newcomers, came down on the issues. Understandably, voters were far less forthcoming than they were with more elementary questions. The mean number of parties designated as either near to or far from the individual's point of view was in all instances less than one (see table 3-13). As with recall and recognition of the parties, participating voters were invariably more knowledgeable than abstainers. There were further differences by issue area (with the questions about president and parliament getting less of a reaction than those about economic transition and social protection) and between positive matches and negative mismatches (matches outnumbering mismatches for all three issues).

For each of the three cardinal issues, and for each of the eight parties under scrutiny, I have constructed an issue proximity variable.[35] It takes the value 1 if the respondent said the party's stand harmonized with his, 0 if he saw it as far from his opinion, and .5 all other times. When these measures are deployed as independent variables in a reiteration of the logistic regressions, the results (see table 3-14) are intriguing and more than a little perplexing. The issue proximity scores beget dramatically higher coefficients than raw opinions do (compare with table 3-10) and are vastly more proficient in forecasting electoral choice, as measured by model improvement and percentage of voting decisions correctly specified. The augmentation of explanatory power seems to apply to all parties, even the tiny ones, and to all three opinion dimensions.

The data, although inadequate to sustain a full-fledged explanation, permit reasoned conjecture about this discrepancy. I submit that we have encountered a process of psychological "projection," wishful thinking whereby voters imagine that political parties or candidates whom they favor on some other grounds share their issue preferences when in fact they do not. A citizen engaging in projection may not be aware of the party's or

Table 3-12. Effects of Opinions and Social Characteristics on Party Vote (Logistic Regression Coefficients)

Independent variable	Radical reformist	Moderate reformist			Women of Russia	Centrist		Nationalist		Agrarian	Socialist
	Russia's Choice	Yabloko	PRES	All		DPR	All	LDPR	KPRF		All
State control scale[a]	-1.36*	-.67	-.68	-.95**	.36	-.67	.19	-.16	2.34*	.34	1.72*
Welfarism scale	-.81*	-.47	-.12	-.14	.86**	-.11	.50	.54	.76	.74	.72
Soviet leaders scale	-1.30*	-1.92*	.15	-1.08*	.18	-1.04**	-.30	1.51*	2.37**	.19	1.63*
Presidentialism	.64*	-.08	.18	.13	-.29	-.54	-.42**	-.04	-.52**	-.08	-.44***
Yeltsin approval	1.59*	-.45	.83*	.17	.25	.57	.49*	-1.24*	-1.61*	-1.02*	-1.48*
Social Characteristics											
Community size[a]	.90*	.84*	-.61	.31	-.61	-.94	-.82*	-.83**	.37	-17.20*	-.81**
Manual worker	.10	.16	-.22	-.13	.25	-.08	.07	.14	-.54*	.15	-.24
Family income[a]	.17	.19	.36	.31	-.05	-.63	.12	.06	.08	-.41	-.21
Improvement in living standard[a]	.06	-.10	.27	.16	.48	-1.13*	-.23	.27	-.76**	.26	-.31
Higher education	.08	.51*	-.35	.13	.09	.49	.17	-.61*	.11	.07	.04
Ethnicity[b]											
Titular in republic	-.74**	-.18	1.33*	.70*	-.44	-.05	-.44	-1.58*	.73*	.71*	1.06*
Non-titular in republic	-.29	.34	.96*	.52	-.19	-.77	-.52	-.65**	1.26*	.11	.97*

Russian in republic	-.06	-.08	.86*	.25	-.44	-1.68**	-.44**	-.00	.35	-.67	.30
Non-Russian in oblast[a]	.52**	.19	.10	-.03	.18	-1.86**	-.02	-.10	-.49	.04	-.61
Orthodox[a]	.09	-.37*	-.05	-.27*	.30*	-.14	.11	.24**	-.20	-.16	-.24**
Macroregion[c]											
European North	-.07	.83*	-1.00**	.34	-.05	-1.07**	-.18	.49**	-.46	-.96*	-.78*
European South	-.25	.03	.47	.25	.11	-.22	.03	.18	.17	-.73*	-.28
Urals	.03	.07	.39	.28	.53**	-.46	.16	.34	-.92*	-.77**	-1.04*
East	-.19	.11	-.16	-.01	.55*	-.38	.20	.17	-.27	-.03	-.22
Woman	.24**	.28	.50*	.32*	1.41*	-.43**	.68*	-1.04*	-.01	0.31	-.17
Age[a]	.46	.39	.42	.47	-.17	-.58	-.22	-1.08*	1.00**	.30	.80**
Former CPSU	.17	-.16	.05	-.12	-.04	-.63	-.16	-.82*	.94*	.24	.82*
Constant	-1.04*	-.95**	-3.09*	-.80**	-4.39*	-2.08*	-2.37*	-1.57*	-5.08*	-2.78*	-3.30*
Model improvement[a]	16.8	8.5	6.8	5.2	9.0	7.5	3.6	13.0	25.7	11.6	21.4
Cases correctly predicted[a]	80.0	91.3	93.9	82.9	89.0	95.6	81.6	80.5	90.5	93.1	84.9
Reduction of errors[a]	9.9	1.1	None	0.6	0.9	None	None	2.5	6.7	2.8	12.7

*p <.01
**p <.05
a. Percent.

Table 3-13. *Mean Number of Parties Named as Close to and Remote from the Citizen's Positions on the Issues*

Issue and proximity	Actual voters	Abstainers	All respondents[a]
Oppose transition to market			
Close	.77	.29	.63
Remote	.54	.24	.45
Favor social protection			
Close	.80	.33	.66
Remote	.41	.16	.33
Favor presidential power			
Close	.50	.17	.40
Remote	.31	.12	.25

candidate's true position on an issue, the party or candidate may not have an unambiguous stance, or the citizen may subconsciously override what he does know to reduce cognitive dissonance. Whatever the mechanism, the voter comes to believe that the political group or personage echoes his point of view on the problem.[36]

In light of the tumultuous circumstances of the election, Russians' inexperience with free elections, and the newness and woolly programs of the parties, the theory of projection is as credible a justification as any for the incongruity between table 3-10 and table 3-14. For the two parties for which we have witnessed hefty associations between voter opinions per se and behavior at the polls—Russia's Choice and the KPRF—projection would have served mainly to reinforce the existing linkages. For the rest of the partisan field, however, imputed issue propinquity took on a life of its own. In reconstructing the decision to vote for or against Yabloko, PRES, Women of Russia, the DPR, the LDPR, and the Agrarians, the *substance* of voters' private opinions counted less than their *perception* that the public stands of the parties were in tune with their own. The disconnect seems to have been a good deal greater than what would be found in a general election in an established democracy.

If projection rested on ignorance, pure and simple, then stratification of the electorate by political knowledge and involvement ought to turn up systematic variation in it. If there were other culprits in 1993, attentiveness to politics would make little difference for the tendency to ascribe spurious positions to the parties.

The statistical correlations set forth in table 3-15 bestow some clarity on these questions. The intermingling between normative opinions and self-

Table 3-14. *Effects of Three Issue Proximity Indicators on Party Vote (Logistic Regression Coefficients)*

Issue	Russia's Choice	Yabloko	PRES	Women of Russia	DPR	LDPR	KPRF	Agrarian
Oppose transition to market	3.42*	4.24*	4.19*	2.53*	2.87*	3.46*	2.40*	3.68*
Favor social protection	2.50*	2.64*	2.77*	2.92*	3.42*	3.82*	4.37*	4.16*
Favor presidential power	1.75*	3.02**	2.04*	1.36**	3.60*	1.92*	2.55*	1.04
Constant	-5.98*	-8.26*	-7.93*	-6.01*	-8.68*	-6.54*	-7.67*	-7.51*
Model improvements[a]	30.3	29.6	23.4	11.6	24.0	33.7	35.5	17.4
Cases correctly predicted[a]	85.0	92.4	94.5	89.4	96.0	86.2	92.5	93.4
Reduction of errors[a]	32.2	13.3	9.8	4.5	9.1	31.2	26.1	6.5

*$p < .01$
**$p < .05$
a. Percent.

Table 3-15. *Associations between Issue Proximity and Issue Opinions, by Level of Interest in Politics (Pearson's* r)

Issue	High interest	Medium interest	Low interest	All respondents
Transition to market				
Russia's Choice	−.39*	−.28*	−.23*	−.30*
Yabloko	−.15*	−.19*	−.08*	−.16*
PRES	−.08**	−.08*	−.09*	−.09*
Women of Russia	.03	.02	.03	.03**
DPR	−.04	−.00	.01	−.02
LDPR	.17*	.20*	.14*	.18*
KPRF	.43*	.30*	.16*	.30*
Agrarian	.24*	.01	.02	.08*
Social protection				
Russia's Choice	−.20*	−.09*	−.06**	−.11*
Yabloko	−.09*	−.07*	−.07*	−.09*
PRES	−.08**	−.04	−.05**	−.06*
Women of Russia	.10*	.01	.00	.02
DPR	−.03	−.08*	−.02	−.06*
LDPR	.04	.07*	.05	.06**
KPRF	.29*	.17*	.08*	.18*
Agrarian	.15*	−.00	.04	.05*
Presidential power				
Russia's Choice	.26*	.20*	.02	.17*
Yabloko	.02	−.03	.00	−.01
PRES	.07**	.04	−.04	.03
Women of Russia	.01	−.04	.03	−.00
DPR	−.03	−.05**	−.07*	−.05*
LDPR	−.11*	−.03	−.06**	−.06*
KPRF	−.23*	−.14*	−.02	−.14*
Agrarian	−.15*	−.04	.03	−.06*

*p <.01 (two-tailed test)
**p <.05 (two-tailed test)

assessed issue proximity did generally vary with political interest. The more keenly the voter followed politics,[37] the more likely we can make out some rational relationship between issue preferences and specification of the parties best able to satisfy those preferences. For nineteen out of twenty-four issue party pairings, the correlation coefficient for the most politicized citizens was higher than the coefficient for the most lethargic (and the most ignorant). We may surmise that the projection of policy preferences onto the parties in 1993 was caused at least in part by limitations on voters' knowledge and engagement with the political world.

However, table 3-15 also tells us that the tie between policy desires and appraisal of the parties was conspicuously firmer for two parties—Russia's

Choice and the KPRF—than for all the others. Moreover, perceptions of these parties (and in a somewhat different way of the KPRF's fellow socialists, the Agrarians) also manifested the steepest fall-off in coherence as between high-interest and low-interest voters. By comparison, the distribution for the LDPR, which took in almost as many votes as Russia's Choice and the KPRF combined, is exceedingly flat. These party-by-party differences imply that projection was not rooted in citizen attitudes alone but owed something to the character of the parties themselves. It is no coincidence that it was the KPRF and Russia's Choice that confronted voters with the most sharply etched programs for action, anchored in the most readily comprehensible ideological verities. Had their rivals followed suit, genuine issue voting would have been more prevalent than it was in 1993.

The Leadership Factor

One last piece of the puzzle needs to be solved. In a presidential election, the object of which is to fill a single office, it is hard for the analyst to avoid the personality and unique drawing power of the individual candidates. But in a parliamentary election, in which teams of politicians fight for control over a corporate institution, the head of the ticket is not so natural an interest, even if it is someone of the stature of Margaret Thatcher or Helmut Kohl.[38] By this criterion, we might safely disregard personalities in Russia in 1993 and concentrate wholly on the parties and on the social and attitudinal variables undergirding their support.

I am inclined to be more inquisitive about the leadership factor. If nothing else, culturalist theories and folk wisdom about Russia should pique our curiosity. One often hears it said that tsarism, the tyranny of successive CPSU general secretaries, and the pervasive mistrust of institutions bred by totalitarianism have fostered a mass mentality that personalizes every public choice. Institutional realities in 1993 buttress the presumptive case. Russia's machinery of state already mixed presidential and parliamentary components, and the shift toward presidential dominance, in place since 1991, was to be confirmed by ratification of Yeltsin's draft constitution on December 12. It is appropriate to ask whether there was spillover of personality-centered thinking into the Duma campaign. The primitive organization of the political parties may also have played a part. Of the eight parties that made it over the 5 percent barrier, three—the LDPR (under Vladimir Zhirinovskii), PRES (Sergei Shakhrai), and the DPR (Nikolai

Travkin)—were to all intents and purposes creatures of a founding leader. A fourth—Yabloko—was hatched by and named after an ambitious triumvirate; one of the three, Grigorii Yavlinskii, had senior status from the start. The KPRF, Agrarian party, and Women of Russia had more collective structures, yet the person atop the electoral list of each (Gennadii Zyuganov, Mikhail Lapshin, and Alevtina Fedulova, respectively) spoke with authority for it and was heralded in the mass media accordingly. Even Russia's Choice, its slate packed by cabinet ministers and democratic-movement activists, owed its existence to the initiative of Yegor Gaidar, its kingpin before and after the election.

Although leadership was not a principal focus of our survey work, we did have respondents evaluate—on a feeling thermometer instrument, a picture of which was handed to them during the postelection interview—the paramount leaders of seven of the eight parties treated in this chapter (all except Travkin of the DPR) as well as one chair of a minor party (Arkadii Vol'skii of Civic Union). As stated previously, our research participants were not inhibited about coming to such a verdict, managing to assess more leaders than parties and doing passably well at connecting one with the other.

It is notoriously difficult in any electoral situation to disentangle politicians' reputations from the reputations of the parties they lead,[39] and this campaign is no exception. In countries with well-vested party systems, the analyst would normally use long-term party identification as a control, seeing how short-term personality considerations compare with it in impact on the vote. For Russia in 1993, where partisan sentiments were still so nebulous, such cross-referencing is excluded.

It is possible, the complications notwithstanding, to tease several regularities out of the thin body of information available. One is that leadership can usefully be brought to bear on the aforementioned syndrome of projection of voter wishes onto issue preferences. Why did so many Russians delude themselves in 1993 into drawing false parities between their opinions and the stands of the parties? The answer cannot be partisanship in its Western incarnation, but it might in part be a precursor to partisanship—an affective bond with the person at the helm of a nascent party organization. The survey data give us no sound basis for saying just what it was about leaders that caught voters' fancy: No doubt it varied from leader to leader. What the data provide are recurrent hints that in general the images of the party leaders fed into the projection pattern.

To represent citizen attitude toward the leaders, I created for each of them a variable structured like the issue-proximity indicators; it was coded as 1 if the respondent found that leader to be plainly superior to the rest, 0 if the leader was judged inferior, and .5 otherwise.[40] Table 3-16 presents the correlations obtained when assessments of the respective leaders are juxtaposed to the issue proximity scores for the parties (seven all told) captained by them. The table shows many similarities to table 3-15, which arrays issue proximity against issue opinions, but there are two major dissimilarities. First, the statistical associations in table 3-16 virtually always surpass those in table 3-15, often by a large margin. Evaluation of the leader of a party, in other words, was as a rule *a more capacious predictor of perceived issue proximity in 1993 than the voter's observable opinions on the issues themselves.*[41] Second, the fault line dividing Russia's Choice and the KPRF from all other parties, so starkly visible in table 3-15, disappears in table 3-16. The highest correlations on all three issues pertain, not to Gaidar or Zyuganov, but to Zhirinovskii—the flamboyant leader of a party with the mushiest of programs.

As a final statistical drill, let us try to gauge the unmediated impact of the leadership factor on the party-list vote. Table 3-17 lists logistic regression coefficients for the effects of the constructed leadership indicators on the likelihood of voting for the seven parties. In the absence of the partisan identification that would normally be the control term for a Western election, I have incorporated the issue proximity scores as covariates. These are second-best alternatives to measures of enduring attitudes toward the parties, and as such they serve as markers of what the citizen *thought* about the relationship between his preferences on "the issues" and what the parties had to offer. Leadership-oriented and issue-oriented variables interacted in 1993—precisely how, we cannot say—but the coefficients in this regression ought to estimate which of the two classes of indicators had the strongest direct impact on electoral decisionmaking.

The results of the regression speak with one voice to the importance—if not the overwhelming importance—of leadership. Evaluation of party leaders was strongly associated with citizen choice. Injection of the leadership measures into the regression greatly elevates the goodness of fit of the statistical model. Except for the deviant case of the Agrarian party and its spectacularly uncharismatic leader, Mikhail Lapshin, appraisal of the leader was more highly correlated with the voting decision than any of the issue-proximity variables, although the issue-related factors do not fall out of the equation. In short, leadership mattered in the election of 1993.

Table 3-16. *Associations between Evaluation of Party Leader and Issue Proximity, by Level of Interest in Politics (Pearson's r)*

Issue	High interest	Medium interest	Low interest	All respondents
Transition to market				
Russia's Choice	.48*	.39*	.21*	.34*
Yabloko	.33*	.29*	.16*	.24*
PRES	.22*	.13*	.09*	.12*
Women of Russia	.05	.12*	.14*	.11*
LDPR	.44*	.42*	.25*	.37*
KPRF	.35*	.26*	.19*	.27*
Agrarian	.12*	.07*	-.02	.06*
Social protection				
Russia's Choice	.42*	.31*	.15*	.29*
Yabloko	.26*	.18*	.14*	.17*
PRES	.24*	.11*	.03**	.11*
Women of Russia	.01	.09*	.07*	.04**
LDPR	.44*	.40*	.26*	.35*
KPRF	.33*	.24*	.11*	.22*
Agrarian	.08**	.07*	.07*	.06*
Presidential power				
Russia's Choice	.41*	.30*	.06**	.24*
Yabloko	.27*	.19**	.13*	.17*
PRES	.20*	.07*	.08*	.09*
Women of Russia	.03	.05**	.08*	.05*
LDPR	.36*	.36*	.22*	.31*
KPRF	.33*	.18*	.07*	.20*

*p <.01 (two-tailed test)
**P<.05 (two-tailed test)

Conclusion

Much about the electorate's conduct in Russia's first post-Soviet election is and will continue to be inexplicable. But much, as this chapter has demonstrated, does yield to patient investigation.

Of the most widely touted models of electoral choice, the first, predicated on stable identification with a political party, is the only one that affords no real insight into the 1993 campaign. The most one can say is that the majority of citizens knew something about the parties in the arena, that certain parties had a steadier grip than others on their sympathizers' affections, and that voters who were fickle tended to switch to parties not so far removed ideologically from the ones with which they started.

The second conceptual approach, tracing partisan alignments back to sociological characteristics and divisions, is a better beacon. Receptivity to-

Table 3-17. *Effects of Evaluation of Party Leader and Issue Proximity Indicators on Party Vote (Logistic Regression Coefficients)*

Independent variable	Russia's Choice	Yabloko	PRES	Women of Russia	LDPR	KPRF	Agrarian
Leader evaluation	3.33*	3.56*	4.00*	3.52*	3.79*	3.74*	2.37*
Oppose transition to market	2.77*	3.25*	3.91*	2.11*	2.87*	2.28*	3.58*
Favor social protection	2.25*	2.47*	2.43*	2.92*	3.35*	4.16*	4.14*
Favor presidential power	1.54*	2.80**	1.93*	1.29	1.34*	2.52*	1.12
Constant	-6.43*	-9.19*	-9.22*	-7.41*	-7.13*	-8.99*	-8.50*
Model improvement[a]	42.7	38.7	35.6	20.8	49.8	44.7	19.8
Cases correctly predicted[a]	88.0	93.3	95.1	90.4	89.9	93.5	93.6
Reduction of errors[a]	45.9	25.0	19.7	13.5	49.5	36.3	9.9

*p <.01
**p <.05
a. Percent.

ward the messages of the parties was not randomly strewn across the social landscape. Russia's neophyte parties, incapable though they were of carving out truly well-bounded bases within extensive segments of society, did find pockets and crannies of group support, as we have called them, and that was no mean achievement.

The third school of thought about voting decisions takes up issue opinions and attitudes, which Russians hold unabashedly and in abundance. It, too, contributes to an understanding of the election saga, and especially of the fate of the two parties with the most cohesive and boldly painted programs—Russia's Choice and the KPRF. Issue opinions, influenced in their own right by social variables, were voting inputs to be reckoned with, and projected images of which parties catered to citizens' opinions were more closely tied to the vote.

The noteworthy causal role of a fourth factor, leadership, may be interpreted as a sign of the immaturity and fragility of democratic practices in early post-Soviet Russia. Yet the prominence of personalities should not be entirely an occasion for pessimism. It is probably easier to grow and educate civic-minded politicians in a country in regime transition than it is to build partisan identification from the ground up, to transform social structure, or to inculcate radically new points of view in tens of millions of people. Assuming that Russians retain and gradually enlarge the capacity for making intelligible political choices that they displayed in 1993, we should be alert to the prospect that partisan entrepreneurs straining to enlarge their shares in the marketplace for votes will impart greater coherence to the electorate in impending elections.

Notes

1. This is particularly so in the United States, where the classic statement remains Angus Campbell, Philip E. Converse, Warren E. Miller, and Donald E. Stokes, *The American Voter* (New York: John Wiley & Sons, 1960). Many issues about applicability to other countries are canvassed in Ian Budge, Ivor Crewe, and Dennis Farlie, eds., *Party Identification and Beyond: Representations* (London: John Wiley & Sons, 1976). A landmark in the non-American literature is Philip E. Converse and Roy Pierce, *Political Representation in France* (Harvard University Press, 1986).

2. The leadership questions were all in the postelection interview. We asked respondents to state the party headed by Vladimir Zhirinovskii, Yegor Gaidar, Gennadii Zyuganov, Alevtina Fedulova, Mikhail Lapshin, and Arkadii Vol'skii. The

evaluation question on the 101-point feeling thermometer was given later and included Grigorii Yavlinskii of the Yabloko party.

3. From the 1952 to the 1988 presidential elections in the United States, the highest proportion of voters who reported coming to a decision any time in the last two weeks of the campaign was 26 percent. But late deciders were much less numerous among voters with firm partisan commitments. The Russian figures for last-minute decision are reminiscent of those reported in U.S. presidential primaries. See Samuel L. Popkin, *The Reasoning Voter: Communication and Persuasion in Presidential Campaigns* (University of Chicago Press, 1991), p. 119–21.

4. Fifteen percent of survey respondents who stated they never followed political events said they decided how to vote by one month or more before December 12, compared with 44 percent of voters who paid constant attention to politics. Seventy-six percent of low-interest voters decided in the final days of the campaign or on election day, versus 39 percent of high-interest voters.

5. Presumably because of a carry over of past political commitments, KPRF voters who had once belonged to the ruling Communist Party of the Soviet Union were especially likely to decide early: 58 percent said they chose by no later than one month before December 12. But ex-members of the CPSU were also more likely than average to come to an early decision to vote for parties other than the KPRF. Forty-three percent of former members of the CPSU who voted for some other party reported having made an early decision, 11 percent more than the mean for all voters.

6. One study of the United States and Sweden from the 1950s to the 1980s found within-campaign turnover to average around 5 percent and between-election turnover to lie between 15 and 25 percent. Donald Granberg and Søren Holmberg, *The Political System Matters: Social Psychology and Voting Behavior in Sweden and the United States* (Cambridge: Cambridge University Press, 1988), chap. 8.

7. This option, of course, did not exist for either the LDPR or Russia's Choice, each of which by our definition was coterminous with a party type.

8. Mark N. Franklin and others, *Electoral Change: Responses to Evolving Social and Attitudinal Structures in Western Countries* (Cambridge: Cambridge University Press, 1992), pp. 4–5.

9. Seymour Martin Lipset and Stein Rokkan, "Cleavage Structures, Party Systems, and Voter Alignments: An Introduction," in Lipset and Rokkan, eds., *Party Systems and Voter Alignments: Cross-National Perspectives* (New York: Free Press, 1967), pp. 1–64.

10. Valerie Bunce and Maria Csanadi argue in "Uncertainty in the Transition: Post-Communism in Hungary," *East European Politics and Society,* vol. 8 (Spring 1994), pp. 240–75, that flux has been so great in all the postsocialist countries as to sever almost all connections between social groups and political action. The point is interesting but, in my view, exaggerated.

11. Retired voters were classified on the basis of the last job held. Students and other young voters who could not yet be put in an occupational category were coded as nonworkers.

12. Missing values for both income and change in living standard were recoded at the mean of the distribution.

13. Other religions, especially Islam, are of theoretical interest, but the small number of faithful in Russia impedes statistical analysis from a general sample of the population.

14. In official parlance, these areas, whose boundaries go back to Soviet times, are called "economic regions" (ekonomicheskiye raiony).

15. See Ralph S. Clem and Peter R. Craumer, "The Geography of the April 25 (1993) Russian Referendum," Post-Soviet Geography, vol. 34 (August 1993), pp. 481–96; Darrell Slider, Vladimir Gimpel'son, and Sergei Chugrov, "Political Tendencies in Russia's Regions: Evidence from the 1993 Parliamentary Elections," Slavic Review, vol. 53 (Fall 1994), pp. 711–32; and especially Gavin Helf, "All the Russias: Center, Core, and Periphery in Soviet and Post-Soviet Russia" (Ph.D. dissertation, University of California at Berkeley, 1994). A survey project carried out by British and Russian specialists in connection with the 1993 parliamentary election tested for some of the same social variables as our study but could not consider region because of insufficient sample size. Matthew Wyman, Stephen White, Bill Miller, and Paul Heywood, "Public Opinion, Parties and Voters in the December 1993 Russian Elections," Europe-Asia Studies, vol. 47 (June 1995), pp. 591–614.

16. See the lucid discussion in Franklin and others, Electoral Change, pp. 27–28.

17. One third of 1 percent declined to answer, and 13 percent said they had been CPSU members. Predictably, former Communists were much more plentiful among men, middle-aged and older voters, and the better-educated. Among men aged forty or over with a college-level education, 60 percent had belonged to the CPSU.

18. Logistic regression transforms the dependent variable into a logit, the natural logarithm of the odds of the outcome occurring. This constrains the expected value of the dependent variable to fall between 0 and 1, avoiding the nonsensical values (representing probabilities of less than 0 or more than 100 percent) that may occur with OLS in a like situation. The plot of expected values is an S-shaped curve, not the straight line of OLS.

19. These two categories overlap, as Russian women tend to be more religious than men, but each had independent influence on the propensity to vote for Women of Russia.

20. The DPR, in a variation on this pattern, seems to have created a reputation for itself of being insensitive to vulnerable minorities, thus alienating both Russians in the republics and non-Russians in the oblasts.

21. The improvement referred to is in the "likelihood" (the probability of obtaining the observed results, given the parameter estimates), as captured in the measure -2 times the log likelihood (-2LL). The comparison is between likelihoods estimated using the equation constant alone and those estimated after assimilation of the social-structural variables.

22. Hardly ever did any party's vote share in a social group or stratum within our survey sample exceed 30 percent. Russia's Choice drew 37 percent among respondents reporting a significant improvement in family finances over the preceding year, 35 percent among the inhabitants of urban areas with populations of more than 500,000, and 30 percent among those with a higher education. Because our

sample overreported the Russia's Choice vote by about 6 percent even after weighting for social characteristics, these proportions are probably inflated. Twenty-six percent of manual workers in our sample said they had voted for the LDPR; this probably understates the LDPR's performance among workers by several percentages. Territorially, the highest proportion achieved by any party in a census region (according to the official returns) was the LDPR's 33 percent in the Central Black Earth zone.

23. For the flavor of this literature, see Norman H. Nie, Sidney Verba, and John R. Petrocik, *The Changing American Voter* (Harvard University Press, 1976); Russell J. Dalton, Scott C. Flanagan, and Paul Allen Beck, eds., *Electoral Change in Advanced Industrial Democracies: Realignment or Dealignment?* (Princeton University Press, 1984); and Franklin and others, *Electoral Change.*

24. These categories are necessarily inexact. Unemployment, for example, could be considered a social problem as much as an economic problem. But reclassification of borderline responses would not greatly modify the overall distribution.

25. As a preliminary test for relationships among opinions, I did a factor analysis, a technique designed to uncover latent dimensions underpinning a multiplicity of observable variables. But the "loadings" and "factor scores" produced in factor analysis are ultrasensitive to the quantity and content of the full set of items. For purposes of follow-up analysis, I prefer less complicated reliability scales, which subsume only the subset of questions directly concerned. To conserve observations, I substituted the mean for all missing values in the opinion questions.

26. The scale equally weights and adds answers to questions about the pace of movement toward the market, privatization in general and privatization of factories, trade, and land, foreign investment, the value of Western economic advice, and the desirability of Westernization. Cronbach's alpha, the conventional test of inter-item correlation, was a high .781.

27. Cronbach's alpha for this scale is .529.

28. Cronbach's alpha was .660. In each case, the respondent was asked to rate the historical figure on a feeling thermometer running from 0 to 100 degrees.

29. The highest correlation coefficient in table 3-9, the .54 value between state control with welfarism, would mean that in an ordinary least-squares regression linking the two variables one would explain approximately 29 percent of the variation in the other. For the lowest observed correlation, the -.15 between presidentialism and appraisal of the Soviet leaders, only 2 percent of the variation would be accounted for.

30. The regression coefficient for welfarism and voting Russia's Choice is significant at the .09 level.

31. In addition, some other coefficients come fairly close to statistical significance at the stock .05 level. Yabloko's coefficient for welfarism was significant at the .08 level, and the Agrarians' for welfarism and the Soviet leaders were significant at the .10 and the .11 level.

32. One of the opinion coefficients (relating welfarism to a vote for the KPRF) drops below the significance threshold, but a second (for welfarism and voting Russia's Choice) rises above the threshold, leaving the total unchanged. Five coefficients actually increased in magnitude and two stayed the same.

33. When social factors only are considered (see table 3-7), the logistic regressions generate forty-one significant coefficients. Taking opinion variables into account, they decline to thirty-four.

34. The fourth issue was about the balance of power between Moscow and the regions. I keep it out of the discussion because it had so little to do with voting choice.

35. Because these indicators reflect voter assessments of all the parties simultaneously, they might all be seen as expressions of the same underlying variable. This is important because the regressions that follow should in principle be performed with the same independent variables.

36. Scholarly discussion in American political science dates back to Benjamin I. Page and Richard A. Brody, "Policy Voting and the Electoral Process: The Vietnam War Issue," *American Political Science Review,* vol. 66 (September 1972), pp. 979–95.

37. The question was phrased in terms of frequency of attention to political events. Twenty percent of our respondents answered that they followed politics *all the time,* 40 percent that they did so *sometimes,* 21 percent that they *very rarely followed politics,* and 18 percent that they *never paid attention;* 1 percent did not answer the question. In table 3-15, the *very rarely* and *never* responses are combined in the low-interest column.

38. Two leading authorities express astonishment that, journalistic interest in Thatcher notwithstanding, "the party leaders . . . are simply, for all practical purposes, written out of the script" of scholarly works on British elections. Ivor Crewe and Anthony King, "Did Major Win? Did Kinnock Lose? Leadership Effects in the 1992 Election," in Anthony Heath, Roger Jowell, and John Curtice, eds., *Labour's Last Chance? The 1992 Election and Beyond* (Aldershot, U.K.: Dartmouth, 1994), p. 126.

39. "It goes without saying that personality images and party images are bound to affect each other." Ibid., p. 127.

40. I constructed the variable from the 0-to-100-degree ratings given to each leader on the thermometer, recoding missing values at 50 degrees. I considered a leader to be ranked ahead of his peers if his temperature rating was at least 10 degrees "warmer" than the mean of the other ratings, and ranked lower than the others if his rating was at least 10 degrees "cooler." As with the issue proximity scores, we can conceptualize these variables as being aspects of one underlying variable.

41. To repeat, there exists no measure of identification with the party, as opposed to appraisal of the leader, that could be used as a control in the analysis. We did ask respondents to evaluate the parties, but the scale was four-point only (with values for a positive attitude toward the party, more positive than negative, more negative than positive, and negative), making it hard to compare results with the 101-point scale used to evaluate the leaders. More damaging, the question about the parties was contained in the preelection interview and that about leaders in the postelection interview.

CHAPTER FOUR

Russia's Choice

The Perils of Revolutionary Democracy

Michael McFaul

IN DECEMBER 1993, for the first time since the formation of Russia's anti-communist movement in the late 1980s, advocates of radical economic and political reform—represented in this election by the electoral bloc Russia's Choice—were rejected by Russia's voters. The results shocked Russia's radical reformers. Although public opinion polls suggested that Russia's Choice might capture as high as 40 percent of the popular vote, this proreform and pro-Yeltsin electoral bloc won only 15. 5 percent, well behind the 23 percent garnered by Vladimir Zhirinovskii's Liberal Democratic Party of Russia (LDPR) and not much higher than the 12 percent won by the Communist Party of the Russian Federation (KPRF). This dismal showing was especially surprising considering that President Boris Yeltsin—the leader and symbol of Russia's radical reform movement—had just won majority approval ratings for both his performance as president and his economic reform plan in a nationwide referendum held in April 1993, just eight months before the December parliamentary elections.

In addition to those people cited in the notes, I would like especially to thank Vladimir Bokser, Mikhail Schneider, and Ludmilla Stebenkova from Russia's Choice for providing me with daily interviews and updates on their campaigns and also allowing me to observe the day-to-day operations and activities of the campaign. In addition, I would like to thank Joshua Freeman, Sergei Markov, and Tanya Kovalenko for their assistance in preparing this chapter. None of the opinions expressed in this chapter should be attributed to anyone but the author.

What happened? How do we explain this dramatic difference in electoral outcomes in such a short period of time?

To frame the context for understanding, this chapter begins by tracing the origins of Russia's Choice and then describing the bloc's strategy and tactics during the campaign. The second part of the chapter analyzes how structural variables, institutions, and individual strategic decisionmaking influenced the electoral performance of Russia's Choice in the 1993 parliamentary elections.

The Origins of Russia's Choice

In the December 1993 elections, Russia's Choice was the latest incarnation of Russia's radical reformist forces. Russia's Choice in December 1993, however, neither represented nor was composed of the same reformist forces that mobilized the democratic movement against Soviet communism in 1990 to 1991. During this interval, Russia's "democratic" movement had undergone many ideological and organizational changes. Part of the explanation for the electoral performance of Russia's Choice can be found in this history between 1990 and 1993.

The electoral bloc Russia's Choice was a descendent of Democratic Russia, a wide coalition of parties, civic organizations, trade unions, and individuals that coalesced around their shared opposition to Soviet communism.[1] During the tumultuous last years of the Soviet Union culminating in the August 1991 coup attempt, Democratic Russia played an instrumental role in mobilizing anticommunist sentiment throughout Russia. When communism collapsed in August 1991, the raison d'être for the Democratic Russia coalition also disappeared. Many of Democratic Russia's most prominent leaders quit the movement to pursue either governmental posts or careers in the emerging private sector. With the period of polarization between communists and democrats apparently over, political parties allied under the Democratic Russia umbrella also left the movement in anticipation of a postcommunist period of multiparty politics. In the Congress of People's Deputies, several deputies from Democratic Russia formed new factions, and others became independents. As a social movement, Democratic Russia's profile also waned during this period; it was much easier to organize demonstrations against communism than rallies in support of shock therapy. Perhaps most important, relations between Yeltsin and Democratic Russia soured. In quest of power, Yeltsin needed the grassroots organizational capacity of Democratic Russia to arrange nationwide rallies, coordinate his presidential campaign, and mobilize opposition to the August 1991 putsch. Once in power, however, Yeltsin and his entourage no longer required such services.

During the summer of 1993, democratic leaders both inside and outside the government increasingly recognized the need to consolidate their ranks. As rumors about new elections began to circulate in the spring of 1993, government officials and politicians close to the president began to worry that "reformers" could not be elected to a new parliament running as candidates from a weak and discredited Democratic Russia. For those who had acclimated to the comforts of government power, Democratic Russia looked like an anarchic band of antiestablishment radicals who might be useful as leaflet distributors but who could not be relied on to run their reelection campaign. As a consequence, several senior political figures including Gennadii Burbulis, Aleksei Golovkov, and Arkadii Murashev organized a new political organization to supersede Democratic Russia. Their aim was to found a movement that could still secure support from Democratic Russia's traditional supporters—the urban, liberal intelligentsia—but could also attract new backing from those that had benefited from the postcommunist status quo, including members of Yeltsin's government and presidential staff, Yeltsin-appointed heads of regional administrations, directors of newly privatized enterprises, and the nouveau riche. This kind of electoral bloc was no longer a revolutionary opposition movement but a party in defense of the current order.

As conceived by the original organizers of this new political organization, the fusion of Democratic Russia and Russia's Choice would take place by the dissolution of the former. Organizers of Russia's Choice hoped to buy off the key members of Democratic Russia's apparat; other members of Democratic Russia would then be invited to join Russia's Choice as individuals. Leaders of Democratic Russia, not surprisingly, opposed this formula.[2] Longtime Democratic Russia figures such as Lev Ponomarev, Gleb Yakunin, Il'ya Zaslavskii, and Vladimir Bokser realized that their personal stature in no way compared to that of Yegor Gaidar, Andrei Kozyrev, or Anatolii Chubais. They also acknowledged that Democratic Russia as a political organization did not enjoy widespread support within the Russian electorate. At the same time, they did not want to fully subordinate their movement to a new organizational structure, an obvious first step toward the permanent disintegration of Democratic Russia.

Eventually, on the eve of the founding congress of Russia's Choice in October 1993, the old leaders of Democratic Russia and the new leaders of the Russia's Choice reached a compromise. Instead of being forced to join the Russia's Choice Movement as individuals, Democratic Russia's leaders agreed to join Russia's Choice bloc. In doing so, Democratic Russia Movement and Russia's Choice Movement each retained its individual identity and organizational integrity. On paper, the Democratic Russia Movement and the Russia's Choice Movement constituted the two central components of the new Russia's Choice electoral bloc. This electoral bloc also included several smaller organizations, including the Association of Private and Privatized Enterprises headed by Yegor Gaidar and Aleksei Golovkov; the Peasant Party of Russia led by Yurii Chernichenko; the League of Cooperatives and Entrepreneurs, and the newly created political arm of the organization the New Party of Democratic Initiative headed by Pavel Bunich and Aleksandr Tikhonov; the Organization of Peasants and Farmers of Russia (AKKOR) headed by Vladimir Bashmachnikov; "Living Circle"; and the Movement "Military for Democracy" (*Voennie za Demokratiyu*).[3] It became clear, however, during the proceedings of the founding congress on October 16 to 17 that this electoral bloc was firmly controlled by people from Russia's Choice Movement. Voting on the federal party list was orchestrated according to plan. Of the nineteen people nominated and chosen for the bloc's federal list, none were leaders of Democratic Russia. Instead, the list of federal candidates from Russia's Choice reflected the bloc's new "party of power" image as sixteen of the nineteen federal list candidates were either current or former government officials.

After these nineteen "federal" candidates, Russia's Choice decided to divide its party list regionally. On these regional lists, Democratic Russia members usually appeared second or third behind names proposed by Russia's Choice Movement, meaning that only seven out of forty deputies elected to the Duma from the party list of Russia's Choice bloc were from Democratic Russia Movement.[4]

The disproportionate representation of candidates from Russia's Choice Movement on the party list from Russia's Choice bloc precipitated real friction between these two organizations both in Moscow and among the regions. In the capital, conflict between Democratic Russia (Movement) and Russia's Choice (Movement) had several debilitating manifestations for an effective campaign. Indicative of these divisions, the two movements maintained separate campaign headquarters. This geographic division impeded effective strategic coordination and effectively marginalized Democratic Russia leaders from the bloc's decisionmaking process.

Outside of Moscow, tensions were even greater. In seeking support of leaders of a less radical persuasion, founders of Russia's Choice Movement had courted many regional leaders (heads of administration, presidential representatives, and entrepreneurs) to join their coalition. In many regions, these were the very people against whom local Democratic Russia leaders had been struggling for the past two years.[5] It was not surprising, therefore, that provincial Democratic Russia activists and Russia's Choice regional members proposed very different lists of local candidates for the bloc's regional party lists. When the Moscow apparat of Russia's Choice unilaterally decided to name their candidates for the bloc's federal list, many regional Democratic Russia branches threatened to quit the bloc as they could not support these nomenklatura candidates. A special "Conciliation Commission" was established in Moscow between the two movements, which made rulings on formal complaints from thirty-one different regions.[6] Table 4-1 demonstrates how regional government officials and economic managers—people not affiliated with Democratic Russia—dominated the new bloc's list of candidates.

Excluded from the party list, dissatisfied regional leaders from Democratic Russia instead submitted their own candidates for single-mandate seats. The result of this anarchic competition was disastrous. Remarkably, the Russia's Choice bloc ran two or more candidates in sixteen electoral districts and Democratic Russia candidates ran as independents in several other races.

Campaign Expectations

Despite these internal divisions both in Moscow and throughout Russia, leaders of the Russia's Choice bloc were still confident they would win the largest percentage of the popular vote as well as the largest plurality of seats in the State Duma. This confidence was based on several assumptions that informed and guided their electoral strategy and subsequent campaign activities.[7] First, the configuration of Russia's Choice represented the "party of power." The bloc included the president's chief of staff, the president's former state secretary, five deputy prime ministers, the foreign minister, as well as the ministers of information, science, culture, and the environment. According to bloc strategists, this lineup of senior government officials

Table 4-1. *Candidate Profiles from Russia's Choice*

	Single mandate	Party list
Number of candidates	210[a]	21.2
Average age	46.5	44.5
Men	92.9	91.5
Former RSFSR deputies	3.8	12.3
Science, education, media	19.5	22.3
Senior economic management	21.4	10.9
Middle economic management	12.9	7.6
Party/social activists	11.0	20.3
Russian government officials	2.8	10.0
Regional government officials	20.9	16.1
Military and police	.9	3.3
Other white collar	7.1	8.0
Blue collar	.5	.5
Other	2.8	0

Source: Mikhail Schneider of Russia's Choice provided data.
a. This is the number of candidates supported by Russia's Choice. From Sergei Yushenkov and Arkadii Murashev, press conference, October 18, 1993.

gave Russia's Choice the advantage of incumbency. Second, as the "party of power," leaders of Russia's Choice expected to win roughly the same level of popular support that the president garnered during the April referendum. As both Arkadii Murashev and Sergei Yushenkov stated openly at the bloc's first press conference, "We are the president's party."[8] Third, the bloc assumed that Russia's Choice would represent the only real alternative for those voters interested in continuing economic reform. If, as demonstrated in April 1993, most Russians supported Yeltsin's reform course, leaders of Russia's Choice thought that they stood a good chance of winning a sizable minority as the representatives of this course in this election.

Factors of Defeat

In retrospect, these expectations seem unwarranted, rooted neither in theory nor recent comparative historical experience. Well before the campaign began, the structural and institutional context of this election greatly constrained the electoral prospects of any reform party. Within these limitations, Russia's Choice fared especially poorly by making many strategic mistakes in the campaign.

The Structural Context

Russia is undergoing a social revolution, a rare and distinct moment in history in which the organization of the polity and economy is transformed abruptly and simultaneously.[9] In 1993, Russia was in midstream of such a revolutionary transformation, similar in scale and scope to the régime-transforming processes unleashed in France at the end of the eighteenth century or Russia at the beginning of the twentieth. Different from these past revolutionary transitions, however, Russia's revolutionaries have refrained from using force to remove those associated with the ancien régime. Rather, they tried to bring about revolutionary transformation through peaceful, democratic means.

Like other great social revolutions, the social base for mass mobilization against the ancien régime was very large in Russia as demonstrated both by the level of participation and actual outcomes of the plebiscite-type votes in the spring of 1990 and the summer of 1991, and the scores of public demonstrations, miners' strikes, and protest acts from 1989 to 1991. Popular support against an incumbent regime, however, does not imply that these same forces have a shared vision about a new system. In Russia, Boris Yeltsin and Democratic Russia eventually defined their "ideology of opposition" in terms of democracy and markets. Although an effective ideology for mobilizing resistance to the Soviet regime, these slogans consciously lacked a proactive definition before August 1991.

After the failed coup attempt in August 1991, Russia's revolutionary opposition was suddenly offered the opportunity to seize the state and then implement a program for socioeconomic transformation. As became readily apparent soon after the initiation of the Gaidar reform plan in January 1992, the real social base for this revolutionary agenda—that is, social groups that would immediately benefit from these reforms—was nascent, small, and politically apathetic. At the same time, the vast majority of Russian citizens, including the largest and most important collective identities such as industrial and collective farm workers, directors of state enterprises, military personnel, and pensioners, were adversely affected by the initiation of this transformative economic program. It is significant that those social groups that most actively supported anticommunist activities during the period of opposition in 1990 to 1991—such as engineers, teachers, doctors, and scientific researchers—were the same people who suffered most directly from Gaidar's economic reform plan.

The initial lack of a social base for a future economic system as well as the presence of a large set of social actors opposed to the destruction of the old system is a feature common to all revolutionary transitions. It should not be surprising, therefore, that elections held in the middle of such transitions go against those affiliated with the revolutionary government in power.[10] When considered in the framework of revolutionary transitions and recent experiences within the postcommunist world, what is really surprising is that we expected Russia's Choice to win.

Compared with other East European transitions, the timing and sequence of Russia's elections have been especially poor for radical reformers. Their first electoral victory in March 1990 for the Congress of People's Deputies and local soviets was only a partial one, yet they were held responsible for government policy thereafter. In a similar manner, Yeltsin won a landslide electoral victory in June 1991, but placed liberal reformers in charge of the government for only the first few months of 1992. Yet again, these liberals were blamed for all of Russia's economic hardships. (One also must not forget the economic mess they inherited.) Thus, unlike Poland, the Czech Republic, or Hungary, Russia's liberal reformers have never enjoyed a firm majority in the parliament or total control of the executive.

The most propitious time for Russia's first postcommunist election was immediately after the August 1991 putsch. In East European countries where the first postcommunist elections were held immediately after the fall of communism, liberal democratic forces dominated the political spectrum and captured clear majorities in their new parliaments.[11] Although splits and realliances among these liberal democratic parties have been widespread, these new political forces nonetheless constituted the main menu of choices for voters in second elections. Equally important, parties that did not gain a position in the parliament after the postcommunist election either disappeared altogether or underwent radical change in orientation to survive.

Russia, however, did not have its founding election immediately after the fall of communism. This delay created a different menu of choices as well as a distinct (that is, less euphoric) context for Russian voters than first postcommunist elections in Eastern Europe. With a two-and-a-half-year interval between the fall of communism and the first postcommunist election, almost all of the proreformist political parties founded in 1990 to 1991 had decayed or disappeared by December 1993.

In addition, during this two-year interval, much happened to undermine the electoral prospects of radical reformist parties. Russia's attempt at economic reform in 1992 and 1993 resulted in greater falls in production, higher inflation rates, and more uncertainty about the future than any other East European market transition. Acute economic hardship helped to sustain political groups from the Soviet ancien régime such as the Communist and Agrarian parties. Unlike discredited Communist parties in Eastern Europe, Russian Communists could remain orthodox in these circumstances and still win votes. In addition, the collapse of the Soviet empire combined with economic woes to kindle more extreme nationalist parties and movements during this period than in Eastern Europe. Under these circumstances, it is difficult to think of a worse time for a first postcommunist election than the winter of 1993.

Proximate Variables

When understood in the context of Russia's revolutionary transition, the poor performance of Russia's Choice in December's election should have been expected. As established earlier in this chapter, comparisons with other postcommunist transitions suggest that the defeat of the radicals in an election held midstream in the process of fundamental economic restructuring is the rule, not the exception. Why, then, were expectations of success for Russia's Choice so high? Part of the reason, as already mentioned, was the bloc's own propaganda about the inevitability of its success. Among leaders of the bloc, the result of the April 1993 referendum also fueled high expectations. In this vote, held only seven months before parliamentary elections, Yeltsin won 58.7 percent of the popular vote, and his economic reform program—a program with which Gaidar and other leaders of Russia's Choice were closely associated—won a remarkable 53 percent. This high level of support for reformers sixteen months after the initiation of Gaidar's radical economic reforms confuses the standard assumption regarding the "antireformist" vote in December. If voters in December were rejecting "shock therapy," why did they not reject this program eight months earlier? The question, then, is what factors changed or intervened between April and December to cause this level of support to fall so dramatically?

The Economy

Economic performance might be a possible important factor. After all, the general state of the Russian economy did not improve between April and December of 1993. Inflation continued to hover between 20 and 25 percent, real wages did not increase, and the real exchange rate actually declined over this period.[12] Polls indicate that Russian voters felt the consequences of these indicators. A poll conducted in November of 2,000 people by the Institute of Sociology of Russian Academy of Sciences showed that 31.5 percent of those surveyed thought the general economic situation in Russia had become "considerably worse" since June; 30 percent thought the economy to be "a little worse"; and only 8.5 had noticed an improvement during this same interval.[13]

Although the economy was bad, it did not get appreciably worse between April and December. Of course, the patience and ability of the average Russian citizen to persevere through this sustained economic hardship most likely declined. But were voters so disillusioned with their current economic condition that only 15 percent of them still supported market reforms? This seems unlikely. A November poll from the Institute of Sociology, for instance, indicated that 45.9 percent of those surveyed thought a transition to a market economy was a correct course for Russia, and only 27.4 percent thought the opposite.[14] This poll showed that 44.5 percent supported privatization, and only 34.5 percent opposed the transfer of state property into private hands. If accurate, these numbers suggest that we cannot attribute the poor showing of Russia's Choice to economic decline alone.

The "October Events"

Another obvious intervening event between the April referendum and the December parliamentary elections was the tragic events surrounding the dissolution of the old Russian parliament. In retrospect, the use of military force by one branch of government against the other appears to have generated apathy among Russian voters, because the turnout in December 1993 was considerably lower than either previous or subsequent elections. Moreover, with Yeltsin firmly in control of the Russian state, the importance of a parliamentary election to voters declined considerably. In November, only 15 percent of those surveyed thought that the December election would change anything in their own lives, and 71 percent was sure that it would not.[15]

Even those who voted revealed their disenchantment with the democratic process. Unofficially, "against all" won an average of 19.8 percent in single-mandate races.[16] Spoiled ballots in these same districts averaged 8 percent, meaning that 27 percent of all votes were cast for no one.[17] This level of alienation with the electoral process may help explain why people did not feel the need to support Russia's Choice, even if most still supported the course of market reform.

Institutions

If the intervening role of economy is questionable and the impact of the October events is difficult to measure, the new rules of the game that shaped the kind of election held in December had a direct impact on that electoral outcome. The most obvious difference between April and December was the kind of election held. The vote in April was a referendum, a plebiscite on Boris Yeltsin and his policies. Voters had only two choices: for or against. It is significant to note that the one vote in December that had a similar dichotomous menu of choices—the referendum on the constitution—had a similar outcome to the April plebiscite. Officially, 58.4 percent of the voting population approved the constitution, almost equivalent to the 58.7 percent that supported Yeltsin in the April referendum.

For the parliamentary ballots, however, voters were not limited to either Russia's Choice or, for instance, the Communist Party of the Russian Federation. Rather, this vote was Russia's first genuinely multiparty election, giving voters the opportunity to express more nuanced preferences. Had the December Duma vote been structured by the same rules of the game as earlier Russian votes, the outcome—or perhaps more important, the perception of the outcome—may have been very different. If one artificially divides the party vote into proreform (Russia's Choice, PRES, Yabloko, Russian Movement for Democratic Reform [RDDR], DPR, and Women of Russia) and antireform blocs (KPRF, the Agrarian party, and the LDPR) the outcome would have been 47.8 percent versus 43.3 percent. These numbers are not significantly different from the voter split on question 2 of the April referendum. The divided vote among the proreform electoral blocs, however, created a different perception concerning winners and losers. The 15 percent garnered by Russia's Choice looks significantly smaller than the 23 percent won by the Liberal Democratic Party. Even the sum of the four proreformist parties (Russia's Choice, PRES, Yabloko, and RDDR) would have been greater at 34 percent than the LDPR total of 23 percent. The change in the kind of vote from a plebiscite to a multiparty election greatly affected the perception, if not the actual outcome, of Russia's Choice's performance in the December elections.[18]

Russia's new mixed electoral system constituted a second set of rules that adversely shaped both the actual outcome and the perception of the outcome for Russia's Choice.[19] As in other countries with proportional representation (PR), Russia's PR encouraged party proliferation, undermining Russia's Choice as the only party representing reform. Small parties such as Yabloko, PRES, and RDDR could hope to cross the 5 percent barrier and win a place in the parliament.[20] In a first-past-the-post system, they would have been forced to cooperate with Russia's Choice and each other to have a chance at winning seats in the parliament.[21]

The PR system also decreased the importance of having effective regional organizations and increased the electoral chances of parties led by one charismatic leader. These factors helped Zhirinovskii's LDPR and hindered Russia's Choice. A pure single-mandate system, however, would have greatly disadvantaged the LDPR, making Russia's Choice look better by comparison. Although winning fifty-nine seats in the Duma through the PR system, the LDPR won only five single-mandate races. In contrast, Russia's Choice won thirty-four single-mandate seats for the Duma.[22] Given that those high-name recognition candidates from Russia's Choice won almost everywhere they ran, even in districts that voted for the LDPR on the party ballot, it seems reasonable to conclude that Russia's Choice would have increased both absolutely and relatively its total number of seats in a pure first-past-the-post system.

Strategic Decisionmaking

The electoral loss suffered by Russia's Choice cannot be explained entirely in terms of structural and institutional variables that confined the bounds of the possible. The final set of factors that contributed to the bloc's dismal electoral performance were strategic decisions made during the electoral period. Different decisions regarding both the composition, organization, and leadership of Russia's Choice as well as the conduct of the campaign would have altered the electoral outcome. Several important mistakes stand out.

Yeltsin's Nonparticipation

Yeltsin's absence as the leader of the proreform forces was the single most striking difference between the April and December votes. With no stake in the outcome of the Duma vote, Yeltsin stayed on the sidelines, claiming that he had to remain "above the fight" of party politics.[23] Yeltsin's cabinet members had joined four different electoral blocs, making it difficult for him to endorse one bloc. Moreover, Yeltsin probably shared the expectations of most concerning the electoral outcome. Believing that the proreformist parties and blocs together would capture a majority of all seats, Yeltsin wanted to reserve a role for himself as power broker and mediator between them.

The absence of Yeltsin created several acute problems for Russia's Choice. In terms of the bloc's original campaign strategy, it became more difficult to project a polarized menu of choices without Yeltsin's participation. If Yeltsin and Russia's Choice were regarded as synonymous to Russian voters, then the campaign ploy to posit only two real choices—for the president or against the president—would have been more successful.

A second problem was leadership. Polls conducted in October 1993 revealed that 28.1 percent of potential Russian voters were planning to make their decision on which bloc to support based on their trust of the bloc's leaders.[24] In contrast, only 6.8 percent planned to make their decision based on party programs, and 3.6 percent planned to make their decision based on campaign promises.[25] In terms of leadership qualities, the substitution of Yegor Gaidar for Yeltsin represented a big blow to Russia's Choice. Gaidar had never been elected to public office, had no experience with electoral campaigning, and was a newcomer to Russian "party" politics. Gaidar's most visible achievement from the point of view of Russian voters was shock therapy, a less than laudable record on which to run for office in the winter of 1993. As a candidate, Gaidar had none of Yeltsin's (or Zhirinovskii's) rhetorical flare, discourse, or delivery. On the contrary, his television appearances consisted of long, theoretical treatises on macroeconomic stabilization. Even his short, stout figure played against him.

Without Yeltsin on the campaign trail, Russia's Choice still managed to win a large portion of the so-called proreform vote—the educated, urban voters in Moscow, St. Petersburg, and the Urals, which constituted a part of Yeltsin's electorate in June 1991 and in April 1993. As polling data for our study clearly indicate (see table 4-2), Russia's Choice performed best in cities with populations of more than 500,000 and worst in rural areas. There was also strong correlation between supporters of Russia's Choice and education level; the higher the level of education, the greater support for Russia's Choice.[26] However, Russia's Choice did not attract the so-called anti-status quo vote—the populist, anticorruption, anti-Moscow, uneducated

Table 4-2. *Support for Russia's Choice*

Community size	Support
< 1,000	7
1,000–9,999	13
10,000–49,999	27
50,000–249,999	20
250,000–499,999	27
> 499,999	35

Source: Timothy Colton, "Demographic Characteristics of Supporters of Major Parties in Party-List Voting," mimeo provided to the author, November 8, 1994.

voters from small and medium-sized cities particularly in Siberia and the Far East who had constituted a second part of Yeltsin's electorate in previous elections.[27] The absence of Yeltsin combined with the bloc's new image as the party of the status quo meant that Russia's Choice could not compete for this segment of the electorate.

Division between Reformist Electoral Blocs

A second dramatic change between April and December concerning the composition of the reformist forces was their lack of unity. In April 1993, Democratic Russia had worked closely with senior government officials to organize a single, united campaign in support of Yeltsin and his reform policies. This united front no longer existed by the fall of 1993. Stimulated by the new electoral system, four electoral blocs emerged from the one coalition that had supported the president in the April referendum: Russia's Choice, the Yavlinskii-Boldyrev-Lukin (Yabloko), the Party for Russian Unity and Accord (Sergei Shakhrai), and the Russian Movement for Democratic Reform (Anatolii Sobchak). These divisions had several deleterious consequences. Symbolically, the vote for democratic parties on the PR ballot was split, making the democratic defeat look worse than it really was. The "democrats" also would have acquired an additional ten or eleven seats in the Duma had RDDR and its 4 percent of the popular vote been part of one of the proreform parties that exceeded the 5 percent threshold. Of the 225 single-mandate races, candidates from these four proreformist blocs ran candidates against each other in 122 districts. In roughly forty races, the number of votes cast for candidates from these four democratic blocs was greater than the eventual winner.[28] These splits also influenced the way these parties conducted their campaigns. Gaidar and Yavlinskii spent most of the campaign quarreling with each other rather than criticizing more serious opponents such as Zhirinovskii.

The Ineffective Campaign

The actual campaign conducted by Russia's Choice constitutes a final variable that affected the bloc's electoral performance. Because no survey data yet exists regarding voters' responses to the various campaign techniques, assessing this set of variables is a rather subjective exercise. However, the dramatic drop of Russia's Choice in the polls in the last few weeks of the election—by some estimates from 41 to 15 percent—suggest that campaigning—be it poor campaigning by Russia's Choice or good campaigning by the others' blocs—critically influenced the final electoral outcome.[29] All other variables already described were relatively constant from November to December.

Russia's Choice ran a disorganized, ineffective, campaign. Most strikingly, Russia's Choice had no comprehensive campaign strategy: No electoral calendar was planned, no campaign message was crafted, and no social groups were targeted for special attention. Instead of making campaign promises, defining policy stances, or juxtaposing Russia's Choice with other electoral blocs, campaign strategist Gennadii Burbulis wanted to project the image of Russia's Choice as the party of the status quo: the party of power, the party of action, the party of the president, and the party of continued reform.

The projection of this image as the party of power accorded an arrogant tone to the bloc's campaign. The first set of television ads commissioned by the bloc, in fact, portrayed Russia's Choice as the party that had already won the election. Another television commercial highlighted footage from the "October events" to suggest that Russia's Choice had already won the big battle. Because they were so certain of victory, many senior politicians in Russia's Choice did not bother to campaign and party leaders decided against organizing many public rallies, demonstrations, or town hall meetings with candidates.

Overconfidence also meant that bloc leaders "promised nothing" to voters.[30] Gaidar did on occasion suggest that the most painful stages of economic reform were over, but he and his colleagues nonetheless warned voters that times would still be difficult for the near future. Although an honest assessment, the smug, insolent way in which these economists proclaimed this bleak future marred their electoral prospects.

Another image developed by Russia's Choice, however, contradicted this idea of the need for more sacrifice as other ads portrayed Russia as a prosperous country and Russians as middle class. One particularly famous television spot portrayed a wealthy, well-dressed family of three with a large, well-fed St. Bernard going out to vote Russia's Choice. For the average Russian viewer with no new clothes and no well-fed dog, the ad clearly identified who benefited from a Russia's Choice government. More generally, many ads and message communication techniques used by Russia's Choice suggested that this group of politicians was out of touch with Russian reality. Smiling, happy people singing songs about Russia's greatness was inappropriate for a country going through a painful transitional period.

The abysmal use of television by Russia's Choice deserves special explanation. Although Russia's Choice logged more time on television than any other bloc, they squandered most of it on either long, monotonous, and academic discussions about the macroeconomics of financial stabilization or on overproduced, empty jingles. Unlike Zhirinovskii, Russia's Choice ran no ads targeted at special interest groups. General themes of concern to all voters, such as crime or inflation, were not addressed.

Several factors combined to produce this poor television campaign. First, overconfident bloc leaders thought that the entire campaign process would only marginally affect the electoral outcome. They therefore paid little attention to the message or content of television commercials. Second, and in part as a consequence of this lackadaisical attitude toward the campaign, the production of television ads became decentralized and unfocused. Endowed with abundant funding but little time, leaders from Russia's Choice contracted ten different firms to produce ads.[31] These companies produced clips with no common theme or message among them. There were high incentives for quantity and few incentives for quality. Third, those in charge of television for Russia's Choice were inexperienced. Yulii Guzman, a talented artistic filmmaker, had no previous experience with political propaganda. As a well-to-do member of the Moscow intelligentsia, he (and his staff) had little contact with or understanding of the average Russian voter. Guzman's work starkly underscored the disconnect between Moscow politicians and the rest of Russia.

Strategists from Russia's Choice also misjudged their opponents. To the extent that they spoke about other parties and blocs, Russia's Choice leaders focused their critical remarks on the Russian Communist party, Civic Union, and to a lesser extent, Yavlinskii. Zhirinovskii was not on their radar until the very last days of the campaign. When Russia's Choice finally

did attempt to respond to Zhirinovskii in a panic after his surge in the polls
the week before the election, their plan backfired. After persuading Ostankino to reschedule its Saturday programming, Russia's Choice sponsored the
airing of two films, an artistic film (*Zavershenie Stalina*) about the redis-
covery and rise to power of Stalin's son, and a documentary film (*Yastreb*)
about Zhirinovskii himself. Although Zhirinovskii unleashed may have
scared some Moscow intellectuals into going out to vote against him, these
two films helped to establish Zhirinovskii as the opposition candidate most
feared by the incumbent government.

In addition to poor strategic planning and ineffective message development, Russia's Choice lacked coordination between its constituent parts
and among its leaders. Given the tensions between Democratic Russia and
Russia's Choice Movement, coordination between Moscow and the regions
was extremely poor. Distribution of leaflets and posters from Moscow was
sporadic and minimal, and communication of common themes between the
national and regional campaigns rarely occurred. Russia's Choice also devoted very little effort to winning support from civic organizations. In past
electoral victories, Russia's democratic forces devoted a great deal of energy to forging grand alliances of all proreform social groups. Russia's
Choice had the appearance of another such alliance as several business organizations, trade unions, and social organizations were nominal members
of this electoral bloc. No serious attempt was made, however, to mobilize
these organizations to campaign for Russia's Choice. Organizations such as
the Independent Miner's Union, the Association of Privatized and Privatizing Enterprises, the VIP Club, Memorial, the Committees for Social Reforms, as well as dozens of smaller business groups, women's organizations, and trade unions contributed only marginally to the campaign
process. Even entrepreneurial associations played no visible role in support
of Russia's Choice. Although claiming to be the only real representatives of
business interests in the race, Russia's Choice did little to mobilize their
participation in the campaign process.

Finally, Russia's Choice even failed to coordinate activities between
their members in and out of government. Russia's Choice had all the advantages that incumbent parties in any election enjoy. Television coverage of
deputy prime minister Gaidar served as free advertising for candidate Gaidar. Candidates for Russia's Choice also used government resources—
telephone lines, offices, planes, support staff—for campaign activities.[32]
However, unlike the weeks leading up to the April referendum, Russia's
Choice did not capitalize on its position within the government to buy

votes. Whereas Yeltsin delivered millions of rubles to crucial constituencies to win their favor in April, the government (dominated by leaders from Russia's Choice) actually decreased government spending in November and December in an effort to meet deficit targets set by the International Monetary Fund. The deficit was lowered by simply not paying wage bills and other government debts.[33] Although this policy did lower inflation to 10 percent in December, the lowest monthly figure since August 1992, the policy also helped to bring down Russia's Choice.

Weighing Variables

Without knowing anything about Russian political parties, electoral laws, or campaign techniques, the logic of postcommunist revolutionary transitions would have suggested that Russia's Choice was destined to fail. The revolutionary program unleashed by Gaidar in January 1992 had created only a small minority of new classes, social units, or collective identities that benefited from this socioeconomic transformation. Although perhaps still philosophically committed to market reforms, the vast majority of citizens in Russia had suffered tremendous economic dislocation over the previous two years. Like other elections in postcommunist transitions two or three years into the transformation process, Russian voters used their electoral voice to sound their frustration with the incumbent regime.

The logic of postcommunist revolutions offers a parsimonious and convincing explanation for the defeat of Russia's Choice. However, this level of analysis leaves several questions about the December election unanswered and cannot explain several important paradoxes of the Russian case. For instance, explanation at this level of analysis tells us little about the extent of defeat. Why did Russia's Choice win only 15 percent of the popular vote and not 25 or 30 percent? If the explanation of this electoral outcome is located at the national level (i.e., general economic decline), why was there such sharp differentiation between regions regarding support for Russia's Choice? Why, for instance, did Russia's Choice win 27.1 percent of the popular vote in Perm' oblast, but only 16.7 percent in Samara oblast, two regions with similar economic profiles and geographic location? Even more striking is the comparison between "progressive" Nizhnii Novgorod oblast and "depressed" Chelyabinsk oblast. Russia's Choice won only 14 percent of the vote in Nizhnii, but captured 23.6 percent in Chelyabinsk. Regarding another set of varying indicators, how can we explain the remarkable contrast between the high support for Yeltsin and his economic reforms in April and the low support for Russia's Choice in December? Between these two votes, the economy did not significantly worsen. Nor, if polls are to believed, did popular support for market reforms significantly decline. Finally, how can we explain the "split" between the majoritarian and proportional representation voting. If voters were totally dissatisfied with the course of Russia's economic transformation, why did they only vote against Russia's Choice in the national party election and support candidates from Russia's Choice in single-mandate races? One factor—the pain of economic transformation—cannot provide answers to these kinds of questions.

Recognizing the parameters of the possible as defined by the logic of revolutionary transitions, three more proximate variables seem most important for explaining these narrower questions about the December election: the Russian electoral law, the composition of the democratic forces, and the actual campaign performance of Russia's Choice. Economic changes, the "October events," and other electoral procedures appear to have been less important.

The very measure by which we judge Russia's Choice in this election is structured by the kind of electoral system in place. In fact, 15 percent of the popular vote garnered by Russia's Choice reflects only the level of support for Russia's Choice on the party list, and not the more positive performance of Russia's Choice in the election as a whole. Although this accounts for only a little more than a third of all candidates elected to the parliament, performance in the PR system has dominated our perception of winners and losers in these elections. In addition, the PR system favored parties with charismatic leaders, diminished the importance of regional organizations, and provided few incentives for coalition building among ideologically similar parties before the election.

The composition of the "democratic" forces also influenced the outcome of the December elections. Most important, Yeltsin was not at the helm. The division of reformers into four electoral blocs instead of one split their vote and distracted their campaign efforts. Serious friction and conflict within Russia's Choice also impaired this bloc's ability to run an effective campaign. A unified electoral bloc of proreformist forces led by Yeltsin would have produced a different electoral result. This bloc would have captured the largest percentage (though probably not the majority) of the popular vote on the PR ballot and would have won more seats in the single-mandate races.

Finally, the actual conduct of the Russia's Choice campaign affected the outcome. Russia's Choice ran a bad campaign: arrogant, content free, and impervious to voter concerns. The poor performance by Russia's Choice was in stark contrast to the brilliant campaign run by Zhirinovskii's Liberal Democratic Party of Russia. How would a more strategically focused and well-organized campaign by Russia's Choice have influenced the actual outcome of the election? Without data about voter reactions to campaign techniques, this counterfactual is most difficult to reconstruct. However, the dramatic decline in support for Russia's Choice during November does suggest that the campaign period did make a difference.

Conclusion

Russia's Choice, or Democratic Choice of Russia (DCR) as the party was later named, has continued to weaken as a political and electoral party since the 1993 elections. In 1994, the party opposed Yeltsin's invasion of Chechnya, effectively relinquishing any pretense the party once had as the "party of power."[34] When a new party of power, Our Home Is Russia, coalesced behind Prime Minister Viktor Chernomyrdin in preparation for the 1995 parliamentary elections, many within Democratic Choice of Russia predicted that they would disappear completely as a political party. These predictions were partly true as Yegor Gaidar and DCR won only 3.9 percent of the popular vote and nine single-mandate seats in 1995, less than one third of their 1993 total. Although the party still enjoys strong representation in several city legislatures, including a majority position in the Moscow Duma, the party's long-term future remains uncertain.

DCR's individual decline since 1993, however, does not necessarily represent a radical shift in electoral preferences against reformist parties or candidates. On the contrary, reformist parties in 1995 won approximately the same level of popular support as they did in 1993.[35] Even more dramatically, Boris Yeltsin, the presidential candidate most clearly identified with radical reform and endorsed by DCR, won a resounding electoral victory in 1996. This alleged paradox of DCR decline at the same time that support for other reformist parties and candidates remained constant helps to bring into sharper focus those variables that influenced the electoral performance of Russia's Choice in 1993.

First, the stability of electoral support for reformist parties in 1993 and 1995 suggests that social cleavages or structural variables were important in 1993 and continued to be important in 1995 and 1996. The overall balance of those that support and oppose market reforms has not changed.

Even when analyzed at the regional level, Russia's political geography in 1995 and 1996 demonstrated tremendous continuity with previous elections.[36] Because social and economic transformation is a slow process, we should not be surprised with this finding. This continuity between votes also suggests that the more proximate variables in 1993, such as economic performance or the October events, were not salient.

If the general balance of preferences within Russia's electorate remained relatively constant, the choices offered to voters did not. Again, institutions mattered. As in 1993, the 1995 parliamentary electoral law included proportional representation (50 percent of all seats) and a low registration threshold—real stimulants for party proliferation. In addition, those competing for single-mandate districts received added federal support and more publicity if their party qualified for the party list, thus providing incentives for individuals to form parties even if they had no chance of crossing the 5 percent threshold. The results were amazing. Instead of thirteen parties, forty-three parties made the ballot in 1995, including eight blocs that were direct descendants of Russia's Choice, and an amazing twenty electoral blocs whose leaders were once part of Democratic Russia. This party proliferation, including the most important creation of a new party of power, greatly damaged the electoral prospects of DCR.

At the same time, Yeltsin's electoral victory provides further evidence of the influence of electoral institutions. In a polarized election, support for reform reached 54 percent, strong evidence that Russia's Choice electoral prospects in 1993 and again in 1995 were strongly influenced by the nature of the election and not only electoral preferences or social cleavages. Had the reformists been united behind Democratic Choice of Russia (or anyone else) in 1995, and had the presidential election taken place at the same time, DCR today would be a major faction in the Duma, instead of a small, near extinct party of intellectuals. The timing, sequence, and kind of election influence the outcome, therefore.

The subsequent electoral experiences of 1995 and 1996 tell us little about the role of campaign strategy and execution by Russia's Choice in the 1993 elections. As the party of power, Russia's Choice had considerably more resources in 1993 than in 1995. The bloc's radical electoral decline between elections, especially when compared to the dramatic climb of Our Home Is Russia, suggests that the campaign is an important variable. However, the extent of the campaign emerges as more important than the quality, suggesting that the relationship between campaign spending and electoral results may be as positive and direct in Russia as in other developed democracies.

All of these comparisons between 1993 and subsequent elections did not portend a rosy future for Democratic Choice of Russia. Regarding socio-economic transformation, time is on their side as polls show unequivocally that Russia's youngest generation is also its most liberal.[37] Whether Democratic Choice of Russia will survive to represent these new liberal voters, however, remains to be seen.

Notes

1. Yitzhak M. Brudny, "The Dynamics of 'Democratic Russia': 1990–1993," *Post-Soviet Affairs*, vol. 9 (April–June 1993), pp. 141–70.
2. Author's interview with Lev Ponomarev, October 1994.
3. *Izvestiya*, October 13, 1993, p. 4.
4. *Rossiiskaya gazeta*, December 28, 1993, p. 2.
5. Russko-Amerikanskii Fond Profsoyuznykh Issledovannii i Obucheniya, *Pered Finishem*, no, 7, mimeo (1993), pp. 1–2.
6. Author's interview with Mikhail Schneider (Moscow, March 18, 1994).
7. Information for the following section and other descriptions of the campaign is based on hours of observation of meetings and activities at the headquarters of Russia's Choice, press conferences with officials from Russia's Choice, and interviews and conversations with the following leaders and campaign managers of Russia's Choice: Gennadii Burbulis, Alla Gerber, Vladimir Bokser, Andrei Dubov, Yegor Gaidar, Aleksei Golovkov, Kirill Ignatiev, Grigorii Kazankov, Sergei Kovalev, Vladimir Mau, Arkadii Murashev, Yulii Nisnevich, Lev Ponomarev, Yuliya Rusova, Mikhail Schneider, Andrei Shutov, Aleksandr Sobyanin, Ludmilla Stebenkova, Gleb Yakunin, and Ilya Zaslavskii.
8. Sergei Yushenkov and Arkadii Murashev, press conference, October 18, 1993.
9. This definition comes from Theda Skocpol, *States and Social Revolutions: A Comparative Analysis of France, Russia, and China* (Cambridge: Cambridge University Press, 1979); and Charles Tilly, "Revolutions and Collective Violence," in Fred I. Greenstein and Nelson I. Polsby, eds., *Handbook of Political Science*, Vol. 3: *Macropolitical Theory* (Reading, Mass.: Addison Wesley), pp. 483–555. For explication of this approach to the study of Russian politics, see Michael McFaul, "Revolutionary Transformations in Comparative Perspective: Defining a Post-Communist Research Agenda," in David Holloway and Norman Naimark, eds., *Reexamining the Soviet Experience: Essays in Honor of Alexander Dallin* (Boulder, Colo.: Westview Press, 1996); McFaul, "Russia's Rough Ride," in Larry Diamond and Marc Plattner, eds., *Consolidating the Third Wave Democracies* (Baltimore, Md.: Johns Hopkins University Press, 1997); and McFaul, "Party Formation after Revolutionary Transitions: The Russian Case," in Alexander Dallin, ed., *Political Parties in Russia* (Berkeley: International and Area Studies, University of California at Berkeley, 1993), pp. 7–28.

10. On the timing and sequence of elections during periods of radical economic reform, see Adam Przeworski, *Democracy and the Market: Political and Economic Reforms in Eastern Europe and Latin America* (Cambridge: Cambridge University Press, 1991), pp. 162–80. More narrowly, see Michael McFaul, *Post-Communist Politics: Democratic Prospects in Russia and Eastern Europe* (Washington, D. C.: Center for Strategic and International Studies, 1993).

11. Lazlo Bruszt, "1989: The Negotiated Revolution in Hungary," *Social Research*, vol. 57, no. 2 (Summer 1990): 365–88; Jiri Musil, "Czechoslovakia in the Middle of Transition," *Daedalus*, vol. 121, no. 2 (Spring 1992): 175–96; and Voytek Zubek, "The Threshold of Poland's Transition: 1989 Electoral Campaign as the Last Act of a United Solidarity," *Studies in Comparative Communism*, vol. 24, no. 4 (December 1991): 355–76.

12. For figures on the months April to September, see "O razvitii ekonomicheskikh reform v Rossiiskoi Federatsii (Yanvar'—Sentyabr' 1993 goda)" (Moskva: Goskomstat, 1993).

13. Tsentr Sotsioekspress, Institut Sotsiologii, Rossiiskaya Akademiya Nauk, *Zerkalo Mnenii* (Moscow, 1993), p. 5.

14. Ibid., p. 6.

15. Ibid., p. 14.

16. This number was derived by averaging the "Protiv Vsekh" percentages released by the administration of the president the night of and the day after the election. Only 158 electoral districts had reported and no statistics were available regarding the "against all of the above" vote regarding the party list. The document was called "Vybory v Gosudarstvennyuyu Dumu po Odnomandatnykh Okrugam: Tablitsa Predvaritel'nykh Itogov Golosovaniya," was released by the Organizatsionnyi otdel, Tsentr Operativnoi Informatsii, Upravlenie po rabote s territoriyami i predstavitelyami Prezidenta RF Administratsii Prezidenta RF, Otdel regional'noi politiki, Otdel po Vzaimodeitstviyu s federal'nymi organami predstavitel'noi vlasti i obshchestvennymi organizatsiyami Sovet Ministrov-Pravitel'stvo RF, mimeo, undated, pp. 1–13.

17. Ibid. This number was calculated by averaging the spoiled ballots as reported in 144 districts. It must be emphasized that these numbers were preliminary. Moreover, 8 percent is an average of these 144 districts and not a percentage of the total vote. We do not have the data to derive this percentage.

18. Had elections for president and parliament occurred simultaneously, the polarizing tendency of the presidential election would have influenced the parliamentary vote as well. On the relationship between these electoral cycles, see Matthew Soberg Shugart and John M. Carey, *Presidents and Assemblies: Constitutional Design and Electoral Dynamics* (Cambridge: Cambridge University Press, 1992), chap. 9.

19. See Rein Taagepera and Matthew Soberg Shugart, *Seats and Votes: The Effects and Determinants of Electoral Systems* (Yale University Press, 1989); Arend Lijphart; *Democracies: Patterns of Majoritarian and Consensus Government in Twenty-One Countries* (Yale University Press, 1984); and the discussion by Guy Lardeyret, Quentin Quade, and Arend Lijphart, "PR vs. Plurality Elections," *Journal of Democracy*, vol. 2, no. 3 (Summer 1991), pp. 30–48.

20. All of these parties as well as the Democratic Party of Russia hoped to use this foothold in the parliament for party development after the elections. Author's interviews with Andrei Antonov (RDDR), Vladimir Lepekhin (PRES), Vladimir Lysenko (Yabloko and Republican party), Anatolii Golov (Yabloko), and Valerii Khomyakov and Evgenii Mal'kin (DPR), December 1993.

21. Quade, "PR vs. Plurality Elections," p. 41. Majoritarian electoral laws eventually tend to create two-party systems. See Maurice Duverger, *Political Parties: Their Organization and Activity in the Modern State*, translated by Barbara and Robert North (New York: Wiley,1954).

22. Thirty-nine is the number of winning candidates endorsed by Russia's Choice, though only twenty-five of these were officially identified as bloc members on the ballot. Thirty-four is the number of single-mandate Duma deputies that officially registered as members of the faction on January 13, 1994. See *Federal'noye Sobranie*, no. 4 (Moscow: "Panorama," July 14, 1994), p. 105.

23. Yeltsin, as quoted in *Segodnya*, November 27, 1993. This presidential hostility to party politics is common in new, unconsolidated democracies. See Guillermo O'Donnell, "Delegative Democracy," *Journal of Democracy*, vol. 5 (January 1994), pp. 55–69.

24. Aleksei Levinson, *Predvybornaya situatsiya v Rossii: Otchet o Rezul'takh Oprosa Gorazhan Rossii* (Moscow: Vserossiyskiy Tsentr Izucheniya Obshestvennogo Mneniya, October 1993), p. 25.

25. Ibid.

26. Ibid.

27. Vladimir Bokser, Michael McFaul, and Vasilii Ostashev, "Rossiiskiy Elektorat na parlamentskikh vyborakh, referendume 12 dekabrya, 1993 goda: Motivatsiya Vybora," in *Analiz Elektorata Politicheskikh Sil Rossii* (Moscow: Carnegie Moscow Center, 1995), pp. 92–110; and I. M. Klyamkin, V. V. Lapkin, and V. I. Pantin, "Politicheskii Kurs Yeltsina: Predvaritel'nye Itogi," *Polis*, no. 3 (1994), pp. 148–78.

28. This number is derived from Mikhail Schneider, "Spravka po golosovaniyu 12-12-93," mimeo, December 1994; and "Kratkaya kharateristika kandidatov v deputaty gosudarstvennoi dumy federal'nogo sobraniya rossiiskoi federatsii," mimeo (Moskva: Agenstvo "Poslednie Izvestiya," February 1995).

29. VTsIOM, "Rossiya i Vybory. Situatsiya do i posle so sobitii 3–4 Oktyabrya" (Moscow, 1993), p. 21; and *Moskovskie novosti*, no. 47 (November 21, 1993), p. 9A.

30. In one public address to auto workers at AZLK in Moscow, Boris Fyodorov, by this author's count, used this phrase six times.

31. Presentation by Ludmilla Stebenkova (National Democratic Institute Conference, Moscow, March 14, 1994).

32. *Kommersant' Daily*, December 8, 1993, p. 1.

33. *Rossiya*, December 8–14, 1993, p. 4.

34. On this evolution, see Michael McFaul, "Russian Politics after Chechnya," *Foreign Policy*, no. 99 (Summer 1995), pp. 149–65; and Michael McFaul and Nikolai Petrov, eds., *Previewing Russia's 1995 Parliamentary Elections* (Washington, D. C.: Carnegie Endowment for International Peace, October 1995).

35. Michael McFaul, *Russia between Elections: What the 1995 Parliamentary Elections Really Mean* (Washington, D. C.: Carnegie Endowment for International Peace, 1996); and McFaul, "Russia between Elections: The Vanishing Center," *Journal of Democracy*, vol. 7, no. 2 (April 1996), pp. 90–104.

36. The autonomous republics in the second round of the presidential election constitute a notable exception.

37. Igor Klyamkin, "Elektorat Osnovykh Izbiratel'nikhob''edineniy na Parlamentskikh Vyborakh 1995 g. po Materialm Fonda 'Obshchestvennoe Mneniye'," in *Parlamentskie Vybory 1995 goda v Rossii* (Moscow: Moscow Carnegie Center, 1996), pp. 64–65.

CHAPTER FIVE

Between the Extremes
The Moderate Reformist
and Centrist Blocs

Daniel Treisman

TWO MAJOR surprises struck observers of the 1993 Russian parliamentary election—the large plurality won by Vladimir Zhirinovskii's Liberal Democratic Party of Russia (LDPR), and the virtual collapse of the progovernment Russia's Choice bloc. But another aspect of the results is perhaps even more puzzling. Numerous opinion polls taken around this time suggest that public opinion on issues of economic and political reform was clustered around the "center" of the spectrum. Majorities or large pluralities favored gradual reform, political compromise, social harmony, and a mixed economy with some state regulation and public provision. In 1993, for the first time, Russian voters were given a chance to vote for parties that shared such commitments. Between the radical market reformers of Russia's Choice and the extreme opposition Agrarians, Communists, and LDPR, nine political groupings competed to offer different brands of moderate, democratic opposition or single-issue-focused campaigns.

I would like to thank Vyacheslav Shostakovskii, Yurii Levykin, Mikhail Motorin, Konstantin Borovoi, Viktor Bondarchuk, Roman Pugachev, Yevgenii Malkin, Viktor Mironenko, Viktor Sheinis, and Vyacheslav Shebkii for helpful conversations. I have benefited from thoughtful comments of Timothy J. Colton, Vladimir Gimpelson, and participants in the reporting conference on the 1993 election held at Harvard in April 1994. Special gratitude to Mikhail Leontyev, Pilar Bonet, and Christian Schüller.

Yet, on the party-list ballot, these nine blocs received between them little more than one-third of the votes—less than the 43.2 percent captured by the three extreme opposition parties.[1]

Moreover, these blocs hardly even did better among voters who claimed to *share* their economic and political positions. More supporters of a "gradual transition to the market" voted for the Communists, LDPR, and Russia's Choice than for all nine of these moderate reformist and centrist blocs together.[2] Of voters who said they favored a centrist or moderate reformist bloc when surveyed in the month before the election, nearly one third later chose one of the extreme options (see table 3-5, this volume).

The indifferent performance by the moderate parties was all the more surprising because almost every politician was convinced that the "center" was the most electorally attractive point on the spectrum.[3] All blocs from Russia's Choice to Zhirinovskii's LDPR called themselves "centrists" and tried—with limited success—to brand their rivals as the true extremists. Even among the center blocs, leaders competed to cast themselves as the most moderate of moderates. "We don't see any centrists," Nikolai Travkin, leader of the Democratic Party of Russia, complained in October. "Around us there are only radicals."[4] Such jockeying for the innermost position seems, in retrospect, a little quaint. In the end, far more of the electorate chose to support the ultranationalist, communist, and radical free-market extremes than the various moderates arrayed between them.

In this chapter I attempt to explain this outcome. I shall describe the composition, programs, and strategy of the moderate reformist and centrist blocs. I will then consider possible explanations for their surprisingly weak performance and examine why some did better than others. I will analyze the geographical strengths and weaknesses of the moderate and centrist blocs. Finally, I will draw some conclusions about the meaning of the 1993 election for the development of democracy in Russia.

A few caveats are in order at the outset. First, the chapter will focus mostly on the electoral-list voting for the State Duma, because this offers a more reliable indication of voter preferences and because campaigns for the single-candidate constituencies and the Federation Council were highly decentralized and rarely coordinated at all from Moscow. (Other chapters in the volume redress this omission.) Second, because of space constraints, the primary focus is on the six moderate reformist and center blocs with the strongest results;[5] three of the four single-issue blocs (Future of Russia–New Names, Constructive Ecological Movement of Russia [KEDR], and Dignity and Compassion), each received less than 1.5 percent of the electoral-list vote, and they are thus given less attention in this chapter.[6] Among the single-issue blocs, the Women of Russia performed so strongly that it clearly merits analysis.

The Moderate Reform and Center Blocs

The *center* is an amorphous term in any political system. A residual category, it gathers together the heirs of those who sat in the middle of the revolutionary Assemblée Nationale—all those who reject both "extremes" of left and right. In post-Soviet Russia, the center has been understood to refer to groups and politicians critical of both the democratic reformers and the communists. The 1990 Russian parliament divided into proreform and anti-reform (including communist and nationalist) wings, with a sizeable "marsh" of uncommitted deputies between them. Often, these center parliamentarians were associated with the politics of lobbying rather than the politics of ideology: many represented industrial branches, agriculture, or particular regions, in the competition for central funds and benefits.[7]

By late 1993 the term "centrism" in Russia had reached an apogee of fogginess. There were centrists in favor of free markets and of state regulation, centrists who advocated a strong federal state, and even, improbably, centrists in favor of decentralization (Sergei Shakhrai, of the Party of Russian Unity and Accord: "True centrism in Russia is possible only through the provinces").[8] Journalists were no better than the politicians at defining what exactly lurked in the marsh between the extremes. According to Vitalii Tret'yakov, the editor of *Nezavisimaya gazeta*, centrism connoted "vagueness, a border, a watershed."[9] For the political commentator Maksim Sokolov, it was the refuge of "lobbyists and patriots."[10] The economics columnist Mikhail Leont'ev mapped Russia's political space onto not a spectrum but a circle, with three segments representing liberalism, nationalism, and socialism. In the center Leontyev placed a "point of political idiocy" around which positions became too vague to be understood.[11]

In the December election, thirteen groupings were ruled to have gathered the 100,000 signatures necessary to participate in the electoral-list voting. Between the progovernment Russia's Choice bloc and the parties of the extreme opposition—the Communists, Agrarians, and Liberal Democrats—were three moderate reform blocs and six centrist or single-issue groups (claiming to represent women, the old and invalids, youth, and ecology).

The decision to consider these nine blocs together was based on the practical needs of this research project, rather than on a substantive belief that they shared a distinct identity. However, certain commonalities as well as differences are discernible among the main contenders. I focus on the five broadly political groupings plus the Women of Russia association. These six blocs all supported some kind of market-oriented economic reform and democratic politics but opposed the current government.[12]

Three blocs were viewed by observers at the time as supporters of moderate reform, opposing some aspects of the program and style of Russia's Choice but sharing its essential goals. The first, Yabloko (Yavlinskii-Boldyrev-Lukin Bloc), was patched together at the last minute by the economist Grigorii Yavlinskii. The author of numerous economic reform plans, Yavlinskii had recently achieved some practical success in Nizhnii Norgorod oblast, where the governor was implementing some of his proposals. Yavlinskii enlisted as partners a former state chief inspector, Yurii Boldyrev, and the ambassador to Washington, Vladimir Lukin. The bloc's title—Yabloko, or "apple"—was an acronym built from the first letters of the three leaders' names. To bring organizational experience and local structures to the coalition, the leaders joined forces with the Social Democratic party, the Russian Christian Democratic Union, and the majority of regional branches of the Republican party, part of which chose instead to side with Russia's Choice. Contrary to the expectations of many observers at the time, Yabloko did survive in subsequent years, despite the loss of Yurii Boldyrev. It was one of the four blocs to cross the 5 percent barrier and win seats in the 1995 parliamentary election on the party-list ballot. However, it has remained little more than a personal vehicle for the political ambitions of Yavlinskii.

The Russian Movement for Democratic Reform (RDDR) gathered an eclectic array of celebrities, businesspeople, politicians, and union leaders under the leadership of the former Moscow mayor Gavriil Popov and the mayor of St. Petersburg, Anatolii Sobchak. It was the remnant of a former Union-Level Movement for Democratic Reforms, which had been set up to unite radical democrats and proreform communists in the summer of 1991, but which had disintegrated in early 1992. The RDDR aimed to be not a political party but a "super-party structure," uniting any democratic and reformist groups that wanted to be members.[13] According to Popov, who did not run for parliament himself, its goal was not to attain power but to serve as a "democratic opposition" to whomever did. In its program, the movement promised to cut the federal bureaucracy in half and to give each Russian citizen a small plot of land. How it would accomplish these feats from the opposition benches was, however, left to the voters' imagination.

Third, a new addition to moderate politics, the Party of Russian Unity and Accord (PRES) of Sergei Shakhrai, emphasized cultural conservatism, pragmatic reform, and regional rights. A behind-the-scenes strategist, who like many others had started off in the Russian parliament and been lured over to the president's administration, Shakhrai had early hinted at his own presidential ambitions. In the Russian Supreme Soviet, he had chaired the Committee on Legislation, but failed to get himself elected a deputy chair of the parliament, despite four attempts to do so.[14] Then he joined the president's team, working in a number of positions, most notably setting up the state-legal directorate. As the Yeltsin administration's chief jurist, he led the prosecution in the 1992 case against the Soviet Communist party, which resulted in a mixed verdict. Later, he served as chair of the State Committee for Affairs of the Federation and Nationalities, helping in 1993 to negotiate the shape of new constitutional relations with the heads of the Russian regions and republics. His designs were, however, rendered obsolete by the events of October 3–4, which hardened the president's position in center-region negotiations.

From his contacts with the provincial governments, however, Shakhrai from the summer of 1993 began assembling a "party of the provinces," as a vehicle to contest the next elections. The party's apparatus came, in large part, from the team of lawyers he had assembled in the post of head of the state-legal directorate.[15] Its raison d'être rested on a paradox: provincial elites wanted two things from any government in Moscow—either more autonomy or more resources. For a parliamentary party to press for the first was a recipe for its own irrelevance. The second constituted a zero-sum game, in which the interests of different regions conflicted, therefore rendering them unlikely electoral partners. As the prime minister of Buryatia, Vladimir Saganov put it with unusual directness at the party's founding congress in October 1993 in Novgorod: "Our platform should be flexible, differentiated in different regions. . . . And, in general, after I join this party—what will I get in addition?"[16]

Viewed initially as the more "moderate" element of a two-card strategy of the Russia's Choice forces to increase their vote, Shakhrai worked hard to lose the image of a party of power and appeal to conservative regional electorates. The party's campaigning combined a sometimes wooden use of patriotic imagery with attempts to show its candidates were "normal" people. "Being a great power is the cornerstone of Russia's special path," campaign advertisements announced. PRES benefited from the tacit support of the prime minister, Viktor Chernomyrdin. Gazprom, the state gas concern that Chernomyrdin had headed, provided ten candidates for the party list, helped obtain signatures, and, according to one party worker, provided a corporate jet for Shakhrai to fly to events in the provinces.[17] Other leading members of PRES included the deputy prime minister responsible for foreign economic affairs, Aleksandr Shokhin, and Yeltsin adviser Sergei Stankevich.[18]

These three moderate reform blocs were flanked by two political groupings and four single-issue groups of the center. Of these, the Democratic Party of Russia (DPR) was the oldest. Founded in May 1990, its leader, Nikolai Travkin, was a blunt-spoken former construction engineer who had made his name as a member of Yeltsin's faction in the 1989 Soviet parliament. The party claimed to have a membership of 50,000 and more than 600 local organizations, in every region except Omsk.[19] Like many of his rivals, Travkin had recruited a smattering of celebrities and former government officials to swell the party's ranks before the election. Among these were two former Yeltsin ministers, Nikolai Fedorov and Sergei Glaz'ev, and the film director Stanislav Govorukhin, a dyspeptic critic of the alleged corruption of the democrats in power.

Travkin had led the party through a patchwork of tactical alliances in the previous three years. Originally part of the Democratic Russia movement, he left in November 1991 to protest the organization's acceptance of the Soviet Union's disintegration. Then, in the summer of 1992, he had joined the party of then vice president Aleksandr Rutskoi (the People's Party of Free Russia) and the Union "Renewal" (the political wing of Arkadii Vol'skii's Russian Union of Industrialists and Entrepreneurs) to form a coalition called Civic Union. The group was billed as the first centrist alternative to both radical reform and the communist-nationalist "red-brown" alliance. But it was always a marriage of convenience among the three leaders, supported by ephemeral political circumstances. In the spring of 1992, public discontent at postliberalization inflation and the sharp fall in real wages had combined with a credit squeeze and a payments-arrears crisis, uniting industrial managers and workers against the government. The subsequent softening of central credit policy, the gradual rise in real incomes, the emergence of new divisions related to privatization, and the increasing polarization of the political elite in 1993 undermined this fragile consensus.[20]

Travkin left Civic Union in June 1993 out of unease with Rutskoi's drift to the antireform extremes and concern that his party would do better if it ran in future elections alone. A month earlier he had resigned his post as a people's deputy of Russia, after the public overwhelmingly endorsed the idea of early reelection of parliament in the April referendum. This tactical exit from Moscow politics provided the opportunity to enter the electoral campaign a few months later "from outside." Since early 1992, Travkin had simultaneously served as head of administration of Shakhovskoi, his home district in Moscow oblast, with a population, according to one press report, of "25,000 people and 32,000 cattle."[21]

By the electoral season of 1993, Civic Union was a ship whose crew had either deserted or mutinied: Aleksandr Rutskoi was in Lefortovo prison awaiting trial for his role in the October uprising; Travkin had gone his own way, leaving only Arkadii Vol'skii at the helm. A former Central Committee department head and leader of the Russian Union of Industrialists and Entrepreneurs, Vol'skii was an inveterately careful politician whose reputation had always rested on an aura of behind-the-scenes influence, never on performance in electoral competition. Although he buttressed the group's electoral list with a few celebrities such as Iosif Kobzon, a middle-aged singer sometimes called the Russian Frank Sinatra, he failed to recruit any political figure with the charisma of Rutskoi or Travkin. To distinguish his organization from its previous incarnation, Vol'skii rechristened it Civic Union for Stability, Justice, and Progress.

Besides these two centrist political blocs, four single-issue groups, all unknown before October, were authorized to compete. KEDR (Constructive Ecological Movement of Russia), which chose an acronym that doubled as the Russian word for "cedar," billed itself as a defender of ecological values and drew considerable organizational and personnel support from the nationwide system of sanitary inspectors. It also included among its sponsors the Movement of Soldiers' Mothers of Russia. Dignity and Compassion, formed on the base of several charitable and veterans groups, claimed to represent invalids and the old and ran on a program of more generous pensions and benefits for the disabled and greater funding for social services. Future of Russia–New Names offered little by which to identify itself except its claim to represent youth, an image occasionally rendered questionable by the gray hairs of some of its spokespersons. Its head was a former leader of the Komsomol, and it also included candidates from the youth wing of Rutskoi's Free Russia party.

Finally, the Women of Russia bloc, drawing support from several social organizations and women's groups, preached a combination of social provision and support for education, culture, and health care, without the bitterness of more extreme opposition factions. In addition, its leaders opposed discrimination against women and supported the rights of children. At times the promise seemed to be to civilize the unruly and raucous tone of Russian politics and to introduce *kul'turnost'* into public life. If a woman occupied some high post, the bloc's chair, Alevtina Fedulova, suggested, "maybe then our Russian house would stop resembling a cold bachelor's apartment."[22]

Although various nuances distinguished the programmatic commitments of the six main moderate reform and center blocs (Yabloko, RDDR, PRES, DPR, Civic Union, and Women of Russia), there were also common elements. The main point on which all agreed was the rejection of both the radicals of Russia's Choice and the extreme opposition of the Communists and the LDPR.[23] All six advocated some kind of more gradual and moderate economic reform.[24] Although most programs mentioned financial stabilization (the primary focus for Russia's Choice), the clear priority for Civic Union, the DPR, and RDDR was to halt the precipitous fall in production, to preserve industry, and to prevent mass unemployment. Most were for structural policy, "reasonable protectionism" to protect the domestic market, and state tax breaks and investment funding to boost "locomotive sectors."

A second important theme sounded by all was the need for social harmony and compromise rather than political or economic confrontation. "For them, the goals are more important than the path to these goals," Yavlinskii said of Russia's Choice. "For us, for me personally, the path to the goal is as important as the goal."[25] According to Travkin's campaign manager, Yevgenii Malkin: "Centrists are distinguished not so much by what they do as by how they do it."[26] This was meant to appeal to those voters appalled by the events of October 3–4. In a striking mixed metaphor, Civic Union's program declared, "The ash of the victims of the October events knocks today at the heart of each honest citizen of Russia!" (The same point was made not so subliminally in Civic Union's television ads, in which scenes of the October disturbances were crossed out with a large black X.) The DPR pointed out in its program that it was not stained "with blood, even in our Time of Troubles." Yabloko limited itself to the observation that, "Civil clashes have begun." Such appeals for social accord and inclusion were only helped by the clumsily divisive style of Russia's Choice presentations, which often appeared to target a narrow stratum of the richest urban intelligentsia.[27]

On the question of welfare provision and social services, the six main moderate reform and center blocs all promised more aid to mothers, children, and invalids. (In this they were not alone—even Russia's Choice made similar undertakings, saying reductions in subsidies to enterprises would yield money for social spending; its promises may, however, have been perceived as less credible.) They differed mostly in how specific and extensive their promises were. Yabloko was the only one to place explicit limits on its commitments on grounds of fiscal responsibility: it prioritized medical care for preschool children and investment in schools.

On foreign affairs, these six blocs had few distinctive positions. Most favored expanding ties with the "near abroad," setting up customs unions, cultural associations, and security relations (Civic Union, DPR, RDDR, Yabloko). Civic Union, the RDDR, and Yabloko also mentioned the need to protect Russian minorities in other republics.

Besides these generally shared positions, different blocs focused on different pet themes. On the economy, beyond the general commitment to gradual reform, restoring growth, and state investment, Civic Union placed particular emphasis on state regulation of the economy and control of the export of raw materials and fuels. Yabloko stressed the importance of enhancing competition, without which it believed anti-inflation policy would fail. The RDDR, whose list included the eye surgeon and businessman Svyatoslav Fedorov, included a call for employees to receive profit shares from their enterprises, an idea Fedorov had long championed in his own clinic.

All the blocs' programs included some formula combining commitment to the wholeness and unity of Russia with respect for regional self-sufficiency and rights. But the emphasis varied. Travkin and Vol'skii, both of whom had opposed the breakup of the Soviet Union, were more in favor of a strong, centralized state than Shakhrai, whose party claimed to be a "party of provinces." (It is interesting to note that the DPR's list included the largest share of non-Moscow residents—87 percent, compared with 80 percent for PRES—somewhat weakening the latter's claim to be the true representative of the regions. Both were far more provincial in composition than the other four blocs.) In an original proposal, the DPR suggested Russia's federal structure could be strengthened by decentralizing rights and responsibilities to the level of municipalities, thus bypassing separatist claims at the level of the region. Yabloko also seemed to come down slightly in favor of the federal center, opposing including in the constitution the option for republics to separate. Shakhrai's party, by contrast, wrote of "contractual relations" between regions and center, and hinted at its readiness to act as conveyor for regional lobbying. "We look at the economy, at all other problems, through the prism of regional and provincial interests," the campaign literature stated.

Much campaign time was devoted to the question of Yeltsin's draft constitution, to be voted on in the referendum held simultaneously with the election. Clumsy statements by state officials who were also running for Russia's Choice gave the impression of a conflict of interest, and Yeltsin himself appeared to be trying to stifle debate.[28] The RDDR supported the president's draft but as a constitution for a transitional period. PRES also supported it, though with reservations about its balance of federal and regional powers. The Women of Russia did not take a firm position but reminded voters the constitution could always be amended. In contrast, the DPR and Civic Union flatly opposed it. Yabloko proposed holding a "constituent assembly" to pass a new constitution and electoral code, followed immediately by presidential and local elections and then by new parliamentary elections. However, Yabloko's scruples about presidential power were not expressed as vigorously after the election results became known.

In their structure and organization, the six main moderate reform and center blocs also differed. The first dimension was their age. Although PRES, Yabloko, and Women of Russia had been set up just months—in some cases, just weeks—before, explicitly to contest the forthcoming election, Civic Union, the RDDR, and the DPR were all more than a year old (marking them as dinosaurs in Russian political ecology). From Moscow it was difficult to assess the strength and cohesion of blocs' regional organizations. Most information suggested central organizers adopted an extremely pragmatic approach, with all the blocs from the DPR to Russia's Choice competing to win over the available political activists in the regions. All admitted that coordination was loose, and central party funding was generally not provided to finance individual candidates' campaigns. (Yabloko and the DPR held seminars for local candidates.) Nor is it likely the party leaders could have struck nationwide nonopposition pacts between themselves and made them stick. Sometimes it seemed the blocs' headquarters had little idea what was going on in the field. Leaders of PRES had to admit late in the campaign that they had had to exclude six members from their list because it turned out they had criminal records, mostly for embezzlement and abuse of official position.[29]

Both Travkin and Shakhrai insisted that because their blocs were parties, candidates would be more accountable to the voters; according to Shakhrai, his party's charter gave it a mechanism to punish members who voted against the party line. The RDDR's program seemed to promise just the reverse: "A deputy to the State Duma's belonging to the RDDR parliamentary fraction will not under any circumstances hinder him from conducting open, frank and constructive dialogue with all political forces represented in the Duma."

In addition, several features distinguished the candidates of the various blocs. The Women of Russia differed sharply from the other five in the number of candidates it was able to field (see table 5-1). Its list, with just thirty-six members, was nearly five times shorter than the next most modest (the RDDR), and it endorsed only six candidates in the single-mandate contests. The other five main centrist blocs each endorsed between sixty and ninety single-member-constituency candidates.

Candidates of all blocs—in both the party lists and the single-member constituencies—were, on average, in their mid-forties. Among the six blocs, the DPR seems particularly youthful, with candidates averaging forty-two. This is probably because of its high representation of younger party activists. The Women of Russia and Civic Union were both just slightly older. All blocs except the Women of Russia were overwhelmingly male in their candidates, with Yabloko marginally more mixed than the others. Women of Russia's candidates were 100 percent female.

In occupation, the characteristics of candidates correspond well to the stereotypes of the different blocs—with Yabloko and the RDDR showing a high representation of the intelligentsia (40.7 percent and 37.9 percent of the list candidates, respectively, employed in science, education, the media, and arts) and Civic Union having a high concentration of industrial managers (39.7 percent of list candidates in senior- or middle-level economic management).

The same trends were observable among the single-member constituency candidates. The DPR's candidates, in both contests, had a relatively high showing of political activists because of the party's reliance on its local party organizers. The DPR was also the only party to have even a relatively small representation of blue-collar workers (6.6 percent and 6.5 percent in the party-list and single-candidate races, respectively). The moderate reform blocs had slightly more candidates from the Russian government and administration, though in all cases fewer than 10 percent. Yab-

Table 5-1. *Characteristics of Center Bloc Candidates*

	Yabloko	RDDR	PRES	DPR	CU	WR
Party lists						
Number of candidates	172	153	193	167	184	36
Average age	43	45	44	42	47	45
Percent men	86.6	91.5	96.4	93.4	96.7	0
Percent formerly in						
Russian Congress	3.5	3.3		0.6	6.0	5.6
Percent listing						
membership in						
electoral player[a]	55.2	0	1.0	76	0	0
Occupation (percent)						
Science, education,						
media, arts	40.7	37.9	17.6	18.0	16.8	25.0
Senior economic						
management	2.3	5.2	15.5	9.0	33.7	16.7
Middle economic						
management	1.2	7.2	10.4	9.0	6.0	5.5
Political or social						
organization	12.8	8.5	14.0	21.6	17.4	16.7
Russian govt.	1.7	7.2	7.3	0	1.6	2.8
Local and regional						
govt.	22.7	13.7	29.5	14.4	15.8	19.4
Military or police	2.3	5.2	0	1.8	1.0	0
Other white collar	15.7	15.0	4.7	16.8	4.9	13.9
Blue collar	0.6	0	0.5	6.6	1.0	0
Agriculture	0	0	0.5	1.8	1.6	0
Pensioners or						
unemployed	0	0	0	1.2	0	0
Single-mandate constituencies						
Number of candidates	90	60	70	62	75	6
Average age	43	42	44	42	45	48
Percent men	92.2	93.3	97.1	95.2	98.7	0
Percent formerly in						
Russian Congress	n.a.	n.a.	n.a.	n.a.	n.a.	n.a.
Percent listing						
membership in						
electoral player[a]	1.1	0	0	24.2	0	0
Occupation (percent)						
Science, education						
media, arts	26.7	31.7	18.6	21.0	13.3	16.7
Senior economic						
management	8.9	16.7	21.4	8.1	37.3	16.7
Middle economic						
management	10.0	11.7	11.4	3.2	2.7	0
Political or social						
organization	5.6	8.3	8.6	29.0	16.0	0
Russian govt.	5.6	5.0	7.1	1.6	4.0	0

Table 5-1. *continued*

	Yabloko	RDDR	PRES	DPR	CU	WR
Local and regional govt.	31.1	15.0	25.7	19.4	16.0	50.0
Military or police	0	5.0	0	1.6	0	0
Other white collar	6.7	1.7	2.9	6.5	0	16.7
Blue collar	0	1.7	0	6.5	2.7	0
Agriculture	0	0	0	1.6	2.7	0
Pensioners or unemployed	5.6	3.3	4.3	1.6	5.3	0

Source: Constructed from various party lists published in *Rossiiskaya gazeta*.
a. In case of Yabloko, listing membership in Republican party, Christian Democratic Union, or Social Democratic party.
n.a. = not available.

loko, PRES, and Women of Russia drew more heavily than others on local and regional officials.

Campaign Strategies

How did these blocs conceive their campaign strategies? Which social, economic, or geographical groupings of voters did they target? What methods for reaching and winning over the electorate did they favor? How did they try to position themselves across the political space between the "extremes" and to distinguish themselves from their rivals? With which could they imagine collaborating, before or after the election? From which did they hope to steal votes?

In many respects, the most notable aspect of campaign strategy among the moderate reform and center blocs was the lack of it. Many party officials felt the Russian political landscape was simply too fluid for them to establish lasting ties to particular socioeconomic or demographic groups. As several politicians pointed out, it was difficult for organizations to represent interests during a social revolution for the simple reason that these interests were continually changing. Instead, they hoped to attract all those who shared their political world view, regardless of occupation, education, region, or other characteristics. As a result, campaigning often seemed to lack focus. (Nevertheless, the RDDR and Yabloko were clearly hoping to attract the urban intelligentsia; PRES and DPR aimed at provincial cities and the countryside; and Civic Union at heavily industrialized regions.)

The weakness of parties was both an effect and a cause of their loose links to social groups. A poll in June 1993 found only 26 percent of respondents supported any party.[30] Instead, parties often began as entourages of ambitious politicians, acquired organizational resources through alliances with members of the executive branch, and built up a base of supporters through historical accident and pragmatic coalitions with preexisting organizations and regional constituencies. (The DPR could give a detailed accounting of its geographical strengths—in the south of Russia, the Volga regions, parts of Western Siberia, republics of the North Caucasus—but why it should be strong in these particular regions was a mystery.) Other blocs existed to represent already obsolete elites.[31]

The choice of campaign methods was improvisational for all blocs because of the short time span between the announcement of the election and polling day. Destinations for trips around the country were chosen in a generally haphazard way—depending on where local organizers could guarantee some organized events, where television coverage was likely, or on opportunistic gambles. According to one PRES campaign official, Shakhrai deliberately chose to stop in certain spots, such as Perm, which central politicians visited only rarely.[32] (In this case, the strategy may have worked: in Perm oblast, PRES did poll above the national trend.)

Although the six campaigns attributed different degrees of significance to television communications, the divergence was largely evened out by the two hours of free airtime provided to each bloc. Yavlinskii clearly underestimated the importance of the press, telling one audience: "Those that know about me already know about me," and holding no press conferences for a month during the height of the campaign, despite eighty-seven requests by journalists for interviews.[33] According to Yabloko's campaign manager, Yurii Levykin, in the bloc's council: "They calculated that the more rarely we appeared, the less the electorate would get sick of us. . . . There were practically no fliers, almost no organization of door-to-door campaigning."[34] Such complacence, oddly common among the moderate reform and centrist leaders, may have stemmed from a limited view of the electoral task ahead of them. Both Yabloko and the DPR considered the essential task to be not attracting new voters so much as holding on to those they believed they already had.

Some nuances of difference were suggested by the blocs' preelection conception of potential future parliamentary partners. When I asked officials from each of the blocs during late November and early December with which other groups their bloc could conceivably collaborate after the elections, Yabloko was the only one to rule out the Agrarians. Neither Yabloko nor the RDDR excluded collaboration with Russia's Choice; they were joined by Civic Union, which admitted, albeit unenthusiastically, it would be willing to collaborate with "even Russia's Choice." The RDDR claimed the broadest range of potential partners, because it did not rule out even the Communists, so long as they were willing to support democratic reform.

Some were better able than others to establish a distinct niche. The Women of Russia certainly stood out from the male crowd, though their proposed policies were as vague as any other bloc's. PRES worked hard to earn itself recognition as the "party of regions," though, as already mentioned, this rested on the paradox that all regions could not simultaneously win in interregional disputes. Yabloko was clear about its commitment to economic reform, and thus offered the obvious choice to educated, prereform constituencies already alienated by Yegor Gaidar and his team. But the RDDR, DPR, and Civic Union seemed to believe maximizing vagueness could maximize the range of their support, an odd position to adopt in an overpopulated multiparty system.[35]

A conviction widely held among the center parties was that voters, skeptical about all promises and platforms, would decide in December not based on programs or ideology so much as on the personal image of party leaders. For more obscure reasons, the center blocs believed this would work to their advantage. Travkin encouraged the public to "vote for those you trust." The RDDR's electoral program rounded off a series of promises with the slogan, "Vote not for slogans and promises, but for concrete people." This was a somewhat surprising strategy for leaders whose names in monthly polls attracted the trust of fewer than 15 percent of respondents.[36] The ambivalence about their own party programs was sometimes almost comical. "Don't read the programs, they're all the same," Travkin counseled voters. Only after the election did newspaper readers learn from Travkin that, "The public voted for Zhirinovskii, and not for us or Civic Union, because it doesn't read programs . . . but we write programs."[37]

This emphasis on the personalities of leaders led to a concentration more on style than on content. Shakhrai's candidates tried to distinguish themselves from the "talking heads and professors" and to show that they were "normal people," campaigning with traditional rhymes, *chastushki.* (One on the wall in PRES's campaign headquarters: "The market is not a bazaar/ Whatever might promise Gaidar./ Together, from krai to krai/ Let's all vote for Shakhrai!") Among other nonstandard advertising, one candidate told me that in the constituency where he was running, he promised, as did Zhirinovskii, the speedy return of Alaska.[38]

The Election Results

The tallies of the voting were sobering for all the moderate reform and center blocs except the Women of Russia. All had expected to do better. But how should these results be characterized? Accounts have differed since December 1993. Although some analysts have written of the "diminishing center" of Russian politics,[39] others have interpreted the results somewhat more sanguinely. Jerry Hough, for instance, notes that, "Almost all candidates in the districts claimed to be centrist, and . . . the center is still strong in the Duma."[40]

Any evaluation of electoral performance requires some standard of comparison. Because this was the first parliamentary election in which any of the blocs had run, their results cannot be measured against past successes. One possibility is to look for overlap between the blocs' declared positions on key issues and public opinion, as measured in surveys. How large was the reservoir of potential ideological support for the center blocs, and how successful were they at tapping this reservoir? Three issues were particularly salient in the center blocs' campaigning: the need for moderate economic reform, a commitment to social harmony and political compromise, and an insistence on combining reform with greater state aid and guarantees to citizens in need.

First, about half the Russian public appeared to favor moderate economic reform. According to the representative, nationwide preelection survey of 3,365 voters analyzed by Timothy Colton and his colleagues, 50 percent favored a "gradual transition to the market," compared with 15 percent who thought "the transition to the market should be quick," and 16 percent who said they were "against the market economy." An additional 18 percent did not know. Surveys by other organizations have yielded similar results and have suggested that the popularity of gradual economic reform was gaining in 1990–93 at the expense of both radical reform and categorical opposition.[41]

Second, some evidence suggests widespread support for the center blocs' call for social harmony and political balance. Public disgust at the level of political division was shown by a poll of the urban and rural population of fifteen regions reported in late November.[42] According to the survey, of the 55 percent of respondents planning to vote in the election, 60 percent considered the events of October a "national disgrace" in which all branches of power were guilty. A question on the desirable balance of power between parliament and president was included in the Colton postelection survey. Although 22 percent favored a stronger parliament and 20 percent preferred a parliament weaker than the president, 45 percent believed the two institutions should have equal power.

A second indicator of commitment to a center-style attempt to reconcile social and individual goals could be gleaned from another question in the Colton postelection survey. Respondents were asked whether they agreed or disagreed with the statement: "Society has the right to defend its interests firmly, even if this means that the innocent sometimes suffer." Only 7 percent said they "fully agreed" and 7 percent said they "completely disagreed"; 42 percent said they "disagreed" and 19 percent confessed to "vacillating." Neither old-style Communist appeals to put the interests of society first nor categorical commitment to individual rights could attract more than a handful of voters.

Third, the center blocs, like their rivals to the left, advocated increasing social welfare payments and state guarantees. Polls reveal close to universal public support for state aid. In the Colton postelection survey, 90 percent either "agreed" or "fully agreed" that "the government ought to guarantee a job to everyone who needs one." And 86 percent thought the state should either "regulate" or "strictly control" food prices.

Such survey evidence suggests the existence of a reservoir of moderate-minded voters for parties in the center to mobilize. On each of the questions cited, about 40 percent or more seemed to favor positions similar to those adopted by the center parties. On most questions, more than twice as many voters chose the "centrist" option as chose either of the extremes. Yet, in the election itself, only 37 percent of voters opted for one of the nine central blocs, compared to 43.3 percent for the Communists, Agrarians, and LDPR.

Indeed, many survey respondents who endorsed moderate positions associated with the center blocs nevertheless reported having voted for either the extreme opposition or Russia's Choice. The rate of support for "centrist" positions (gradual economic reform and equal power between president and parliament) was almost as high among Russia's Choice, LDPR, and Communist voters as it was among supporters of PRES, Women of Russia, or the RDDR (see table 5-2). Although the center blocs drew a larger proportion of their support from adherents to the "centrist" positions, these positions were the modal choice for supporters of all blocs but the Communist party.

The puzzle is why an apparently overwhelmingly centrist electorate would vote so reluctantly for the official centrist blocs and so enthusiasti-

Table 5-2. *Policy Attitudes of Voters toward Respective Parties*
Percent

	Moderate reform				Center				
Attitudes	Yabloko	RDDR	PRES	DPR	Civic Union	Women of Russia	KPRF	LDPR	Russia's Choice
Transition to market economy									
Should be quick	17	23	11	20	4	12	3	11	27
Should be gradual	62	56	54	59	78	44	41	48	51
Against market economy	6	9	16	8	9	13	38	22	6
Constitutional division of powers									
Parliamentary supremacy	18	11	21	23	27	19	44	24	11
Equal powers	51	47	43	56	51	47	38	46	44
Presidential supremacy	20	33	24	16	16	16	6	15	33

Source: Postelection survey of 2,623 voters. Figures provided to author by Timothy Colton

cally for the extreme parties. It is even more puzzling in light of the relatively strong performance of many independent, moderate candidates, often running on their regional notability, in the single-candidate constituencies. Twenty-four of the 225 seats allocated in single-mandate races went to candidates running under the banner of the six main center blocs. But another 136 candidates won as nonparty independents; many of them were ideologically somewhere between the two extremes. Combining the list and single-member constituency voting, the nine center blocs received 101 seats, fewer than one quarter of the 450 in the State Duma—a less than inspiring result.

Explaining the Center's Performance

Why were the parties of the center unable to attract greater numbers of the Russians who supported gradual economic reform, seemingly opposing radical democrats, communists, and extreme nationalists alike? Why did so many of those who favored a balance of political institutions vote for those blocs clearly committed to either presidential or parliamentary dominance?

A number of explanations sometimes proposed for the center's faltering performance do not seem fully adequate. Both during and after the campaign, the center blocs were accused by leaders of Russia's Choice of divisiveness. The poor showing for proreform parties in the center was attributed to the failure of the reform wing to unite against the radical opposition.[43] The logic, however, was somewhat obscure. Before the election, the claim was usually made regarding the single-member races: because only a plurality was necessary to win, reformers risked splitting the reform vote and losing to a single opposition candidate. The logic in proportional representation is just the opposite: representing a broader range of different positions is likely to attract more rather than fewer voters to a coalition. But, in fact, it was precisely in the single-member constituencies that Russia's Choice performed better. Whereas the LDPR, Communist Party of the Russian Federation (KPRF), and Agrarians received almost three times as many seats as Russia's Choice in the electoral list voting, they only just beat Russia's Choice in the one-candidate constituencies (with thirty-one seats to Russia's Choice's twenty-five).

It thus seems unlikely that reformist parties of the center would have received more votes if they had allied with Russia's Choice rather than opposing it. A more plausible version of the argument would emphasize not the division of the reform camp, but the splits between different center blocs. Voters may have been alienated by the mutual accusations, personal ambition, and feuding and by the confusing inability of the center parties to explain the essential distinctions in their positions. A united center grouping, with a clear commitment to gradual reform, democracy, stability, and increased social welfare provision might have been able to inspire more voters.

Such divisions were particularly embarrassing for the center blocs. Unlike the extreme opposition, which could claim ideological conviction and the imperatives of struggle, the "centrist" ethos they all endorsed was one of social harmony, compromise, unity, and cohesion. Yet they found themselves appealing to the electorate from six adjacent camps, while studiously ignoring or snubbing each other. Their very number undermined the image of social integration they hoped to project. Few found a convincing principle to explain their fractiousness; instead, most simply disparaged their rivals quietly on ad hominem grounds.

Second, though some centrists argued that the electoral rules were designed to benefit Russia's Choice, this does not appear to have made much difference in practice. Campaign officials complained about the frequency with which the Central Electoral Commission changed the rules, improvising as it went along. Yevgenii Malkin said the changes in the form of voting papers and rules for the use of TV time made it difficult to plan ahead: "What's annoying is not so much that they change in the interests of one side as that they change constantly."[44] The periodic interjections of television moderators into the free air time of blocs when they grew too critical of government policies probably only increased sympathy for the speakers. The requirement that blocs gather 100,000 signatures of support in a short period led to the elimination of twenty-two out of thirty-five blocs. Had these been allowed to contend the election, few appear likely to have topped the 5 percent barrier, though including less extreme nationalist groupings might have sapped a certain amount of support from the Communists, LDPR, and Agrarians. In this sense, the reduction in destructive competition on the extreme opposition side of the spectrum worked directly *against* the interests of the radical and moderate reformers. By and large, however, this does not explain the center's weak result.

A third factor that some thought might disproportionately affect electoral outcomes was money. Despite concerns that the election might be bought, in the end what is striking is the low efficacy of money for securing political goods, at least in the electoral-list part of the contest.[45] Published figures on the campaign spending of the blocs bear no obvious relationship to the results. Although these figures may have been inaccurate, it seems unlikely that the blocs that did relatively well with low reported spending (for example, Women of Russia, the KPRF) did so because of concealed expenditures. There was very little evidence of lavish spending by these blocs during the campaigns. More plausibly, the figures for Russia's Choice, already the highest spender, may have been underreported.[46]

Several characteristics of the campaign process limited the effectiveness of money. First, the speed with which the election was called found most parties unprepared either for rapid fund raising or rapid campaigning. This was particularly problematic for those blocs without a financially experienced and well-connected staff that could break through the logjams of the banking system. According to Yabloko's campaign manager, Yurii Levykin, the bloc's official bank account was only opened one week after it registered. Money transfers even within Moscow took five to ten days to clear. Contributors knew the account would be frozen by the Central Electoral Commission on December 11. All this left a narrow window of opportunity to get money in and out before the campaign was over.[47] Some campaigns presumably used other bank accounts to pay for their expenses.

Second, the two hours of free television time provided more advertising opportunity than many blocs knew how to use to their advantage. Many feared excessive or clumsy advertising could have a counterproductive impact, prompting viewers simply to turn off the television. Indeed, there is no evidence that more ad time per se increased a bloc's vote. No correlation exists between commercial advertising time on the two main TV channels and the results (see chapter 7 by Laura Roselle Helvey). Third, the underdeveloped market for political consultancy, polling, and campaign services meant money was difficult to convert into advantage. Effective use of finance was limited by the unreliability of contracts and of large organizations based on money. Principals could not monitor agents or punish them for opportunism.

This was strikingly demonstrated during the race to gather the 100,000 signatures necessary for a bloc's inclusion on the ballot. All three business-led blocs—the Transformation bloc, Aleksandr Tikhonov and Valerii Neverov's Consolidation party, and Konstantin Borovoi's August bloc—failed to gather the required number of authentic signatures in the allotted time.[48] Like various other blocs, they paid gatherers from 100 to 500 or more rubles a signature. But the sheets they received included too many forgeries or incomplete listings. Those blocs that succeeded had not just money but tested political organizations with committed members (for example, Yabloko's Republican party and Social Democratic party), or bureaucratic organizations with hierarchical authority (for example, the Agrarians' networks of collective farms). Often they had diversified organizational supports, which could cover for unexpected areas of weakness. According to one campaign official for PRES, for instance, the party obtained 50,000 signatures from Gazprom; about another 100,000 from those oblasts, krais, and republics whose leaders were supporters; besides some from member Konstantin Zatulin's association of entrepreneurs and the Union of Russian Cities, which unites local administrators, mayors, and chairs of city councils.[49]

Entrepreneurs had better luck obtaining places on lists. Of the candidates for the State Duma, 22 percent were entrepreneurs and industrial directors, the largest occupational group. For the Federation Council, they were the second largest, with 15.5 percent. Certain businesses also financed campaigns, most notably commercial banks. The most visible was Most, which hedged its bets, contributing to all four of the reform blocs. (During the campaign, Gaidar advocated protection for Russian banks against foreign competition.) Shakhrai's PRES received support from Bank Imperial, a member of the Gazprom consortium.[50]

If disunity, unpredictable rules, and lack of finance only partially explain why the center blocs did not perform better, what other factors were important? Two hypotheses suggest themselves from survey data that have been published since the elections.

On each issue a large plurality of respondents seems to have favored moderate positions, but there appears to have been little constraint over how voters combined reformist, centrist, and opposition opinions. Commitment to a "centrist" position on one issue did not necessarily entail commitment to the "centrist" position on others. Operating in a confusing, rapidly changing political environment, in which the logic of political cause and effect was highly unclear, voters were relatively free to construct often incongruous portfolios of apparently inconsistent positions on different questions. Few parties offered an integrated and convincing *Weltanschauung* that could explain Russia's current situation and suggest a strategy for effective change.

As a result, although pluralities favored the "centrist" position on most important issues, any individual voter might have some moderate and some extreme positions on different issues. Her voting would thus depend largely on *which* issue she thought about as she decided for whom to vote. According to Hough, among those survey respondents who favored gradual reform—the "centrist" position on economic policy—only 48 percent favored equality of power between parliament and president—a "centrist" position on political institutions.[51] This implies that only 23 percent of all respondents favored the "centrist" position on *both* of these issues. Some combinations of views were held by a significant fraction of respondents, even when apparently contradictory. Thirteen percent of those in favor of rapid reform favored a strong parliament rather than a strong presidency, despite the parliament's recent obstruction of reform measures. Another 13 percent of those categorically against economic reform nevertheless favored a presidency stronger than the parliament, despite President Yeltsin's battles to get reform measures past the Supreme Soviet.[52] This lack of party-rooted packages of coherent beliefs left predominantly "centrist" voters unusually free to choose on what basis they would place their vote.[53]

When voters' commitments come in unstructured, idiosyncratic packages, it is important to consider how voters decide on what issue to vote. What policy question is the ballot asking? The 1993 vote could be conceived as a referendum on each of three alternative questions. First, voters might choose to view it as a poll on what Russia's political *goals* should be—democracy and market reform, communism and central planning, authoritarian dictatorship. Second, voters might see it as a referendum on *methods* of political action, on procedural rules and the character of the institutional process. Third, they might view it as a referendum on current *performance* of the economy and incumbent regime.

Preferences of voters for electoral blocs may cycle on these three issues. Some evidence suggests that a majority of voters may have simultaneously favored Western-style market democracy as an ideal or goal of political development; supported compromise, consultation, balance of powers, and the search for social consensus as preferred methods of reaching political outcomes; and yet agreed with the extreme opposition parties in rejecting the performance of the reformers during the previous two years.[54]

If this is true, victory in the 1993 election depended on framing the election in the voters' minds as a referendum on one of these questions rather than the others. One interpretation of the strong peformance of the extreme opposition is that the incumbent reformers of Russia's Choice and their moderate reformist counterparts failed to convince enough swing voters that the election was in fact a referendum on the ideals and goals of political development. The centrist blocs and the moderate reformists failed to convince the electorate that the vote was in fact a referendum on what mode of conflict resolution and decisionmaking should structure government action. The extreme opposition succeeded in casting the election as a referendum on the performance of the incumbent reformists in power. On this issue, the majority wished to express as extreme a protest as possible.[55]

Had the center blocs been able to cast both Russia's Choice and the Communists and LDPR as "Bolsheviks of the left and of the right," extremists forcing their positions on a reluctant population, and to arouse resentment at the authoritarian style of decisionmaking, they might have been able to get voters to declare a "plague on both their houses." Had Russia's Choice been able to portray the Communists and LDPR as committed to some sort of antidemocratic, state-controlled authoritarian regime, and to paint the centrists and moderate reformers as their stooges, it might have been able to persuade more voters to vote their ideals and to support the most definite supporters of market democracy.

Not only was the lackluster performance of the moderate reform and center blocs a disappointment to many of their organizers, the relative performance of the parties was not as observers had predicted. Earlier polls underestimated the performance of some centrist blocs and overestimated the vote of some of the moderate proreform blocs. It is not clear whether this indicated a higher education and occupational status bias in polling, misrepresentation of preferences by respondents, or a change in opinion during the campaign. The high support for the Women of Russia took many observers by surprise. Why did some moderate reform and center blocs do better than others? Although data does not permit any rigorous conclusions, it is possible to suggest some qualified judgments.

As in the case of the center as a whole, the amount of campaign spending and television time do not seem to bear any clear relationship to blocs' votes. Women of Russia, the lowest spender of the six, did best, and the highest spender, PRES, came in only third. Was name recognition important? The percentage of survey respondents who could recall the names of the parties followed quite closely their order in the final tallies on the party-list voting (see chapter 3 by Colton). More than half remembered the Women of Russia, whereas only about one in eight recalled Civic Union. However, because this survey was taken in part after the election, it is hard to know whether to interpret this as suggesting that those who recognized a party's name were more likely to vote for it or that those who voted for a party were more likely later to recognize its name. There was a somewhat looser match between the percentages who claimed to be fully or partially familiar with the programs of the blocs and their vote totals. Distinctiveness may have helped—the Women of Russia stood out clearly from the predominantly male crowd, and Yabloko was the most clearly proreform. But on these grounds, the distinct issue-orientations of blocs such as KEDR, with its ecological program, should have stood out too. If they did, it did not help.

Did blocs whose leaders were particularly popular or respected do better than others? It is interesting how little this seemed to determine the vote in the case of the center blocs. Overall, only about one-quarter of respondents reported that they voted for a particular slate in the party-preference ballot because it contained authoritative politicians. About two-thirds of those who evaluated the leaders of the Women of Russia, PRES, and Yabloko first in a ranking of party leaders nevertheless chose to vote for a different bloc (see chapter 3).

Was the nature of the bloc's program a decisive factor? An overwhelming 55 percent of voters claimed to have made up their mind in the list ballot on the basis of the blocs' programs. This, of course, does not mean they made up their mind to vote for the same program. The two strongest center performers—Yabloko and Women of Russia—came from opposite ends of the center spectrum, the former favoring radical economic reform and the latter endorsing paternalist state regulation and welfare provision.

Another possible factor is, oddly enough, the age of the electoral organization. By and large, it was those blocs most recently founded that performed best. The longer established blocs—Civic Union, the RDDR, and the DPR—were the poorest three performers of the six main centrist blocs. Perhaps the older groupings had become discredited through past publicity, whereas the newer groups could still hope to be taken more seriously. (Of course, such an effect did not extend to the also recently formed minor single-issue campaigns.)

The Geography of Center Support

How was support for the center blocs spread across Russia's territory? Geographers have for several years noted a sharpening political divide between the more liberal and proreform North, East, and metropolitan areas, and the conservative, agrarian South and Southwest.[56] Where does support for the center fit into this political map?

Support for the nine blocs in between Russia's Choice and the extreme opposition increases as one moves from West to East. There is a correlation (at $r = .33$, $p = .002$) between the nine center blocs' total vote and the regional capital city's longitudinal location (see table 5-3). In the twenty-nine regions to the east of Tyumen oblast, the mean center vote was 46.3 percent. In the sixty regions to the west, the mean share for the nine center blocs was only 38.6 percent. The easterly increase in center votes seems to have come at the expense of the three opposition parties (these have a correlation of $r = -.30$, $p = .005$ with longitudinal location), rather than at the expense of Russia's Choice (whose vote is not correlated to east-west location). Political polarization appears to be less extreme in the East, and voters there are somewhat more eager to find alternatives to both the radical reformers and their extreme opponents. By contrast, the center blocs performed worst in the agricultural heartland of the Central and Central Black Earth regions, where the opposition did particularly well.

The regional profiles of particular moderate reform and center blocs differed. Some blocs had much greater variation in support across regions, and others had a more evenly spread electorate. Among the nine blocs, the coefficient of variation across regions ranged from .32 for Women of Russia, indicating a dispersed electorate, to 1.07 for the DPR, indicating a relatively regionally concentrated electorate (see table 5-4).[57]

Different center blocs had strengths in different regions. The Women of Russia did particularly well in the East (correlation with regional capital's

Table 5-3. *Correlation Coefficients between Regional Bloc Vote (December 1993) and Selected Characteristics of Region*

	Nine moderate reform and center blocs	Yabloko	RDDR	PRES	DPR	Civic Union	Women of Russia
Eastern longitudinal location	.33 (.002)	.01 (.90)	.19 (.07)	.25 (.02)	.18 (.11)	.10 (.34)	.44 (.00)
Per capita subventions in 1992	.26 (.01)	−.05 (.65)	−.07 (.52)	.35 (.00)	.22 (.04)	.19 (.08)	.22 (.04)
Regional budget spending per capita 1993 (January–August)	.47 (.00)	.19 (.08)	.42 (.00)	.13 (.22)	.33 (.00)	.17 (.11)	.39 (.00)
Proportion of enterprises loss-making 1993	.40 (.00)	−.15 (.18)	.04 (.70)	.44 (.00)	.18 (.11)	.22 (.05)	.33 (.00)
Russia's Choice vote	.22 (.04)	.42 (.00)	.74 (.00)	−.16 (.13)	.09 (.39)	.11 (.30)	.28 (.01)
Urban share of population	.01 (.95)	.35 (.00)	.59 (.00)	−.34 (.00)	.17 (.11)	.01 (.92)	−.04 (.72)
Republics	.35 (.00)	−.01 (.91)	−.22 (.05)	.42 (.00)	−.11 (.33)	.30 (.01)	.02 (.85)
Support for Yeltsin in April 1993 referendum	.28 (.01)	.39 (.00)	.73 (.00)	.02 (.86)	.24 (.02)	.13 (.22)	.50 (.00)

Source: Voting data are available in Michael McFaul and Nikolai Petrov, eds., *Politicheskii al'manakh Rossii, 1995* (Moscow: Moscow Carnegie Center, 1995). Other data are available from various Goskomstat publications.

Note: In calculating these correlations, the extreme outlying case of Ingushetia (where the DPR received 71 percent of the vote) is excluded from the data for the DPR. This result cannot be explained by nationwide trends.

Table 5-4. *Characteristics of Regional Vote for Moderate Reform and Center Blocs*

	Nine moderate reform and center blocs	Yabloko	RDDR	PRES	DPR	Civic Union	Women of Russia
Mean	41.16	7.84	3.79	8.26	5.84	2.20	9.42
Standard deviation	11.12	6.15	1.68	6.11	1.18	1.14	3.06
Coefficient of variation	0.27	0.78	0.44	0.74	1.07	0.52	0.32

Source: Regional voting data are available in Michael McFaul and Nikolai Petrov, eds., *Politicheskii al'manakh Rossii, 1995* (Moscow: Moscow Carnegie Center, 1995).
Note: The coefficient of variation, a measure of dispersion, is a statistic's standard deviation divided by its mean. The higher is the coefficient of variation of a party's support, the more uneven was its geographical concentration.

longitudinal location at $r = .44$, $p = .000$), and PRES also did well there (correlation of $r = .25$, $p = .02$). Yabloko was particularly strong in industrial centers and large cities—St. Petersburg, Moscow, Nizhnii Novgorod—as well as in certain regions of the North and East—Murmansk, Kamchatka, Magadan. The RDDR, besides the cities of Moscow and St Petersburg, had a burst of support in the center of the country, stretching roughly from the Urals to Lake Baikal and centered on Kemerovo, apparently because of the bloc's alliance with the Independent Union of Mineworkers, which had strong representation in the coal-mining centers of the Kuzbass. The DPR won a remarkable 71 percent of the vote in Ingushetia, but had relatively even support in most of the rest of the country. Civic Union did particularly well in Ivanovo—a center of the depressed textile industry—and in a few republics, such as Kalmykia, and autonomous formations, such as the Nenetskii Autonomous Okrug.

It is interesting to note that although both the radical reformers and the extreme opposition did worse in the most industrially unprofitable regions, center blocs performed better in such areas. There was a positive correlation between the proportion of enterprises in a region that were insolvent and the center vote.[58] There was also a positive correlation between the center bloc vote and regional receipt of subventions in 1992 (at $r = .26$, $p = .014$).[59] Apparently, the most unprofitable and dependent regions were more likely to reject both the radical reformers and the extreme opposition in favor of the center blocs, which emphasized the need for continued subsidies, state welfare provision, and industrial policy. Meanwhile, both Russia's Choice and the center blocs seemed to benefit from higher spending by the regional government. Per capita regional spending was positively correlated with the Russia's Choice and the center votes, but negatively correlated with the extreme opposition vote (at $r = -.50$, $p = .000$).[60]

Some early observers interpreted the opposition victory in December as an "expansion of provincial subconsciousness" in which the countryside mobilized while city voters stayed home.[61] The opposition blocs polled particularly strongly—and Russia's Choice weakly—in rural areas. However, the center blocs apparently spanned the urban-rural divide. There was no overall correlation between the center vote and urbanization. Although the most proreform centrists (Yabloko and RDDR) did strictly better in urban regions, PRES did better overall in rural regions.[62] The other three blocs' results were not significantly correlated with urbanization.

Overall, the center blocs polled higher in the republics than in oblasts and krais. But this is explained mostly by the performance of PRES and Civic Union. PRES, if it did not completely establish its claim to be a "party of regions," did earn a place as a party of republics.[63] (The party did not poll significantly higher, however, in regions in which its local list included a member of the regional administration or parliament.) Yabloko, the DPR, and Women of Russia did not do significantly better either in republics or nonrepublics, and the RDDR did worse. In nonrepublics, support for the center blocs was correlated with support for Yeltsin in the April 1993 referendum; but in republics, there was no relationship with recent support for Yeltsin. Even in republics more hostile to Yeltsin, voters might still turn to PRES, Yabloko, or Civic Union.[64]

Several blocs demonstrate an interesting split in the nature of their support in the two types of region. In the nonrepublics, PRES performed as a typical moderate proreform bloc, polling higher in urban regions and ones in which support for Yeltsin was stronger (correlation at $r = .45$, $p = .000$). But in the republics, there was no relationship between the PRES vote and support for Yeltsin. Apparently, although its fate was tied to that of the democratic reformers in the oblasts and krais, Shakhrai's party had succeeded in forging an independent basis for support in the republics. The Women of Russia's vote exhibited exactly the opposite discontinuity. In oblasts and krais it appears to have been perceived as a moderate opposition bloc, with a commitment to continuing subsidies. But in the republics, it was in the most pro-Yeltsin, prosperous, and urbanized regions that the Women of Russia did better.

Conclusion

In December 1993, a skeptical and querulous voting public chose over-whelmingly to reject the incumbent governing coalition. In the process, it also gave only a lukewarm endorsement to the moderate reformers and centrists who claimed to stand in the middle of the political spectrum. Each unhappy campaign was unhappy in its own way, and it would be easy to list for each a series of blunders, miscalculations, organizational and strategic errors, inspired by overconfidence, ignorance, and political inexperience. However, these were not unique to the moderate reform and centrist blocs. For all his postelection reputation as a gifted television communicator, Zhirinovskii's campaign appearances were not always on target (his rambling lecture on sexual hygiene was considered by observers at the time to have been a gaffe). The Communists and Agrarians were simply turgid. Inexperience, weak organization, intense time pressure, scarce resources, unpredictable crises, and sheer bungling were universal phenomena, and do not explain why some blocs enjoyed spectacular success and others failure.

So why the result? This chapter has hypothesized that the best explanation has to do with the poorly integrated political beliefs and commitments of the Russian public. The result turned not just on the content of voters' opinions but on the choice of issue on which they voted. The radical reformers failed to cast the election as a referendum on ultimate goals (democracy and a market economy); the centrists failed to turn it into a vote on preferred styles of political action and social conflict resolution. The extreme opposition won because ultimately voters chose to use their ballots to express their anger at current economic hardship and political chaos. In their normative ideals, the majority of Russians were arguably radical reformers, committed to democracy and markets; in their choice of political styles and procedures they lined up more closely with the positions of moderates and centrists; but in their rejection of the incumbent regime's performance they stood in December 1993 clearly on the side of the extreme opposition.

What determines on what basis voters choose to vote in a given election? Why do they at different times see the vote as a referendum on ideals, on procedures, or on performance? Why does the protest vote sometimes go to the extreme opposition and sometimes to the center? These are questions for more systematic comparative analysis. Here, I can only make four conjectures for future testing. First, voting on abstract ideals is likely to be more widespread in the first election after an authoritarian regime either collapses or liberalizes. This offers an unusually unstructured choice between the performance of the past and the promises of previously excluded—and so less discredited—outsiders. Second, center blocs may do better when the economic crisis is not too severe. In the presence of very high inflation or unemployment, the tendency for voters to express extreme protest against current government performance may be greater. Third, the prospects for a moderate alternative may be brighter in cases in which the nationalist card has already been played decisively by the anticommunist coalition that took over in the first postcommunist election (as was the case in the Baltic states). Fourth, the center may lose more to the extremes when the question of "stateness" has not yet been resolved, with the country's borders in dispute.[65] Perhaps the center would also have received more votes in Russia if it had united under a charismatic leader, in clear but moderate opposition to the government, though there is no decisive evidence for this.

The 1993 election was Russia's first post–postcommunist election, and as happened in other East European states, it saw the rejection of the first anticommunist coalition. This was a vote of protest against current government performance rather than a transfer of support to any particular alternative. Geographically, Russia's Choice did worst not where any other bloc's vote was high but where support for Yeltsin and reform was low.

Unlike Russia's Choice, however, the moderate reform and center blocs were clearly in competition for votes with the opposition groupings. They did worst where support for Yeltsin had fallen most between 1991 and 1993 and in regions in which Zhirinovskii had been strong in the 1991 presidential election. The televised campaigns communicated effectively to angry voters the choice of extreme blocs available, and a last-minute official panic over the Zhirinovskii threat conveyed to such voters how to make the most dramatic statement. Judging from polls taken during the campaign, voters seem ultimately to have converged on blocs in the last weeks of the campaigns at rates proportional to the blocs' ideological distance from the government.

According to President Yeltsin, interviewed in *Izvestiya* the following spring, the parliamentary elections had "taught all of us a lesson."[66] What exactly leaders of the moderate reform and center blocs should have learned from them, however, is unclear. Spending on the campaigns, political advertising, travel, and organization seem to have made only a marginal contribution to the differences between the blocs' performance. Divisions may have lowered their vote, as did the failure to provide convincing, integrated packages of beliefs about political means and ends. With a large proportion of the population holding dissonant views about appropriate public goals, methods of social action, and current economic and political realities, an ideology that could harmonize such views, even at the cost of logic and consistency, would have considerable electoral appeal.

Notes

1. This argument refers to the *national* center blocs. The single-member constituency voting did return a large number of non–party-affiliated deputies who subsequently joined a newly formed centrist faction, New Regional Policy. This does not alter the fact that the results were surprisingly poor for the blocs that ran on center platforms.

2. Of the 1,319 voters from a representative, nationwide postelection survey who said they favored a "gradual transition to the market," 537 reported having voted for one of the nine center and moderate reform blocs, and 652 reported having voted for either Russia's Choice, the LDPR, or the Communist Party of the Russian Federation (Colton-Hough survey).

3. A similar vogue was evident in Poland after the 1991 parliamentary elections, when all but two of the numerous parties insisted on being seated in the center of the chamber. See Krzysztof Jasiewicz, "From Solidarity to Fragmentation," *Journal of Democracy*, vol. 3 (April 1992), pp. 55–69, at p. 64.

4. *Segodnya*, October 16, 1993, p. 2.

5. These were Yabloko, the RDDR, PRES, Women of Russia, the DPR, and Civic Union.

6. They also received only four seats in the single-mandate constituencies between them.

7. For more on the politics of lobbying, see Daniel Treisman, "The Politics of Soft Credit in Post-Soviet Russia," *Europe-Asia Studies*, vol. 47, no. 6 (September 1995), pp. 949–76.

8. Press conference, November 25, 1993, Dom Druzhby, Moscow.

9. *Nezavisimaya gazeta*, December 8, 1993, p. 1.

10. *Kommersant'*, no. 46, 15–21, November 1993, p. 4.

11. *Segodnya*, November 27, 1993, p. 3.

12. This section draws on the parties' programs and campaign materials, television addresses, and personal interviews with campaign officials and candidates from the parties, in particular: Vyacheslav Shebkii, press secretary of the RDDR; Yurii Levykin (campaign manager), Mikhail Motorin (candidate), Vyacheslav Shostakovskii (leader of the Republican party); Yurii Boldyrev (leader) of Yabloko; Roman Pugachev, delegate to the Central Electoral Commission of PRES; Yevgenii B. Malkin, campaign manager of the DPR; and Viktor Mironenko (cochair of the Union Renewal) of Civic Union.

13. Author's telephone interview with Vyacheslav Shebkii, press secretary of the RDDR, Moscow, December 14, 1993.

14. Nikolai Troitskii, "Kabinetny strateg, kotory mechtaet stat' liderom," *Stolitsa* (1993) no. 45, pp. 6–8.

15. Author's interview with Roman V. Pugachev, delegate to the Central Electoral Commission of PRES, Moscow, November 27, 1993.

16. *Segodnya,* October 19, 1993, p. 2.

17. Author's interview with Roman V. Pugachev, Moscow, November 27, 1993.

18. Although PRES continued to exist in 1996, it was little more than a collection of Shakhrai supporters and cronies.

19. Author's interview with Yevgenii B. Malkin, campaign manager of the DPR, Moscow, 23 November 1993.

20. For a thoughtful interpretation of the rise and fall of Civic Union, see Michael McFaul, "Russian Centrism and Revolutionary Transitions," *Post-Soviet Affairs,* vol. 9, no. 3 (1993), pp. 196–222.

21. *Argumenty i fakty,* no. 24 (December 1993), p. 2. Travkin was later expelled from his party's leadership after he accepted a job as minister without portfolio in Yeltsin's regime. He has largely disappeared from sight.

22. *Moskovskiye novosti,* November 21, 1993. The Women of Russia is the only one of the four single-issue groups not to have disappeared from the public arena since 1993. The Women of Russia, nevertheless, failed to clear the 5 percent barrier to receive seats in the party-list voting in December 1995.

23. The RDDR was the exception, saying that as an umbrella proreform group, it could work with anyone committed to reform, even the Communists.

24. Reforms must make "life easier" and require "no . . . new shock!" (Civic Union); be evolutionary and based on "nationwide agreement" (DPR); be "not a goal, but a means of improving life" (Women of Russia); be "reoriented to people's needs" (RDDR); and take place "from the bottom up" (Yabloko). Taken from program and campaign materials of the various blocs.

25. Grigorii Yavlinskii, press conference, Moscow, Parliamentary Center, December 7, 1993.

26. Author's interview with Yevgenii B. Malkin, Moscow, November 23, 1993.

27. Most notable was a much-repeated television ad with a small boy sitting on the well-polished parquet floor of a clearly opulent apartment, pinning a Russia's Choice button to his denim overalls and explaining to his well-fed, shaggy dog that no one would take them to vote for Russia's Choice because they were "too little." Even the usually unflappable Andrei Kozyrev said later that every time he saw this ad it aroused in him "nothing but class hatred." *Segodnya,* December 17, 1993, p. 1.

28. See, for instance, "Meddling in Campaign Must Stop," *Moscow Times,* December 1, 1993, p. 8.

29. *Moskovskiye novosti,* December 8, 1993, p. 2.

30. VTsIOM (Russian Center for Public Opinion Research), *Economic and Social Change: Bulletin of Information,* vol. 4 (August 1993), p. 46).

31. McFaul argues that Civic Union of 1992 came into being to "represent the *new* interests of *old* identities," the directors of state enterprises and official trade unions (McFaul, "Russian Centrism and Revolutionary Transitions," p. 207).

32. Author's interview with Roman V. Pugachev, Moscow, November 27, 1993.

33. Yavlinskii meeting at Dom Kino, December 9, 1993; press conference at Parliamentary Center, December 7, 1993.

34. Author's interview with Yurii Levykin, campaign manager of Yabloko, Moscow, December 14, 1993.

35. One rationale for such a strategy is offered in Barbara Geddes, "A Comparative Perspective on the Leninist Legacy in Eastern Europe," *Comparative Political Studies*, vol. 28, no. 2 (July 1995), pp. 239–74.

36. For instance, in VTsIOM's June poll, when respondents were asked to pick from a list the names of those politicians whom they most trusted, Yavlinskii received 12.5 percent, Shakhrai 11.4, Travkin 6.5, Vol'skii 2.3, and Popov 1.9. (VTsIOM, *Economic and Social Change: Bulletin of Information*, p. 46).

37. *Segodnya*, December 18, 1993, p. 2.

38. Author's interview with Roman V. Pugachev, Moscow, November 27, 1993.

39. For example, Wendy Slater, "The Diminishing Center of Russian Parliamentary Politics," *RFE/RL Research Report*, vol. 3 (April 29, 1994), pp. 13–18.

40. Jerry F. Hough, "The Russian Election of 1993: Public Attitudes toward Economic Reform and Democratization," *Post-Soviet Affairs*, vol. 10, no. 1 (January–March 1994), pp. 1–37, at p. 34.

41. *Izvestiya*, November 27, 1993, p. 8.

42. *Komsomol'skaya pravda*, November 24, 1993, p. 1.

43. This argument was endorsed by some analysts. See, for example, Alexander Rahr, "The Implications of Russia's Parliamentary Elections," *RFE/RL Research Report*, vol. 3 (January 7, 1994), pp. 32–37.

44. Author's interview with Yevgenii B. Malkin, Moscow, November 23, 1993.

45. In the single-mandate constituencies, it may have been more effective.

46. According to official figures published later by the Central Electoral Commission, the blocs' campaign spending was as follows: Russia's Choice: 1.92 billion rubles; PRES: 830 million; Yabloko: 380 million; LDPR: 100 million; KPRF: 100 million; DPR: 98 million; Agrarians: 90 million; and Women of Russia: 63 million. Fifty million rubles were provided by the state to each registered electoral list. See *Byuleten' Tsentral'noi Izbiratel'noi Komissii RF*, vol. 4, no. 15, 1994, p. 23. For an analysis of the impact of money on the results of the 1993 and 1995 elections, see Daniel Treisman, "Dollars and Democratization: The Role and Power of Money in Russia's Transitional Elections," *Comparative Politics*, forthcoming.

47. Author's interview with Yurii Levykin, campaign manager of Yabloko, Moscow, December 14, 1993.

48. Borovoi said that although his bloc had raised the required number of signatures, it chose not to submit them because some had apparently been obtained from lists in enterprise personnel departments, where names are kept along with the nec-

essary passport data (author's interview with Konstantin Borovoi, Moscow, November 29, 1993).

49. Author's interview with Roman V. Pugachev, Moscow, November 27, 1993.

50. Pilar Bonet, written communication (dispatch to *El Pais*), Moscow, December 8, 1993.

51. Jerry F. Hough, "The Russian Election of 1993: Public Attitudes toward Economic Reform and Democratization," p. 17.

52. In the Colton postelection survey, 47 percent of those who had voted for the radical promarket Russia's Choice bloc said the state should "strictly control food prices," 20 percent did not support the purchase and sale of land, 9 percent thought that privatization should be stopped or reversed, and 6 percent said they were "against the market." One in ten Russia's Choice voters either *agreed* or *fully agreed* that "Stalin gets accused of things that he never did." Meanwhile, 17 percent of Communist voters said the state should not limit the incomes of rich citizens, a position that would certainly have surprised Marx or Lenin. And an amazing 29 percent of LDPR voters fully agreed with the statement that "human rights should be very well defended, even if this allows someone to escape punishment" (information from Colton postelection survey).

53. Other scholars have noted "incoherent or inchoate patterns of interest articulation and belief structure" in postcommunist societies, as well as a lack of understanding of tradeoffs between conflicting principles. Geoffrey Evans and Stephen Whitefield, "Identifying the Bases of Party Competition in Eastern Europe," *British Journal of Political Science*, vol. 23, no. 4 (October 1993), pp. 521–48, pp. 529–30.

54. Whitefield and Evans, in a survey of 2,030 respondents in fifty Russian regions taken in the summer before the 1993 election, found that although 49 percent of respondents expressed commitment to "the ideal of democracy," only 19 percent gave a positive evaluation of "performance in advancing [this] ideal in Russia so far." And although 62 percent were committed to the market as an ideal, only 14 percent had a positive view of performance to date in advancing toward it (ibid., pp. 46–47). They conclude that while a majority or large plurality of voters have a "*normative* commitment to markets and democracy in principle," their "current preferences" are "against marketization and privatization as it has been pursued." Stephen Whitefield and Geoffrey Evans, "The Russian Election of 1993: Public Opinion and the Transition Experience," *Post-Soviet Affairs*, vol. 10, no. 1 (January–March, 1994), p. 41). For evidence that a majority simultaneously favored moderate or centrist modes of decisionmaking and conflict resolution, see the polls cited in the previous section.

55. Some indirect evidence for this can be inferred from the particularly high volatility of early procenter or moderate reform voters. Of those who said in the preelection survey that they planned to vote for one of the centrist blocs, one-third later reported actually having voted for Russia's Choice, the LDPR, the KPRF, or the Agrarians. Of those who before the election planned to vote for a "moderate reformist" bloc, 30 percent in fact chose one of the radical reformist, nationalist, or socialist options (see chapter 3, table 3-5).

56. For example, see Elizabeth Teague, "North-South Divide: Yeltsin and Russia's Provincial Leaders," *RFE/RL Research Report,* vol. 2 (November 26, 1993), pp. 7–23; Darrell Slider, Vladimir Gimpleson, and Sergei Chugrov, "Political Tendencies in Russia's Regions: Evidence from the 1993 Parliamentary Elections," *Slavic Review,* vol. 53 (Fall 1994), p. 711.

57. This high indicator of regional concentration is entirely a result of the surprisingly high vote for the DPR in Ingushetia, where it received 71 percent. If the DPR's outlying performance in Ingushetia is excluded from the data, the value of its coefficient of variation falls to 0.20.

58. The vote of the nine center blocs was correlated with the proportion of loss-making enterprises at $r = .40$, significant at .000; correlation with Russia's Choice vote at $r = -.21$, significant at $p = .06$; correlation with three opposition blocs' vote at $r = -.37$, significant at $p = .001$.

59. This may explain, in part, the center's strength in eastern regions, which were developed in ways that make them heavily dependent on imports from other regions. Transport and energy costs are generally higher in the East. The correlation between subsidies and center support was particularly strong in the twenty-eight easternmost regions taken separately; meanwhile, there was no relationship with subventions in the Western regions taken separately.

60. For a more detailed analysis of the relationship between regional spending and the evolution of political opinion in Russia, see Daniel Treisman, *After the Deluge: Regional Crises and Political Consolidation in Russia* (forthcoming, University of Michigan Press).

61. See, for example, *Segodnya,* December 15, 1993, p. 2.

62. This, however, reflects PRES's performance in the republics, many of which are rural. Among 58 nonrepublics, the PRES vote was actually stronger in *urban* than in rural regions (correlation with urban proportion of the population at $r = .25, p = .063$).

63. The correlation between republic status and PRES vote was .42, significant at p = .00.

64. *Segodnya,* December 15, 1993, p. 2.

65. See Juan J. Linz and Alfred Stepan, "Political Identities and Electoral Sequences: Spain, the Soviet Union, and Yugoslavia," *Daedalus,* vol. 121 (Spring 1992), pp. 123–39.

66. Alexander Rahr, "Yeltsin's Interview," *RFE/RL Daily Report* (March 28, 1994).

CHAPTER SIX

Right and Left in the Hard Opposition

Evelyn Davidheiser

THE MOST startling result of the 1993 election was the victory of the right-wing Liberal Democratic Party of Russia (LDPR) under the leadership of Vladimir Zhirinovskii. By midnight December 12, just two hours after the polls closed in Moscow, it was clear that the radical reformers had not produced the win expected. Instead the LDPR was in a strong first place in the party-list race. By the time the votes were counted, the LDPR had indeed won a plurality of the party-list votes, but in the overwhelming attention devoted to Zhirinovskii's victory, most ignored the equally important strength of the left opposition—the Communist Party of the Russian Federation (KPRF) under Gennadii Zyuganov and the Agrarian Party of Russia under Mikhail Lapshin. These two parties had promised a post-election coalition from the beginning and together they came in a close second to the LDPR. More important, in the single-mandate races, the KPRF and Agrarian party did far better than the LDPR, winning nine and sixteen seats, respectively, to the LDPR's five seats. Both the spectacular showing of the LDPR and the very solid showing of the KPRF and Agrarian party point to a strong vote of opposition to Boris Yeltsin and the government, but the variation in the performances of the parties in the two types of races points to the more subtle ways in which Russia's emerging party system is being shaped. The distribution of seats across these three parties—and especially between the parties on the left and the LDPR on the right—was influenced both by external constraints and by constraints internal to the opposition parties themselves.

Two external constraints influenced the performance of the opposition parties—popular opposition to Boris Yeltsin and his policies and the extent of competition among the parties of the hard opposition. External constraints effectively limited the hard opposition to the three electoral blocs considered in this chapter. They competed for a well-established pool of opposition votes, particularly in those regions of the country where Yeltsin and his policies had been having trouble all along. The opposition parties reacted to these external constraints by developing campaign strategies that reflected their internal assets. Two internal constraints were most important: organizational capacity (including the pool of candidates) and command of the media, which was strongly affected by campaign funding. The LDPR relied on the high profile of its leader, Zhirinovskii, and high levels of funding to wage a nationwide campaign that exploited the media, especially television. In contrast, the Agrarian party and the KPRF were limited by scarce funding and forced to rely more heavily on the depth of their organizations. External and internal forces interacted to produce support for the LDPR, which had breadth but lacked depth, and more concentrated but narrower support for the Agrarian party and the KPRF. This was reflected in the LDPR strength in the party-list race and the successes in the single-mandate districts of the Agrarian party and the KPRF.

In this chapter I explain the performance of the parties of the hard opposition by developing the popular opposition to Yeltsin within the electorate, profiling the parties that were competing for this vote and examining the internal resources available to these parties. I conclude with a brief comparison of 1993 to subsequent Russian elections. Although a careful comparison is beyond the scope of this chapter, it is useful to highlight factors that help to explain the 1993 outcome. Comparing the results of the 1993 and 1995 parliamentary elections emphasizes the importance of the *interaction* of external and internal constraints. Between 1993 and 1995, external constraints changed in significant ways. Both opposition to Yeltsin and competition among parties of the hard opposition increased. Internal constraints, however, changed only marginally. The result was an overall increase in support of the hard opposition, but a much different distribution, with the KPRF outperforming the LDPR by better than two to one in the party-list race, while simultaneously winning a plurality of single-mandate seats.

External Constraints

External constraints defined the environment in which the parties competed. Antipathy toward Yeltsin's program set the boundaries on competition amongst the parties of the hard opposition. The speed of the campaign and rules of the game limited the extent of competition within these boundaries.

Opposition to Yeltsin and His Policies

The LDPR, the KPRF, and the Agrarian party were in competition for the vote of opposition against Yeltsin and his policies. Certainly they expected those portions of the population that had suffered under Yeltsin's economic reforms to provide a heavy opposition vote. One of the most striking stories I heard in Moscow involved a doctor at the morgue where the bodies were taken after the conflict in October. As the doctor walked down the rows of corpses, he commented that there was not one new pair of shoes among the lot of them. Yet the results of the April 1993 referendum had persuaded many Yeltsin advisers that opposition to his government and its policy within the population was minimal. Even on question 2 in the referendum—Do you approve of the president's policy?—Yeltsin had scored a victory.

The results of the referendum had followed a regional pattern of political attitudes already clearly established in the 1990s. The popular vote for president in 1991 and the voting behavior of deputies in all ten Congresses concentrated support for Yeltsin in the more heavily urbanized regions of the country as well as on the country's northern and eastern rims. Yeltsin's opposition by contrast was concentrated in the southern agricultural regions of the country. The central industrial zones fell somewhere in the middle. The December election results also followed this pattern. Support for the opposition parties was concentrated in (though not limited to) the Black Earth and North Caucasus regions, with more diffuse support in central industrial regions. December's strong opposition showing in those same regions of the country where opposition to Yeltsin had a history confirms that the vote was one of protest.

Survey data support this. In chapter 3 of this volume Timothy Colton finds important relationships between the voter's location in Russia's social fabric, attitudes on the pressing issues of the day, and support for one party list over all others. Although the election results and the survey data indicate that the opposition parties were successfully targeting an established opposition vote, this does little to explain the distribution. Party programs as well as the survey results show that the real opposition party was the KPRF. Attitudes on policy issues, as well as economic misery, were more strongly correlated with attitudes toward the KPRF than with any of the other parties of the hard opposition. Perhaps the biggest mystery of the election is not why the opposition parties did so well, but why the vote was distributed across them the way it was. Why did the KPRF lag so far behind the LDPR when attitudes on policy issues showed the KPRF to be the clear alternative to Yeltsin? Given the rapidity of the election and the low level of party identification among voters, the constraints on competition and internal party resources were responsible for this surprising outcome.

Opposition Competition: Profiles of the Parties

Until Yeltsin dissolved the parliament, it seemed that opposition to his policy was fairly united. Many spoke of the "red-brown coalition" in parliament or what one deputy more ominously referred to as the "coalition of former communists and future fascists." Yeltsin's actions that fall were aimed at these groups and significantly influenced both the number of opposition blocs as well as which opposition blocs were included in the race. After the violence of October 3 and 4, the activities of sixteen political organizations—including the KPRF—were banned by presidential decree. When the state of emergency ended on October 18, ten of these groups were free to resume activities, but a presidential decree of October 19 banned the six most extreme of the potential opposition organizations from registering for the election. These included the National Salvation Front (Il'ya Konstantinov and Al'bert Makashov), the Officers Union (Stanislav Terekhov), Shchit (Shield; Vatalii Urazhtsev), the Russian National Unity party (Aleksandr Barkashov), the Russian Communist Youth League (Igor Malyavov), and the Russian Communist Workers Party (Viktor Anpilov). The last was one of a number of opposition organizations that declared a boycott of the election in any case, claiming it was illegal.[1]

Whereas left-wing parties were either banned outright from participating or chose to boycott the election, nationalist parties had difficulty raising the requisite 100,000 signatures for entering the party-list race. The most notorious case was Sergei Baburin's Russian National Union, which submitted petitions with the required number of signatures but was disqualified after a number were proven invalid. The circumstances surrounding this incident were controversial. The Union's offices were ransacked shortly before the deadline for submitting petitions, and when a number of the signatures submitted were found invalid, Baburin's party claimed it could not produce replacement signatures because they had been stolen. In the end, Baburin ran successfully as an independent candidate in his home oblast, Omsk. A number of other conservative candidates also were successful with independent candidacies in single-mandate races, but in the party-list race the conservative opposition was effectively limited to three.

Banning the most extreme opposition groups gave the three remaining parties increased legitimacy with the voter. Moreover, Yeltsin's actions served to concentrate the vote for the hard opposition. There was only one nationalist party and only two communist parties, which promised to unite after the election in any case. Concentrating the vote on so few parties was especially significant given the 5 percent threshold required for seating a bloc in the Duma. Had the 12.4 percent of the vote won by the KPRF been spread across, say, four of the rival communist groups, it might have been difficult for any one to win the requisite 5 percent. The implications were especially significant on the right, where the nationalist vote was concentrated on the LDPR. Baburin was quite bitter about this. As the only member of his Russian National Union to win a seat, he placed Zhirinovskii's victory squarely at Yeltsin's feet. "By throwing the patriotic opposition out of the electoral campaign the present ruling gang set the conditions in which the resulting political vacuum was filled by a more radical-nationalist and Communist opposition."[2]

Although the pressures placed on the opposition forces by the government may have helped concentrate the vote, there were government actions that made the campaign more difficult for the opposition. This was especially true for the left, which Yeltsin—at least initially—seemed to take more seriously than the right. Not only were the activities of the KPRF temporarily banned by presidential decree, in the aftermath of October's conflict, its newspapers—its key means of communication—were forced to suspend publication until November 2. Restrictions were also imposed on the ability of opposition forces to meet. For example, Moscow's Lenin Mausoleum, an important gathering place for both the left and right opposition, was closed in the fall. When representatives of opposition organizations continued to congregate in front of the building, barriers were erected and militia wearing flak jackets and combat helmets were posted on Sundays.[3]

The parties of left and right faced similar constraints, but those contesting the election presented very different programs to the voter. As the left-right division of the opposition indicates, there were two aspects to the hard opposition in Russia, one economic and the other nationalistic. Though they were not wholly independent issues, the parties aligned on them in different ways. For the parties of the left (the KPRF and the Agrarian party) economic issues were paramount. In contrast, the LDPR gave more emphasis to issues of nationalism and was quite far from the left on issues of domestic economic policy. Only on the issue of foreign economic policy were questions of the economy and nationalism merged in a way that marked the common ground of left and right in the hard opposition.

KPRF

Undoubtedly the KPRF represented the bloc farthest left on the ballot. The party was officially registered with the Russian Ministry of Justice only in July 1993, but it could boast a high level of political experience and a much longer political legacy than any other group contesting the election. Although it would be incorrect to label the KPRF the sole heir of the Communist Party of the Soviet Union (CPSU) in Russia, most of the party's leadership previously held CPSU membership and Zyuganov was a member of the Secretariat of the Communist Party of the Russian Soviet Federative Socialistic Republic (CP-RSFSR). Indeed, the origins of the KPRF can be traced to the conflict over the creation of the CP-RSFSR in 1989–90. Unlike the other republics of the former Soviet Union, the RSFSR did not have its own republican party organization. As Mikhail Gorbachev's reforms proceeded and the position of the party was weakened, conservative party members within the RSFSR began a drive for the creation of republic party institutions. Gorbachev consented to the creation of a Russian Bureau within the CPSU, but the Russian Party Conference of June 1990 transformed itself into "the founding Congress of the CP-RSFSR" and elected Ivan Polozkov first secretary. The second portion of the founding Congress was held in September, after the Twenty-Ninth Party Congress of the CPSU, and elected a central committee and secretariat that included Zyuganov. In August 1991, just before the coup, Polozkov resigned without explanation and was replaced as first secretary by Valentin Kuptsov. Zyuganov was one of three nominated to replace Polozkov, but he and Yurii Prokof'ev withdrew their names in favor of Kuptsov.[4] In the wake of the August 1991 coup, Yeltsin suspended the activities of the CP-RSFSR and confiscated its assets. In December 1992 the Constitutional Court overruled Yeltsin, and the party's Second Congress was held in February 1993, voting to change the party's name to the KPRF and electing Zyuganov first secretary.

Zyuganov represented the key link between the KPRF and the CP-RSFSR of the past. He figured prominently in the party's politics from its founding through the registration of the KPRF in the summer of 1993. Gennadii Andreevich Zyuganov followed a career path typical of someone engaged in party work for the CPSU. Born in 1944 in a small village in Orel oblast, he joined the CPSU at age twenty-two and began Komsomol work in Orel, gradually working his way up to the position of secretary of the Orel Komsomol obkom. He followed Komsomol work with a series of positions in the Orel party apparat, serving as head of the agitation and propaganda department of the obkom from 1974 to 1983. In 1983 he was promoted to the central apparat in Moscow, where he worked in the CPSU Central Committee department for propaganda. In 1989 he became deputy head of the ideology department, and in 1990 he became both a member of the Politburo and a Central Committee secretary in the newly created CP-RSFSR.[5]

Despite Zyuganov's role and the party's history, more radical communist organizations have challenged the inheritance of the KPRF, showing the link between the CP-RSFSR and the KPRF to be weaker than one might expect. The party's Second Congress was organized not only by members of the central committee of the CP-RSFSR but also by representatives of the Socialist Workers party, the Union of Communists, and the Russian Party of Communists. Of the eighteen CP-RSFSR Politburo members profiled in *Sovetskaya Rossiya* in September 1990, only two appeared on the party list in 1993: Zyuganov at number one and V. V. Chikin, editor of that paper, at number five. A third, A. S. Sokolov, ran on the Agrarian party list. Others active in the CP-RSFSR in 1990 and 1991 were either not included on the party list or situated near the bottom. Neither Polozkov nor Kuptsov was included on the list. Extremist organizations such as Nina Andreeva's All-Union Communist Party of Bolsheviks and Viktor Anpilov's Russian Communist Workers' party were highly critical of the KPRF for its moderate position on both economic and political questions, describing the KPRF as the "soft communists," and before the 1993 election the KPRF had never championed joint organization with the more hard-core leftists.[6]

Despite its relatively moderate position, if the economy had been the only issue in the campaign the Communists would have been the clearest choice for those opposed to the Yeltsin government. The KPRF was quite clear about who it was and on what its opposition to Yeltsin was based. It had established this position well before the elections were called, and the official program of the KPRF was just a few typewritten sheets titled "Program of the Communists—Simple but Effective." The program committed the party to establishing basic socioeconomic guarantees for the population as well as protecting the population from the pressures of the marketplace. The KPRF called for an end to compulsory privatization and an investigation of the legality of privatization that had already taken place. Though not excluding the possibility of privatization, altogether the KPRF clearly had a very different image from the Yeltsin government about the process. The KPRF opposed voucher privatization, a system that allowed shares in an enterprise to be bought by anyone holding a sufficient number of the vouchers that had been distributed to the population earlier that year. KPRF candidates warned of firms' being bought by outsiders with no stake in the enterprise or the community. Instead they advocated giving enterprise workers a say in the form that process should take, even if it meant rejecting privatization all together. Although critical of an excessively centralized economy, the KPRF nevertheless argued that it would be just as bad to fall into the trap of "primitive capitalism." In addition, the party maintained that the government needed property to guarantee citizens' economic rights. The platform was not clear on how limited privatization would square with the claim that state property is necessary to ensure the capacity to meet social welfare needs. During an interview with an economist from Moscow State University who was running on the KPRF ticket, I raised this issue. His response emphasized the importance of establishing a mixed economy in which state and private enterprises could operate side by side, much as they do in many other industrialized countries.[7]

Opposition to Yeltsin was not voiced on economic grounds alone. A separate document, oriented more toward politics than economics, was produced to accompany the economic program. This "Appeal to Communists, Workers, and all Patriots of Russia" decried "Yeltsin's dictatorship" and sharply attacked the Yeltsin constitution as undemocratic. The same document laid out the KPRF's own three-stage plan for turning Russia around. The first stage would establish the rule of law; the second would transform (perekhod) the economy and stabilize the political situation; and the third would move to establish a new constitution for the country. That constitution would create a parliamentary system consistent with the communist belief in "all power to the soviets."[8]

Agrarian Party

The Agrarian party program differed from the Communist program more in emphasis than in substance, but the party differed markedly from the KPRF in its origins. Whereas the KPRF represented the attempt of the old party structures to convert themselves into an electoral organization, the Agrarian party represented the attempt of a professional association to transform itself into a successful electoral party.

The decision to create a party based in the agricultural sector was taken at the January 1992 All-Russian Congress of collective farm workers. The congress elected an organizational committee to develop a party program and organize a founding congress. This congress was held on February 23, 1992, and 219 delegates from forty-six regions of the country were present, representing a variety of agricultural organizations. The most important of these were the Agrarian Union faction from the Russian Congress of Peoples Deputies, the extraparliamentary Agrarian Union, headed by Vasilii Starodubtsev (who at the time of the election still faced charges for his participation in the August 1991 coup), and the trade union of workers from the agroindustrial complex (APK).[9]

Though the Agrarian party included mass-based organizations, it was at heart a parliamentary organization. The Agrarian Union faction in the Congress of Peoples Deputies had been the largest and best-organized group in the legislature, but it was really a professional organization rather than a party with deep roots in the electorate. Most of the faction's members were collective farm chairmen who had been elected in 1990 by virtue of either name recognition or the ability to control rural voting. The Agrarian Union had effectively dominated the agriculture committee and monopolized the legislature's treatment of land reform.

In order to transform itself into an electoral party, the parliamentary faction strengthened its existing ties with mass-based agricultural organizations. The party was headquartered in the building that housed the Ministry of the Agroindustrial Complex and the APK trade union. Aleksandr Davydov, head of the APK trade union, was number two on the party's list in December. Links to the extraparliamentary Agrarian Union were also clear. In that same building, Starodubtsev's name remained on the door of the office being used by Ivan Rybkin, which was a hub of campaign activity. However, attempts to emphasize the mass-based organizational components of the Agrarian party were often lost in the dominance of the party by Moscow-based elites. For an opposition party, the Agrarian party claimed a remarkably strong presence in government. Six of the party's candidates held positions in the government of the Russian Federation, and 19 percent held posts in local and regional governing bodies. Number three on the list was Aleksandr Zaveryukha, first deputy Prime Minister in charge of agriculture, and Mikhail Lapshin, chair of the Agrarian Union in the Congress, continued as leader of the Agrarian party, heading the party's list in the December election.

Like Zyuganov, Lapshin followed a typical Soviet-era career path. Born in 1934, he graduated from the Moscow Agricultural Academy and later earned a candidate of science degree in economics. He spent his entire career working in the agricultural sector, first as an agronomist, then as the director of a sovkhoz in the Stupinskii raion of Moscow oblast. He was elected to the Congress of Peoples Deputies in 1990 from Stupinskii, served on the powerful agriculture committee, and became the leader of the Agrarian Union.[10] Although Lapshin and Zyuganov both followed career paths typical of the Soviet era, differences in their careers had different implications for the campaign. While Zyuganov had worked in agitation and propaganda, acquiring campaign skills, Lapshin was an administrator with a colorless personality. His career had been built on efficient deal making, not on popular mobilization, and his temperament seemed better suited to the former. He was an adept legislator, capable of defending agrarian interests in the parliament, but he was ill suited to generating popular enthusiasm for his cause. He appeared older than his fifty-nine years, delivered speeches in a consistent monotone, and looked like what he was—a relic of an era that Russia was fast leaving behind.

Despite their different origins, on the issues that defined the campaign, the KPRF and the Agrarian party were relatively close. Most members of the parliamentary Agrarian Union had been CPSU members in the past. The Agrarians cooperated closely with the Communists in the previous legislature and promised to do the same once the Duma was convened. The Agrarian party program showed many similarities with the program of the KPRF. The Agrarians sided with the Communists in opposing the draft constitution, criticizing the strong presidency, and, like the KPRF, the Agrarian party was fond of making the argument that it favored economic reform but opposed "shock without the therapy." However, the Agrarian party naturally emphasized agricultural rather than industrial issues. In its program, the Agrarian party blamed the country's economic conditions for the social confrontation in the country, but it was even more critical of the hardships that agriculture and related industries (APK) suffered under

Yeltsin's economic policy. The Agrarian party attacked the government for withholding payment to the peasants for grain and other products already delivered, attacked speculators for price gouging, and called for parity in prices of agricultural and industrial goods. It attacked government policy for its unwillingness to invest in agriculture and claimed that the party had already prepared legislation to introduce in the Duma that would provide the funds for infrastructure to improve agricultural productivity. On television, the party used a farmer, who was among the party's more dynamic speakers, to highlight the plight of his class. Though prices were rising in the stores, he argued, the "mafia"—not the tiller of the soil—was enjoying the profits.[11]

Certainly the most sensitive issue for the Agrarian party was land reform. Agrarians argued that the unrestricted sale and purchase of land would be a tragedy for the peasantry, placing land in the hands of speculators rather than those who work it. The Agrarian party was quite clear in expressing its position that the free sale and purchase of land would be wrong, but it allowed the possibility of land for the peasants, emphasizing the importance of ownership by those who actually labor on the land, as well as talking about multiple forms of ownership in the economy (*mnogoukladny*). Peasants could sell land to one another, but not even peasants should be permitted to sell to nonproducers. Land, Lapshin argued, should be strongly regulated by the government. Other civilized countries—France, the United States—regulate agriculture; Russia should do likewise, according to Lapshin. Despite the room for private ownership acknowledged in theory, in practice the Agrarian party was less enthusiastic. I was told repeatedly by party members that all of the private farmers in Russia produced only 1 percent of the country's agricultural output, yet they used 10 percent of the land.[12]

The real challenge for the Agrarians was moving from a single-issue interest organization to a broader based electoral organization. Though the platform included attempts to broaden its appeal, these were weak at best. They argued that the concerns of agriculture should be the concerns of the country as a whole. Problems of the Moscow milk supply, the need to feed the country, and the role of agriculture as a consumer of industrial products were all used to establish the universality of agriculture's interests.

In the end, however, the party could justify its existence only in terms of its sectoral base. Though the KPRF would have been quite content to run with the Agrarians as a single united party, the Agrarians were determined to preserve autonomy in the campaign. The leadership clearly believed that the only way to preserve the interests of the agricultural sector was to launch an independent list that placed rural interests at the forefront. They pointed to the mistake the Peasant party had made in joining Russia's Choice for the campaign. Where, they asked, were rural interests in that bloc's program? By running independently, the Agrarian party intended to be in a stronger position to press agricultural issues in the Duma. To maintain a parliamentary alliance, the Communists would be forced to make concessions on agricultural questions.

LDPR

The LDPR was the only nationalist opposition party to field a list and looked very different from the parties of the left on both the issues and in its roots. It was a party based on the charisma of its leader, with established electoral experience. It lacked links to the previous parliament, to the government, or to the old regime. The party's leader, the charismatic Vladimir Zhirinovskii, had established a name for himself during the 1991 presidential race but had not previously held a governmental position. He was born in Alma-Ata, Kazakhstan, in 1946 to a Russian mother and a Jewish father, who died while Zhirinovskii was still a baby. His childhood in Kazakhstan was unhappy, and he often felt discriminated against because he was Russian. He was educated at Moscow State University in the Institute of Asian and African Countries and worked as a translator for the State Committee for Foreign Economic Relations. He later earned a law degree from Moscow State and worked for the Mir publishing house. His bid for the presidency in 1991 catapulted him to fame.[13]

Zhirinovskii together with Vladimir Bogachev founded the LDPR in the summer of 1989 to further Russian rights within the Union and to establish itself as the first true opposition party in the USSR. The party's founding congress was held in December 1989, and its first full congress was held at the end of March 1990 in Moscow. The congress elected Zhirinovskii party chair, and Bogachev as chief coordinator. In October 1990 Bogachev sharply attacked Zhirinovskii, and the former was driven from the party, leaving Zhirinovskii in sole command. In April 1991 the party's second congress nominated Zhirinovskii for the Russian presidency. From that point on, Zhirinovskii injected himself into the Russian political arena. During the August coup, he appeared on the balcony of the Moskva Hotel to proclaim his support for the coup. Though not an active participant, this declaration was enough to get Moscow mayor Gavriil L. Popov to demand that the party be banned. The request was rejected by the Moscow Procuracy, but the controversy surrounding the party continued. In August 1992 the party's registration was challenged by the Ministry of Justice, when an investigation of the registration documents turned up evidence that membership numbers had been falsified. The party presented new registration materials and was able to continue its activities, but membership estimates are unreliable. At the time of the third congress in May 1992, the LDPR claimed a membership of more than 80,000; it increased the claim to 100,000 members at the time of the December election, though others put the actual number closer to 1,500. None of its candidates had served in the previous parliament, and only one—Vladimir Gusev—had previous governmental experience.[14]

The LDPR was just as critical of the state of the Russian economy as were the parties of the left, but more confident about its ability to fix those problems. For the LDPR the real problem for the Russian economy was foreign influence. To solve the country's economic problems, all the government needed to do was to control this influence. The LDPR promised to fix the economy in four months, "through an altered foreign policy." Although not supporting shock therapy, the LDPR clearly differed from the parties of the left on the role of the market. Though most observers highlighted the party's misnomer, emphasizing its lack of liberalism on social issues and questionable democratic credentials, the Russian parties on the left took the LDPR's economic liberalism quite seriously. The LDPR emphasized the wealth of Russia's natural and human resources and attacked not just the Yeltsin system but also the Soviet system for weakening them. On the whole the LDPR was far more supportive of privatization and marketization than either the KPRF or the Agrarian party. In essence, the economic policy of the LDPR was one of classic populism, opposing both foreign influence and large-scale government intervention and claiming to place economic power in the hands of the average citizen. It rejected the big government of the communists and the big business of the Yeltsin-Gaidar reforms. It rejected worship of Western economic models in favor of relying on Russia's own resources. As one LDPR candidate put it, "Russia should not be the seat of an economic and social experiment." The party called for a gradual approach to economic reforms, placing control in the hands of the producer.[15]

Nationalism was the key theme underlying the whole of the LDPR program including its economic policy. Not only was foreign aid and advice rejected; the program also called for an end to immigration into Russia, an end to the education of foreign students in Russia, and restriction of trading privileges to Russian citizens alone. The nationalist component of LDPR policy also had implications for Russia's relations with "the near abroad." The LDPR was vehemently opposed to the Commonwealth of Independent States, which Zhirinovskii described as an artificial creation. Even within Russia itself nationalism played a role. The party opposed autonomous republics within the federation, calling for a return to the tsarist system of guberniia with equal powers. In a similar fashion, the LDPR program devoted much more attention to foreign policy issues than did the programs of the Agrarian party or the KPRF. The most important issue was, of course, the rights of Russians in the former Soviet republics, but foreign policy concerns for the LDPR went well beyond this. For the LDPR, the world was one of spheres of interests. Russian interests lay to its south, not in Europe. Russia had no place in Europe; it was geopolitically unique. Likewise, so the argument went, no other country should meddle in Russia's natural sphere of influence—Afghanistan, Iran, or Turkey.[16]

Finally the LDPR took a very different position from the KPRF and Agrarian party on the draft constitution. Although Zhirinovskii criticized the document for guaranteeing the rights of non-Russian ethnic groups and for giving too much power to the republics at the expense of the Russian oblasts and krais, he supported the strong presidency at the heart of the document. Appearing on television, Zhirinovskii called for the adoption of the constitution, arguing that all countries required a basic law in order to make other laws.[17]

The LDPR was pushing a very different economic policy from the parties of the left, and this brought attacks from the communists. Although the KPRF was eager to enter an alliance with the Agrarian party, from the beginning it attacked Zhirinovskii and his policy as too liberal. This attack became more intense as the campaign progressed. The day before the election an article by Zyuganov that appeared in *Pravda Rossii* soundly criticized the LDPR for supporting privatization.[18] The same day, KPRF activists were handing out scraps of paper in front of the Lenin Mausoleum that warned voters against supporting Zhirinovskii. The handouts acknowledged it was all right to vote for the Agrarian party, but under no circumstances should voters support the LDPR, arguing that Zhirinovskii supported marketization just as Russia's Choice did.

On only one policy issue did the left and right opposition parties speak with a common voice: foreign economic policy. The attack on Western influence and the call for protection of the Russian economy were key elements in the programs of all three parties. All three programs called for protection of domestic industries, control over foreign investment in Russia, strict limits or outright prohibitions on the export of raw materials, and restrictions on the use of foreign currency within Russia. For the LDPR foreign economic policy was clearly a part of the economic nationalism at the heart of the program, but all three parties blamed Russia's economic problems on the West. For Zhirinovskii, the West and its economic institutions had brought "Russia to its knees." The Agrarian party blamed trade liberalization for destroying uncompetitive enterprises and paving the way to mass unemployment. In an article published the day before the election, Zyuganov dramatically laid out his party's line, proclaiming "There is only one question: to follow the reform scheme of the IMF [International Monetary Fund] or not."[19]

Internal Constraints

The ability of the parties to convey their programs to the electorate and to translate programmatic appeal into votes depended on each party's pool of candidates and organizational capacity on the one hand and its financial strength and ability to use media resources effectively on the other. External constraints defined the arena in which the parties played, determining the pool of potential voters for the hard opposition and the scope of competition for them. Internal constraints, however, determined how the parties would compete within that arena. Not only did the programs of the left parties differ from the program of the right LDPR; the memberships and roots of the three parties also presented very different profiles. The LDPR boasted a strong and dynamic leader but a narrow and inexperienced list of candidates. The Agrarian party and the KPRF in stark contrast lacked charismatic leaders but could claim more experienced candidate lists. These differences had profound implications for the campaign. Although the parties of the left held the advantage in the organizational assets, the LDPR commanded superior financial strength and better use of the broadcast media. The three parties based their campaign strategies on the resources available. The Agrarian party and the KPRF adopted strategies designed to exploit their organizational strength and to target established pockets of support. The LDPR in contrast adopted a strategy designed to exploit the charismatic appeal of its leader and to blanket the country with his image and message. These different strategies, reflecting different resources, contrib-uted significantly to the distribution of votes across these three parties.

Organization and the Candidate Pool

Comparison of candidates for the three parties, both on the party lists and in the single-mandate district races, shows clear differences in the depth and breadth of the three parties (see table 6-1). The Agrarian party boasted the oldest and most experienced candidates, and the LDPR had the youngest and least experienced candidates. The KPRF was much more similar to the Agrarian party, though in some areas its candidate pool shows important similarities with the LDPR. The three parties ran lists of similar size (Agrarian Party of Russia [APR] = 145, LDPR = 147, KPRF = 151) and included virtually every single-mandate candidate on the party's list.[20] All three candidate pools were also dominated by men. The KPRF, which included the largest number of women among the hard opposition, barely reached the 10 percent mark for the party list, though it did somewhat better in single-mandate races. In almost every other respect there were important differences between the pools of candidates that reflected the different roots of the parties.

The Agrarian party, with the shortest list of the three, ran more candi-dates in the single-mandate races than either of the other two parties. The KPRF ran the fewest single mandate candidates of the three, but the per-centage of party members running in single-mandate districts shows the much deeper organization of the KPRF. Although 76 percent of the KPRF single-mandate candidates listed party membership, only 15 percent of LDPR single-mandate candidates claimed to be members of the party. For the Agrarian party, the 36 percent of its single-mandate candidates listing party membership was offset by the importance of occupational criteria for inclusion. Reflecting the origins of the Agrarian party as a single interest organization, 45 percent of the Agrarian party candidates in the okrugs (and 40 percent of the party-list candidates) listed their occupation as director or chair of an economic enterprise. Of the fifty-eight candidates who fit this category, seventeen were clearly identified as director of a kolkhoz or sovk-hoz. The others all managed enterprises in the agroindustrial complex. (For example, G. V. Chernikov, who ran in Moscow city okrug 194, was the di-rector of a champagne factory.) In contrast, KPRF and LDPR candidates were more diverse. For the Communists, education and the media were es-pecially well represented on the list. The LDPR also drew a number of edu-

Table 6-1. *The Hard Opposition: Candidate Characteristics*

	LDPR List	LDPR SMD	KPRF List	KPRF SMD	APR List	APR SMD
Number of candidates	147	59	151	55	145	67
Average age	42	41	48	51	51	53
Percent men	94	97	90	87	94	90
Percent CPD	0	0	8	18	10	9
Percent party members	11	15	62	76	35	36
Percent science, education, arts, media	29	32	40	46	11	18
Percent senior economic management	1	2	7	2	40	45
Percent middle economic management/engineer	12	12	6	6	5	3
Percent full-time political activity	5	5	3	7	12	6
Percent Russian government	0	0	0	0	4	3
Percent local and regional government	1	0	0	0	19	13
Percent military and police	7	9	1	2	0	0
Percent other white collar	31	27	28	24	6	8
Percent blue collar	12	9	13	11	1	2
Pensioners and students	2	2	3	4	0	0

Source: Compiled from candidates' biographies appearing in *Rossiiskaya gazeta*, November 12, 1993, for party lists and November 30, 1993, for single-mandate candidates. Corrections to the single-mandate candidate lists were made on the basis of a file compiled by Timothy Colton, based on unpublished data located and kindly supplied by Michael McFaul.

SMD = single-mandate races.

cators, but other white-collar occupations were even more heavily represented. Chief among this group were lawyers (*yurist*). The law and order theme of the LDPR was also reflected in the inclusion of ten candidates from either the armed forces or police.

Finally, the Agrarian party candidates—and to a lesser extent those of the KPRF—showed a much stronger reserve of political experience than did those of the LDPR. Although none of the LDPR candidates had served in the Russian parliament previously, the party lists on the left both included a small but noticeable contingent of deputies from the former Russian Congress (twelve candidates on the KPRF list; fourteen on the Agrarian party list; and, from the old USSR Congress, three and six, respectively). All three on the KPRF list had also served in the Supreme Soviet, including Anatolii Luk'yanov as the chair. There were no LDPR candidates from the Union parliament.[21]

Similar differences emerge when one examines candidate's experience as full-time political activists. Although the LDPR list boasts a slightly higher percentage than the KPRF list, there are telling differences between the two. The LDPR activists were all engaged in party work, whereas the KPRF activists included both party workers and trade-union activists. The 12 percent of Agrarian party candidates listing full-time political work reflects the even stronger presence of trade-union activists on this party list, underlining the party's attempt to forge parliamentary with extraparliamentary organizations.

Finally the Agrarian party stands out from both the KPRF and the LDPR in its presence in government. Neither the KPRF nor the LDPR list included a single candidate from the Russian Federation government. The Agrarian party included six individuals, four percent of the party list candidates, ranging from the high-ranking First Deputy Prime Minister Zaveryukha to a department head in the Ministry of Fisheries (S. A. Muradova). Another 19 percent of the Agrarian party list held full-time local or regional governmental jobs. Only one LDPR candidate fit this category, and none of the KPRF candidates was employed in local governmental structures at the time of the election.

These variations reflect the different histories of the three parties and also the different strategies used by the parties for filling out their list of candidates. Agrarian party officials reported that candidates were chosen for their professional skills, intellectual potential, and to provide adequate geographical representation. Although two candidates listed their occupations as "farmer" (*fermer*), amazingly not a single candidate on this peasant party list claimed to be a peasant! In contrast, the KPRF attempted, at least in principle, to choose candidates according to old criteria of social representation. One representative explained that the party wanted to balance representation across workers, intellectuals, men, and women. He admitted that there was no real effort to recruit peasants because the KPRF was not trying to be a peasants' party. Peasants, I was told, could and should vote for the Agrarian party. The LDPR representatives I interviewed could not articulate an overarching strategy for selecting candidates. The thinness of the organization and the inexperience of the candidates suggests that the party ran whomever was available.[22]

Differences in the strength of the organizations were reflected in differences in the candidates fielded and this had dramatic implications for the success of the three opposition parties in the single-mandate races. Difficulties in acquiring information about candidates placed the advantage with local notables, and—at least in the regions in which the opposition stood to make the greatest inroads—local notables if affiliated with any party were most likely to be either Agrarians or Communists. Of the sixteen Agrarian party candidates who won in single-mandate races, nine were directors of kolkhozy or other agricultural enterprise, and another three held local or national government posts. Communist victors in the okrugs were less illustrious, with the exception of Lukyanov, but they still held visible positions in education, the media, or local government. In contrast, most LDPR candidates were unknowns in their okrugs. One of the five okrugs won by the LDPR was won by Zhirinovskii himself. Without party affiliation on the ballot, there was little reason to vote for unknown LDPR candidates.

The depth of the candidate pools on the left in contrast to that of the LDPR also reflects the strength of party organization. At the time of the election the KPRF claimed to have the largest membership of any of the blocs running, citing the 500,000 members at the party's Second Congress in February 1993. It also boasted the most extensive regional organization, tapping into the old organizational structure of the CPSU at the local level to collect signatures, raise funds for local candidates, pass on the party's program, and get out the vote. This ability was not absolute, of course. It varied across the country. According to officials at KPRF headquarters, the party had very little organization in the far North and far East. The strongest organizations were in the Black Earth zone. The KPRF also faced criticism for running from more hard-line communists who also attempted to manipulate old CPSU structures. Still, the KPRF claimed eighty-nine regional organizations, and eighty-five of these backed the party's decision to field candidates in the December election.[23] The experience with widespread regional organization on the one hand and an established central organization on the other gave the KPRF a strong start in preparing for the December election.

The Agrarian party could also boast a large membership—100,000— and an extensive network of regional organizations through the collective farm system. Like the KPRF, the Agrarian party was a strong hierarchical organization arranged along territorial lines, but the Agrarian party accorded more autonomy to its local organizations, allowing them to write their own rules and to control their own membership. Testifying to the strength of regional organizations, the Agrarian party submitted more signatures than any of the other blocs running (500,000).[24]

The LDPR's organization, in contrast, was much weaker. Like the other two parties, the LDPR was hierarchically organized along territorial lines, but a local organization required only three members, and only thirty party members were required for a quorum at the Congress.[25] Membership has been more of a problem for the LDPR than votes, and all of the party papers as well as the program included membership applications.

Financing and the Media

Although the Agrarian party and KPRF enjoyed the advantages of organizations that were both deep and strong, they lacked the advantages of a superior funding and a charismatic leader who could make good use of the media available to the LDPR.

The LDPR began the national campaign with tremendous advantage in name recognition. Zhirinovskii's 1991 bid for the presidency, though unsuccessful, had established him as a national political figure, and voter awareness of the LDPR, even at the start of the campaign, was higher than for any of the opposition blocs (73 percent to 47 percent for the Agrarians and 61 percent for the KPRF).[26] Voter awareness was especially problematic among potential opposition voters. As Colton points out in Chapter 9, voters in less urban areas (where the opposition audience was concentrated) had the lowest levels of media consumption and associated low levels of knowledge about the blocs contesting the election. Given the low rates of voter awareness, especially within the opposition audience, simply informing the voter became a key part of the campaign. I asked representatives of each of the three blocs how they conveyed their message to the voters and received two very different answers. For the LDPR, television and the image of Zhirinovskii himself were all important. The Agrarian party and KPRF in contrast reported more dependence on the print media and local organizations. The difference in strategies reflected both different leadership assets and different resources for campaign financing.

The leadership styles of the three parties could not have been more different. Zhirinovskii was the youngest of the three heading the opposition party tickets and undoubtedly the most charismatic. The LDPR relied heavily on Zhirinovskii's personal appeal, even publishing a pamphlet titled "The Zhirinovskii Phenomenon," which was sold along with his autobiography and the LDPR program. Though the Western media tended to portray him as a lunatic, he came across much differently in Russia in 1993. His speaking style was dynamic and fiery and generally admired. Zhirinovskii also played the populist card well. One issue of the LDPR newspaper, *Yuridicheskaya gazeta,* carried not only the party list but also a two-page spread of photos of Zhirinovskii and various family members including grandmother and grandfather, under the title "I am one of you. I am just like you." (*Ya odin iz vas. Ya takoi zhe, kak vy.*)[27] The styles of Lapshin and Zyuganov were very different from that of Zhirinovskii. Lapshin, who was fifty-nine at the time, had been successful in turning the Agrarian Union into a formidable force in the parliament, but this kind of elite coalition building did not play nearly as well with the electorate as did Zhirinovskii's dynamism. Lapshin's plodding style was more likely to put the television viewer to sleep than to drum up support for the Agrarian party. Zyuganov was younger and a more dynamic speaker than Lapshin, but he too lacked the charisma of Zhirinovskii.

Not only did the LDPR have a more appealing leader; unlike the Agrarian party and the KPRF, the LDPR represented something new. The Agrarian party had a double problem to overcome. It was viewed by many as the party of the collective farm chairs—a bastion of the old system. At the same time, however, it was difficult for the Agrarian party to portray itself as completely in opposition to the Yeltsin government, when the party's list featured six candidates working in the federal agricultural apparat, including two high-ranking members of the government, Zaveryukha and Shcherbak. The KPRF had to distance itself from the discredited CPSU without losing its core base of support. It had to combat the calls of more radical communists for a boycott of the election, but at the same time, the KPRF had to create the impression that it was something new. In short, the KPRF had the problem of being too red for some and too pink for others. Some candidates in single-mandate races who were sympathetic to the Agrarian party or KPRF dealt with the problem by running as independents and later joining the parliamentary faction. In contrast, it was quite important for LDPR candidates to show affiliation with Zhirinovskii, and no new members were added to the faction in January 1994.

The LDPR clearly began the campaign with a series of advantages over its rival opposition parties: name recognition, charismatic leadership, and the clearest break with past and present politics. The LDPR was able to use these assets to its advantage over the course of the short campaign, largely because of superior funding. The issue of finance was undoubtedly the most sensitive issue during the campaign. Questions on the subject elicited little useful information from party workers or candidates, nor were official reports helpful. Each bloc was allocated 100 million rubles and was required to produce documents on sources of funding for review by the Central Electoral Commission by January 6, 1994. But the Commission's bulletin reported that six blocs—including all three of those analyzed in this chapter—used only the funds allocated by the state and had no money from "physical or juridical individuals."[28]

This claim is more reasonable in the cases of the KPRF and Agrarian party than in the case of LDPR. Both the KPRF and Agrarian party claimed to have almost no money other than that allotted them by law. When I interviewed Ivan Rybkin, then one of the leaders of the Agrarian party, he complained bitterly that, because the government was not paying agriculture for products already delivered, local organizations were completely unable to raise money for the campaign. All of the funds allocated to the party were being used for the central campaign. Candidates were on their own in the single-mandate races. During the interview he took a call from a candidate in Kaliningrad oblast who was waging his entire campaign with 100,000 rubles (then less than $100)! But links to the trade unions and to the government meant that alternative sources of support, such as office space, were available. KPRF activists were aware of the problems associated with running a viable campaign given the nature of their support base—pensioners, those who had been disadvantaged by Yeltsin's reforms, and the like. In an interview published in *Pravda* early in the campaign, Zyuganov spoke to this issue: "Certainly we need means—we will be thankful to those who can help, we also need cadres."[29] The local cadres proved to be the key to the KPRF campaign, especially in single-mandate districts.

The LDPR presence on television clearly indicated that it had money to spend, and the rumors about where the money was coming from were wide ranging and far-fetched, including the KGB, Iraq, East German communists, and even Russia's Choice itself! One of the more plausible stories was one that claimed funding was coming from the Stolichnii and Menatep banks.[30] Russian banks had previously supported legislative attempts to limit the advantages enjoyed by foreign banks, and it is plausible that they would fund a nationalist candidate. However, when I asked LDPR officials about the source of the party's funding, I was told that ordinary Russians contributed to rescue their country. Undoubtedly the truth is somewhere between the two extremes. In the months following the election, evidence began to emerge that the LDPR had less money than opponents initially claimed. Agrarian party officials complained that television stations were allowing the LDPR to buy time on credit, while demanding that the Agrarian party and others pay up front. During the election Zhirinovskii himself complained that the party had borrowed more than 200 million rubles for its election efforts. The independent daily *Segodnya* reported in March that radio *Galaktika* was accusing the LDPR of paying for radio time with forged payment orders.[31]

Visits to the headquarters of the three parties helped provide an impressionistic sense of the funding available. The Agrarian party was headquartered in a government building at number 3 Orlikov Pereulok, which also housed the Russian Federation Committee for the Food and Food Processing Industry and, ironically, the association of private farmers. The offices were well maintained and typical of government buildings. In contrast, the KPRF was relegated to a few rooms in a small building on Komsomolskii Bolshoi Pereulok near Staraya Ploshchad'. This building was set aside to provide free office and meeting space to qualified social organizations. The Socialist Workers Party also had offices there, as did a variety of nationalist organizations, and the American Carnegie Foundation. The KPRF was the only electoral bloc that was housed in this building.

Finally, the LDPR had a wholly independent location, occupying the entire top story of number 1 Rybnikov Pereulok. Though its office space was not grand, it was more extensive than KPRF headquarters and clearly free of state influence, unlike the Agrarian party. The first floor of the building was home to "Rok Magazin," which sold black leather jackets and black t-shirts sporting the logos of rock bands. Rather than an official demanding a "propusk" like at Agrarian party headquarters, getting into LDPR headquarters required getting past two groups of party activists. Six large fellows in their twenties politely, but aggressively, barred the way upstairs. When I gave the name of someone at the headquarters, they let me pass.[32] I met with a similar reception at the door to the headquarters but was allowed to enter after giving the same name.

Differences in organizational strength and differences in funding translated into very different campaign strategies, especially in the realm of advertising. Both the KPRF and Agrarian party were far more dependent on the print media, whereas the LDPR focused its efforts on broadcast media. Neither the Agrarian party nor the KPRF relied on advertising that they had to pay for. Both limited their use of the broadcast media (radio and television) to the free time allocated to each bloc. In contrast, the LDPR bought more broadcast time than any other bloc involved in the campaign. Neither the Agrarian party nor the KPRF paid for advertisements in the print media, either. The Agrarians could count on considerable "free" space in specialized agricultural newspapers—*Sel'skaya zhizn, Zemlya i lyudi, Sel'skii kommersant,* and even *Dachniki,* as well as local newspapers in rural areas, which provided substantial coverage of Agrarian party activities. The party's October congress, which was responsible for election preparations, was widely reported in these sources, and many carried the Agrarian party list of candidates after November 12. Lapshin and other party leaders were frequently interviewed in the agricultural press. The party also received favorable coverage in the communist press (for example, *Pravda, Sovetskaya Rossiya*), though reliance on this could be problematic, given the uncertainty of publication (see the discussion later in this section).

In addition to widespread use of agricultural newspapers, the Agrarian party produced professional looking pamphlets dealing with agriculture's problems and expounding the party program.[33] These were in ample supply at party headquarters. Though too long to be effective in communicating the party's position to the average voter, their distribution to candidates ensured that those running on the party ticket would have ample data at their fingertips to back up claims that the Yeltsin government was destroying the country's agricultural base. Voters could be courted with calendars featuring either a bouquet of flowers or a fuzzy kitten and bearing the single line "The Agrarian Party of Russia—To the Federal Assembly." There were no posters featuring Lapshin or other members of the leadership. Posters promoting individual candidates in single-mandate districts depended on the ability of those candidates to find funding for their printing.

The KPRF advertising effort was beset with problems. Although the Agrarian party could use trade papers, the KPRF had only the communist press to provide free coverage. However, the two key newspapers, *Pravda* and *Sovetskaya Rossiya*, were shut down after the conflict of October and reopened only on November 2. *Pravda* was forced to close again on November 19 for lack of funds, and *Sovetskaya Rossiya* published only sporadically. *Pravda* finally reopened on December 10—only two days before the election. Viktor Trushkov at *Pravda* complained that the paper's absence after the 19th was devastating to the party and abetted Zhirinovskii's victory. There was virtually no way for the KPRF to have a national presence without the paper. The party never had the opportunity to publish either its program or even its party list.[34] In part this reflected bad choices by the party. When *Pravda* reappeared at the beginning of November it printed an interview with Lapshin on November 3 and one with Zyuganov conducted on November 4. From November 10 through 12 it published portions of the draft constitution. Between the 12th (when registration of candidate lists was complete) and the 19th (when the paper disappeared again) it never published the list of party candidates, nor did *Pravda* publish the party's program.

The party's program was far more accessible in style than that of the Agrarian party, however. It consisted of two short Xeroxed handouts, *Obrashchenie k kommunistam, trudyashchimsya, vsem patriotam Rossii* and *Programma Kommunistov—Prostaya no Effektivnaya.*[35] These were produced by typewriter not computer and the print quality was not good. There were no posters for the KPRF list, but candidates in single-mandate races often produced their own posters or flyers. These too testified to the low-budget campaign being waged. Most were $8\frac{1}{2}$" $\times$ 12" flyers giving the candidate's biography, his or her goals as a deputy, and a small picture of the candidate. Like the program, these were typewritten and photocopied. The KPRF also relied on small flyers—really slips of paper—that were distributed by hand. In Moscow, one such flyer identified KPRF candidates running in single-mandate districts. In addition the KPRF used flyers calling on voters to oppose specific parties. One urged voters to oppose the lists of Russia's Choice and Party of Unity and Accord (PRES) as "parties of the Ministers" and to oppose the Russian Movement for Democratic Reform (RDDR) as the party that destroyed the Soviet Union and opened the door to Western economic influence. On the reverse side of the flyer it urged voters to oppose the draft constitution. A similar hand out, produced more hastily and distributed two days before the election, urged voters to oppose the LDPR. Both flyers advised voters to support the list of the KPRF *or* the Agrarian party.

Printed material was of far less importance to the LDPR. Zhirinovskii's autobiography and the LDPR program were for sale on the street, as were several party papers: *Yuridicheskaya gazeta, Pravda Zhirinovskogo, Sokol Zhirinovskogo,* and *Liberal.* The last, which claimed to be the party paper, was woefully out of date. The most recent copy I could find during the campaign—even at party headquarters—was October 1992. *Yuridicheskaya gazeta* claimed to be a weekly paper, but issues after number 40–41, which published the party list, could not be found. These papers focused on building the persona of Zhirinovskii rather than explicating the party platform. The Zhirinovskii photo album that appeared in *Yuridicheskaya gazeta* (discussed previously) was just one example. Another featured a crossword puzzle in which the clue to number 3 across read "He will always defend Russia." The answer, of course, was Zhirinovskii.[36]

Posters were more important to the LDPR campaign than they were to the Communists or Agrarians, and all prominently featured Zhirinovskii.

These posters were more professional than the small xeroxed flyers that the KPRF candidates used, but, in contrast to posters of many of the reformist blocs, Zhirinovskii's posters had a distinctly Russian flavor. His favorite venues for the photo were the Kremlin and Red Square—symbols of Russian power that could be featured as a back drop to a sober-faced Zhirinovskii. There were no catchy slogans but only simple promises or exhortations: "I will raise Russia from her knees" or "Vote for the list of the LDPR." Candidates in single-member districts took these posters and attached their own name and district, associating themselves with the party's leader rather than establishing an individual identity.

Though there were clear differences in use of print media, the biggest difference in campaign style was to be seen in the parties' use of television. Although the Agrarian party and KPRF were restricted to the free television time allocated by law, the LDPR bought a total of two hours and forty-four minutes on the two national channels (Ostankino and Rossiya). When news coverage of the parties is added to the free time and bought time, the LDPR had more time on television than the Agrarian party and KPRF combined. Variation in the use of print versus broadcast media reflects not only the funds available to the parties but also differences in leadership style.

Electoral blocs could use their free broadcast time as they chose, and a variety of different techniques were used. Zhirinovskii preferred to focus the camera on himself and spend the time—free or purchased—addressing the voter directly. His usual style was to begin by calmly addressing the problems facing Russia—the decaying economy, declining international status, rising crime, and the like. As he continued the pitch increased until he reached a righteous rage. He pounded the table with his fist but, at the same time, gave the distinct impression that he was in control. In some broadcasts Zhirinovskii included an interviewer (usually a woman) who would provide the questions to start his diatribe. In others, Zhirinovskii appeared with other candidates from the party list. In virtually every broadcast, however, Zhirinovskii was in the spotlight.

The KPRF strategy on television evolved during the course of the campaign. In its earliest appearances Zyuganov appeared with other KPRF candidates, chosen to demonstrate the representative nature of the party list. For example one night a doctor, a teacher, and a technical worker appeared with Zyuganov.[37] The interviewer was chosen by the party and posed sympathetic questions that allowed the candidates to criticize the government and to express the party program. These responses were offered in a matter-of-fact manner, without the emotion so important to Zhirinovskii's appearances. Toward the end of the campaign, however, shorter presentations by Zyuganov or other candidates were accompanied by a brief campaign film eliciting more emotional responses. The film contrasted images of past greatness with current problems—rocket ships and cosmonauts on the heels of riot police bashing workers, *Soviet Culture* newspaper in the gutter, Boris Yeltsin followed by a drug addict, money changers, and McDonald's. In contrast, the Agrarian party never produced a prepared clip for broadcast during its allotted time nor did it bring its own interviewer to the studio. Party candidates appearing during the two national election shows were questioned by employees of the television station. This left the Agrarian party open to constant interruptions from hostile moderators.

Variations in internal assets influenced campaign choices. Differences in media usage contributed to the different outcomes in party-list and single-mandate races. In chapter 9, on the media, Colton points to the strong positive relationship between interest in the campaign, media consumption, and knowledge. Those who voted but evidenced only moderate interest and knowledge were more likely to get the bulk of their information from television. This group evidenced many of the same social characteristics that Colton found associated with support for the LDPR (e.g., lower levels of education, residence in less urban areas). Although television was effective in winning support from those with fewer political skills in the national race, it was less effective in local races. Opposition parties on the left relied on their organizational capacity and the inclusion of local notables to support their candidates in single-mandate districts. In the brief 1993 campaign, however, organizational capacity was not sufficient to make up for a weak media presence in the party-list race. The LDPR was able to exploit this advantage in the national contest but showed its organizational weakness in the single-mandate races.

Campaign Results

Was it program or campaign strategy that was responsible for the electoral outcome? Were the three opposition parties taking votes away from each other? The results are conflicting. The dramatic difference in performance in the party-list and single-mandate races suggests that campaign strategy must have been the critical factor, but the survey of the electorate shows different types of voters were supporting different parties. Likewise the final distribution of the party-list vote across the country suggests that the left and right were appealing to different portions of the electorate. Undoubtedly there was an interaction between campaign strategy and audience that accounted for the final outcome. Both sets of factors suggest that the LDPR appealed to a broadly spread but thin audience, whereas the appeal of the Agrarian party and KPRF was more highly concentrated. The breadth of the LDPR versus the concentration of the Agrarian party and KPRF is also clear in oblast-level results in the party-list race. The coefficient of variation is much smaller for the LDPR (31.11) than for either the KPRF (55.13) or the Agrarian party (58.20). In other words, there was less variation in the percentage of vote that the LDPR won in each oblast, republic, and krai than there was in the percentages given to either the KPRF or the Agrarian party.[38]

Although the party-list race seems to indicate that the right and left were appealing to different audiences, the results from the single-mandate races are less clear. There were only eleven okrugs in which all three parties ran candidates with clear party affiliation. Three of these went to an opposition party candidate (27 percent), and the other eight were in regions in which all three parties had weak appeal (Moscow oblast, Moscow city, and Nizhnii Novgorod). In the sixty-five races contested only by a single opposition party, the performance in terms of percentages was only slightly worse. Opposition candidates won only 16 or 25 percent of these races. Performance was only slightly better in races in which two of the three parties were contesting the seat. Here opposition candidates won eleven of thirty-nine seats (28 percent; see table 6-2). In those races in which the vote was split, adding together the vote for the hard opposition would have produced victories in only eleven cases (31 percent). In eight cases this would have required a left-right coalition of voters that was highly unlikely. These results suggest that organizational factors were critical in candidate success rather than a systematic causal relationship between the number of opposition candidates and the success of those candidates. Interviews confirmed that local organization was critical in winning support for district candidates. This was particularly true for the Agrarian party. Although the LDPR and the KPRF won single-mandate races only in oblasts in which the party list garnered more than the national average, the Agrarian party won 38 percent (six seats) of its single-mandate races in oblasts where the party scored below the national average.

Table 6-2. *Single-Mandate Races*

Hard opposition contesting	LDPR wins	KPRF wins	Agrarian party wins	Other candidate wins	Total
Only LDPR	4			18	22
Only KPRF		3		11	14
Only Agrarian party			9	20	29
LDPR and Agrarian party	0		0	10	10
LDPR and KPRF	1	3		11	15
KPRF and Agrarian party		3	4	7	14
All three	0	0	3	8	11

Source: Compiled from cndidates' biographies appearing in *Rossiiskaya Gazeta*, November 12, 1993, for party lists and November 30, 1993, for single-mandate candidates. Corrections to the single-mandate lists were provided by the Carnegie Foundation. Also from Byulleten' Tsentral'noi Isbiratel'noi Komissii Rossiiskoi Federatsii, 1994, no. 1 (12), pp. 68–225.

Lessons from the Campaigns of the Hard Opposition

When Yeltsin disbanded the parliament in September he hoped to rid himself of a strong communist-nationalist coalition. Despite the engineering efforts of his advisors, the 1993 elections produced strong opposition on both the left and right, but opposition that was less unified than before. The hard opposition split between leftists and nationalists on programmatic grounds. At the national level external and internal constraints interacted to produce campaign strategies that resulted in a unified vote for the right opposition while tending to split the vote for the left opposition. Paradoxically, the concentration of Agrarian party and KPRF support as well as the experience of these two parties later facilitated their promised postelection coalition. In contrast, the lack of depth for the LDPR and the election of other nationalists in single-mandate races meant that the right entered the Duma more fragmented. To fill the fifty-nine seats it won in the party-list race, the LDPR had to go far down its list. Maintaining party discipline proved to be a challenge, and there were several instances of LDPR deputies opposing Zhirinovskii in the Duma and even leaving the party. In contrast the KPRF and Agrarian party worked well as a parliamentary coalition. This was clear in the choice of Ivan Rybkin as chair of the Duma. Rybkin was a coordinator of the communist faction in the Russian Congress of People's Deputies but ran on the Agrarian party list. In January 1994, Rybkin personified the Agrarian party–KPRF coalition and was a good choice given the plurality of seats won by that coalition.

The campaign tells us much more about the nature of the left and right opposition than simply what kinds of coalitions would emerge in the parliament, however. As electoral politics in Russia have continued to evolve, it points to the important interaction of external and internal constraints in determining the outcome of the election. All aspects of the opposition campaign underlined the stark contrast between the broadly spread support for the right, the LDPR, and the more concentrated support for the left, Agrarian party, and the KPRF. Because the LDPR was able to distance itself from both the current regime and from the old Soviet regime, it offered the clearest break from the past. The KPRF, by contrast, represented a clear break with the policies of the current government but raised the specter of the Soviet past. This conservatism played well in less urban areas and served local notables well. Thus the party of the proletariat found itself transformed into a peasant party. Ironically, the KPRF during the campaign was willing to allow the Agrarian party be the "peasant party." The Agrarian party, however, was unable to distinguish itself fully from the current government or to broaden its appeal beyond the countryside. Together these factors weakened its support.

Program and image alone were insufficient in winning votes, however. Communicating with the voter was critical, and the method depended on internal assets. The 1993 election suggests that a strong media presence, which requires a charismatic leader, is essential to successfully waging a nationwide campaign but that organizational capacity is the key to local electoral victories. In retrospect, however, these conclusions are less clear-cut. In 1995, the KPRF fulfilled its potential as the true opposition party, running strong in both national and local contests, while changing its campaign strategy only marginally. The key differences between 1993 and 1995 were the external constraints: Competition was more intense and the campaign was longer. The nationalist field was much more crowded in 1995, making dominance of the media more difficult and undermining Zhirinovskii's ability to use this tool. His charisma was also challenged by a growing reputation for foolishness and the presence of other charismatic nationalist candidates. Without the atmosphere of crisis that prevailed in 1993, organization became more critical than media presence. This preliminary conclusion about the interaction of external and internal constraints would seem to be confirmed by the 1996 presidential election. The field was narrowed once again, and media presence overwhelmed organizational capacity in determining the outcome in this national contest.

No doubt as Russian electoral politics continue to evolve and parties continue to develop, these constraints will have a significant impact on the process. In a country as vast and complex as Russia, both the national reach of media presence and the local penetration of strong organizations will play an important role in determining election outcomes, but their relative importance will be influenced by the arena in which the parties compete.

Notes

1. "Six Parties to Remain Barred from Elections," *Interfax*, October 30, 1993, in Foreign Broadcast Information Service, *Daily Report: Central Eurasia*, October 21, 1993, p. 35 (hereafter FBIS, *Central Eurasia*); "Communist Parties Announce Boycott of Elections," Interfax, October 28, 1993, in FBIS, *Central Eurasia*, October 29, 1993, p. 36.

2. Baburin press conference on December 17, 1993, quoted in the *Moscow Times*, December 17, 1993, p. 5.

3. *Izvestiya*, October 19, 1993, p. 4.

4. *Pravda*, August 7, 1991, p. 2. For an interesting discussion of the creation of the CP-RSFSR and the role of grassroots organizations see John Gooding, "The XXVIII Congress of the CPSU in Perspective," *Soviet Studies*, vol. 43, no. 2 (1991), pp. 237–53.

5. *Kto est' kto Rossii i v blizhem zarubezh'e* (Moscow: Novoe vremya, 1993), 262–63, and *Sovetskaya Rossiya*, September 9, 1990, p. 1.

6. *Sovetskaya Rossiya*, September 9, 1990, pp. 1–2; *Kto est' chto, Rossii* (Moscow: Catallaxy, 1993), pp. 147–54, 162–69, 351–57, 467–73; A. Ostapchuk, E. Krasnikov, M. Meier, *Spravochnik politicheskie partii, dvizheniya i bloki sovremennoi Rossii* (Nizhnii Novgorod: Leta, 1993), pp. 26–38.

7. "Programma Kommunistov—Prostaya no Effektivnaya," unpublished, November, 1993; *Sovetskaya Rossiya*, September 7, 1993; Channel 2, November 29, 1993, 7:15 P.M.; interview with Grigorii Rebrov, candidate in Moscow okrug no. 194, December 6, 1993.

8. KPRF Central Executive Committee, "Obrashchenie k kommunistam, trudyashchimsya, vsem patriotam Rossii" (Moscow: October 26, 1993).

9. *Spravochnik*, p. 17. *Agrarnaya Partiya Rossii* (Moscow: 1993), pp. 29–30.

10. *Sel'skii Kommersant*, no. 35–36, November, 1993: 3; INDEM software, (Moscow: June 1, 1993).

11. Channel 2, November 29, 1993, 7:45 A.M.; *Agrarnaya Partiya Rossii*, p. 45; V. F. Vershinin on channel 5, December 3, 1993; *Sel'skaya zhizn'*, December 7, 1993, p. 1.

12. *Agrarnaya Partiya Rossiya*, pp. 46–68; Lapshin on "Chas Izbiratelei," December 1, 1993, 10:25 P.M.; and November 26, 1993, 10:36 P.M.; interview with Ivan Rybkin, December 2, 1993.

13. Vladimir Zhirinovskii, *Poslednii Brosok na Iug* (Moscow: 1993).

14. Gusev served as first secretary of the Saratov obkom and later as a deputy chair of the USSR Council of Ministers. *Spravochnik*, pp. 84–86. *Kto est' chto*, p. 233.

15. *Obrashchenie Vladimira Zhirinovskogo Predsedatelya Liberal'no-Demokraticheskoi partii Rossii k chlenam LDPR i sochuvstvuyushchim* (Moscow: n.d.), p. 1. In the publication Zhirinovskii promises to fix the economy in short order. On television he promised to fix it in four months. "Electoral Bloc Leaders Comment on Plans," Ostankino, Channel 1, October 27, 1993, in FBIS *Central Eurasia*, October 28, 1993, pp. 24–26; Channel 2, December 9, 1993; *Rossiiskaya gazeta*, October 15, 1993, p. 2.

16. *Programma Liberal'no-Demokraticheskoi partii Rossii* (Moscow: n.d.), pp. 7–10; "Chas Izbiratelei," December 7, 1993.

17. "Chas Izbiratelei," November 29, 1993.

18. "V chem sut' vybora?" *Pravda Rossii*, December 11, 1993, p. 2. *Pravda Rossii* was published as a series of special election issues of *Sovetskaya Rossiya*.

19. *Agrarnaya Partiya Rossii*, p. 23; *Rossiiskaya gazeta*, December 3, 1993, p. 1; Gennadii Zyuganov, "V chem sut' vybora?" *Pravda Rossii*, December 11, 1993, p. 2.

20. The only exception was one Agrarian party candidate, A. P. Dorogovtsev, who ran in okrug 73 in Vologda. He was one of two Agrarian candidates contesting that seat. The other Agrarian won the race.

21. Although the percentages may seem small, it is important to recognize that very few of the former deputies were interested in running for reelection. This was especially true for conservative deputies, frustrated with the legislature's lack of authority. Only two Agrarian party candidates from the Union Congress won election to the Duma in 1993, but one was A. Ye. Vorontsov, who had served in the Supreme Soviet. Among the three former USSR deputies on the KPRF list, only Lukyanov was elected in December.

22. This impression is borne out by Mikhail Savin and Aleksandr Smagin at the Institute for Socio-Political Research. They conducted a survey of delegates to the LDPR Congress in April 1993. Results were reported in *Nezavisimaya gazeta*, December 18, 1993, pp. 1–2.

23. Interviews at KPRF headquarters, December 6, 1993; *Pravda*, November 4, 1993, p. 1.

24. *Pravda*, November 3, 1993, p. 1; *Agrarnaya Partiya Rossii*, pp. 38–39.

25. *Ustav LDPR*, (no publication information given), pp. 13–14.

26. Jerry F. Hough, "The Russian Election of 1993: Public Attitudes toward Economic Reform and Democratization," *Post-Soviet Affairs*, vol. 10 (January–March 1994), p. 31.

27. *Yuridicheskaya gazeta*, no. 40–41 (1993), p. 8–9.

28. *Byulleten' Tsentral'noi Izbiratel'noi Komissii Rossiiskoi Federatsii*, no. 1 (12), 1994, pp. 30–31.

29. *Pravda*, November 4, 1993, p. 1.

30. *Rossiiskaya gazeta*, October 15, 1993, p. 2.

31. "Chas Izbiratelei," December 7, 1993; *Segodnya*, March 3, 1994, p. 1.

32. These "nationalists" were drinking Fanta soda and smoking American cigarettes.

33. For example, *Agrarnaya Partiya Rossii* (Moscow: 1993); Nikolai Petrovich Radugin, *Problemy Agrarnoi Reformy v Rossii* (Moscow: Finansy i Statistika, 1993); and A. P. Orlenko, *Shokovaya Terapiya ili Reforma dlya Naroda?* (Moscow: 1993).

34. Interview with Viktor Trushkov, December 14, 1993.

35. Appeal to communists, workers, all patriots of Russia and Program of the Communists—simple but effective.

36. *Sokol Zhirinovskogo*, no. 8 (1993), p. 7.

37. Channel 2, November 29, 1993, 7:15 P.M.

38. The coefficient of variation provides a standardized measure of the distribution of data and thus allows comparison across different units. Coefficients were computed using the official data on election results. *Byulleten'*, no. 1 (1994), pp. 52–66.

CHAPTER SEVEN

Television and the Campaign

Laura Roselle Helvey

THE DECEMBER 1993 Russian parliamentary election provides a unique opportunity to study and assess the role of television in the Russian political process. Before one can study the relationship between media message and vote choice, one should understand what messages are presented and how they were shaped in the first place. This chapter analyzes the rules for and the content of television campaign programming during the 1993 parliamentary elections and argues that to understand television coverage one must distinguish among party agendas, government agendas, and journalistic agendas. It is too simple to argue that, "the State Television Company, Ostankino, headed by [Vyacheslav] Bragin of Russia's Choice, much resembled in its political reporting one long 'infomercial' for the 'governing party.'"[1]

Careful analysis shows that this was not the case. Advertising and free time rules were not biased in favor of Russia's Choice. What differed was the manner in which parties exploited the opportunities for media coverage of particular agendas or themes. Even in television news, where one *can* argue that government could shape coverage to support Russia's Choice, the primary themes were legitimation of the processes of democratic election and the adoption of the constitution. Support for Russia's Choice was sec-

I am grateful to Timothy Colton and Jerry Hough for the opportunity to participate in their national election survey. Elon College also supported this research in the form of a Faculty Research and Development Grant, Summer 1994. Sarah Oates at Emory University contributed with assistance in taping and coding television broadcasts. Catherine Shapiro gave helpful comments on earlier drafts.

ondary. Attention to the connection between the party, government, and journalistic agendas and the content of media coverage tell us much more than what was covered in any particular campaign period and speak to the broader issue of democratic reform in Russia.

Agendas and Agenda Setting

Agenda-setting research has a long history.[2] Although much of this research has focused on the link between media content and public opinion or agendas, some work has focused on how media content is shaped to begin with.[3] After all, journalists and news organizations are not the only actors who can shape media coverage; politicians also have the incentive and may have the opportunity to influence coverage. According to David Weaver, "It is not quite accurate . . . to speak of the media as setting agendas if they are mainly passing on the priorities and perspectives of prominent news sources such as politicians and their campaign managers."[4] During an election campaign research of this nature presents questions such as, Who sets the agenda for media coverage? Can parties or candidates get their themes across via media? What role do journalists play in this process? The answers to these questions will say much about the structure of the political system and the election process itself.

An American-British research team headed by Holli Semetko typologizes relevant levels of influence that journalists and politicians have in setting campaign agendas using the 1984 American presidential election and the 1983 British general election as case studies.[5] They conclude that both macropolitical and micro variables are important in explaining media content. Macro variables include the strength of the political party system, whether the media system is public or commercial, the degree of professionalization of the campaign, and cultural differences. These variables highlight the importance of the broader political, social, and cultural environment in shaping media content. Microlevel conditions of importance include journalistic norms, partisan leanings of specific media, the status of candidates, and the amount of space or time devoted to campaign coverage.[6]

The conclusion reached by the British-American comparison is that, "in the case of Britain it is difficult to speak of the media *setting* agendas, whereas even in the U.S. case it is clear that the major news media do not have unlimited discretion to set agendas."[7] The authors suggest a scale

ranging from agenda setting to agenda shaping, agenda amplifying, and finally agenda reflecting:[8]

> Strength of journalists and news organizations
> *High* .... *Low*
> Setting   Shaping   Amplifying   Reflecting

Where journalists and news organizations are most powerful, they have
the ability to set much of the media agenda—in other words, what is presented by the media. Where news organizations are not powerful, there is
more opportunity for politicians to influence the content of media coverage.
This framework seeks to allow for comparative analysis of media agenda
setting in countries where there are varying levels of political or governmental influence on that agenda.

It is clear that Russia is not Great Britain or the United States. During the
1993 Russian parliamentary election television was state controlled and
highly centralized, the party system was in a formative stage, and journalists lived with the legacy of one-party control. One would assume that because of the characteristics of the Russian system that media would be
agenda reflecting. That is, one would expect that Russian media would reflect the agenda of the government-favored party (Russia's Choice). Useful
as the Semetko typology is, it fails to account for the effects of transition of
the political system on the rules and themes of election coverage. In Russia,
democratic elections were not the norm. President Boris Yeltsin and his
government supported Russia's Choice, of course. But there was more at
stake in the election. The government had to legitimize the election process
itself, which required permitting differing parties and candidates the ability
to express and advertise their views through the mass media. Thus, the government had two often conflicting agendas: (1) to promote the democratic
process and (2) to have people vote to support Russia's Choice.

Soviet Television: Control and Effectiveness

The power of television has long been acknowledged in Russia. During
the 1970s the Soviets built an elaborate television system that pervaded the
eleven time zones of the Soviet Union.[9] Satellite technology, developed in
the 1970s and 1980s, allowed television to reach a large percentage of the
population. At the same time, television production increased. The purpose

of television in Soviet society was no different than the purpose of other media in the Soviet Union—to educate the masses and to contribute to the socialization of the Soviet man, woman, and child.

The State Committee for Radio and Television, Gostelradio, controlled television. In addition to issuing specific directives about what could or could not be shown on Soviet television, Communist party leaders controlled budgets and job advancement within Gostelradio. As a consequence, television presented the leadership view or agenda and did not cover events the party leadership preferred to suppress. "Vremya," the evening news program, was shown on Program or Channel One every night at 9:00 P.M. on all networks, across all time zones.[10] It had an audience of 150 million people. "Vremya" was believed to be so vital to party interests that an armed guard was stationed outside the "Vremya" studio. An armed guard symbolized the power of the state that directed the presentation of all news to the Soviet people.

Communist party control meant that journalists did not develop norms of fairness or presentation of opposing sides. Television and television journalists presented the official line. Thomas Remington notes that during the Soviet period, "Journalists [did] not regard their institutional status as being poised between the political elite, on the one hand, and the public interest, on the other, the social position that fosters the emergence of an ethic of professional objectivity. Success for journalists derive[d] from becoming part of the ruling elite, from acting as an extension of the party apparatus."[11] Journalists were taught, both in journalism schools and on the job, that they were to serve the interests of the leadership and follow the party line.

Strict central control has ramifications for the effectiveness of the media system. First, control did not guarantee that the party leadership would use television effectively. Effective television, as perceived by the Soviet leadership, involved simply reaching the population with the message of the leader or the party. This is the so-called hypodermic model of media effect that falsely assumed "the immediate and unaltered reception of all new information carried by the media system, much as a hypodermic needle inserts its dosage into the human organism."[12] To a great degree the audience was undifferentiated. There was a growing, but still inadequate, understanding of the individuals who made up the viewing audience.[13] Second, widespread knowledge of control lessened the credibility of television as a tool of the party. Citizens knew that media were controlled and therefore did not believe their messages.

Mikhail Gorbachev's policy of glasnost reflected an understanding of the deficiencies of the previous approach to media, giving momentum to the process of change in television coverage of both domestic and foreign affairs.[14] The visual nature of television was acknowledged, leading to changes in the content and format of coverage. More reports from correspondents in the field with film of events were aired. Even the graphics began to change. Soviet television began to use computer graphics to present a slicker look. More frequently political or military leaders would answer questions from reporters at press conferences. Gorbachev and others hoped that more appealing visuals on Soviet television would increase its effectiveness. In addition to a change in formatting and visuals, television began to present different opinions on issues. For example, the number of foreigners on Soviet television increased.[15] These foreigners could and did present opinions contrary to the official Soviet position. The changes in formatting reflected a greater understanding of the audience and what constitutes effective television. It had become clear to the Soviet leadership that the audience had not understood or had not accepted what media were offering.[16]

Gorbachev's new policy would remedy many of the problems and create new ones of its own.[17] Soon those who worked in television began to test the extent of tolerable criticism. New programs that tested the boundaries, including "Vzglyad" (View) and "Kto yest kto," (Who's who), aired stories on such topics as political corruption, economic inefficiency, and social problems. Some argue that the policy of glasnost, particularly with regard to the media, fundamentally changed the political environment in the Soviet Union and contributed greatly to the collapse of the country because it undermined the totalitarianism of the state.[18] Glasnost allowed more than the official story to be told: "When glasnost changed the informational and value content of all means of communication it did more than break the party's monopoly over communications. It also destroyed the underpinnings of the single official ideology."[19] One defining characteristic of Soviet rule was an official ideology expressed through a controlled media system. This was undermined by glasnost.[20]

Television became a battleground for the acquisition of political power, spurring attempts by leadership, particularly by early 1991, to crack down on television by placing censors in editing rooms.[21] The August 1991 coup, which led to the demise of the Soviet Union, focused attention on the central role of television and media style in the political changes.[22] The State Committee on the State of Emergency took over Gostelradio, but its subsequent broadcasts to the Soviet people were in the pre-1985 style, which was not an effective or legitimate way to communicate.[23] Long decrees of the Emergency Committee were read in droning voices, and the Committee's press conference was an utter failure. Meanwhile CNN, which reached a sizable audience in Moscow, covered Yeltsin atop a tank cheering on those who would challenge the coup. And even though CNN had a relatively small audience throughout the whole of Russia, Yeltsin emerged as the leader, thanks, in part, to television.

Russian Television: A Political Battleground

When the Soviet Union ceased to exist, central television, now called Ostankino, came under the jurisdiction of the Russian government. The battle for control of television, however, was not over by any means. The period from 1992 through October 1993 was marked by conflict between the president and parliament over television. Both Yeltsin and parliamentary leaders saw the media, and particularly television, as crucial to gaining support, and there was political conflict between the two sides over who exactly should have more or less control over television. When, in September and October 1993, the situation heated up, television was fought over with guns and tanks as the Ostankino building was attacked.[24]

After the changes brought by glasnost, government control remained, even if there was conflict over which branch of government would maintain that control. Journalists were unprepared and untrained for a situation in which the party line changed drastically and ultimately fell apart. Some came to see the need for journalists to take an active part in shaping the media agenda. For some journalists this meant not "objective" journalism as defined in the West but advocacy of his or her own ideas or views.[25] The rules set up to govern media coverage of the 1993 election speak to control, the role of journalists, and the process of democratic transition.

The Rationale for Media Rules

Yeltsin issued degrees on the rules for media coverage of the December election beginning in early fall of 1993. On September 21 Yeltsin issued regulations for the election that included requirements for equal media opportunities for candidates and for allocation of one hour of free time to candidates on work days during the three weeks before the election. On October 29, a full explication of "information guarantees" was approved by Yeltsin. The rationale for the information guarantees included the following:

—to guarantee free democratic elections;
—to recognize the right of blocs and candidates to set out their programs and views without hindrance by using media;
—to protect against interference in the editorial offices of media;
—to take account of recommendations of the International Radio and Television Policy Commission;[26]
—to ensure unimpeded campaigning.

The purpose of the regulations—to contribute to the conduct of free and fair elections—is clearly spelled out in the statute itself.

These regulations have a number of stated or implied goals: to provide some sort of basic equity in access to radio and television among the qualified parties, to *limit the cost* of television and radio as an element in political campaigning, to *minimize bias* by the state-owned or managed broadcast systems, and to *reduce the impact of differences in wealth* among competing blocs by limiting the amount of television and radio that any bloc can use.[27]

By reducing bias, providing equity of access, and limiting the cost, the regulations on information guarantees were also designed to legitimize the election process in general. If the candidates and public perceived the rules to be fair, the results of the election were less likely to be contested. Of course this creates a dilemma for the executive. Fair rules may encourage acceptance of the election results, but fair rules also may benefit the government's adversaries by allowing their views to be expressed.

To achieve the goal of free and fair elections, regulations addressed advertising, free time for candidates, news restrictions, mechanisms for addressing conflicts or challenges, and rules for journalists. The regulations of October 29 served as a basis for the structure of election coverage. However, some regulations changed during the election campaign process, and different interpretations of the regulations had to be reconciled throughout the campaign. At times the objective of promoting a free and fair election conflicted with the desire to support particular positions on issues. Still, the government set up a system that allowed conflicting views to be presented.

The Structure of Free Time, Advertising, and News Coverage

The new rules guaranteed that parties would have access to venues to present platforms and views. Parties were given free time and the ability to buy time on television. The regulations on information guarantees stipulated that, for the three weeks prior to the election, there would be one hour of free time to be devoted to each party on both Ostankino and Russian Television.[28] Russian Television aired this hour from 6:45 to 7:45 P.M. every weekday, and Ostankino from 7:45 to 8:45 P.M.[29] On Ostankino, this came before the nightly news broadcast ("Novosti") at 9:00 P.M. The time was allocated by lottery. Some parties chose to use two separate thirty-minute periods; others chose three twenty-minute segments. Although there were conflicts during this period, mostly the parties were able to use their time as they wished.

Paid political advertising was carefully defined and rules for its use were clearly established in the regulations on information guarantees. Parties and candidates were free to pay for political advertising from the time of registration until November 20. Advertising allowed access to television beyond the free time given to the parties. The extent of advertising was carefully defined, however. Paid airtime could not exceed "2 minutes per 24-hour period for political advertisements, but not more than 10 percent of total airtime received by the candidate or electoral bloc for a fee; 70 minutes a week for the broadcast of speeches, press conferences, and interviews; 350 minutes for the broadcast of election debates and round tables."[30]

Political advertisements meant short spots or ads. Parties could buy additional time for speeches, interviews, and other presentations. Restrictions on advertising were designed to reduce the impact of differences in the assets of parties by disallowing the purchase of an unlimited amount of time on television. However, it was difficult to keep track of spending because parties and candidates did not have to disclose campaign financing.[31]

Paid political advertising was supposed to end on November 20. Vyacheslav Bragin, the head of Ostankino, confirmed this as late as November 18.[32] However, the cessation of advertising on November 20 was objected to by, among others, the Information Arbitration Tribunal, which will be discussed later in the chapter. The tribunal ruled that television managers could decide whether or not to sell further time to candidates or blocs, and advertising did continue.[33]

Many ads were aired during the day and during a special bloc of time following the 9:00 P.M. news program. The reader (anchor) was careful to remind the audience, before this bloc of advertisements, that these were paid advertisements, that varying points of view would be presented, and that each person had to make his or her own choice. The cost of advertising was between 600,000 and 750,000 rubles per minute, roughly $600 to $750 per minute.[34] The regulations themselves stated, "In order to limit monopolistic activity in the sphere of distribution of election campaign communications, the Council of Ministers of the Government of the Russian Federation may establish maximum levels of payment for the distribution of television/radio programs containing election campaign communications for the period of the election campaign."[35] The regulations stipulated that political advertising clearly identify the person or party "in whose interest it is being distributed" and identify who is liable if the advertisement breeches any of the election information regulations.[36]

News reporting did not escape the regulations placed on free time and advertising. News stories about the campaign were to be grouped together in a clearly designated manner, and no journalist commentary was allowed. The regulations on campaign information (October 29) stated: "During newscasts, information regarding the election campaigning of candidates and electoral blocs should be presented exclusively in the beginning of the program as a separate segment. In newscasts, this information shall not be the subject of commentary. These segments shall not be paid for by candidates or electoral blocs."[37] Journalists and parties were limited in their ability to shape news, whereas the government was not necessarily so limited. News coverage of governmental agendas will be discussed in the next section.

The Information Arbitration Tribunal

The leadership realized that there would be disputes over the application of the new information rules and set up the Information Arbitration Tribunal to monitor the use of media during the election and to rule on complaints. The tribunal also served as a mechanism for legitimizing the election and its result. The tribunal was made up of nine members who were appointed by President Yeltsin and were not allowed to be "members of any electoral bloc, nor candidates for deputy to the State Duma or Council of the Federation, nor their official representatives."[38] The arbiters were expected to suspend their memberships in all public associations. According to the editors of the *Post-Soviet Media Law and Policy Newsletter*, "the makeup of the tribunal seems fairly designed to provide the fact and appearance of independence."[39]

Although the tribunal was charged with adjudicating election-coverage complaints, it was not granted legal authority to set sanctions on those who did not obey the election rules. The government may have rejected a powerful independent body for a number of reasons, including the desire to maintain some control over the election process. However, the tribunal could publicize its findings and, in that way, pressure candidates or blocs to obey the rules. State media were required to carry announcements of the decisions made by the tribunal.[40] The tribunal issued resolutions from its first meeting on November 11, 1993, through the rest of the campaign, and in many cases its decisions were influential. The course of the campaign was marked by periodic attempts by government to control how parties and candidates used television; however, at times the tribunal played an important role in lessening this control.

Some resolutions related to local matters and others related to complaints brought on a national level.[41] At times, the resolutions of the tribunal affected the rules of the campaign by taking stands that were contrary to government positions. For example, during the December 1 meeting, the tribunal ruled that First Deputy Prime Minister Vladimir Shumeiko could not ban the Russian Communist party and the Democratic Party of Russia from the election.[42] Shumeiko had claimed that they should be removed from the ballot because they had criticized the draft constitution on television. The leader of the Democratic Party of Russia, Nikolai Travkin, said in a released statement that Shumeiko "openly tries to rob his political opponents of their right to take part in the elections."[43] The government clearly supported passage of the constitution. Yeltsin threatened to "block parties from the airwaves if they criticized the constitution, [leading] to criticism that he was trying to neutralize opponents."[44] After Shumeiko's remarks and the ruling of the tribunal, Yeltsin's government and Russia's Choice leaders softened their criticism of those who would criticize the constitution. So, although Yeltsin did try to influence the content of media coverage, he gave in to pressure from the monitoring body he had set up to legitimize the election.

Rules for Journalists

A final set of regulations were designed to define the role of journalists in the election process and placed limits on journalists who were candidates for parliamentary seats. The regulations stated that a journalist who was a candidate "must suspend his or her journalistic participation in the preparatory work of television or radio programs."[45] This regulation caused some to question the candidacy of Vyacheslav Bragin, the head of Ostankino. Many complained that his position constituted a direct conflict of interests and violated Yeltsin's stated goal of trying to "minimize bias by the state owned or managed broadcasting systems."[46] The pressure for Bragin to choose between being head of Ostankino and being a candidate was great. On November 18, Bragin abandoned his campaign.[47]

The regulations also explicitly outlined the role of journalists during this period in their coverage of the election: "During the election campaign, journalists, in their own programs, as well as when participating in other television or radio programs which are distributed by state television/radio companies, must refrain from supporting one or another of the candidates, electoral blocs, or election programs or platforms."[48] Journalists could be punished for violating these rules by suspension from preparing or broadcasting election-related material. These rules, of course, were designed to reduce actual bias or the perception of bias.

The application of the rules went beyond restricting a journalist from imposing his or her own opinions or views into election coverage. Journalistic neutrality was interpreted by many television officials to mean that journalists were not allowed to ask difficult questions of the candidates or blocs. Vsevolod Vilchek, director of the Ostankino Sociological Center, criticized this view when he said that "what has not been protected is the interest of one participant of the forthcoming elections: the voter."[49] Candidates, through use of free time and political advertising, were able to present unchallenged messages, ideas, accusations, and promises. Television presented few roundtables or debates during which candidates could confront each other. Even the debates that were televised on the last two nights before the election contained too many participants for the audience to clearly separate the issues and candidates.

It is easy to say that journalists should have asked hard questions of the candidates and bloc representatives in spite of the way television officials interpreted the regulations. However, there are reasons why this was difficult. The state controlled the salaries and advancement of journalists, making it harder for journalists to ask probing questions of progovernment candidates. In addition, if difficult questions were asked of opposition parties or candidates, it could have left the perception that the questioners were biased against that opposition. Furthermore, journalists simply were not trained to be objective and to ask difficult questions. The ramifications of this are clear. Journalists did not have the ability to significantly shape coverage of the December 1993 parliamentary election in Russia. This left room for party and governmental agendas to shape the content of television coverage of the campaign.

Party Agendas: Free Time and Advertising

The information guarantees were set up so that parties had the opportunity to present their views through the use of free time and advertising. However, opportunities can be exploited or lost. So the question is raised: How well did each party use television to present an effective message to the electorate? That is, how well did each party convey its own agenda by projecting specific themes and policies? A review of free time and advertising use shows a wide range in the way different parties used their time. Analysis of free-time presentations shows that most parties used a variety of formats and did give information on positions and themes, even if there were few policy specifics.

Analysis of one free-time presentation by each party gives an idea of the various formats used.[50] A large majority of the presentations used filmed messages for the voters that included strong visual images. About half of the parties used an interview format, at least in parts. Usually these interviews were staged and were used to bring out party agendas. A quarter of the presentations used in-studio discussions, and a quarter used music videos. Almost all parties used a number of formatting techniques. The Yabloko free time in this sample is an exception to the rule. After a brief filmed piece of Grigorii Yavlinskii walking through the snow, the candidate spent the rest of the time as a talking head, speaking directly to the camera. In spite of the use of various formats, Russians complained about the sheer boredom of watching some of the presentations during the free time. Vsevolod Vilchek, head of Ostankino's sociological service, reported a 15 to 20 percent drop in viewership during the free-time programs.[51] This drop might have been a result of the excessive amounts of free-time presentations shown on Ostankino and Russian Television.

Various types of formats were used by parties, but how well did they present information about party themes or agendas? Specific policy proposals were not often found in the free-time presentations. Sarah Oates's analysis of campaign agendas and television transmission of these agendas concludes that Women of Russia and the Liberal Democratic Party of Rus-

sia (LDPR) were the most successful at presenting "concrete policy sugges-
tions that reflected their campaign platforms."[52] That is not to say that the
audience did not learn about the parties and their positions from television.
Analysis of the free time does show that most parties set out general goals
and distinguished themselves from other parties, at least to some degree.
Table 7-1 gives a brief summary of themes presented by the various parties.
Many parties set out their stands on the pace of reform and the role of government in the transition of the economy. Some made explicit their support
for or opposition to the proposed constitution. Russia's Choice and Yabloko criticized the LDPR, at least implicitly, and many of the other parties
explicitly criticized Yeltsin, Yegor Gaidar, and administration policies.

In addition to free time, parties had the opportunity to present their own
themes or agendas through advertising. There is no agreement on the
amount of money spent on advertising or even the amount of time each
party advertised, and data from one source often do not match data from another source. For example, according to data from the Russian-American
Press and Information Center, Russia's Choice bought more than one and a
half hours of time on Ostankino between November 9 and December 11
and more than three hours on Russian Television.[53] On Ostankino and Russian Television combined, the top four advertising blocs were Russia's
Choice (four hours and fifty minutes), PRES (three hours and twenty-two
minutes), Civic Union (three hours and eight minutes), and the Liberal
Democratic Party of Russia (two hours and forty-four minutes). But according to an article in *Izvestiya*: "Russia's Choice purchased 180 minutes
of time on Ostankino and 44 minutes on the network Rossiya [Russian
Television]. The comparable figures for its two nearest competitors in this
category, PRES and LDPR, were 77 and 77 minutes, and 90 and 59 minutes, respectively."[54]

This highlights a very important issue. When making assertions about
the content of broadcasting one must be careful. There are many ways to
conduct content analysis, and the specific coding instrument and time period must be extremely clear. And those who watched television during the
election campaign know that at times it was difficult to distinguish between
paid time and public affairs or editorial time.[55]

Although there is no definitive record of the amount of time and money
spent on broadcasting, we know that those who chose to buy time could do
so. Some ads were short "Western style" ads, featuring the top leaders of
the party list. Some focused on the party itself. In one ad by Russia's
Choice, a young boy with his dog bemoaned the fact that they were not big

Table 7-1. *Presentation of Themes during Free Time*

Party	General goals	Comments about/comparison to others
Russia's Choice (12/8/93)	Need for a stable economy. Need order and stability. Need for a stable constitution, power, government, and legal basis.	Warns against demagogues. (Indirect reference to Zhirinovskii).
Yabloko (12/8/93)	Need faster reform, the development of competition. Against the constitution.	Warns against leader of LDP and demogoguery.
PRES (12/3/93)	Need reform of parliament and effective reform.	Vague
RDDR (12/8/93)	Need to be more effective in reforms, less costly. Need for smaller government, law-based system.	RDDR deals with mistakes of government. Yavlinskii wants to be administrator of government. Fight is over what type of reform is needed.
Women of Russia (12/3/93)	Laws should provide practical support for common people. The market economy can't take care of everything. Need to protect the interests of all groups, including women, youth, veterans.	There has been much talk about democratization but little real communication with the people.
DPR (11/29/93)	Need to fight crime, which is supported by state infrastructure. Western loans generated bureaucracy and corruption.	President has too much control.
Civic Union (12/6/93)	Need for measured reform. Government must regulate the switch to a market economy.	Gaidar and his team were destructive, destroying the country, destroying production. Shock therapy was wrong.
Future of Russia (12/6/93)	Need to address the problems of youth, soldiers, including education and jobs.	Government has not worked on the issues of education.
KEDR (11/29/93)	Need to focus on ecology and health.	Vague
Dignity (11/29/93)	Need to protect the rights and interests of veterans, disabled, women, children, victims of nuclear and environmental disaster.	Authorities (Gaidar) have not fulfilled promises.

Table 7-1. *continued*

Party	General goals	Comments about/comparison to others
LDPR (12/7/93)	Need to focus on issues that concern common people, including education, work, money, and food.	Zhirinovsky tells the audience that the people are being deceived—that there is money for the relief or their problems. He will tell them the truth.
KPRF (12/7/93)	Against the constitution. Need for collective type of power, ties with Ukraine, Belarus, and Kazakhstan.	Claims the government has destroyed the security of the country.
Agrarian (12/3/93)	Concern for the agricultural sphere made clear—favors private ownership of land. Narrative by Aleksandr Zaveryukha emphasizes experience/background in dealing with agricultural issues—implicit comparison to those in different parties.	

Source: Party Free Time, Ostankino. Dates as indicated. Coding by Sarah Oates and Laura Helvey.

enough to vote for Russia's Choice. In addition, parties were allowed to pay for longer periods of time during which they could present their views. It is interesting to note that not all parties chose to buy the time. Some candidates and parties, including the Communist party, the Agrarian party, and Yabloko, chose not to advertise. Grigorii Yavlinskii of Yabloko was quoted as saying that he had decided not to use political advertising "on principle."[56]

The effects of advertising during this election are difficult to assess because of the availability of free-time party presentations that did provide general information about party positions. Colton's survey data show that those who were exposed to television were more likely to know about the parties and electoral issues in general terms than those who did not watch television.[57] The data on issue knowledge, however, do not separate exposure to types of television coverage (that is, free time or advertising).

Government Agendas: News Coverage

Although free time and advertising provided an opportunity for parties to present their views, the presentation of the news was shaped by government ownership of and control over television. Government was able to influence news coverage for two reasons. First, the state controlled the purse strings for television. Second, high-level Ostankino management was staffed by progovernment personnel, including Bragin, who gave up his candidacy to remain the director of Ostankino. The European Institute for the Media (EIM) reported that "the situation renders people susceptible to pressure in a way which makes the formal guarantee of non-intervention by the President in daily duties devoid of substantive meaning."[58] The content of television news provides an opportunity to assess the executive's agenda. The data show that news coverage was used to promote legitimate elections and passage of the constitution. The promotion of individual candidates or parties was secondary.

This is not to say that Russia's Choice did not receive significant airtime in news and public affairs programming during the election campaign. Results compiled by the Russian-American Press and Information Center show that progovernment parties dominated the news and public affairs programming on both Ostankino and Russian Television throughout the campaign.[59] Russia's Choice received more than five and a half hours of news and public affairs coverage on Ostankino from November 9 to December 11 and three and a half hours of coverage on the news and public affairs on Russian Television from November 12 to December 11.[60] This is in contrast to the exposure given to other parties, which was significantly less. In this coding, the news time of candidates and parties was determined over the entire news broadcasts, not simply the designated election coverage. One would expect that candidates who are also governmental leaders, as many Russia's Choice candidates were, would get more coverage. Likewise, public affairs time was determined by the presence of Russia's Choice candidates, whether or not they were presented as candidates at all. Thus, a significant amount of time, particularly in the public affairs programming, was not necessarily directly related to the election. Still, this afforded those candidates more exposure to the electorate and should be considered.[61]

A closer look at the themes of coverage allows a more subtle analysis of campaign coverage and government agendas. For this reason a two-week period of the 9:00 P.M. news, "Novosti" on Ostankino, was analyzed for thematic content, as well as time spent covering each party. "Novosti" was chosen because it was shown regularly on Channel 1 and had the widest viewing audience of all news broadcasts. In the two weeks prior to the election, the news spent a total of about one hour on election coverage. Stories found in the election segment of the broadcast and any others that directly addressed the election by discussing particular parties or candidates, the need to vote, the constitution, or related issues were included in the analysis. Themes were coded for each election news story within the sample. Party-related stories were coded as those stories that focused on party-candidate meetings, news conferences, campaigning, and presentation of party or party leaders' views on political issues. When stories focused on the proposed constitution they were placed in the constitution category, including stories showing who supported or opposed the constitution. Stories were coded as promoting the general election process if their primary theme included the following topics:

1. How to vote. These included encouraging people to vote and make their vote count through an understanding of the ballots.

2. Rules of the election and voters' rights during the election.

3. The presence of foreign observers to monitor the election. In other words, outsiders who could vouch for the fairness of the election, thereby adding to its legitimacy.

4. Public participation. These included stories usually showing ordinary people saying they would definitely vote.

In addition, a category was developed for those stories that directly addressed for whom or for what to vote. The results from the thematic coding are presented in table 7-2. The time spent on specific parties is found in table 7-3.

The single most important theme of the election news coverage was legitimation of the election in general. In the "Novosti" coverage from November 29 through December 10, 47 percent of all election stories were primarily about the voting process. Thus almost half of all stories were about how to vote, the rules of the election itself, the presence of observers to monitor the elections, and the participation of the public in the process. In addition to news coverage, television focused on the elections during announcements similar to public service spots, which encouraged participation in the election and explained the voting procedure. Television spots discussed each ballot and showed voters what to look for and how to properly fill in the ballots. The news, in its election stories, promoted the election and attempted to legitimize the process.

The data in table 7-2 show that less than a quarter (still a significant amount) of the news coverage focused on the parties. Table 7-3 shows that

Table 7-2. *News Themes, November 29–December 10, 1993,*
"Novosti," Ostankino[a]

Theme	Number of stories	Time	Percent of total time
Party-specific story	15	7:23	12.2
Parties story	5	6:19	10.4
Total party coverage	20	13:42	22.6
Constitution	13	12:15	20.2
Voting process (rules, how to, participation)	32	28:22	46.8
Direct government statements on what to vote for; necessary results	4	2:58	4.9
Polls	2	1:48	3.0
Media	3	1:34	2.6
Total	74	60:39	100.1

Source: "Novosti," Ostankino.
a. Stories were coded for their primary emphasis or the most important theme.

it was Russia's Choice that received the most coverage in total time on "Novosti" from November 29 through December 10. Stories included those that focused on the party exclusively plus those stories in which Russia's Choice was either grouped with or compared to other parties. Russia's Choice could be found in more than half that time devoted to parties (almost fourteen minutes). However, that accounts for only 11.5 percent of the total news time within this sample. Russia's Choice received ample television time on the news, but it cannot be said that the news was an infomercial for Russia's Choice.

The constitution was another important theme in television news, with a little more than 20 percent of news stories focused on it. Yeltsin clearly supported the constitution, but it is important to distinguish between support for the constitution and support for Russia's Choice. After all, Zhirinovskii's LDPR supported the constitution as well. In addition to news stories, television spots were also used to promote the new constitution. Even in public service announcements designed to educate voters on the exact procedures of voting, government officials clearly supported passage of the new constitution. In one spot, Nikolai Ryabov, who was in charge of organizing the elections, told the audience to "make the right choice in favor of the [C]onstitution."[62] In addition, Yeltsin personally supported the constitution and he used television to champion its cause. On Thursday December 9, he made a televised speech in which he said that the constitution was needed in order to avoid civil war in Russia.[63]

Table 7-3. *Party Time on "Novosti,"*[a] *November 29–December 10, 1993*

Party	Stories about this party solely		Stories with other parties		Total time[b]	Percent of total time
	Number	Time	Number	Time		
Russia's Choice	2	:38	5	6:19	6:57	50.7
Yabloko	4	1:35	2	3:31	5:06	37.2
Communist	1	:41	2	2:51	3:32	25.8
RDDR	1	:54	2	1:57	2:51	20.8
LDP	2	:55	1	1:25	2:20	17.0
PRES	4	2:05	0		2:05	15.2
Agarian	0		1	:50	:50	6.1
Civic Union	1	:25	0		:25	3.0
Democratic	0		0		0	0
Dignity and Compassion	0		0		0	0
Future of Russia	0		0		0	0
KEDR	0		0		0	0
Women of Russia						

Source: "Novosti," Ostankino.
a. All parties mentioned within a story were coded.
b. Minutes and seconds.

The government agenda, as shown through television news coverage, emphasized the process and rules of democratic election, the constitution, and to a lesser degree, the promotion of Russia's Choice candidates. The results of the election show more clearly than anything else the conflict among these competing agendas.

A New Political Year?

The government had promised election night coverage of results to supply information to the public and legitimize the election and its results. Ostankino planned to broadcast live from the Kremlin, reporting the results of the election. The show was scheduled to run all night and to finish at 6:00 in the morning of the 13th and was designed to combine election results and entertainment. This would be a modern, information- and entertainment-packed television show, including performances for the members of the different parties, all assembled at banquet tables. However, when it became clear that Zhirinovskii's Liberal Democratic party was doing much better than expected and that Russia's Choice was doing much worse than expected, the results ceased to be aired. Legitimation of a free and fair election collided with an unwanted election result—always a possibility in such an election. The program was taken off the air about 3:20 A.M. The program's presenter, Tamara Maksimova, later "said she was not sure who had made the decision to go off the air."[64] After the Ostankino show went off, the next hours were a retreat to television of the past. There was little information about the election results on television.

Electoral Results and Legitimation of Democratic Processes

The results of the parliamentary election were not expected or desired by Yeltsin. When it was finally announced that Zhirinovskii's party had won the highest percentage of the party vote, many blamed television. Interfax reported that the "secret to Zhirinovskii's success appears to have been his aggressive television campaign, financed from a war chest of almost 1 billion rubles ($815,000)."[65] In addition, Yeltsin seemed to blame television, quickly firing Vyacheslav Bragin, the head of Ostankino. Bragin was let go on December 16, and a replacement, Aleksandr Yakovlev, was announced on December 20. Radio Free Liberty reported that "in the aftermath of the elections, Bragin had also been criticized by both journalists and members of the government for allowing Zhirinovskii to appear so often on his station."[66] TASS reported that Bragin was "accused of complete incompetence for his role in the electoral campaign which gave excessive coverage of ultra-nationalist Zhirinovskii."[67] The implication was that Zhirinovskii's Liberal Democratic party won as a result of the amount of time he appeared on television. This is a simplistic conclusion reminiscent of the hypodermic model of media effect. As the Soviet leadership learned, access to television does not guarantee effective communication. Russian leaders, including Yeltsin, were quick to go back to a discredited understanding of television effect.

If one studies television coverage of the 1993 parliamentary election more closely, a more optimistic conclusion can be reached. Television promoted the acceptance of democratic procedures during this election. First, television supplied information that was needed by the people to make vote choices, including information about important issues and the positions of the various contenders. The national election survey data discussed by Colton in chapter three in this volume show that people *did* gain general information from exposure to campaign information via the mass media. Second, television educated the public about the rules of the electoral process and encouraged them to participate. By fulfilling these important functions, the medium promoted the legitimacy of the process. A University of Glasgow poll reports a 20 percent "rise during the campaign in the number of people who thought that the elections were 'free and fair.'"[68] Although no correlation with television viewing was done, this suggests a possible relationship between television attention to the legitimation of the election process and public opinion. The rules for and content of television coverage of the December 1993 parliamentary election, although not perfect, did set the stage for future elections that took place on schedule. For example, during the 1995 parliamentary election campaign, all of the forty-three parties were given free time on national television.[69]

That is not to say that the tension between legitimation of democratic processes and the promotion of particular candidates or parties has ebbed. This was particularly evident during the 1996 presidential election. Yeltsin was accused of controlling television coverage during the campaign by placing his own supporters in positions of power at the various television stations. This included the replacement of Oleg Poptsov by Eduard Sagalayev at Nezavisimoye Televideniye (NTV-Independent Television).[70] Careful analysis of the 1996 Vremya election news coverage does show clear support for Yeltsin's reelection. Interestingly, themes that addressed legitimation of the election process itself were also evident. This time, however, Yeltsin's victory was presented as crucial for the continuance of free and fair elections in the future.[71]

Conclusion

Analysis of the the December 1993 parliamentary election is particularly important because it was during this campaign that the structural foundation for media use and expectations and rules for parties, government, and media professionals were set out. In 1993 specific structures were designed that were guided by stated principles of support for free and fair democratic elections. These structures included the use of free time, paid advertising, and a means for addressing disputes. Parties and candidates were guaranteed access to media and journalists were expected not to campaign or promote specific policies on air. Of course, there were conflicts and problems. Journalists complained that they could not ask difficult questions. The news still reflected government priorities. It has been argued here that the most important theme supported by government was the legitimation of the election process itself. This was shown through coding of election news stories themselves. The outcry over Yeltsin's use of media during the 1996 election shows the conflict inherent in promoting free and fair elections and supporting particular candidates or parties. The future of election coverage in Russia will have much to do with the level of commitment to the principles set out in 1993 and how the established system is refined to address the challenges that arose in 1996.

Notes

1. Michael Urban, "December 1993 as a Replication of Late-Soviet Electoral Practices," *Post-Soviet Affairs*, vol 10, no. 2 (April–June 1994), p. 139.
2. Everett M Rogers, James W. Dearing, Dorine Bregman, "The Anatomy of Agenda-Setting Research," *Journal of Communication* vol. 43, no. 2 (Spring 1993), pp. 68–84; Gerald M. Kosicki, "Problems and Opportunities in Agenda-Setting Research" *Journal of Communication*, vol. 43, no. 2 (Spring 1993), pp. 100–27.
3. Holli A. Semetko and others, *The Formation of Campaign Agendas: A Comparative Analysis of Party and Media Roles in Recent American and British Elections* (Hillsdale, N.J.: Erlbaum, 1991).
4. David Weaver, "Media Agenda Setting and Elections: Voter Involvement or Alienation?" *Political Communication*, vol. 11 (October–December, 1994), p. 349.
5. Semetko, and others, *Formation of Campaign Agendas*, p. 178.
6. Ibid., pp. 178–79.
7. Ibid., p. 179.
8. Ibid., p. 179.
9. For a discussion of Soviet television see Ellen Mickiewicz, *Media and the Russian Public* (New York: Praeger, 1981); Ellen Mickiewicz, *Split Signals: Television and Politics in the Soviet Union* (New York: Oxford University Press, 1988)
10. Mickiewicz, *Split Signals*, p. 5.
11. Thomas F. Remington, *The Truth of Authority: Ideology and Communication in the Soviet Union* (Pittsburgh: University of Pittsburgh Press, 1988), p. 170.
12. Mickiewicz, *Split Signals*, pp. 180–81.
13. David Wedgwood Been, *Persuasion and Soviet Politics* (Oxford: Basil Blackwell, 1989), pp 133–83; Mickiewicz, *Split Signals*, pp. 179–203.
14. It should be made clear that an understanding of the deficiencies did not come with Gorbachev. Mickiewicz has shown that there was a growing concern with the effectiveness of television even before Gorbachev came to power. Mickiewicz, *Split Signals*, p. 50.
15. Mickiewicz, *Split Signals*, pp. 52–56.
16. Ibid, pp. 179–203.
17. There are a number of studies of the changes in television under glasnost. See Mickiewicz, *Split Signals*; Linda Jensen, "The Press and Power in the Russian Federation," *Journal of International Affairs*, vol. 47, no. 1 (Summer 1993),

pp. 97–125; Jonathan Eisen, *The Glasnost Readers* (New York: New American Library, Penguin Books, 1990); James Dingley, "Soviet Television and Glasnost," in Julian Graffy and Geoffrey A. Hosking, eds., *Culture and the Media in the USSR Today* (New York: MacMillan, 1989); Marsha Siefert, ed., *Mass Culture and Perestroika in the Soviet Union* (New York: Oxford University Press, 1991).

18. Rasma Karklins, "Explaining Regime Change in the Soviet Union," *Europe-Asia Studies*, vol. 46, no. 1 (1994), p. 45.

19. Ibid., p. 34.

20. This point is also made by William E. Odom, "Soviet Politics and After: Old and New Concepts," *World Politics*, vol. 45 (October 1992), pp. 66–98.

21. Jensen, "The Press and the Power," p. 105.

22. Ibid., pp. 105–06; Victoria E. Bonnell and Gregory Freidin, "Televorot: The Role of Television Coverage in Russia's August 1991 Coup," *Slavic Review*, vol. 52, no. 4 (Winter 1993), pp. 810–38.

23. Bonnell and Freidin, "Televorot," p. 813. The contempt of some of the journalists during the press conference by coup leaders was obvious.

24. Jensen, "The Press and the Power," pp. 115–18.

25. These views were expressed at a briefing by media representatives at a meeting of the International Republican Institute, December 10, 1993. Moscow representatives were present from *Izvestiya, Moskovskii Komsomolets,* and Ostankino.

26. The Commission on Television Policy, to which Yeltsin's decree refers, includes experts from the independent countries of the former Soviet Union and the United States. It is chaired by former president Jimmy Carter and Eduard Sagalayev, chair of the Confederation of Journalists' Unions and former president of Russia's newly independent Channel 6. The commission's study of and debate on the role of television in elections is presented in Ellen Mickiewicz and Charles Firestone, *Television and Elections* (Queenstown, Md.: Aspen Institute and the Carter Center, 1992).

27. "Media Law and the December Election," *Post-Soviet Media Law and Policy Newsletter*, vol. 1, no. 2 (November 17, 1993). Emphasis added. See this issue for a full reprint of the decree and a thorough discussion of its contents.

28. Ostankino broadcasts on Channel 1 and reaches approximately 200 million people in Russia and the former Soviet republics. Russian Television broadcasts on Channel 2 and reaches 140 million people. Laura Belin, "Wrestling Political and Financial Repression," *Transition*, vol. 1, no. 18 (October 6, 1995), p. 59.

29. With morning repeats each party received four hours of free time on Ostankino and Russian Television combined.

30. "Regulations on Information Guarantees in the Election Campaign," *Post-Soviet Media Law and Policy Newsletter*, vol. 1, no. 2 (November 17, 1993), p. 8.

31. *Moscow Times,* December 3, 1993, p. 1.

32. "Novosti," Ostankino, November 18, 1993.

33. "Novosti," Ostankino, November 25, 1993.

34. "Media Law and the December Election," p. 3. The final report of the European Institute for the Media states that there were varying reports on the price of a minute of airtime—from 150,000 rubles to 6 million rubles. See EIM, "Monitoring

of the Election Coverage in the Russian Mass Media," *International Affairs*, no. 5 (1994), pp. 3–78.

35. "Regulations on Information Guarantees in the Election Campaign," p. 9.

36. Ibid., p. 9.

37. Ibid., p. 10.

38. Ibid., p. 10.

39. "Media Law and the December Election," p. 5.

40. Ibid., p. 4.

41. In the last days of the election, the tribunal complained that local mass media councils had not been set up. The tribunal handled all media complaints, including those that might have been handled at a local level. See "Yakovlev to Head Ostankino, Media Institutes Reshuffled," *Post-Soviet Media Law and Policy Newsletter*, vol. 1, no. 3 (December 22, 1993), p. 2.

42. Communique of the work of the tribunal from November 2 to December 7, 1993, p. 4.

43. *Moscow Times,* December 1, 1993, p. 1.

44. "Prezident RF protiv ispolzovanie pressi dlya napadok na konstitutsiyu i vlast," *Vybory ezhednevnii vypusk,* November 25, 1993, p. 1; *Moscow Times,* December 2, 1993, p. 3.

45. "Regulations on Information Guarantees in the Election Campaign," p. 10.

46. "Media Law and the December Election," p. 1.

47. "Novosti," Ostankino, November 18, 1993.

48. "Regulations on Information Guarantees in the Election Campaign," p. 10.

49. *Izvestiya*, November 24, 1993, p. 1.

50. The following free-time presentations were coded for formatting techniques used: Russia's Choice on December 8, 1993; Yabloko on December 8, 1993; PRES on December 3, 1993; RDDR on December 8, 1993; Women of Russia on December 3, 1993; DPR on November 23, 1993; Civic Union on December 6, 1993; Future of Russia on December 6, 1993; KEDR on November 29, 1993; Dignity on November 29, 1993; LDPR on December 7, 1993; KPRF on December 7, 1993; Agrarian on December 3, 1993.

51. Press Conference at the Russian-American Press and Information Center (RAPIC), December 7, 1993.

52. Sarah Oates, "The Importance of Party Strategy in Developing Democracies: Formation and Transmission of Campaign Agendas in the 1993 Russian Duma Elections," paper prepared for the Conference on Party Politics in the Year 2000, University of Manchester, United Kingdom, January 1995, p. 12.

53. Press Release, RAPIC, Moscow, December 15, 1993, charts 1 and 2.

54. *Izvestiya,* December 19, 1993. Quoted in Urban, "December 1993 as an Application of Late-Soviet Electoral Practices," p. 142.

55. The European Institute for the Media conducted content analysis of election coverage and makes this very point. It reports that "those parties who made the heaviest use of [advertising] . . . were the Russia's Choice bloc, the Party for Russian Unity and Accord and the Liberal Democratic Party." "The Monitoring of the Election Coverage in the Russian Mass Media," p. 17.

56. Press Release, RAPIC, Moscow, December 15, 1993, p. 2.

57. This was true even when interest in the campaign and other relevant individual characteristics are taken into account.

58. EIM, "The Monitoring of the Election Coverage in the Russian Mass Media," p. 19.

59. Press Release, RAPIC, Moscow, December 15, 1993, charts 1 and 2.

60. The data came from coding of all newscasts (not only the 9:00 P.M. newscast).

61. For an example, see Press Release, RAPIC, Moscow, December 15, 1993, pp. 3–4.

62. This spot was shown frequently during the campaign.

63. "Novosti," Ostankino, December 9, 1993.

64. *Moscow Times,* December 14, 1994, p. 1.

65. Ibid., p. 2.

66. "Ostankino Chief Dismissed," *RFE/RL Daily Report,* no. 240 (December 16, 1993).

67. Quoted in "Yakovlev to Head Ostankino, Media Institutions Reshuffled," p. 2.

68. Matthew and others, "Public Opinion, Parties and Voters in the December 1993 Russian Elections," *Europe-Asia Studies,* vol. 47, no. 4 (1995), p. 602.

69. For a summary of media regulations during the December 1995 election, see European Institute for the Media, "Monitoring the Media Coverage of the 1995 Russian Parliamentary Elections: Final Report," Dusseldorf, Germany, February 15, 1996.

70. NTV is Russia's largest private network and began broadcasting in January 1994. It has received recognition for its coverage of the war in Chechnya and has been pressured by the government to modify coverage at various times since its inception. See Belin, "Wrestling Political and Financial Repression," p. 59.

71. Sarah Oates and Laura Roselle Helvey, "Russian Television's Mixed Messages: Parties, Candidates and Control on 'Vremya,' 1995–1996" (paper prepared for 1997 annual meeting of the American Political Science Association, Washington, D.C., August 28–31, 1997).

CHAPTER EIGHT

The Press and the Campaign

Comprehensive but Fragmented Coverage

Joel M. Ostrow

THE RUSSIAN national print media provided uncensored, wide-ranging, and lively coverage of the 1993 parliamentary election campaign. Taken together, the eight national newspapers surveyed for this study—*Izvestiya, Komsomol'skaya pravda, Trud, Krasnaya zvezda, Pravda, Nezavisimaya gazeta, Segodnya,* and *Argumenty i fakty*—offered comprehensive coverage and represented a wide range of political views. *Pravda*, as expected, strongly supported the Communist party and other centrist and antireform opposition groups. *Krasnaya zvezda* had no clear favorite. The other six papers divided their support among three proreform blocs—Russia's Choice, Party of Russian Unity and Accord (PRES), and Yabloko.

In this chapter I attempt to answer one question: did these newspapers provide the voter with the information necessary to make an informed choice on election day? Collectively, they provided an abundance of news and analysis of the major electoral blocs[1] and their campaign platforms to enable the electorate to make an informed decision. But the key word is "collectively."[2] Coverage by particular newspapers was fragmented. With

I would like to thank the Berkeley-Stanford Program in Soviet and Post-Soviet Studies for permission to participate in this project while in Moscow on a dissertation research fellowship; Andrei Sayenko for research assistance; Irina A. Andreyevna and the Parliamentary Library of the Federal Assembly for their kind and attentive assistance; and Brian Taylor and Valerie Sperling for insightful comments on earlier drafts of this chapter.

the possible exception of the small, independent *Segodnya*, no single paper provided high-quality, comprehensive campaign coverage. A voter would have to have read several of these newspapers to obtain such coverage. But a number of factors, including changes in the structure of the Russian press and the state of the Russian economy, meant only the rare voter would have read more than one or two, if any. Therefore, although taken together the newspapers provided comprehensive campaign coverage, severally they did not, and this fact denied most readers the information needed to make a fully informed decision on election day.

This chapter opens with a discussion of the transformations that have shaken the former central newspapers since the collapse of the Soviet Union, outlining the declining influence and continuing evolution of the Russian national print media and introducing the newspapers included in the study sample. The analysis of their campaign coverage follows, first with an examination of the rules under which the newspapers operated during the campaign and the restrictions they faced. These were in fact few, particularly compared with those faced by the electronic media; in fact, the response of the newspapers to the campaign on television was in many cases the source of their most important and informative coverage. The heart of the chapter—two sections examining the strategies the papers employed in covering the campaign and their allocation of space to the competing electoral blocs and the bias in their coverage—demonstrates the diversity among the papers and the need to have read several of them to have obtained comprehensive coverage. Two final sections discuss the papers' reactions to the election results and their broader influence in the campaign.

The Newspapers

The disintegration of the Soviet Union has rendered the concept "central press" an obsolete remnant of Soviet politics and Sovietology. But the newspapers that used to be thought of, and used to think of themselves, as "central" continue to publish. If they are no longer "central," then what are they? How do they see themselves? Which papers are most important today from the standpoint of Russian politics?

The daily newspapers traditionally thought of as the Soviet central press—*Pravda, Izvestiya, Trud, Komsomol'skaya pravda, Krasnaya zvezda*, and *Sovetskaya Rossiya*—all used to have daily circulation rates in the millions, *Komsomol'skaya pravda* leading the way with 22 million readers. These papers carried the gospel of the ruling Communist party to the farthest corners of the Soviet Union, where they were available and read. And used for toilet paper.

However, in post-Soviet Russia, as in most countries, toilet paper is readily available and far less expensive than its equivalent in newspaper. As *Izvestiya* political editor Nikolai Bondaruk noted, a person who once subscribed to ten papers now can afford only one, if any. This is particularly so in the provinces, where transportation costs from Moscow have raised newspaper prices to levels even loyal former readers are unwilling or unable to pay, and where the papers arrive up to a week late, rendering their "news" obsolete. These two facts spell a dramatic decline in the circulation and influence of the former central press.[3] Moreover, kiosks would rather "sell two cartons of American cigarettes or a couple of bottles of drink and have a big day" than struggle to sell Moscow newspapers.[4]

The impact of the higher costs of newspapers is dramatic. As late as 1989, a single issue of *Izvestiya* cost 2 kopeks, or a miniscule 1/15,000th of an average monthly salary of 300 rubles. During the 1993 campaign, an issue of *Izvestiya* cost 90 rubles, or roughly 1/800th of a monthly salary of 75,000 rubles. The cost of a newspaper in relation to income has thus risen nearly twentyfold.[5] (In relation to the dollar, the cost has risen by a factor of 50![6]) Circulation rates for these papers have thus dropped dramatically (see table 8-1), and "central press" has lost its meaning. The editors have eliminated the term from their vocabulary, all opting for "national press" as a more accurate label. "Mostly as a result of inertia," as Bondaruk put it, these former central newspapers are still distributed all across Russia, in spite of the difficulties already mentioned.[7] At least three editors said only one-third of their print run remains in Moscow. But this is bound to change, for willingly or grudgingly they all also acknowledge the advantages of concentrating on Moscow circulation—being located in the capital, it is cheaper to distribute the papers there and the potential earnings are greatest. The current structure of the Russian print media is thus extremely unstable and may be expected in the near future to develop in a direction familiar in the West—toward city-based publications.[8]

What is clear is that these newspapers did not have the influence in 1993 that they enjoyed in the Soviet era. With circulation down, and availability difficult at best for most individuals and scarce in most regions, these newspapers are printing far fewer copies and are distributed less widely. They are less important, and the smaller regional press is more important than ever before. By contrast, today one can assume more safely that those who

Table 8-1. *Circulation Rates of the Major Central Newspapers (in millions)*

Newspaper	1975[a]	1985[b]	1988	1989	1990	1991	1992	1993
Argumenty i fakty	—	3.0	9.5	22.1	32.9	24.1	26.2	5.8
Komsomol'skaya pravda	9.9	13.2	17.6	18.3	21.9	17.9	12.8	1.6
Krasnaya zvezda	n.a.	n.a.	n.a.	n.a.	n.a.	1.1	0.4	0.5
Izvestiya	8.0	6.7	10.5	11.0	10.1	4.7	3.8	0.7
Pravda	10.6	10.5	10.9	10.7	7.7	3.2	1.4	0.5
Trud	8.2	16.7	18.7	20.4	21.6	18.5	12.6	2.5

Source: All figures (except as noted specifically below) were obtained directly from the newspapers or their circulation departments. The author thanks Andrei Sayenko for research assistance.

a. *Letopis' perevodicheskikh i prodolzhayushchikhsya izdaniya*, ch. 2, "Gazety, 1971–1975gg." Gosudarstvenniy Komitet SSSR po pechati (Moscow: Kniga, 1981).

b. *Letopis' perevodicheskikh i prodolzhayushchikhsya izdaniya*, ch. 2, "Gazety, 1981–1985gg." Gosudarstvenniy Komitet SSSR po pechati (Moscow: Knizhnaya palata, 1989).

n.a. = not applicable.

do purchase the newspapers discussed in this study do so to read them, whether or not they use them afterward for other, more mundane purposes.

The newspapers selected for the study sample reflect the changes the Soviet press is undergoing and represent the most important across a spectrum of types (see table 8-2). The older newspapers claiming roots in the Soviet-era were closer to pamphlets than true newspapers. Normally four to six pages long, each publication was directed to a targeted readership. *Pravda* was the organ of the Central Committee of the Communist party, and the most authoritative mouthpiece of the Kremlin leadership for the party rank and file. Although officially run by the paper's worker's collective, it is to this day the paper of what remains of the Communist party and the main voice of the "irreconcilable opposition" hostile to the political and economic reforms of the post-Soviet leaders.[9] Indeed, during the election campaign it was the only such voice. This study does not include *Sovetskaya Rossiya* because President Yeltsin banned it, along with "nationalist-patriotic" pamphlets and papers such as *Den'*, after the October uprising. *Izvestiya* was the official organ of the Soviets, the nominally representative bodies with the USSR Supreme Soviet Presidium at the top of the hierarchy. It focused on information from and about government institutions and the nomenklatura at various levels. *Izvestiya* is now run by its journalists' collective and has been a strong backer of the president and the government. *Komsomol'skaya pravda* was formerly the organ of the Communist Youth League, and is now run by its journalists' collective. It took a strong

Table 8-2. *Background and Profile of the Major Central Newspapers*

Newspaper	Year founded	Old publisher	New publisher	Subsidy	Political orientation
Izvestiya	1917	Soviets	Journalist collective	no	Propresident, progovernment, pro-reform
Pravda	1912	—	*Pravda* worker's collective	until July 1993	Procommunist, oppositionist, reform without reducing strd of living
Komsomol'skaya pravda	1925	Communist Youth League	Journalist collective	yes	Proreform, mostly propresident
Argumenty i fakty	1980	—	Journalist collective	yes	Propresident, gives space to wide range of views
Trud	1921	Professional unions	*Trud* workers collective	yes	No clear political line, generally supports Yeltsin
Nezavisimaya gazeta	1990	—	Editorial collective	no	Liberal opposition to president and government
Segodnya	1993	—	Financial group "Most"	no	Proreform, generally supportive of government
Krasnaya zvezda	1924	Armed forces of the Soviet Union	Russian armed forces	yes	Promilitary, politically neutral, cautiously supportive of the president

Source: Information compiled by the author.

proreform line in the Gorbachev era. *Trud* was the newspaper of the professional unions. Although it walks a fairly neutral yet pro-Yeltsin political
line, it retains a pro-union tone. *Krasnaya zvezda* was the publication of the
Soviet armed forces and remains the official organ of the Russian military.
Trud and *Krasnaya zvezda* were chosen for this study because I assumed
that they are read widely by members of the military, elderly citizens, labor-
ers, pensioners, and others who may be considered to fall in the category of

centrists or opponents of radical reform. *Trud*, it should be noted, was the least expensive of these dailies and had the largest circulation at more than two million.

In addition to these five core newspapers, *Nezavisimaya gazeta* is included as a leading independent daily with extensive political coverage, as is *Segodnya*, a new independent and continually expanding, multisection daily that is arguably the most objective and highest quality Russian-language newspaper published today. It is quickly becoming the most widely read newspaper among Russian intellectuals.[10] Still, these two papers have circulations of around 100,000 and outside of Moscow are only available in a few of the largest cities. Finally, *Argumenty i fakty* is included as the most widely circulated news weekly in the country.[11] As its name suggests, it provides arguments and facts representing a wide range of views.

Although some of the content in these official newspapers overlapped in the Soviet era, particularly the first two pages when the general secretary made a speech, many people read several of them. No less so today, one must read several of these papers, along with the sports newspaper, a local city paper, and a classified paper to obtain a range of news roughly similar to that published in a single typical Western newspaper. However, as already indicated, unlike the past this is now beyond the means of the average Russian. The papers have simply become too expensive. Indeed, only *Izvestiya*, *Komsomol'skaya pravda,* and *Argumenty i fakty* retain substantial readership in the provinces; the rest restrict their distribution to the Moscow region.[12] According to one survey of Yaroslavskaya oblast, the average family, which subscribed to between four and ten newspapers in 1991, now subscribes to one or two. Roughly 80 percent of the respondents in this survey said they read a regional or city newspaper, and this figure is confirmed by a broader national survey. The implication is that "the sinking and crumbling 'universal' monolith . . . is giving way to a different structure of communication," one giving greater emphasis to regional publications.[13]

Although the national newspapers have become less accessible to the average Russian citizen, they remain highly partisan, and it is a much more diversified partisanship than in the Soviet era. There is no such thing as an "objective" Russian newspaper.[14] The print media clearly reflect and actively reproduce the "*kto kogo*" (who from whom) underpinnings, the intensely zero-sum basis of Russian political thought. Each paper has its line, its readers, its patrons, and its enemies. As already suggested, the papers in this survey presented the entire spectrum of politically relevant views in the campaign, ranging from *Izvestiya*'s strong pro-Russia's Choice stand to *Pravda*'s scathing contempt for that bloc and unabashed support for the Communists. The other papers filled every shade in between. Bias in their campaign coverage is discussed later. It is sufficient here to say that there is no question that these newspapers, taken together, made all views available to the public during the campaign.

The metamorphosis of the former Soviet central press means few voters were likely to read more than one or two of the papers in this sample, if indeed they read any at all. But the partisanship of these papers means a voter reading only one or two of them, with the possible exception of *Segodnya*, would have received highly skewed and fragmented coverage, lacking the depth and objectivity necessary to enable a fully informed decision on election day. Only taken collectively did the papers provide such information.

The Rules

That they were able to provide comprehensive coverage of the election even collectively is in large part thanks to the rules under which the newspapers operated. As one analysis put it, the rules were acceptable, "especially considering that such conditions in the past were completely lacking and the time to develop them was severely restricted."[15]

In contrast to the electronic media, the print media were relatively unrestricted in the methods and strategies available to them for covering the campaign. The single glaring exception was President Yeltsin's October 5 banning of *Sovetskaya Rossiya* after the October uprising. Even those who favored the closing of radical nationalist publications such as *Den'* and *Pamyat'* found this difficult to justify, particularly after a court ruled on November 23 in favor of a suit filed by the paper that the ban violated the Law on the Press.[16] Even after the court decision the paper did not print for more than two weeks, reportedly because the government failed to lift a freeze on the paper's accounts.[17]

Although the banning of *Sovetskaya Rossiya* may be deplored, its absence left no major void in the campaign coverage—collectively, the newspapers that did publish covered the full spectrum of views embodied by the candidates and electoral blocs. There was no evidence of direct political pressure against their editorial content. This is certainly true for the financially independent publications in this survey—*Izvestiya*, *Nezavisimaya gazeta*, and *Segodnya*. As Bondaruk of *Izvestiya* said, "There is no way for any outside party to influence our work." Even the others, which still receive government subsidies, were free of direct pressure. "We are independent as never before," Valery Simonov of *Komsomol'skaya pravda* said.[18] Subsidies, introduced in January 1992 to help ease the burden of increased prices for newsprint and other costs, were available to all of these newspapers, and *Komsomol'skaya pravda, Trud,* and *Argumenty i fakty* were among those receiving the largest support.[19] Although the European Institute for the Media correctly observes that such subsidies at least theoretically create a degree "of dependence on state authorities," and that the situation is far from ideal, it is important to note that the subsidies have not resulted in control over editorial content.[20] *Sel'skaya zhizn',* a newspaper targeted toward the agricultural sector, receives one of the largest subsidies, but strongly supported the Agrarian party and the Communist party that were far from sympathetic to either the Russian president or the government. *Pravda,* the leading opposition newspaper, also received a subsidy in 1993.[21]

Several papers, including *Pravda* and *Komsomol'skaya pravda,* temporarily ceased publication beginning November 20, but this was for strictly financial not political reasons. They were in arrears to their common printer.[22] *Komsomol'skaya pravda* resumed publishing November 24 after receiving its fourth-quarter subsidy, having missed two issues.[23] *Pravda* had more serious problems. On its own initiative, it had not requested a subsidy after the second quarter of 1993, counting instead on support from its Greek "partner." However, the latter proved, to a somewhat irritated *Pravda* editor-in-chief Viktor Linnik, to be "a lightweight in a league for heavyweights . . . unable to keep the financial monster" *Pravda* on its feet.[24] *Pravda* remained closed until December 10, two days before the election, and missed the critical last weeks of the campaign. But it bears repeating that the paper's own financial disarray, not arbitrary political rule or censorious distribution of subsidies, caused the closure. Linnik steadfastly insisted that "there is no direct link between some kind of political pressure and our financial problems." Communist party leader Gennadii Zyuganov's charges as election day neared that President Yeltsin and Russia's Choice were responsible for closing *Pravda* were therefore nothing short of lies. As *Segodnya* put it, there was no "organized informational blockade"; the paper and party were simply broke.[25]

The only specific government control over information in the print media was a ban on the publication of opinion polls within ten days of the election.[26] An official from the Central Electoral Commission (TsIK) stated the official reason for the ban: "The people ought to be given at least ten days to make up their minds without being influenced by these bothersome polls."[27] Some analysts interpreted the ban as a government attempt to protect Russia's Choice by preventing potential challengers from gaining momentum as election day neared. "The government is using all methods to try to protect [Russia's Choice]," Simonov said. "It demonstrates their lack of confidence in their strength."[28]

If this was the reasoning behind the ban, in retrospect it failed and may even have backfired. One sociologist argued the ban helped Vladimir Zhirinovskii by enabling him to make claims, which had to remain unchallenged, that he would capture more than 45 percent of the vote. And indeed, support for Zhirinovskii did swell. Without the ban, the argument goes, both the figures Zhirinovskii presented and growing support for him could have been countered by more concerted efforts by the other electoral blocs.[29] This argument, however, is weakened by the fact that the ban also allowed Civic Union candidate Oleg Rumyantsev to claim, again unchallenged, that only 10 percent of voters would support the constitution and the referendum would fail miserably. This did not come to pass; the constitution was adopted by 58.4 percent of the voters. Moreover, several papers sought ways around the ban by publishing general trends rather than specific results.[30] *Segodnya* even got its hands slapped by the special arbitration court for going too far in stretching the rules, but the information was published the day before the election and the judgment rendered long after. The public got the information.[31]

The most notable additional attempts to control information in the press were those of several government members, including President Yeltsin himself, to ban criticism of the draft constitution and of the president. Press Minister Vladimir Shumeiko even demanded that TsIK ban parties speaking out against the draft constitution. The newspapers in this sample, particularly *Nezavisimaya gazeta*, *Komsomol'skaya pravda*, and *Segodnya*, universally condemned all such efforts, and even Shumeiko's own colleagues roundly criticized his actions.[32] The TsIK rejected his demand.

Perhaps more significant than attempts to control information in the newspapers were rules against preventing the publication of information. Although the newspapers could essentially determine the amount and content of editorial space on the campaign and the candidates, according to several editors interviewed they were required to run any paid political advertisements received. Newspapers could not reject advertisements on political grounds, nor were they allowed to play games with advertising rates.[33] The advertising departments are generally independent from the editorial staff, and, given the dire economic straits elaborated on previously that faced all of the publications, it would be hard to imagine any rejecting millions of rubles in advertising revenues. I am not aware of any complaint by any candidate or bloc about the advertising policies of any of the papers in this sample. Those who wanted to run political ads and had the money to pay for them could do so. The fact that a page in *Izvestiya* and *Komsomol'skaya pravda* cost more than 16 million rubles, a page in *Trud* 12 million, and a page in the smaller papers between 2 and 5 million rubles explains the absence of advertising by the majority of parties in these papers. Only PRES and Russia's Choice ran daily ads for several weeks in all of these papers. As election day neared, the number of ads from smaller parties increased. Most interesting, however, is that the Liberal Democratic Party of Russia (LDPR) did not purchase a single ad in these papers. Its strategy was clearly to spend its money buying as much television time for its leader as possible, and, whether consciously or not, it correctly anticipated the lack of influence of the newspapers.

Informing the Voter: Responding to Television

Not only did the newspapers have, as suggested previously, greater freedom in covering the campaign than television had, the most important role they played was as a counter to television. The campaign rules denied television journalists the ability to take an active and professional approach in covering the campaign, and the papers universally condemned television for failing in its duty to inform the electorate. In so doing, the newspapers raised the quality of information available to the voter and filled what would otherwise have been a gaping information void.

As *Segodnya* sarcastically observed, try watching two hours of party programming "from November 22 through December 8, four to six parties each day." Try to imagine coming out of that with a "healthy intellect," not to mention any interest in politics. "It is impossible!"[34] *Trud* quipped that Ostankino's "Voter's Hour" was misnamed—it was in fact a "candidate's hour."[35] But although these papers criticized the format of the television campaign, which gave each electoral group two hours of free time to do with as they pleased and denied television journalists the ability to ask questions or challenge the candidates, they only irregularly addressed the content of candidates' television presentations.

Izvestiya did so more systematically, determining to do its own challenging of the television monologues and making this a central part of its strategy for covering the campaign.[36] "Zhirinovskii is trying to introduce fascism in the country, and [television] journalists cannot express their opinion or ask him questions," Bondaruk said. "This is not normal."[37] *Izvestiya*'s daily column regularly questioned economic figures presented by Civic Union and the Democratic Party of Russia, exposed the fallacy of "tirades" by Communist party leader Zyuganov about foreign agents stealing Russia's wealth, and condemned various "rantings" of Zhirinovskii aimed at "lulling the voter to sleep."[38] It is worth noting, however, the conspicuous absence in *Izvestiya*'s criticisms of challenges to statements by Russia's Choice candidates.[39]

Similarly, *Nezavisimaya gazeta* criticized all thirteen electoral blocs for "wasting their allotted time" paid for by the taxpayers, condemned the shallowness of television news coverage, and denounced the candidacies of Ostankino chairs Vyacheslav Bragin and Kirill Ignat'ev on the Russia's Choice list.[40] Even the normally staid *Krasnaya zvezda*, which the Russian-American Press and Information Center cited as "the most detached and objective of all newspapers"[41] in the sample, was harsh in its critique of the "boring" nightly monologues. "There can be little doubt that the overwhelming majority of potential voters simply turned off the programs in search of the next segment of 'Santa Barbara' . . . (someone mercifully put this on the air as an alternative.)"[42]

The newspapers thus tried to fill the information void created by the poor format of the television campaign. Their critical analyses and challenging questions raised the quality of information reaching the public domain. To the extent that the candidates and parties failed to provide constructive and detailed responses, the newspapers are hardly to blame.

Informing the Voter: Strategies for Coverage

Important as were their reactions to the campaign on television, the newspapers of course also provided independent coverage. Their strategies for doing so varied widely, resulting in a wide array of published information. These strategies included both covering raw news and actively seeking to present information about the candidates.

Izvestiya provided the most thorough coverage of the older, established papers. At the outset of the campaign, the editorial board held a strategy session to assign a different correspondent to cover each of the registered election blocs. Correspondents were assigned based on "who knows whom best." They were charged with attending press conferences, following the leaders, and publishing information "when something important happened."[43] In a concrete sense, then, *Izvestiya* sought to provide coverage of all electoral blocs and all sides of issues. But this did not necessarily mean equal coverage to all. As Bondaruk explained, *Izvestiya* decided "not to overplay formalistic equality" in its coverage. "Why exaggerate the influence" of the smaller groups, he rhetorically asked. "If they pass the 5 percent barrier, we'll write about them." Although it neglected none of the registered blocs, this approach focused attention on those realistically competing for predominance in the parliament. The smaller blocs thus tended to get lost in the newspaper coverage, in contrast to television, where each bloc was given an equal two hours of free time.[44]

Izvestiya was the only paper in the sample to systematically interview the leaders of the electoral blocs, although, despite its offer to meet with a representative from all thirteen, only seven interviews took place. Those left out "either had no interest in appearing before *Izvestiya* readers, or couldn't meet in time" for publication, the paper explained.[45] These interviews all appeared on page 4, were of identical length, and included brief biographical sketches of the leaders and outlines of the main points of the program of their electoral bloc. As discussed later in the chapter, however, they were not carried out with equal objectivity.

The other papers were less systematic in their coverage and, as a result, less exhaustive. Simonov geared *Komsomol'skaya pravda*'s coverage toward deciding "who our readers are more interested in," not to providing balanced coverage of all candidates. Much the same can be said of *Pravda*, although its readers were apparently interested in different candidates![46] *Komsomol'skaya pravda* regularly published material in the form of reader call-ins to candidates. *Trud*'s main campaign feature was publishing letters and commentary from readers. These papers also ran stories on issues of the campaign, but none had any clear systematic approach to the organization and publication of such material. The same may be said of the two remaining newspapers, *Nezavisimaya gazeta* and *Argumenty i fakty*. However, as discussed in greater detail later, *Nezavisimaya gazeta* geared its coverage toward discrediting President Yeltsin and the electoral bloc Russia's Choice, while *Argumenty i fakty* sought to promote Yeltsin and Russia's Choice.

Krasnaya zvezda was the most "detached and objective" of these news-papers[47]—detached in the sense that except for the one-liner quotations from the candidates, more in-depth articles on the campaign were sporadic at best. And perhaps not surprising, the theme of these articles was fairly uniform—of eleven articles devoted to the campaign, six were devoted to the specific issue of the interests of the Armed Forces. Two days before the election, the paper published submissions of the nine electoral blocs that re-sponded to its solicitation, and seven of these focused on military issues.[48] Four of the other five articles in *Krasnaya zvezda* were straight presentation of statistics on the registration of candidates and electoral blocs. Each of the papers in the sample published such statistical information as the number of candidates submitting applications for registration, the number registered, their profile, and so on, as the TsIK made such information available. They generally sought to provide objective coverage of the campaign rules and procedures.

Izvestiya and *Komsomol'skaya pravda* also made use of their regional networks of correspondents to report on violations of campaign rules and other generally scandalous news from the provinces. The other papers that addressed regional aspects of the campaign at all—*Segodnya*, *Nezavisi-maya gazeta*, and, to a lesser extent, *Trud*—relied exclusively on wire serv-ice reports for such material, or, in the latter case, on readers' letters.

But of all the papers in the sample, *Segodnya* provided the most thor-ough and objective information on the campaign platforms of the electoral blocs. In some respects, *Segodnya*'s approach mirrored *Izvestiya*'s. It cov-ered all blocs, focused on the major ones, and assigned correspondents to cover categories of electoral blocs—reformist, centrist, opposition, and the-matic. *Segodnya*'s coverage was more exhaustive and the highest quality of all the papers in this sample. The best examples of this materialized out of the paper's general criticism of all electoral blocs for having "failed to an-swer the main questions" in voters' minds—namely, "how and why they differ from each other and what they plan to do if they come to power." *Segodnya* attempted in the final week of the campaign to present this infor-mation itself, both graphically and textually, in two detailed and extremely informative encapsulations, first of the ideological orientations of each electoral bloc and its main leaders, and second on the positions of each bloc on eight major issues in the campaign.[49] For presenting and comparing the positions of each electoral bloc, these items were the two most informative pieces published in any of these newspapers during the campaign. It is also significant that of all these papers, only *Segodnya* endeavored to publish a special Monday issue with early results of the referendum to adopt the country's new constitution and of the first multiparty parliamentary elections in Russian history.[50]

Informing the Voter: Space to and Bias toward the Candidates

As discussed previously, the Russian press is highly partisan. All the more perplexing, then, that not one of the newspapers in the sample issued an open endorsement. The expressed desire by the editors of all of these papers to strive for greater objectivity than they were allowed in the Soviet era may in part explain this. Be that as it may, the result was that each more covertly pushed its preferences, in both the amount and the quality of the space it devoted to various blocs.

The struggle between objectively covering and actively supporting candidates was perhaps played out most dramatically in *Izvestiya*, which tried simultaneously to cover every bloc while resolutely supporting Russia's Choice. As noted previously, *Izvestiya* offered to interview the leaders of each electoral bloc, and seven of the thirteen accepted. Although Bondaruk maintains the interviews provided each leader equally with "the right to a direct and clear voice, without commentary by us," the tone of the interviews varied dramatically.[51] For example, the questions of Communist party leader Zyuganov were so belligerent, including a long string beginning "Do you or do you not. . . ." and "Did you or did you not . . . ." that Zyuganov shot back, "Even the prosecutor addressed me with more respect. I come here to a paper I've read for years and feel as if I am being interrogated."[52] He had a point. The biographical sketch introducing Zhirinovskii at the beginning of its interview with him was bitterly derogatory, calling his program "typical propaganda designed to lull the voter," and the questions were hostile.[53] A detailed commentary published directly after the interview linked Zhirinovskii to Hitler, argued his promises were "lies," and warned against the threat to Russia's fragile democracy posed by his party and by the Communists.[54] The tone of these interviews sharply contrasted to those with members of proreform groups and was a world away from the cheerleading questions addressed to Russia's Choice leader Yegor Gaidar.[55]

But Bondaruk was astounded by criticism that such interviews were laced with hostile commentary. "This reflects a different approach," he said. "The questions express our feelings about the candidate." *Izvestiya*, he argued, showed objectivity by merely publishing these interviews. But, he said, "It is a very dangerous thing when Americans try to hold us to their standards under our conditions." He called Zhirinovskii a "fascist who may get too many votes in our troubled society and times. Our democracy is too fragile to risk this simply in the interests of journalistic genre. Journalists have a responsibility to influence as much as possible to prevent this."[56]

Indeed, *Izvestiya* carried out nothing short of a crusade against Zhirinovskii. It was the first to recognize the potential power of his populist message, beginning its relentless criticism of him November 26, the day after his first television broadcast. From discrediting his credentials as both a "liberal" and a "democrat," to branding him alternatively a "Bolshevik" and a "Nazi," to detailed attacks on his economic promises, *Izvestiya* sought to counter in print Zhirinovskii's dominance of the airwaves.[57]

Izvestiya's coverage of Russia's Choice in particular, and proreform blocs in general, was categorically different. It published its interview with Gaidar closest to election day, and throughout the campaign its analyses and op-ed pieces were overwhelmingly pro–Russia's Choice. "We have already offered everyone an interview, but beyond this we are not going to give a tribunal to those whose views are antithetical to ours," Bondaruk said.[58] Endless examples from virtually every issue reveal *Izvestiya*'s pro–Russia's Choice bias. The most glaring point was noted previously: in its daily responses to candidates' statements on television, *Izvestiya* took to task every electoral bloc *except* Russia's Choice.[59]

After *Izvestiya*, *Argumenty i fakty* and *Komsomol'skaya pravda* were the papers most overtly biased toward the proreform blocs. Of the fifteen articles in *Argumenty i fakty*, one was about the Communist party and who supported it, one a sharp criticism of the Democratic Party of Russia (DPR) leader Nikolai Travkin, and one an interview with a leader of Future of Russia—New Names. The other twelve were interviews with or sympathetic articles about the four reformist parties—five on Russia's Choice, three on PRES, two on Yabloko, and two on the Russian Movement for Democratic Reform (RDDR). The figures alone reveal the paper's bias, particularly given the editors found it "hard to distinguish" between Russia's Choice and PRES.[60] In *Komsomol'skaya pravda*, all four reader call-in features, and all four long interviews, were with Russia's Choice or PRES candidates. Although the paper was critical of the activities of Russia's Choice leaders Shumeiko and Filatov, like *Izvestiya* its preelection issue carried critiques and caricatures of the alternative reform blocs, with coverage clearly supporting Gaidar and Russia's Choice.[61] More than any other papers, *Argumenty i fakty* and *Komsomol'skaya pravda* ignored the centrist and antireform blocs.[62]

Coverage in the other papers was qualitatively different. *Trud* and *Segodnya* were both proreform in their editorial positions, but they were far more muted than the cheerleading tone of the papers discussed previously. *Trud* was most likely concerned not to offend its more conservative readership, and was extremely subtle in its editorial line. Although the paper ran a long article by an independent economist defending Russia's Choice from attacks by the other reformist blocs, it also ran an equal number of articles and interviews by the alternative reformist groups.[63] *Trud* did save its interviews of Russia's Choice leaders Gaidar and Boris Fedorov for the last days of the campaign, but it also ran interviews with Civic Union and PRES leaders in these same issues.[64] Moreover, *Trud* did not clearly support any one bloc—although its editorial tone was sympathetic to reform, it was rather ambivalent when it came to distinguishing among the four options.

Segodnya, meanwhile, was one paper whose support could not be deduced simply from space allotted, for the paper provided substantial coverage on all of the major contenders. Indeed, even though the paper only began daily publication two days before the election, its 143 election-related items exceeded even *Izvestiya*'s coverage, the most comprehensive of the dailies, by 20 percent.[65] Its coverage of DPR's early surge and later sputter was the only extensive coverage of this party in these papers, and *Segodnya* was often the only paper to report on the press conferences and campaign strategies of other centrist and conservative blocs like Civic Union and the Agrarian party.[66] Still, as mentioned previously, there is no such thing as an objective Russian newspaper. *Segodnya*'s editorial line quite vocally favored the proreform blocs in its editorials and in the overall tone of its coverage, although its attitude among these seemed to be to pick any one of the four.[67]

Two papers in the sample, *Nezavisimaya gazeta* and *Pravda*, were scathingly critical of the government, the president, and even of the elections themselves. It is not surprising that *Nezavisimaya gazeta* was somewhat less uncompromising in its criticism than *Pravda*. But the tone of the editorial line of both papers is testimony to the freedom and independence the newspapers had in determining and propounding their editorial line.

Nezavisimaya gazeta published a barrage of hostile attacks on President Yeltsin and Russia's Choice in virtually every issue from November 9 through December 10. Its editorial line evolved from early support for the centrist blocs DPR and PRES to later sympathy for Yabloko.[68] Although the paper never issued a formal endorsement, two front-page editorials just before the election combined scathing criticism of the other major blocs with thinly disguised sympathetic references to Yabloko.[69] The switch to Yabloko is best explained by three factors: incoherent public ranting by two of DPR's leaders on television that reversed its early momentum in the polls; PRES's announced support for the existing government; and Yabloko leader Grigorii Yavlinskii's increasingly vicious attacks on Gaidar and Yeltsin, to which the editorial board was highly sympathetic.[70] Unlike its counterpart *Segodnya*, this independent paper made no pretensions to objective reporting.[71] The one clear goal of each issue was to criticize Russia's Choice and the president, not necessarily to provide comprehensive information on the candidates for election.[72]

Pravda, after resuming publication, dropped all earlier pretensions of objectivity in casting its support for the Communist party.[73] Before ceasing printing, its daily column *"Dumai Narod, Dumu Svoyu"* ("Think People, the Duma is Yours") featured interviews with leaders of DPR, Civic Union, the Russian National Union, and Dignity and Compassion, all centrist and antireform blocs.[74] But after returning to press, *Pravda* ran seven items about and supporting the Communist party and its candidates, accompanied by a lone interview with the leader of Civic Union. All mention of the other blocs was in the form of epithets in these articles.[75] And an apparent informational piece explaining how to fill out the complicated ballot was in fact a poorly disguised endorsement: "Don't pay attention to those who aren't likable to you. Find the one true association which you want to support. We say this is the Communist party of the Russian Federation. Put a check next to it."[76] Throughout the campaign, *Pravda* leveled scandalous attacks at Russia's Choice, accusing it in lead articles of everything from "buying" the people with bribes during its registration petition drive[77] to "stealing from the people" in its economic program.[78]

Krasnaya zvezda was the only paper with no discernible line. Its brief, factual articles on the registration process provided statistics on all registered blocs, and as noted earlier, its column of quotes of the day excerpted from the leaders of every bloc. In-depth articles almost exclusively focused on the interests of the military, and without exception offered no guidance about who best served those interests. Two clear editorial opinions emerge from *Krasnaya zvezda*'s articles during the campaign: first, the army needs "its man" in parliament, and second, the electoral blocs without exception presented "too little information to say exactly what they think on military matters."[79] Other than this parochial interest, the paper truly was "detached" from the politics of the campaign and published the least material on the elections of the papers in the sample.

As for Zhirinovskii's LDPR, the eventual victor in the PR vote, the newspapers, like the electoral blocs, appear to have been taken completely by surprise by his impressive showing at the polls. Indeed, except for *Izvestiya*, they seemed to take him for a clown with little hope of increasing his popularity beyond a few percentage points. The papers whose strategy was to focus on those blocs with popularity ratings over the 5 percent barrier thus simply ignored him until a few days before the election. When they did write about him, the coverage was universally negative, albeit to differing degrees.[80] Even *Segodnya*, which did comment periodically on Zhirinovskii's more controversial television broadcasts, did not publish in-depth coverage of his campaign until December 10, two days before the vote.[81] On December 11, the paper appeared shocked that his support had risen "from 3 percent to 15 percent" and that he "could finish second." *Nezavisimaya gazeta* mocked Zhirinovskii's use of free television time to make long-winded speeches as a "waste of time," and never really took him seriously.[82] *Trud*'s singular coverage of Zhirinovskii, again late in the campaign, suggested he triggered a brawl at a rock concert and made jokes suggesting the paper did not consider him a serious contender.[83] Typical of its general coverage, *Krasnaya zvezda*'s only coverage of Zhirinovskii was to run a few sentence-long excerpts from his speeches.[84]

It should be noted, however, that Zhirinovskii in turn virtually ignored the print media. In contrast to the other major electoral blocs, he did not run a single advertisement in the papers in this sample, and his only newspaper interview was with *Izvestiya*. If the papers wrote about him less, this is in part because he sought them out less, focusing his media efforts almost exclusively on television. Still, the papers as a whole can be faulted for their late recognition of the serious challenge posed by Zhirinovskii, particularly given the amount of attention they paid to the television broadcasts that he dominated. The press reactions to the election results are discussed at length in the next section.

Two additional general assessments of the campaign coverage in the papers sampled must be noted. First, this discussion has focused on coverage of the electoral blocs in the nationwide PR vote, because this is what the papers themselves focused on. They decided, quite reasonably, to let the regional press cover the campaigns in the single- and two-mandate majority-vote districts. But as election day neared, the papers worried that the vote on election day would be "random," that the public had no idea who or what they would be voting for.[85] The most colorful explanation was given by an industrious *Izvestiya* reporter, who discovered to his horror, on surveying his journalist colleagues a mere four days before election day, that "not one had any idea who the competing candidates even were" in their districts. "And these are journalists, who should be politically aware and active! What about the rest of the citizenry? . . . The vote will hardly be informed."[86]

Second, the papers paid little attention to the smaller blocs, particularly to the thematic blocs such as the Constructive Ecological Movement (KEDR), Women of Russia, and Dignity and Charity. The reasons for this have already been mentioned—they lacked evidence of popular support to warrant spending scarce editorial space on them. This is in sharp contrast to television, where each of the thirteen blocs was allotted an equal two hours of free time. When this television exposure helped them increase their support, as, for example, it did DPR early and LDPR late in the campaign, or decrease it, as with DPR later in the campaign, the papers played a reactive role by adjusting accordingly both the quantity and quality of their coverage of these blocs.

From this review of the campaign coverage in the Russian national press, it would be difficult to sustain the argument that any legal and politically relevant point of view was absent from the major print media. Even when *Pravda* was not publishing, its editor was satisfied that *Nezavisimaya gazeta* was "filling the void that we've left."[87] Although the tone and coverage of the campaign would have been richer had *Pravda* not closed and had *Sovetskaya Rossiya* not been banned, the papers that did publish covered the full spectrum of political views in the campaign.[88]

It should also be clear from the analysis that the voter who read only one of these papers would not have been a very informed voter on election day. One could not, for example, have read only *Komsomol'skaya pravda* and gone to the polls feeling informed about the positions of, say, the Agrarian party. The same is true of *Izvestiya*, for although it was the only paper to offer interviews to leaders of all the blocs, it published little objective material on the candidates it did not like.

Because the Russian press is such a highly partisan and fragmented press, therefore, a voter could not have read just one or two papers and come away with an objective information base from which to judge the candidates. However, the newspapers were free enough and diverse enough so that, taken collectively, they presented the positions and views of all the major contenders for parliament and provided a wealth of information and analysis to the public domain. The fact that the papers were either physically unavailable or fiscally inaccessible for the vast majority of people, combined with the unfortunate nature of the television broadcasts that made them virtually unbearable to watch, explains the general impression that most people felt they had no idea who or what they were voting for.

The Results

None of the papers welcomed Zhirinovskii's election-day success. Their specific reactions followed quite predictably from their coverage of the campaign more generally. *Izvestiya* and *Komsomol'skaya pravda* were loudest in their dismay, and warned of the danger of pending fascism; *Trud* was more muted in its assessment; *Segodnya* expressed surprise but oriented its coverage primarily toward explaining the reasons for the vote; *Nezavisimaya gazeta* blamed President Yeltsin and Russia's Choice; *Krasnaya zvezda* presented the statistics without commentary; and *Pravda* trumpeted the strong showing of the Communists.

The headlines in *Izvestiya* and *Komsomol'skaya pravda* reflected their analyses: *Izvestiya*'s "Country, What Have You Voted For?" expressed embarrassment over the results, and *Komsomol'skaya pravda* lamented, "Monday the 13th: A Gloomy Morning in Russia." *Izvestiya* renewed its comparison of Zhirinovskii to Hitler and national socialism and warned of a Russian version of the "catastrophe of 1933." *Komsomol'skaya pravda* quipped, "They fired boomerangs at the White House" in reference to the October 4 storming of the Supreme Soviet. Its coverage took the form of a search for answers, concluding, "One thing has stayed the same in Russia—it remains painfully unpredictable." Both blamed the reformist blocs for the result: *Izvestiya* argued that they were too complacent in believing the demise of communism meant they could turn their sights on each other; *Komsomol'skaya pravda* accused them of making "every mistake they could possible make."[89]

Segodnya, meanwhile, focused on the reactions of the candidates and blocs themselves. In doing so, it managed to convey its own editorial line of surprise and supported the idea of creating a national, antifascist coalition. A related, and significant point, is that the paper presented less of a panicked tone than the other papers. It rejected the notion that the vote was a catastrophe, suggesting instead that fascism was "only a possible occurrence," and time remained to prevent it.[90]

All three of these papers criticized the reformist blocs for not unifying and for not taking Zhirinovskii seriously.[91] They could easily have leveled the latter criticism against themselves. They all also eagerly and approvingly covered subsequent results showing the reformist blocs would control more parliamentary seats than Zhirinovskii, including a huge majority in the Federation Council.[92]

Trud, meanwhile, perhaps out of concern not to offend its readers, avoided attacking Zhirinovskii. Although also critical of the reformist blocs, *Trud* reasoned that Zhirinovskii "promised the people what they wanted to hear." *Krasnaya zvezda* also demonstrated concern for its readers in the week after the election. Its main concern seemed to be in defending the military against rumors that the army voted overwhelmingly for Zhirinovskii, noting as did the Defense Ministry that the vast majority of the military voted in open, civilian polling places and that real statistics on the military vote are thus not available.[93]

Nezavisimaya gazeta, not surprisingly but somewhat incoherently, blamed the "totalitarian" President Yeltsin and Russia's Choice for the strong LDP showing![94] The paper called the government "inept to protect democracy, and politically incompetent," arguing the people do not want fascism, but the Kremlin is "pushing people in this direction." It argued that hysteria and panic were out of place, as Zhirinovskii was only elected a member of parliament, not Russia's president, and, in keeping with its antigovernment line, even saw some good—that Russia's Choice would not control the parliament.[95]

Finally, *Pravda* was predictably satisfied with the Communist party's strong showing. The paper's response to Zhirinovskii's success was to quote approvingly Zyuganov's statement that the Communists were prepared to cooperate with any bloc in opposition to the government, including Zhirinovskii's, but that they would not cooperate with or support extremists calling for recreating the Soviet Union by force of arms. Given some of Zhirinovskii's campaign statements, this would seem to leave cooperation with him up in the air. But Zyuganov made it clear, and *Pravda* readily approved, that he was willing to cooperate with nonextremists in the LDPR.[96]

Conclusion

The fact that Zhirinovskii did so well in spite of a rush of negative material in the print media in the final days of the campaign is testimony, at least in part, to the limited influence of the print media. When reading a newspaper such as *Pravda* or *Izvestiya*, one gets a strong impression that it is preaching to the choir. A *Nezavisimaya gazeta* columnist put it best, arguing, "It is self-evident that the overwhelming majority of publications and journalists do not inform about the election campaign, but participate in it."[97] Although statistical evidence is difficult to come by, the editors of these papers all seem to agree that readers, given the high costs of the papers, tend to buy papers whose opinions they agree with. Long before the campaign began, *Pravda* already had its readers who supported the Communists and a general antireform line, and *Izvestiya* had its readers who supported radical economic and political reforms. A highly partisan press has partisan readers, and, although over the broad sweep of time there is certainly give and take between readership opinion and editorial orientation, when viewing a single instance such as an election campaign, one must agree with Linnik that "papers like *Pravda* probably tend to solidify the views of those who were pretty much set," rather than winning significant numbers to its side.[98] Perhaps this explains why the editors decided not to issue endorsements—the act would have been redundant.

It might also be added that it would be unfair to charge the newspapers with responsibility for the personalization of the campaign. The candidates took care of that themselves. "What can these parties differ in," Simonov said when discussing the campaign tactics of the electoral blocs. "These are people from a single background, similar education, similar experience. Shakhrai and Gaidar, these are not that different people—so personality is the only way they can differentiate themselves."[99] Such an impression hardly required confirmation by opinion poll statistics and analyses.[100] The candidates themselves referred to the blocs as "partiya Gaidara," "partiya Shakhraia," "blok Yavlinskogo," even "partiya Zyuganova," reflecting their recognition that these are not in fact parties but competing personalities and ambitions.[101] Indeed, the more insistent a bloc was that it really was a party, the more evident that it was personality driven. DPR, for example, made no attempt to organize its campaign around programmatic principles—its ads both on television and in print flashed the images of its three leaders in front of the statement, "It's better with us." Similarly, Shakhrai by early December had abandoned ads of a programmatic nature and centered around the party title, in favor of large photos of himself with the appeal, "For Shakhrai!" References to PRES became insignificant and often nonexistent.

The newspapers therefore did not need to personalize the campaign. They merely reflected the personalization of politics and the campaign as conducted by the politicians themselves. To this extent they may have helped reinforce this tendency, but their coverage presented an accurate picture of the campaign.

If the average voter felt uninformed on election day with regard to the programs and orientations of the various electoral blocs, the newspapers are not to blame. As *Segodnya* lamented as the campaign drew to a close, "We, like all voters, expected that the thirteen participants in the campaign would explain to us, in a short and comprehensible form, first, how they differ from the competition, and second, what they would do if they came to power. Alas, these expectations were in vain."[102] It is the press's function to present the information the candidates provide and to report on it, not to create that information.

As this chapter has demonstrated, the newspapers collectively presented the entire range of views embodied by the candidates themselves. But two factors combined to deny most voters access to the entirety of this information. First, the structure of the Russian press, which is highly partisan and fragmented in the form of a large number of small publications, meant the information and views were scattered across a number of papers. Second, the state of the Russian economy made it impossible for most voters to have access to the entirety of this information. The papers have become too expensive for most people to purchase them in the numbers they were accustomed to in the Soviet era, and they arrive outdated in most provincial areas.

On the first of these factors, the press is only partly to blame; on the second, it is as much a victim as is the rest of society. Most important for this study, these two factors combined to severely limit the influence of these newspapers in the 1993 election campaign. We will never know how the vote might have differed had the average Russian voter watched less television and read more, for example, of *Segodnya, Izvestiya, Nezavisimaya gazeta*, and even *Pravda*. All this analysis can argue is that by not reading all of these papers, the average voter lacked the most comprehensive coverage of the campaign.

Notes

1. This chapter uses *electoral bloc* and *reformers* in place of *party* and *democrats*, respectively. I believe the latter pair to be misleading or misused in contemporary Russia.

2. I do not mean to imply that the newspapers worked as a collective, but that one had to read the entire collection of papers to get complete information on all electoral blocs.

3. *Vestnik Moskovskogo Universiteta. Seriya 10. Zhurnalistika*, no. 1 (1994), pp. 10–23; and *Vestnik Moskovskogo Universiteta. Seriya 10. Zhurnalistika*, no. 2 (1994), pp. 16–27. See also *Svobodnaya mysl'*, no. 2–3 (1994), pp. 122–26; and *Segodnya*, January 2, 1994, p. 7.

4. Interview with Nikolai D. Bondaruk, deputy editor-in-chief, *Izvestiya*.

5. In fact, I have deliberately chosen figures that underestimate the increase. The average monthly salary during the campaign was probably closer to 50,000 rubles.

6. Calculating at rates of 10 rubles to the dollar in 1989, when *Izvestiya* still cost 2 kopeks (one-five hundredth of a dollar), and 1,000 rubles to the dollar in 1993, when it cost 90 rubles (roughly one-eleventh of a dollar).

7. Interview, Bondaruk.

8. Although these editors claim that about two-thirds of their circulation goes outside Moscow, this clashes with the overwhelming impression of the lack of availability of these papers in the provinces. Each editor predicted that within three to four years, the high cost of printing in multiple locations and of delivering across Russia's long distances will force their papers to abandon their national aspirations and focus on Moscow. One can expect a dynamic period of closings and mergers, with a small number of large papers replacing the large number of four- to six-page papers. Interviews with Bondaruk, *Pravda* editor-in-chief Viktor A. Linnik, and Valery P. Simonov, deputy editor-in-chief of *Komsomol'skaya pravda*.

9. *Irreconcilable opposition* was adopted by *Segodnya*, November 9, 1993.

10. Some may challenge including these in a study of national papers. They each reported circulation of 100,000, and even this may be inflated. But they are the best examples of the new, independent newspapers in the country, and the editors of the established papers all cite them as their primary competitors in the future. But the point that in 1993 they lacked a mass readership is well taken, and *Segodnya* is included primarily because I consider it the highest quality Russian-language newspaper available.

11. In many provincial cities, such as Vladivostok, *Argumenty i fakty* is the most widely read Moscow publication among those who read any Moscow newspaper.

12. *Moskovskiye novosti*, no. 26 (June 26–July 3, 1994), p. 10. See also *Kommersant Daily*, July 22, 1994. p. 2.

13. *Svobodnaya mysl'*, no. 2–3 (1994), pp. 122–26; and *Segodnya*, January 2, 1994, p. 7. See also *Vestnik Moskovskogo Universiteta. Seriya 10. Zhurnalistika*, no. 1 (1994), pp. 10–23; and *Vestnik Moskovskogo Universiteta. Seriya 10. Zhurnalistika*, no. 2 (1994), pp. 16–27.

14. I do not mean to impose an American standard on the Russian press. The discussion seeks only to point out that Russian newspapers more closely follow the European tradition of a fragmented, partisan press.

15. "Parlamentskiye Vybory v Rossii: Monitoring osveshcheniya vyborov Rossiyskimi sredstvami massovoy informatsii" (Parliamentary Elections in Russia: Monitoring the coverage of elections by the Russian mass media), *Report of the European Institute of the Mass Media* (February 1994), pp. 18–19.

16. See *Trud*, November 24, 1993. Also interview with Simonov, who said the banning of *Sovetskaya Rossiya* and *Pravda* was a mistake because "a huge mass of people are for these papers." *Pravda* resumed publishing November 2, after meeting President Yeltsin's demand that it replace its editor-in-chief. *Sovetskaya Rossiya* refused a similar demand.

17. See the report in *Nezavisimaya gazeta*, December 1, 1993.

18. Bodaruk and Simonov, interviews.

19. *Delevoy mir*, March 2, 1994, p. 1. This article reports that from January 1992 to December 1993, the price of paper had increased 360 times and printing by 150 times. Of the 33 billion rubles in subsidies issued in 1992–93, the three papers named along with *Sel'skaya zhizn'* and the weekly *Ogonek* received more than 30 percent.

20. "Parlamentskiye Vybory v Rossii," p. 12.

21. See "Parlamentskiye Vybory v Rossii," pp. 35–38, for further details on the finances of the Russian press. The progovernment publications receiving subsidies were *Argumenty i fakty* and *Komsomol'skaya pravda*; the centrist *Trud* also received a subsidy, as did *Pravda* in early 1993. *Rossiiskaya vesti* and *Rossiiskaya gazeta* are government publications financed from the state budget.

22. The government publication *Rossiiskaya gazeta* also temporarily closed.

23. Simonov admitted that accepting a subsidy can lead to pressure. He bristled at "occasional phone calls from members of the president's administration." Although these do not play "a major role" in *Komsomol'skaya pravda*'s content, they are discussed at meetings of the editorial board and "taken into account," he said. But tension between editorial boards and public officials over what the former print of the latter is hardly unique to Russia.

24. The newspaper entered into the partnership of its own accord, and, Moscow rumors notwithstanding, there is absolutely no evidence of complicity between the Russian government and the Greek partner. The paper's decision to decline further subsidies reflects its desire to gain financial independence from a government it opposes. Linnik, interview.

25. *Segodnya*, December 11, 1993, p. 2.

26. See *Polozheniye o vyborakh deputatov Gosudarstvennoy dumy v 1993 godu* (Regulations on the Elections for Deputies to the State Duma in 1993).

27. *Moscow Times*, December 2, 1993. Many countries limit publication of poll results, but the limits usually range from 2 to 3 days before election day. Ten days is unusually long.

28. Simonov, Interview.

29. *Segodnya*, December 11, 1993, p. 1.

30. *Izvestiya, Komsomol'skaya pravda*, and *Segodnya* all published such information after December 2, the day the ban took effect.

31. See *Segodnya*, December 11, 1993. Even Sergei Filatov, Yeltsin's chief of staff, told journalists the results of an opinion poll. *Komsomol'skaya pravda* tweaked him, saying, "We, however, are law-abiding," and published comments but not results on December 9, 1993, p. 1.

32. See all issues of these papers from December 1 through December 4. Because Shumeiko was press minister, some regional papers reportedly acted as if his wishes were commands.

33. The editors of *Izvestiya, Komsomol'skaya pravda*, and *Pravda* all stated that selective acceptance of campaign ads was not allowed. Although I was unable to find this provision in any law or decree, Article 28 of *Polozheniye o vyborakh* stated that any publication having the government as a founder or receiving government financing "is required to provide equal access to candidates." Presumably, this would include equal access to advertising space. In any case, as suggested throughout this chapter, the financial situation of all Russian newspapers is such that virtually any advertising revenue is considered a blessing.

34. *Segodnya*, November 20, 1993, p. 3.

35. *Trud*, November 24, 1993.

36. The Russian-American Press and Information Center (RAPIC) reports that *Izvestiya* alone published twenty articles on this subject during the campaign. See RAPIC Report, "Zhirinovsky Received Most TV Exposure during Campaign according to New Study by Russian-American Press and Information Center," December 15, 1993.

37. Bondaruk, interview. The chair of Russian Television, Oleg Poptsov, told *Izvestiya*, "It is more difficult for TV journalists to keep silent than to speak," arguing that the papers were too critical of television. But *Komsomol'skaya pravda* editor Simonov noted that the print media fight when pressured by the government and said the print journalists were justly criticizing their television colleagues for not fighting government restrictions on their work.

38. The quotes are from *Izvestiya*, November 25, 1993, p. 1; November 26, 1993, December 1, 1993. The column "Tsitaty telekampanii" appeared daily beginning November 25, p. 1.

39. *Izvestiya*, November 27, 1993.

40. *Nezavisimaya gazeta*, November 19, 1993, p. 1, and December 7, 1993, p. 2. See also the RAPIC Report, "Coverage of the Election Campaign by the Russian Media," December 2, 1993. Television news particularly during the first week of the campaign was blatantly pro-Russia's Choice. The officials soon withdrew their candidacies.

41. See RAPIC Report, "Zhirinovkii Received Most TV Exposure," December 15, 1993.

42. *Krasnaya zvezda*, November 27, 1993, p. 1.

43. Bondaruk, interview.

44. Of course, in terms of overall television exposure the smaller blocs had less money to buy additional time. But the proportion of time a relatively insignificant group received was far greater than what would be provided minor parties in, say, American election campaigns.

45. Bondaruk, interview. *Izvestiya*, December 9, 1993, pp. 1–4. Those interviewed were the leaders of PRES, Yabloko, the Communist party, DPR, LDPR, the Agrarian party, Women of Russia, and Russia's Choice. Those not interviewed were the leaders of RDDR, Civic Union, KEDR, Future of Russia–New Names, and Dignity and Compassion. There is no pattern of favoritism in evidence.

46. Both editors were quite persuaded that their strategy for covering the campaign was one of "absolute objectivity," as Simonov put it, rather than support for one or another party.

47. See RAPIC Report, "Coverage of the Election Campaign by the Russian Media."

48. *Krasnaya zvezda*, December 10, 1993, p. 2.

49. *Segodnya*, November 27, 1993, p. 3, and December 7, 1993, p. 3. The first of these was a "graphical interpretation" of each electoral bloc's ideological orientation and that of its top leaders. The second was a table of their "basic views" on major issues: national-state formation (federation, confederation, unitary state, etc.); type of federal authority (presidential, parliamentary); orientation toward private property; economic model; external economic orientation (open, protectionist); solutions for inflation; relations to former Soviet states (preserve CIS, re-integration); and foreign policy orientation. Women of Russia was left out because it declined to provide the necessary information.

50. *Segodnya*, December 13, 1993, p. 1.

51. Bondaruk, interview.

52. *Izvestiya*, November 19, 1993, p. 4.

53. *Izvestiya*, November 30, 1993, p. 4.

54. See *Izvestiya*, November 29, 1993, p. 4; November 30, 1993, December 2, 1993, and almost daily commentaries thereafter. One article responding to statements of members of DPR and LDPR on television was titled, "*Gospoda Zhirinovskiy i Govorukhin Derzhat Izbirateley za Polnykh Idiotov*" ("Mr. Zhirinovskii and Mr. Govorukhin Take the Voters to be Complete Idiots"). *Izvestiya*, November 26, 1993, p. 1.

55. *Izvestiya*, December 8, 1993, p. 4.

56. Bondaruk, interview. Coincidentally, the author's interview with Bondaruk took place after Bondaruk emerged from a meeting with his correspondents, at which he was blasted for publishing the interview with Zyuganov "without commentary"!

57. See in particular *Izvestiya*, November 29, November 30, and December 9.

58. Bondaruk, interview. He was responding to complaints by DPR candidate Oleg Bogomolov, who complained that *Izvestiya* denied him the right to publish an article, after having run an op-ed by Russia's Choice candidate and military advisor

to President Yeltsin, Dmitri Volkogonov. "Volkogonov's view is *Izvestiya*'s view," Bondaruk explained.

59. For two examples, see *Izvestia* issues of November 19, 1993, and December 1, 1993. As election day neared, references to all other blocs were associated with the communist past, or with warnings of economic collapse as in Ukraine, or of approaching Nazi-style dictatorship.

60. *Argumenty i fakty*, nos. 46, 47, 48 (1993).

61. See *Komsomol'skaya pravda*, December 9, 1993.

62. I found no items in *Komsomol'skaya pravda* coverage of the programs of any "centrist" or antireform blocs. Their mentions were almost exclusively limited to references to their appearances on television and critiques of specific statements. The Communist party is another matter, but articles on it were in the form of warnings to support the reformist blocs.

63. See *Trud*, November 19, November 23, December 1, December 4, and December 9.

64. *Trud*, December 8, December 9, December 11.

65. The figures are from the RAPIC Report, "Coverage of the Election Campaign." See *Nezavisimaya gazeta* on November 9, November 11, November 12, November 19, November 25, December 7, December 8, and December 9. The November issues were heavily pro-PRES; the later issues focused on Yabloko.

66. See *Segodnya*, November 18, November 20, November 25, November 27, December 4, and December 11.

67. I was persuaded that *Segodnya* leaned toward favoring PRES. Others, though, felt it supported Russia's Choice, and still others that it supported Yabloko.

68. For attacks on Russia's Choice and President Yeltsin, see the November 25 and November 30 issues.

69. See the front-page editorials on December 8 and December 10.

70. See *Nezavisimaya gazeta* on November 9, November 11, November 12, November 19, November 25, December 7, December 8, and December 9. The November issues were heavily pro-PRES; the later issues focused on Yabloko.

71. *Segodnya* formed in early 1993 when several *Nezavisimaya gazeta* journalists walked out in protest over the editorial line and lack of objective reporting.

72. What existed on the other blocs was buried in short items in the middle pages.

73. Linnik had said his paper would not issue a formal endorsement of any bloc. Although his paper would only present material sympathetic to the Communist party, Civic Union, the Agrarian party, and DPR, "to single out any one opposition leader doesn't make any sense to me," he said. "The opposition is much broader than communists." Linnik, interview.

74. See *Pravda*, November 13, November 17, November 18, November 19.

75. See *Pravda,* December 10, December 11. In a review of all electoral blocs on the eve of the election, *Pravda* even ran a paragraph sympathetic to Zhirinovskii, the single such item in the entire sample during the campaign.

76. *Pravda*, December 10, 1993.

77. *Pravda*, November 13, 1993. Even *Nezavisimaya gazeta* conceded that other than the Communist party, Russia's Choice was probably the single bloc that

did *not* resort to such illegal tactics. *Nezavisimaya gazeta*, November 9 and November 11, 1993.

78. *Pravda*, November 16, 1993, pp. 1–2.

79. See especially *Krasnaya zvezda* December 7, p. 2, and December 8, 1993, p. 2.

80. The sole exception is the one paragraph mentioned above in *Pravda*.

81. *Segodnya,* December 11, 1996.

82. In its last preelection issue, the editor-in-chief published a rambling front-page editorial, riddled with nonsequitors, that argued Russia's Choice caused Zhirinovskii's rise.

83. *Trud*, December 9, 1993, p. 1. "Zhirinovskii on December 12 will still only be considered an injured, wounded victim," the article concluded.

84. Zhirinovskii was one of the nine who submitted material on the paper's solicitation for the December 10 issue, discussed previously. However, this was essentially free advertising space offered to all blocs and hardly counts as professional journalistic coverage.

85. See *Segodnya*, December 4 and December 7; *Komsomol'skaya pravda*, December 7 and December 9; *Izvestiya*, December 8; and *Nezavisimaya gazeta*, December 2.

86. *Izvestiya*, December 8, 1993, p. 4.

87. Linnik, interview.

88. Interestingly, *Sovetskaya Rossiya* reopened on December 11, the day before the election, without a single election-related item in the paper.

89. See *Investiya,* December 14, 1993, p. 1, and *Komsomol'skaya pravda*, December 14, 1993, p. 1.

90. *Segodnya*, December 14 and December 15, 1993, p. 1.

91. See, for example, the article in *Segodnya*, December 25, 1993, p. 2.

92. These results trickled out of the TsIK and the president's office over the course of the next fourteen days. Final results were not published until December 28.

93. See the papers from December 14 through December 17. Reports about the military vote continued for weeks after the election. Apparently, statistics showing that one-third of the military vote went to Zhirinovskii come from data in the few closed polling places and from exit polls. I thank Brian Taylor for keeping me abreast of his research on this controversy.

94. *Nezavisimaya gazeta*, December 10, 1993.

95. *Nezavisimaya gazeta*, December 14 and 15, 1993.

96. *Pravda*, December 14, 1993.

97. *Nezavisimaya gazeta*, December 2, 1993.

98. Linnik, interview.

99. Simonov interview

100. See *Segodnya*, November 30, 1993, for one such statistical analysis.

101. This reflects a better understanding of the candidates than of many Western observers, who see political parties where there are none.

102. *Segodnya*, December 7, 1993.

CHAPTER NINE

The Mass Media
and the Electorate

Timothy J. Colton

THE EFFECTS of mass media on the elections were examined from the top down by Laura Roselle Helvey in chapter 7 and Joel Ostrow in chapter 8; they analyzed the conduct of the television and press establishments and the information product they generated. This chapter approaches the phenomenon from the bottom up, charting and assessing regularities in the electorate's consumption of and responses to media output during the 1993 campaign.

Although the news media are all but unreconnoitered territory for students of post-Soviet elections, they have attracted attention in the United States and other mature democracies for a half-century. Interest in the theme has always been normative as well as scientific. There was always an underlying unease among the pioneers of election scholarship, writing out of Columbia University during and just after World War II, about the potential of modern communications technology to manipulate—something many scholars and critics feared was augured in anti-utopian fiction and in Adolph Hitler's real-world subversion of German democracy by radio propaganda. These scholars were struck and rather reassured by the degree to which they found press, radio, and, eventually, television information to be mediated by interpersonal networks and other filters.[1]

The media have of late roused renewed concern among specialists on public opinion and voting in the West. Recent work revisits some of the core issues of the early studies, as it puzzles over the domination and seeming trivialization of vote seeking by the television screen and by the "sound bites" and reductive "horse race" images it exudes. The repercussions for democracy are grand and the debates unresolved. Despite a mountain of learned books and articles, a leading expert can lament about U.S. electoral research that, "we have not adequately examined the implications for society and campaigning of the transitions from face-to-face to electronic communities."[2]

If Americanists and Europeanists feel they have handled the subject inadequately, pity the poor Russianists: they have barely *raised* the issue during the historical instant that competitive elections have been on their agenda. This chapter shall contribute to an empirically grounded discussion and identify some basal realities about media exposure and effects in the parliamentary campaign of 1993. The study draws chiefly on individual-level data from a two-wave survey of a national probability sample of 3,905 eligible voters, interviewed across the Russian Federation before and again after election day. I open by discussing the relative importance of the mass media and by mapping quantitative and qualitative patterns of media intake. I then profile the audience for mass media information during the campaign. In subsequent sections of the chapter I link media consumption to political knowledge and sophistication and to the ballot box decisions registered on December 12. I conclude with brief observations about media bias.

The Campaign as a Mass Media Event

A fascinating and at times baffling hallmark of Russian democratization has been the distortion of developmental sequences historically observed in the West. Electoral campaigning is a case in point. In the early democratizing countries, parties spawned as legislative factions or political clubs were off and running before the suffrage was broadened and possessed national and local machines, structurally ramified and reliant on oral and simple print communication, decades in advance of instantaneous communications. In Russia, by contrast, the universal franchise arrived in one fell swoop in the 1990s, by which time its subjects-become-citizens were long before wired in to television.[3] The media revolution preceded rather than followed the emergence of parties and of the other institutional tissue of an orderly mass politics.

The 1993 Russian election manifests this inversion in spades. Face-to-face communication about the campaign was abundant, as 73 percent of the respondents in our preelection interviews—carried out in late November and early December—reported having talked about politics with family or friends at least once in the preceding week (see table 9-1).[4] Because of the rudimentary nature of political organization, though, direct contact with the parties, with nominees for the State Duma and the Federation Council, and with their agents was negligible. Four percent of our survey respondents had attended a candidates' meeting or political rally during the week, and merely one third said they had seen an election poster.[5] The mass media were far and away the principal conduit to the political arena. More than 85 percent of informants indicated some exposure to the campaign the preceding week via one or more of the newspapers, magazines, radio, and television. Approximately one fifth had obtained some information from one mass medium, around 30 percent from two media, and an equal portion from three media; 4 percent had partaken of all four media.

Of the quartet, it was television, technically the most advanced medium and the most recent to saturate Russian households, that overshadowed all in 1993. Seventy-seven percent of the individuals my colleagues and I que-

Table 9-1. *Involvement with the Election during One Week of the Campaign*[a]

Percent

Activity	Frequency
Attended a candidates' meeting or rally	
No	96
Yes	4
Saw election posters	
None	66
A few	29
Many	5
Discussed politics with family or friends	
Never	27
Once or several times	33
Almost daily or daily	40
Obtained information from newspapers, magazines, radio, and television	
No information	15
Information from one medium	22
Information from two media	31
Information from three media	28

a. *Don't knows* and *refusals to answer* are excluded from behavioral indicators, including measures of media consumption, in this and all other tables in the chapter. As a rule, only several percent of respondents were unable to give answers to such questions.

Table 9-2. *Exposure to the Campaign through the Respective Mass Media*

Percent

Frequency in week before interview	Newspapers	Magazines[a]	Radio	Television
Never	55	94	39	23
Once	6	—	4	6
Several times	24	—	24	31
Almost daily	8	—	14	18
Daily	7	—	19	22

a. Because magazines are published monthly or, less commonly in Russia, weekly, respondents were not asked about more frequent exposure to them.

ried during the campaign had watched a television program containing information about the election the preceding week, nearly twice as many as had netted any materials from a newspaper (see table 9-2). For exposure at daily or almost-daily frequency, the asymmetry between television and newspapers was even greater—40 percent to 15 percent. Radio occupied a middle position between the two of them, and magazines were consulted by only 6 percent—a telling difference between Russia and, say, the United States or Germany, where news magazines packed with political reporting and gossip have enormous readerships.

To say that television had the widest reach is not to say it was the only game in town or that it had its viewers all to itself. Media markets intermingle in the Russian Federation, as in any industrial society, and so they did during the 1993 election. As can be read from the correlation matrix in table 9-3, levels of exposure to the respective news media were highly interrelated. Especially large correlations are evident among the three main mass media—that is, between television use and radio use ($r = .40$), television and newspapers ($r = .39$), and newspapers and radio ($r = .34$). Magazine readership was fairly well connected with use of the other print medium, newspapers ($r = .26$), but less significantly, by comparison, with exposure to television and radio.

The cross-cutting of media subaudiences is depicted more concretely in table 9-4. Few consumers, even in the television market, were prisoners of any one medium in November and December 1993. The small set of magazine readers had the most catholic tastes, as only 5 percent of them confined themselves to magazines and two thirds paid some attention to all three media alternatives. Newspapers were next in order of exclusiveness, followed by radio and television. In each category, regular consumers (who came across campaign information in that medium every day or almost every

Table 9-3. *Correlation Matrix (Pearson's* r) *for Frequency of Exposure to the Campaign through the Four Media*[a]

	Magazines	Radio	Television
Newspapers	.26*	.34*	.39*
Magazines	—	.12*	.09*
Radio	—	—	.40*

a. Frequency measured on a three-point index for newspapers, radio, and television (0 for no exposure; 1 for exposure once or twice a week; 2 for daily or almost daily exposure) and on a two-point index for magazines (0 for no exposure; 1 for some exposure).
*p <.01 (two-tailed test)

day) had much more recourse to the other media than did occasional consumers (who used the medium once or several times a week). Even in the television subaudience, the most insular of the four, 87 percent of regular watchers and 75 percent of occasional watchers acquired at least some campaign information from one of the other media, and 43 percent of regular television viewers and 30 percent of the occasional viewers were exposed to two of the other media.

Quantitative and Qualitative Consumption

Media use comes into crisper focus if we scrutinize its quality as well as its quantitative extent. Persons who had availed themselves of presentations about the campaign from one medium or another were asked in the preelection interview whether they had done so closely, not very closely, or not closely at all.[6] For three of the four media, the modal response, given by about 40 to 50 percent of the respondents, was the in-between category, "Not very closely" (see table 9-5). It is fair to say that, on the whole, campaign-relevant information rubbed off on the Russian electorate in 1993 more than it was eagerly sought out.[7]

There was a pronounced differentiation among the mass media in the qualitative dimension, just as there was in the quantitative dimension. The advantage here was with the print media, not the electronic media. Sixty-two percent of magazine readers insisted that they had carefully read the campaign materials they came across in that medium. Newspaper readers, a much more numerous group than magazine readers, came next with 44 percent, and the two most extensive subaudiences, for radio and television, trailed, with 37 and 34 percent, respectively, saying they were attentive to what they heard and saw. On the face of it, the subaudiences for the elec-

Table 9-4. *Overlaps in Mass Media Audiences for Campaign Information*

Percent

Medium and frequency of exposure[a]	Number of other media to which exposed[b]			
	None	One	Two	Three
Newspapers				
Occasional readers	4	28	62	6
Regular readers	2	15	67	17
Magazines				
Readers	5	6	22	67
Radio				
Occasional listeners	13	40	42	5
Regular listeners	7	35	49	9
Television				
Occasional viewers	25	41	30	4
Regular viewers	13	36	43	8

a. *Regular consumers* took in information about the campaign through the given medium almost daily or daily; *occasional consumers* did so once or several times a week. This distinction does not apply to magazine readers.

b. At least one reported exposure in week before preelection interview.

tronic media, wider by far than the print media's, were also typified by shallower involvement with the electoral process. The newspaper and magazine subaudiences, to judge by our respondents' self-assessments, were both narrower and deeper in their election involvement.

The quantitative and qualitative aspects of media exposure did not contradict one another but were mutually reinforcing in Russia in 1993, a not uncommon thing in the developed democracies, too. With respect to each medium for which we can distinguish regular from occasional users—newspapers, radio, and television—there was a pronounced association between the quantity of the citizen's intake and its quality. Correlation coefficients between measures of quantity and intensity were practically identical across media: .34 for newspaper reading, .35 for radio, and .36 for television.[8] Russians with heftier appetites for political information were thus doubly privileged in that they also tended to be more alert to what they were digesting. As for mass media grazers, according to the data, they were both more intermittent and more casual users.

The Audience

Just who made up the audience for mass media information about the election? What kinds of people were overrepresented and what kinds un-

Table 9-5. *Self-Reported Quality of Consumption of Mass Media Information about the Campaign*

Percent

	Attention to materials		
Medium	Not close at all	Not very close	Close
Newspapers	16	40	44
Magazines	11	27	62
Radio	14	49	37
Television	15	51	34

derrepresented in the auditorium? Who ingested the most and the best information?

Statistical analysis establishes that the intensity of the subjective interest taken in the political world was by far the heartiest predictor of Russians' attentiveness to the news media on the eve of the 1993 election. More than anything, it was curiosity about, and a sense of engagement with, public affairs that seem to have impelled citizens to switch on the television or radio (or not switch it off) when it came time for news or partisan broadcasts, or to break open the pages of a newspaper or magazine. To illustrate from raw proportions, a mere 6 percent of those who claimed no interest in the parliamentary election regularly read stories about the campaign in the press and only 19 percent took in such information from television; at the opposite pole, 33 percent of individuals who reported being very interested in the election took in information about it regularly from newspapers and 72 percent from television.

As the correlation coefficients in table 9-6 reveal more systematically, interest in politics in general and interest in the 1993 parliamentary campaign specifically went hand and hand with greater media use, and the effect is visible for political signals emanating from *each* of the news media (most weakly for magazines,[9] most strongly for television) and from all four combined. Of the two measures of interest, the one targeted on the 1993 election was the more powerful influence, undoubtedly because of its direct link to the drama and stakes of the campaign. The causal relationship between subjective interest and media consumption was in all likelihood a reciprocal one: exposure to political news and advertising in the media would have stimulated interest in the campaign (if not in politics in the abstract) as well as being stimulated by it.[10]

Table 9-6. *Association between Exposure to Campaign Information and Political Interest (Pearson's* r*)*[a]

Medium	Interest in politics	Interest in election
Newspapers	.37*	.40*
Magazines	.11*	.11*
Radio	.29*	.35*
Television	.38*	.48*
All media combined	.45*	.53*

a. Frequency of exposure is measured on the same index for individual media as in table 9-3. The combined media score is the sum of the values for the four individual media, and ranges from 0 to 7. Interest in politics is measured on a three-point index (0 for no or very rare attention to politics; 1 for attention sometimes; 2 for constant attention). Interest in the campaign is also a three-point index (0 for no interest; 1 for some interest; and 2 for a good deal of interest).
*p <.01 (two-tailed test)

Over and above subjective interest, the level of exposure to political messages in the mass media varied noticeably among different segments of the population. Standardized regression coefficients for five pertinent sociodemographic variables are given in the top panel of table 9-7. By a wide margin, the most efficient predictors of high media exposure were age and education. Older and better-educated electors sought out conspicuously more information in all four of the news media. Education proved to be more tightly related than age to newspaper stories, a natural enough finding given the greater intellectual investment required to read a newspaper; age was better tied than education to radio listening and television viewing, forms of activity that make fewer mental demands than perusing a newspaper and that also pose no accessibility problem for the elderly, who may have a harder time than younger persons in affording newspapers and will not see them in a work setting.[11] Gender, ethnic origin, and community size also account for some of the variation in media consumption in 1993, although the regression coefficients are much lower than for age and education and cross fewer significance thresholds. Men were more apt than women to learn about the campaign from the media, especially from newspapers. Ethnic Russians made somewhat more use than non-Russians of the broadcast media, in which non-Russians have fewer options to consume the product in their native languages than they do for the print media. And residents of rural and small-town communities had more exposure than inhabitants of the big cities.

Incorporation into the regression of the two indicators of political interest—in general and in the 1993 campaign—doubles or triples explanatory power, as can be seen in the bottom panel of table 9-7. Felt interest in poli-

Table 9-7. *Influence of Sociodemographic Variables and Political Interest on Exposure to Campaign Information (OLS Beta Coefficients)*

Independent variables	Newspapers	Magazines	Radio	Television	All media
Sociodemographic variables only					
Age	.26*	.05*	.33*	.27*	.37*
Education[a]	.31*	.11*	.16*	.22*	.30*
Male	.10*	.03**	.03	.03	.07*
Ethnic Russian	.02	−.04**	.07*	.05*	.05*
Community size	−.04*	−.01	.01	−.07*	−.04*
Adjusted R²	.103	.011	.097	.073	.139
Sociodemographic variables and political interest					
Age	.13*	.01	.23*	.11*	.20*
Education	.19*	.08*	.06*	.07*	.14*
Male	−.05*	.02	−.01	−.03**	.01
Ethnic Russian	.01	−.04*	.06*	.05*	.04*
Community size	−.03	−.00	.02	−.05*	−.02
Interest in politics	.19*	.06*	.16*	.22*	.25*
Interest in election	.29*	.08*	.24*	.36*	.38*
Adjusted R²	.246	.023	.195	.288	.387

a. Education measured on a three-point index (with values for elementary or incomplete secondary education, secondary or secondary specialized education, and higher education).
*p <.01
**p <.05

tics and, more emphatically, in the parliamentary election per se obviously surpass all of the sociodemographic characteristics in impact on attentiveness to the media. Nonetheless, most of the relationships between social factors and media intake do survive in diminished form the control for the effects of political interest. Age and education level stay positively associated with media exposure throughout; Russian ethnicity keeps its positive relationship with openness to the broadcast media; and community size remains negatively correlated with media use.

When social characteristics and political interest are brought into the picture in combination, the cumulative shaping effect on the political audience can be formidable. For example, when age, education, and ethnicity simultaneously assumed their most consumption-favorable values (that is, when the voter had the equivalent of a college education, was sixty years of age or older, and was an ethnic Russian), intake of campaign information from each of the mass media was dramatically higher than when these values were at their most consumption-unfavorable (when the citizen did not have a secondary school diploma, was younger than forty, and belonged to a minority national group). Under triple-favorable conditions, 72 percent reported receiving campaign information from television daily or almost daily, whereas only 19 percent of triple-unfavorable citizens had this much exposure. Among triple-positive persons who also evinced maximum interest in the election campaign, a commanding 85 percent reported regular reception of election information from television.

Another question of theoretical interest is whether the 1993 campaign audience contained pockets of concentrated activism. Researchers in the West have discovered that a stratum of "opinion leaders" there serves as a crucial link between rank-and-file electors and the wellsprings of political information, mainly the mass media. In this "two-step flow of communications," as Paul Lazarsfeld and his Columbia colleagues wrote in their seminal study of the 1940 presidential election, "ideas often flow from radio and print to the opinion leaders and from them to the less active sections of the population."[12]

According to our survey research, this configuration was part and parcel of the 1993 Russian campaign. A substantial minority of our respondents, when asked after the election whether they had at any time during the campaign attempted to convince others of "the merits of one or another bloc [party or quasi party] or candidate," replied in the affirmative. Twenty-three percent had exercised opinion leadership vis-à-vis family members and the very same fraction, 23 percent, vis-à-vis nonfamily members.[13] These two behaviors were intimately interrelated ($r = .56$), and they were also influenced by socioeconomic status and by interest in the campaign.[14]

Although we cannot ascertain in minute detail how opinion leaders interacted with nonleaders, we can pull out of the data that they brought to the transaction markedly more exposure to the campaign via the mass media than the nonleaders. Opinion leadership within the family setting was associated with higher levels of exposure in each medium except magazines and with a summary measure for all media; nondomestic opinion leadership went with higher exposure to each separate medium and to the four in sum (see table 9-8). The relationships were sturdiest for television and newspapers.

Media Exposure and Political Knowledge and Sophistication

To get at the function of the mass media in the campaign, it is necessary to consider not only the contours of the audience but the cognitive and behavioral consequences of any individual's placement in it. A fundamental question to pose regards information transfer. Were media-attentive citi-

Table 9-8. *Association between Exposure to Campaign Information and Opinion Leadership (Pearson's r)*

Citizens	Newspapers	Magazines	Radio	Television	All media
Opinion leaders within family	.14*	.03	.12*	.17*	.18*
Opinion leaders outside family	.15*	.06*	.10*	.15*	.18*
Combined index[a]					

a. This index combines positive responses to the questions about in-family and out-of-family opinion leadership.
*p <.01 (two-tailed test)

zens more knowledgeable about the campaign and the issues being fought out in it than their compatriots who consumed less media output? If they were, was it a result of media exposure in and of itself or a result of some other cause or causes?

Let us begin with some elementary yardsticks of political knowledge. A battery of questions about political players and issues were put to respondents in the preelection and the postelection interviews. Among other things, they were asked at various points: (1) whether they recognized the names and programs of the thirteen political parties that contested the State Duma election; (2) to identify the parties headed by seven national leaders (Alevtina Fedulova of Women of Russia, Yegor Gaidar of Russia's Choice, Mikhail Lapshin of the Agrarians, Sergei Shakhrai of the Party of Russian Unity and Accord [PRES], Arkadii Vol'skii of Civic Union, Vladimir Zhirinovskii of the Liberal Democratic Party of Russia [LDPR], and Gennadii Zyuganov of the Communist Party of the Russian Federation [KPRF]; (3) to recall the names of the individual candidates standing for the State Duma and the Federation Council in their electoral district; and (4) on five major issues, to name up to three parties whose policy positions were closest to his or her viewpoint and three whose positions were the most distant.

Comparison of means, as displayed in table 9-9, is enough to get across the point that political knowledge did very much rise with rising levels of media consumption. The relationship shines through for all four measures of knowledge employed and for all four mass media. Occasional readers of campaign information in the press, for instance, recognized 2.9 times as many political parties as those with no exposure to the election in the media; they also identified 2.1 times as many leaders, recalled the names of 2.5 times as many individual candidates, and volunteered 3.5 times as many spatial locations for the parties. Regular press readers had commensurately

Table 9-9. *Political Knowledge by Level of Exposure to the Campaign through the Mass Media*

Medium and frequency of exposure	Parties recognized	Leader identified	Candidates recalled	Parties located
Newspapers				
Occasional readers	5.7	3.6	2.7	3.9
Regular readers	7.2	4.2	3.3	5.4
Magazines				
Readers	6.3	4.0	3.0	5.1
Radio				
Occasional listeners	5.1	3.3	2.3	3.4
Regular listeners	6.2	3.5	2.7	4.2
Television				
Occasional viewers	4.7	3.1	2.2	3.1
Regular viewers	6.4	3.7	2.7	4.4
All citizens	4.9	3.4	2.2	3.3
Citizens with no media exposure	2.0	1.7	1.1	1.1

higher scores—3.6 times the baseline of no-exposure citizens for party recognition, 2.5 times for leader identification, 3.0 times for recall of candidates' names, and 4.9 times for placement of parties' positions. The count can be repeated for magazines, radio, and television, with broadly similar results.

The story told in table 9-9—that the higher the exposure to the campaign through the mass media, the more competent the citizen—is an important one. It casts cold water on a staple of the criticism and self-criticism of the Russian media in 1993 that held that media content was so paltry, or the message so deformed by government intimidation or by media wizards like Zhirinovskii, that usable political information and cues did not penetrate to the ordinary voter. Our data point in a very different direction: Moderate consumers of media information knew more about the electoral contest than nonconsumers and avid consumers more than moderate consumers. Generally speaking, media exposure coincided with political knowledge, not political ignorance.

As a guide to cause and effect, table 9-9 must be treated with caution. For one thing, the varieties of exposure to political information in the respective mass media are interrelated, as we saw in tables 9-3 and 9-4. The great majority of regular users of any given medium were at the same time users of one or several other media. Eighty-seven percent of the regular watchers of television, who graded so high on our political competence tests, also absorbed campaign information from other media; 98 percent of the heavy newspaper readers tuned in to other media. Without statistical controls for the effects of other media exposure variables, it is impossible to disentangle the separate influence of any one of them. The second limitation of the data presented in table 9-9 is that more remote variables that may, in principle, exert some concurrent and perhaps confounding influence on levels of political information and on levels of media exposure were excluded. It has already been noted that interest in political affairs and in the election contest, and to a lesser extent demographic traits such as age and education, were associated with differing levels of media exposure in the 1993 campaign. It might well be that some such variables would also contribute directly to political knowledge and sophistication, without being routed through systems of mass communication.

Multiple regression analysis, which takes overlap among explanatory variables into account, helps resolve this double bind. The upper panel of table 9-10 puts forth standardized regression coefficients for the media-use indicators only, run conjointly as independent variables against the four measures of knowledge as dependent variables. Twelve of the sixteen coefficients are statistically significant at an exacting level ($p < .01$), meaning that it was most unlikely that these associations could have occurred through chance alone; both exceptions are for magazine use.

Unlike the cross-tabulation in table 9-9, this exercise makes allowance for the tendency of various kinds of media use to go together: the regression coefficients estimate the information value added per unit of use of the particular medium identified, holding consumption of the other three media constant. As can be seen, newspaper use is more predictive of knowledge on two measures, television watching is best for one knowledge measure, and these two media are in a dead heat for a fourth measure.

The regression model permits us, moreover, to discriminate among the differential effects of particular media on citizens' comprehension of various kinds of political phenomena. The results for the two leading media, television and the press, make good intuitive sense. It is eminently reasonable that television would be the more knowledge-inducing medium for the softest indicator of knowledge, brand-name recognition of the parties. It is equally plausible that for the tougher tests of identification of party leaders and unprompted recall of individual candidates' names, exposure to the printed word would come out ahead.

Table 9-10. *Influence of Media Exposure and Political Interest on Political Knowledge (OLS Beta Coefficients)*

Independent variables	Parties recognized	Leaders identified	Candidates recalled	Parties located
Media only				
Newspaper exposure	.19*	.23*	.20*	.17*
Magazine exposure	.01	.03**	.02	.05*
Radio exposure	.12*	.04**	.07*	.07*
Television exposure	.24*	.20*	.13*	.16*
Adjusted R^2	.180	.146	.102	.103
Media and political interest				
Newspaper exposure	.11*	.13*	.14*	.07*
Magazine exposure	.00	.03**	.02	.05*
Radio exposure	.07*	-.00	.04**	.02
Television exposure	.14*	.09*	.05*	.05*
Interest in politics	.22*	.33*	.23*	.40*
Interest in election	.15*	.08*	.06*	.03**
Adjusted R^2	.244	.245	.151	.235

*$p <.01$
**$p <.05$

The bottom panel of table 9-10 shows what happens when we round out the model by injecting our two indicators of political interest, which were shown previously to have a major effect on voter exposure to the news media. It turns out that they also have an important effect on all four of our measures of knowledge about the campaign. Of the two interest indicators, it is general interest in politics—not just interest in this one election—that plays the more potent role again and again, dwarfing campaign interest in all four cases. The more exacting the knowledge test—they are arrayed from left to right in table 9-10 in ascending order of difficulty—the greater the predictive power of overall political interest, as opposed to election-specific interest.

But the most suggestive finding is about the media variables themselves. Even when interest in politics and in the campaign are properly taken into the reckoning,[15] *exposure to campaign information through the mass media is robust enough to retain explanatory power.* Although the values of the regression coefficients are in nearly every case lower than when media variables in isolation are used to run the regression, most of the coefficients for the media-use variables—eleven out of sixteen—remain positively signed and statistically significant. The array of differential effects on discrete measures of knowledge remains largely as it was before the introduction of the political interest variables. In other words, the data tell us in no uncertain terms that information intake from the mass media raised levels of citizen knowledge about the campaign, regardless of other factors. For all four of our measures of knowledge, at least one media coefficient was higher than the coefficient for interest in the election.

Media Exposure and the Voting Decision

Analysis of the media factor would be most satisfactory if it were pushed a step or two further. It is beyond controversy that exposure to the campaign via the mass media helps explain mass knowledge about the 1993 election. The question remains: were there implications for what Russians ultimately did in the polling booth?

One factor, hardly surprising, has to do with whether the citizen entered the booth at all. Our survey found exposure to media coverage of the campaign to be correlated with the exercise of the right to vote. On our eight-point summary index for media use, participating voters (those who reported having cast a ballot in the party-list portion of the race for the State Duma) had an average score of 3.1; for abstainers, the mean score was 2.0.[16] For use of individual media, differences in intake between civic-minded voters and apathetic nonvoters were steepest for newspaper readers and smallest for magazines.[17]

The volume of media intake was related not only to the choice to vote or abstain but to the degree of assuredness with which citizens went about pursuing their options. The point comes through in table 9-11, based on the preelection survey. The gradation in reception of mass media information corresponds neatly to vote intention. Intended no-shows scored lowest in media exposure, with respondents uncertain about whether they would take part in the election next in line, but that is less interesting than what we learn about the Russians who had made up their minds to cast a vote.[18] Those who had decided to vote but did not yet know which party list they would back ranked higher than the intended abstainers in media absorption but lower than all others; would-be voters who had arrived at a party preference but admitted it might change thereafter came next; and the highest rating for media use was for the most firmly committed voters, individuals who had selected a party and took the attitude that this decision was final.

We see here an ironic maldistribution of access to campaign materials. Among men and women who planned to vote, in any case, it was the very ones who were in the direst need of illumination about the election bat-

Table 9-11. *Media Exposure and Voting Intention*[a]

Intention	Combined media index
Intends to abstain from vote	1.7
Unsure whether will vote	2.2
Intends to vote, but undecided about which party to support	2.8
Intends to vote and has decided which party to support,[b] but says decision is not final	3.4
Intends to vote, has decided which party to support,[b] and says decision is final	3.7
All citizens	2.8

a. Concerns only party-list portion of election to State Duma.
b. Includes 1.2 percent of all respondents who said they intended to vote against all the parties.

tle—undecided about party or with a partisan choice subject to revi-
sion—who devoted the slightest attention to campaign information in the
mass media. The individuals who lavished the most attention, and thus
made the fattest deposits in their personal information banks, were the least
needful—the dutiful citizens who had *already* reached closure on what
they would do on election day.

What can we say about media consumption and the bottom line of the
election, the substance of what voters did on December 12? Did having
more exposure to mass communications or less predispose them for or
against candidates of specific ideological hues? Does the media factor help
account for, say, the disappointing showing by Westernizing liberals or the
unexpected successes racked up by Zhirinovskii's LDPR?

There definitely were some associations in 1993 between voting preference and the political competence that attention to the mass media fostered.
Employing a summary index of knowledge about the election, and cluster-
ing the thirteen parties into five programmatically defined groups (see table
9-12), we find positive and statistically significant correlations between
knowledge and a vote for the radical reformists in Russia's Choice, for any
of the three moderate reformist parties, and for the two socialist parties; a
negative correlation with a vote for the nationalist LDPR; and no relationship to a vote for the six centrist parties. These correlations do not control
for other explanatory variables and are nowhere near sufficient to model
the voting decision (see chapter 3, which attempts this). The correlations do
suggest, at a minimum, that about half of the warring parties won the support of electors who on average were perceptibly above or below the mean
level of informedness about the campaign and its issues.[19]

Table 9-12. *Association between Political Knowledge and Partisan Choice (Pearson's r)*[a]

Party grouping voted for	Correlation
Radical reformist	.08*
Moderate reformist	.10*
Centrist	.03
Nationalist	−.12*
Socialist	.06*

a. The index of political knowledge was constructed by adding and equally weighing the four knowledge items given in table 9-10.
*p <.01 (two-tailed test)

If we turn to the mass media themselves, however, we see that connections with the thrust of the voting decision are fewer and farther between. As the upper panel of table 9-13 indicates, a statistically significant positive correlation between overall media exposure and voting choice can be estimated for two of the five party groups (centrist and socialist) and a negative correlation for a third (nationalist). But the magnitudes of the coefficients are small, noticeably smaller than for political knowledge and the party vote, and there are relatively few associations, positive or negative, between voting behavior and exposure to any one of the mass media. And, as can be seen in the lower panel of table 9-13, statistical control for the effect of three of the sociodemographic variables that other evidence (see chapter 3) shows to be related to voting choice in 1993—age, education, and community size—washes out a number of the relationships that appear in the zero-order correlations. Looking at the impact of summary media exposure (in the last column), we see only a negative relationship with voting Russia's Choice and a positive relationship with voting for one of the centrist parties. The patterns are faint indeed.[20]

The reader should bear in mind what Helvey in chapter 7 and Ostrow in chapter 8 establish about the informational content of the mass media. The government's desire to twist state television to its advantage notwithstanding, it did not keep paid advertisements, feature programs, or news items about the opposition parties off the airwaves during the campaign. And the printed press, even allowing for the chilling effect of the bloodshed and temporary state of emergency of the October days, was quite pluralistic and often openly sectarian. With the possible exception of the extremist movements banned from the hustings, no major voice in Russia's election debate was screened out of the mass media.

Table 9-13. *Association between Media Exposure and Partisan Choice (Pearson's* r *and Partial Correlation Coefficients)*

Party grouping voted for	Newspapers	Magazines	Radio	Television	All media
Correlation coefficients					
Radical reformist	.00	–.00	–.01	–.05**	–.03
Moderate reformist	.03	–.04**	–.03	.02	.01
Centrist	–.01	.02	.06*	.04**	.05**
Nationalist	–.04**	–.01	–.03	–.02	–.04**
Socialist	.03	.04**	.01	.05*	.04**
Partials, controlling for age, education, and community size					
Radical reformist	–.02	–.00	–.02	–.06*	–.05*
Moderate reformist	.01	–.05**	–.03	.03	–.00
Centrist	–.01	.01	.06*	.04	.04**
Nationalist	.00	–.00	.01	.00	.01
Socialist	.02	.05*	–.03	.02	.01

*p <.01 (two-tailed test)
**p <.05

None of this should be mistaken for a belief that the media did not matter in the election. As the workhorse information-bearing pipelines of the campaign, they clearly counted for a lot, and politically astute Russians at the time knew so perfectly well. Time constraints kept my colleagues and I from interrogating our survey respondents about precisely which media outlets they patronized—which newspaper they read, which television channel they watched, and so forth. Insofar as individual newspapers, magazines, and radio and television stations had distinct political personalities, we can conjecture that voters relied most on the one or ones that were most congruent with their predilections. Some of the pretenders to power—the demagogic Zhirinovskii is the obvious example—to all appearances exploited their media opportunities more adroitly than others.

The survey research does not negate any of these observations, but it does caution us about hasty generalization concerning the global impact of the mass media. Almost never, we can take from table 9-13, did the level of exposure to any one medium or to the media combined do much to define the electorate's political outlook. Neither high nor low media intake *as such* seems to have made it more or less amenable to the messages of the party of power or its principal critics.

Many election postmortems took it as self-evident that television somehow propelled Zhirinovskii and the LDPR to their stunning showing. The polling data compel skepticism about claims such as this, for we see in the mirror of table 9-13 that nationalist voters, far from having gorged themselves on on-screen propaganda, took in marginally less television programming on the election, and marginally less campaign information in all four media, than the median Russian voter. When controls for sociodemographic factors are introduced, there is absolutely no statistical connection between media exposure and a proclivity to vote for or against the LDPR. And support for Russia's Choice, the main victim of Zhirinovskii's vote-winning prowess, is, contrary to folk wisdom about the campaign, negatively related to media consumption, even though that party received preferential treatment in many publications and broadcasts. In sum, although the election of 1993 was in certain senses a mass media event, degree of attentiveness to the media did not noticeably affect the tendency of voters to go along with most of the major political players clamoring for their support.

The Question of Media Bias

One might well say that the party-neutral role of the mass media was achieved in spite of rather than because of the intentions of the media's managers, who were anything but indifferent to the outcome of the election. It is natural to wonder, then, whether political access to the media hit home as an issue in the minds of the voters.

As a matter of fact, media bias was not a burning question in 1993. Nearly half of the persons our project surveyed declined to express an opinion about its presence or absence on centrally controlled television, and more than 60 percent could not do so for local television and the local press (see table 9-14). Of those who harbored a view, a sizable plurality believed that these media had treated all parties and candidates evenhandedly. About one quarter of all citizens perceived inequities in coverage of the campaign by national television and about one eighth in local television and newspapers. Among the minority who detected some bias, six or seven times as many saw the media as prejudiced against hard- and soft-opposition candidates as recognized an antigovernment bias, and about one quarter could not identify the direction of the bias.

Popular perceptions of media bias fluctuated in a subtle way with level of contact with the media. As table 9-15 brings out for television and newspaper consumption, increased media exposure brought with it a higher incidence of both the conviction that the media were treating the parties unjustly *and* the contrary view—that the media were acting equitably. We can

Table 9-14. *Perception of Mass Media Bias in Campaign*

Percent

Perception	Central television	Local television and press
All citizens		
Parties treated unequally	23	12
Parties treated equally	31	26
Hard to say	46	61
Citizens who perceived some bias		
Against supporters of Yeltsin		
and government	10	11
Against opposition to Yeltsin	46	42
Against other groups	22	23
Hard to say	22	25

read this as further evidence of the sophistication and confidence encouraged by media use. It was inability to answer the question that declined sharply with exposure to television and the press, and it was possession of an opinion, be it pro or con, that ascended with exposure.

Attitudes toward media fairness were related also to partisan position (see table 9-16, which is for central television only). As might have been expected, citizens who eventually voted for either the nationalist or the socialist opposition, and especially the latter, were more inclined than Russia's Choice voters to impute bias to the mass media and to see the opposition to Yeltsin's government as the target of that bias. Supporters of the moderate reformist parties were, in fact, slightly harsher in their assessments than centrist voters, perhaps because of the fierceness of the rhetorical exchanges between Russia's Choice and the parties ideologically least distant from it.

What is maybe unexpected is the slenderness of the differences between partisan groups. For example, only 15 percent of the Russia's Choice voters who acknowledged the existence of bias in central television claimed that it was directed against progovernment candidates—a position that surely would have been hard to uphold on factual grounds—and this was barely 3 percent more than the LDPR voters and 6 percent more than the socialist voters who reported the same view. What these data hint at is a reservoir of fair play and common sense that on questions of political control may have been closer to Western liberal norms than the attitudes of the governmental and nongovernmental stewards of the Russian media were.

Table 9-15. Perception of Mass Media Bias by Media Exposure

Percent

Medium assessed	Frequency of exposure		
	None	Occasional	Regular
Television exposure			
Central television			
Biased	10	21	32
Unbiased	9	34	42
Hard to say	81	44	26
Local television and press			
Biased	6	12	16
Unbiased	7	27	38
Hard to say	87	60	46
Newspaper exposure			
Central television			
Biased	17	28	36
Unbiased	27	36	44
Hard to say	57	36	20
Local television and press			
Biased	9	16	20
Unbiased	18	34	43
Hard to say	73	50	37

Conclusion

The bulk of the Russian electorate experienced the 1993 election vicariously, through the mass communications media. Television was the individual medium that connected with the largest number of political consumers, and yet no medium had anything like a monopoly on transmittal of ideas or on suasive power. The contours of the mass media audience were shaped by the interest taken in politics and in the campaign and by personal characteristics such as age, education, and size of community of residence.

The mass media, for all their limitations, did contribute significantly to voters' understanding of the election process, to their sense of involvement in it, and to their awareness of how they might exercise their franchise rights. Although those with the most to learn from the mass media tended to be the last to be heedful to them, even a smattering of exposure helped. Media intake, so strongly predictive of citizen knowledge, was but feebly predictive of partisan preference. And media bias impressed but a small minority as being of serious moment. In the final analysis, it is not the communications media but the political elites who contrived the clashing

Table 9-16. *Perception of Bias in Central Television by Partisan Choice*

Percent

	Radical reformist	Moderate reformist	Centrist	Nationalist	Socialist
Bias detected					
Yes	20	26	23	27	31
No	42	38	39	32	26
Hard to say	37	37	37	41	43
Direction of bias[a]					
Antigovernment	15	8	11	12	9
Antiopposition	45	50	42	50	58
Anti-other groups	21	19	32	17	21
Hard to say	19	23	15	21	12

a. Among those who perceived bias in coverage of the campaign by central television.

partisan messages of 1993, and the mass of newly empowered citizens who tried to make sense of them, who must bear responsibility for the outcome of Russia's first post-Soviet election, for better or for worse.

Notes

1. See especially Paul F. Lazarsfeld, Bernard Berelson, and Hazel Gaudet, *The People's Choice: How the Voter Makes up His Mind in a Presidential Campaign*, 2nd ed. (Columbia University Press, 1948), and Elihu Katz and Paul F. Lazarsfeld, *Personal Influence: The Part Played by People in the Flow of Mass Communications* (Glencoe, Ill.: The Free Press, 1955).

2. Samuel L. Popkin, *The Reasoning Voter: Communication and Persuasion in Presidential Campaigns* (University of Chicago Press, 1991), p. 217. On the neglect of media effects in American election studies of the 1950s and 1960s, see Herbert F. Weisberg, "Model Choice in Political Science: The Case of Voting Behavior Research, 1946–1975," in Herbert F. Weisberg, ed., *Political Science: The Science of Politics* (New York: Agathon Press, 1986), pp. 297–98. An excellent recent study from outside the American field is Scott C. Flanagan, "Media Influences and Voting Behavior," in Scott C. Flanagan and others, *The Japanese Voter* (Yale University Press, 1991), pp. 297–331.

3. Ninety-three percent of the Soviet population regularly viewed television in 1986, versus 5 percent in 1960 (and 98 percent in the United States in the 1980s). Radio use, on the other hand, declined in the late Soviet period, and in 1979 there were only 54 radio sets per 100 population (versus more than 200 in the United States). Ellen Mickiewiecz, *Split Signals: Television and Politics in the Soviet Union* (New York: Oxford University Press, 1988), pp. 3, 17.

4. The figures cited here are means for all respondents. Reported levels of activity were higher for voters polled late in the campaign than for voters questioned early in the campaign.

5. We asked about campaign canvassing in the postelection interview. Only 1 percent of our respondents remembered being contacted at their doors or on the telephone by representatives of any of the thirteen parties. Two percent said they had been canvassed in the course of the campaign by representatives of an individual candidate for the State Duma or State Federation, and a fraction of 1 percent remembered a contact but could not recall if it came from a party or an individual candidate.

6. This question, standard fare in studies of Western elections, proved difficult to render in Russian. The word used for "closely" was *vnimatel'no*, which may be more narrowly translated as "attentively."

7. The "rubbing off" image was used by Bernard R. Berelson, Paul F. Lazarsfeld, and William N. McPhee in their classic study *Voting: A Study of Opinion Formation in a Presidential Campaign* (University of Chicago Press, 1954), p. 244.

8. Quantity was measured on the same 3-point scale employed in table 9-3, but an index of 0 for quantity had to be treated as missing data in computing the correlation because there was no corresponding qualitative measure. Quality was also expressed in a 3-point scale (0 for inattentive consumption, 1 for not very close, and 2 for close). All correlations are significant at the .01 level. To illustrate the point a different way, 69 percent of regular readers of the press devoted close attention to what they had read about the campaign, yet only 31 percent of occasional readers did so. For regular and occasional viewers of television, these proportions were 49 and 18 percent, respectively.

9. The measure for consumption of campaign information in magazines was binary, as we could not distinguish between regular and occasional use. A weaker statistical association with any predictor variable might thus be expected. If, however, we collapse regular and occasional use into a single category for newspaper, radio, and television consumption, the correlation coefficients relating to interest in the campaign are still much higher than for magazines—.38 for newspapers, .31 for radio, and .39 for television.

10. Early studies of voting referred to this as a "spiral effect": "Mass-media exposure affects mediating variables like partisanship, interest, and discussion that in turn lead back to mass-media exposure." Berelson, Lazarsfeld, and McPhee, *Voting*, p. 248.

11. For a similar finding for Japan, see Flanagan, "Media Influences and Voting Behavior," pp. 306–07.

12. Lazarsfeld, Berelson, and Gaudet, *The People's Choice*, p. 151.

13. The Russian word for family used in the question (*sem'ya*) describes the nuclear family, not the extended circle of relatives. Five percent of respondents said they did not have such a family and were therefore excluded from the statistical analysis.

14. Fifteen percent of our respondents had engaged in both kinds of opinion leadership and 32 percent had done one or the other. Pearson's *r* for the relationship between in-family opinion leadership and interest in the campaign was .18; for

nonfamily opinion leadership it was .19. Coefficients for level of education and opinion leadership in the two spheres were .16 and .19, respectively. Age, gender, and community size were not significant predictors of opinion leadership.

15. I also ran the regression with the sociodemographic factors given in table 9-7 as additional independent variables. This yielded low coefficients and had marginal effect on the coefficients for the other variables.

16. Information about media consumption was solicited in the preelection survey; voting or nonvoting, it goes without saying, could only be ascertained retrospectively, in the postelection survey.

17. If the ratio of the average score for voters to the average score for nonvoters was 1.57:1 for the four media combined, it was 2.09:1 for newspapers, 1.49:1 for television, 1.42:1 for radio, and 1.26:1 for magazines.

18. Behavior on December 12 did not always correspond to the voter's intention declared in the preelection survey. Forty-five percent of the respondents who said before the election that they would not vote told us after the election that they had voted; 78 percent of those who said they would vote but who were without a party preference reported later that they voted, and 89 percent of the intended voters with a declared party preference voted. This makes the media inattentiveness of the intended nonvoters an even more serious problem than if none of these persons would have voted in the end.

19. For individual parties other than Russia's Choice, knowledge was positively related to a vote for Yabloko (a moderate reformist party), the KPRF (socialist), and Civic Union (centrist). It was negatively related to a vote for the LDPR (nationalist), Women of Russia (centrist), or against all the parties.

20. When the correlations are estimated by individual party, there are statistically significant positive relationships between media exposure and a vote for the KPRF and Civic Union. When the test is repeated for the four separate news media, reliable coefficients come through in a mere three of the fifty-two cells.

CHAPTER TEN

Public Opinion and the Constitutional Referendum

Timothy J. Colton

IT WAS the vicious quarrel over how to recast its Soviet-era constitution that killed the so-called First Russian Republic and dragged the country to the verge of civil war in 1993. The "step-by-step constitutional reform" Boris Yeltsin unveiled September 21 foisted the problem on the soon-to-be-elected Federal Assembly. This "wholly unprecedented or at least highly bizarre procedure"[1] carried mountainous risks: were the assembly *not* to adopt a constitutional bill with dispatch and in language palatable to Yeltsin, it would strand him, Russia, and itself in legal limbo. In the aftermath of the military showdown with the outgoing parliament and its defenders two weeks later, the president executed a hairpin turn and concluded he would rather wager on public opinion than on a future parliament.[2] He decreed October 15 that a binding national referendum on a draft constitution would take place to coincide with the general election on December 12. Having to pause for his constitutional convention to reconvene, he did not promulgate a finished text until November 10, a mere thirty-two days before the dual event.

The edict of October 15, skirting the requirement of Russia's statute on referendums that a simple majority of the electorate affirm any question put before it, stipulated that the new constitution would go into effect so long as turnout reached 50 percent and half of those participating—25 percent of all eligible voters—concurred.[3] It transpired that turnout December 12 was 54.8 percent, by tally of the Central Electoral Commission, and the assenting votes 58.4 percent of the votes cast. The consent of a shade under one third of the citizenry was more than adequate for passage under Yeltsin's custom-tailored quorum rules. On December 25, two years to the day after the Russian tricolor replaced the Soviet hammer and sickle on the Kremlin flagstaff, Yeltsin proclaimed the charter to be in force. The president's brainchild, under which the Second Russian Republic has been governed ever since, is so amendment-proof that not one comma in it has yet been changed.[4]

The constitution broke sharply with Soviet symbols and principles, declaring in its preamble that Russia was henceforth to be "a democratic, federative, law-based state with a republican form of government." Its 137 articles went on to entrench the norm of free election of leaders and a thick catalog of human rights and liberties. The two most contentious provisions, each hotly disputed since the collapse of the USSR, covered the allocation of powers between the executive and legislative branches and between the central government and the eighty-nine republics, oblasts, and krais making up the federation. On the first score, the constitution has rightly been labeled a "superpresidential" scheme,[5] as it vests the head of state with prerogatives as lavish as imaginable in any political system anchored in representative institutions and the rule of law. In the same spirit of concentration of authority, its makers also tried to halt the trickle of influence from Moscow down to the regions, the twenty-one ethnically defined republics among them.[6]

Scholarly analysis of the referendum, its regime-consolidating function notwithstanding, has been sparse. Although the election study my colleagues and I conducted did not focus on the constitution, we unearthed enough for me to report briefly on the mass politics underlying its ratification.[7]

Popular Awareness of the Constitution and Related Issues

The constitution was Yeltsin's supreme priority from October to December 1993. Maintaining statesmanlike distance from the bare-knuckled campaign for the State Duma and Federation Council, he touted it as Russia's best bulwark against anarchy. "It is for you to decide," he told the populace in a television address December 10, "whether or not there will be peace and calm in Russia." Reminding his audience that a national blood-letting had been narrowly averted two months before, he warned that "until the new constitution is adopted this threat will hang over the country and over each of us."[8]

Russian citizens' minds, however, lay elsewhere. Almost three out of four of those quizzed in our nationwide survey, as noted in chapter 3, identified inflation, the decline in output, or some other economic problem as the most wrenching issue facing the Russian Federation. A mere 6 percent mentioned any sort of political or constitutional problem; a little more than 1 percent believed legislative-executive friction to be Russia's worst difficulty, one fifth of 1 percent cited threats to the territorial unity of the country, and a trifling one tenth of 1 percent the constitution explicitly.

Rampant apathy, governmental improvisation, and the tardy release of the wording of the constitution all made for slender public knowledge about the debate. A little more than 30 percent of the respondents disclosed in the preelection interview that they were acquainted with *(znakomy s)* the charter, and fewer than 40 percent when reinterviewed subsequent to December 12 said they had read it (see table 10-1). Awareness varied with personal interest in current affairs and was two or two-and-a-half times higher among participant voters than among abstainers.[9] Nonetheless, it hardly inspires confidence in the deliberative quality of the process to realize 51 percent of all those who *voted* in the referendum had never read the historic document. The same holds for the regularity that "yes" voters were marginally less likely to have perused it (or to have alleged familiarity with it before the election) than "no" voters.

This is far from saying that Russians were devoid of opinions about constitutionally germane issues, as distinct from the clauses of the bruited con-

Table 10-1. *Public Awareness of Draft Constitution*
Percent

Respondents	Acquainted with draft (preelection interview)	Had read draft (postelection interview)
All	31	38
By level of interest in politics		
High	55	65
Medium	33	44
Low	16	18
By participation in referendum		
Voted Yes	35	48
Voted No	40	50
Abstained[a]	21	19

a. Includes persons who could not say whether they had voted or not.

Table 10-2. *Opinions about Constitutional Issues*
Percent

Question	Response
Distribution of power in central government	
President stronger than parliament	21
Equal balance	41
Parliament stronger than president	19
Don't know	18
Distribution of power between center and regions	
Center stronger than regions	21
Equal balance	34
Regions stronger than center	31
Don't know	14
Declarations of sovereignty by republics	
Strongly disapprove	19
Disapprove	20
All the same	16
Approve	12
Strongly approve	10
Don't know	22

stitution. As table 10-2 shows, the bulk of the citizens we surveyed were not shy about answering three questions in the preelection interview dealing with concrete aspects of the constitutional imbroglio. Eighty-two percent volunteered a perspective on the distribution of power in Moscow, 86 percent on relations with the regions, and 77 percent on the recent assertions by the republics of the privileged status of "sovereignty." Ninety-five percent of respondents replied on one or more constitutional issues and 63 percent on all three. Ability to respond was anywhere from several to approximately 10 percentage points higher among persons who took part in the referendum than among ones who declined.[10]

On the presidential-parliamentary tussle and the devolution of power to the provinces, a plurality of Russians fancied a balanced solution. The compromise mood was plainest on the former topic, where there was as much enthusiasm for juridical equality between president and parliament as for the hard-line presidentialist and parliamentarist positions combined. Only over republican sovereignty was there polarization away from the midpoint of the spectrum. Copiously more voters were either congenial to or (twice as frequently) hostile to the republics' ambitions than professed neutrality.[11]

All of this is to say that the electorate did not fly blind on things constitutional in 1993. Many more individuals harbored convictions on the substance of the cardinal issues than grasped chapter and verse of the draft of the basic law.

Social Structure and the Referendum

Yeltsin's twin goals in the referendum gambit were to fulfill the 50 percent quorum and to bag a majority of the votes cast. His key to getting the first job done was to piggyback the referendum onto a legislative election with barriers to entry sufficiently low for all major parties and political movements to hurdle. This shrewd device restrained elite-level foes of the constitutional blueprint—the only exceptions were the handful of banned parties and the fringe factions that sat out the election—from attempting to obstruct it through boycott. At the mass level, Russians who trooped to precinct polling stations December 12 picked up ballot slips printed by the Central Electoral Commission for both the president's referendum and the election; the overwhelming majority dutifully ticked off boxes in each.[12] Temporal coincidence and conjoint administration render it virtually impossible to unsnarl the reasons for participation in either exercise from the reasons for participation in the other.

If we scan, for example, the sociological profile of participants in the referendum, the survey data reveal a pronounced overrepresentation of better-educated persons in white-collar occupations, males, and, especially, of middle-aged and elderly citizens. Not only are these identical to the social-structural correlates of participation in the Duma election, they are also in modified form the personal traits that go with most civic involvements in an industrial society, and hence say nothing much about the dynamics of this referendum.[13]

The challenge, therefore, is to lay bare the determinants not of participation in the constitutional vote but of the choices the participants came to—for or against the president's state-building project. We might hypothesize that social factors would play some role, as we saw them doing in the campaign for the State Duma (see chapter 3). We would want to know further whether voter opinions—about constitutional and nonconstitutional issues alike—impinged on choice. And it is prudent, in light of the fact that 1993 was Russia's inaugural multiparty election, to inquire into the repercussions of partisan sentiment.

Beginning with sociodemographic variables, table 10-3 presents coefficients for the logistic regression of a positive referendum vote on the same

Table 10-3. *Effects of Social Characteristics on a Positive Vote in Referendum (Logistic Regression Coefficients)*[a]

Social characteristic	Coefficient
Community size	.76*
Manual worker	.13
Family income	–.11
Improved living standard	.98*
Higher education	–.12
Ethnicity	
Titular in republic	-.91*
Nontitular in republic	–1.29*
Russian in republic	.16
Non-Russian in oblast	.53**
Orthodox	.10
Macroregion	
European North	.50*
European South	–.07
Urals	.75*
East	.40*
Woman	.10
Age	.97*
Former CPSU	–.58*
Constant	.11
Model improvement[b]	6.3
Cases correctly predicted[b]	72.9
Reduction of errors[b]	2.5

*p <.01
**p <.05
a. Analyzes only respondents who participated in the constitutional referendum and recalled how they voted.
b. Percent.

indicators employed in chapter 3. Of the six attributes statistically associated with a "yes" vote, we encountered four of them—urbanization, trend in the family's standard of living, ethnicity, and region of residence—as cogent predictors of a vote for the "party of power," Russia's Choice, in the Duma race.

Thus big-city dwellers and economic winners were inclined to say "yes" to the referendum question, just as they were to vote for a government party whose leaders supported the constitution; the inhabitants of villages and small towns and economic losers were inclined to be nay-sayers on the referendum and to select a party other than Russia's Choice to represent them in the Duma. In terms of ethnicity, the cleavage in the referendum, as in the parliamentary vote, was not between Russians and non-Russians, inasmuch as members of the country's dozens of national minorities acted differently in different demographic and institutional contexts. Non-Russians in the oblasts and krais towed the line on the constitution even more than ethnic Russians there, in all probability out of a gut feeling that the powers it assigned to Moscow would protect them and their cultures against encroachment by local Russian majorities. But non-Russian residents of the republics, for whom a puissant center was a potential threat instead of a shield, tended to oppose the draft.[14] Geographically, the European South macroregion was a vulnerable zone for the constitution as well as for Russia's Choice, with the difference that in the referendum denizens of the European North and the eastern reaches of the country were more cordial toward the government than voters from the heartland of European Russia, the omitted category in the regression equation.

Two of the sociological correlates of advocacy of the constitutional initiative—past membership in the Communist Party of the Soviet Union and age—were not predictive of a Russia's Choice preference for the State Duma, although both were positively related to a vote for the Communist Party of the Russian Federation (KPRF) and the socialist opposition. That one-time members of the CPSU would be biased against the constitution bears witness to the way the question tapped passions rooted in the Soviet past. If that will not turn any heads, the sign and magnitude of the generational variable surely should. Senior age cohorts were more apt than the young to vote for the KPRF, the most scalding critic of Yeltsin's government; in the constitutional plebiscite, they disproportionately *supported* the powers that be. My conjecture is that the same ingrained antipathy toward the unfamiliar and disruptive that bred dissent in the Duma election predisposed older men and women to sanction Yeltsin's constitution in the referendum, on the intuition that without a settlement turmoil was going to deepen and further invade their everyday lives.

Opinions

An alternative explanation of citizen conduct in the referendum, as in the parliamentary election, would rest on political attitudes and beliefs rather than on social background and group reflexes. Whatever Russians' credentials to judge the draft constitution per se, it is vital to know whether their normative opinions shaded their actions on it.

We have already learned that Russians had likes and dislikes on specific constitutional controversies over the division of powers, intergovernmental relations, and republic rights. These could plausibly have figured in the calculus of deciding on the draft broached by Yeltsin, so long as voters had the minimum knowledge needed to draw action implications from their preferences. For this purpose, bare-bones information about the gist of the text—that it made the president more powerful than parliament, for example, but not in detail how the two would handle appointment of a prime minister—would probably have sufficed.

But it is by no means self-evident that constitutional notions, strictly speaking, would have been the only ones relevant to the referendum question. The president's grafting of the poll onto the parliamentary election leaves no doubt that he, for one, foresaw and welcomed a spillover of politics writ large into the constitutional battleground. This could have come about in three ways.

The first would have stemmed from voter ignorance of the fine print or, worse, of the essence of the draft. In this pattern, constitutional semiliterates or illiterates, pressed to make up their minds, would have taken guidance in the referendum from their ideas on extraneous matters. A second option would have been for citizens indifferent to the referendum's intrinsic stakes but not necessarily uninformed about it to eye the vote instrumentally, reasoning consciously or assuming subconsciously that the outcome would aid or hinder realization of their other dreams and fears in life. Someone who desired, say, a market economy (but who did not care about the constitution per se) would have voted "yes"; a devotee of economic planning, by the same logic, would have voted "no." As a third possibility, the intimate identification of the constitutional plan with a single politician might have tempted some to personalize the referendum choice. It would have been a natural enough reaction under the circumstances to perceive it as foremost a vote of confidence or no confidence in Boris Yeltsin and his record in office and to treat constitutional niceties as secondary.

Individuals' outlooks on constitutional and nonconstitutional issues and on Yeltsin's presidency interacted in elaborate ways, as the correlations in table 10-4 bear out. The indicators here for the constitutional opinions (presidentialism, centralism, and rejection of republic sovereignty) embody the responses to the three survey questions delineated in table 10-1. For core nonconstitutional attitudes, the yardsticks are the multi-item scales I constructed for the investigation of party-list voting in chapter 3 for positions on state control of the economy, welfarism, and the Soviet leaders. The Yeltsin approval score, also used in that chapter, comes from a four-way question about stance toward his performance as president.[15]

Table 10-4. *Correlation Matrix (Pearson's* r*) for Constitutional and Nonconstitutional Opinion Variables*

	Centralism	Anti-sovereignty	State control	Welfarism	Soviet leaders	Yeltsin approval
Presidentialism	.04**	–.02	–.23*	–.16*	–.15*	.31*
Centralism		.04*	.15*	.17*	.14*	–.02
Antisovereignty			.16*	.05*	.05*	–.04*
State control				.54*	.42*	–.40*
Welfarism					.36*	–.24*
Soviet leaders						–.22*

*p <.01 (two-tailed test)
**p <.05 (two-tailed test)

One lesson of table 10-4 is how precious little overlap there was among attitudes toward the assorted constitutional issues. The bivariate correlations between the indicators for presidential power, the center's grip on the regions, and republic sovereignty are all minuscule, and one of them (for the pairing of centralism with antisovereignty) does not attain statistical significance by the usual rule of thumb.[16] Almost universally, constitutional opinions cohered more tenaciously with nonconstitutional opinions than they did with one another.

Note also that the signs for the coefficients involving the presidentialism value invariably point in the opposite direction from the coefficients linking centralism and republic sovereignty with the nonconstitutional variables. Presidentialism correlates negatively with acceptance of state control of the economy, welfarism, and admiration of the Soviet dictators and positively (and quite heartily) with approval of Yeltsin as president. For centralism and revulsion at republic sovereignty, it is the other way around: the coefficients joining these variables to state economic control, welfarism, and Sovietism are positive, whereas with approval of Yeltsin as leader they are negative. It follows that the effects of the three constitutional preferences on behavior in the referendum, if any, may not be uniform or mutually reinforcing.

The impact of individuals' sundry opinions on the likelihood of voting "yes" in the referendum is estimated in the logistic regression coefficients listed in table 10-5. To help isolate the consequences of knowledge of the constitution, I iterated the regressions consecutively for the minority of survey respondents who said in the preelection debriefing that they were ac-

Table 10-5. *Effects of Opinions about Constitutional and Nonconstitutional Issues on a Positive Vote in Referendum (Logistic Regression Coefficients)*

Opinion	Acquainted with draft constitution	Not acquainted with draft constitution	All voters
Constitutional issues only			
Presidentialism	1.42*	1.28*	1.34*
Centralism	.46**	−.04	.14
Antisovereignty	−.02	.07	.02
Constant	−.02	.39**	.24
Model improvement[a]	4.1	2.6	3.0
Cases correctly predicted[a]	71.8	73.7	72.2
Reduction of errors[a]	1.1	2.4	None
Nonconstitutional issues only			
State control scale	−1.77*	−2.19*	−2.04*
Welfarism scale	1.00**	1.10*	1.05*
Soviet leaders scale	−1.34*	−.75*	−.89*
Yeltsin approval	2.53*	1.69*	1.95*
Constant	.76**	1.28*	1.09*
Model improvement[a]	16.4	9.4	11.4
Cases correctly predicted[a]	73.5	75.2	74.1
Reduction of errors[a]	7.0	8.1	6.8
Constitutional and nonconstitutional issues			
Presidentialism	.15	.68*	.56*
Centralism	.67*	.15	.33**
Anti-sovereignty	.36	.25	.27
State control scale	−1.98*	−2.12*	−2.05*
Welfarism scale	.94**	1.07*	1.03*
Soviet leaders scale	−1.34*	−.76*	−.89*
Yeltsin approval	2.47*	1.54*	1.81*
Constant	.38	.77**	.60**
Model improvement[a]	17.3	10.1	12.2
Cases correctly predicted[a]	73.8	76.4	74.7
Reduction of errors[a]	8.1	12.8	9.0

*$p < .01$
**$p < .05$
a. Percent.

quainted with the draft constitution submitted, for the larger subset not acquainted with it, and for all participants in the referendum.

The table contains three horizontal panels. In the topmost, the variables used to forecast the referendum vote are the three constitutional opinions by themselves.[17] One indicator—of receptivity toward presidential hegemony over parliament—does indeed occasion a positive and rather large coefficient for the entire sample, savvy and uninitiated voters included, signifying a neat congruence between personal belief and course of action in the referendum.[18] Only for citizens familiar with the draft charter is a second opinion, the preference for central over regional power, also correlated with a proconstitution vote. Viewpoints on a special niche for the republics are not systematically related to citizen choice for either subgroup or for the sample as a whole—this in spite of the aforementioned coolness of ethnic non-Russians in the republics against the constitution.

The middle panel of table 10-5 displays the influence of the nonconstitutional positions, with no controls for other factors. It is striking that all four parameters are large and highly significant, and consistently so for constitutionally informed and constitutionally uninformed voters. Over the whole population, two indicators—the ideological measure of economic statism and the individualized measure of approval of President Yeltsin—spin off amply higher coefficients than either presidentialism or centralism does from the cluster of constitutional opinions. Goodness of fit of the statistical model is manifestly superior with these opinions alone than with constitutional opinions alone.

Be that as it may, the genuinely discriminating test, recognizing that Russians possessed opinions on *both* the constitutional and the nonconstitutional agendas, ought to be for the two broad categories of attitudes in tandem. A simultaneous regression is reported in the bottom panel of table 10-5. Proof of the explanatory value added is that the merged analysis improves statistical fit over analysis relying solely on either class of attitudes.

So far as constitutional opinions are concerned, the combined regression paints a mixed picture. Across the board, presidentialism is robustly enough related to referendum choice to survive inclusion of the nonconstitutional variables, although the coefficient sags to less than half of its initial magnitude. Folding in the panorama of opinions also enlarges the parameters for centralism and antisovereignty feeling and bumps centralism above the conventional .05 boundary of statistical significance.[19]

Notice, however, the contradictory and counterintuitive ramifications of constitutional sophistication. For voters acquainted with the actual clauses of the constitution before December 12 (in the first column of table 10-5), the centralism indicator significantly influenced the referendum decision; for those unacquainted with them (in the second column), it did not. The contrast is a telling sign of a sophistication effect.

At the same time, presidentialism, the most potent of the constitutional attitudes in the electorate at large, had no effect on the referendum choices of voters in the know, once allowance is made for nonconstitutional attitudes, whereas it had a substantial effect on voters not conversant with the text of the constitution. The primary reason for this anomaly seems to be the tighter mental connection between presidentialism and approval of Yeltsin among individuals who had bothered to gather intelligence about the constitution.[20] Oddly, these model citizens, typically more engaged in all facets of the political world than their compatriots, were less capable of detaching their estimation of the law of the land in the long term and the abstract from their appraisal of one human being in the here and now.

The fascinating revelation in the bottom part of table 10-5, though, is about the relative contributions of constitutional and other attitudes to citizen choice. Across the board, the coefficients for economic statism, approbation of President Yeltsin, welfarism, and the Soviet leaders are altered much less by the admission of constitutional opinions than those for constitutional variables are altered by the extraconstitutional opinions. For all four gauges of general opinion, the parameters exceed the coefficients for the properly constitutional indicators; those for economic statism and rating of Yeltsin dwarf them. The finding applies to well-informed and poorly informed voters without much discrimination. Russia's climactic constitutional referendum, in short, *hinged far less on opinions about constitutional issues as such than on opinions about other, more politically salient issues.* We cannot be sure of the exact structure of citizens' motivations—to what extent they either consciously calculated the costs and benefits of their votes or acted on the basis of tacit premises and instincts. But we can be sure of the strength of the association between opinions on public issues and behavior.

For three of the four nonconstitutional attitudes highlighted, the referendum mirrors the voting for party slates. That is to say, personalized confidence in Yeltsin, a philosophical attraction to a market economy, and disapproval of Soviet ways were conducive to a "yes" vote on the constitution, much as they were to voting Russia's Choice for the State Duma. Conversely, unhappiness with the president, socialist economic beliefs, and warm memories of Soviet rule turned people against the constitution, just as it led them into the arms of the Communist party in the parliamentary contest.

In one crucial regard, the nexus between opinion and behavior was peculiar in the constitutional arena. Espousal of the bundle of redistributive and social security policies I denote as "welfarism" went hand and hand with a parliamentary vote for, among others, the KPRF and the socialist opposition and with a low likelihood of voting Russia's Choice. In the constitutional plebiscite, by contrast, resistance to the shredding of the social safety net lined up with a *positive* decision on the Yeltsin draft. The inversion of the expected relationship is reminiscent of what was remarked on previously for one particular sociological attribute—the person's age. The phenomenon, I would surmise, originated in the same craving for continuity and equilibrium found in a sizable segment of the population. Flawed and dimly understood as it may have been, the proposed constitution was for a lot of Russians the best bet available in the autumn of 1993 for stabilizing the country's politics and keeping at bay the chaos glimpsed in the streets of Moscow and on Russia-wide television October 3 and 4.

The Role of the Parties

From the matrix of attitudes in table 10-4 and the regression results laid out in table 10-5, it should be obvious that many voters were painfully cross-pressured by the referendum. Pro-welfarist individuals, for instance, would have leaned toward statist economics and disapproval of Yeltsin; their welfarism would hence have prodded them to vote "yes" in the referendum and their statism and dislike of Yeltsin pushed them to vote "no." The end point of the tug of war in any one citizen's case would have depended on intensity of feeling on the issue dimensions, interactions among attitudes, and the influence of other factors and of random variation.

A wellspring of additional and novel complexity was the system of political parties taking preliminary shape in the Russian Federation in 1993. Popular orientations toward them were colored by many of the considerations that bore on the constitutional question. The selfsame causes of citizen A's vote for Russia's Choice might have prejudiced him in favor of Yeltsin's constitution; for citizen B, the upshot might have been votes cast for the socialist opposition and against the constitution. But choices in the two forums did not have to be arrived at independently. Most of the parties stumping for seats in the State Duma, in fact, did not want this to happen. Ten of the thirteen entrants took public stands on the constitution and exhorted their sympathizers—and anyone else who would listen—to fill out their referendum ballots accordingly. Recommending ratification were the radical reformist Russia's Choice, two of the moderate reform parties (Party of Russian Unity and Accord [PRES] and the Russian Movement for Democratic Reform [RDDR]), the centrist Constructive Ecological Movement of Russia [KEDR], and the nationalist Liberal Democratic Party of

Russia [LDPR]; spurning it were the moderate reformist Yabloko, two centrist factions (the Democratic Party of Russia [DPR] and Civic Union), and both socialist parties (Communist Party of the Russian Federation [KPRF] and Agrarians).

The final question to consider becomes, then, did the experience of voting for a given party affect the individual's assessment of the constitution? Insofar as many of the causal factors already scrutinized would have exerted a parallel influence on both decisions, what we need to discern is whether and how much of a difference party preference made over and above these factors.

The newness and immaturity of the Russian parties in 1993 rule out any role for habitual party loyalties in the Western sense. But that exclusion does not exhaust the possibilities. Again, the paucity of information about the constitution at the grassroots must have made some citizens receptive to input from other sources. We have seen how values and political opinions on nonconstitutional subjects such as the economy and social programs fed into citizens' decisions on the Yeltsin project. There is no *a priori* reason to say that cues could not have flowed from the parties and quasi parties as well, regardless of the shallowness of the emotional attachment to them as organizations. The parties and their platforms were much more visible in the campaign period than the constitutional draft—the opponents of which were not allowed to form an organizing committee or to mount a concerted attack in the mass media. Praise or vilification of the text by the harried citizen's chosen political party might have served him or her as an "information shortcut," lightening the burden of learning about and making the referendum decision.[21] The convenience would have been greatest, one would think, for those voters most in the dark on the subject. Moreover, the voter, once having come to a verdict on the State Duma, could have wanted to transfer that preference into the second contest, sniffing an opportunity to extend his favored party's influence or to foster institutional and political conditions in which its program would be implemented.

Table 10-6 sets forth the results of the regression of a positive referendum choice on ten dummy variables representing a vote for each of the parties that had a constitutional position in 1993. Because we are interested in ascertaining the influence of party preference at the margin, I use constitutional and nonconstitutional opinions as statistical controls. As with the foregoing analysis of the opinion variables, I divide participant voters into those who claimed familiarity with the constitutional text and those who did not.

Table 10-6. *Effects of Party Vote and of Opinions about Constitutional and Nonconstitutional Issues on a Positive Vote in Referendum (Logistic Regression Coefficients)*

Independent variable	Acquainted with draft constitution	Not acquainted with draft constitution	All voters
Voted for party that supported constitution			
Russia's Choice	1.56*	.97*	1.17*
PRES	−.07	.37	.22
RDDR	.15	−.34	−.23
KEDR	−.30	−.44	−.41
LDPR	−.11	−.60*	−.45*
Voted for party that opposed constitution			
Yabloko	−.57	.10	−.24
DPR	−1.05*	−1.41*	−1.27*
Civic Union	−.09	−.33	−.26
KPRF	−1.77*	−1.49*	−1.63*
Agrarian	−.45	−.55**	−.54*
Opinions			
Presidentialism	−.12	.54**	.34
Centralism	.59**	.13	.29
Antisovereignty	.21**	.38	.30
State control scale	−1.44**	−1.77*	−1.68*
Welfarism scale	.93	1.24*	1.19*
Soviet leaders scale	−.97**	−.39	−.53**
Yeltsin approval	1.88*	1.38*	1.53*
Constant	.56	−.55**	.48
Model improvement[a]	25.5	17.9	20.1
Cases correctly predicted[a]	77.2	78.6	77.5
Reduction of errors[a]	25.2	18.6	19.1

*p <.01
**p <.05
a. Percent.

Did party choice have anything to do with behavior on the referendum question? The statistical evidence says unambiguously that it did. Among all participating voters, table 10-6 demonstrates middling to large relationships for five parties—the LDPR, Russia's Choice, the KPRF, the Agrarians, and the DPR. These parties finished first, second, third, fifth, and eighth in the proportional-representation race and between them garnered 64 percent of all votes cast. Among the parties that crossed the 5 percent threshold for seating in the Duma, only Yabloko demonstrates no effect.[22] Incorporation of the party variables produces markedly higher goodness of fit with the data, as measured by model Chi-square improvement and cases correctly predicted. It also renders statistically insignificant all coefficients for the effects of constitutional opinions on the referendum vote.[23] It is clear that the party factor must be appreciated as an integral part of the explanation for the referendum outcome, not a minor addendum.

Party influence played itself out in different ways for different parties in 1993. For four of the five parties where it was consequential—all except the LDPR—the effect achieved was consistent with the objectives of the party's leaders. For the two parties with the most forthright positions on the constitution, Russia's Choice and the KPRF, the higher coefficient in the first column than in the second column suggests some premium from sophistication. Voters conversant with the draft were more likely than voters not conversant with it to have their referendum choice affected by the experience of voting for either of the parties with polar positions on ratification. For the centrist DPR, which fought ratification almost as tenaciously as the KPRF, the estimates in both columns are high and negative; the small number of DPR voters in the sample makes it impractical to compare them further.

The puzzling rows in table 10-6 concern two parties, the Agrarians and the LDPR. The Agrarians opposed the constitution, but in polite tones and without giving up the several portfolios leaders of the party held in Viktor Chernomyrdin's Council of Ministers. Voting Agrarian had a negative effect on the odds of a "yes" choice for both sophisticated and unsophisticated voters; for the sophisticated the magnitude was slightly smaller and statistically invalid. Conceivably, the connection was diluted among citizens cognizant of the constitution because they were also aware of the party's continued cooperation with Yeltsin and Chernomyrdin.

For the LDPR, whose showing in the party-list vote was the biggest sensation on December 12, the aberration lies in the fact that it was the only party whose following made constitutional choices contrary to the party's position. Vladimir Zhirinovskii, the LDPR strongman who spoke out several times in favor of the draft constitution, later boasted he had helped ensure its confirmation. The data testify that he did no such thing. Other factors held constant, an adherent of the party was more likely, not less likely, than the average voter to turn thumbs down in the referendum. Zhirinovskii's soothing words on the constitution were drowned out in an overall message of alienation and inchoate protest at the status quo. The same angry voters who bought into the LDPR's demagoguery did not and perhaps could not bring themselves to vote in the next breath for Yeltsin's charter for Russia. All we can say for Zhirinovskii's proconstitution rhetoric is that it appears to have offset the antigovernment impulse among those voters who were well versed in the constitution—and presumably relatively well versed in party politics, too. In such urbane circles, the net effect was a lack of systematic connection between support of the Liberal Democrats and the referendum choice. Among constitutional unsophisticates, though, there was a palpable negative correlation, and it is this that creates the total effect.

Conclusion

Of all the acts of political engineering attempted by Yeltsin's government in 1993, the constitutional referendum was the most audacious and the most successful. It succeeded because its initiator managed to piece together the kind of winning coalition that eluded him and his friends in the parliamentary election. The coalition for ratification was informed by skimpy public knowledge about the intricacies of the constitution but by widespread and reasonably discerning knowledge about constitutionally charged issues. Although sociological and economic variables such as community size, living standard, ethnicity, and age were predictive of citizen choice,[24] attitudes were far more so. Strangely for a constitutional referendum, public opinion about nonconstitutional subjects mattered more than opinion about constitutional subjects, even among constitutional sophisticates. And surprisingly for a poll coinciding with the country's first multiparty election, the untried political parties were also able to serve as a compass to many participants in the referendum.

Russians, in sum, granted Yeltsin his fondest political wish at the same time that they frustrated the partisan plans of his most fervent partners and backers. The governing charter they put in place has allowed him and his associates to rule ever since by executive fiat, relegating the new parliament to a largely subsidiary role. The referendum founded both the relative political stability of the mid-1990s and rank uncertainty about the future of politics after Yeltsin, when the superpresidential machinery he crafted and the electorate accepted may yet fall into the hands of leaders pursuing nondemocratic ends.

Notes

1. Stephen Holmes, "Superpresidentialism and Its Problems," *East European Constitutional Review*, vol. 2/3 (Fall 1993/Winter 1994), p. 125.

2. In his memoir describing this period, Yeltsin is strangely silent about what went into the decision. His description of the referendum of April 25, 1993, in which "the people gave a clear sign of their support for me," hints at confidence. But he also admits he was "seized" by psychological depression after the fighting in downtown Moscow, which conveys desperation more than optimism. Boris Yeltsin, *The Struggle for Russia*, trans. Catherine A. Fitzpatrick (New York: Times Books, 1994), pp. 247, 285. Speaking on national television on the eve of the election, he defended his decision to take ratification away from the Federal Assembly on two grounds: (1) The new deputies would have little parliamentary experience and so would need "precise and clear rules" from a constitution to guide their conduct, and (2) there would be "a new spiral of struggle" within the Federal Assembly over the constitution, and "we are already weary of this sort of thing." *Rossiiskiye vesti*, December 11, 1993, p. 1.

3. As mentioned in chapter 1, Yeltsin got around the referendum law, passed in October 1990 when he was chair of parliament, by ruling the procedure a "vote" rather than a referendum.

4. Under the main procedure for amendment, outlined in Articles 108 and 135, a constitutional change would have to be approved by three quarters of the membership of the Federation Council, two thirds of the State Duma, the president, and two thirds of the regional governments.

5. Holmes, "Superpresidentialism and Its Problems," pp. 123–26.

6. The constitution omitted the "federative agreements" signed in 1992, violating a commitment Yeltsin made at the time, and any reference to the "sovereignty" of the republics. It also opened many policy areas in which the regions sought residual powers to "joint jurisdiction" by Moscow.

7. The fullest discussion thus far is in Stephen White, Richard Rose, and Ian McAllister, *How Russia Votes* (Chatham, N.J.: Chatham House, 1996), chap. 5 (analysis of public opinion and the referendum at pp. 102–06). See the same book, chap. 4, for informative discussion of earlier Soviet and Russian referendums.

8. *Rossiiskiye vesti*, December 11, 1993, p. 1.

9. Knowledge of the constitution was also associated with interest in the 1993 election campaign, though less strongly so than with interest in politics in general. In addition, it was positively related to exposure to political news in the mass media, especially in the press. In our preelection interviews, familiarity with the draft grew slightly as the campaign progressed. Thirty-three percent of those questioned after December 4 stated they were familiar with the document, as compared to 27 percent before November 27 and 30 percent from November 28 to December 4.

10. Eighty-four percent of individuals who in due course voted in the referendum volunteered a response on the division of powers in Moscow, 87 percent on relations with the regions, and 80 percent on the sovereignty declarations; 96 percent had an opinion on at least one of the three questions and 66 percent on all three. For abstainers, these proportions were 75, 83, 74, 92, and 58 percent.

11. It is possible that more would have chosen a neutral response if we had found a way to verbalize it other than to ask if the respondent thought it was all the

same *(bezrazlichno*—meaning "indifferent"). Our inability to come up with such wording reflects the inherent divisiveness of the issue.

12. Official figures show a slight discrepancy between votes cast in the election and in the referendum. In our national sample, 97.5 percent of those who said they voted in the constitutional referendum reported having also voted in the party-list portion of the State Duma election, whereas 1.9 percent said they had not voted for the Duma and .6 percent could not recall whether they had. It is interesting to note that 7.7 percent of respondents who said they voted for the Duma said they had abstained in the referendum and .9 percent could not remember abstaining or voting in the referendum.

13. Cross-tabulations do show some differences across macroregions and turn up somewhat higher participation among rural and small-town dwellers and former members of the Communist Party of the Soviet Union (CPSU). But when regression analysis is used to control for the concurrent effects of all social variables, only educational level, occupational status, gender, and age are significant predictors of participation.

14. Somewhat mysterious is the intense animosity to the constitution by members of the nontitular nationalities in the republics. It seems to reflect a sense on their part that an overbearing central government was more of a danger than overbearing republic governments. For most such persons, of course, there was a republic designated as the ethnic homeland of their own ethnic group somewhere in Russia—usually nearby—but the same point could be made of non-Russians in the oblasts and krais.

15. In order to conserve observations for analysis, I recoded missing values on the opinion questions at the mean of the distribution on the question.

16. This lack of coherence of constitutional issues occurred despite the frequent linkage of them in politicians' rhetoric. For example, Yeltsin in his preelection speech to the nation tied the division of powers in Moscow to containment of centrifugal tendencies in the federation, saying a strong presidency "would personify all Russia and be the main guarantee of its unity" (*Rossiiskiye vesti,* December 11, 1993, p. 1).

17. As I have done elsewhere, I rescaled the opinion indicators to run from 0 to 1, which makes it easier to compare the coefficients computed.

18. Even among "yes" voters, though, the most popular position was to support equality between the two branches. Sixteen percent of "yes" voters favored parliamentary supremacy, 43 percent equality, and 26 percent presidential supremacy, with 16 percent undecided; for "no" voters the proportions were 30, 45, 12, and 13 percent.

19. It is mostly integration of the measure of approval of Yeltsin that reduces the coefficient for presidentialism, and addition of the scales for state control, welfarism, and the Soviet leaders enlarges the coefficients for centralism and antisovereignty opinion. Approval of Yeltsin was positively related to a "yes" vote in the referendum; high scores on the core opinion scores were negatively related to a "yes" vote.

20. Pearson's *r* for presidentialism and approval of Yeltsin, .31 for the entire sample (see table 10-4), is .42 for participants in the referendum who said they were acquainted with the draft and .26 for participants unacquainted with the draft.

21. See Samuel L. Popkin, *The Reasoning Voter: Communication and Persuasion in Presidential Campaigns* (University of Chicago Press, 1991).

22. For the sixth-finishing Yabloko, the relationship with a "yes" vote is negative and close to statistical significance ($p = .09$) among voters acquainted with the draft constitution.

23. The coefficients do not stray far below significance ($p = .06$, .06, and .10, respectively).

24. When the social characteristics given in table 10-3 are incorporated into a logistic regression using the opinion and party-support variables given in table 10-6, four sociological variables remain highly significant predictors of choice in the referendum: ethnicity, macroregion, age, and former membership in the CPSU. The age coefficient is in fact much larger than in the regression using only social variables as predictors. The reason for the difference is that older Russians tended in 1993 to have more conservative opinions on issues like the transition to the market and assessment of the Soviet past. Once the impact of these opinions is taken into account, the positive effect of age on receptivity toward Yeltsin's constitution comes through all the more sharply.

CHAPTER ELEVEN

Preserving the Radical Stronghold

The Election in Moscow

Judith S. Kullberg

ON DECEMBER 12, 1993, Moscow reaffirmed its support for fundamental reform. Just as in 1989, 1990, and 1991, Muscovites overwhelmingly supported democratic candidates and parties. Badly beaten in the country as a whole, radical and moderate reformist parties triumphed in Moscow, garnering 60.5 percent of the vote on the party-list ballot. Support for the radicals was particularly impressive: Russia's Choice received 34.7 percent of the Moscow vote, its highest plurality in any region of the country and more than twice its share of the national vote. Candidates nominated or supported by Russia's Choice also won eleven of the city's fifteen single-seat races and dominated in the contests for seats in the new Moscow City Duma. Parties and candidates of the extreme opposition were overwhelmed by the democratic landslide. The combined total for the Liberal Democratic Party of Russia (LDPR), the Communist Party of the Russian Federation (KPRF), and Agrarian Party of Russia was only 25.3 percent. Although the LDPR led on the national party-list ballot with 22.9 percent, it gathered only 12.8 percent of the Moscow vote, its fourth worst showing in all the regions.

How did radical reformism prevail in Moscow, as well as a few other large cities and northern regions, against the tide of support for the opposition? The standard economic explanation for the 1993 results is that the

311

Moscow Oblast

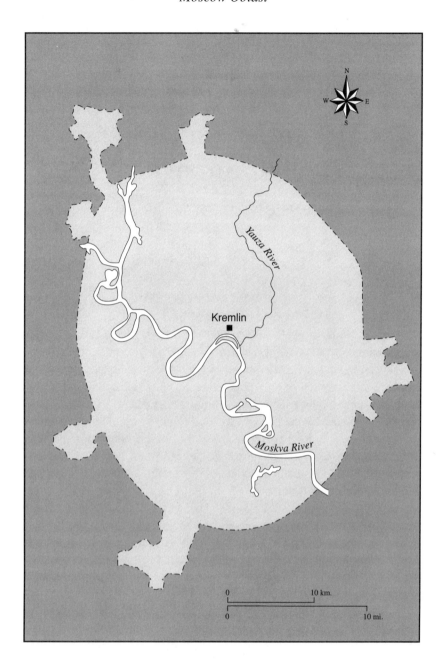

N
W · E
S

Yauza River

Kremlin
■

Moskva River

0   10 km.

0   10 mi.

"costs" incurred by the Gaidar "shock therapy" program of monetary stabilization and budgetary restraint fueled electoral support for opposition parties. This argument suggests that the reformists won where the costs of reform were lower—in other words, where regions and their populations were less harmed in the reform period.[1] Thus, we would expect that a relatively robust local economy produced the proreform Moscow vote. Yet, by almost all measures the Moscow economy was hit at least as hard as other regional economies. All through 1991 and 1992, industrial production in the city fell 25 percent, capital investment 19 percent, and retail trade 34 percent, compared with respective national declines of 18 percent, 39.7 percent, and 3.5 percent.[2] This economic decline severely affected the city's residents. By the end of 1992, 36 percent of Muscovites were living at or below the consumption minimum or absolute poverty level, compared with 28.2 percent of the Russian population as a whole. Further deterioration in the Moscow standard of living took place in 1993.[3]

The citizens of Moscow thus had as much cause as voters elsewhere to "throw the rascals out," yet they did not. Why? The answer is that a distinctly reformist political configuration had taken root in the capital. This configuration—made up of liberal voters, radical parties and politicians, and a proreform, probusiness power structure—was sufficiently established by 1993 to withstand the counterreformism that swept the country in the wake of economic decline. Although unique in several respects, the liberal Moscow configuration is just one example of the diverse, regionally based political climates that have emerged across Russia since the collapse of communism. To the extent that these climates can be explained only partially by differences in the performance of regional economies,[4] they reveal the insufficiency of simple or pure economic approaches to Russian electoral behavior and highlight the need for alternative theories and approaches.

An alternative explanation for the considerable political diversity across Russia's regions can be found in the contextual theory of electoral behavior. In contrast to economic theories of electoral behavior, which assume that voters are isolated monads who choose parties and candidates purely on the basis of calculations of expected utility,[5] the contextual approach conceptualizes voters as situated in, and influenced by, specific, geographically, and temporally bounded social contexts.[6] Contextualists argue that the political preferences and voting decisions of citizens are affected by the opinions and attitudes of the people with whom they live and work and the political information they receive.[7] The distribution of public opinion in a community and the content of political information are in turn heavily shaped by the presence and activities of social and political organizations, particularly political parties. To mobilize and sustain support, parties appeal to voters not only through programs and ideologies, but also by resurrecting memories of past conflicts or exploiting current tensions in the community or nation. If these strategies are successful, parties create or mold mass political identities and engender long-term patterns of voting behavior.[8] In sum, contextualists assert that voting is less a product of individual self-interest and calculation than of social influence, communication flows, and the activity of political organizations.[9]

This chapter adopts a contextualist framework to analyze the 1993 elections in Moscow. It explains the vote as a consequence of the sociodemographic character of the Moscow population, the character and ideology of the new political organizations and actors that arose in the late Soviet period, the content of political communications in the capital since the reform era, and the structure of political power in the city at the time of the elections. The analysis traces the persistent electoral reformism of Moscow to the city's demographics and to the broad-based democratic movement in the late 1980s that successfully mobilized millions of citizens to participate in rallies and to support democratic candidates in the first competitive elections in Soviet history. Reformist parties, the direct descendants of the democratic movement, won the 1993 elections by once again mobilizing substantial segments of the city's electorate with calls for radical transformation and destruction of the old order.

Electoral mobilization in 1993 was assisted considerably by the power structure that emerged in the city after the collapse of communism. The Moscow city and Russian state administration, in alliance with the developing business community and the capital's liberal mass media, directly and indirectly assisted reformist candidates and parties. In so doing, they created an uneven playing field on which centrist and extreme opposition parties found it difficult to compete.

Thus the 1993 reformist victory in Moscow was secured not only by the durable liberalism of Muscovites, but also by the direct involvement of the state in the campaign and the weak position of opposition parties in the city's power structure. The paradoxical combination of competition and state intervention is indicative of the complex character of postcommunist Russian politics and the continued centrality of the state in postcommunist political life. The conclusion to this chapter generalizes from the specific features of the Moscow case to consider the dynamics of Russian electoral politics and the long-term prospects of radical reformism in the country.

The Democratic Upsurge: 1986–91

As both the capital and the largest city of the Soviet Union, Moscow was the headquarters of the enormous state and Communist party bureaucracies, a major center of technology and advanced industry, and the home of the country's premier scientific, academic, and cultural institutions. Most significant developments in Soviet science, culture, and the arts took place in Moscow. With its numerous foreign embassies and large numbers of international visitors, Moscow was also the Soviet city in which foreign influences and ideas were most strongly felt. In comparison to the rest of the country, the cultural and intellectual life in Moscow was vital and intense.

The people who lived this richer and somewhat freer life constituted a relatively elite segment of the Russian population. Because of the capital's status as political, economic, and technological center, a large segment of the Moscow workforce, 42.2 percent, comprised higher status professionals and specialists, compared with 31 percent of all employed Russians. As we might expect from these statistics, proportionally fewer Muscovites were employed in the industrial sector, 24.1 percent versus 33.2 percent of all Russian workers, but many more in science, 19.8 versus 4.3 percent. An even clearer indication of the elite status of the Moscow population was its educational attainment. By the late 1980s, 26.4 percent of the Moscow population aged fifteen or older had completed a higher education, a proportion 2.3 times greater than in the same segment of the Russian population.[10]

By concentrating well-educated specialists in Moscow and a few other cities, rewarding them with high social status and according them a special role, the Soviet regime contributed to the emergence of a conscious social group—the intelligentsia. Dependent on the intelligentsia for the attainment of its production and development goals, yet chronically concerned about its tendency to bridle against restrictions on freedom of information and thought, the regime used a mixture of incentives with intellectuals that included rewards and privileges but also intimidation and repression. In reaction to the brutality of the Stalin era and the state's close supervision of and interference in their work across the entire Soviet period, many intellectuals harbored anger and resentment toward the regime. Although conditioned to mask their discontent, specialists and intellectuals were much more critical of the Soviet order than other social groups.[11]

Prevented from establishing independent organizations, the Moscow intelligentsia was arranged informally in a dense web of hundreds and perhaps thousands of small, intimate circles of friends and colleagues. With the relaxation of repression in the post-Stalin era, these circles spawned clandestine study and discussion groups, many of which were attracted to liberalism and saw democracy as the solution for the various problems plaguing society. From such groups came the dissidents and human rights activists of the late 1960s and 1970s.[12]

With Gorbachev's repeal in 1986 of the decades-long ban on nonstate civic organizations, the informal circles and hidden groups produced scores of new social and political organizations, the *neformal'ny* or nonformals. The political nonformals introduced tens of thousands of Muscovites, most of whom were highly educated professionals, to civic activism.[13] Initially supportive of Gorbachev's goal of democratizing state socialism, many nonformals quickly moved into open opposition to the Soviet regime. These "radical" democrats advocated the total, revolutionary destruction of the old order and its immediate replacement with liberal democracy.

The introduction of competitive elections for the Soviet Congress of People's Deputies in 1989 provided an incentive for the diverse Moscow nonformals to pool their resources, establish alliances, and support common lists of democratic candidates.[14] In January 1990, an election committee dubbed "Democratic Russia" was formed in Moscow for the express purpose of electing a national slate of democrats to the new Russian Congress of People's Deputies.[15] Democratic Russia rapidly blossomed into a mass movement that incorporated nonformals and voters' clubs from across Russia. This loose alliance was held together by a common commitment to fundamental social and political transformation and the establishment of liberal democracy.[16] The coalition successfully elected democrats to represent Moscow in the Soviet and Russian parliaments, and deputies adhering to the Democratic Russia platform took control of the new Moscow city soviet in 1990.

The elections created a new Moscow political elite, the most popular member of which was Boris Yeltsin. Yeltsin had been brought to Moscow from Sverdlovsk by Gorbachev in 1985 to revitalize the city party organization. Yeltsin lost his position as first secretary of the Moscow Communist Party Committee and was expelled from the Politburo when he began to attack the privileges of party officials and expose corruption within their ranks. Yeltsin's expulsion only enhanced his popularity and strengthened his image in Moscow as a reformer and a radical democrat.[17] Thwarting the attempts of the leadership to exclude him in the nomination process, Yeltsin ran in the national-territorial election District 1 of Moscow, gathering an impressive 89.44 percent of the vote.[18] With a popular mandate for fundamental reform, Yeltsin and the Moscow "progressive" contingent of deputies at the first Congress of People's Deputies organized other independent and radical deputies into the Interregional Group of Deputies (IRG). The IRG raised uncomfortable issues and pushed for more radical change at the Congress. In so doing, it undermined Gorbachev's control over the reform process and stole from him the agenda of radical transformation and democratization.[19]

The easy victories of Moscow's democrats in the 1989 parliamentary elections considerably weakened the Moscow Communist party committee's authority. When democrats took control of the city soviet and councils in the raions and microraions in 1990, the party was forced to largely withdraw from city politics. Losses at the polls precipitated the resignation of more than half a million members from the city party organization.[20] As the party withered at its base, Democratic Russia grew: Democratic Russia "cells" formed in more than two hundred work collectives, in some cases actually replacing the primary organizations of the party.

Contributing considerably to the weakening of the party and growing influence of Democratic Russia was the liberal Moscow press. Initially encouraged by the policy of glasnost, many established Moscow newspapers adopted an explicitly proreform position, and new stridently anticommunist newspapers and journals proliferated.[21] As a consequence, Muscovites were exposed more than most Russians to the basic tenets of liberal ideology and the radicals' harsh critiques of Soviet communism.

Genuinely mass in character, the democratic movement successfully mobilized millions of citizens to participate in rallies, marches, and election campaigns. Although solid evidence of the effects of the democratic movement on mass political orientations is limited, there can be little doubt that it altered the political loyalties of Muscovites. A survey conducted in early 1991 indicated that 51 percent of Muscovites "trusted" Democratic Russia, as compared with 13 percent who felt similarly about the Communist Party of the Soviet Union.[22] It is safe to assume that the democratic upsurge produced not only such broad, diffuse support for Democratic Russia but also commitment to democratic values, particularly among the most active participants.

The Postcommunist Crisis: 1991–93

Although the democratic upsurge of 1986 to 1991 fundamentally transformed Moscow politics, it did not lead directly to democratic consolidation. After the attempted August coup hastened the destruction of the party and the dissolution of the Soviet Union, sustained intraelite and interinstitutional conflict led to the fragmentation of the democratic movement and impeded the development of political parties and representative institutions in the city. At the heart of this conflict was a struggle over the political and economic resources of the socialist state. A few democrats, disentangling and distancing themselves from the democratic movement, strengthened the power of the city bureaucracy, undermined the Moscow city soviet, and established the basis for a new powerful political "machine" in the capital. They justified this course of action, and their unwillingness to compromise and work with moderates and social democrats, as necessary to destroy the last vestiges of communism.

The troubles of the postcommunist era actually began before the communist collapse. Democratic control of the Moscow city soviet and city government in 1990 led almost immediately to a power struggle and a scramble for the financial resources and property of the city government and the Communist party. Early "privatization" involved the transfer of state resources into the hands of politicians and their close allies. The ease with which political office could be used for material gain provided a powerful incentive for actors to pursue their own individual interests and to be less concerned with collective goods and goals, such as political and economic reform and the development of the city soviet. As Boris Kagarlitskii, a social democratic deputy of the soviet, describes the situation in 1990–91, "Most democratic politicians were concentrating on shoving their rivals away from the feeding trough."[23]

While the city soviet floundered in endless debates and its sessions degenerated into rowdy shouting matches, Gavriil Popov, the elected chair of the soviet, Sergei Stankevich, the deputy chair, and Yurii Luzhkov, a longtime city bureaucrat appointed by Popov to head the city administration, quickly expanded their power and that of the city's bureaucracy. In part, this expansion appears to have been a conscious move to maximize their autonomy and to prevent the soviet from overseeing or interfering with their business activities. Their power was also enhanced greatly by the fact that as the top officials of the new government, they had acquired control of tremendous resources—the city bureaucracy, the vast public wealth of the city, and influence over the mass media. With such assets, their preeminence was virtually guaranteed. They did not need to rely on the soviet to exercise authority, a fact they made sure to point out to the deputies.[24] The deputy corps' attempts to resist the leadership's practice of bypassing the council and ignoring its decisions were largely ineffective. The deputies' lack of political experience, their reliance on the soviet leadership for salaries and other material benefits, and the incoherence of the Democratic Russia faction hampered the exercise of the powers formally allocated to the soviet.[25]

In early 1991, Popov sought to institutionalize his preeminence by proposing an amendment to city law that would establish the position of a directly elected mayor of Moscow. This move was coordinated with the proposal by Boris Yeltsin, Popov's ally, who was at that time chair of the Russian Congress of People's Deputies, for the creation of the office of president of Russia. Yeltsin and his advisors apparently believed that centralizing the power of Moscow government into the hands of an individual allied with Yeltsin would strengthen Yeltsin's power once he became president of Russia.[26] (This assumption was to be proven correct in October 1993.) The creation of an independent executive intensified intraelite conflict and transformed it into interinstitutional power struggle. After Popov was elected mayor, he, the soviet and the soviet's new chair, Nikolai Gonchar, were continually at odds.

This conflict paralleled and was exacerbated by the national presidential-parliamentary fight, which by late 1992 had engulfed all major actors in the capital. Caught in the crossfire were the new and still fragile political organizations that had emerged in the city during the democratic upsurge. Democratic Russia was immediately harmed. Its leaders quarreled and split over the relations the movement should have with the Yeltsin government.[27] Democratic Russia's member parties, such as the Democratic Party of Russia, were similarly rent. Some actors, such as Mayor Popov, withdrew from political life when they perceived that events were leading the country off the democratic path (Luzhkov replaced Popov as mayor in June 1992). Others sought to form a loyal opposition to the Yeltsin government. The most prominent opposition organization, the Civic Union, set up a Moscow branch that united a small group of local officials, including city soviet chair Gonchar, and leading figures in the Moscow organizations of the Democratic Party of Russia and Vice President Aleksandr Rutskoi's Peoples' Party of Free Russia.[28] It is not surprising that the conflict and fragmentation in the democratic camp effected a rapid demobilization of Moscow's rank-and-file democratic activists.

As the democratic movement ruptured, the extreme opposition gained strength. The rise of conservative Communist and nationalist groups, which had been practically invisible in the city during the democratic upsurge, posed an additional threat to the Russian and Moscow governments. Their rallies and marches drew significant numbers of elderly, unemployed, and otherwise marginalized and materially disadvantaged individuals. As tensions increased between the opposition and the government, the protests of the extreme opposition became violent. In the particularly ugly 1993 May Day demonstration, about six hundred people were injured and one Interior Ministry officer died four days later as a result of injuries sustained during the demonstration.

Yeltsin's dissolution of the Russian parliament through decree on September 21, 1993, triggered severe civil violence in the capital. Many deputies of the Moscow soviet sided with the Russian parliament and established bases for resistance to the government in several raion soviets. The activity in these centers intensified after the White House was cordoned off by special forces troops and surrounded by tanks on September 28. The ultimate escalation of the conflict on October 3rd and 4th to armed violence and the shelling of the White House by tanks left hundreds dead, many of them Muscovites.[29]

The loyalty of Mayor Luzhkov to the Yeltsin government was a crucial factor in the suppression of the opposition "uprising." The city militia helped to restore order and disperse the remaining bands of oppositionists left in the city after the capture of the White House. Luzhkov declared a state of emergency, and tens of thousands were arrested as the city was "cleaned up" of protesters, "criminals," and people from the Caucasus, particularly Chechens, lacking resident permits. Using his emergency powers, Luzhkov also dissolved the city soviet and raion soviets on October 6. Opposition parties and papers were banned, and other newspapers and television broadcasts were censored.[30] With the opposition crushed and representative institutions dissolved, the mayor and his bureaucracy, in alliance with the Russian government, stood as the unchallenged masters of Moscow.

The Field of Competition

The denouement of the postcommunist crisis profoundly affected the position of Moscow's political forces and actors in the election campaign. It strengthened those attached to or supportive of the Yeltsin government, primarily Russia's Choice, and destroyed or severely weakened those linked to the Russian parliament, the city soviet, or the centrist and extreme oppositions. A central feature of Moscow's political landscape at the time of the election campaign was a political machine headed by Mayor Yurii Luzhkov. The machine was not a single coherent organization, but rather an alliance consisting of the city bureaucracy, banks and businesses, and remnants of Democratic Russia linked to the city administration through representatives in the mayor's office.[31] The combined efforts of these allies did much to preserve Moscow as a reformist stronghold in the 1993 elections.

Because of its effect on electoral competition, the relationship between the Moscow government and the emergent business sector deserves careful examination. As a major supplier of property to the burgeoning real estate market in the city, Luzhkov and the Moscow city administration developed close ties with construction firms and financial organizations.[32] These firms were directly beholden to the state for their wealth and dependent on it for future inputs of resources. A fine illustration of the relations between the local state and Russian capitalists is Most Bank. Most was founded with Luzhkov's direct assistance and headed by his friend and ally, Vladimir Gusinskii. The city deposited a large share of its annual budget in Most, but allegedly received no interest while Most used the money to finance its development projects. Fifty percent of the bank's capital holdings reportedly consisted of privatized Moscow real estate.[33] At the time of the election campaign, Most was even housed in the *meriya* (city hall). Thus, in a very real sense, Most and firms like it were extensions of the Moscow city bureaucracy.

Given the dependence of business on the local state, it is hardly surprising that Most and other Moscow banks and financial institutions made significant contributions to the campaign funds of the democratic election associations. According to a political consultant at Most, banks preferred Russia's Choice although they also supplied smaller sums of money to Yabloko, Party of Unity and Accord (PRES), and the Russian Movement for Democratic Reform (RDDR).[34] The campaign provided Moscow banks and other types of enterprises an excellent opportunity to further strengthen their relations with the government and advance their interests.[35]

A major asset for the Luzhkov machine and the ruling party was the Moscow mass media. The newspaper *Kuranty*, which had been the official organ of the Moscow soviet, fell under the control of the city administration after the soviet was dissolved and became a mouthpiece for city government. The major independent newspapers in Moscow, particularly *Moskovskii komsomolets* and *Segodnya*, also clearly favored the ruling party during the campaign. Considerable attention was paid by the press to Russia's Choice candidates and other prominent liberals, but very few reports about the centrist parties and their candidates, and even fewer about the extreme opposition, appeared in newspapers during the campaign. If the opposition was mentioned at all, it was with disdain. Opposition candidates were depicted as unreformed Communists or rabble-rousing rebels who were somehow responsible for the October uprising.[36]

In part, the open partisanship of newspapers was the natural continuation of the reformist, anticommunist orientation they had adopted in the period of the democratic upsurge. However, their proreform position was now reinforced by rubles spent on advertising, much of it from firms with strong connections to the Moscow and Russian administrations. Direct ownership of the press by new capitalists also played a role in ensuring favorable coverage for the ruling party. By late 1993, Most Bank's expanding empire of business firms, the MOST Group, owned the newspaper *Segodnya*, the "independent" television station NTV, and the radio station *Ekho Moskvy*, all major sources of information for Muscovites.[37]

The Election Campaign

Despite the unevenness of the playing field and the highly unequal distribution of resources among contenders, electoral competition did take place. Complete control over election outcomes was rendered impossible by the realities of fragmentation and divisiveness among democrats, structural weaknesses in the Russia's Choice organization, and the inability of the ruling clique to entirely block the flow of resources to its competitors. These holes in what might otherwise have been an impenetrable offense established a basis for competition.

The opposition, however, was unable to take full advantage of these weaknesses because of its own state of disarray. The call for elections found the nonstate parties and blocs in Moscow woefully unprepared for a campaign. Most were poorly organized, lacked coherent strategy and plans, and had limited human and financial resources. With about two and a half months to election day, parties and candidates raced to put together staffs, recruit volunteers, develop strategy and tactics, and raise funds. Participants complained that the race was more of a "sprint" than a "marathon."[38] As Grigorii Rebrov, a Communist Party of the Russian Federation (KPRF) candidate in District 194, commented wryly, "The tempo of the campaign is such that only Communists can do well under such circumstances. Only Bolsheviks can triumph in such a campaign."[39]

The first stretch of the sprint was devoted to registration. As undoubtedly foreseen by those who wrote the rules, Russia's Choice had little difficulty gathering signatures in Moscow. It activated the extensive network of Democratic Russia activists and supporters in the city to quickly gather the maximum number of signatures possible in one region, while other parties struggled to reach the minimum.[40] The bloc also used the state-owned media to appeal for signatures. On November 10, five days before the registration deadline, *Kuranty* published a front-page article by Yegor Gaidar asking Muscovites to rapidly collect 35,000 signatures for Yurii Chernichenko's candidacy in the Federation Council race. The appeal was also broadcast on the state radio station *Mayak*.[41] Additional evidence suggests that the state bureaucracy was also used by Russia's Choice to gather signatures for itself and its allies[42] and that the police may have been called on to block the registration of an opposition party. In early November, a special security force of the Moscow militia raided the Russian People's Union (RPU) headquarters, after which the party reported that signature lists had been taken. The RPU was subsequently denied registration on the grounds of a shortfall of signatures.[43]

Lacking the resources possessed by Russia's Choice, the contending parties and independent candidates found other means of gathering signatures. The most common tactic was the exchange of money or gifts for signatures. Falsification of signatures also appears to have been rampant in Moscow. It proved to be an effective means of gaining registration, because the election commissions were so poorly staffed and funded that they could not possibly verify the validity of all the signatures collected.[44] As a consequence, the intended effect of the registration requirements to weed out competitors of the ruling party was not entirely achieved.

Players and Strategies

At the end of the registration period, thirteen political parties and blocs were left to vie for a share of the huge Moscow vote on the single national party-list ballot. One hundred sixty-six party and independent candidates stood for election in the fifteen single-seat State Duma districts and the two-seat Federation Council district. The strength of the contenders, as well as their strategies and the character of their campaigns, varied considerably. This variation affected the ability of the parties to communicate with voters and mobilize support.

Radical and Moderate Reformists

Of all the contending blocs, Russia's Choice occupied the most advantageous position in Moscow. The bloc was partially based in the machinery of the Russian and Moscow government, possessed good connections with Moscow's banking and entrepreneurial elite, and received favorable coverage from the press. As the chief beneficiary of the uneven postcommunist playing field, Russia's Choice used the resources at its disposal to squeeze out the opposition and mobilize the democratic electorate.

However strong the general position of the reformist camp, it had one major weakness: it was divided. Rather than pooling their resources and efforts, reformist politicians competed with one another. In so doing, they risked splitting the democratic vote. This division appears to have been largely a product of elite ambition, since it was not paralleled by deep divisions among rank-and-file democratic activists. Svetlana Bol'shego, organizer of the RDDR's Moscow campaign, observed that "The same people gathered signatures for RDDR, for Shakhrai [PRES], for all the candidates of a democratic orientation. And they gave help alike to all. And the same for the flyers. They came to us to distribute them, and they went to Russia's Choice...."[45]

Although elite ambition was certainly a factor, the reformists were also riven by disagreement over the correctness of Yeltsin's handling of the Russian parliament and the ensuing September–October crisis. The October crisis was a source of friction between the two components of the Russia's Choice Moscow organization—the Moscow political "establishment" (the presidential administration, segments of the Russian government, and Luzhkov's machine) and the Moscow Democratic Russia organization. The founding of the bloc prompted a withdrawal in late October from

Democratic Russia by groups that would not tolerate a formal electoral alliance with a government that had violated the constitution in dissolving the parliament.[46] Democratic Russia's leaders were acutely aware of the tenuous support for the alliance among their remaining members and repeatedly stated during the course of the campaign that Russia's Choice was merely a temporary alliance.[47]

The possible benefits accruing from the alliance outweighed whatever distaste each side had for the other. In particular, the establishment needed Democratic Russia. By allying with Democratic Russia, it hoped to mobilize the huge Moscow electorate, thereby adding substantially to its share of the national vote on the party-list ballot and acquiring most of the city's single-member district seats.[48] Democratic Russia could provide candidates with great popular appeal, the stars of the Moscow democratic and human rights movements, most of whom had ridden the first waves of anticommunism into office in 1989 and 1990 (figures such as Sergei Kovalev, Lev Ponomarev, Alla Gerber, and Yulii Nisnevich). Furthermore, Democratic Russia still possessed a grassroots organization. Although considerably diminished by the general decline in participation after 1991, substantial remnants of the loose alliance of voter's clubs and raion-level organizations of the democratic movement remained. The establishment turned to Democratic Russia to carry out the entire election campaign in Moscow, counting on its networks of activists to gather signatures, distribute campaign material, and get out the vote.[49]

For its part, the establishment provided overall strategy and brought invaluable resources to the campaign. It did most of the fund raising, relying on its connections with Moscow's banks and commercial structures. The money thus raised was used primarily for mass media advertising in the city. The establishment also made use of government facilities and employees in the campaign.[50] Other crucial resources, such as the control of state-owned media and influence over the independent Moscow press, were provided by the establishment. Augmenting the Russia's Choice lineup were several well-known government officials and actors, such as Boris Fedorov, the Minister of Finance, and Andrei Makarov, lawyer and former head of a special presidential committee that had been established to investigate corruption within the government and parliament.

In contrast with the extensive, if loose, networks and operations of Russia's Choice, PRES had a limited presence in Moscow. Although Deputy Prime Minister Sergei Shakhrai claimed in mid-November that his party had a "strong" Moscow organization, the evidence indicates that PRES's

Moscow organization connected several elite groups within various structures of the Russian government, the disbanded city soviet, and a few other institutional and personal networks.[51] According to Telman Gdlyan, chair of the People's Party, the groups that made up PRES were united not by a coherent ideological position but by desire for power.[52] PRES's selection of candidates betrayed the bureaucratic origins of the party: Of the ten who stood for election in Moscow's single-seat districts, six held positions in government administration, three of those in the Russian state bureaucracy.[53] Not surprisingly, reports indicated that the party also used state resources and staff in the campaign.[54]

PRES's official national strategy was to work in tandem with Russia's Choice, focusing its efforts on the various regions of the country to "squeeze out" the Agrarian party, while leaving Russia's Choice to go after the Communists and nationalists in Moscow and other "big industrial centers."[55] However, this strategy did not prevent PRES from attempting to wrest a piece of the Moscow vote away from Russia's Choice. Compensating for its shallow organization, the party engaged in an extensive media campaign on local radio and in city newspapers.[56] Furthermore, Shakhrai's national video clips, which featured him exchanging views with cultural and intellectual figures, had a surprisingly distinct Moscow flavor for a politician with eyes on the "regions." PRES also conveyed its intentions to carve out a place in Moscow politics by nominating eighteen candidates in the thirty-five districts to the new City Duma.[57]

Almost completely unconnected to government structures and in a much more adversarial position to the government was the Yavlinskii-Boldyrev-Lukin bloc (Yabloko). In founding the bloc, Yavlinskii made direct appeals to Moscow groups that had split off from Democratic Russia because of the alliance with Russia's Choice, appearing, for instance at the founding Congress of the League of Independents in mid-October to gather supporters.[58] Yabloko was relatively successful in attracting disgruntled Democratic Russia activists by criticizing the government's authoritarian behavior and disregard for the democratic rules of the game.[59]

Accepting the impossibility of actually defeating Russia's Choice on its home turf, Yabloko strove simply to do as well as possible in Moscow, and in the process, to construct an organization that could be used in the 1996 presidential election.[60] Yabloko's campaign effort relied on the bloc's component parties, particularly the Republican party, several civic organizations, including the Russian Ecological Union, the Independent Women's Forum, and the Academy of Sciences Voters' Club, and the personal networks of Yabloko's leaders and candidates.[61] Although each party occupied separate office space and maintained separate staffs and operations, this did not seem to hinder the bloc's campaign. Indeed, the Yabloko campaign effort in the city was impressive. In the last week before the election, the bloc, relying partly on paid campaign workers, distributed tens of thousands of pieces of campaign literature daily.[62] This literature and the programs adopted by the bloc's candidates in the Duma district races emphasized the necessity of adhering to democratic rules, strengthening representative institutions, checking arbitrary power of officials, and protecting society from the ravages of marketization.

Similar to Yabloko in its minimal ties to the Russian state bureaucracy and also adopting a critical stance on the government's policies and behavior, albeit much more muted than Yabloko's, was the Russian Movement for Democratic Reform (RDDR).[63] Originally founded by former mayor Gavriil Popov and others in 1991, RDDR had fairly good connections with city government. Although current mayor Luzhkov refrained from participating in the 1993 campaign, city deputy premier Aleksandr Braginskii ran (and won) as an RDDR candidate in District 201, and some city personnel worked in the RDDR campaign.

RDDR's campaign strategy was to rely on an extensive grassroots organization with branches and coordinators in each district of the city. However, after the election, staffers complained that the movement's resources had been inadequate for mounting such a campaign and that the party had attracted fewer volunteers than anticipated.[64] In retrospect, it appears that RDDR counted too heavily on its reputation as a "prestigious" organization of reformist intellectuals and overestimated its support within the Moscow electorate. To the extent that RDDR's program and strategy emphasized grassroots activism, and relied very little on the mass media, the movement seemed nostalgically stuck in the period of democratic upsurge.[65]

Centrists

Centrist parties and blocs were in poor condition in Moscow in autumn 1993, and none more so than those that had been involved in the conflict between the president and the parliament. Having failed in their attempt to defend parliamentary democracy against the encroachments of the executive, they were disorganized and discouraged. Not only were their organizations weak, but they were either ignored or ridiculed by the Moscow press. A sur-

vey of the campaigns of the most viable centrist contenders reveals just
how negligible the centrist presence in the city was.

A shadow of its former self, the Democratic Party of Russia conducted
an extremely limited campaign, sponsoring only three candidates in Moscow's fifteen Duma districts. Weakened by a precipitous loss in membership because of the DPR's involvement in the presidential-parliamentary
battle, the city organization was further harmed in the autumn by a rift with
the party's leader, Nikolai Travkin, over the quality of its nominees and its
conduct of the campaign.[66] Travkin's criticism of the operation appeared
justified—the Moscow organization seemed to be barely functioning and
had no coherent campaign strategy.[67] Most of the space in the party's poorly
heated headquarters was rented to a private business, in contrast to the preceding year when the entire building was occupied by the DPR. Hand-
painted signs and blurry mimeographed handbills attested to the organization's poor finances.

The Civic Union, to which DPR had belonged, was scarcely in better
condition. It nominated one candidate for the Federal Assembly, three candidates in the single-member districts, and thirty-five candidates (one in
each district) for the City Duma. The Civic Union operation was heavily
dependent on what was left of the Moscow branch of Rutskoi's People's
Party of Free Russia and its youth auxiliary. The factor that gave some hope
to the Civic Union in Moscow was the general popularity of its Moscow
leader, Nikolai Gonchar, former chair of the dissolved Moscow city soviet.[68] However, early predictions by the Civic Union's political consultants
that its candidates would be viable contenders against Russia's Choice candidates in the single-seat districts proved to be wildly optimistic, because
the bloc suffered a crushing defeat in the city and throughout the country as
a whole.[69] Yet all was not lost: Gonchar won one of the two seats to the Federal Assembly, and two other Civic Union candidates won in the City
Duma.

Although it did not have a separate Moscow campaign organization or
coordinator, the Women of Russia bloc managed a respectable showing in
Moscow. Such returns on a very thin organization were made possible by
the bloc's effective use of the mass media. Much less successful in compensating for minimal organization with mass media appeals was the Constructive Ecological Movement of Russia (KEDR), an ecological party organizationally based in the "sanitary and epidemiological supervision"
administrations of Moscow and the oblast. Housed in a few rooms of a
former research institute in Moscow's *Kitai gorod,* KEDR nominated ten

candidates in the city races but did little more than distribute flyers and calendars on the streets during the last few days of the campaign.[70]

Socialists and Nationalists

Although the extreme opposition was also severely damaged in the interelite conflict, the KPRF and the LDPR managed to campaign in Moscow. Their success in actually competing in the elections can be attributed to their relatively well-developed organizations and the commitment of their activists.

Despite the perception of the national KPRF leadership that Communists faced a hostile environment in Moscow and other large cities, the heads of the Moscow organization were less negative about their position in the city.[71] Their optimism does not appear to be entirely unfounded. Analysis of survey results in the following section shows that although workers and pensioners were the core supporters of the KPRF in Moscow, they were also able to attract voters from the intelligentsia. A KPRF organization at Moscow State University was quite active and visible during the campaign, and Communist candidates held meetings there that were well attended by faculty and students.[72]

Although confident and proud of the strength of its organization, the Moscow KPRF leadership admitted that it felt handicapped by limited resources and an unsympathetic press. Lacking money to mount a mass media campaign, the Communists relied on traditional agitation, which was facilitated by the party's solid and disciplined organization.[73] Operations at KPRF headquarters were rather primitive but efficient.

The LDPR was better organized and better prepared for the elections. In part, this was because the party had stayed out of the September–October fray between the president and the parliament. As a consequence it could not be blackened by the Moscow press as a counterrevolutionary group, although it was never treated as a respectable contender to the ruling party.

Most explanations for the LDPR's national victory have focused on the impact of Zhirinovskii's television appearances, ignoring the considerable organizational work conducted prior to the election that transformed a small fringe group into a genuine party. As the home of the party, Moscow was the site in which most of this work had been done. In the two years before the elections, Zhirinovskii staged weekly Sunday afternoon rallies near the Sokolniki metro station, which drew crowds numbering in the thousands. The party also published two newspapers in Moscow, *Pravda Zhiri-*

novskogo, Zhirinovskii's Truth, and *Sokol Zhirinovskogo*, Falcon of Zhirinovskii, which propagated the party's ideology and the ideas of its leader. Long before the call for early elections, the LDPR began to prepare for the campaign by recruiting qualified individuals for positions within the party and as candidates.[74] Although most of the LDPR's candidates in Moscow's single-member districts were political neophytes, they were generally well educated, and a few were respected intellectuals or had been previously active in Moscow politics.[75]

The 1993 LDPR campaign in Moscow relied on the tried-and-true meetings at Sokolniki and a few other locations. At the meetings, just as in the LDPR's media campaign, Zhirinovskii was the main attraction. Filled with vivid images and jokes, his speeches were both passionate denunciations of the post-Soviet order and entertaining performances. At their conclusion, people surged forward to touch Zhirinovskii, shake his hand, or ask for his autograph. At one rally, people mobbed a truck blaring the LDPR campaign song for Zhirinovskii posters. In the post-October climate of political apathy and pessimism, the excitement surrounding Zhirinovskii was impressive.

Electoral Mobilization

Judging solely from the vote on the party-list ballot, the returns to parties corresponded quite well with their relative position on the playing field and expenditure of effort and resources in the campaign. Russia's Choice, the bloc with the strongest organization, candidates, finances, and other resources accruing to it from its status as ruling party, received the largest percentage of the vote. The vote shares taken by other parties also correlated closely with their resources, effort, and level of organizational development.

Electoral victories are not simply "bought," however, by the expenditure of resources, but also generated by appeals to established political identities and loyalties. The national election study data provide compelling evidence that the Moscow electorate, with its long exposure to liberal ideas and past support of radical and reformist candidates, was particularly responsive to reformist appeals, particularly radical appeals. Tables 11-1 and 11-2 compare the preelection-day party preferences of the Moscow subsample and the rest of the Russian sample. They reveal significantly higher levels of support for Russia's Choice across all educational and occupational groups in Moscow. Although the strongest support for Russia's Choice was ex-

Table 11-1. Party Preference by Level of Education, National and Moscow Samples[a]

First figure in each cell is the number of cases; the second is the column percentage

Party preference	Illiterate and elementary		Incomplete secondary		Complete secondary		Secondary specialized		Incomplete higher		Complete higher	
	National	Moscow	National	Moscow	National	Moscow	National	Moscow	National	Moscow	National	Moscow
Russia's Choice	24	19	55	15	43	23	84	32	20	11	64	58
	17	73	15	26	17	37	20	37	32	38	30	46
Other reformists	21	0	56	15	49	14	82	24	17	13	54	31
	15	0	15	26	19	22	20	28	27	45	25	25
Centrists	19	2	91	14	65	11	116	13	12	2	52	19
	14	8	25	25	25	18	28	15	20	7	24	15
KPRF and Agrarian party	43	0	85	3	39	5	50	7	7	1	35	10
	30	0	23	5	15	8	12	8	11	3	16	8
LDPR	35	5	83	10	61	10	79	10	6	2	10	7
	25	19	23	18	24	16	19	12	10	7	5	6
Total	142	26	370	57	258	63	411	86	62	29	206	125
	100	100	100	100	100	100	100	100	100	100	100	100

Source: National election study, November 1993.

a. The table does not include respondents who were undecided as to their party preference (about 50 percent of respondents who indicated they intended to vote) and the small percentage of voters who indicated they would vote against all parties.

Table 11-2. Party Preference by Occupation, National and Moscow Samples[a]

First figure in each cell is the number of cases; the second is the column percentage

Party preference	Administrators and managers		Technical specialists		Natural sciences and humanities specialists		Clerical workers		Skilled workers		Unskilled workers	
	National	Moscow	National	Moscow	National	Moscow	National	Moscow	National	Moscow	National	Moscow
Russia's Choice	40	30	25	18	33	28	44	20	65	24	39	9
	24	44	20	38	27	49	21	42	15	33	23	28
Other reformists	32	16	38	12	27	17	43	13	66	15	35	13
	20	23	31	24	22	30	21	28	16	21	21	41
Centrists	41	11	28	13	33	7	53	6	101	12	45	2
	25	16	23	28	27	12	26	14	24	17	20	6
KPRF and Agrarian party	31	9	22	1	18	2	32	3	67	7	22	3
	19	13	18	3	15	4	16	6	16	10	13	9
LDPR	20	3	11	4	12	3	35	5	128	14	30	5
	12	4	9	8	10	5	17	11	30	20	18	16
Total	164	69	124	48	123	57	207	47	428	72	171	32
	100	100	100	100	100	100	100	100	100	100	100	100

Source: National election study, November 1993.
a. Excluding undecided and those who indicated they would vote against all parties.

pressed by those groups that made up the backbone of the democratic movement—the well-educated, higher ranking managers and the non-technical intelligentsia—the bloc also drew voters from the rest of the socioeconomic spectrum. Levels of support for Russia's Choice among citizens lacking a higher education, technical specialists, office workers, and skilled workers were 1.5 to 2 times greater in Moscow than in the rest of Russia.

Additional evidence that the preexisting liberalism of the electorate contributed to the reformist victory is the relative immunity of Muscovites' loyalties to the ravages of economic downturn. Table 11-3, which displays individual party preference by reported change in family financial situation, shows that in comparison to other Russians, the preferences of Muscovites were not as affected by deterioration in family material well-being. Although reported family financial position was strongly associated with support for reformist parties in the non-Moscow sample, the relationship was markedly weaker and flatter among the Moscow respondents. Only among those Muscovites who reported their situation to be much worse do we see a substantial drop in support for reformist parties.

The national election survey data also provide clear evidence that the radical and moderate reformists appealed to the democratic commitments and loyalties of the Moscow population. Results of logistic regression presented in table 11-4 show that anti-Soviet and proreform attitudes were strongly associated with an intention to vote for the reformists. Support for the rapid transition to the market, a belief that the collapse of the Soviet state had benefited Russia, and a perception that Western nations had only good intentions in their relations with Russia were all strong predictors of a preference for reformists. Positive assessment of Yeltsin's performance in office was also a good predictor of a reformist preference.

The survey data thus provide compelling evidence that the strength of liberal commitments was an important fact in the reformist victory. They also support the claim made earlier that the reformist parties' near monopoly on the Moscow mass media and political communications assisted in the mobilization of the reformist vote. Exposure to newspaper articles during the campaign was strongly and positively associated with an intention to vote for the radicals ($r = .15$, $p .01$), even when controlling for age and education ($r = .143$, $p .01$), but was not correlated at all with an intention to vote for moderate reformist, centrist, or opposition parties. The absence of a relationship between exposure to newspaper coverage of the campaign and support for other parties can be explained by the liberal bias of the print media.

Table 11-3. Party Preference by Reported Change in Family's Financial Situation in the Past Year, National vs. Moscow Samples

First figure in each cell is the number of cases; the second is the column percentage

Party preference	Much better		Somewhat better		Unchanged		Somewhat worse		Much worse	
	National	Moscow	National	Moscow	National	Moscow	National	Moscow	National	Moscow
Reformists	26	18	104	58	158	77	141	61	135	47
	52	85	53	83	48	70	38	78	27	44
Centrists	9	2	48	6	67	15	92	8	133	23
	18	9	24	9	20	14	25	11	27	22
Antireformists	15	1	45	6	105	19	137	9	228	36
	30	7	23	8	32	17	37	11	46	34
Total	50	21	197	70	330	111	370	78	496	106
	100	100	100	100	100	100	100	100	100	100

Source: National election survey, November 1993.

Table 11-4. *Logistic Regression Model of Party Preference*[a]

Variables	Coefficients
MARKET[b]	
Transition to market should be quick	−.9707
Transition should be gradual	−1.6823
Against the market economy	−2.2429
WEST[c]	−.6669*
YELTSIN[d]	−.7333*
SOVSTATE[e]	−.6669*
Constant	7.2289
Model improvement (percent)	14.42
Cases correctly predicted (percent)	80.13

Source: Moscow sample of the national election survey, November 1993.
a. Reported intention to vote for a reformist party was coded 1, for a centrist or opposition party, 0.
b. "What do you think about the transition to a market economy in Russia?"
c. "Is the West pursuing the goal of weakening Russia with its economic advice?" Possible responses were "Yes, certainly," "Probably yes," "Probably no" and "No, certainly not." Coding of this variable was reversed for the analysis.
d. "Do you approve of B. N. Yeltsin's activity in the post of president of Russia?" Responses ranged along four categories from completely approve to completely disapprove.
e. "How do you assess the disintegration of the Soviet Union?" Respondents were given four possible response categories, ranging from "It was beneficial," to "It was harmful."
*p <.01.

The beneficial effects accruing to Russia's Choice from newspaper bias were partially balanced by television coverage of the campaign. For example, exposure to television broadcasts was positively correlated with an intention to vote for the LDPR, even controlling for age and education ($r = .13$, $p < .01$). This finding can be explained by the fact that television coverage of the campaign, due to the legal mandate of an equal amount of free airtime for all parties and the LDPR's purchase of large blocs of time, was considerably less biased against the LDPR than the Moscow print media.

In sum, data gathered by the survey of the Moscow population support the central claim of the chapter that reformists triumphed in Moscow in large measure because they managed to mobilize an already existing liberal electorate. Survey responses also provide evidence that the opposition parties, because of the pervasiveness of liberal views and the uneven playing field, were unable to benefit in the capital as fully from economic decline as they did in many other regions of the country.

The Vote in the Single-Member Districts

However durable the liberalism of the Moscow electorate and firm its attachments to reformists, examination of the vote in the single-member district races suggests that the fragmentation of the political elite and inattention to organizational development in the postcommunist era threatened reformist dominance in the city. Competition among democrats and weak campaigns in the districts reduced margins of victory, thus enhancing the chances of independent candidates and increasing the probability that nationalist or socialist opposition candidates could be elected to the Duma, even in radical democratic Moscow.

The threat to reformist dominance can be seen clearly in the performance of Russia's Choice in the districts. Although Russia's Choice managed to emerge as the hands-down victor on the party-list ballot, its control over outcomes in the single-member districts was much more tenuous. While it gathered nearly 35 percent of the vote on the party-list ballot, the average share of its candidates in the districts was only 20.4 percent (table 11-5).[76] Furthermore, Russia's Choice candidates faced serious competition in more than half the districts. They lost four races and squeaked through five others with a margin of victory that averaged only 3.8 percent.[77]

A number of factors contributed to the competitiveness of the district races. First, the large number of candidates—an average of eleven per district—inevitably fragmented the vote and reduced margins of victory. Faced with such long lists, approximately 20 percent of voters cast their ballots against all candidates. The extent of negative voting was such that in six of Moscow's fifteen districts the percentage of ballots cast against all candidates actually exceeded the percentage cast for the winner.[78] As a consequence of fragmentation of the vote and negative voting, victors were sent to the Duma with the support of only a small minority of the voters in their districts. For example, Finance Minister Boris Fedorov, a Russia's Choice candidate, trounced his opponents in District 205, but he actually received only 12 percent of the eligible vote in the district.

A second factor that eroded the position of Russia's Choice in the districts was competition from other reformist parties. By facing off against one another in the district races, the reformists split the democratic vote and enhanced the chances of independent and opposition candidates. In each of the districts in which a Russia's Choice candidate won with a margin of less than 5 percent, competition from other reformist candidates, particularly those from Yabloko and PRES, heightened the closeness of the race. Where democrats lost, it was also at least partially a result of the competition from other democrats.

The best example of the dire consequences from head-to-head contests among democrats was the victory of nationalist Yurii Vlasov in District 200. Vlasov won with 24.5 percent of the vote, narrowly surpassing the

Table 11-5. Results in the Single-member State Duma Districts, City of Moscow, December 1993

District	Number of candidates	Average per candidate share of vote	Winner	Party or bloc	Winner's share of vote	Percent of votes cast "against-all"
191	10	7.3	Nisnevich.	Russia's Choice	15.5	27
192	11	7.5	Kovalev	Russia's Choice	25.1	18
193	11	7.6	Zadonskii.	Russia's Choice	22.1	20
194	10	8.0	Khakamada	Independent[a]	29.6	20
195	9	8.2	Mironov	Independent[a]	20.5	27
196	11	7.2	Volkov	Independent	18.9	21
197	13	5.7	Osovtsov	Independent[a]	16.8	25
198	8	9.9	Zhukov	Dignity and Compassion[a]	25.1	21
199	13	6.1	Gerber	Independent[a]	19.6	21
200	9	9.8	Vlasov	Independent	24.5	12
201	13	6.3	Braginskii	RDDR	23.2	19
202	16	5.3	Tarasov	Independent	14.9	16
203	11	7.1	Makarov	Russia's Choice	29.4	22
204	9	9.6	Medvedev	Independent[a]	23.8	14
205	9	8.4	Fedorov	Russia's Choice	25.7	24

Source: Tsentral'naya Izbiratel'naya Komissiya Rossiiskoi Federatsii. Russian Central Electoral Commission. "Resul'taty golosovaniya na vyborakh v Gosudarstvennuyu Dumu po odnomandatnym izbiratel'nym okrugam."

a. Indicates candidates who were not nominated by Russia's Choice, but were supported financially by the bloc or endorsed it in the last few weeks of the election.

22.5 percent cast for the liberal Konstantin Borovoi, founder of the Party of Economic Freedom. If just one of the candidates from the reformist blocs—Russia's Choice's Aleksei Surkov, Yabloko's Yurii Shatalov, or the RDDR's Igor' Glinka—had withdrawn from the race and thrown his support to Borovoi, Vlasov undoubtedly would have been beaten.

Why did democrats fail to cooperate in such races? Public and private ruminations by politicians on the subject emphasized the considerable mistrust and ambition among reformist politicians. Yabloko's Besnisko asserted that the rivalry among democrats in Moscow was such that many "would rather see a Communist win than allow another democrat through."[79]

The weaknesses of the parties also reduced the likelihood of cooperation. Once candidates had been nominated, the only way party cooperation could occur was for candidates to withdraw in favor of candidates from other parties. In their weak and decentralized condition, parties had few means of eliciting such self-sacrifice.[80] District campaigns were at least partially financed, and almost always managed, by candidates themselves: asking candidates to withdraw was equivalent to asking them to take an immediate loss on the considerable resources and effort they had already invested.[81]

To their credit, the blocs did cooperate in a few districts, possibly forestalling additional defeats. After much anxious talk about the dangers of competition and the necessity of cooperation, agreements were reached at the last minute resulting in the withdrawal of four candidates, PRES's Vladimir Tumanov (District 191) and Anatolii Sliva (District 195), and Yabloko's Valerii Borshchev (District 197) and Viktor Sheinis (District 204). In only one case, that of Sheinis, was withdrawal publicized. Each withdrawal was in a close contest narrowly won by a Russia's Choice candidate.[82] Because the only known withdrawal of a Russia's Choice candidate in Moscow was by Vasilii Selyunin in favor of Alla Gerber, another Russia's Choice candidate, we can assume that Russia's Choice either withdrew one or more of its candidates in close races outside of Moscow or that it rewarded PRES and Yabloko in other ways.

The decentralization of the Russia's Choice district campaigns may also have weakened the performance of the bloc's candidates and heightened the competitiveness of the races. Apart from the distribution of large amounts of campaign literature for its candidates in the last week of the campaign, there was little evidence of a concerted effort by Russia's Choice in the district races. The bloc apparently did not provide much assistance in the way of advice or resources to the district candidates. Mikhail Shneider, coordinator of the campaign in the Moscow region, admitted that very little "advance work" had been done with candidates and that as a consequence they were "a bit incompetent, raw."[83] Candidates were responsible for much of their own fund raising. Those who wanted television time had to purchase it themselves.[84]

The Russia's Choice decision to delegate the actual conduct of the campaign in Moscow to Democratic Russia may also have resulted in rather incoherent district campaigns.[85] Lev Ponomarev described how the reliance on Democratic Russia's primary organizations affected his campaign.

> Well, a [Democratic Russia] structure exists in every prefecture, and they have preserved their old structures across the raions, basically. Because they formed within raions, they therefore think of themselves, understand themselves better by raion. I work with several of these organizations . . . therefore it is difficult to establish a unified headquarters.[86]

The defeat of Ponomarev, one of the founders and leaders of Democratic Russia, by Andrei Volkov, a reform-minded independent, on Ponomarev's home territory is a good example of how decentralization negatively affected the Russia's Choice campaign in Moscow. With better funding, organization, and direct assistance from the central Russia's Choice organization, Ponomarev might have been able to fend off the challenge from Volkov.

The participation of strong independent candidates also enhanced the competitiveness of the district races. Independents were the sturdiest challengers to Russia's Choice candidates, averaging a greater share of the vote than candidates of any of the other reformist or opposition parties. One ingredient in the relative success of independents was their nonpartisanship. Independents attracted the votes of citizens who either did not identify with a party or were generally suspicious of parties and politicians. Such voters composed a significant proportion of the Moscow electorate. Playing to the antiparty sentiment of the electorate, almost 30 percent of independent candidates specifically mentioned their disconnection from parties in the campaign programs filed with the district election commissions. This tactic appears to have had some effect in drawing antiparty voters: the average vote share taken by independent candidates who emphasized their lack of affiliation with a party was 9.45 percent versus 7.82 percent for those who made no mention of it.

Independent candidates differed considerably from one another in background, political experience, and the quality and quantity of resources they brought to the campaign. There were three main types of independents in the 1993 elections: those with ties to political parties and organizations that failed to meet the registration requirements or were banned from participation; those holding minor office or advisory positions in Moscow and Russian government but not allied, at least formally, with one of the democratic "circles"; and new entrepreneurs whose primary occupation was business rather than politics. Although the benefits from party activism and officeholding were not negligible—such candidates averaged 10.4 percent and 12.8 percent of the vote—they paled in comparison with the electoral reward for a successful business career. Two entrepreneurs, Artem Tarasov (District 202) and Irina Khakamada (District 194), won Duma seats. Four—Nina Milyukova (District 191), Grigorii Kovalenko (District 193), Borovoi (District 200), and Aleksandr Ishchenko (District 204)—finished in second place and one in third, Mikhail Bocharov (District 204), very close behind the victor and the second-place challenger. The average share of the vote for these seven candidates was 18.4 percent, only slightly lower than the 20 percent averaged by the Russia's Choice candidates.

Examination of the backgrounds and activities of these entrepreneurs provides some clues to the causes of their electoral success. All were self-made business people. Young and well educated, they seized the advantages present in Moscow at the beginning of the reform period to accumulate capital, invest it, and quickly build enterprises. After establishing themselves in the business world, they became involved in social organizations, business associations, or philanthropic activity, in the process attaining a high degree of visibility in the city.

Although the financial resources and connections possessed by these candidates undoubtedly bolstered their chances for success, their knowledge of marketing also served them well. Rather than developing programs and promises, entrepreneurs marketed themselves, claiming that the personal qualities that had contributed to their business success could be applied to solving the country's problems.[87] In particular, the campaigns of Khakamada and Tarasov were fine examples of entrepreneurial campaigning in contemporary Russia. Tarasov's slogan, "The country doesn't need party, but smart, people," succinctly conveyed the pitch made by independent entrepreneurs.

The moderate positions of the entrepreneurs, which contrasted sharply with the disregard for the social consequences of reform conveyed by the leadership of the Russia's Choice bloc, may also have added to their appeal. Although they strongly supported development of the market, they avoided market radicalism. They called for destatization but also asserted that the government was obligated to provide social welfare programs and economic opportunity for the average citizen. This right-centrist political stance corresponded well to the general liberalism of the Moscow public but also acknowledged the growing popular expressions of dissatisfaction and concern over spreading poverty and the fate of the elderly, disabled, and young families.

Conclusion

The contextual analysis has sought to explain the victory of radical and moderate reformists in the capital as the outcome of a specific path of political change. Although the goal of the analysis has been to elucidate the factors that produced particular results, the factors thus identified can be used to examine other regions as well. Knowing why Moscow is liberal tells us quite a bit about why other regions are conservative or "red."

First and foremost, the study of Moscow highlights the importance of a city or region's economic profile and the accompanying social structure for the long-term character of its electoral politics. The world view, desires, and proto-organizations of the Moscow population, particularly its intelligentsia stratum, were the essential ingredients of the democratic movement. The democratic movement recruited reform-oriented candidates who competed successfully in elections. These new elites powerfully strengthened the movement, radicalized public discussion, undermined the position of the Communist party, protected liberal Moscow newspapers and journalists, and thus deepened the liberalism of the mass public. Deep public attachment to liberal values and reformist goals and candidates was a crucial determinant of reformist victories in the capital, not only in 1993 but also in the parliamentary elections of 1995 and the presidential elections of 1996.

In addition to social structure, the Moscow case illustrates the significance of the configuration of political actors and parties and the postcommunist power structure for regional election outcomes. The denouement of the postcommunist crisis inflicted serious damage on political parties, particularly those of the centrist and extreme opposition parties. By autumn 1993 the city executive and his bureaucracy, in alliance with the

Russian government, were firmly in control of the city. By selectively distributing resources, Mayor Luzhkov was able to create a political "machine" that encompassed the bureaucracy, remnants of the democratic movement and some of its former leaders, and the new business interests. This machine and the interests attached to it were extremely important in the election campaign and powerfully benefited Russia's Choice and reformists in general by providing them organizational and financial resources and guaranteeing them positive coverage by the mass media.

Awareness of the factors that combined over time to produce reformist victories in Moscow assists us in explaining the weak support for reformists, particularly of the radical variety, in most other regions of Russia, as well as the strength in such places of the socialist and nationalist opposition. In smaller cities, towns, and the countryside, the proportion of the population made up of the intelligentsia was much smaller than in Moscow. In such places, the democratic upsurge consequently either did not occur at all or was ephemeral.[88] Reformist candidates did not compete or did not win the first elections in such regions; rather, existing communist elites tended to persist and govern much as they had before. We can assume that this elite continuity, and a much more conservative regional and local press, contributed significantly to the emergence of conservative voting patterns. Just as in Moscow, officials were able to use the powers and resources of various parts of the government apparatus to advance themselves and their allies in the 1993 and subsequent elections. Rather than a proreform stance however, they articulated either a distinct nationalist or socialist, anti-Moscow, antiliberal stance and sought to protect the economic interests of the regions and their political autonomy against Moscow's directives.

The logical conclusion to be drawn from this argument is that reformists did not lose the parliamentary elections because of economic downturn, although economic performance certainly was a factor, but because by 1993 the configuration of liberal voters, liberal mass media, and radical democratic and reformist elites had developed in so few cities and regions. We know from the examination of Moscow that even in the reformist strongholds, serious divisions among reformists and weak organizations provided gaps through which opposition parties and independent candidates could penetrate. The isolation of reformists, and their internal weaknesses, does not bode well for the survival of Russian liberalism over the long run.

Notes

1. For example, see Stephen Whitefield and Geoffrey Evans, "The Russian Election of 1993: Public Opinion and the Transition Experience," *Post-Soviet Affairs*, vol. 10, no. 1 (January–March 1994), pp. 38–60.

2. "Sotsial'no-ekonomicheskoye polozheniye Moskvy v 1992 godu," in *Rossiiskaya Federatsiya, Moskva i oblasti tsentral'nogo eknomicheskogo raiona v 1992 g.* (Moscow: Respublikanskii informatsionno-izdatel'skii tsentr, 1993), pp. 179–80, and *Rossiiskaya Federatsiya v tsifrakh v 1993 godu* (Moscow: Goskomstat Rossii, 1994), pp. 8, 13-14.

3. "Sotsial'no-ekonomicheskoye polozheniye Moskvy," pp. 184, 190; *Rossiya—1993, ekonomicheskaya kon'yunktura* (Moscow: Tsentr Ekonomicheskoi Konyunktury i Prognozirovaniya, 1993), pp. 71–74, 82, 89–92; and *Finansovye izvestiya* (November 19–25, 1993), p. 6.

4. Ralph S. Clem and Peter R. Craumer, "A Geographical Analysis of the Russian Election and Constitutional Plebiscite of December 1993," *Post-Soviet Geography*, vol. 36, no. 2 (1995), pp. 67–86.

5. Anthony Downs, *An Economic Theory of Democracy* (New York: Harper and Row, 1957), pp. 36–50.

6. Robert Huckfeldt and Paul Allen Beck, "Contexts, Intermediaries, and Political Behavior," in Lawrence C. Dodd and Calvin Jillson, eds., *The Dynamics of American Politics: Approaches and Interpretations* (Boulder, Colo.: Westview Press, 1994), pp. 252–76.

7. Classic contextual analyses include Herbert Tingsten, *Political Behavior: Studies in Election Statistics* (London: P. S. King 1937), and V. O. Key Jr., *Southern Politics* (New York: Vintage Books, 1949), pp. 4–7, 318–21.

8. Seymour Martin Lipset and Stein Rokkan, *Party Systems and Voter Alignments: Cross-National Perspectives* (New York: Free Press, 1967).

9. See Adam Przeworski and John Sprague, *Paper Stones: A History of Electoral Socialism* (University of Chicago Press, 1986), pp. 1–11, 45–56; and Robert Huckfeldt and John Sprague, "Political Parties and Electoral Mobilization: Political Structure, Social Structure, and the Party Canvass," *American Political Science Review*, vol. 86, no. 1 (March 1992), pp. 70–86.

10. Percentages were calculated from the following official sources: Goskomstat RSFSR, *RSFSR v tsifrakh v 1989 g.* (Moscow: Finansy i statistika, 1990), pp. 31–32, 35, 103; Moskovskoye gorodskoye upravleniye statistiki, *Moskva v tsifrakh 1990: Stat. Ezhegodnik* (Moscow: Finansy i statistika, 1990), pp. 28–31, 36.

11. V. Khoros, "Drama Intelligentsii," in A. I. Prokopenko, ed., *SSSR: Demograficheskii Diagnoz* (Moscow: Progress, 1990), pp. 197–212.

12. Ludmilla Alexeyeva, *Soviet Dissent: Contemporary Movements for National, Religious, and Human Rights* trans. by Carol Pearce and John Glad (Middletown, Conn.: Wesleyan University Press, 1987), pp. 10–11, 283–300.

13. Timothy J. Colton, *Moscow: Governing the Socialist Metropolis* (Cambridge, Mass.: Belknap Press of Harvard University Press, 1995), pp. 586–99; and V. N. Berezovskii and N. I. Krotov, *Neformal'naya Rossiya: o neformalnykh politizirovannykh dvizheniyakh i gruppakh v RSFSR (opyt spravochnika)* (Moscow: Molodaya Gvardiya, 1990).

14. The first organization to appear was the Moscow Popular Front in 1988, followed by the Moscow Association of Voters later in the year, and the group "Elections 90" in late 1989. V. N. Berezovskii, N. I. Krotov, and V. V. Chervyakov, *Rossiya: partii, assotsiatsii, soiuzy, kluby* (Moscow: RAU-Press, 1991), pt. 1, pp. 61–63, and pt. 2, pp. 189–90, 192–93.

15. *Ogonek*, vol. 6 (February 3–10, 1990), pp. 17–18.

16. See M. Steven Fish, *Democracy from Scratch: Opposition and Regime in the New Russian Revolution* (Princeton University Press, 1995).

17. Boris Yeltsin, *Against the Grain: An Autobiography* (New York: Summit Books, 1990).

18. *BBC Summary of World Broadcasts*, TASS, March 28, 1989.

19. Giulietto Chiesa with Douglas Taylor Northrop, *Transition to Democracy: Political Change in the Soviet Union, 1987–1991* (Hanover, N.H.: Dartmouth College, 1993), pp. 74–77, 92–94.

20. *BBC Summary of World Broadcasts*, Soviet television, 1840 GMT, July 23, 1991; Brendan Kiernan and Joseph Aistrup, "The 1989 Elections to the Congress of People's Deputies in Moscow," *Soviet Studies*, vol. 43, no. 6 (1991), pp. 1049–69.

21. David Remnick, *Lenin's Tomb: The Last Days of the Soviet Empire* (New York: Random House, 1993), pp. 376–83.

22. *Vechernaya Moskva*, April 29, 1991, p. 3.

23. Boris Kagarlitskii, and others, *Square Wheels: How Russian Democracy Got Derailed*, trans. by Leslie A. Auerbach and others (New York: Monthly Review Press, 1995), p. 36.

24. Ibid., p. 95.

25. Colton, *Moscow*, pp. 663–69.

26. Kagaritskii, *Square Wheels*, pp. 110–11.

27. *Nedelya*, no. 45, November 1991, p. 3; *BBC Summary of World Broadcasts*. All-Union Radio, Radio-I 1700 GMT, November 9, 1991.

28. Interview with Aleksandr L. Gorbachev, first secretary of the Moscow City committee of the Russian Union of Youth, November 15, 1992.

29. Alexander Buzgalin and Andrei Kolganov, *Bloody October in Moscow: Political Repression in the Name of Reform*, trans. by Renfrey Clarke (New York: Monthly Review Press, 1994), pp. 179–81.

30. Buzgalin and Kolganov, *Bloody October*.

31. M. Malyutin and A. Yusupovskii, *Rasstanovka politicheskikh sil v Rossii i prognoz ikh roli v blizhaishei perspektive* (Moscow: Fond "In-t razvitiya," 1993), pp. 10–11.

32. *Stolitsa*, vol. 12, March 19, 1995, pp. 30–32; *Kommersant*, March 16, 1995, p. 2.

33. *Izvestiya*, December 7, 1994, pp. 1, 4; *Argumenty i fakty*, vol. 48, November 29, 1994, pp. 1–3.

34. Interview with Igor Dergunov, political consultant of Most Bank, December 9, 1993.

35. *Izvestiya*, November 19, 1993, p. 4; *Kommersant Daily*, December 2, 1993.

36. *Moskovskii komsomolets*, December 11, 1993, p. 2.

37. Reuters News Service-CIS and Eastern Europe, May 6, 1995.

38. Interviews with Sergei K. Obzarkhanov, Moscow organizer of the Constructive Ecological Movement of Russia (KEDR), December 13, 1993; Valentin Fedorovich Kornilov, Agrarian party candidate in Istrinskii okrug (District 116) and chair of the Moscow oblast organization of the Agrarian party, December 14, 1993; Oleg Besnisko, Moscow organizer of the "Yavlinskii-Boldyrev-Lukin" bloc, December 7, 1993; and Yurii Chernichenko (by telephone), leader of the Peasant party and a subsequent member of the Soviet of the Federation, December 14, 1993.

39. Interview with Grigorii K. Rebrov, KPRF candidate in Kashirskii okrug, December 10, 1993.

40. *Reuters*, October 30, 1993.

41. *Kuranty*, November 10, 1993, p. 1; and Radio Mayak, November 9, 1993. Chernichenko's late entrance into the race was prompted by Luzhkov's decision to withdraw.

42. *Moskovskii komsomolets*, November 13, 1993, p. 1.

43. *Kuranty*, November 9, 1993, p. 1.

44. *Izvestiya*, November 5, 1993, p. 1; *Rossiiskaya gazeta*, November 18, 1993, pp. 1–2; *Segodnya*, November 23, 1993, p. 2; *Moskovskii komsomolets*, November 20, 1993, pp. 1–2.

45. Interview with Svetlana Bol'shego, December 15, 1993.

46. Interview with Lev Ponomarev, December 8, 1993.

47. "Press Conference by Lev Ponomarev and Other Leaders of Democratic Russia," *Official Kremlin International News Broadcast*, October 29, 1993.

48. Interview with Mikhail Schneider, December 8, 1993.

49. Interviews with Lev Ponomarev (December 8, 1993) and Mikhail Schneider.

50. "Key Blocs Rely on Analytic Centers for Campaigning," *Kommersant-Daily*, December 11, 1993, p. 4, in Foreign Broadcast Information Service, *Daily Report: Central Eurasia*, December 13, 1993, p. 38 (hereinafter FBIS, Central Eurasia.) I also witnessed the distribution of large amounts of campaign literature from the Moscow city administration building a week before the elections.

51. "PRUC to Cooperate with Russia's Choice," Interfax News Agency, November 18, 1993, in FBIS, *Central Eurasia*, November 19, 1993, p. 29.

52. Interview with Telman Gdlyan, December 11, 1993.

53. Two of the latter were close associates of Shakhrai.

54. "Key Blocs Rely on Analytical Centers," FBIS, *Central Eurasia.*

55. *Rossiiskiye vesti*, November 18, 1993.

56. Interview with Alla Karpova, PRES director of information, November 25, 1993.

57. *Moskovskii komsomolets*, November 24, 1993, p. 1.

58. "Osnovnye dokumenty uchreditel'nogo s''ezda obshchestvenno-politicheskogo dvizheniya soyuz nezavisimykh," October 16–17, 1993, Moscow.

59. Interview with Besnisko.

60. Interview with Besnisko.

61. *Kuranty*, October 29, 1993; and author's conversation with Viktor Vasil'evich Parshutkin, press secretary of Vladimir Lukin, December 7, 1993.

62. Interview with Besnisko.

63. Interview with Vadim Vadimovich Masalkov, vice chair of the RDDR executive committee, December 15, 1993.

64. Interview with Bol'shego.

65. "Aims at Democratic Reforms Movement Outlined," *Rossiiskaya gazeta*, November 17, 1993, p. 2, in FBIS, *Central Eurasia*, November 18, 1993, pp. 36–37.

66. "Urals Local Reforms," *Izvestiya*, November 24, 1993, p. 4, in FBIS, *Central Eurasia*, November 26, 1993, p. 30.

67. Interview with Eduard Stankevich, vice chair of the DPR Moscow organization, November 30, 1993.

68. *Nezavisimaya gazeta*, November 3, 1993, p. 2.

69. *Rossiiskiye vesti*, November 17, 1993, p. 1.

70. Interview with Obzharkhanov.

71. *Segodnya*, December 11, 1993, p. 2.

72. Interview with Arsenii Chanyshev, December 8, 1993.

73. Interview with Rebrov. See also *Segodnya*, December 11, 1993, p. 2; and press conference by Gennadii Zyuganov, *Official Kremlin International News Broadcasts*, November 17, 1993.

74. *Sokol Zhirinovskogo*, no. 6, 1993, p. 1.

75. Interview with Gdlyan. See also the account by former democratic activist Vitaly Zhuravlev, a former democratic activist, of his recruitment into the LDPR: "My," *Oppozitsiya*, no. 8 (1994), p. 4.

76. Analysis based on tabulations contained in the Central Electoral Commission document "Resul'taty golosovaniya na vyborakh v Gosudarstvennuyu Dumu po odnomandatnym izbiratel'nym okrugam."

77. Districts 191, 193, 195, 197, and 199.

78. Districts 191, 195, 196, 197, 199, and 202.

79. He also thought that divisions had emerged among the democrats because of the desire of democratic leaders to distinguish themselves from one another. Besnisko, interview.

80. Interview with Masalkov.

81. In an interview with me on December 1, 1993, Dmitirii Glinskii, a democratic activist who had been approached by Yabloko to run in the elections, claimed that Yabloko expected its candidates to raise eight million rubles on their own for campaign ads.

82. According to the Central Electoral Commission (CEC) report of the Moscow results, Tumanov withdrew on November 23, Sliva on December 9, Borshchev on December 10, and Sheinis on December 8. One outcome of these withdrawals was an increase in the number of ruined ballots and votes cast against all candidates. Across Moscow the average vote against all candidates was 19.3 percent and in the districts where withdrawal occurred it was 22.8 percent.

83. Schneider, interview.

84. Ponomarev claimed problems with funding.

85. The extent of the bloc's reliance on local DR and voters' organizations is exemplified by the fact that only eight candidates in Moscow's fifteen single-seat districts were directly nominated by Russia's Choice, although it claimed seven more as its own by December 6. See *Argumenty i fakty,* no. 49 (December 1993), p. 9.

86. Interview with Ponomarev.

87. See, for example, the programs of Milyukova, Khakamada, Tarasov, and Borovoi.

88. Gavin Helf and Jeffrey W. Hahn, "Old Dogs and New Tricks: Party Elites in the Russian Regional Elections of 1990," *Slavic Review*, vol. 51, no. 3 (Fall 1992), pp. 511–30.

Leningrad Oblast

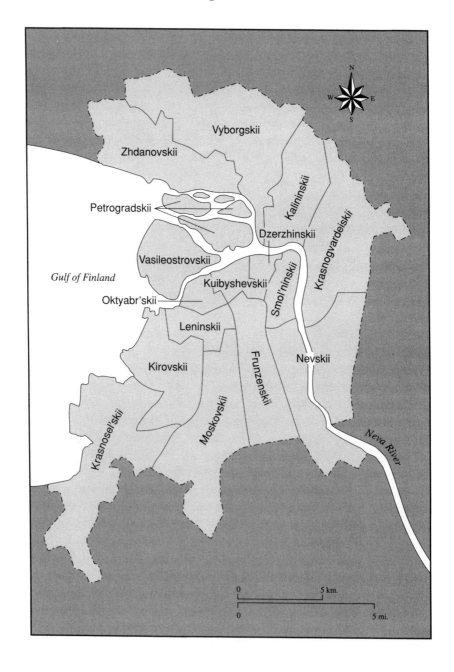

Vyborgskii

Zhdanovskii

Petrogradskii

Kalininskii

Dzerzhinskii

Krasnogvardeiskii

Vasileostrovskii

Gulf of Finland

Kuibyshevskii

Smol'ninskii

Oktyabr'skii

Leninskii

Nevskii

Kirovskii

Frunzenskii

Krasnosel'skii

Moskovskii

Neva River

0	5 km.
0	5 mi.

CHAPTER TWELVE

St. Petersburg

The Election in the Democratic Metropolis

Yitzhak M. Brudny

THE LITERATURE analyzing the process of transition from authoritarian to democratic rule puts great emphasis on the inaugural election that ushers in the democratic regime. This election, therefore, is called a "founding election."[1] Although a series of parliamentary and presidential elections took place in Russia between 1989 and 1991, no founding election ever occurred. Instead the executive and legislative institutions formed during the transition period continued their existence in the postcommunist era. The December 12, 1993, parliamentary election was, therefore, both the first postcommunist election and the first multiparty election in Russia.

Called roughly two and a half years after the collapse of communism, this election was dominated by issues typical to postcommunist societies: the pace of transition to the market economy and the cost associated with it; the nature of the division of power between executive and legislative branches of government; and the extent of the territorial boundaries of the nation-state.[2] The December 1993 election took place under a very different

I would like to acknowledge Dr. Aleksandr Duka and Dr. Yelena Zdravomyslova of the Institute of Sociology, Russian Academy of Sciences, for their invaluable assistance in researching this project; Professor Joel Fetzer of Pepperdine University, for his help in analyzing the survey data; and Dr. Mary McAuley of Ford Foundation and Professor David Mayhew of Yale University for their comments on an earlier draft of this paper.

set of political and socioeconomic conditions than those that prevailed during the 1989, 1990, and 1991 elections.

This chapter seeks to determine whether electoral results in postcommunist societies are consequences of hardship and dislocation caused by the radical economic reform or whether the results were determined by political, institutional, and cultural factors. Based on an analysis of the December 1993 campaign and election in the city of St. Petersburg, I break this discussion into five key analytical points that address campaign and voting behavior: first, whether developmental indicators, such as degree of urbanization, educational levels, saturation of mass media, and so forth, which are often cited as causes for the collapse of communist regimes, continue to determine political trends in the postcommunist period;[3] second, to what extent "social characteristics determine political preferences," as was postulated by the authors of *The People's Choice,* or to what extent worsening economic conditions led to "pocketbook voting";[4] third, to what extent the campaign made a difference in the first multiparty election in which voters had still not developed a clear identification with one party, which is viewed by the authors of *The American Voter* as the key variable for explaining electoral behavior, and how important organizational resources and the preexisting organizational networks were to the success of the parties' campaign efforts;[5] fourth, to what extent change of the electoral system from two rounds to one, significant increase in the size of the electoral districts, and other changes in the rules affected the electoral results of the single-member district races; and fifth, the characteristics and qualifications of successful candidates.

In this chapter I argue that the St. Petersburg campaign and election illustrate the greater importance of political, cultural, and institutional factors over economic ones.

The first part of this chapter presents the socioeconomic and the political profile of St. Petersburg. The next two parts analyze the campaign and election to the State Duma, the lower house of the Russian parliament. The second part in particular examines the party-list (proportional representation) vote, and the third part, the single-member districts vote. The fourth part analyzes the campaign and election to the Council of the Federation, the upper house of the Russian parliament. The fifth part examines the constitutional referendum called by Boris Yeltsin to approve the new Russian constitution. The chapter relies heavily on the St. Petersburg section of the 1993 national election survey, which polled 1,000 city residents during the last three preelection weeks.

Profile of a Democratic Metropolis

St. Petersburg, like Moscow, has the status of "subject of the Federation"—in other words, it constitutes one of the eighty-nine regions of Russia. As an administrative unit of Russia, St. Petersburg comprised in 1993 seventeen urban raions and eight suburban towns with the status of city raions, which are subordinated to the city government. With a population of approximately 4.9 million—of which 3.7 million were registered voters in December 1993—St. Petersburg is the third most populous region of Russia (after Moscow and Moscow oblast) and its second largest city.

St. Petersburg is first and foremost a major industrial center: in the early 1990s, 33 percent of its workforce was employed in industry, compared with only 23 percent similarly employed in Moscow. Moreover, the city had an extremely high concentration of giant enterprises, mostly belonging to Russia's military-industrial complex, specializing in electronics, high-precision optical equipment, and ship and machine building. In fact, in the early 1990s, 170 such enterprises (out of total of 500) produced 70 percent of the city's entire industrial production. This has a tremendous impact on the city social structure: a high concentration of skilled labor and of scientific and technical intelligentsia live and work in the city.

In addition to the scientific and technical intelligentsia, there is a high concentration of professional and liberal arts intelligentsia in St. Petersburg. This is largely because of the thirty institutes of the Russian Academy of Sciences; thirty-four institutions of medical training and research; forty-one institutions of higher education; arts organizations, including twenty theaters and sixty-five museums; thirty publishing houses; five mass-circulation newspapers; and a television station that functions as one of Russia's national channels. The educational levels of the city residents reflect this economic and cultural presence. According to the 1989 census, 25 percent of St. Petersburg residents had higher and incomplete higher education, almost twice the national average. Moreover, the city had 4,734 students enrolled in its institutions of higher education per 100,000 residents, 2.5 times the national average.[6]

This great concentration of highly educated people has made the city the most receptive to Western cultural and political influences. It also led to a high level of independent political activity during the perestroika period. By the spring of 1990, there were eighty-four independent political and cultural organizations in Leningrad; only Moscow had more, with 127.[7]

Most of these organizations had a strong democratic and anticommunist orientation. They demonstrated their ability to successfully mobilize voters against the Communist Party of the Soviet Union (CPSU) in the 1989 and 1990 elections. In the 1989 elections to the USSR Congress of People's Deputies, a coalition of democratic organizations, "Elections-89," handed the CPSU its most humiliating defeat: the oblast first party secretary and candidate member of the Politburo, Yurii F. Solov'ev, as well as six other leading party and government officials, failed to gain seats in the new Soviet parliament.[8]

The 1990 elections to the RSFSR Congress of People's Deputies and the city soviet resulted in a resounding victory for the candidates of the alliance of democratic organizations, "Democratic Elections-90." This coalition won 25 out of 33 seats in the RSFSR Congress of People's Deputies and 240 out of 400 in the Leningrad city soviet. Gaining the absolute majority in the city soviet allowed reformers to elect Anatolii A. Sobchak, a dean of the Leningrad University Law School and a prominent reformist member of the USSR Supreme Soviet, as chair of the soviet.

In 1991 St. Petersburg continued to be, together with Moscow, the center where the drive for radical political and economic reforms enjoyed the strongest popular support. The presidential and mayoral elections of June 12, 1991, as well as the local referendum on the city name, clearly showed the radical bent of the city electorate. Boris N. Yeltsin's candidacy to the post of Russian president was supported by 68 percent of city voters (refer to table 12-3, later in the chapter). At the same time, in the city mayoral election, Sobchak defeated the CPSU candidate, Yurii K. Sevenard, with a 66 to 26 percent margin; and 55 percent of the voters, to emphasize their rejection of the city's communist past, approved the proposition to return the city its original name, St. Petersburg.[9]

In 1992 to 1993, support for Yeltsin and the politics of radical reform declined somewhat among members of the St. Petersburg delegation in the Russian Congress of People's Deputies. In May 1990 the delegation scored 84 on the Sobyanin Rating of pro- and anti-Yeltsin roll-call votes; in April 1992, this score declined to 45; and in March 1993, it stood at 34. However, this last score still made the St. Petersburg delegation the second most supportive of Yeltsin and his reforms.[10]

The April 25, 1993, referendum demonstrated that popular support for Yeltsin and his reform policies also remained strong. Thus 72.8 percent of city voters expressed their confidence in Yeltsin (58.7 percent nationwide), and 65.6 percent of voters supported the Yeltsin government's socioeconomic policies (53.1 percent nationwide). However, in the aftermath of the forceful dissolution of the parliament, Yeltsin's approval rating deteriorated: according to a survey of city voters done under the auspices of our election project, 56 percent approved of Yeltsin's performance, which represented a decline of 17 percent compared with the April referendum but was still considerably higher than the national average.

With such strong continuous popular support for radical reform, combined with the fact that the reformers controlled both the mayor's office and the city soviet, one would have expected harmonious relations between the two branches of the city government. However, the contentious nature of city politics in 1992 to 1993 closely mirrored the national political arena. Yeltsin's power struggle with the Supreme Soviet in Moscow was replicated in St. Petersburg in Sobchak's incessant fighting with the city soviet—and especially with its most active part, the thirty-eight member Small Soviet—over power to run the city. Predictably, during the fall 1993 crisis Sobchak endorsed Yeltsin's dissolution of the parliament, and the Small Soviet condemned the president's actions as an attempted coup d'état.[11]

After the October 3 to 4 events, Sobchak attempted to dissolve the city and district soviets. Although he faced little resistance in dissolving the district soviets, he failed to eliminate his main nemesis, the city soviet. The November 16 session of the soviet rejected Sobchak's request to dissolve itself. Thus, during the period leading up to the December 12 election, the St. Petersburg city soviet was one of the few functioning soviets in the country.[12] More important, two years of confrontation with the soviet, as well as Sobchak's attempt to disband it, had one major consequence in the December 12 election: the largest and most successful group of candidates in the single-mandate district elections were deputies of the city soviet. However, Sobchak failed to attract even one of them to run as a candidate of his own party, the Russian Movement for Democratic Reforms (RDDR), which represented a very weak slate of candidates that fared poorly at the polls.

Another factor that played a significant role in the December 12 election in St. Petersburg was the impact of economic reforms. The city was both victim and beneficiary of the economic reforms; while the backbone of the city's economy, the military-industrial sector, sank into deep crisis because of the drastic reduction in state orders, the private sector of the economy experienced tremendous growth.

Thus, between 1990 and 1993, the volume of industrial production declined by 27 percent, and the number of people employed in city industrial enterprises also declined by 27 percent. The crisis of the military-industrial complex was the main cause of increased unemployment in the city. According to the city statistical agency, 52 percent of those who lost their jobs in 1993 were employed in military-industrial enterprises. This accounted for the fact that people with higher education constituted a disproportionate number of the unemployed in the city: whereas nationwide people with university-level education constituted 10 percent of the unemployed, in St. Petersburg this category constituted 22 percent. Overall, in 1993, 12.2 percent of the city's economically active population were either unemployed or worked part time, which was 5.6 percent higher than in Moscow and 2.2 percent higher than the national average.[13]

Although the city's state-owned military-industrial complex was in deep crisis and laying off workers, the private sector was growing. Privatization of small business in St. Petersburg was among the fastest in Russia: by January 1993, 28 percent of retail stores and 78 percent of restaurants were privatized. The financial sector was growing as well: in mid-October 1993, the city had 39 voucher investment funds, the second highest number after Moscow, as well as 18 local banks and 200 branches of Russian and foreign banks. All this led to rapid growth of employment in the service sector. Between 1990 and 1993 the number of St. Petersburg residents employed in the service sector increased by 54 percent.

Hand in hand with the fast growth of the service sector came fast growth of joint ventures. In 1991 the city had 98 joint ventures that exported and imported goods and services worth $85 million; in 1993 there were 985 such enterprises that exported and imported goods and services worth $269 million.[14]

The process of private capital formation and the advanced pace of privatization and growth of the nonstate and service sectors of the economy led to the emergence of two new major institutional players in St. Petersburg politics: the city branch of the Association of Private and Privatized Enterprises and the Association of St. Petersburg's Commercial Banks, both of which became important financial backers of the Russia's Choice campaign.

Finally, a dramatic increase in crime and ethnic tension in the city became an issue in the campaign and helped Vladimir V. Zhirinovskii's Liberal Democratic Party of Russia at the polls. Between 1990 and 1993, the crime rate in St. Petersburg rose by 54 percent, which in turn led to the proliferation of support for law and order.[15] Along with a rise in the crime rate came an upsurge of ethnic tension between Slavs and Azeris, who by the late 1980s effectively controlled all the major food markets in St. Petersburg. This contributed to a sharp rise in anti-Azeri sentiment. In a poll conducted in September 1992, 83 percent of city residents endorsed the view, "the less people of Caucasian origins in St. Petersburg, the better it is for the city."[16] Thus Zhirinovskii's anti-Caucasian rhetoric, which played a prominent role in his campaign, reached a receptive audience in St. Petersburg.

Election to the State Duma: The Party-Lists Vote

This section argues that the party-list vote in St. Petersburg was the result of a combination of social cleavages and the effectiveness of the parties' campaign effort. To be more precise, the socioeconomic and political profile of St. Petersburg was responsible for the division of power between democratic and communist-nationalist blocs of parties, while the organizational resources and effective campaign strategies were responsible for the division of power among parties within each bloc. The preexisting organizational networks played a major role in the parties' ability to organize an efficient campaign and thus affected their electoral success.

Actors and Their Organizational Capacities

In the late 1980s Leningrad, along with Moscow, was a central location where parties of all political orientations were established and most active. When the decision was made to hold elections on December 12, 1993, many of the political parties and alliances already had in place organizational structures to mount an electoral campaign, as well as a core group of leaders that was ready to join the party lists and compete in the single-member districts.

Between 1991 and 1993, St. Petersburg reformers coalesced around the city chapter of the political movement Democratic Russia, the umbrella organization of Yeltsin's supporters. The main organizational components of Democratic Russia were local branches of the Social Democratic Party of Russia, the Republican Party of Russia, and the Free Democratic Party of Russia, the latter being the strongest democratic organization in St. Petersburg (with a weak presence in other Russian cities). Each of the parties had a large number of activists with experience from the 1989, 1990, and 1991 electoral campaigns.

The formation of electoral parties led to a split within the St. Petersburg Democratic Russia chapter, with the Social Democratic party and the Republican party leaving to join Yabloko, while the Free Democratic party became the organizational backbone of the city's Russia's Choice chapter. An important faction in the St. Petersburg city soviet, the so-called Regional Party of the Center, also had a strong organizational structure, politicians experienced in running successful campaigns, and substantial financial resources. Regional Party of the Center joined Yabloko and was an active participant in its campaign.

RDDR had virtually no official party structure in the city. However, the head of the party, Sobchak, was also the mayor of St. Petersburg, and he could rely on the city administration to help organize the party's electoral campaign. Deputy Mayor Valerii I. Malyshev, who was unofficially running the RDDR campaign in the city, did not hesitate to give orders to the heads of the raion administration to assist the party's campaign efforts. Moreover, Sobchak had special access to media as a result of his position as mayor of the city: the St. Petersburg television channel was run by his appointee, Bella A. Kurkova, who was careful to present a positive image of the mayor. This became especially easy after October events, when Kurkova banned the "600 Second" investigative reporting program produced by Russian nationalist journalist Aleksandr G. Nevzorov, who missed no opportunity to criticize Sobchak and his policies. Finally, Sobchak also controlled the city's main newspaper, *Sankt-Peterburgskiye vedomosti* (St. Petersburg Gazette), which he used to promote himself and his party.

In St. Petersburg, Sergei Shakhrai's Party of Russian Unity and Accord (PRES) had neither the Russia's Choice or Yabloko-type organizational foundations to build on nor RDDR's advantage of control of the city government. PRES had to build its organization from scratch, and did so during the campaign. Its poor showing at the city's polls had much to do with this lack of an organizational foundation.

The centrist parties were traditionally weak at the city level and this was still the case in the fall of 1993. The St. Petersburg chapter of the Democratic Party of Russia (DPR) had existed since 1990 and once had been a major mainstay of the local Democratic Russia chapter. However, after DPR broke with Democratic Russia in late 1991, most of the members of the St. Petersburg branch resigned, an act that virtually destroyed the DPR organization in the city. Thus from mid-1992 on, only a handful of party loyalists constituted the St. Petersburg chapter of DPR. This had a significant impact on the DPR's ability to run an effective campaign, and resulted in an electoral showing that was significantly worse than in Moscow, where the party organization was much stronger.

The institutional mainstay of St. Petersburg's Civic Union chapter was the Association of Industrial Enterprises of Transportation and Communication, an umbrella organization of the city military-industrial enterprises that had existed since 1989. It cooperated with Sobchak in an effort to obtain government subsidies for the city's defense industries but was not ready to support his party in the December election. Instead, in mid-October 1993, the association reached an agreement with the local Federation of Trade Unions to support the Civic Union. However, the unions got involved only marginally in the campaign, leaving the association to do most of the organizing work.[17]

Essentially a lobbying group, the association had neither the experience of running an electoral campaign nor a clue as to how to do it. Moreover, the military-industrial enterprises, the backbone of the association, were in economic crisis and could not provide funds necessary to run an effective campaign. These handicaps led the association's leaders to be pessimistic about support for the Civic Union in St. Petersburg even before election day.[18]

The Women of Russia movement had no organizational foundation in St. Petersburg and made no effort to create one. Even though it received the highest number of votes among the centrist parties in the city, this lack of an organizational foundation certainly contributed to a showing in the St. Petersburg polls that was well below its national average.

The political parties and movements of socialist and nationalist orientation were much better organized than the centrist parties but were no match for the reformers. On the eve of the December election, there were two main communist organizations in St. Petersburg: the reconstituted Communist Party of the Russian Federation (KPRF) and the militant Russian Communist Workers' party (RKRP). In St. Petersburg, KPRF had a much weaker organizational base compared with RKRP but benefited from the ban imposed on the RKRP for its active role in the October 3 to 4, 1993, uprising in Moscow. KPRF's main rival was thus unable to run, and there was no danger of a split within the communist constituency. This, combined with the realization that the city's democratic orientation was unlikely to yield strong support, led KPRF to invest little effort in St. Petersburg.

Since 1988 St. Petersburg had been an important center of activity for a variety of Russian nationalist organizations, including the Liberal Democratic Party of Russia (LDPR), although all the organizations played a marginal role in city politics. On the eve of the December election, the strongest Russian nationalist organization in St. Petersburg was the National Republican Party of Russia. It attempted to gain a slot on the December ballot but failed to gather the required number of signatures because it had little organizational structure outside St. Petersburg, where the party was founded. The party leader, St. Petersburg resident Nikolai N. Lysenko, who was mindful of his 1990 failed attempt to become a RSFSR People's Deputy from the city, chose to run in the single-mandate district race in Saratov oblast and was absent from the city during the campaign. The main beneficiary of this development was the local LDPR chapter, which was able to attract many of the National Republican party's activists to participate in its campaign effort. But even with such reinforcement, the St. Petersburg LDPR was incapable of conducting an aggressive city-wide campaign. As will be shown later, its subsequent success in the city had much more to do with Zhirinovskii's masterful television campaign than with the efforts of his local organization.

Formation of the Party Lists

There were sixty-nine candidates from St. Petersburg on the national party lists.[19] However, the size of St. Petersburg's representation differed substantially from party to party. As table 12-1 shows, the size of the representation was related either to the party's organizational strength in St. Petersburg or to its expectation of electoral support in the city. Thus Russia's Choice, Yabloko, Civic Union, and RDDR had the largest representation, whereas the Agrarian Party of Russia (APR) included only one St. Petersburg resident on its list. The table also indicates that most of the blocs had St. Petersburg politicians in the top part of their lists, reflecting both the recognition of the important role the city plays in national politics and the parties' strategy to attract voters from the third most populous region of the country.

Russia's Choice and Yabloko had deepest roots in the city's democratic politics and had, therefore, the greatest reservoir of well-known politicians from which to choose. This made formation of each party's list a complicated affair for Anatolii B. Chubais (Russia's Choice) and Yurii Boldyrev (Yabloko), prominent national politicians from St. Petersburg who were entrusted with the task of determining the city's delegation and where he or she would be placed on the list. The composition of the Russia's Choice list

Table 12-1. *St. Petersburg Candidates on the Parties' National Lists for the State Duma*

Parties	Size of the St. Petersburg representation	Among top 20 on the list
Yabloko	13[a]	4
Russia's Choice	12	1
Civic Union	11	2
RDDR	10	3
PRES	6	—
DPR	5	1
LDPR	5	2
KPRF	3	2
KEDR	2	—
Women of Russia	1	—
Dignity and Compassion	1	—
Agrarian Party of Russia	—	—
Future of Russia	—	—
Total	69	15

Source: Byulleten tsentral'noi izbiratel'noi komissii Rossiiskoi Federatsii, no. 6 (November 1993).
a. Includes Yurii Boldyrev, who withdrew his name in order to run for a seat on the Council of the Federation.

was decided in a three-way negotiation between Chubais, the leaders of Democratic Russia, and Kirill V. Smirnov, the chairman of a major St. Petersburg bank, who represented the interests of the private entrepreneurs. Chubais, who was a senior official in the city government in 1990 to 1991, pushed for the inclusion of senior officials from the city administration and the exclusion of radical democratic activists; the leaders of Democratic Russia promoted prominent city intellectuals and the leaders of political parties and organizations; Smirnov insisted on including the people who could effectively represent the interests of the city's business community.

After two weeks of intense bargaining that became so acrimonious that Chubais was forced to pay a personal visit to St. Petersburg to resolve the issue, a compromise was reached. The regional part of the list was headed by Democratic Russia's candidate Mikhail M. Molostvov, a former political prisoner and a respected intellectual. The second slot was given to Chubais's candidate, Grigorii A. Tomchin, the deputy head of the city branch of the State Property Committee. The third, fourth, and fifth slots went to Democratic Russia representatives. Two other candidates of the business community, Aleksei L. Kudrin, deputy mayor and head of the financial department of city government, and Sergei A. Popov, president of the Association of Commercial Banks of St. Petersburg, were given the sixth and seventh positions on the list.

Smirnov and other leaders of the business community did not find the compromise entirely satisfactory, probably because of the low position given to Kudrin and Popov. Before and during the negotiations they promised to contribute 450 million rubles ($361,000) to the Russia's Choice campaign in St. Petersburg, and after the list was finalized they gave only 150 million ($120,000). However, even this amount was regarded as sufficient for an effective campaign, and certainly no other party in the city had at its disposal anything approaching this figure.

The Yabloko list was also a result of a three-way negotiation involving Boldyrev, chairman of the Social Democratic party, Anatolii G. Golov, and the leaders of the Regional Party of the Center. Golov opposed the strong anti-Yeltsin and anti-Russia's Choice rhetoric of Boldyrev and in particular opposed putting Boldyrev's candidate, Yurii M. Nesterov, at the top of the Yabloko regional list. Regional Party of the Center had no political disagreements with Boldyrev, but demanded greater representation on the list. The parties ultimately reached a compromise, according to which the "federal" part of the Yabloko list would have two Boldyrev candidates (in addition to Boldyrev and Golov), and the Regional Party of the Center was given four (out of nine) slots on the regional list, including the top position. Nesterov was placed third on the regional list, which was widely regarded to be an "unsafe" position.[20] Nesterov's low placement on the list would play a major role in the single-mandate district race in which he was running.[21]

In other democratic parties, formation of the regional list was a much simpler matter. Sobchak, eager to receive the widest possible support of the city's intelligentsia, put the popular St. Petersburg theater actor, Oleg V. Basilashvili, in the third slot of RDDR. The remaining eight St. Petersburg representatives on the RDDR list (which had no regional sublists) were placed low, largely in order to allow them to run in the single-mandate district races without gathering signatures.

With his emphasis on the provinces, Shakhrai made no effort to place any well-known St. Petersburg politician on the "federal" or regional sections of the PRES list. The absence of well-known city figures on the party list was also an implicit recognition that PRES had given up on the city even before the campaign began.

The St. Petersburg candidates on the Civic Union list were determined by Petr G. Semenenko, director of the giant Kirov Works, who was slotted in the fourth position on the Civic Union list. The list made no effort to appeal to any constituency other than industrial managers; the top six (out of nine) slots on the regional section of the list were given to directors of the city's major military-industrial enterprises.

Zhirinovskii regarded the city as crucial to his overall campaign strategy. Accordingly, Vyacheslav A. Marychev, the head of the St. Petersburg branch of LDPR, was placed third on the party list. Marychev hand picked the remaining members of the city candidates on the LDPR list with the goal of appealing to the Russian nationalist intelligentsia, the military, and nationalist businessmen: it included a naval officer, a Russian nationalist writer, and a private entrepreneur. However, all of the St. Petersburg candidates, including Marychev, were little-known figures and, as the single-member district races demonstrated, attracted an insignificant number of voters.

The Campaign: The Blocs' Strategies

The impact of campaign efforts on electoral outcomes is notoriously difficult to assess. Donald E. Stokes argues that "it is all too easy after the fact to attribute to strategy and organization the shifts of party strength that are due to broader conditions prevailing in the country." However, more recent research provides empirical evidence to support the thesis that campaigns do have a significant impact on electoral behavior.[22] The St. Petersburg case supports the argument that the campaign probably affected the voters' decision to vote for a party within a given ideological bloc of parties (for example, Russia's Choice or Yabloko) rather than to switch from one bloc to another (for example, to vote for LDPR instead of Yabloko).

Party strategies in St. Petersburg were largely determined by their organizational strength, availability of financial resources, existence of local leaders with name recognition capable of attracting voters, and a general assessment of the party's popularity in the city. Russia's Choice had the best organization and the largest sum of money to spend on the campaign. It, however, did not have a local leader with wide name recognition capable of attracting voters. As a consequence, its campaign was largely impersonal in nature and relied heavily on the distribution of leaflets in populous city areas; renting large billboards on Nevskii Prospekt, the city's main avenue; and buying significant advertisement time on local television. In the final days of the campaign, Russia's Choice distributed to virtually every residential mailbox 1.5 million leaflets calling for voters to support the party, its Duma and Council of the Federation candidates, and the new constitution.[23]

The personal aspect of Russia's Choice campaign was limited to the December 7 visit of Yegor T. Gaidar to St. Petersburg. This visit, despite the wide coverage it received in the local media, hardly affected the electoral outcome, because Gaidar was not as popular in St. Petersburg as he was in Moscow. In fact, during the campaign, local Russia's Choice strategists regarded Gaidar as more of a liability and refused to post the large posters featuring his picture that were sent from Moscow.

Ultimately, it was intense street and media campaigning that increased Russia's Choice prospects in the city. The survey findings show that three weeks before the election, Yabloko held a slim lead over Russia's Choice (22 percent against 21 percent); in the last week of the campaign, Russia's Choice pulled ahead of Yabloko (21 percent against 17 percent).

Yabloko did not possess the financial resources of Russia's Choice. However, it had one significant advantage over Russia's Choice in the figure of Boldyrev, who, according to a local poll, was the city's most trusted politician.[24] In order to bolster the party's support in St. Petersburg, Boldyrev gave up his safe second position on the Yabloko list and decided to run for the Council of the Federation seat. In essence, the Yabloko campaign in St. Petersburg was run through Boldyrev's campaign, which largely relied on personal appearances at enterprises and research institutes, as well as newspaper interviews. His eventual success created a coattail effect, boosting the party's performance in St. Petersburg though not its Duma candidates in the single-mandate districts.

Like Yabloko, RDDR had the advantage of the most important city politician heading the party list for the Duma. However, this precluded Sobchak's running for the Council of the Federation seat, which could have helped to create a coattail effect for RDDR, as it did for Yabloko. Moreover, he campaigned throughout Russia on his party's behalf and was often absent from the city during the campaign. This weakened his party's prospects because Sobchak remained not only the city's most recognized politician but also the second most popular one after Boldyrev. The RDDR campaign, nevertheless, was highly personalized and focused on Sobchak. Party leaflets distributed in the city called on citizens to vote for Sobchak and portrayed his achievements as the city's mayor. Sobchak also used the time allotted to RDDR on the local television channel to present his record and explain the platform of his party.

The availability of substantial financial resources combined with the lack of an organizational structure and of a local politician with name recognition dictated PRES's electoral strategy. It relied heavily on the distribution of leaflets and advertisement in local newspapers, radio, and television. PRES's version of a personality-oriented campaign was to erect thirty stands with Shakhrai's portrait near major subway entrances. However, because of bad weather conditions these stands were covered with snow for most of the campaign period and few passersby could read their message. Overall, PRES's electoral campaign was the most ineffective of all the reformist blocs, despite the availability of substantial financial resources.

The centrist, socialist, and nationalist parties were hardly visible on the streets of St. Petersburg during the campaign. Of the centrist parties, only Civic Union had the organization and resources to campaign in the city. However, it chose to limit its campaign to industrial enterprises in the hope that managers could influence their workers to vote for the party. The only plan to take the bloc's campaign outside the factory gate was an attempt to distribute 500,000 leaflets on the eve of the election, but the plan was never carried out.

The Agrarian party did not campaign in the city, and the campaign of KPRF was hardly visible. KPRF chair Gennadii A. Zyuganov visited the city in mid-November, before the campaign really had begun, and maintained an exceptionally low profile. It is likely that following this visit, the socialist leadership decided not to expend much effort on campaigning in St. Petersburg. In fact, leaflets urging a vote for the party appeared in the city only in the closing days of the campaign.

With the exception of Zhirinovskii's visit, the LDPR campaign was virtually invisible. The party claimed to have brought several truckloads of leaflets from Moscow and to have distributed them in the city, as well as to have organized visits to industrial enterprises and city hospitals by party activists. However, the only place I was able to find LDPR leaflets was at Zhirinovskii's rally. Moreover, party activists were not allowed into any of the city's major enterprises and had to be content with the small factories whose managers were sympathetic to Zhirinovskii.[25]

The only political rally that took place in St. Petersburg during the electoral campaign was during Zhirinovskii's visit to the city on December 8. This rally could not have had a serious impact on the electoral results because it took place during working hours and attracted no more than several hundred people. The chief reason for Zhirinovskii's visit, however, was not the rally but an opportunity to appear on local television in the prime-time, hour-long slot allocated to his party. This again demonstrates that the main focus of the LDPR campaign was on the electronic media.

The Campaign: The Role of the Media

As a British media specialist once noted, "to a large degree, television coverage *is* the electoral campaign."[26] The campaign broadcasts improved the electorate's knowledge of the parties on the December ballot: on the eve of such broadcasts (three weeks before the election), 41 percent of the respondents knew ten parties or more, and 13 percent knew three parties or fewer; one week later, the share of those who knew ten or more parties rose to 52 percent, and the share of those who knew three parties or fewer fell to 8 percent. The survey also shows that LDPR's television campaign was the most effective: a week after the campaign began, support for the party jumped three times, whereas support for all other parties changed only insignificantly, if at all.

The effect of local print media on the St. Petersburg electoral results corroborates Stokes's argument that "the partisan press is far more effective in reinforcing existing opinion and mobilizing the faithful than it is in making new converts."[27] The situation in the print media was virtually one-sided; out of seven city main newspapers, six had a strong proreformist orientation. The city's main opposition newspaper, the RKRP-sponsored weekly *Narodnaya pravda* (People's Truth), was banned following the October events and it did not appear during the electoral campaign period. With its absence, only a few small-circulation, irregularly published Russian nationalist and communist newspapers appeared in the city.[28]

The six liberal newspapers showed little sympathy to the opposition parties and had only minimal coverage of their activities (see table 12-2). This coverage would have been even less if *Sankt-Peterburgskiye vedomosti,* as an official publication of the city government, had not been obliged to give space to present their views to all political parties listed on the December ballot. However, the dearth of coverage hardly affected support for LDPR because, as the survey shows, LDPR voters were not avid newspaper readers: 67 percent of the party's supporters were reading election-related material no more than once a week; 27 percent, several times a week; and only 3 percent read election-related material on a daily basis. KPRF voters read newspapers more regularly: 46 percent once a week, 36 percent several times a week, and 18 percent on a daily basis. However, the party had a sta-

Table 12-2. *Coverage of Parties in the St. Petersburg Press,*
November 11, 1993–December 11, 1993

Party	Number of articles[a]
Russia's Choice	34
Yabloko	4
RDDR	14
PRES	6
DPR	4
Women of Russia	2
Civic Union	2
KEDR	2
LDPR	5
KPRF	2
Agrarian Party of Russia	2
Future of Russia	1

Source: Author's calculations.
a. Include interviews with and essays by party leaders or their supporters, as well as reports concerning the party's activities.

ble constituency of mostly older people who were not swayed by the liberal press's ravaging treatment.

According to the survey, voters of the four reformist parties on the ballot read election-related material quite regularly: 53 percent once a week, 37 percent several times a week, and 9 percent on a daily basis. Positive press coverage was, therefore, crucial to the efforts of these parties' campaigns. Although none of the six main city newspapers officially endorsed any of the competing parties, Russia's Choice had a decisive advantage over its rivals. Four newspapers—the dailies *Smena* (Shift) and *Vechernii Peterburg* (St. Petersburg at Evening) and the weeklies *Chas pik* (Rush Hour) and *Sankt-Peterburgskoye ekho* (The St. Petersburg Echo)—supported Russia's Choice, and the remaining two—the dailies *Nevskoye vremya* (The Neva Times) and *Sankt-Peterburgskiye vedomosti*—were sympathetic to Yabloko and RDDR, respectively. This advantage was reflected in the disproportionate coverage Russia's Choice received in the city's press. In fact, there were more publications concerning Russia's Choice than the other three democratic parties combined (see table 12-2). With a tight race between Russia's Choice and Yabloko, strong support by the city's press may well have played a role in the eventual victory of Russia's Choice.

The Results

The democratic orientation of the majority of city residents manifested itself in the electoral results: Russia's Choice and two out of three moderate reformist parties (Yabloko and RDDR) did much better in St. Petersburg than in the country as a whole, and only one moderate reformist party (PRES) fared worse. The 26 percent of the vote received by Russia's Choice's,Yabloko's 20.4 percent, and RDDR's 8.7 percent represented respectively the third, the first, and the second best showing of these parties in the country. The four reformist parties together received 58.7 percent of the vote, which was 25.4 percent higher than their combined national average and constituted their best showing in Russia.

In sharp contrast to the strong showing of reformist parties stands the weak performance of the centrist, socialist, and nationalist parties. Each of them received less support in St. Petersburg than in Russia as a whole, and only two (KPRF and LDPR) passed the 5 percent threshold. The combined total of the six centrist parties (Women of Russia, DPR, Civic Union, Future of Russia, KEDR, and Dignity and Compassion) was 12 percent, which constituted their second worst showing in the country, and the combined strength of three socialist and nationalist parties (APR, KPRF, and LDPR) was 25.7 percent of the vote, which constituted their third worst showing.

The 1993 election illustrates the stability of St. Petersburg voter alignments. A comparison with the June 1991 presidential election indicates that despite three years of painful economic reform and a decline in voter turnout, there was virtually no change in support for the socialist and nationalist opposition (in fact a decline of 0.2 percent) and only a minor decline (1.2 percent) in support for the reformist and centrist parties (see table 12-3).

The national election survey data support the conclusion that the political preferences of the St. Petersburg electorate remained largely unchanged: an analysis of the 1993 preferences of supporters of Yeltsin and Vadim V. Bakatin, the 1991 presidential candidates who held reformist and centrist positions still undifferentiated at that time, shows that 90 percent of voters intended to vote for democratic and centrist parties, whereas only 6 percent of them said that they intended to vote for LDPR or KPRF.

All this begs the question of why reformist parties did so well in St. Petersburg. The survey data suggest a combination of strong support among all the main social groups, and especially strong support among educated voters, as well as the failure of pocketbook voting to take place, as the explanation of the reformers' success. Russia's Choice, Yabloko, RDDR, and PRES together received support from 35 percent of the skilled and unskilled workers, 32 percent of clerical workers, and 50 percent of the technical, scientific, and liberal arts intelligentsia. In comparison, KPRF and

Table 12-3. *June 1991 and December 1993 Elections in St. Petersburg: A Comparison*[a]

Percent

June 12, 1991, presidential election		December 12, 1993, parliamentary election	
Candidates	*Support*	*Parties*	*Support*
Reformist and centrist candidates	71.9	*Radical reformist, moderate reformist, and centrist parties*	70.7
Boris Yeltsin	68.4	*Radical Reformist*	26.0
Vadim Bakatin	3.5	Russia's Choice	26.0
		Moderate Reformist	32.7
		Yabloko	20.4
		RDDR	8.7
		PRES	3.6
		Centrist parties	12.0
		Women of Russia	4.9
		Democratic Party of Russia	3.8
		Civic Union	1.8
		Future of Russia	0.6
		KEDR	0.5
		Dignity and Compassion	0.4
Nationalist and Socialist candidates	25.9	*Nationalist and socialist parties*	25.7
Nationalist candidates	5.8	*Nationalist parties*	17.4
Vladimir Zhirinovskii	5.8	LDPR	17.4
Socialist candidates	20.1	*Socialist parties*	8.3
Nikolai Ryzhkov	10.8	KPRF	7.4
Albert Makashov	5.2	Agrarian Party of Russia	0.9
Aman Tuleyev	4.1		
Against all candidates	2.4	Against all parties	3.7

Source: Various publications.

a. Results are calculated as the percentage of valid votes

LDPR were supported by 9 percent of skilled and unskilled workers, 5 percent of clerical workers, and 4 percent of the technical, scientific, and liberal arts intelligentsia. Moreover, the reformist parties held a decisive edge over the socialist and nationalist parties among educated people: 54 percent of people with higher education and 32 percent with incomplete higher education intended to vote for the democratic parties. At the same time, only 2 percent of people with higher education and 8 percent with incomplete higher education intended to vote for the socialist and nationalist parties.

The pocketbook voting phenomenon did not occur in St. Petersburg. According to the survey, 24 percent of the respondents claimed that their personal situation had improved in the preceding year, 26 percent declared that their situation had not changed, and 50 percent said their situation had worsened. On the basis of these findings one could anticipate stronger support for the opposition parties. This did not happen because 39 percent of those who said that their situation had worsened planned to vote for the reformist parties and only 8 percent of the people in the same economic category planned to vote for the socialist and nationalist parties.

This supports the conclusion that in St. Petersburg strong support for reforms was translated into strong support for policies advocated by reformist parties. This support was not restricted to the well-educated stratum (although this group was certainly the core of the reformist electorate) but was widely shared by members of all social groups. Moreover, the commitment to such policies was strong enough to prevent pocketbook voting among those who were victimized by the economic reforms.

Although the preelection survey showed strong support for reformist parties among all major social groups, it also revealed that there were significant differences in *relative* support of these groups for different parties. Because of the different social composition of various city districts, the raion-level electoral results (see table 12-4) help to confirm the survey's finding concerning the relations between social cleavages and voter alignment in St. Petersburg.

Dzerzhinskii and Kuibyshevskii raions (administrative districts) are situated in the historic center of St. Petersburg and are home to many of the city academic and cultural institutions. In both raions there is a higher concentration of the liberal arts intelligentsia and students (there are nine institutions of higher education in both) than in other parts of the city. At the same time, concentration of the scientific and technical intelligentsia, Yabloko's main social base, and workers, LDPR's primary social base, is lower here than in the rest of the city.

Survey data show very strong support for Russia's Choice among the liberal arts intelligentsia: 33 percent of the members of this group intended to vote for Russia's Choice, whereas only 21 percent intended to vote for Yabloko. Russia's Choice also held a significant advantage among young people: 22 percent of people aged eighteen to twenty-nine intended to vote for Russia's Choice and only 11 percent intended to vote for Yabloko. These political preferences were reflected in the raion-level results: support for Russia's Choice in both raions was the strongest in the city, support for

Table 12-4. Vote for the Party Lists in Eight City Districts

Percent of support

Raion party	Kuibyshevskii raion	Dzerzhinskii raion	Kalininskii raion	Vyborgskii raion	Nevskii raion	Town of Pushkin	Town of Kolpino	Town of Kronstadt	St. Petersburg
Russia's Choice	30.7	30.3	27.5	27.4	24.6	21.5	19.7	17.4	26.0
Yabloko	20.0	19.9	21.2	21.4	18.7	18.2	17.3	13.9	20.4
RDDR	8.6	10.3	9.0	8.5	8.5	6.6	7.3	6.2	8.7
PRES	3.1	2.9	3.2	3.4	3.7	4.2	4.1	4.6	3.6
Women of Russia	4.5	4.0	4.4	4.7	5.4	4.9	6.6	6.6	4.9
DPR	4.0	3.8	3.9	3.7	3.9	4.1	4.1	3.6	3.8
Civic Union	1.6	1.7	1.6	1.5	1.9	1.6	1.4	1.8	1.8
LDPR	13.6	13.1	15.7	16.0	21.1	21.1	26.3	29.9	17.4
KPRF	6.1	6.8	7.5	7.5	6.7	8.7	6.7	7.7	7.4
Agrarian Party of Russia	0.6	0.8	0.8	0.9	0.8	3.1	0.9	0.7	0.9
Others[a]	1.3	1.6	1.5	1.4	1.4	1.7	1.6	2.3	1.6
Against all	3.3	3.8	3.6	3.6	3.4	4.5	4.0	5.4	3.7
Percentage of votes cast	47.0	49.5	53.5	53.1	50.0	57.1	52.2	53.8	52.5

Source: Unofficial protocol, Central Electoral Commission of St. Petersburg.
a. Includes Future of Russia, Dignity and Compassion, and KEDR.

Yabloko was below the city average, and support for LDPR was the lowest in the city (see table 12-4). The heavy presence of students in both raions also explains why electoral turnout here was the lowest in the city: The survey shows that people aged eighteen to twenty-nine planned to vote in significantly smaller numbers than older voters.[29]

Kalininskii and Vyborgskii raions, the Northern residential districts, have the highest concentration of scientific and technical intelligentsia in the city. Within these two adjacent raions are located twenty-eight technological and scientific research institutions and eighty-eight industrial enterprises.

The scientific and technical intelligentsia, affected by the plight of the military-industrial sector and sharp cuts in budgets of scientific institutes, was strongly dissatisfied with the course of economic reform and held Russia's Choice responsible. At the same time, however, the scientific and technical intelligentsia did not embrace LDPR or KPRF. It was Yabloko that received the majority of the protest vote of this group. According to the survey, 25 percent of the scientific and technical intelligentsia was planning to vote for Yabloko, 19 percent for Russia's Choice, and only 6 percent for LDPR and KPRF. These preferences are corroborated by the voting results in Kalininskii and Vyborgskii raions. Here the support for Yabloko was the highest among the city's twenty-four districts.

The distinctive feature of Nevskii raion and the town of Kolpino is a high concentration of skilled and unskilled workers in both districts: 18.6 percent of personnel of the city industrial enterprises worked in both districts. This is because Nevskii raion has the highest concentration of industrial enterprises (sixty) within the city limits, whereas the town of Kolpino is an industrial suburb of St. Petersburg with all the characteristics of a factory town because most of its residents work at the Izhorskii Works, which produces reactors for nuclear power stations.

According to the survey, LDPR in St. Petersburg relied largely on working-class support: 46 percent of LDPR's voters were skilled and unskilled workers; 4 percent, clerical workers; and 14 percent, scientific, technical, and liberal arts intelligentsia. In comparison, 30 percent of Russia's Choice voters were skilled and unskilled workers; 10 percent, clerical workers; and 34 percent, scientific, technical, and liberal arts intelligentsia. The raion-level data support the notion of LDPR as a working-class party: the 21.1 percent support for the party in Nevskii raion was the strongest showing within the city limits, whereas the 26.3 percent support for LDPR in Kolpino was the party's second best result in metropolitan St. Petersburg after Kronstadt.

Finally, the survey data and electoral results in Nevskii raion and Kolpino also prove that the Communists had ceased to be the working-class party. The survey found that only 13 percent of KPRF supporters were skilled and unskilled workers; 38 percent, clerical workers; and 50 percent, scientific, technical, and liberal arts intelligentsia. Support for the party in these two working-class districts was also among the lowest in the city. In fact, similarly low support for KPRF appeared only in Dzerzhinskii and Kuibyshevskii raions, the strongholds of Russia's Choice.

The town of Pushkin is a nonindustrial suburb of St. Petersburg and as such has a different social profile than Kolpino or the city itself. The tourism industry provides most of the employment, which translates into a much lower concentration of industrial workers than in Kolpino. Thus, Pushkin's share of the city industrial personnel was only 0.2 percent. Moreover, because of its clean air the nonindustrial suburbs tended to have more retired people than Kolpino or the city. Thus, pensioners constituted 28.3 percent of Pushkin's residents, whereas in Kolpino and the city the same social group constituted 22.8 percent and 24.7 percent of residents, respectively.[30]

This combination of characteristics makes Pushkin as conservative as Kolpino: in both places LDPR, KPRF, and APR together received 32.9 percent and 33.9 percent of the vote, respectively. However, in Pushkin support for LDPR was weaker than in Kolpino, whereas the support for KPRF and APR was stronger. In fact, the Pushkin vote for both parties was the strongest in metropolitan St. Petersburg. This fits well with survey findings that indicate that the percentage of clerical workers as well as people aged 55 and older among KPRF and APR supporters was much higher than among LDPR supporters.

Kronstadt, located on an island in the Gulf of Finland, is a garrison town, which serves as the home port of the Baltic Fleet. Thus, the vote of Kronstadt provides a clear indication of the electoral behavior of the military in general. LDPR received its strongest support in Kronstadt with 29.9 percent of the vote, and Russia's Choice's 17.4 percent and Yabloko's 13.9 percent were their worst electoral performances in St. Petersburg. In short, the military rebuffed the reformist parties in favor of Zhirinovskii.[31]

Election to the State Duma:
The Single-Member Districts Vote

This section argues that the political affiliation of a candidate, his or her name recognition, and his or her experience in running earlier political campaigns proved to be crucial elements in a candidate's success in winning a single-member district seat in the State Duma. The section also argues that electoral laws and last minute changes in them did significantly affect the election results.

Actors and Their Organizational Capacities

Based on its population, St. Petersburg had been allotted eight single-member seats in the State Duma. Accordingly, St. Petersburg's thirty-one electoral districts in the 1990 election for the RSFSR Congress of People's Deputies were amalgamated into eight single-member districts for the purposes of the Duma election. In the process of drawing up the single-member districts, the Central Electoral Commission's requirement that differences in population between the largest and smallest districts within the same federal unit be no more than 15 percent was violated; St. Petersburg's smallest single-member district had 414,822 registered voters and the largest had 516,513 voters, a difference of 20 percent. Nonetheless, the Central Electoral Commission approved the proposal for St. Petersburg's single-member districts and there were no complaints that the redistricting favored any particular political interests.

The intense nature of party life in St. Petersburg was reflected in the mix of candidates in the single-member districts: 53 percent of all candidates belonged to various political parties active in the city. The parties on the December ballot were the major beneficiaries of the electoral rule, which allowed them to place candidates in the single-member district races without gathering signatures from the required 1 percent of a district's registered voters. These parties used this rule to nominate 80 percent of their candidates in the single-member district races (see table 12-5).

The strength of the reformist parties in the city found its expression in their domination of the party-affiliated candidates in the single-member district election: the four reformist parties together had twenty-seven candidates, the centrist parties had eleven candidates, and the socialist and nationalist parties (including the extremist local parties not on the December 12 ballot) had ten candidates.

Table 12-5. *St. Petersburg Candidates in the Single-Mandate Districts*

Totals

Parties	Candidates nominated from party list	Candidates who collected signatures for nomination	Total candidates	Districts
Russia's Choice	6	5	11	8
Yabloko	7	1	8	7
Civic Union	4	3	7	6
LDPR	4	—	4	4
RDDR	5	—	5	5
Democratic Party of Russia	4	—	4	4
PRES	3	—	3	3
KPRF	2	—	2	2
Total	35	9	44	8
Parties not on the December ballot	—	4	4	3
Independents	—	42	42	8
Total	35	55	90	8

Source: Author's calculations based on Central Electoral Commission's bulletin.

Of all the parties, only Russia's Choice competed in all eight districts. Its main competitor, Yabloko, had candidates in seven districts. Because of the large pool of potential candidates, Russia's Choice placed two people on the ballot in three districts, with the understanding that polling results would determine which candidate ultimately would be the bloc candidate on election day and which would drop out of the race. The significant organizational resources of Russia's Choice also allowed it to place five candidates on the ballot through signature gathering. This was more than all other parties combined.

Representatives of two occupational groups, professional politicians and private entrepreneurs, provided 55 percent of all candidates. The politicians were the USSR and Russian Federation People's Deputies, as well as deputies in St. Petersburg city and Leningrad oblast soviets, and accounted for 37 percent of the candidates, while private entrepreneurs made up 18 percent. A comparison between these two groups and their degree of affiliation with political parties reveals that the deputies were more likely to be affiliated with political parties: 66 percent of deputies running in the single-member districts had a party affiliation, whereas only 25 percent of private entrepreneurs had such an affiliation. This is not surprising given the fact that most of the deputies had been involved in politics since the late 1980s and had played a major role in the formation of political organizations or factions in local or federal legislatures. Moreover, most deputies lacked the financial resources to run independently and this greatly increased their incentive to secure a party affiliation. Private entrepreneurs did have the needed financial resources to run independent campaigns and this lessened their incentive to seek party affiliation. Moreover, most entrepreneurs were political novices with little knowledge of political parties and their programs. Finally, few parties made significant recruiting efforts to attract private entrepreneurs with political ambitions.

The Campaign: The Strategies of the Parties

Elections in the single-member districts posed more of a problem for the parties than the Council of the Federation elections because the great majority of the party-nominated candidates competing in the single-member districts did not have wide name recognition. Establishing name recognition during a short campaign period required substantial organizational effort and financial resources. Moreover, the single-round election required significant cooperation between parties of similar political orientation in order to elect a mutually acceptable candidate.

Substantial financial and organizational resources allowed Russia's Choice to make promotion of its candidates in the single-member districts an integral part of its electoral campaign effort. In order to create a coattail effect, the bloc printed leaflets that clearly identified its candidates and bought television time to promote them. Russia's Choice also benefited from its close connection with the city's business community, which helped to promote the party's candidates in a variety of its own publications.[32]

The other parties could not offer any substantial organizational or financial assistance and limited their efforts to informing their candidates about the party platform and advising them on campaign strategy. Russia's Choice was subsequently far more successful in establishing the name recognition of its candidates, and ultimately this accounts for their stronger performance than the candidates of all the other parties combined.

A single-round election with an average of 11.3 candidates per district made fragmentation of the vote a likely outcome. This required parties of a similar political orientation to cooperate in order to place a single candidate per district on election day. The problem was especially acute for Russia's Choice and Yabloko because they were competing against each other in seven out of eight districts. Moreover, Russia's Choice had the additional problem of having two candidates in three different districts, and Yabloko faced a similar situation in one district.

Both parties succeeded in solving the second problem in three out of four cases because candidates with lower poll ratings voluntarily dropped out of the race. However, where candidates did not want to withdraw in favor of another candidate of their party, the party had no means of removing them from the ballot. This happened to Russia's Choice in District 207, in which neither of the party's candidates agreed to drop out of the race in favor of the other because each employed different pollsters who presented conflicting poll results.

Yabloko faced a similar situation in District 206. The party had two candidates, Igor Artem'yev and Sergei M. Nikiforov. Artem'yev ultimately removed himself from the race in favor of Nikiforov. However, Artem'yev's withdrawal announcement was made at the last possible moment, and this meant that many voters were not aware of his withdrawal and that many precinct committees failed to strike him from the ballot sheets. Artem'yev received 3.7 percent of the vote, thus helping the Russia's Choice candidate win the district. This situation was hardly surprising because both parties were hastily formed on the eve of the election and were too weak to impose discipline on their members.

Russia's Choice and Yabloko failed to cooperate in the single-member district elections because there was no tradition of electoral agreements between parties. The best illustration of this was electoral District 210, in which candidates from both blocs had to face a strong independent opponent, Aleksandr Nevzorov, a popular television journalist with militant Russian nationalist views. Moreover, on the eve of the ballot, Zhirinovskii forced his party candidate in the district to withdraw in favor of Nevzorov.

District 210, in the center of St. Petersburg, included five raions which indicated the highest level of support for Russia's Choice in preelection polls. However, the party's candidate, Yurii I. Vdovin, was running neck and neck with Nevzorov in opinion polls. Arguing that he had the best chance to defeat Nevzorov, Vdovin and Russia's Choice pressured Yabloko's candidate, Yurii M. Nesterov, who trailed both Nevzorov and Vdovin in the polls, to withdraw from the race. Nesterov refused to withdraw because he had been assigned an "unelectable" position on the Yabloko regional list. His decision was backed by Boldyrev, who opposed any preelection deals with Russia's Choice.

Failing to convince Yabloko to remove Nesterov, Russia's Choice tried to convince RDDR to remove its candidate, a little known former deputy of the oblast soviet, Gennadii I. Shuklin, who was running a distant fourth in the polls. However, Sobchak held a grudge against Vdovin, who as chairman of the city soviet committee on mass media had been critical of the mayor's policies in this area and refused to remove Shuklin from the race. The democratic parties' failure to cooperate allowed Nevzorov to beat out Vdovin by a 1.5 percent margin.

Zhirinovskii's assistance in electing Nevzorov was an exception rather than the rule as far as the cooperation between the nationalist and socialist parties was concerned. In District 207, these parties had a good chance of repeating Nevzorov's success because the reformers were even more fragmented than in District 210. Indeed, not only did Russia's Choice have two candidates in the district but Yabloko, RDDR, and PRES also had their own candidates. The logical step for the opposition parties was to unify behind the KPRF candidate, Yurii P. Belov, who did very well in preelection polls. However, neither the LDPR candidate nor the candidates from other opposition parties agreed to withdraw from the race. In this case, the lack of cooperation between the socialist and nationalist parties resulted in a victory for the independent reformist candidate, Mikhail M. Kiselev, with a mere 8.7 percent of the vote, with Belov finishing 2.2 percent behind.

The inability of opposition candidates to cooperate was most striking in District 212, which included the conservative districts of Nevskii and Kolpino. Because of its conservative nature, Russia's Choice was the only reformist party to field a candidate in the district. The LDPR's candidate, Yurii P. Kuznetsov, was running strongly in the polls but his victory was dependent on his ability to convince three independent opposition candidates to withdraw from the race. Despite his efforts, all three remained on the ballot, allowing the Russia's Choice candidate, Sergei Popov, to win.

The Results

Strong support for Russia's Choice certainly helped its candidates in the single-member districts; they won in four out of eight races. In fact, one can argue that Russia's Choice won in five districts because Kiselev, the winner in District 207, although officially an independent candidate, was very close to the party in his political orientation, used its logo during the campaign, and ultimately joined the radical-reformist Union of December 12 faction in the Duma, whose members largely came from Russia's Choice.

Yabloko, RDDR, and PRES officially did not win in any district. PRES nonetheless was still able to secure a seat in St. Petersburg because Mark L.

Goryachev, a wealthy businessman who was on the federal list of Civic Union but campaigned as an independent in the single-member district race, joined the party faction in the Duma. The only centrist victory came in District 211. The winner, the chairman of the city soviet finance and budget committee, Aleksandr K. Yegorov, an independent candidate whose main campaign promise was to fight for a greater allocation of federal resources for the city, joined the centrist New Regional Policy faction in the Duma. Despite the crucial help of Zhirinovskii, Nevzorov did not join his faction in the Duma, preferring instead to belong to another Russian nationalist faction, the Russian Path.

Electoral rules had an important impact on the electoral outcomes. As was shown in the previous section, the single-round election format and a lack of cooperation between candidates with similar political positions led to a victory by an opposition candidate in the most reformist district and by a reformer in the most conservative district. Equally important was a last-minute change in the regulations that eliminated a provision invalidating the election results in those districts in which the number of votes cast against all candidates was higher than the number of votes cast for the winner. This happened in four districts (see table 12-6). Both Nevzorov and reformist candidates benefited from this rule change. Reformers benefited because they won in all four districts (three official Russia's Choice candidates and Kiselev). Nevzorov benefited from the rule change because it scuttled an agreement between Vdovin, Nesterov, and Shuklin in which all three were to have withdrawn from the race and asked their supporters to vote against all candidates. This would almost certainly have invalidated the results in District 210. The change in rules rendered this strategy irrelevant and kept all three candidates on the ballot.

Previous electoral experience and name recognition were more important factors in election victories than the availability of financial resources. Six out of eight winners were either deputies in the city soviet, Russian Federation People's Deputies, or well-known media personalities. In comparison, only one of the winners was a private entrepreneur.

Finally, dissatisfaction of voters with candidates in the single-member districts was very high. The average share of votes cast for winning candidates in the single-member districts was 16.6 percent, whereas the average share of votes cast against all candidates was 19.3 percent. This high dissatisfaction with the pool of candidates can be explained by the fact that the short electoral campaign time made it difficult for candidates to establish themselves in the minds of the public. This lack of information, in turn,

Table 12-6. *Vote in the St. Petersburg Single-Member Districts*

Candidate and percent of support

District affiliation	West #206 candidate	North #207 candidate	Northeast #208 candidate	Northwest #209 candidate	Central #210 candidate	South #211 candidate	Southeast #212 candidate	Southwest #213 candidate
Russia's Choice	Savitskii*12.9	Leverovskii 6.2 Sungurov 5.5	Rybakov* 26.7 Soshnikov**	Aleksandrov* 19.5	Vdovin 27.1 Chernov**	Gladkov 8.3	Popov*18.8	Pustyntsev 8.3
Yabloko	Nikiforov 8.0 Artem'yev** 3.7	Drozdov 5.1	Nikiforenko 4.4	Amosov 6.9	Nesterov 8.4	Gubanov 6.4	No candidate	Vinnikov 3.1
RDDR	No candidate	Murashev 3.2	Filimonov 2.2	Kutenev 1.8	Shuklin 7.5	No candidate	No candidate	Arutyunov 3.1
PRES	Dmitriev 10.5	Zubik 2.9	No candidate	Kalinin 2.3	No candidate	No candidate	No candidate	No candidate
DPR	No candidate	Khodyachenko 0.7	Talanov 2.3	No candidate	No candidate	No candidate	Evdokimov 4.6	Spitsa 3.9
Civic Union	Shcherbakov 11.0	Tereshchenko 0.4 Derbin 1.8	No candidate	Karmanovskii 7.3	No candidate	Gapanovich 6.6	Zanin 12.0	Goryachev*a 20.0
LDPR	No candidate	Tuinov 3.0	M. Ivanov 11.3	No candidate	Marychev**	No candidate	Kuznetsov 12.9	No candidate
KPRF	No candidate	Belov 6.5	No candidate	No candidate	No candidate	No candidate	No candidate	Krasnitskii 2.7
RKRP	No candidate	Turetskii 3.6	Tyul'kin 7.3	No candidate	No candidate	No candidate	No candidate	No candidate
Local nationalist parties	No candidate	Bondarik 3.8	No candidate	Onegin 4.9	No candidate	No candidate	No candidate	No candidate

Independent	Semenov 10.5 Solov'yev 9.3 Istomin 6.5 Konstantinov 6.3 Antonov 4.3	Kiselev*[b] 8.7 Selivanov 6.8 Glagovskii 6.7 Bogatov 5.8 Novolotskii 5.1 Yurchenko 4.1 Smirnov 3.1 Linchenko 0.5	V. Ivanov 7.1 Kravchenko 6.4 Pomeshchikov 6.3 Matorin 5.5 Perchik 3.5	Yag'ya 9.4 Ryabchikhin 7.4 S. Yegorov 6.5 Rudenko 4.8 Tsvetkov 3.8 Shesteryuk 1.4	Nevzorov*[c] 28.6 Shutov 5.9	A. Yegorov*[d] 17.2 Drapeko 15.8 Levashov 11.3 Zorin 6.2 Yemets 5.2 Chibisov 5.0 Toper 1.2	Cherezov 8.8 Lutsenko 8.5 Serdyukov 5.9 Yurkan 5.4 Gukov 3.9	S. Andreyev 15.9 A. Andreyev 15.7 Kol'tsov 9.6 Volotskoi 0.9
Against all	20.7	16.6	17.0	24.2	22.5	16.9	19.2	17.0
Percentage of votes cast	54.2	52.1	53.6	51.5	50.2	54.2	50.7	52.3
Number of registered voters	476,460	516,513	477,630	430,654	483,574	414,822	481,500	468,922

Source: Given to the author by the St. Petersburg Central Electoral Commission.

* Marks the winning candidate; ** marks withdrawn candidate.

a. Joined the PRES faction in the Duma.
b. Joined The Union of December 12 faction in the Duma.
c. Was endorsed by LDPR on the eve of the ballot; joined the Russian Path faction in the Duma.
d. Joined the New Regional Policy faction in the Duma.

prompted many either to vote for the best-known candidate in the district or against all candidates.

Elections to the Council of the Federation

This section argues that the key element for success in the Council of the Federation race was wide name recognition of the candidate and his ability to align with one of the two political parties most popular in the city, Russia's Choice and Yabloko.

Actors and Their Organizational Capacities

The election of the Council of the Federation, the upper house of the Russian parliament, was modeled on the U.S. Senate with each region given two seats on the Council regardless of its size. Because elections for both seats were to take place simultaneously, Russia's eighty-nine regions became, in effect, two-member districts in which the top two finishers were to be elected into the chamber.

In most of Russia's regions heads of the regional administration ran for a seat in the Council of the Federation. The main difference between St. Petersburg and the rest of Russia was the absence from the race of the head of the regional administration (in this case, the mayor of St. Petersburg). By deciding to head the RDDR list for the Duma election, Sobchak opened up the race for both of St. Petersburg's seats in the Council of the Federation. However, like elsewhere in Russia, the St. Petersburg elections to the Council of the Federation attracted only a few leading local politicians. The reason was simple: only politicians with wide name recognition and substantial organizational and financial resources could place themselves on the ballot and campaign effectively in a constituency of 3.7 million registered voters. The elections to the Council of the Federation, indeed, taught the political parties the crucial importance of aligning themselves with well-known politicians. At the same time, it also demonstrated to local politicians the importance of affiliation with political parties that have significant organizational resources.

This all became clear as early as the candidate-selection and the signature-gathering stage of the campaign. As was mentioned earlier, the

Achilles' heel of Russia's Choice was its lack of prominent local politicians capable of attracting votes. This problem was especially acute in the case of the Council of the Federation election. In an effort to compensate for this weakness, leaders of the bloc negotiated with Yeltsin's representative in the city, Sergei A. Tsyplyayev, and the chairman of the St. Petersburg city soviet, Aleksandr N. Belyayev. Although the negotiations with Tsyplyayev fell through, Russia's Choice reached an agreement with Belyayev resulting in an endorsement of his candidacy. Belyayev, however, wanted to minimize his commitment to Russia's Choice and negotiated similar endorsement agreements with RDDR, PRES, and DPR. Russia's Choice continued to search for its own candidate and finally selected Russian People's Deputy Nikolai M. Arzhannikov. Despite the fact that Arzhannikov was one of the leaders of the well-publicized 1989 Leningrad police officers' strike, he was not a well-known figure in the city. This handicap turned out to be major liability during the campaign.

The dearth of politicians with wide name recognition willing to run for the Council of the Federation affected the other parties as well. Yabloko was in a far better position than the rest after Boldyrev joined the race. However, it could not find a suitable second candidate and refused to endorse Belyayev or Arzhannikov. RDDR and PRES did not have candidates of their own and finally endorsed Belyaev. Both refused to endorse Boldyrev or Arzhannikov.

Of the centrist parties, only Civic Union had its own candidate—the head of the city tax inspectorate and former obkom secretary for industry, Dmitri N. Filippov. DPR could not find candidates of its own and endorsed Boldyrev and Belyayev. The socialist and nationalist parties had no official candidates in the race. However, the vice mayor of St. Petersburg, Vyacheslav G. Shcherbakov, a retired rear admiral who had openly sided with Ruslan I. Khasbulatov and Aleksandr V. Rutskoi during the October crisis, was publicly supported by various socialist and nationalist organizations.

The importance of name recognition and organizational resources was highlighted during the signature-collecting phase of the campaign. Unlike in the Duma election, the parties could not place candidates directly on the ballot and had to collect signatures in order to qualify their candidates for the race. Only six candidates—Arzhannikov, Belyayev, Boldyrev, Filippov, Shcherbakov, and Tsyplyayev—were able to gather the required 25,000 signatures. Tsyplyayev, however, was forced to withdraw his candidacy after a validity check revealed a massive falsification of signatures.

The Campaign: The Strategies of Parties and Candidates

Arzhannikov was the least known of the five candidates on the ballot. According to a public opinion poll taken on November 21–22, Arzhannikov was not among the top fifteen public figures whose names were mentioned as deserving to represent the city in the new parliament. All of his competitors were named.[33]

The situation dictated the campaign strategy of Russia's Choice. The main goal was to create a coattail effect wherein support for the bloc could significantly improve Arzhannikov's chances. Toward this end, the party made the promotion of Arzhannikov's candidacy one of the main elements of its campaign. Virtually every Russia's Choice leaflet contained an explicit call to vote for Arzhannikov. Moreover, Russia's Choice designed a special promotional booklet for Arzhannikov that provided his biography and sported an endorsement by the city's most prominent intellectual, academician Dmitri S. Likhachev. More than 1.5 million copies of this booklet were distributed on the eve of the election. Finally, Russia's Choice bought time on the local television channel to run Arzhannikov's ads featuring a full account of his record.

As was the case for Russia's Choice in general, the intense campaigning significantly improved Arzhannikov's rating by the end of the campaign. However, the party's weakness in the conservative suburbs, as well as the brevity of the campaign, worked against Arzhannikov. He finished third with 6,611 votes behind Belyayev and 21,003 votes behind Boldyrev.

Unlike Arzhannikov, Belyayev had strong name recognition, and as the highest ranking city politician competing in the election, he had two significant advantages over his competitors. First, he had substantial financial resources as a result of contributions from entrepreneurial groups that he had helped in the past or that wanted him to promote their interests in Moscow. Second, he was the only competitor who could make concrete promises concerning the material well-being of city residents.[34] This became an important facet of Belyayev's electoral strategy. In his appearances at enterprises he promised to sell state-owned housing for a lower-than-market price to people on the waiting list and to provide free housing for those unable to purchase apartments. In light of the fact that 22.4 percent of the city's population still lived in communal apartments, this was, indeed, a very significant promise.

For the intelligentsia, Belyayev's strategy was to position himself on the ideological spectrum between Arzhannikov and Boldyrev. On the one hand, he tried to garner backing from the intelligentsia by expressing support for the new constitution and by securing the endorsement of Likhachev and other prominent liberal intellectuals. He also prepared a leaflet that emphasized his record as a committed supporter of radical reform and had it distributed in the central raions of the city. At the same time, he cultivated the image of an independent reformer by seeking and receiving endorsements from PRES, RDDR, and DPR. In particular, he tried to appeal to the scientific and technical intelligentsia by emphasizing his disagreement with Russia's Choice on the issue of economic reform. For this purpose he distributed a different leaflet in the areas with a heavy concentration of technical intelligentsia. He pledged to support Russia's science and technology even if this meant a continuation of subsidies to the military-industrial complex enterprises.[35]

Contrary to Arzhannikov, who relied heavily on the electronic media, Belyayev relied primarily on the print media, believing that the press could play a crucial role in winning the intelligentsia's vote. In particular, he aligned himself with one of the city's most popular liberal dailies, *Smena*. *Smena* advertised his campaign schedule and his bank account number for campaign contributions, reported his promise of affordable housing, and even published his income declaration that indicated that he was an honest person living exclusively on his official salary. More important, Belyayev paid more than 20 million rubles for a special issue of the newspaper, published on December 7, which included two long articles outlining his positions in detail and an essay that contained a devastating attack on Filippov. *Smena* printed 560,000 copies of this special issue, 430,000 copies above its usual run. The additional copies were distributed by Belyayev's campaign staff throughout the city.[36]

Belyayev's strategy worked; he came in a very close second (0.8 percent behind) by winning substantial support among all the main social groups. He won in the city's working-class raions; finished second after Arzhannikov in those raions with a heavy concentration of liberal arts intelligentsia; and second after Boldyrev in raions with a heavy concentration of scientific and technical intelligentsia.

As mentioned earlier, Boldyrev was the city's most popular political figure. His image as a leading radical democrat was largely shaped in the years 1989 to 1991. In 1989, he caused one of the major upsets of the elections to the USSR Congress of People's Deputies by defeating the gorkom first secretary, Anatolii N. Gerasimov. He was a prominent reformist politician in the Soviet parliament and later headed the Control Directorate of the Russian presidential apparatus charged to fight corruption. However, in March 1993, he was abruptly removed from his post and subsequently became a vocal critic of Yeltsin.

In his campaign, Boldyrev attempted to present Yabloko as the reformist alternative to Russia's Choice. He harshly attacked Yeltsin for provoking the October crisis, the new constitution for instituting an all-powerful executive, and Russia's Choice for what he dubbed as "vulgar [economic] liberalism" (in a radio braodcast on December 2, 1993). This strategy was popular among the scientific and technical intelligentsia and also helped him to gain substantial support among conservative social groups. As will be shown in the following section, both of these groups were key to his electoral victory.

This strategy, however, undermined Boldyrev's image as a radical reformer and cost him the support of many members of the intelligentsia. His vicious attacks on the new constitution, which enjoyed strong support in the city, also eroded his popularity. He won the race with 34.4 percent of the vote, but with Belyayev and Arzhannikov very close behind. The brevity of the campaign worked to his advantage, because a longer campaign would probably have further eroded his support and cost him a seat in the Council of the Federation.

A fourth candidate for the Council of the Federation, vice mayor Shcherbakov, had played in local politics a similar role to that of Rutskoi at the national level. A retired rear admiral, he was chosen by Sobchak to be his running mate in the June 1991 mayoral election in an effort to gain the support of the military and the military-industrial complex. During the August 1991 coup, Shcherbakov played a crucial role in negotiations with the commanders of the Leningrad military district, preventing the army's move into the city. He subsequently moved away from Sobchak politically and associated himself with the anti-Yeltsin opposition. During the fall 1993 crisis, Shcherbakov sided with Rutskoi and Khasbulatov, but refused to endorse the military insurrection in Moscow.

Although supported by a variety of socialist and nationalist organizations, Shcherbakov realized that this support was an electoral liability in a city like St. Petersburg. His electoral strategy, therefore, was to present himself as a centrist and disassociate himself from Rutskoi and Khasbulatov. He emphasized his role in foiling the 1991 coup and in preventing a violent uprising in St. Petersburg in October 1993, as well as his involvement in the conversion of the city's military-industrial enterprises. However, he had no resources to mount a large-scale campaign and was negatively treated by the city's main newspapers, which portrayed him as a communist-nationalist extremist. All this forced Shcherbakov to focus his campaign efforts on the LDPR and KPRF core constituencies—the military, retirees, and workers—in hope that their strong support would enable him to win a seat. The fact that he finished only 5.3 percent behind Belyayev suggests that this strategy was not unrealistic.

Filippov's name would never have been on the ballot had he not been fired from his post as the head of the city tax service on October 9, 1993. Filippov was a former obkom secretary for industry, and in 1990 he was invited to organize the city's tax service. By all accounts he turned it into one of the best in Russia. However, Sobchak removed him from his post because of the heavy fines his tax service imposed on the city's large joint ventures for concealing illegal foreign bank accounts. Filippov's firing caused an uproar in the local and national press and this gave him instant name recognition and the image of a courageous fighter against rampant tax evasion.

Out of a job and trying to capitalize on his image and name recognition, Filippov decided to run for the Council of the Federation as the unofficial candidate of the Civic Union. However, his campaign suffered from lack of experience in organizing an effective city-wide campaign. Like the Civic Union's general campaign, he assumed that industrial workers would follow their managers' advice and vote for him. He focused his campaign efforts on distributing leaflets in industrial enterprises. This proved to be a crucial strategic error. His high position in the former regional hierarchy of the CPSU was also not an electoral asset in a city in which anticommunist sentiments were still very strong. Finally, in the last week of the campaign, the city's liberal press made a concerted effort to tarnish his image. The combined impact of these factors explains why Filippov finished last.

The Results

The results indicate what a tight race the Council of the Federation election was; only 5.3 percent separated the first- and fourth-place finishers. Despite this, support for the different candidates varied greatly from one city district to another. As in the case of the vote for the party lists, social cleavages found their expression in electoral behavior. This becomes especially clear if one analyzes the geographic distribution of votes for Arzhannikov and Shcherbakov and if one compares this to the geographic distribution of the vote for Russia's Choice and LDPR.[37]

The raion-level results of the Council of the Federation vote suggest a high degree of consistency in voter preferences. Thus, strong support for Russia's Choice went hand in hand with strong support for Arzhannikov, and strong support for LDPR went hand in hand with strong support for Shcherbakov (see table 12-7). Thus, in the districts such as Dzerzhinskii or Kalininskii, Arzhannikov came in first or second and in the districts such as Pushkin or Kronstadt, Shcherbakov came in first or second. Ultimately, Arzhannikov finished first or second in twelve out of fifteen city districts in which Russia's Choice received 24.6 percent or more. Shcherbakov finished fourth in each of these fifteen districts. At the same time, he finished first or second in nine out of the ten districts in which LDPR received 18.6 percent or more. In nine of these ten districts, Arzhannikov finished fourth.

By positioning himself in the center of the St. Petersburg political spectrum, Boldyrev was able to draw strong support from both the reformist and antireformist electorate. He came in first in districts supporting reformist parties, such as Vyborgskii, and in such conservative strongholds as Pushkin and Kolpino. He also came in second in five other conservative suburbs, including Kronstadt. However, Boldyrev's attack on Yeltsin and Russia's Choice was costly; although he was one of the top two finishers in nine out of the ten districts in which LDPR received 18.6 percent or more, a similar result occurred in only four out of twelve districts in which Russia's Choice received 26.5 percent or more.

The Constitutional Referendum

This section argues that the constitution passed largely as a result of the support of voters who had backed the democratic and centrist parties, including those parties that urged their voters to oppose its approval. At the same time, despite Zhirinovskii's personal support for the new constitution, LDPR supporters voted against it.

The Campaign

Acceptance of the new constitution with as wide a margin as possible was a matter of personal prestige for Sobchak because he was one of its principal authors. He ordered the media subordinate to the city government to promote acceptance of the new constitution. Between November 22 and December 10, the St. Petersburg television channel broadcast a series of

Table 12-7. *Vote for Council of the Federation in Eight City Districts*

Percent of support

Raion candidate	Kuibyshev-skii raion	Dzerzhinskii raion	Kalininskii raion	Vyborgskii raion	Nevskii raion	Town of Pushkin	Town of Kolpino	Town of Kronstadt	St. Petersburg
Boldyrev	34.6	34.2	32.7	33.6	31.1	33.2	32.9	25.6	34.4
Belyayev	37.5	36.9	33.3	33.6	33.1	27.0	29.7	22.1	33.6
Arzhannikov	37.8	40.9	33.6	33.2	31.2	24.0	23.6	21.1	32.8
Shcherbakov	28.1	26.6	28.1	27.3	29.1	32.3	32.8	33.6	29.1
Filippov	16.8	17.1	17.3	17.9	17.6	18.8	19.3	19.9	18.2
Against all	9.6	9.7	9.7	10.3	10.8	14.7	14.7	19.5	10.8
Percentage of votes cast	46.5	49.4	53.5	53.1	50.2	55.4	52.0	53.9	52.3

Source: Unofficial protocol, Central Electoral Commission of St. Petersburg.

programs titled "Discussing the Project of the Constitution of Russia," which strongly supported the draft. The city government's newspaper, *Sankt-Peterburgskiye vedomosti,* published only articles that supported adoption of the new constitution.

Sobchak was not alone in his efforts to convince city residents to vote for the constitution. In fact, there was an informal alliance to promote the new constitution, an alliance that included, in addition to Sobchak, Belyaev, prominent city liberal intellectuals, the city's main newspapers, and Russia's Choice, which conducted its aggressive street campaign under the slogan "Vote for Russia's Choice and the Constitution." It is not surprising, therefore, that the rise in the city polls of Russia's Choice coincided with an increase in support for the new constitution. The survey's findings reveal that two weeks before the election, 58 percent of respondents said that they would vote for the new constitution, 19 percent opposed it, and 23 remained undecided; in the last week before the ballot, support for the constitution rose to 73 percent, opposition declined to 13 percent, and only 13 percent remained undecided.

The drive against the new constitution was led by Boldyrev, who made this issue one of the prominent elements of his electoral campaign. In addition to Boldyrev, various extreme nationalist and communist organizations actively campaigned to persuade citizens to boycott the vote on the new constitution altogether or, failing a boycott, to vote against it. However, the organizational resources of the opponents could not match those of the constitution's supporters, and Boldyrev's personal popularity turned out to be insufficient to affect the vote in a radical way.

The Results

The new constitution received strong support in St. Petersburg. The city's support at 71.6 percent was 13.2 percent higher than the national level. This was a consequence of strong support on the part of most of the city's main social groups: survey preelection findings reveal that 57 percent of the scientific, technical, and liberal arts intelligentsia; 65 percent of clerical workers; and 66 percent of skilled and unskilled workers intended to vote for the new constitution.

The survey's findings also suggest that the constitution passed largely because of the support of voters supporting the reformist and centrist parties: 97 percent of Russia's Choice voters, 75 percent of Yabloko voters, 89 percent of RDDR voters, 100 percent of PRES voters, 78 percent of

Women of Russia voters, and 50 percent of DPR voters expressed their intention to vote for the constitution. Raion-level results of the constitutional referendum corroborate these findings: strong support for the previously mentioned six parties goes hand in hand with strong support for the constitution (see table 12-8). Thus Kuibyshevskii and Dzerzhinskii raions in which combined support for these six reformist and centrist parties was the strongest in the city (70.9 percent and 71.2 percent, respectively) also demonstrated the strongest support for the new constitution (74.7 percent and 74.0 percent, respectively).

In sharp contrast to the support of reformist and centrist party voters stands the socialist and nationalist parties' adherents. Despite widespread speculation, the new constitution was not supported by LDPR voters. The survey findings show that despite Zhirinovskii's personal support for the new constitution, 68 percent of LDPR supporters intended to vote against it. The raion-level results also show that strong support for LDPR coincided with weak support for the new constitution. In seven out of the eleven districts where support for LDPR exceeded 18 percent, support for the new constitution was less than 70 percent.

Among KPRF supporters, opposition to the new constitution was even stronger: survey findings show that 86 percent of the party's voters opposed it. The results of the constitutional referendum in the town of Pushkin support the survey data: the party received 8.7 percent of the vote, its highest in St. Petersburg. At the same time, the 66.3 percent support for the new constitution in Pushkin was the lowest of all twenty-four city districts.

Conclusion

The main argument of this chapter is that the December 1993 election demonstrated that despite a severe industrial recession, rise of unemployment and crime, the reformist parties, politicians, and causes continued to enjoy strong support in St. Petersburg as they did between 1989 and 1991. The election also confirmed the consistency of the reformist preferences of the city electorate: four reformist parties received nearly 60 percent of the city vote; the new constitution received almost 73 percent support in the city; and both victors in the Council of the Federation ballot and six out of eight winners in the single-member district races belonged to the reformist parties or had a reformist orientation.

Table 12-8. *Constitutional Referendum in Eight City Districts*

Percent of support

Do you support the adoption of the Constitution of the Russian Federation?	Kuibyshevskii raion	Dzerzhinskii raion	Kalininskii raion	Vyborgskii raion	Nevskii raion	Town of Pushkin	Town of Kolpino	Town of Kronstadt	St. Petersburg
"Yes"	74.7	74.0	72.0	71.7	72.3	66.3	69.7	68.3	71.6
"No"	25.3	26.0	28.0	28.3	27.7	33.7	30.3	31.7	28.4
Percentage of votes cast	46.9	51.8	53.6	53.1	50.2	57.1	52.2	54.3	52.4

Source: Unofficial protocol, Central Electoral Commission of St. Petersburg.

Victory for reformist parties was not predetermined by the social composition of the population because those parties received strong support from all the main social groups. The victory also demonstrated that adverse personal economic conditions were not sufficient to lead people to abandon the reformist parties. Preexisting organizational networks and the availability of significant financial resources were critical to the victory by Russia's Choice in St. Petersburg. These networks supplied Russia's Choice with a core of activists with experience in conducting electoral campaigns and candidates who could successfully contend in tight races.

The single-member district elections exposed dominance of the reformist candidates who won six out of eight races. The single-member district ballot also illustrated the importance of rule changes in comparison to the 1990 election. The elimination of runoff necessitated cooperation between parties and candidates with similar political orientations. However, both reformist and opposition parties demonstrated little interest in or ability to cooperate, and this resulted in surprising losses in safe districts. The last-minute elimination of the rule that invalidated the results in races in which the number of votes cast against all candidates outnumbered the votes cast for the winner had a significant impact on the election because without the rule change, new elections would have been forced in five districts—four of which were won by reformers. Finally, although the rule changes had an impact on individual races, they did not change the political profile of the city's parliamentary delegation in comparison to 1990.

The Council of the Federation ballot illustrated the crucial importance of name recognition and of prior experience in running for elective office. The Council of the Federation ballot results indicated that the organizational and financial power of Russia's Choice was not sufficient to make Arzhannikov, a candidate with weak name recognition before the campaign, a winner. In the case of single-member district elections, the failure of the private entrepreneurs to gain more than one seat, combined with the success of local soviet deputies, indicated that political experience was a more valuable asset than money.

The result of the December 1993 constitutional referendum ballot was closely tied to the party-list vote. The new constitution was adopted by voters supporting the reformist and centrist parties. Contrary to the impression created by the mass media and Zhirinovskii himself, LDPR voters played no role in the success of the constitutional referendum as far as St. Petersburg is concerned. As both survey findings and raion-level results show,

LDPR voters opposed the new constitution despite Zhirinovskii's personal support for it.

Epilogue

The electoral trends we observed in the case of the December 1993 election fully manifested themselves again in the December 1995 parliamentary election and the June to July 1996 presidential election. In December 1995, reformist and centrist parties received 64.2 percent of the city vote, 22.4 percent above their national average, whereas the socialist and nationalist parties received 31.2 percent of the city vote, 22.2 percent below their national average. The primary difference between the 1993 and 1995 ballots was the emergence of Yabloko as the city's main reformist party and of KPRF as the main opposition party. In the second round of the 1996 presidential election, Yeltsin received 73.9 percent of the city vote, which was 20.2 percent above his national average, and Zyuganov received 21.1 percent of the city vote, 19.3 percent below his national average.

These results occurred despite the continuous decline of industrial production, a rise in unemployment, chronic delays in the payment of wages and pensions, and a growing gap between rich and poor. The key characteristic of this voting behavior remained the same as in 1993—namely, the absence of pocketbook voting. According to a November 1995 survey, 57 percent of respondents declared themselves to be below or well below average income. Of this group 65 percent intended to vote for reformist and centrist parties, and 35 percent intended to vote for socialist and nationalist parties.[38]

The December 1995 election demonstrated again the dominance of the reformist candidates in the single-member district races. This time they won all eight districts. As in 1993, the most popular reformist party won the majority of the city's single-member seats. In December 1995, Yabloko won in six single-member districts, whereas Russia's Choice won only one district.

Continuation of the first-past-the-post system meant that the incentive for cooperation between parties of similar ideological orientation remained strong. Yet, as in 1993, this did not happen. The dominance of the reformist candidates was strong enough to defeat socialist and nationalist candidates in every single-member district.

The 1993 Federation Council election was Russia's only federal-level experiment with two-member districts. The 1993 constitution left the formation of the Federation Council to be determined by legislation at a later time. The law adopted in December of 1995 replaced the principle of the formation of the upper chamber through election with the principle that heads of the executive and legislative branches of Russia's regional governments would become ex officio members of the Federation Council. Thus no election to the Federation Council took place in St. Petersburg in December 1995.

The 1996 equivalent of the Council of the Federation elections was St. Petersburg's mayoral election, in two rounds that took place on May 19 and June 2. In this race, the incumbent mayor, Sobchak, won in the first round but lost to another reformist candidate, his former deputy Vladimir Yakovlev, by 1.7 percentage points (47.5 percent to 45.8 percent) in the runoff election. Election results from 1993 through 1996 demonstrate that the city remains Russia's most democratic metropolis.

Notes

1. Guillermo O'Donnell and Philippe Schmitter, *Transitions from Authoritarian Rule: Tentative Conclusions about Uncertain Democracies* (Johns Hopkins University Press, 1986), pp. 61–64. Huntington prefers to use the term "stunning elections" to describe the same phenomenon. See Samuel P. Huntington, *The Third Wave: Democratization in the Late Twentieth Century* (University of Oklahoma Press, 1991), pp. 174ff. For the survey of the founding elections in eastern Europe, see Kimmo Kuusela, "The Founding Electoral Systems in Eastern Europe," in Geoffrey Pridham and Tatu Vanhanen, eds., *Democratization in Eastern Europe : Domestic and International Perspective* (London: Routledge, 1994), pp. 128–50.

2. Claus Offe, "Capitalism by Democratic Design? Democratic Theory Facing the Triple Transition in East Central Europe," *Social Research*, vol. 58, no. 4 (Winter 1991), pp. 865–92.

3. For an argument that links development to the collapse of communism, see Lucian W. Pye, "Political Science and the Crisis of Authoritarianism," *American Political Science Review*, vol. 84, no. 1 (March 1990), pp. 3–19.

4. The "pocketbook voting" theory postulates direct relationship between personal economic conditions and voting behavior. For a discussion, see Morris P. Fiorina, *Retrospective Voting in American National Elections* (Yale University Press, 1981), pp. 25–32; Samuel L. Popkin, *The Reasoning Voter: Communication and Persuasion in Presidential Campaigns*, 2d ed. (University of Chicago Press, 1994), pp. 31–34; Paul Lazarsfeld, Bernard Berelson, and Helen Gaudet, *The Peo-*

ple's Choice: How the Voter Makes up His Mind in a Presidential Campaign, 3d ed. (Columbia University Press, 1968).

5. Agnus Cambell and others, *The American Voter* (New York: John Wiley, 1960).

6. *Itogi vsesouyznoi perepesi naseleniya 1989 goda* (Results of the All-Union population census, 1989), vol. 6, part 1 (Minneapolis: East View Publications, 1993), pp. 18, 76; *Narodnoe khozyaistvo Rossiiskoi Federatsii. 1992* (Economy of the Russian Federation, 1992) (Moscow: Respublikanskii informatsionno-izdatelskii tsentr, 1992), p. 257.

7. Zinaida Sikevich, *Politicheskie igry ili politicheskaya borba?* (Political games or political struggle?) (Leningrad: Lenizdat, 1991), p. 48.

8. On the role of democratic organization in the 1989 electoral campaign, see Yelena Zdravomyslova and Anna Tyomkina, "Izbiratel'naya kampaniya i obshchestvennoye dvizheniye v Leningrade" (Electoral campaign and social movements in Leningrad) in *Vybory 1989* (Moscow: Panorama, 1993), pt. 2, pp. 1–17.

9. On St. Petersburg politics between 1989 and 1992, see Robert W. Orttung, *From Leningrad to St. Petersburg: Democratization in a Russian City* (New York: St. Martin's, 1995).

10. Aleksandr Sobyanin, Aleksandr Gel'man, and Oleg Kayunov, "Politicheskii klimat v Rossii 1991–1993 gg," *MEIMO* (Mirovaya Ekonomika i Mezhdunarodnye Otnoshenie), no. 9 (1993), p. 21.

11. *Sankt-Peterburgskiye vedomosti*, September 23, 1993, p. 2.

12. The city soviet was ultimately dissolved on Yeltsin's orders on December 22, 1993.

13. Philip Hanson, *Regions, Local Power and Economic Change in Russia* (London: Royal Institute for International Affairs, 1994), p. 45; *Sankt-Peterburg i Leningradskaya oblast v 1994 godu* (St. Petersburg and Leningrad oblast in 1994) (St. Petersburg: Peterburgkomstat, 1995), pp. 32–33.

14. *Delovye lyudi*, July 1993, p. 58; *Delovoi mir*, November 15–21, 1993, p. 3; *Kommersant*, March 15, 1994, p. 44; *Sankt-Peterburg*, pp. 11, 87.

15. *Sankt-Peterburg*, p. 42.

16. *Kachestvo naseleniya Sankt-Peterburga* (Quality of population of St. Petersburg) (St. Petersburg: Institut sotsiologii RAN, 1993), pp. 208, 216.

17. *Edinstvo*, November 10, 1993, p. 2.

18. Interview with Anton Sidorenko, Civic Union coordinator, St. Petersburg, December 5, 1993.

19. These figures are based on the list of candidates published by the Central Electoral Commission in mid-November 1993; see *Byulleten' tsentral'noi izbiratel'noi kommissii Rossiiskoi Federatsii*, no. 6 (November 1993).

20. Interview with Valentina Terekhova, Yabloko coordinator, St. Petersburg, December 8, 1992; interview with Golov, December 12, 1993.

21. I received the information on the formation of the party list by Russia's Choice and Yabloko from activists and Duma candidates of both parties.

22. Donald E. Stokes, "What Decides Elections?" in David Butler, Howard R. Penniman, and Austin Ranney, eds., *Democracy at the Polls: A Comparative Study of Competitive National Elections* (American Enterprise Institute, 1981), p. 279;

Shaun Bowler and others, "The Informed Electorate? Voter Responsiveness to Campaigns in Britain and Germany," in Shaun Bowler and David M. Farrell, eds., *Electoral Strategies and Political Marketing* (New York: St. Martin's, 1992), pp. 204–22.

23. Interviews with Igor' Soshnikov, the manager of Russia's Choice campaign in St. Petersburg and his staff; numerous occasions.

24. According to this December 2, 1993, poll, Boldyrev was fully trusted by 22 percent of the respondents and fully mistrusted by 16 percent. Sobchak, the next local politician on the list, was fully trusted by 18 percent and fully mistrusted by 32 percent of the respondents; see *Ekspress-otchet po oprosu obshchestvennogo mneniya naseleniya Sankt-Peterburga* (Sankt-Peterburg: Natsionalnyi institut vnutrenipoliticheskikh issledovanii, December 2, 1993), p. 6.

25. Interview with Vera Fradkova, LDPR coordinator, St. Petersburg, December 16, 1993.

26. Anthony Smith, "Mass Communications," in Butler, Penniman, and Ranney, *Democracy at the Polls*, p. 177.

27. Stokes, "What Decides Elections?" p. 280.

28. Of such publications, the three that appeared regularly during the campaign were *Nashe Otechestvo* (Our Fatherland), *Rossiyanin* (Russian), and *Vechernii Leningrad* (Leningrad at Evening). *Nashe Otechestvo* called to boycott the elections altogether, and the other two did not endorse any political party.

29. According to RES, intention to vote went up with age: 49 percent of people aged 18 to 29; 61 percent of people aged 30 to 49; and 81 percent of people aged 50 and older planned to vote. The predicted turnout was 62.7 percent, 10.2 higher than actual.

30. *Itogi vsesoyuznoi perepisi*, pp. 76–79; *Raiony Sankt-Peterburga v 1994 godu* (St. Petersburg's administrative districts in 1994) (St. Petersburg: Peterburgkomstat, 1995), p. 17.

31. Because the RES sample of the military people was too small to be representative, I rely only on the raion-level results in analyzing the vote of the military.

32. See, for example, *Vygodnoye delo*, November 25, 1993, p. 6; *Novyi Peterburg*, December 10, 1993.

33. *Ekspress-otchet*, December 2, 1993, p. 5.

34. Shcherbakov could not make such promises since Sobchak had suspended him from the post of vice mayor.

35. Interview with Belyayev's aide, Dmitri Dolgovet, December 7, 1993. Two types of leaflets are on file.

36. *Smena*, November 26, 1993, p. 1; November 27, 1993, p. 1; November 30, 1993, p. 2; December 7, 1993, pp. 1, 3–6.

37. Because most of the people interviewed for the RES project were undecided about their Council of the Federation candidates, my analysis relies exclusively on the raion-level results.

38. The survey, administered by St. Petersburg's Independent Analytical Center, interviewed 9,646 city residents on November 15–16, 1996. My analysis is based on the survey data kindly provided to me by the Center.

Sverdlovsk

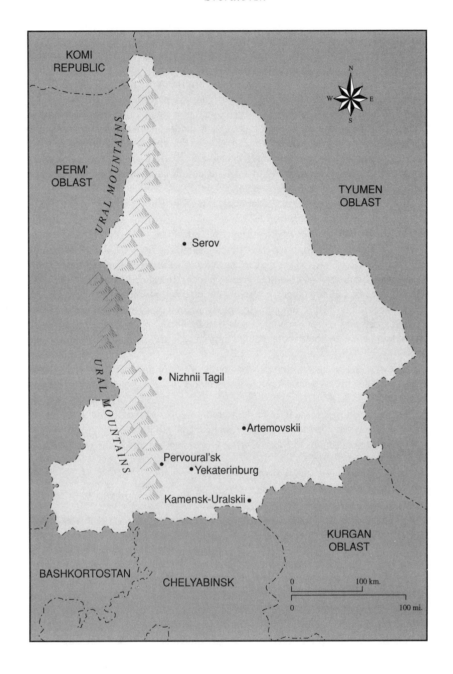

KOMI
REPUBLIC

PERM'
OBLAST

URAL MOUNTAINS

• Serov

TYUMEN
OBLAST

URAL MOUNTAINS

• Nizhnii Tagil

•Artemovskii

Pervoural'sk
•Yekaterinburg

Kamensk-Uralskii•

KURGAN
OBLAST

BASHKORTOSTAN

CHELYABINSK

N
W   E
S

0   100 km.

0   100 mi.

CHAPTER THIRTEEN

Sverdlovsk

Mixed Results in a Hotbed of Regional Autonomy

Robert G. Moser

NOWHERE WERE expectations for victory of reformist forces higher in December 1993 than in Sverdlovsk oblast. This native region of President Boris Yeltsin has been the most consistently proreform region in Russia outside of Moscow and St. Petersburg, providing Yeltsin with his highest level of support both in the June 1991 presidential election and the April 1993 referendum.[1] Sverdlovsk thus provided a best-case scenario for Yeltsin's constitutional project and the electoral fortunes of the reformers, particularly Russia's Choice. If they could not win in Sverdlovsk oblast, Yeltsin's homebase, they could not win anywhere.

By any numerical criterion, reformers won the 1993 elections in Sverdlovsk oblast. Russia's Choice gained the most votes in the party-list election with 25.2 percent of the vote, ten points higher than its national average. If one compares the percentages for all radical and moderate reformist blocs to the total for antireformist and centrist blocs, the reformers came out with a relatively comfortable victory. Reformist blocs gained a total of 52.6 per-

I would like to acknowledge Boris Bagirov, Yelena Markelova, and Rima and Timor Menadzhiyev for their help and kindness during fieldwork in Sverdlovsk oblast.

cent of the proportional representation (PR) vote compared to 27.5 percent for antireformers and 20.0 percent for centrists.[2] Individual candidates in the single-member district races and in the dual-member constituencies to the upper house were predominantly reformers. Five out of seven single-member district winners were proreform according to Sobyanin ratings, with four of these scoring among the radical reformers. Only two deputies were antireform, and only one (Tamara Tokareva of the Agrarian party) was a clear representative of the irreconcilable opposition. A similar result was found in the Federation Council race. The two winners were firmly in favor of continued market reform. The constitutional referendum was supported by almost 80 percent of the voters (the highest proportion in Russia), although the requisite 50 percent turnout was not accomplished for passage in Sverdlovsk oblast.

Although Russia's Choice and reformist forces in general registered an impressive victory, on closer inspection the results from Sverdlovsk provide a mixture of often contradictory implications. As this chapter will demonstrate, the real victor in December 1993 was not Russia's Choice or even Yeltsin and his constitution. Rather, it was the regional governor, Eduard Rossel, who used the election to stage a remarkable comeback after being removed as head of administration by Yeltsin only a month before over the issue of the Urals Republic (the attempt of Sverdlovsk oblast to upgrade its federal status from oblast to republic, discussed later in this chapter). With hindsight one can see that Rossel used the 1993 election as a springboard to build the regionally dominant Transformation of the Urals *(Preobrazheniye Urala)* electoral bloc. Transformation of the Urals has since gone on to capture the governorship for Rossel in a hard-fought gubernatorial election in 1995 and win a plurality of votes in Sverdlovsk in the 1995 parliamentary election as Transformation of the Fatherland *(Preobrazheniye Otechestva)*, a national electoral bloc emphasizing regional interests led by Rossel. Rossel's bloc has been even more dominant in regional parliamentary elections, capturing a working majority in the oblast duma after winning more than 35 percent of the PR vote in regional parliamentary elections in April 1996.[3] Meanwhile, Russia's Choice disintegrated in the region after 1993, losing 80 percent of its support in Sverdlovsk in the 1995 parliamentary elections and vanishing as an electoral force in regional elections. This balance of power in the region in which Rossel and his bloc dominated the region's reformist camp remained intact during the 1996 presidential elections as the oblast administration under

Rossel's control led Yeltsin's very successful regional reelection campaign.

Moreover, a superficial rendering of the results in Sverdlovsk as simply overwhelming support for reform misses other signs of voter disillusionment. Sverdlovsk had the lowest voter turnout (not counting Tatarstan, which had an organized boycott of the election) of all the regions examined here (refer to chapter 1 and to table 1-8). This relatively low voter turnout, which continued in the 1995 parliamentary elections, and a high incidence of voting against all candidates (averaging 20 percent in single-member district races) show an electorate plagued with a deep sense of apathy and disenchantment. This disenchantment was also showcased in a surprising second-place finish by Vladimir Zhirinovskii's nationalist Liberal Democratic Party of Russia (LDPR) in the PR balloting, suggesting that even voters in Yeltsin's home region were growing impatient with the Yeltsin regime and were frustrated with the electoral process in general.

What accounts for this mixture of regionalism, reform, and voter apathy in the 1993 vote in Sverdlovsk? How was it that both Yeltsin's constitution and a former governor vanquished by Yeltsin for touting regional autonomy could capture the imagination of Sverdlovsk's voters? How does one reconcile strong support for the status quo as manifested by the victory of the party of power (Russia's Choice) and signs of voter dissatisfaction in low voter turnout and a high incidence of voting against all candidates? Given the mixed results, what effect did the 1993 elections have on democratic development in the region?

It will be argued that the region's election results were caused by three major determinants: the region's socioeconomic environment; the "rules of the game," which influenced and channeled these structural influences; and the actions and strategies of individual political actors.

The region's socioeconomic profile as a heavily industrialized and urbanized region along with its political legacy as an anticommunist stronghold strongly advantaged reformist blocs. It has been shown that one of the major cleavages in Russian politics is urban-rural, with urban areas being generally more reformist and rural areas voting more heavily for opposition parties.[4] Being one of the most urbanized regions of Russia, Sverdlovsk oblast lacked the rural agricultural areas that have been the mainstay of opposition (particularly socialist) support.

The mixed electoral system reinforced these structural advantages of the reformists. As other contributors to this volume have noted, the 1993 election was actually a collection of several discrete electoral contests, each with its own set of actors and each prioritizing certain electoral resources over others.[5] The PR election had more of a national character in which unionwide electoral blocs campaigned on national issues of economic reform, social welfare, and national pride using primarily mass media, in particular television. The single-member district election and the dual-member election to the Federation Council were more local in nature, with individual candidates campaigning on local name recognition and issues of local importance. These two electoral arenas demanded very different resources to gain success. The PR election showcased the bloc leader and allowed for a party with very little local organization to still do well as demonstrated by the success of the LDPR, Yabloko, Russian Movement for Democratic Reforms (RDDR), and Party of Russian Unity and Accord (PRES) in Sverdlovsk. The single-member district races hinged mainly on name recognition and local organization. Therefore, parties needed a strong local cadre of well-known candidates and a grassroots organization to contest these elections effectively. The predominance of independent candidates and the failure of all parties with the partial exception of Russia's Choice in the single-member district elections demonstrate the influence of the rules.

Finally, strategies of individual actors had a significant impact on the results. One reason that Russia's Choice was so strong in Sverdlovsk was because almost all local reformist groups joined the regional branch of the bloc and gave Russia's Choice the most formidable grassroots organization in the region. Other reformist blocs with the potential to capture significant support in Sverdlovsk were simply locked out of the race because there was no regional political elite and no grassroots organization to manage their regional campaign. Regionalism was a powerful force in Sverdlovsk not only because it struck a chord among voters in this "donor region" (which pays more taxes to Moscow than it receives in state subsidies) but more important because it had the region's most charismatic politician as its torchbearer, former governor Rossel.

The Social and Political Environment of Sverdlovsk Oblast

Sverdlovsk oblast, with a population of 4.7 million, lies in the heart of Russia in the Ural Mountains marking the border between Europe and Asia. Along with the other six subjects of the Urals's socioeconomic region, Sverdlovsk oblast serves as a center of Russian heavy industry, mineral and

energy extraction, and the defense industry. Its social and political character has been greatly influenced by the large state enterprises that dominate
its economy. It is one of the most urbanized districts in the federation, with
87 percent of its population living in urban areas. Huge factories dealing in
metallurgy, chemical production, manufacturing of heavy machinery and
supplying Russia's arsenal dominate the landscape and have ruined the region's environment. The sensitive nature of work in weapons manufacturing closed the area off from outside influences until 1990. Yekaterinburg, a
city of 1.3 million, is the political, cultural, educational, and manufacturing
center of the region. Some of the largest factories in Russia, such as the
heavy machinery and vehicle manufacturing conglomerate Uralmash, lie
on its outskirts. The city's university and numerous institutes and polytech-
nics are oriented toward supplying the huge enterprises with the needed
technical specialists.

Geographically, the oblast can be divided roughly in half. The northern
half is less heavily populated and possesses large deposits of mineral resources and lumber. Mining interests are predominant in the north, making
politics there similar to other mining regions such as Vorkuta. Because of
its sparse population, one electoral district encompassed the whole northern
portion of the oblast. Unlike the other electoral districts, which had no
shortage of candidates, this northern electoral district could produce only
two candidates capable of fulfilling the signature requirements for nomination, with the second joining the campaign very late in the nomination process. Moreover, a miners' strike protesting the state's failure to pay regional miners disrupted part of the campaign.[6] By contrast the southern
portion of the oblast is more densely populated, containing the remaining
six electoral districts. It is in this area that the oblast earns its reputation as
the industrial center of Russia. Even in areas that are referred to as "rural,"
such as Artemovskii electoral district in the eastern part of the oblast, only 5
percent of the population engages in agriculture.[7] Smaller cities and towns
are often dwarfed by the factories they feed with workers.

The status of industrial interests as a political and electoral force and in
relation to other political forces is difficult to discern. According to one
specialist, before market reforms and democratization the political power
wielded by state directors was more visible. State directors or their chosen
representatives held positions in the regional and national soviets themselves. With the advent of competitive elections state directors lost many of
these elected positions.[8] This is born out in the occupational profile of the
region's legislative delegations coming out of the 1990 and 1993 parlia-

mentary elections. In the 1990 parliamentary elections to the Russian Congress of Peoples' Deputies, enterprise and agricultural directors made up the second largest group in the region's delegation, sending nine representatives or 28 percent of the region's national legislators.[9] In the 1993 parliamentary election not a single member of the corps of state directors was elected to the State Duma or Federation Council. Electoral organizations declaring themselves the representatives of these interests, namely Arkadii Vol'skii's Civic Union, remain weak in the area.[10] Nevertheless, directors of large state enterprises still wield great power behind the scenes and demand attention and cooperation from elected officials because of the vast economic resources at their command.[11] As a result, the corps of state directors have long been strongly tied to elected officials and was considered to be a powerful source of financing and influence behind former oblast head of administration Rossel's campaign.[12]

The distribution of political organizations reflects this mixture of different elite political orientations. A plethora of reform-oriented organizations grew out of the more radical political community of Yekaterinburg during the struggle to reform and eventually bring down the Communist Party of the Soviet Union (CPSU). In late 1989, Democratic Choice originated out of a number of voters and discussion clubs in Yekaterinburg under the leadership of future Yeltsin aide Gennadii Burbulis. In 1990, the movement won eight out of thirty-two seats in the elections to the Russian Congress of Peoples' Deputies. It was even more successful in local contests, winning about forty seats in the oblast soviet, sixty seats in the Yekaterinburg city soviet, and electing one of its own, Yurii Samarin, as speaker of the Yekaterinburg city soviet. In August 1990, the movement joined the Democratic Russia movement as a collective member and changed its name to Democratic Choice–Democratic Russia (DC–DR).[13]

This conglomeration of reformist organizations has remained a relatively close-knit political community. This has allowed regional reformist forces to resist much of the infighting that has plagued reformist movements throughout Russia. Reformers in Sverdlovsk oblast have managed to consolidate into relatively cohesive movements during electoral periods. The first such coalition, known as the People's Concern, was formed in 1991 as a loosely structured union of democratic forces supporting the president. In March 1993 the DC–DR and the Fund for the Support of the First President of Russia (FSFPR) initiated the formation of the Center of Social Initiative, which brought together reformists in support of President Yeltsin's call for an all-national referendum.[14] Later, a new coalition of reformist forces initiated by DC–DR in July 1993, appropriately called Urals' Choice, formed the basis for the regional branch of Russia's Choice.

A similarly cohesive political community has existed among the various Communist, agrarian, and nationalist political organizations of the area. The close coordination among regional conservative organizations has been vital to the survival of this end of the political spectrum. Conservative organizations allowed to legally operate tended to absorb and support elites from organizations banned by the Yeltsin regime.[15] Several all-union conservative organizations have had well-established regional organizations in the area, including the Communist Party of the Russian Federation, the Socialist Party of Labor, the Russian Communist Worker's party (Viktor Anpilov), and Zhirinovskii's Liberal Democratic Party of Russia. In 1992 the patriotic movement, Motherland, united the area's nationalists and Communists from the LDPR, Russian Communist Workers party, the Socialist Party of Labor, and the Russian National Union, among others. Stanislav Nekrasov, a member of both the LDPR and Communist party, spearheaded this drive to unite the area's nationalists and Communists.[16] In the same way, efforts to unite the conservative community came from the regional branch of the Communist Party of the Russian Federation. Valerii Novoselov, secretary of the oblast Communist party, was instrumental in forming the oblast's Agrarian party as a corollary to the KPRF in rural areas. Furthermore, Novoselov heads the Union of Workers, Peasants, and Intelligentsia of the Central Urals, a movement that unites a dozen parties, movements, and trade unions from all elements of the conservative camp.[17]

Like Moscow, by the beginning of 1993 the political environment in the region evolved into a battle between two polarized political forces. Organizations espousing a centrist position began losing influence and were pushed to choose sides as an increasingly polarized elite brought the country to the brink of chaos and violence. Nevertheless, centrist parties and organizations carved a significant niche in the political landscape of Sverdlovsk oblast. The Democratic Party of Russia was the most established and active of these groups. Established locally in 1990, the party operates throughout the oblast and managed to elect six members to the Yekaterinburg city soviet and two to the Sverdlovsk oblast soviet.[18] According to one survey done in April 1993, the DPR was the most popular party in Yekaterinburg with 12.8 percent of respondents supporting it.[19] Aleksandr Rutskoi's People's Party of Free Russia also had a local branch in the region but was not as well known or as popular as DPR. Both of these parties remained more closely tied to the democratic camp than the conservatives in the region. Although the regional DPR branch followed Travkin's lead and left the Democratic Choice–Democratic Russia movement in December 1991, both DPR and the local branch of Rutskoi's party continued to participate in broader coalitions of reform-oriented organizations such as the Center of Social Initiative.[20]

Despite this rich variety of ideological tendencies in the region's developing civil society, Sverdlovsk oblast remained solidly reformist in its political orientation. The region stood fast behind Yeltsin during the August 1991 putsch. The presidium of the oblast soviet quickly denounced the putschists' emergency rule as unlawful and supported the declaration of Yeltsin. An extraordinary session of the oblast soviet on August 21 reiterated this support for Yeltsin and announced the region would support Yeltsin's call for a general strike. Meanwhile, strikes protesting the coup swept the large manufacturing conglomerates in Yekaterinburg and several mines up north.[21] The September to October 1993 crises were much more controversial and sparked more critical local assessments. Almost immediately following the dissolution of the Congress of Peoples' Deputies, there was a heated debate over the president's actions in the Yekaterinburg city soviet with a majority of the legislators calling the action unconstitutional. The oblast soviet concluded that both the executive and legislature were acting outside the constitution and called for a compromise in which there would be simultaneous presidential and parliamentary elections held in February 1994. Nevertheless, the Sverdlovsk executive leadership remained behind Yeltsin. After the September 21 declaration, then head of administration Rossel issued a declaration calling for calm and order and the continuation of normal governmental functions in the oblast. After the October events, Rossel and chair of the oblast soviet, Anatolii Grebenkin, sent a telegram to Yeltsin expressing their support of his actions. The oblast soviet adopted a similar resolution in the wake of the street violence presumably initiated by opposition forces.[22]

The Formation of Electoral Blocs and the Nomination of Individual Candidates

The formation of local branches of all-union electoral blocs in Sverdlovsk oblast manifested all of the dynamics and difficulties that have marked party-building efforts in Russia since the beginning of democratic reform. In general, local development of electoral blocs was accomplished in one of two ways. Several of the thirteen electoral blocs were previously existing organizations that established their local existence in the region over time. These included the Democratic Party of Russia, the Liberal Democratic Party of Russia, and the Communist Party of the Russian Federation. The other blocs tended to be creations of the moment, coalitions of various organizations and individual leaders cobbled together through negotiations surrounding the call for parliamentary elections. For these blocs the key to manifestation in the provinces lay in the ability to capture a section of the already existing local elite. Indeed, political entrepreneurs, such as Yegor Gaidar and Grigorii Yavlinskii, had this in mind when courting organizations with some form of local structure across the federation. Democratic Russia was to provide this for Russia's Choice, whereas the Republican and Social Democratic parties were to undergird Yavlinskii's bloc. Sergei Shakhrai's PRES followed neither of these two strategies, choosing instead the virtually impossible route of building a party based on regional interests from scratch.

Some of the major electoral blocs, namely Yabloko, PRES, and Civic Union, failed to establish any significant local presence. This is hardly surprising given the short time period of the campaign and the difficulty of establishing a new political organization in an already crowded political community. Moreover, local manifestations of the electoral blocs often varied significantly from their counterparts in Moscow. The boundaries between organizations—in other words, the splits and coalitions that occurred amid the political intrigue of Moscow—rarely survived the long trip to Yekaterinburg intact. As a consequence, some parties that entered into one electoral bloc in Moscow entered a different bloc in Sverdlovsk oblast or refused to participate in any bloc at all. As will be seen, this phenomenon benefited some blocs, namely Russia's Choice, at the expense of others, such as Yabloko. Moreover, because of the close ties between elites in the regional political community, there was great coordination between electoral blocs of similar political orientation, particularly between the Communist and Agrarian parties.

The main beneficiary of the local constellation of democratic organizations was Russia's Choice, which managed to absorb the latest in a series of local coalitions of democratic forces. This was a result of the relative cohesion of the democratic movement around the principle of supporting President Yeltsin as the embodiment of democratic reforms. As noted previously, reformist organizations retained a level of consensus that allowed them to consolidate into a relatively united coalition for special mobilizational tasks such as elections. Therefore, it was quite natural for the majority of local democratic forces to consolidate into one coalition and join the bloc most closely associated with Yeltsin, Russia's Choice. Already in July 1993, there began a consolidation of political parties, social organizations, potential candidates, and activists with the intention of uniting reformers from different levels of government in anticipation of the possibility of early parliamentary and presidential elections. On September 3, the Urals Choice coalition was formed that included the major reform-oriented organizations of the area such as Democratic Choice–Democratic Russia, the Republican Party of Russia, the Fund for the Support of the First President of Russia, the Social Democratic Party of Russia, and the Liberal Club.[23] Throughout September, the group worked out common principles regarding organizational structure and policy stances. By the end of September, Urals Choice decided to join the Russia's Choice electoral bloc. The local chapter of Gaidar's bloc was expanded even more on October 10 when Gaidar himself came to Yekaterinburg for its founding congress. Twenty-seven local organizations attended the congress including Memorial, the Union of Local Self-Government, and a number of youth and veteran organizations in addition to the organizations listed previously.[24]

Russia's Choice managed to coopt almost all of the local reformist organizations of any significance including the Republican Party of the Russian Federation and the Social Democratic Party of Russia, which were both officially part of Yabloko. As a consequence, there was little room for other democratic blocs to establish themselves locally. Without the Republican and Social Democratic parties, Yabloko was left with virtually no local organizational base. The bloc's local campaign consisted of a visit from Yavlinskii himself and a single individual, Sergei Martyushov, a scientific researcher with no previous political experience, who ran unsuccessfully for a seat in a single-mandate district under the Yabloko label. In a similar way, the Party of Russian Unity and Accord's (PRES) Sergei Shakhrai attracted large crowds when he campaigned in Yekaterinburg but had little local organization to carry on the campaign in his absence. PRES had only two individual candidates, one of which also ran under the Civic Union bloc. The Russian Movement for Democratic Reforms also had a minimal local organization that was originally formed out of dissatisfied members of DPR, the Republican party, and the People's Party of Free Russia.[25]

The antireform blocs and DPR had an easier time establishing local branches because they had previously existing organizations. On the calling of elections, these organizations built on already established foundations of popular support and political influence. The LDPR possessed a charismatic and controversial local leader, Vyacheslav Sen'ko, who reflected Zhirinovskii's flamboyant political style in the regional arena. The Communists and Agrarians had their own noteworthy local candidates and extensive connections with local power bases. Valerii Novoselov, first secretary of the KPRF, tapped his extensive connections with rural trade unions, state farmers, and agribusiness through his position as head of the Oblast Trade Union of Workers of the Agribusiness Complex. The Agrarian party had noteworthy local candidates in Vladimir Isakov, former member of the Russian Congress of People's Deputies, and Tamara Tokareva, former head of the Standing Commission on Land in the oblast soviet.

The nomination and campaign of individual candidates followed a different dynamic than the party-list contests. Party affiliation did not appear in the candidate's biographical description on the ballot, significantly reducing the opportunity for voters to base their decision among individual candidates on party identification.[26] Furthermore, local public opinion polls showed that party affiliation was not a major factor in determining the support of an individual candidate. Respondents stated that a candidate's political and economic program and professional position mattered more than party affiliation.[27] Because of the virtual absence of significant party identification among the population, candidates with any real chance of garnering popular support had to rely on an individual power base or charismatic appeal.

Nevertheless, the elite community in the area was sufficiently permeated by parties, movements, and social organizations that most candidates were nominated by one of the electoral blocs. Out of thirty-one candidates for seats in the State Duma, twenty-one were nominated by an electoral bloc. However, all three candidates in the race for the oblast's two seats in the Council of Federation ran as independents. Several features of individual candidate nominations illustrate the persistently weak nature of incipient electoral organizations and political parties in the area. First, no electoral bloc was strong enough to run a candidate in each of the region's seven electoral districts. The Democratic Party of Russia came closest with five candidates but none of its candidates went on to win his or her district. Second, despite the fact that most candidates were party nominees, many of the most well-known and powerful candidates shunned party affiliations, preferring to run as independents. Those running without party labels tended to have an independent power base. Oblast and raion-level heads of administration, state directors, and wealthy entrepreneurs made up the bulk of independent candidates. Independent candidates made much of their freedom from all party affiliations and used it as a campaign tool, indicating a persistent antiparty sentiment that has plagued party-building efforts since the beginning of democratic reforms.

Russia's Choice was particularly hard hit by defections and candidates who preferred to run as independents rather than as nominees of the bloc. Galina Karelova, the eventual winner of one of the Council of Federation seats, was originally a member of Russia's Choice. She participated in the bloc's regional congress and was even on its party list but abandoned the bloc just before announcing her independent candidacy for the upper house. Another eventual winner, Leonid Nekrasov, left Russia's Choice because of a conflict between his party, Konstantin Borovoi's Party of Economic Freedom, and Russia's Choice. Instead, he also ran as an independent. A number of other strong candidates ran as independents, although they were known to have close ties to Russia's Choice and the bloc supported them in the campaign. Two candidates, Mikhail Anan'in, a state director in Pervoural'skii district, and Yurii Brusnitsyn, head of administration of a raion in Yekaterinburg, were supported by Russia's Choice without being officially nominated by the bloc. According to a regional specialist on parties, party affiliation was a "very private matter" and these candidates wanted to keep their ties to Russia's Choice secret.[28]

Most of those who eventually made it onto the ballot in the candidate-centered elections to the Federal Assembly came from the local governing or economic elite. Out of thirty-four candidates for the State Duma and Council of Federation, eleven held positions in the state. Eleven more were directors of state enterprises or private entrepreneurs. The rest of the field was made up of professionals (doctors, lawyers, teachers), academics, and leaders of parties, trade unions, or other social organizations. The field was dominated by older men. Only four women ran for office (three of whom won) and only eight of the candidates were under the age of forty.[29]

It appeared that two factors were decisive in where candidates chose to run. First, not surprisingly, candidates tended to run in the districts in which they lived. Second, there was some degree of shopping around for districts that matched a candidate's ideological orientation. This tended to segment the political elite along electoral district lines and limit the ideological choices of voters in single-member district races. There was very little direct competition between clearly reformist and staunchly conservative candidates in single-member districts. The Yekaterinburg districts tended to attract more reformist candidates (with the exception of Agrarian party member Vladimir Isakov), whereas the strongest conservative candidates were concentrated in the more rural Artemovskii electoral district (District 160). The region's other districts featured more independents and were dominated by local political and economic elites.

The Electoral Campaign

The issue of the Urals Republic dominated the electoral campaign. This was the most covered issue in the local press, which tended to be sympathetic to the republicanization of the oblast. Although candidates and electoral blocs preferred to discuss ways of ending the economic crisis and breakdown of social order, each competitor also had to address the issue of the region's relationship with the center.

Moreover, the issue was seized by a charismatic candidate, the embattled former head of administration, Rossel, who capitalized on the public's sympathies after his removal as oblast head of administration. After his removal, Rossel decided to run for a seat in the upper house on a platform centered around the protection of regional interests and the eventual achievement of republican status for Sverdlovsk oblast. He proved to be the most popular politician in the oblast and a new regional political movement, Transformation of the Urals, formed around his charismatic campaign.

The idea of a Urals Republic had been discussed long before the oblast soviet's declaration in July 1993. In its latest manifestation, the attempted republicanization of the oblast began as a question added to the April 1993 referendum. More than 80 percent of voters favored the change in status of the oblast.[30] In July 1993, citing this nonbinding plebiscite, the regional legislature declared the establishment of the Urals Republic as a way of making the status of the region equal to non-Russian republics such as Tatarstan, Udmurtiya, and Bashkortostan. However, President Yeltsin responded negatively, issuing decrees in November that declared the Urals Republic void, dissolving the local legislature, and removing Rossel as head of administration.[31] The new constitution also pointedly rejected the notion of the Urals Republic by maintaining the status and name of the region as Sverdlovsk oblast in its list of subjects of the federation.[32]

The local press closely followed the crisis, usually from the regionalist perspective. *Oblastnaya gazeta,* the organ of the soviet and the oblast administration, was a virtual mouthpiece of Rossel, publishing stinging in-

dictments of President Yeltsin's actions and personal messages from Rossel to the president and the oblast's citizens.[33] The oblast's three other major
dailies also gave extensive coverage to the events surrounding the dissolution of the regional legislature and the removal of Rossel. Moreover, all the
major newspapers made the status of the oblast the centerpiece of their coverage of the debate over the new constitutional project.

The issue became a central part of the local campaign with the candidacy
of Rossel. Rossel turned his removal from office into a campaign weapon,
portraying himself as the local defender of the region's rights, undaunted
by persecution from higher authorities. The phenomenon of Rossel's popularity was reminiscent of Yeltsin himself in his battles with Soviet authorities during his days as a leader of the democratic opposition. His campaign
propaganda reinforced this perception of a persecuted local hero. Campaign flyers were often set against the backdrop of a map of the oblast and
contained slogans such as, "He left in order to return, he is coming back to
stay." Rossel also had a number of other electoral resources. He had name
recognition and even a level of international notoriety following the controversy over his removal. His tenure as head of administration provided him
with contacts within the regional administration structure. This structure
served as an informal network of support across the oblast. Moreover, he
was backed by powerful economic interests that bankrolled his campaign
through the Transformation of the Urals movement. No other individual
candidate enjoyed the level of media exposure or amount of campaign agitation and propaganda. His election as a member of the Council of Federation was virtually ensured. The only question was who would fill the other
seat.

The controversy over the Urals Republic also influenced the electoral
battle in the party-list race. The issue caused problems for reformist and antireformist contenders alike. For reformers it undermined local support for
Yeltsin (and Russia's Choice by implication) because he removed the
popular head of administration; dissolved the local parliament; and declared the establishment of the Urals Republic null and void, supposedly
without even examining the content of the region's declaration. The fact
that Yeltsin built his career in the oblast made his actions all the more inex-
cusable. The issue was a source of tension within the democratic camp in
general and the local chapter of the Russia's Choice coalition in particular.
Some influential reformist groups and politicians, such as the Fund for the
Support of the First President of Russia and Yurii Samarin, speaker of the
Yekaterinburg city soviet, were strongly against the idea of the Urals re-

public.[34] However, many of the local deputies who voted for the declaration were reformists. In the end, the reformists managed to soft-pedal the issue by generally supporting regional interests without specifically supporting the Urals Republic as recently formulated.[35] Most individual candidates in the single-member district races took similar stances regarding regional autonomy. A common campaign platform was the vague promise of increased regional autonomy within a united Russian Federation. The stand of Boris Guseletov, Future of Russia–New Names candidate in Yekaterinburg, was typical: "I stand for the establishment of reasonable economic, financial, and political independence for all Russian regions within a united federal Russian state."[36] As will be shown, the final results from the oblast suggest that voters did not necessarily choose between reformist and regionalist forces. Both reformists and Rossel enjoyed widespread support. This is hardly paradoxical. Support for economic reform and greater regional autonomy is actually a common feature of postcommunist Russian politics. Survey data shows that contrary to the long-held assumption that local power structures are bastions of conservatism, residents of Russian oblasts look to provincial governmental structures to pursue economic reform. Thus it is common for Russians to simultaneously hold anti-Moscow and proreform sentiments.[37]

One reason the Urals Republic issue was not more damaging for Russia's Choice and Yeltsin's constitution was that their competitors could not capitalize on the issue. The opposition desired increased centralization of power and feared the disintegration of Russia and therefore could not support a Urals Republic, with its call for increased regional autonomy. Thus, there was no electoral bloc willing to take up the issue and run with it. Centrist and conservative electoral blocs came out against the proposed change.[38] Even the bloc most associated with expanding the powers of the regions, PRES, came out against the declaration of the Urals Republic. In an interview with *Oblastnaya gazeta* during his campaign stop in Yekaterinburg, Sergei Shakhrai stated that he supported the idea of a Urals Republic only as a regional economic association that included all of the oblasts and republics of the Urals economic region.[39]

The national campaign between the electoral blocs was conducted primarily over the television and radio airwaves and through the print media. Only when several bloc leaders (the Communist party's leader Gennadii Zyuganov, Yabloko's Grigorii Yavlinskii, and PRES leader Sergei Shakhrai) made campaign stops in Yekaterinburg was this contest brought directly to the voters of Sverdlovsk oblast. Only those blocs with some kind of regional organization or candidates running in the single-member constituencies had any real local campaign. Even this did not guarantee a visible local presence because some candidates were more active and loyal to their blocs than others. Russia's Choice was the best organized electoral bloc in the region. It had a seemingly endless supply of campaign paraphernalia, a headquarters in the city soviet building staffed by a full-time director, and several full-time volunteers.[40] The local LDPR campaign featured the party's local leader, Vladimir Sen'ko, filling the airwaves with the LDPR's nationalist rhetoric and trying to replicate Zhirinovskii's aggressive campaign style. The Communists and Agrarians closely coordinated their local campaign activities, putting out propaganda featuring candidates from both parties and conducting joint meetings with voters.[41]

In the single-member district races, the campaigns of local candidates varied widely according to the resources at the candidate's command. Entrepreneurs, particularly from the private sector, tended to have more money for staff, flyers, and had the ability to spend more time away from the job campaigning. One entrepreneurial candidate, Oleg Dolganov running in a district of Yekaterinburg, went so far as to buy tickets to a popular concert to distribute to supporters. Another, Vladimir Lobok also running in Yekaterinburg, constructed telephone lists of voters in his district and had volunteers call prospective voters to solicit support and invite them to one of two campaign headquarters for more information.[42] Aside from such exceptions, however, campaigning remained restricted mainly to small meetings with voters in factories, mines, collective farms, and town halls and the distribution of handbills with the candidate's picture, biography, and major policy stands. Policy stands remained vague and candidates tended to concentrate on their personal appeal to the voters—in other words, how their past personal, political, and occupational experience made them particularly suited to represent their district. A candidate's "professionalism" was a big issue; voters tended to favor candidates who could point to previous experience in elected or appointed positions in the state.

Election Results

Unlike much of the rest of the country, voters in Sverdlovsk oblast did not overwhelmingly reject the policies of Gaidar and Yeltsin. The government's party, Russia's Choice, controlled the area, enjoying a level of support ten percentage points higher than its national average. Other reformist blocs such as the Russian Movement for Democratic Reforms (RDDR) and PRES performed much better in Sverdlovsk than in the rest of the country. Moreover, if support for the constitution is taken as a referendum on Yeltsin's presidency, then Yeltsin's personal popularity in his home region remained intact. Despite the fact that a low voter turnout meant the constitutional plebiscite did not pass in the oblast, regional support for the constitution ran about 20 percent higher than the national average.

The PR Race

As stated in the introduction of this chapter, three major factors influenced the results of the 1993 elections in Sverdlovsk: socioeconomic composition of the electorate, "rules of the game," and individual actors' strategies. In the PR portion of the election, socioeconomic factors such as the level of urbanization and the professional profile of the electorate seemed to play a more substantial role than in other parts of the election. As will be shown, despite the fluidity of the Russian party system, relatively stable voting patterns among electoral districts within the region suggest that social groups within Sverdlovsk oblast do indeed provide somewhat predictable and stable constituencies for blocs representing various parts of the political spectrum.

The institution of a PR party-list election affected this campaign by highlighting certain resources that were effective in winning support in the PR but not important in securing victory in the single-member districts. Thus, because the PR race was a national campaign waged primarily over the airwaves, parties without substantial grassroots organization or a well-known local cadre such as the LDPR, PRES, or Yabloko could still do well in the region in the PR race. A charismatic national leader who could use television effectively, such as Zhirinovskii, was more important for success in the PR race than organization. This was not the case in the candidate-centered single-member district races.

Finally, the actions of political actors came into play but not so much in campaign tactics or strategies. Such factors were probably only of marginal importance to the final result of the PR race. More important was party building prior to the 1993 balloting. The fact that Russia's Choice could rally the support of the vast majority of Sverdlovsk reformist elite including the tacit support of the existing regional power structures gave it an advantage over its reformist competitors and thus consolidated the reformist vote behind Russia's Choice. A cursory examination of the 1995 parliamentary election results shows the difference a more fractionalized reformist camp makes. Transformation of the Fatherland gained a plurality of votes because of Rossel's regional popularity and support from regional power structures. However, Rossel's winning bloc managed to receive only half that of Russia's Choice in 1993 (12 percent) mainly because it faced stiffer competition from other reformist blocs.

The success of all the reformist blocs suggests that in this region the failure to present voters with one united coalition of reformers did not undermine overall support for the reformist position. In fact the increased number of reform-oriented blocs may have actually expanded popular support for the reformist camp. Because of the personalization of politics, voters who disliked Russia's Choice but remained sympathetic to market reform could turn to a different reformist bloc. However, if there was only one reformist bloc then voters who hated Gaidar would have no other choice but to turn to centrist or antireformist blocs, vote against all the blocs, or not vote at all.

Besides showing general support for Yeltsin-Gaidar policies, the area also displayed an unwillingness to return to past solutions to Russia's problems. Anticommunist sentiment remained strong in the region. The Communist party and its rural counterpart the Agrarian party, which after the LDPR were the other surprise success stories of the national campaign, did significantly worse in Sverdlovsk oblast than in the rest of the country. The Communists registered a 5.8 percent showing in Sverdlovsk, under half their total nationwide. The same was true of the Agrarian Party of Russia, which managed only 4.0 percent in Sverdlovsk, also half of its nationwide support. The protest voter instead turned to Zhirinovskii's brand of nationalism. Although the LDPR's total in Sverdlovsk was also lower than its national average (17.7 percent in Sverdlovsk versus 22.9 percent nationwide), its solid second-place showing in the region suggests that Zhirinovskii was the recipient of Sverdlovsk's protest vote. Zhirinovskii's appeal to regain Russia's international prestige as a great power obviously hit a chord in this area so closely tied to the military and the military-industrial complex.

Only regional support for centrist blocs followed the national average. As in the rest of Russia, the Democratic Party of Russia barely overcame the 5 percent barrier in Sverdlovsk. Women of Russia achieved close to its national average in Sverdlovsk, receiving more than 8 percent of the vote. Support for Civic Union and Russia's Future–New Names were negligible in the area, just as in the rest of the country. Despite the predominance of large state enterprises in the economy, Vol'skii's bloc supposedly representing state directors could barely muster 2 percent of the vote. This poor showing plus the failure of any regional state director to win a seat in the individual candidate races suggests that large industrial interests have little potential as an electoral force in the area. Instead, these interests will have to continue to lobby behind the scenes. As mentioned previously, regional state directors seemed to have turned to Rossel and the Urals Republic movement as a conduit to state power.

A breakdown of the PR vote in Sverdlovsk oblast by electoral district appears in table 13-1. In the absence of individual-level survey data it is not possible to engage in systematic analysis of the voting patterns of the Sverdlovsk electorate by social and economic groups based on age, gender, occupation, or income. However, the breakdown of the PR vote by electoral district provides some distinguishable patterns of the socioeconomic influences on PR voting in the region.

The most important distinction that can be made in Sverdlovsk oblast is between urban areas of the provincial capital and the region's one rural agricultural area. Four blocs seemed most influenced by this urban-rural division: Russia's Choice, RDDR, Yabloko, and the Agrarian Party of Russia. Support soared for Russia's Choice and RDDR in the two districts of Yekaterinburg. Yabloko enjoyed its largest success in these two districts as well but did not have as great a difference between its vote share in Yekaterinburg and the rest of the region. Clearly, Yekaterinburg as the one true metropolitan area of the region contained the most reformist electorate. The provincial capital witnessed the most positive changes of Yeltsin's economic reforms such as more foreign and domestic goods in the shops. Also the city contained those citizens most likely to vote for continuation of the current market reforms—professionals and the urban intelligentsia concentrated in the center, not to mention a high concentration of state employees indirectly beholden to Yeltsin. The correlation of high concentration of support for Russia's Choice and RDDR in Yekaterinburg also indicates that, at least for Sverdlovsk voters, these two blocs represented the clearest option for continuation of the Yeltsin-Gaidar economic policies. Yabloko could also be categorized as a member of this reformist group based on its higher than average support in Yekaterinburg. But its more even distribution across the region suggests that the bloc also had a slightly different appeal as the democratic opposition to the party of power, as Yavlinskii had intended.

Table 13-1. *1993 PR Results by Electoral District*

Percent of total in italics

Electoral bloc	#160	#161	#162	#163	#164	#165	#166
Reformists	77,456	145,874	103,469	114,032	126,550	96,833	103,800
	31.7	*57.4*	*44.0*	*46.7*	*57.7*	*40.4*	*45.1*
Russia's Choice	33,260	72,245	47,414	56,249	61,631	48,003	51,156
	13.6	*28.4*	*20.1*	*23.0*	*28.1*	*20.0*	*22.3*
PRES	20,293	18,892	22,589	21,326	16,421	21,932	20,428
	8.3	*7.4*	*9.6*	*8.7*	*7.5*	*9.2*	*8.9*
RDDR	12,514	31,146	16,780	18,428	26,805	13,801	17,501
	5.12	*12.2*	*7.1*	*7.5*	*12.2*	*5.8*	*7.6*
Yabloko	11,389	23,591	16,686	18,029	21,693	13,097	14,715
	4.7	*9.3*	*7.1*	*7.4*	*9.9*	*5.5*	*6.4*
Centrists	36,766	29,322	36,676	34,496	26,048	34,717	36,093
	15.0	*11.5*	*15.6*	*14.1*	*11.9*	*14.5*	*15.7*
Women of Russia	20,504	12,018	20,177	19,180	11,210	20,418	19,631
	8.4	*4.7*	*8.6*	*7.9*	*5.1*	*8.5*	*8.5*
Democratic Party of Russia	12,227	12,529	11,646	11,004	10,983	10,435	11,808
	5.0	*4.9*	*5.0*	*4.5*	*5.0*	*4.4*	*5.1*

Civic Union	4,035 *1.7*	4,775 *1.9*	4,853 *2.1*	4,312 *1.8*	3,855 *1.8*	3,864 *1.6*	4,654 *2.0*
Opposition	91,199 *37.3*	43,180 *17.0*	54,942 *23.3*	54,604 *22.4*	37,044 *16.9*	67,238 *28.1*	55,232 *24.0*
Liberal Democratic Party of Russia	50,576 *20.7*	28,073 *11.1*	36,528 *15.5*	41,185 *16.7*	24,026 *11.0*	39,644 *16.6*	40,235 *17.5*
Communist party	16,072 *6.6*	12,142 *4.8*	11,765 *5.0*	9,723 *4.0*	10,549 *4.8*	13,796 *5.8*	10,926 *4.8*
Agrarian party	24,551 *10.1*	2,965 *1.2*	6,649 *2.8*	3,696 *1.5*	2,469 *1.1*	13,798 *5.8*	4,071 *1.8*
	8,425 *3.4*	7,214 *2.8*	8,687 *3.7*	7,419 *3.0*	5,705 *2.6*	8,694 *3.6*	7,414 *3.2*
Against-all	12,629 *5.2*	12,425 *4.9*	13,185 *5.6*	13,213 *5.4*	9,846 *4.5*	12,112 *5.1*	12,652 *5.5*
Voter participation	50.3	47.2	50.4	48.3	45.1	51.5	49.3

Source: Sverdlovsk Electoral Commission.

The 1995 parliamentary election witnessed a great reshuffling in the relative strength of reformist blocs in Sverdlovsk with Rossel's Transformation of the Fatherland bloc winning a plurality of votes in the region followed by the new party of power, Our Home Is Russia. Although Yabloko managed to hold on to most of its vote share, Russia's Choice virtually vanished from the electoral map, failing to even overcome the 5 percent barrier in the region. Nevertheless, general voting patterns for reformist blocs remained relatively stable. Gaidar's Democratic Russia's Choice almost doubled its regional vote average in the two Yekaterinburg districts and Yabloko and Our Home Is Russia were particularly strong in Yekaterinburg as well. Rossel's more moderate Transformation of the Fatherland had a very different voting distribution, similar to Shakhrai's PRES, which will be discussed later in this chapter.[43]

The situation was exactly opposite in the more rural Artemov District 160. This was definitely the stronghold of Communist, nationalist, and agrarian forces. It was the only district in the oblast in which Russia's Choice lost. This rural district, with its concentration of state farms and agro-industrial enterprises, meshed well with the power bases of the conservative camp—agrobusiness trade unions and state farm directors. It is not surprising that this district also showcased the leaders of the conservative blocs, Vyacheslav Sen'ko (LDPR), Valerii Novoselov (KPRF), and Tamara Tokareva (Agrarian party) in the single-mandate contest for the State Duma. The Agrarian party was the chief beneficiary of the socioeconomic environment in Artemovskii in which the party garnered 10 percent of the vote as opposed to its rather pathetic 1 percent to 2 percent showing in the rest of the region. Closer examination of the vote at the raion level shows the extent to which the Agrarian party's electorate was concentrated in rural areas. There was a sharp distinction within the Artemov district between more rural raions in which the Agrarian Party of Russia averaged more than 16 percent of the vote and raions of small towns and cities in the district in which the Agrarians averaged only 4.5 percent. This same stark distinction in the Agrarian Party of Russia's raion-level voting occurred in Pervoural'sk district (District 165), which also had some rural agricultural areas. In three rural raions of Pervoural'sk district the Agrarian Party of Russia averaged almost 20 percent of the vote, whereas in the rest of the district the party averaged only 3 percent of the vote.[44] The same type of voting distribution occurred in the 1995 parliamentary elections with the Agrarian Party of Russia getting 8 percent of the vote in rural Artemov district but between 1 percent and 3 percent of the vote in the region's other districts. This suggests a stable underlying socioeconomic basis for the Agrarian vote in Sverdlovsk. Thus the vote distribution of the Agrarian party suggests that its support in Sverdlovsk oblast was strongly influenced by socioeconomic factors. The Agrarian Party of Russia only received significant support in areas in which its natural constituency, large state farms and agrobusiness firms, existed in significant numbers. This runs counter to the experience in Bashkortostan where, Henry Hale argues in chapter 18, the Agrarian party was able to extend its support even to urban areas.

The other PR blocs had less distinctive patterns of support than Russia's Choice, RDDR, Yabloko, and the Agrarian party. In the opposition camp, both the Communist party and LDPR had relatively even distributions across the region, although both had their best showing in rural Artemovskii District 160 and their worst performance in the two districts of Yekaterinburg (Districts 161 and 164). Neither the Communists nor the LDPR seemed to draw their support exclusively from rural areas like the Agrarians. The LDPR was particularly strong in Serovskii District 166 in the north where Zhirinovskii's charisma and nationalist rhetoric may have appealed to disillusioned workers in mineral extraction there who had gone on strike during the campaign for payment of back wages. The districts of defense towns such as Nizhnii Tagil (District 163) also showed considerable support for the LDPR, which suggests that workers and soldiers from the military-industrial complex in Sverdlovsk may have voted for Zhirinovskii in substantial numbers. Zhirinovskii's message of national rebirth hit a nerve among a portion of the whole population tired of the hardship and disorder accompanying market reform and the dismantling of the Soviet Union. In 1995 the Communist party supplanted the LDPR as the most popular opposition party in Sverdlovsk. The increased support for the KPRF clearly came from other opposition parties such as the Agrarian Party of Russia and LDPR. However, the voting patterns described previously for 1993 remained relatively intact. All opposition parties did best in the rural Artemovskii district and worst in Yekaterinburg. The Communists and LDPR once again had relatively evenly distributed strength across the region. Communist support was a bit more concentrated in the rural areas of Artemovskii and Pervoural'skii districts, suggesting a migration of support from the Agrarian Party of Russia to the Communists. The LDPR once again had its greatest support (after Artemov) in the northern Serov District 166 and then in Nizhnii Tagil.

Regional support for PRES, the moderate reformist bloc of Sergei Shakhrai that emphasized regional autonomy, was perhaps the most interesting of all. Of all the reformist blocs, support for PRES was the most evenly distributed across the oblast, suggesting that this bloc may have captured a different segment of the reformist electorate that favors economic and political reform but is disillusioned with the shock therapy economic policies associated with the rest of the reformist blocs. Most interesting is the fact that support for PRES, although quite evenly distributed across the region, was lowest in the two districts of Yekaterinburg, precisely where the other three reformist blocs did best. PRES did best in the districts of large industrial cities such as Kamensk-Uralsk (District 162) and in the north (District 166) away from the urban intelligentsia of Yekaterinburg that seemed to form the basis of support for the rest of the reformist blocs. This corresponds with Shakhrai's itinerary when he visited the oblast during the campaign. He spent the day meeting with heads of local administrations, leaders of heavy industry, and the military. His voters' rally in Yekaterinburg was attended en masse by soldiers. Yavlinskii's campaign tour through the region, by contrast, concentrated more on the academic community in addition to the oblast and economic power structure. His voters' meeting was held at Urals State University and was attended by academics, students, and younger voters.[45] PRES collapsed as an electoral bloc in 1995 all across Russia and did not receive more than 1 percent of the vote in Sverdlovsk in the next parliamentary election. However, the unique electorate of PRES seemed to find a home with Rossel's Transformation of the Fatherland, a bloc that, like PRES, emphasized a more moderate program of reform and regional autonomy. The pattern of support for Rossel's Transformation of the Fatherland in the 1995 parliamentary election bears an almost uncanny resemblance to the support for PRES in 1993. Unlike the other reformist blocs, Rossel's bloc also received its lowest support in the reformist stronghold of Yekaterinburg and did best in medium-sized industrial cities and the north.

The PR race in Sverdlovsk oblast demonstrates the predominance of socioeconomic factors in determining the party-list vote. Although in the absence of individual-level survey data one cannot make definitive judgements about the voting preferences of segments of the region's electorate, voting patterns within the oblast suggest an identifiable constituency for all parts of the political spectrum. Yekaterinburg was the center of reformist support, particularly for the radical reformist Russia's Choice. Rural Artemovskii district was the center of opposition support. Although the Agrarian party's (and to a lesser extent Communist) constituencies have been restricted to predominantly rural agricultural districts, the LDPR was able to broaden its electorate across the region, excluding Yekaterinburg. The districts of medium-sized industrial cities and the northern Serovskii district (District 166) are harder to classify but seem to be most attracted to moderate reformers as demonstrated by the success of PRES in 1993 and Transformation of the Fatherland in 1995.

Single-Member District Races and the Federation Council

The same three factors (socioeconomic structure, rules of the game, and individual actors' resources and strategies) influenced the results in the single-member district and Federation Council elections, only in different ways and to different extents. Although the socioeconomic composition of the electorate seemed most important in the PR race, candidate resources and, most important, local name recognition were the most important determinants of the single-member district results. The institution of the plurality elections contested on a nonpartisan ballot made very different resources vital for success in the single-member district races. Unlike in the PR contest, a well-known local cadre and grassroots organization were vital ingredients for single-member district success. A charismatic national leader, which was the key to success for the LDPR and even Yabloko, did not help these blocs at all in the single-member district elections in which partisan affiliation did not appear on the ballot. Without this cue, voters were much less likely to cast so-called "straight-ticket" votes, reinforcing their PR vote with a vote cast for a single-member district candidate of the same bloc or even a bloc with a similar ideology. Thus, the coattails of successful PR blocs in Sverdlovsk did not extend to the single-member district election because the rules worked against it. This situation gave the advantage to well-organized parties with a strong local cadre and greatly disadvantaged blocs without a regional organization or well-known candidates. Most of the national blocs fell in the latter category and therefore had little chance of gaining a seat in the single-member districts. Only Russia's Choice had the organization and local cadre to effectively contest single-member district races across the region in 1993. However, although Russia's Choice did manage to use this advantage to win one single-member district seat in Yekaterinburg, the real winners in the single-member contests were independent candidates from the regional political power structure.

In candidate-centered elections to the State Duma and the Federation Council, political power—in other words, the holding of a position within the state apparatus—was the most important determinant of electoral success. Table 13-2 shows the winners of the single-member district and Federation Council elections. Of the nine winning candidates, seven held positions in local, oblast, or national government bodies at one time. Government office bestowed the most important resources on a candidate—name recognition and a claim to professional government experience. Moreover, government office often supplied valuable logistical resources such as office space and the symbolic resource of being able to claim knowledge of the region's potential problems in order to be better prepared to fight for regional interests in Moscow. Thus, the local political elite was able to retain its position of control over the state apparatus despite the mostly negative social and economic developments that occurred during its tenure in office. Those who voted did not seem to blame the economic and social hardships they were experiencing on their locally elected officials or wish to replace the seasoned politician with new personnel. Rather, voter disenchantment seemed oriented toward the center or the political process as a whole as reflected in low voter turnouts.

The local economic elite continued to suffer from an inability to translate economic power into electoral success. Entrepreneurs from both the large state enterprises and the private sector did surprisingly poorly. Only one member of the business community won, Leonid Nekrasov, a banking executive in Pervoural'skii District 165. The younger entrepreneurs who built their fortunes in the private sector faced considerable obstacles because the public associated them with the fast-growing Sverdlovsk mafia. The failure of state directors is harder to explain. They suffered from a loss of legitimacy as large enterprises began closing and laying off workers. Moreover, this group had not adapted well to the new demands of electoral politics and suffered from an inability to conduct an effective campaign and put forward attractive, charismatic candidates.

The low incidence of winning candidates affiliated with electoral blocs shows two weaknesses in party development in the area. First, the poor performance of party-nominated candidates demonstrates that political parties and electoral blocs continue to have little influence over voters' decisions and weak ties to society in this oblast. A local opinion poll conducted during the campaign showed that respondents considered a candidate's positions on social and economic problems to be the most important factor in determining their voting preference. Party affiliation was deemed least important.[46] The failure of party nominees from relatively well-organized electoral blocs such as the Democratic Party of Russia and Russia's Choice

Table 13-2. *Winners in Single-Member District and Federation Council Elections*

District	Winning candidate	State duma affiliation	Occupation	Percent of vote
160	Tokareva	Agrarian Party of Russia	Deputy in regional legislature	36.8
161	Mishustina	Russia's Choice	Deputy in national legislature	36.4
162	Mikheyev	Independent	School director	38.9
163	Veyer	Independent	Assistant city head of administration	31.3
164	Brusnitsyn	Independent	Raion head of administration	26.2
165	Nekrasov	Independent	Entrepreneur	35.5
166	Selivanov	Independent	City administration official	67.2
		Federation	*Council*	
66	Karelova	Independent	Deputy in regional legislature	48.5
66	Rossel	Independent	Former oblast head of administration	61.9

Source: *Byuleten* (Moscow: Central Electoral Commission, 1994).

reinforces this observation. Second, electoral blocs failed to coopt the most popular and well-known elements of the local elite into their structures. Even Russia's Choice with its strong foothold in the reformists' political community could not field strong enough candidates to win more than one seat in the single-member constituency contests. The strongest candidates continued to shun party affiliations. Well-known candidates were able to achieve independently the grassroots mobilization and campaign financing that political parties afford candidates in other political systems. The failure of electoral blocs to play a dominant role in who was elected in the candidate-centered elections in the oblast was also a result of the weakness of local party organizations themselves. Electoral blocs failed to provide sufficient benefits, in the form of mass mobilization or financial and logistical assistance, to outweigh the costs of affiliating oneself with a party label that could restrict political maneuvering and alienate a portion of the electorate.

The absence of effective party labels in candidate-centered contests had detrimental effects on the voters' ability to make an informative choice. Of course, the electoral blocs themselves ran personalized campaigns and did not provide voters with well-defined options or clear policy programs. However, they did provide a shorthand that allowed the average voter to

make some distinctions between competitors' general political orientations. In single-member constituencies this generally was not the case.
Most voters in Sverdlovsk oblast, like much of the rest of the country, did
not even know the names of the candidates running in their district, much
less their policy stands. The high number of invalid ballots and votes cast
against all candidates in the single-member district contests suggests that
voters were quite frustrated and confused by the choices confronting them
in these elections. Voting for "against all" tended to be high in Sverdlovsk
oblast, averaging 20.0 in the region and reaching 28.5 percent in Ordzhonikidze District 164 in Yekaterinburg, which far out-distanced the
winning candidate's 16.7 percent of the vote. When compared to the
party-list vote in the oblast, the difference in the numbers rejecting all
candidates is striking. Only 5 percent to 6 percent of voters rejected all the
electoral blocs in the oblast. This suggests that voters were more confused
and frustrated with their choices among the individual candidates than
among the electoral blocs. Part of this frustration must have resulted from
the more difficult task of differentiating between lesser-known local personalities with no party affiliations on the ballot to help identify their political leanings.

The victory of well-known, nonpartisan local political elites in the
single-member districts does not mean that political ideology and socioeconomic interests played no role in the outcome of these races. The plurality
races in the single-member districts did produce candidates and winners
that roughly matched their ideological and socioeconomic makeup despite
the threat that like-minded candidates would split the vote and allow a candidate from the opposite ideological camp to win with a small minority of
the vote. There was a sort of self-selection among candidates in which the
conservative candidates tended to concentrate in the conservative districts
and reformist candidates tended to gravitate toward the reformist-oriented
districts. This generally made for less ideological races that were contested
based on candidates' personal characteristics and professional credentials
rather than strong ideological or policy programs. Thus, in Artemovskii
District 160, an Agrarian party member and oblast soviet deputy won in a
race that was contested almost exclusively by candidates from the antireformist opposition. In Yekaterinburg's Verkh-Isetskii District 161, a member of Russia's Choice and deputy in the Russian Congress of Peoples'
Deputies won election in a race dominated by reformist politicians. In
Yekaterinburg's other district (Ordzhonikidze District 164), a raion head of
administration who was supported by Russia's Choice but ran as an inde-

pendent won even though the challenge by a Yabloko candidate almost si-phoned off enough of the reformist vote to allow Agrarian party member and well-known member of the irreconcilable opposition in the Russian Congress of Peoples' Deputies, Vladimir Isakov, to win. The less starkly ideological districts of medium-sized defense and industrial cities were usually won by well-known local notables either from government circles or, in the case of Pervoural'sk District 165, the economic sphere.

Ideology and social interests played a role by providing broad bounda-ries of acceptable candidates. Thus a staunchly conservative candidate was not going to have much luck in Yekaterinburg, and radical reformists were not going to do well in rural Artemov district. Candidates typically read these signals and did not run in ideologically unfriendly districts. After this general socioeconomic constraint, resources of name recognition and local organization determined the winners. This conveyed great advantage to the local political elite who tended to shun partisan identification and run as in-dependents. Where these two determinants came into conflict—that is, where well-known candidates ran in inhospitable ideological districts such as Agrarian Party of Russia candidate Vladimir Isakov in Yekaterin-burg—there was some uncertainty about outcome. In 1993 a reformist in-dependent candidate managed to beat off Isakov's conservative challenge. However, in 1995 this trend was reversed, and well-known candidates managed to win in inhospitable districts. In conservative Artemovskii dis-trict a Yabloko candidate, a well-known deputy in the oblast duma, man-aged to capture the opposition stronghold with an energetic campaign in part because opposition candidates split their electorate.

Conclusion

The outcome of the 1993 elections in Sverdlovsk oblast was a result of environmental factors, the rules of the game, and individual actors' re-sources. The development of political forces in the region during per-estroika produced a relatively favorable environment for Russia's Choice within the democratic camp. The reformist camp had been heavily oriented toward favorite son Yeltsin and naturally gravitated toward the bloc most closely associated with him, Russia's Choice, eclipsing the remaining re-formist blocs.

Sverdlovsk oblast's socioeconomic environment also favored reformist blocs. Its highly urbanized population tended to be oriented more toward political and economic reform, especially in the provincial capital, Yekaterinburg. The lack of substantial rural areas dominated by collective farming interests deprived the antireformist forces of their strongest constituency. The fact that the one rural area dominated by agricultural and agroindustrial interests was the only district in the oblast in which antireformist blocs won the majority of votes and the single-member district seat reinforces this point. The high level of urbanization may also help to explain the relatively low level of voter participation in the oblast. Put simply, the urban voter was more likely to stay home on election day, and this oblast had a predominance of urban voters.

A second important factor in the campaign was regionalism. The issue of the Urals Republic was the most discussed issue throughout election coverage, and it dominated electoral debates. However, no national bloc took up the issue for fear of weakening the center's already fragile hold over the regions. One consequence of this neglect was the birth of a non-party regionalist movement, Transformation of the Urals, led by the popular former head of administration, Rossel. In retrospect we can see that Rossel managed to use his victory to the Federation Council in 1993 to build a powerful regional electoral bloc. Only three years later, Transformation of the Urals had established itself as the predominant bloc in Sverdlovsk oblast. Rossel is firmly in control of the now popularly elected governorship, and Transformation of the Urals controls the regional legislature. Moreover, the movement has made an attempt to use its message of regional autonomy on the national level. Although Rossel's Transformation of the Fatherland did not succeed in securing a national following, it was able to solidify its hold on the regional political scene. This development demonstrates the powerful influence that a popular politician can have when he or she sets about building a party structure.

The conduct and outcome of the 1993 elections in Sverdlovsk oblast provided a mixture of both positive and negative signs of democratic consolidation in Russia. On the positive side, elites showed a general acceptance of the basic rules of free and fair electoral competition for political power. All electoral blocs and candidates conducted their campaigns according to the electoral law and rules handed down by the electoral commission with few irregularities. This occurred despite the fact that these rules were handed down by a president who violently dissolved the national parliament, dissolved several prominent opposition parties, disbanded local governing bodies, and was ruling by decree. Those members of organizations excluded from competition either accepted their fate, were absorbed by organizations that met official requirements, or were able to compete as independent candidates. No significant elite groups boycotted the elections. There was no use of violence or the threat of violence to affect the election results. Corruption was minimal and restricted mostly to questions surrounding the collection of signatures for nomination. Even antisystem parties and candidates participated, perhaps with too high a degree of success.

Although elites seemed to accept the basic principles of electoral competition, the 1993 elections in Sverdlovsk oblast did not see the establishment of strong local electoral organizations or the integration of the mass public in the political system. The party-list contest thrust electoral organizations onto the political stage. However, these organizations remained little more than personal vehicles of ambitious elites. As a result, electoral blocs failed to differentiate themselves according to programmatic appeals, and the contest between electoral blocs became a popularity contest between the various bloc leaders. Moreover, electoral blocs failed to establish themselves adequately on the local level. Although candidates in Sverdlovsk's single-member constituencies were predominantly nominees of one of the thirteen electoral blocs (twenty-two out of thirty-one), electoral blocs remained marginal actors in individual candidate races. Despite an elite community that tended to organize itself along party lines, the strongest candidates tended to remain independents, depriving nascent parties of strong, charismatic leaders.

Mass participation was also problematic. Voter apathy produced a low turnout in the region, failing to reach even the 50 percent national threshold required to pass the constitutional plebiscite. Voters knew very little about the constitution they were asked to vote on; in most cases they did not even know the names of the candidates they were asked to choose among in the candidate-centered elections to the lower house. Widespread disenchantment with all choices was manifested in a high incidence of voting against all of the choices offered.

In the final analysis, the victory of reformist forces in Sverdlovsk oblast does not hide the fragile nature of Russian democracy even in this traditionally progressive area of the federation. The reformist organizations that won have fragile organizational bases and little status within the community. They did not seem to become more consolidated from the electoral experience. The local power structure, with its personal networks and strong informal ties to the large state enterprises that still dominate the economy, has remained firmly in control.

Notes

1. For voting results by oblast since 1989, see L. V. Smirniagin, managing ed., *Rossiiskiye regiony nakanune vyborov-95* (Moscow: Yuridicheskaia literatura, 1995).

2. This follows roughly the five-tiered categorization of parties and blocs used by Timothy Colton in chapter 1, this volume, with the caveat of combining the radical reformist and moderate reformist categories in a single reformist camp and the nationalist and socialist categories in a single antireformist camp.

3. Sverdlovsk's 1996 regional parliamentary elections were modeled after the national elections, with half of the seats going in a PR party-list election in one regionwide district and the other half of the seats going in twenty-one single-member districts.

4. See Ralph S. Clem and Peter R. Craumer, "The Politics of Russia's Regions: A Geographic Analysis of the Russian Election and Constitutional Plebiscite of December 1993," *Post-Soviet Geography,* vol. 36, no. 2, pp. 67–87.

5. See chapter 14, this volume.

6. "Zabastovka v Severoural'ske," *Na Smenu,* December 3, 1993.

7. Personal interview with Valerii Novoselov, candidate in State Duma elections in Artemovskii electoral district and first secretary of the Sverdlovsk oblast Communist Party of the Russian Federation, November 1993. According to the 1989 census, only 2 percent of the population worked on collective farms for Sverdlovsk oblast as a whole, which was the lowest in the Urals region and among the lowest in the federation. *Gosudarstvennyi Komitet RSFSR postalistike, Kratkaya Sotsial'no-demograficheskaya Kharakteristika Naseleniya RSFSR, vol. 2: Istochniki sredstv senshchestvovaniya, obshchestvennye gruppy* (Moscow: Respublikanskii informatsoye-izdatel'skii tsentr, 1991), pp. 100–01.

8. Personal interview with Valerii Sartakov, head of the Sverdlovsk Oblast Administration Information–Analytical Center, December 1993.

9. Occupational profiles of 1990 deputies were taken from a data set supplied by Jerry Hough.

10. Personal interview with Oleg Podverezin, general director, Sverdlovsk Oblast Union of Industrialists and Entrepreneurs, December 1993.

11. A. D. Kirillov claims that, despite the proliferation of political organizations in the area, real political influence remained in the hands of large state enterprises and agricultural interests. A. D. Kirillov, *Ural: Tendentsii Politicheskogo Razvitiya, 1991–1993* (Yekaterinburg: Urals Cadre Center, 1993), p. 21.

12. Personal interview with Valerii Sartakov, Sverdlovsk Oblast Administration Information–Analytical Center; Boris Bagirov, dean of the philosophy faculty, Urals State University; and Aleksandr Khuzin, head of Sverdlovsk oblast Administration Commission of Social Organizations. Both Sartakov and Bagirov stressed the influence state enterprise directors had over Rossel and his network of city and raion level heads of administration. Khuzin claimed that the movement for a Urals Republic and protection of regional economic interests tended to take a centrist position toward economic reform, preferring a slower movement toward a market economy that favored the interests of state directors.

13. Nikolai Privalov, *Osnovnye obshchestvenno-politicheskiye organizatsii Urala* (Yekaterinburg: Center for Democracy and Human Rights, 1995), pp. 9–10.

14. Ibid., pp. 9–10, 31–32.

15. Numerous examples substantiate this claim. Both the Socialist Party of Labor and the Russian Communist Workers' party provided an outlet and temporary structure for the regional Communist party after it was banned following the August coup up until the ban was nullified by the Constitutional Court. Kirillov, *Ural: Tendentsii politicheskogo razvitiya,* pp. 20–21.

16. Personal interview with Stanislav Nekrasov, chair of the History of Culture Department, Urals Polytechnic Institute, Yekaterinburg, December 1993.

17. Personal interview with Valerii Novoselov, first secretary of Sverdlovsk Oblast Communist party, Yekaterinburg, November 1993. See also Kirillov, *Ural: Tendentsii politcheskogo razvitiya,* pp. 19–20.

18. Privalov, *Osnovnye obshchestvenno-politcheskiye organizatsii Urala,* pp. 10–11.

19. Ibid., p. 42.

20. Kirillov, *Ural: Tendentsii politicheskogo razvitiya,* pp. 10–11. Tamara Alaiba, chair of the Republican party and Democratic Choice–Democratic Russia, also emphasized the closer ties DPR has to reformist organizations in Sverdlovsk oblast than in Moscow. Personal interview, Yekaterinburg, November 1993.

21. E. V. Rasshivalova and N. S. Seregin, eds., *Putch: khronika trevozhnykh dnei* (Moscow: Progress, 1991), pp. 45, 156, 158.

22. Nikolai Privalov, "Reaktsiya obshchestvenno-politicheskikh sil Urala na Ukaz Prezidenta ot 21 Sentyabrya 1993 i krovavyye sobytiya v Moskve 3–4 Oktyabrya 1993." Unpublished manuscript.

23. These groups were all signatories of the Urals' Choice movement. Kirillov, *Ural: Tendentsii politicheskogo razvitiya,* p. 119.

24. Privalov, *Osnovnye obshchestvenno-politicheskiye organizatsii Urala,* pp. 11–12.

25. Kirillov, *Ural: Tendentsii politicheskogo razvitiya,* p. 97.

26. An important exception to the exclusion of party affiliation on the ballot occurred when the candidate's professional occupation was leader or activist of a party's local branch. Thus the short descriptions included on the ballot for Vyacheslav Sen'ko, leader of the LDPR, and German Karelin of the DPR included party affiliation. This is not to say that an individual candidate's party affiliation was not in the public realm. Descriptions in the press and on campaign flyers included party affiliations.

27. "A ty za kogo?" *Na Smenu,* November 26, 1993, p. 1.

28. Personal interview with Alexander Khuzin, head of Sverdlovsk Oblast Administration Commission on Social Organizations, Yekaterinburg, December 1993.

29. This breakdown is based on an analysis of the registration results prepared by B. Yu. Berzin, chair of the Committee on Ties with Social Organizations and the Study of Public Opinion. Unpublished manuscript.

30. "Udar, eshche udar!" *Ural'skii rabochii,* November 12, 1993, p. 1.

31. These decrees were published in *Oblastnaya gazeta,* November 12, 1993, p. 1.

32. "Constitution of the Russian Federation," chapter 3, article 65, *Izvestiya*, November 10, 1993, p. 3.

33. *Oblastnaya gazeta*, November 10, 1993, p. 1.

34. Personal interview with Yurii Samarin, former speaker of the Yekaterinburg city soviet, Yekaterinburg, December 1993.

35. Nikolai Privalov, "Predistoriya i obosnovaniye provozglasheniya ural'skoi respubliki." Unpublished manuscript, pp. 10–11.

36. Vladimir Lobok, running under Civic Union and PRES, supported "Unity of the Russian Federation. Priority of interests of regions before the Center. A united economic structure. Free development of cultural and national traditions." Vladimir Isakov of the Agrarian party supported reform of the Federation and "the removal of economic inequality and difference in political status of its subjects." The Communist party's Vladimir Novoselov called for a "Russia undivided, its subjects equal. . . . " (These statements were all collected from campaign posters.)

37. See Josephine Andrews and Kathryn Stoner-Weiss, "Regionalism and Reform: Evidence from the Russian Provinces" (paper delivered at the American Political Science Association Meeting, New York City, September 1–4, 1994), pp. 6–9.

38. For example, in an interview, Gennadii Zyuganov came out against the Urals republic and self-government for the regions. *Ural'skii rabochii,* November 30, 1993, p. 1. Sergei Glaz'ev of the DPR condemned Yeltsin's dismissal of Rossel as uncivilized but did not favor the Urals Republic out of fear that the process could lead to separatism similar to the experience of the former Soviet Union and Yugoslavia. "Zakon, ne dychle," *Ural'skii rabochii,* November 18, 1993, p. 2.

39. "Pod znamenem mestnogo samoupravleniya," *Oblastnaya gazeta*, December 3, 1993, p. 2.

40. Personal interview with Alya Panacheva, head of the Fund for the Support of the First President of Russia and regional director of the Russia's Choice Urals regional campaign, Yekaterinburg, December 1993.

41. Personal interview with Valerii Novoselov, first secretary of Sverdlovsk oblast Communist party, Yekaterinburg, November 1993.

42. Personal interview with volunteers at the campaign headquarters of Vladimir Lobok, Yekaterinburg, December 1993.

43. For a discussion of the 1995 parliamentary campaign in Sverdlovsk oblast see Robert G. Moser, "Reform and Regionalism: Continuity and Change in the 1995 Parliamentary Elections in Sverdlovsk Oblast" (paper presented at the annual meeting of the American Political Science Association, San Francisco, California, August 28, 1996).

44. I managed to get a copy of the results by raion produced by the Sverdlovsk Electoral Commission from contacts who wish to remain anonymous.

45. This is based on personal observation of these events.

46. *Krasnaya zvezda*, December 3, 1993, p. 2.

CHAPTER FOURTEEN

Nizhnii Novgorod
The Dual Structure of Political Space

Nigel Gould-Davies

THE MOST WIDELY accepted general conclusion about the Russian election of December 1993 is that it was a crushing defeat for reformers in power, caused primarily by mass discontent with the consequences of the economic policies that they had introduced during the previous two years. While it requires elaboration and refinement, there is much to be said for this view. It also throws into sharp relief the outcome of the election in Nizhnii Novgorod. Here, too, a group of young democrats had taken power in late 1991 and introduced a far-reaching program of reform. They, however, waged an overwhelmingly successful campaign that returned strongly proreform candidates almost throughout the region.

The central question addressed by this chapter is how, in the background of electoral revolt against reformers in power at the national level, those at the local level in Nizhnii Novgorod not only succeeded in retaining power but actually secured a near monopoly on legislators representing the region. The answer to this question is a complex one, but its essence can be stated briefly at the outset. Two distinct electoral arenas emerged during the cam-

I would like to thank all the candidates who agreed to be interviewed for this study and to express my gratitude to Viktor Lysov of the Public Relations Department of the Regional Administration, Tat'yana Khlebnikova of the Oblast Soviet Information Department, and Anatolii Nekrasov of the Regional Election Commission for their great helpfulness and willingness to share information. I am especially indebted to Yuliya Fadeyeva for her invaluable assistance during the election campaign.

Nizhnii Novgorod

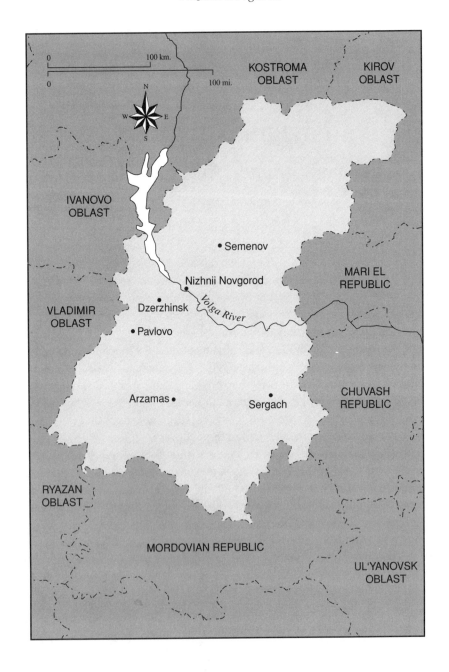

paigns: a national one in which parties competed, whose outcome was determined by broad demographic factors; and a local one in which candidates competed, whose outcome was decisively influenced by the preponderance of resources held by an alliance of local elites. Crucially the local arena was insulated from national trends by a combination of interrelated factors: the weakness of party structures, the design of electoral rules, and the political strategies adopted by candidates. This insulation enabled the Nizhnii Novgorod reform-led coalition, unlike its national counterpart, to mobilize its resources both effectively and legitimately—winning the election not by writing rules to engineer a victory but by exploiting the advantages of incumbency in a normal way.

I will begin with a brief discussion of the main characteristics of Nizhnii Novgorod as an electoral subsystem and suggest how they influenced the starting point of the election campaign. Second, I will discuss the brief but hectic precampaign for registration in order to examine the character and determinants of the political supply that was to face the electorate. Third, I will trace the course of the election campaign itself, paying particular attention to the programs and strategies of candidates and parties and to the demands and responses of the electorate. Finally, I will analyze the results of the election, and consider the broader implications of these findings for the future of electoral politics in Russia.

The Historical Backdrop

Nizhnii Novgorod is the name of a region (oblast)—a subject of the Russian Federation—and its capital city, the third largest city in the country, located 250 miles east of Moscow.[1] The oblast, about the size of a small Western European country, is one of the most economically developed (seventh largest by industrial output), one of the most urbanized, and one of the most ethnically homogeneous regions in Russia.[2] Its distinctiveness as an electoral subsystem in 1993 was defined by three interrelated factors: economic, political, and center-periphery. Together these shaped the circumstances in which the elections were held: they helped to determine the range of potential participants—both candidates and interest groups—in the elections; they determined the initial distribution of political, social, and economic resources among those seeking power or representation; and they shaped the set of concerns, fears, interests, and values of the electorate that had the potential to become electoral issues. But while these contextual

factors did predispose the campaigns in important respects, they determined neither their course nor their outcome. Much was to depend on the
effectiveness with which potential participants mobilized and deployed
their resources in appealing to voters' preferences and in emphasizing those
issues of greatest electoral benefit to themselves.

The economic structure of the region epitomizes the fundamental problems faced by reform in Russia as a whole. Nizhnii Novgorod is a center of
heavy industry, especially the military-industrial complex that is responsible for one-third of all production in the region; for this reason Nizhnii
Novgorod was a closed city until 1991. By the time of the election campaign many larger factories were coming close to bankruptcy and operating
on a three- or four-day week or, in some cases, putting their workforce on
unpaid leave. Although several sectors of local industry face a bleak economic future, the region has suffered significantly less than the country as a
whole from the economic crisis.[3] Special mention must also be made of the
huge GAZ automobile plant and the unique place it occupies in the city.
This monument to Soviet gigantism not only employs about 100,000 workers but also owns and operates a comprehensive social infrastructure of
schools, housing, and medical facilities; consequently its economic, social,
and potential political influence is very great. Beyond Nizhnii Novgorod
city, the most important centers in the regions are Dzerzhinsk, formerly a
center of chemical weapons production; Arzamas and Pavlovo, large industrial cities specializing in machine building, light engineering, and
transportation; and Arzamas-16, the first and still the most important of the
ten closed "nuclear cities" in Russia.[4] But while the oblast as a whole is
highly developed, there remain significant contrasts between the industrial
cities and a still backward countryside undergoing rapid depopulation.

These typically Soviet problems of industrial gigantism and rural decline have since April 1992 been the setting for the most significant regional economic reform initiative in the country, a focus of national and international attention. This program, elaborated by Grigorii Yavlinskii, the
young economist who later founded and led the Yabloko bloc, has focused
on the small-scale privatization *(malaya privatizatsiya)* of shops, enterprises, transport, and land. More generally, an active policy of opening up
the region to foreign commerce has helped to create an entrepreneurial environment and restore the region's prerevolutionary reputation as the
"pocket of Russia," a national center of trade and finance.

While much Western attention has been devoted to the technical aspects
of these reforms, the elections provided the opportunity to explore their *po-*

litical consequences and raised important questions about their influence on perceptions of interest and forms of political participation of economic groups affected in different ways by reform. What role was played by those groups that had been created by or had benefited from reforms (the natural "reform constituency") and those that had suffered from them? And what was the economic basis of this cleavage: property form, setting state enterprises against private commercial structures; relations to the means of production, setting managers against workers; or level of income, setting those who had become wealthier against those who had become poorer?

The introduction of economic reform in Nizhnii Novgorod has been led by the young governor, Boris Nemtsov, who entered national politics in 1990 as part of the Democratic Russia insurgency in the major Russian cities. He defeated the Communist establishment in his district in the March parliamentary elections of that year and was appointed presidential representative after the 1991 coup and governor in November. On coming to power Nemtsov, with considerable skill, constructed a broad coalition of political elites, and in particular was able to introduce reform-minded personnel without alienating the former party nomenklatura.[5] As a consequence, Nizhnii Novgorod has enjoyed unusually stable and harmonious relations both between branches of government (the regional administration and oblast soviet) and between levels of government (the oblast and city organs).[6] The close political relationship between Governor Nemtsov and the chair of the oblast soviet, Yevgenii Krest'yaninov, has been the key element in this arrangement, and Nizhnii Novgorod was one of the few regions in which the oblast soviet was not dissolved during the October to December interregnum. Furthermore, the governor succeeded in attracting a formidable array of local forces, including the wealthy heads of new commercial structures and influential figures from the local television stations, to strengthen his own political position in the oblast as a whole. This new elite had governed effectively for two years and in December faced its first political test. How, lacking strong roots in established nomenklatura networks of the Soviet era, would it fare in electoral competition? How effectively would it make political use of the advantages of incumbency and of the support and resources of those who had benefited from the reforms it had introduced?

Political and economic factors have also influenced the character of relations between Nizhnii Novgorod and the central government. Although the region's strategic significance had assured it a position of special importance in the Soviet Union,[7] the political affinity between regional and national reformers has more recently created strong ties between Nizhnii Novgorod and the central government. Nemtsov himself stayed with Yeltsin in the White House during the August 1991 coup and was subsequently appointed presidential representative and then governor.[8] These links have thickened and spread, and Nizhnii Novgorod officials have a voice in influential chambers of counsel in Moscow,[9] a fact that was to be confirmed in March 1997 with Nemtsov's appointment as first deputy prime minister. However, while the population has shown itself to be slightly, though not significantly, more reform-minded than the country as a whole,[10] evidence suggests that the popular mood has been steadily turning against the central government since 1991. Support for Boris Yeltsin in the June presidential election of that year was 72.2 percent, twelve points higher than the national average; by the April referendum two years later, approval of the president had fallen by seven points in Nizhnii Novgorod, whereas in Russia as a whole it actually rose slightly. Indeed, it was the only region located above the 55th parallel (which demarcates the consistently conservative south) in which support actually fell during this period.[11] Furthermore, the regional administration has shown itself ready to challenge or resist federal actions perceived to damage local interests.[12]

The nature of center-periphery relations is particularly significant if it is recalled that *four* elections were held in December 1993: two primarily regional (the single-mandate races to the Duma and the bimandate elections to the Federation Council) and two primarily national (the competition between party lists and the constitutional referendum). How much did reformers at national and local levels try to coordinate their efforts? To what extent were moral and material resources channeled between them? In short, to what extent were the four campaigns conducted separately and how much did they interact with each other?

In sum, three sets of local factors provided the setting for the electoral contest in Nizhnii Novgorod. First, the economic structure combined an old, military-industrial base, dependent on subsidies from the center, with a vibrant, newly privatized trade and financial sector sponsored by local reforms—contrasts that were potential sources of new electoral cleavages. Second, local political structures were largely united around these reforms, whereas opposition forces were weak and unorganized. Particularly notable was the fact that the political elite was not sharply divided by conflicts of personality or principle, by standing political feuds or grievances, around which the elections could become polarized. Third, a tension existed between the solid links of local and national reform leaders and the growing distance that the region was traveling from the center.

These distinctive features of the local electoral subsystem were overlain by a broader set of national influences, common to all regions, whose effects were nonetheless refracted through local structures. These include the protracted conflict between the president and the legislature, the worsening economic situation and the new inequalities to which this gave rise, and the perceived decline of Russia's position in world affairs. Together these evoked a complex response, generating new sources of resentment and anger even as they contributed to a large-scale demobilization and withdrawal from political activity. But the national factor that had the most significant and direct impact on the local electoral environment was the political crisis—the dissolution of the Supreme Soviet on September 21 and the bloody events of October 3 to 4—in which the elections were called. The bitter ironies of this situation—a president acting illegally in order to call free elections, deputies with no particular commitment to democracy defending the sanctity of the constitution—were also felt on the local level. They briefly threatened to strain relations between Governor Nemtsov and the oblast soviet. The latter passed a resolution on September 22 declaring the president's decree invalid in the region. Nemtsov protested against this action, arguing that the soviet had exceeded its authority in doing so, and the soviet subsequently issued a partial retraction of its resolution.[13] It appears that Nemtsov, who sharply criticized the presidential decree and who was known to be in contact with Aleksandr Rutskoi, one of the leaders of the anti-Yeltsin opposition, strove to maintain a broadly neutral position in the confrontation. This deliberate distancing from the president, in sharp contrast to August 1991, further illustrates the distance that had arisen between local and national reformers.

The Candidates

The first stage of the electoral process on which these contextual factors made their influence felt was the precampaign for registration, which in turn determined the range of political choices that were to face the voters. Who put themselves forward as candidates, which of them succeeded in registering, and why? It is clear that several politicians had been planning their candidacies and marshaling their resources in anticipation of elections even before the September–October crisis. Almost a year earlier the organization Fond Vybor (Choice Foundation) had been set up to unite the components of Governor Nemtsov's political coalition on a systematic basis.

Chaired by the head of a local television station, Georgii Molokin, and generously financed by local businesspeople, Fond Vybor was to play a key role in the elections. On September 18, on the eve of the Moscow crisis, the Nizhnii Novgorod Bloc of Centrist Forces was established as a response to Fond Vybor, with the explicit intention of contesting future elections. It brought together a range of local social organizations and regional branches of political parties (including the Social Democratic party and Rutskoi's "People's Party of Free Russia") under the leadership of the deputy chair of the Nizhnii Novgorod city soviet, Yevgenii Sabashnikov.[14]

It was natural for Nemtsov, as governor and former Supreme Soviet deputy, and Krest'yaninov, as chair of the oblast soviet, to stand for the Federation Council. Indeed, Krest'yaninov had been one of the principal advocates of such a chamber prior to the crisis in Moscow.[15] With the resources of high office and Fond Vybor behind them, they had no difficulty in collecting the 25,000 signatures necessary for registration. The sheer preponderance of their material resources and political support, however, created an interesting problem. According to electoral law, every race had to be contested; that is, at least three candidates had to take part in an election returning two deputies. But the very large number of signatures proved a formidable barrier to the far weaker opposition forces. Four serious attempts to register were made. The extreme Communist Workers' Council—part of the so-called irreconcilable opposition—began collecting signatures, but gave up. The regional branch of the Democratic Party of Russia (DPR) and the Bloc of Centrist Forces both came close to achieving registration, each collecting signatures right up to the deadline. The latter actually submitted its documents for the registration of Sabashnikov, but in circumstances that remain obscure he withdrew his application, ostensibly in protest at the unfairness of the conditions in which the elections were to be held. Only the chair of the local student trade union, Misha Mirnyi, was able to register, and even his campaign team was surprised at this success. Throughout the subsequent campaign there were persistent rumors that the governor's team had facilitated the collection of these signatures in order to secure the participation of the necessary third candidate. Certainly, Mirnyi was the ideal political opponent: inexperienced, largely unknown, and lacking any real organizational or financial support, he ran a thoroughly friendly, nonconfrontational campaign that stressed the problems of higher education. From the moment of his registration there was no serious doubt that Nemtsov and Krest'yaninov, the two best-known politicians in the oblast, running on a joint platform, would win.

The precampaign for registration in the Duma elections was conducted by a much larger number of politicians in a far greater variety of conditions, which makes it possible to draw more significant comparisons and more general conclusions about the determinants of political "supply" in the elections. The oblast was divided into six single-member districts (okrugs): two (Avtozavod and Kanavin) in the city of Nizhnii Novgorod itself; two (Arzamas and Dzerzhinsk) of mixed urban-rural character, each centered on a major city devoted primarily to military-industrial production; and two very large, almost entirely rural districts that between them make up nearly five-sixths of the total oblast by area (Semenov and Sergach). Although the 1 percent requirement (about 5,000 signatures) was clearly easier to surmount than in the Federation Council race, it still constituted a real barrier, especially because of the widespread reluctance among voters to give the necessary passport data. From the experiences of the candidates it is possible to draw some conclusions about the factors that determined success in registration. Four by no means mutually exclusive devices were used: first, prior familiarity and a network of established local contacts, usually enjoyed by virtue of holding local political office; second, a senior position in a large factory or enterprise, where it was relatively easy to collect signatures among the large concentration of workers; third, private wealth that enabled otherwise unknown candidates to pay (in some cases up to 1,000 rubles) for each signature; fourth, association with Fond Vybor, which sponsored, and in some cases actively supported, one candidacy in each district.

Altogether, out of thirty-six who submitted registration papers (and several more who began collecting signatures but gave up), thirty-one candidates succeeded in registering. The collection of signatures in general was a hectic affair, with almost all the candidates completing the process within three days of the November 14 deadline. An additional twenty earned their right to compete by virtue of their inclusion on a national party list. Of the total of fifty-one candidates, only two were women and nineteen were aged forty or younger. The fact that only two of the twenty-four deputies of the old Congress of Peoples' Deputies chose to stand for the Duma ensured an almost complete turnover of the legislative elite from the region.

Almost every successfully registered candidate belonged to one of four categories. To a large extent, this classification corresponds to the resources that they had at their disposal to achieve registration and that they were to use in the course of the election campaign.[16] The first and largest category, about eighteen candidates, comprised professional politicians and political professionals. These included elected representatives—principally oblast deputies but also two deputies of the disbanded Supreme Soviet—and full-time party officials. A small but important subset comprised Communist party apparatchiki, among them the former obkom first secretary, Gennadii Khodyrev, and the former gorkom first secretary of Nizhnii Novgorod city, Aleksandr Mal'tsev. Khodyrev and Mal'tsev ran in the two most rural districts where the older population there remains more sympathetic to the Communist party, although, significantly, they did not do so as official Communist party candidates.[17]

The second category included twelve administrators of state companies. In four of the six districts a leading official, usually a director, of a large industrial enterprise stood as a candidate.[18] The most striking examples were Aleksandr Tsapin, the deputy general director of the giant GAZ plant, and Valerii Lisitsyn, who occupied a similar position at the historic Krasnoye Sormovo Shipbuilding Works (the second largest enterprise in the area after GAZ). Each of these candidates stood in one of the districts in Nizhnii Novgorod city. A special case of this phenomenon was the candidacy of a research scientist from the nuclear city Arzamas-16.

The third category of candidates consisted of chairs or directors of commercial structures. This was a relatively small group (about ten candidates) that nonetheless reflected the diversity of the new private sector. Among the most significant of such candidates was Yevgenii Bushmin, a financial expert who headed one of the two stock exchanges *(birzhi)* in the city, as well as the Nizhnii Novgorod Confederation of Entrepreneurs whose endorsement Bushmin naturally received. Another type of business was represented by Vladimir Danilov, a director of Russkii Klub, a large and diverse trading company. Danilov became an obedient but by no means willing political initiate when the chair decided that he was to become the company's candidate.[19] Also, there was the mercurial Gennadii Gabov, a twenty-one-year-old entrepreneur who three years earlier had become Russia's youngest millionaire and who during the registration campaign had paid so handsomely for his signatures. A final category of candidates was a residual one that included intellectual and cultural workers and local administrators.

Nearly every district included at least one member of each of these four groups of candidates, so it is possible to compare their fortunes in different social and economic settings across the oblast. These four categories constitute a rather broad array of local interests—that is, of those groups that could be expected to seek political representation and who possessed resources to mount a plausible campaign. The most significant exception was organized labor. The poorly funded and demoralized trade unions were almost completely inactive during the elections. They did not put forward a single candidate of their own, and gave their endorsement to only two: the GAZ director, Tsapin, and, in the Federation Council election, the "third candidate," Misha Mirnyi, who, although chair of the student trade union, could hardly be said to represent the interests of labor. Furthermore, not a single candidate was by profession a worker.

Most of the main political parties ran at least two candidates in the Duma races. Significantly, however, Vladimir Zhirinovskii's Liberal Democratic Party of Russia (LDPR) had only a single representative, the chair of the regional party branch, who was far down in his party's list; and the Communist party ran no official candidates at all in the region.[20] By contrast, the Democratic Party of Russia (DPR) emerged as the most well-organized party, running one candidate in each district, many of whom were full-time local party workers. Indeed, the DPR was the only political bloc to exhibit a recognizably Western-type party identity. Elsewhere, the haste with which party lists were assembled ensured that the relationship between a party and the candidates running on its platform was often tenuous and even arbitrary. The whole question of party membership, in particular whether it should be considered an advantage or a disadvantage in a candidate, was to become an issue during the campaign itself.

Finally, a special group of candidates ran together, not as a national party but rather as a local team. The governor and his electoral organization Fond Vybor supported and actively campaigned on behalf of one independent candidate in each district. Indeed, in the case of Tat'yana Chertoritskaya, an ethnographer with no previous political experience, the governor himself suggested that she stand as a candidate.[21] Her campaign against the former obkom first secretary Khodyrev was to be one of the most interesting aspects of the elections.

Thus was the political cast assembled on November 20. With one exception the six single-mandate races were from the start open ones, whose outcome could not be confidently predicted. Each included at least five candidates from a range of parties and a wide variety of backgrounds; and although conservative opposition parties were clearly underrepresented, the candidates included several forceful critics of the regional administration. Each participant started with a local base of support, and while some were initially better known than others, few could claim district-wide prominence. Different candidates had access to different resources in order to familiarize a larger circle of voters with themselves and their programs, but it was far from clear which means, in which combination, would prove most effective in doing so.

The partial exception was Avtozavod district, where the position of Aleksandr Tsapin, the deputy director of the GAZ factory that employed 20 percent of his electorate, was very strong from the start. He was clearly the factory's candidate and had been the first of the fifty-one candidates in the oblast to register. Nonetheless, even his victory was by no means a foregone conclusion. It could not be assumed that factory workers would give political support to their bosses, as the fate of other such director-candidates was to show. Even here, the outcome of the election was to depend on how candidates presented themselves to the large mass of undecided voters. Only the race for the Federation Council, where the inequality in resources between Nemtsov and Krest'yaninov on the one hand and Mirnyi on the other was simply enormous, was to lack a genuinely competitive campaign.

Opening Lines

Three important aspects of the election campaign may be distinguished, although they are in practice intimately related: the views presented by the candidates to the voters; their campaign strategies—that is, the way they used their resources to maximize electoral support; and the way voters responded, both during the campaign and ultimately in their voting decisions on December 12.

What political choices did the successfully registered candidates offer the electorate, and how can these be explained? What issues did they choose to emphasize, and which policies did they propose? The arguments and rhetoric of political suppliers help to shape the terms of political discourse—the language and concepts used to articulate political problems and solutions—in any election campaign. But it may be argued that the influence of this candidate-led discourse on the way potential voters define and interpret political issues will be especially great during periods of systemic transition and widespread disorientation, as in Russia, where robust conceptions of identity and interest are lacking. The absence of a strong party system that normally helps to fulfil important stabilizing functions—to organize political interests, socialize voters, and present coherent political choices—can only increase the significance of the programs articulated by individual candidates.[22]

The issues raised by the candidates can be divided, not always cleanly, into socioeconomic, moral, and political. Nearly every candidate laid the greatest emphasis on socioeconomic issues, and all except those associated with Russia's Choice criticized, to greater or lesser extent, current government policy. In its place, most candidates proposed a series of highly general objectives, with little analysis either of the cause of the present economic crisis or the means by which it was to be alleviated. Thus, for example, all were in favor of stimulating production *and* controlling inflation *and* fighting unemployment; all claimed to support economic reform while ensuring adequate social guarantees for the poor; all supported a variety of property forms while opposing corruption in the privatization process; all were pledged to fight crime, to work for a clean environment, and to tackle the housing problem (which is especially acute in Nizhnii Novgorod).

There were, however, differences of emphasis. Factory directors such as Tsapin and Lisitsyn predictably stressed the problems of heavy industry and the value of "practical experience" and affected disdain for "abstract ideas."[23] Those with an economic or legal background tended to emphasize the need to secure adequate protection for property and establish a working financial system. Interestingly, perhaps the sharpest expression of these differences appeared in views on foreign policy. By itself an insignificant issue in the Duma elections, it was raised by several candidates in the context of economic policy. Factory directors, in particular, linked the economic revival of the country with the strengthening of links with other Commonwealth of Independent States (CIS) countries and with the reduction of much-resented economic subordination as a "raw-material appendage" to the West.[24] Furthermore, a somewhat greater hostility to property reform could be detected in the rural districts, a question made locally relevant by the introduction of the first land privatization program in Russia on the eve of the campaign.

Relatively few candidates outlined a *policy* as well as a *program*—that is, a strategy for achieving their declared objectives that recognized the relationships between means and ends and the trade-offs that must be made between different objectives. Those who did, however, were far more likely to belong to political parties or blocs. Despite the haste with which party lists were assembled, the electoral platforms worked out in the central campaigns provided a more sophisticated basis for political campaigning than those offered by most independent candidates. And the right of a member of a party list to run in a single-member district had the effect of transferring these programs—and the competition between party organizations—onto the campaigns between individual candidates. This was responsible for the only two significant disagreements on socioeconomic issues between candidates. Against the otherwise unanimous call for tax cuts to stimulate industrial production, the representatives of Russia's Choice insisted on grounds of fiscal responsibility that this was currently impossible.[25] And the single LDPR candidate, Igor' Veletminskii was almost alone in calling for a halt to military conversion, in accordance with his party's program. In a region where the defense sector accounted for one-third of total production, this was a significant issue.

One of the distinctive features of the electoral discourse was its moral component. Again, this was not a divisive issue (as it has been in, say, Poland). Rather, candidates shared a concern, even anxiety, over the need to revive the country's moral and spiritual foundations. Indeed, *vozrozhdeniye* (rebirth), with an unmistakable spiritual component, was the term most widely used during the election. It may be added that this did not in any way imply the reassertion of a distinctly *Russian* identity; the ethnic homogeneity of the region ensured the absence of nationality issues during the campaign.[26]

Thus, despite the depth and seriousness of the socioeconomic situation in the country and the widespread concern about it among voters and candidates alike, the candidates as a rule did not help to structure political space in a coherent way. They did not present a clear choice of alternative priorities or solutions, even when one might have predicted this from their backgrounds. Entrepreneurs, in particular, differed little in their explicit statements from other economic groups, and indeed were as likely to emphasize moral issues as economic ones. In short, debate was framed by *valence* rather than *position* issues: most goals were shared by candidates who each claimed to be the most reliable guarantor of their fulfillment, with the goals themselves not being disputed.[27]

It was on more narrowly political issues that the candidates were most clearly distinguishable, in particular in their analyses of the September–October events and in their attitude to the draft constitution. Both introduced real bitterness into a campaign otherwise lacking passion. Views about the actions of the president that had led to the calling of elections ranged from those who considered them illegal but necessary to those who considered him no less responsible than Khasbulatov and Rutskoi for the bloodshed in Moscow. The paradox of unconstitutional actions making possible the holding of free elections cast a long shadow over the campaign and thus potentially over the new political system they inaugurated. In part it generated skepticism, even cynicism, among sections of the electorate, and raised the question of the legitimacy of the entire process, of whether voters should feel obliged to participate in the elections or be bound by their results. It also exacerbated divisions among forces otherwise committed to reform, with candidates who were far from sympathetic to the old Supreme Soviet criticizing, on impeccably constitutional grounds, the president's actions.

In an even more direct way the constitutional referendum forced candidates to take an unambiguous stand on a controversial issue, thereby introducing an inescapably position issue into a largely valent campaign. Most candidates did not explicitly include their attitude to the draft constitution in their programs, though a significant majority of those who did so came out against it. Those who were initially silent on this issue were soon compelled to articulate their position in response to persistent questions from voters. And the local television debates on the constitution occasioned the most lively exchanges between candidates.

In conclusion, the systemic character of the economic and political transition in the country gave rise to a broad range of issues, but only the immediate political context of the elections—the events that preceded them and the simultaneous constitutional referendum—served to distinguish clearly the views of candidates. It might be said that while much ground was covered by the campaign, little territory was contested.

The Campaign

As elsewhere in Russia, the campaigns conducted by parties and candidates were shaped by the brevity of the contest and the apathy of the voters. Political actors had barely three weeks to make themselves known to an electorate, much of which was preoccupied with the increasingly difficult daily struggle of simply getting by. The national parties established almost no direct presence on the local level and presented themselves instead through centrally organized television advertisements. This was true also of those parties that had chosen to divide into regional groups; this provision of the electoral law, designed to create incentives for local activism, proved almost entirely ineffective. Only the well-organized DPR (which did not divide into regional parts) ran a vigorous campaign not only for its own party list and single-mandate candidates but against the constitution and against the Federation Council race (in which they urged people to vote "against all candidates"). Their activities were the nearest thing to traditional European campaigning: strongly worded campaign leaflets distributed in the streets by party workers with megaphones.

Somewhat more surprising, and significant, was the weakness of party presence in the individual candidate elections. Not only did the majority of candidates run as independents, but many considered this an electoral asset, emphasizing that their independence meant freedom from party discipline, although they sometimes expressed their support for a particular party. This ambivalent attitude to parties among candidates, and consequent attempts to reap the benefits of both political independence and party association, sometimes gave rise to elaborate formulations. The ex-obkom first secretary stood "independently" of the Communist party to which he belonged. Bronislav Puchkov declared himself to be "nonparty [who] shares the electoral platform of the Agrarian Party."[28] The minority of candidates who were party representatives naturally campaigned on their parties' platforms, although many emphasized their party leader (especially Travkin, Yavlinskii, and Zhirinovskii) in order to fix party identity in the minds of voters.[29]

In the absence of strong party identities among candidates and of sharp differences between their individual programs, campaigns tended to emphasize the candidates' personal qualities and experience. They were in a sense not campaigns at all, lacking the interactions—attacks, criticisms, and rebuttals—between political rivals that are the staple of electoral combat elsewhere. They more resembled parallel exercises in self-publicity that, given the conditions of brevity and apathy in which they were conducted, sought above all simply to acquaint voters with the candidates. These background conditions also influenced the methods that were used to achieve this. Most candidates decided early not to organize public meetings or rallies, assuming that few people would bother to attend, and the few meetings held between candidates were poorly advertised and sparsely attended. Candidates did, however, visit factories, an efficient way to meet a large number of people. This tends to confirm the important political role of such large economic units: they served both as bases of support for factory directors seeking political office and as important campaigning sites. Of course, where a candidate actually administered a factory, then access was denied to political rivals; consequently, such meetings were sometimes held surreptitiously.[30] Campaign leaflets were widely distributed, including, in the case of richer candidates, lavish color posters whose ostentation evoked disapproval in many voters. But when they could afford to, candidates put greatest emphasis on the mass media, especially television. While local television stations allotted half an hour free to each candidate, including two "telemarathons" at the beginning and the end of the campaign, additional air time for political commercials could be bought at an average cost of 80,000 rubles a minute, which only the wealthier candidates could afford.[31]

Given that the candidate campaigns were focused on the personality and backgrounds of the individuals taking part, the response among voters was highly significant: they persistently sought to link these locally specific contests to those being fought simultaneously on a national scale. Voters tried to establish candidates' party affiliation, including whether they had been members of the Communist Party of the Soviet Union. This behavior suggests that in the absence of strong cues for choosing between individual candidates, voters attempted to apply those that were being formed in the more informative and highly structured national party competition. Several candidates also reported that one of the most frequently asked questions was how to vote in the constitutional referendum,[32] which a significant majority of them opposed. Here it seems the direction of causation was reversed: that is, voters were seeking guidance from candidates about the constitution rather than choosing between candidates according to their attitudes. Thus, while the candidates themselves conducted their campaigns in relative isolation from the other elections simultaneously taking place, voters sought to establish connections between different kinds of campaigns being fought at different levels and thus to integrate their voting decisions into a single, consistent political orientation.

Nonetheless, the local candidate races remained largely insulated from the national party and referendum campaigns. It was this phenomenon, carefully managed by Governor Nemtsov, that enabled him to mobilize the local resources of Fond Vybor and his own popularity in implementing by far the most effective electoral strategy in the region. This strategy was much more significant in the open Duma races than in the race for the Federation Council, in which victory for the popular Nemtsov-Krest'yaninov ticket ("From the rebirth of Nizhnii to the rebirth of Russia") could be assumed. Even here, however, both were careful to distinguish themselves from the party campaigns, choosing to run as independent candidates despite being approached by several parties[33]—although this did not prevent Nemtsov from announcing his support for Yabloko, headed by his friend Grigorii Yavlinskii who had worked on the Nizhnii Novgorod reforms or from urging voters to approve the draft constitution.[34] Nemtsov also maintained his distance from the government, voicing criticism of the conditions in which the elections were being held and of economic policy,[35] thus helping to distinguish his own position from that of a reformist government with which he otherwise enjoyed close links.

On the one hand, Nemtsov sought to reinforce the insulation of the local electoral arena from the national one. On the other hand, he sought to *strengthen* the connections between the two elections conducted on the local level by campaigning not only on his own behalf in the Federation Council race but for one candidate in each of the six single-mandate Duma districts, all of whom were also independents. Fond Vybor helped to organize and finance these campaigns, help that included the production of "troiki"—leaflets picturing Nemtsov, Krest'yaninov, and the chosen candidate together—and especially, long and superbly produced television commercials. In addition, the local television stations used their discretion to promote certain candidates, especially those favored by Governor Nemtsov. These efforts were concentrated particularly in two districts: strongly conservative Arzamas, where the twenty-six-year-old Sergei Voronov, the oblast's representative in Moscow, was competing in a field that included Boris Pevnitskii, the representative from the nuclear facility Arzamas-16; and in Semenov, where the ethnographer Chertoritskaya faced the ex-obkom First Secretary Khodyrev. This latter race was perhaps the most symbolically significant in the entire region: an academic without political experience, supported by the governor and by "new money" competing against a former apparatchik turned businessperson whose glossy leaflets also implied the support of the governor, even as he used Communist networks to build electoral support.[36] It also produced the only serious controversies in the elections.[37] In each of these districts the governor's candidate won by a margin of less than 3 percent over the nearest rival in the two tightest races in the region. There is every reason to believe that the governor's support and Fond Vybor's resources played a decisive role in these victories.

Voting

Four questions can be asked about the election results. Who voted? Did they understand the system? How satisfied were they with the political choices available to them? How did they vote? There are no survey data for Nizhnii Novgorod, but within two months the Regional Election Commission published complete election results down to the raion level—the only region known to the researchers in this volume to have done so.[38] The first and last questions can thus only be answered somewhat impressionistically (incurring the risk of ecological fallacy) by comparing the results across raions and districts. However, answers to the second and third, less frequently asked, questions are suggested by the election data, from which some striking conclusions can be drawn.

It is helpful to begin by reconstructing the sequence of events that occurred when a voter went to the polls. First, he or she had to decide to vote. The average turnout in the region, 51.9 percent, was marginally lower than in the country as a whole. Participation exhibited a strong inverse relationship to urbanization: whereas only 46 percent voted in Nizhnii Novgorod city itself, turnout was double that in the most rural raions.

Second, having decided to go to the polling station, the voter actually had to vote, and this presupposes that he or she understood the electoral system. This can be measured by the number of invalid ballots, for which statistics also exist. In Western countries, spoiling a ballot is often a means of expressing political protest, but in the Russian elections the possibility of voting "against all candidates" suggests that ballot spoilage was accidental and a consequence of not understanding how the system works. There were two reasons why a Russian voter might have been confused by the electoral system. It was the first time that voters were required to put a cross in a square by the preferred candidate, rather than cross out all the alternatives. More significant, the sheer number of choices (thirteen in the case of party lists) might have proved disorienting. The results, indeed, show that the number of invalid ballots rose steadily with the number of political choices available: on average, 2.9 percent in the referendum, 5.1 percent in the Federation Council race, 8.1 percent in the single-mandate districts, and 9.1 percent in the party-list election. This ordering holds within each district. These figures are very high by European and American standards.

Third, those voters who understood the electoral system had to decide whether to vote for a candidate or party or to vote against them all as a gesture of dissatisfaction with the available choice, or perhaps more fundamentally with the political system itself. The first trend that emerges is that the figures "against all parties" are much lower than "against all candidates." The relevant figures are 4.6 percent "against all" in the party lists, 12.9 percent "against all candidates" in the Federation Council race, and an average of 15 percent "against all candidates" in the single-mandate districts. There is some irony in the fact that although many candidates saw their "independent" status as an asset, the overall level of voter dissatisfaction with parties was much lower than with individual candidates.

In addition, there was considerable variation among the districts in the level of dissatisfaction with candidates. The mean figure of 15 percent conceals considerable variation: a low of 11.6 percent in Dzerzhinsk and an astonishing 23.2 percent in Kanavin district. Indeed, "against all candidates" actually came first in the latter contest. According to the original electoral rules, the contest should have been considered invalid (Article 38.2.z of the election statute). But a subsequent decree (No. 1846, November 6, 1993) annulled this provision and, after some initial confusion, Vadim Bulavinov, who trailed "against all candidates" by 3 percent, was declared the winner. In the other district in Nizhnii Novgorod city, Avtozavod, "against all candidates" came second, with nearly 14 percent of the vote. These are very high levels of dissatisfaction, manifested in precisely those areas in which turnout was lowest. Furthermore, they occurred in those districts that offered the largest number of candidates (ten and thirteen, respectively) to choose from, suggesting not merely dissatisfaction with the available choice but a deeper disaffection with the political system as a whole.[39]

Fourth, once a voter had decided to vote for a candidate or party, rather than against all of them, he or she had to decide for whom to vote. As elsewhere in Russia, there is evidence that a large proportion of voters had not done so by the last week of the election and that many were still unsure even as they stepped into the polling booth and read the ballot paper on which was written some biographical information about each candidate. It was not much to go on—year of birth, place of residence, and occupation—but for undecided voters it provided crucial clues to how they should vote. Any candidate not resident in the oblast was instantly rejected.[40] More significant, certain professions—in particular, those with legal and economic training—were widely seen as appropriate preparation for a deputy, and certain others were by contrast treated with suspicion.[41] This helps explain Bulavinov's surprising success. One of the least-known candidates, he was identified on the ballot with his profession (lawyer) written below his name. The way professions were thus described had been a minor source of controversy at the beginning of the campaign, and a degree of haggling took place between candidates preparing to register and the local election commissions. It seems clear that in conditions in which a large proportion of the electorate remains undecided about its voting intentions up to the day of the elections, the "politics" of getting information on the ballot has an influence on the result.

Russian ballots provided more information than is typical of their Western counterparts, but in one crucial respect they provided less: they did not include party affiliation. Even if a candidate ran for the Duma by virtue of his inclusion on a party list, this was not indicated to the voter. The evidence suggests that this omission, by reinforcing the insulation of local candidate campaigns from party competition at the national level, had significant electoral consequences. For example, the sole LDPR candidate, Igor' Veletminskii, received only 7.3 percent of the vote,[42] whereas his party came first with 18.3 percent in the same district. The fact that the Regional Election Commission received many calls from voters asking who the LDPR candidate was tends to confirm the impression that voters were seeking to identify candidates according to party membership.[43] The absence of such information on the ballots deprived them of the possibility of doing so, ensuring that the two elections proceeded according to different logics and their outcomes determined by different factors.

The Results

As in Russia as a whole, the LDPR came first and Russia's Choice second in Nizhnii Novgorod. Zhirinovskii's party swept all but the main electoral district in the oblast capital, although it received 3.7 percent less than its national average.[44] Although conservative opposition parties as a whole (nationalists and Communists) did slightly worse (4.3 percent) than in the country as a whole, and reform parties as a whole did marginally better (a result consistent with the April referendum that showed the region to be 3.6 percent more proreform), the results in Nizhnii Novgorod mirror those in Russia more closely than any other region in this volume. The same is true of voting in the constitutional referendum, with virtually identical proportions of the population supporting the draft law.

One highly distinctive feature of local party voting, however, does emerge. Although reformers did slightly better in Nizhnii Novgorod, the leading reform party, Russia's Choice, itself did worse. This is because a significant share of the reform vote went instead to Yabloko, which received over 50 percent more of the vote in Nizhnii Novgorod than in the country as a whole (12.2 percent compared with 7.9 percent) and did better in only six other regions. While some of this support was probably a consequence of Yabloko leader Yavlinskii's earlier involvement with Nizhnii's reform program, a compelling explanation can be offered in orthodox spatial terms. Like his friend Nemtsov, Yavlinskii had impeccable reformist credentials yet could be strongly critical of government policy. Daniel Treisman, in chapter 5 of this volume, reminds us of the importance of understanding the "destination" of the antigovernment opposition vote. The destination of the *pro*reform vote—of those who support fundamental economic transition but not necessarily the present government—is no less significant. Yabloko was the only credible destination of voters who supported reform but not the current reformist government.

While the distribution of support within the reform camp reflects the distinctive character of Nizhnii Novgorod's recent development, as a region both supportive of economic reform and increasingly disaffected with the central government, the results of party and referendum voting are otherwise consistent both with national trends and with earlier patterns of voting in Nizhnii, suggesting that local factors played little part in these contests. Furthermore, the distribution of such voting across the six districts in the oblast shows that support for the constitution and for reform parties was strongest in urban areas and weakest in rural ones. Together, these factors—the consistency of regional and national results, the stability of results, and the distribution of support within the region— confirm the impression that both contests were fought at the national level, largely on television, and were determined primarily by large-scale demographic factors.[45] As will be seen, however, none of these statements holds for the other two, locally centered, parts of the election.

Unlike the constitutional referendum and party-list campaigns, the contest among candidates to the Federation Council was fought only within Nizhnii Novgorod (although, of course, each subject of the Federation held such an election). To no one's surprise, Governor Nemtsov and oblast soviet chair Krest'yaninov won easily, receiving respectively 80.2 percent and 68.7 percent, with the young Mirnyi getting 20.4 percent. But while these two leading reformers were many times more popular throughout the region than were reform parties, the distribution of that support is somewhat unexpected: while support for reforming *parties* was highest in Nizhnii Novgorod city, support for the reforming *governor* was lowest.

Four out of the six single-mandate races were won by the candidate backed by the governor and the formidable Fond Vybor. This support appears to have been especially important where it was most concentrated, in conservative Arzamas, where Voronov beat Pevnitskii from Arzamas-16, and in rural Semenov, where Chertoritskaya beat Khodyrev, both by less than 3 percent. In each case, however, the replacement of a French-style runoff system with a single election helped to split the preponderant conservative vote: destructive competition among conservative candidates enabled more liberal ones to win. The other two races were won somewhat more comfortably by Mikhail Seslavinskii, a liberal and popular Supreme Soviet deputy in Dzerzhinsk, and the local financier Yevgenii Bushmin in Sergach (results of the candidate races are given in table 14-1). Voting patterns within large districts show that almost every candidate had a local base of support, particularly in their native raion, where they polled very well, but performed poorly in the rest of the district. It thus seems that victory went to the candidate who by the end of the campaign was best known overall in the district and that this in turn was most effectively achieved by Fond Vybor's political advertising that linked candidates to the popular governor. Particularly striking was the fact that such name recognition was not only enjoyed by local notables but could be *created* at exceedingly short notice.

Nemtsov's candidates lost both elections in the city of Nizhnii Novgorod itself. In Avtozavod district, Tsapin won the easiest victory of any candidate, but only by virtue of his directorship of the GAZ factory, in whose raion he gained a massive 68.4 percent of the vote; in the rest of the district he was not even first. And in the peculiar Kanavin election, Bulavinov won despite gaining fewer votes than "against-all candidates." With the exception of Tsapin, no state enterprise directors won, and with the exception of Bushmin neither did any private entrepreneur. No candidate of any party was successful, nor was any member of the old nomenklatura, with the ex-party officials Khodyrev and Mal'tsev coming second in their respective races. Support from the governor was by far the strongest predictor of electoral victory. Furthermore, the success of both Nemtsov and his candidates ran directly counter to national demographic trends linking support of reform with degree of urbanization. Remarkably, the governor not only did better outside Nizhnii Novgorod city than in it but was more successful in projecting electoral influence into the more rural areas of the surrounding region than his counterparts in Moscow and St. Petersburg were in Moscow and Leningrad oblasts.

The political consequences of the governor's influence may be seen by comparing the six deputies elected from Nizhnii Novgorod to the Duma in December 1993 with their twenty-four predecessors who had been returned to the much larger Congress of Peoples' Deputies in March 1990. The latter

Table 14-1. *Winners of Duma and Federation Council Elections in Nizhnii Novgorod, December 1993*

Okrug	Candidate	Nominated by	Vote received (percent)
117	Tsapin	Independent[a]	43.4
118	Voronov	Independent (supported by Fond Vybor)[b]	
119	Seslavinskii	Independent (supported by Fond Vybor)	40.1
120	Bulavinov[c]	Independent	26.2
121	Chertoritskaya	Independent (supported by Fond Vybor)	32.5
122	Bushmin	Independent (supported by Fond Vybor)	39.8
Nizhnii Novgorod	Nemtsov	Independent (supported by Fond Vybor)	80.2
Nizhnii Novgorod	Krest'yaninov	Independent (supported by Fond Vybor)	68.7

Source: Calculated from A. I. Nekrasov, N. P. Emel'yanov, and Yu. D. Artamonov, *Vozvrashcheniye Gosudarstvennoi Dumy* (Nizhnii Novgorod, 1994).
a. Tsapin ran as an independent, but subsequently joined the Yabloko parliamentary group.
b. Fond Vybor was the regional electoral organization that supported the governor.
c. Bulavinov received more votes than any other candidate, but less than "against all candidates."

were almost wholly and equally divided between ten "conservatives" (seven of whom were "extreme conservatives") and ten "radicals" (seven of whom were "extreme radicals"). By contrast, five of the six deputies elected in 1993 were "extreme radicals," with the sixth (Tsapin) a "radical."[46] A politically polarized group of legislators became an overwhelmingly radical one, in striking contrast to national trends. While some of this shift can be accounted for by the greater competitiveness of the 1993 elections, thus enabling reformist electoral sentiment to be more accurately reflected, there is no evidence that the population of Nizhnii Novgorod itself had become significantly radical during those three years. In the party list competition the region showed itself, as before, to be 3 percent to 5 percent more reform minded than the country as a whole. Yet it elected among the most radical deputies in the country and the most radical of any of the regions studied in the present volume.[47]

This finding confirms in a most striking way a hypothesis that the course of the campaign and the results had already suggested: two distinct political spaces coexist on a single territory, possessing distinct properties and producing radically different outcomes yet operating largely independently of each other. Centrally organized campaigns, such as party contests and referenda, are conducted primarily through the national mass media and their results largely determined by historical and demographic factors; the main features of the party results in Nizhnii Novgorod could have been predicted from a knowledge of recent trends in the region and of national voting figures. But although parties are able to mount relatively coherent and informative campaigns, their organizational weaknesses prevent them from projecting their influence downward to the candidate races. This insulation of regionally based campaigns from nationally based campaigns, reinforced by the governor's deliberate weakening of electoral links between periphery and center, created the conditions in which local resources could play a decisive role. Detached from party competition, candidate races became contests between individuals, with victory going to the one who had become most widely known by election day. The strong alliance of political, economic, and media elites enjoyed an overwhelming preponderance of the means necessary to achieve name recognition. In the absence of strong national electoral structures, Fond Vybor and the candidates it supported functioned as a dominant local "party."

Thus two distinct electoral campaigns emerged in Nizhnii Novgorod during November and December 1993: a national party competition won by conservatives and a local candidate competition won by reformers. These two political spaces were fully sealed off on election day by the absence of party affiliation on candidates' ballots. There is clear evidence that voters persistently tried to use the more informative and popular party system to guide their decisionmaking in the candidate elections. The withholding of this information deprived them of the possibility of doing so and perpetuated the underdevelopment of a truly national party system. It seems that a simple change in this "rule of the game"—the possibility of including party membership on the ballot—would have a significant impact on the Russian political system by meeting the voters' evident need to anchor their political choices in party labels.

Conclusion

The reforming Russian government waged an electoral campaign that was disastrous almost everywhere, including Nizhnii Novgorod. The reforming administration of Nizhnii Novgorod waged a campaign that was almost entirely successful. How can this sharp contrast in the fates of reformers in power be explained and what does it tell us about the evolution of the Russian political system? It is useful to begin by recalling the three sets of questions concerning the economic, political, and center-periphery features of Nizhnii Novgorod that together distinguish it as an electoral subsystem.

First, the elections reveal some surprising things about the political consequences of local economic reforms: economic issues were *not* more salient in this "reform capital" than elsewhere in the country. In particular, there was little evidence of a crystallization of political interests around new economic cleavages. Economic problems were emphasized by all candidates but did not sharply divide them. There were, however, significant variations in levels of participation among economic interests. Industrial workers, one of the groups most threatened by further reform, remained strikingly unorganized and underrepresented, showing solidarity neither with each other nor, for the most part, with their own factory directors who stood as candidates. By contrast, the new private commercial and financial interests that had emerged under economic reform played a significant, though largely indirect, role. Although few businesspeople actually stood as candidates, they donated large sums of money to Fond Vybor and helped Nemtsov and those he supported to win elections.

Second, this strong alliance between "new money" and the regional administration, in which wealth created under reform policies supported reform politicians, was perhaps the most significant political consequence of regional economic reform.[48] It was a key element in the new administration's capacity to mobilize the advantages of incumbency to win elections at the local level. The coalition it formed with business and media elites endowed it with a combination of resources unmatched by political rivals. Old established political networks that proved decisive in more conservative parts of European Russia could not bring victory when divorced from incumbency, as the defeat of former apparatchiki showed.[49] Nor could wealth alone buy votes as it had registration signatures, as the defeat of business candidates showed. "I will buy the voters," declared Gennadii Gabov, the wealthiest of them all; he bought 8,000 registration signatures but only 2,300 votes. Only Tsapin's directorship of one of the largest factories in Russia provided an alternative base for electoral victory.

Third, in two distinct ways the weakness of the links between center and periphery in Russia enabled regional leaderships like that in Nizhnii Novgorod to wage effective campaigns. The significant diffusion from 1991 of political authority and economic control to the provinces of a traditionally highly centralized country gave local incumbents considerable advantages in electoral combat. But their success depended also on a more contingent and less irreversible *electoral* decentralization that ensured that locally and nationally based contests would be largely immune from each other. On the one hand, the popularity of a regional reform administration did not dispose the Nizhnii Novgorod voter much more than the average Russian to support national reform parties, a result confirmed by subsequent elections to the Duma in December 1995 and the presidency in June 1996. On the other hand, and more significant, national parties were unable to reach down into the district races and translate antipathy toward national reformers into a similar attitude toward their provincial counterparts. Sheltered behind this relatively impermeable barrier to national forces, the governor's alliance of elites was thus able to deploy its preponderance of local power to impressive effect. Nemtsov carefully distanced himself from government reformers as well as national parties, even as he ran on his own successful record as a local reformer—a strategy that itself partly reflected the strong secular decline in support for national reformers among the local population. This testifies to the current weakness of center-periphery electoral links in Russia, for if such links were important anywhere, it would be in Nizhnii Novgorod. Indeed, Nizhnii Novgorod stands out as a most vivid illustration of the argument that provincialism, rather than being conservative in nature, is fully compatible with support for reform.[50]

It follows that the capacity to convert regional incumbency into electoral power in *national* legislative elections (especially on behalf of other candidates) will be retained only to the extent that provincial, territorially organized bases of mobilization remain stronger than national, vertically integrated ones. There is already evidence that the balance may be shifting in favor of the latter, leading to the emergence of a more unified electoral space. One important source of local insulation has already gone: the electoral law governing the parliamentary election in December 1995 for the first time stipulated the inclusion on ballots of candidates' party affiliation. As predicted above, this had a significant effect. In that more recent election, incumbents in the three most rural okrugs, all supported by Fond Vybor in 1993, lost their seats: the former apparatchiki Khodyrev and Mal'tsev got their revenge on Chertoritskaya and Bushmin; and the nuclear city Arzamas-16 finally got one of its own elected. The results of candidate races thus came to resemble more closely those of party voting, a trend observed elsewhere in Russia, particularly in the individual seats captured by the Communist party. As discussed earlier, there is evidence that the voters themselves want to use party competition to inform their choices about individual candidates; if electoral laws and the fractiousness of politicians do not prevent parties from responding, then a more robust party system may emerge that will tend to unify the bases of voter choice and hence electoral outcomes across types of election. For the moment, however, whether the dual character of electoral space proves to be a birth pang of the Russian political system or a birthmark remains to be seen.

Notes

1. Both oblast and city were named Gorky between 1932 and 1991.

2. See the report by Grigorii Yavlinskii's EPItsentr team, *Nizhegorodskii Prolog: ekonomika i politika v Rossii* (Nizhnii Novgorod: Tsenovaia Politika, 1992).

3. For example, industrial production fell by only 4.2 percent in 1993 compared with 16.2 percent in Russia as a whole, one of the smallest declines in the country. "O Khode Ekonomicheskoi Reformy v Nizhegorodskoi Oblasti," vol. 2 (Nizhnii Novgorod: Nizhegorodskii Oblastnoi Komitet po Statistike, 1994).

4. For a discussion of the challenges facing this city in the post-Soviet era, see Kimberly Marten Zisk, "Arzamas-16: Economics and Security in a Closed Nuclear City," *Post-Soviet Affairs*, vol. 11, no. 1 (January–March 1995), pp. 57–80.

5. This phenomenon is described, in the comparative context of other Russian regions, by A. Magomedov, "Politicheskiye Elity Rossiiskoi Provintsii," *Mirovaya Ekonomika i Mezhdunarodniye Otnosheniya*, no. 4 (1994), pp. 72–79.

6. For a discussion of the problems that have arisen from conflicts between these institutions in other regions, see Jeffrey W. Hahn, "Conclusions: Common Features of Post-Soviet Local Politics," in Theodore H. Friedgut and Jeffrey W. Hahn, eds., *Local Power and Post-Soviet Politics* (Armonk, N.Y.: M. E. Sharpe, 1994), p. 272.

7. Gorky, as it was after 1932, became known as a "school for cadres," a region where promising young party officials were sent to gain experience. Lazar Kaganovich and Andrei Zhdanov, for example, both served time as obkom first secretary there.

8. Another reason for the political stability of the region, therefore, is the absence of conflict between the holders of these two positions.

9. These links were confirmed after the elections when Krest'yaninov was repeatedly urged—and declined—to stand for the position of deputy speaker in the new Federation Council.

10. Approval of the government's social and economic policies (question 2) in the April 1993 referendum was 3.6 percent higher than in the country as a whole.

11. Comparison of the 1991 presidential election with the 1993 referendum shows that Nizhnii Novgorod was one of only twenty-nine regions—and the only one north of the 55th parallel—where support for Yeltsin fell between the two elections. A. Sobyanin, E. Gel'man, and O. Kayunov, "Politicheskii Klimat v Rossii v 1991–1993," *Mirovaya Ekonomika i Mezhdunarodniye Otnosheniya*, no. 9, 1993, pp. 26–27. Local polls also show that after mid-1992 voters increasingly distinguished between the reformist

president, whose popularity fell substantially, and the reformist governor, whose approval rating remained very high. Yavlinskii, *Nizhegorodskii Prolog*, p. 74.

12. For example, in April 1992 Nizhnii Novgorod successfully took the central government to court over nonpayment of wages—under the Soviet-era labor code! "Yavlinskii Tries His Reform in One Province," *Current Digest of the Post-Soviet Press*, vol. XLIV, no. 34 (September 23, 1992), p. 9. The region has also clashed with Moscow over its privatization program. Kathryn Elizabeth Stoner, "Local Heroes: Political Exchange and Governmental Performance in Provincial Russia" (Ph.D. dissertation, Harvard University, 1994), pp. 159–60.

13. *Nizhegorodskii rabochii*, September 29, 1993.

14. *Delo*, no. 36, September 24–30, 1993; *Nizhegorodskiye novosti*, October 14, 1993.

15. Interview with Krest'yaninov, December 22, 1993.

16. Some candidates can be classified in more than one way. In such cases, I have chosen the criterion that seemed most politically relevant in their campaign.

17. The tendency for Communists to stand in rural areas for this reason had been noted by local sociologists as early as 1990. See V. O. Rukavishnikov, ed., *Vybory-90: Itogi issledovanii v Gork'ovskoi oblasti* (Moscow: Institut Sotsiologii, Akademiya Nauk SSSR, 1990).

18. State enterprise here also means those enterprises currently in the process of becoming joint-stock companies (aktsionnernoye obshchestvo).

19. *Birzha*, no. 47, November 1994. The candidature of Sergei Maslagin, running in Dzerzhinsk district, was also reportedly decided for him by his enterprise. These cases point to an intriguing phenomenon of "company candidates," an especially direct way of trying to convert economic resources into political ones.

20. Where party lists chose not to divide into regional sections (as provided for in art. 38:4 of the election statute), a candidate's position on the party list served to rank his or her importance in that party. Igor Veletminskii was 119th on the LDPR list.

21. Interview with Chertoritskaya, December 9, 1993.

22. A. I. Nekrasov, N. P. Emel'yanov, and Yu. D. Artamonov, *Vozvrashcheniye Gosudarstvennoi Dumy: Perviye posle 1917 goda mnogopartiiniye vybory v Rossii* (Nizhnii Novgorod: Gipp "Nishpoligraf," 1994) provides excellent summaries of the candidates' programs. It is also a unique source of election statistics.

23. *Delo*, no. 46 (December 3–9, 1993). Tsapin expressed similar sentiments graphically, if inelegantly: "You can write as many laws as you like according to legal theory, but if they do not take into account the realities of things, then their paragraphs will grasp life like hooks, constantly hindering it . . . 'even a little practice is worth a big theory.'" Nekrasov Emel'yanov, and Artamanov, *Vozvrashcheniye Gosudarstvennoi Dumy*, p. 101.

24. This phrase was used in one of Tsapin's leaflets. Sergei Maslagin, director of a large factory and a candidate in Dzerzhinskii district, declared that "from a 'super-power' our country is becoming a 'raw-material appendage' of Western states, that votes for any proposals of the USA." *Nizhegorodskiye novosti*, November 30 1993. By contrast, Vladimir Danilov, the representative of the private trading company Russkii Klub, openly declared himself satisfied with Russian foreign policy. Nizhnii Novgorod Television, 20.00 [10:00 p.m.], November 23, 1993.

25. For example, Yevgenii Zagriadskii's address during the first election telemarathon.

26. There was only one explicitly Russian nationalist candidate, and he received less than 7 percent of the vote in his district.

27. Valence and position issues are discussed in David Butler and Donald Stokes, *Political Change in Britain: The Evolution of Electoral Choice*, 2d ed. (New York: Macmillan, 1974), p. 292.

28. Nekrasov, Emel'yanov and Artamanov, *Vozvrashcheniye Gosudarstvennoi Dumy*, p. 109.

29. This was hardly avoidable by the representatives of Yabloko, which must be one of the few political movements in the world whose title consists of the names of its leaders.

30. Most candidates assembled a "team" to organize their campaign. One interesting consequence of this was the emergence of a local infrastructure of political advisers, poll-takers, and "politologists" who were paid to give information and advice.

31. Even money was not enough. The television stations owned the best technical facilities, which they put in the service of candidates favored by the governor; as a result, his commercials were slick and professionally made. Others had to make do with inferior means: the commercials of the fabulously wealthy Gennadii Gabov resembled home videos.

32. Interview with Bushmin, December 24, 1993; interview with Veletminskii, January 20, 1994.

33. Interview with Krest'yaninov, December 22, 1993.

34. Krest'yaninov wrote a series of articles in the local press supporting the constitution. *Nizhegorodskiye novosti*, nos. 131, 133, November 1993. Yevgenii Sabashnikov wrote against it. *Delo*, no. 44, November 19–25, 1993.

35. *Nizhegorodskiye novosti*, no. 133, November 1993; Jerry F. Hough, "The Russian Election of 1993: Public Attitudes toward Economic Reform and Democratization," *Post-Soviet Affairs*, vol. 10 (January–March 1994), p. 5.

36. Chertoritskaya, an expert on the Old Believers (a schismatic religious group dating from the Niconian reforms of the mid-seventeenth century), also benefited from the support of the significant Old Believer population in Semenov district, with which her research had made her familiar. In Russia's only previous multiparty election in December 1917, the Old Believer party did better in Nizhnii Novgorod and Perm' regions than anywhere else in the country. Oliver H. Radkey, *Russia Goes to the Polls: The Election to the All-Russian Constituent Assembly, 1917* (Cornell University Press, 1989), pp. 154–56.

37. Khodyrev took up the allegation made in *Moskovskiye novosti*, November 21, 1993, p. A10, that Andrei Kliment'yev, a prominent local businessperson and close friend of the governor, had donated 100 million rubles to Chertoritskaya's campaign. Khodyrev himself was accused of including the governor's photograph in a campaign leaflet, implying that he enjoyed Nemtsov's support. The fact that the former obkom first secretary sought to link himself with the reforming governor is itself significant.

38. Nekrasov, Emel'yanov, and Artamanov, *Vozvrashcheniye Gosudarstvennoi Dumy*.

39. Removal of the original provision rendered the act of voting "against-all candidates" practically meaningless. It did have one curious consequence, however: such votes are considered legitimate acts of electoral participation, and thus contribute to the attainment of the 25 percent turnout threshold necessary for an election to be valid.

40. Thus Sergei Kapterev, a well-known entrepreneur with a potentially good chance of winning, came last because he was registered as living in Moscow, even though he worked and lived in Nizhnii Novgorod.

41. See, for example, the poll in *Nizhegorodskii rabochii*, November 23, 1993, which showed that 46 percent of people wanted to see economists and 38 percent, jurists, elected to the Duma.

42. Percentages of the vote gained by candidates and parties are calculated as a proportion of total votes cast for candidates and parties, excluding those cast "against all."

43. Interview with Aleksandr Kokhas', chair of the Kanavin district election commission, March 23, 1994.

44. These comparisons draw on statistics supplied by the Regional Election Commission, as those published centrally do not take into account votes cast "against-all candidates."

45. A notable exception was Arzamas, a mixed urban-rural district that was by far the most hostile both to reform parties (Russia's Choice came only fourth) and the constitution (where a majority opposed it). Some unexpected local factor outweighed broader trends. A comparison may be drawn with the district of Engels in Saratov oblast, which similarly displays a distinct local conservatism. See chapter 15 of this volume.

46. This classification of deputies is borrowed from A. Sobyanin, whose ratings measure the degree of deputies' reform-mindedness by their voting records. For purposes of comparison I have collapsed his 200-point scale used in evaluating deputies elected in 1993 into the 8-point scale used in 1990. The 1993 ratings are from A. Sobyanin, E. Gel'man, and O. Kayunov, *Golosovaniya deputatov Gosudarstvennoi Dumy* (1994).

47. With the exception of Moscow city and a handful of small, peripheral regions (Adygeia, Karelia, Kamchatka, Astrakhan, Chitinsk), only Tomsk oblast returned a more radical group of deputies. The *increase* in reform-mindedness of deputies elected in 1993 in comparison with their 1990 counterparts is even more striking: their average Sobyanin score rose by 59 points, whereas across Russia it fell by 20 points.

48. Unlike the alliance of "new money" with *insurgent* reformers in Kursk, its alliance with reformers *in power* in Nizhnii Novgorod never looked likely to disintegrate. See chapter 16 of this volume.

49. Compare chapters 15 on Saratov and 16 on Kursk in this volume.

50. See Josephine Andrews and Kathryn Stoner-Weiss, "Regionalism and Reform in Provincial Russia," *Post-Soviet Affairs*, vol. 11, no. 4 (1995), pp. 384–405.

Saratov

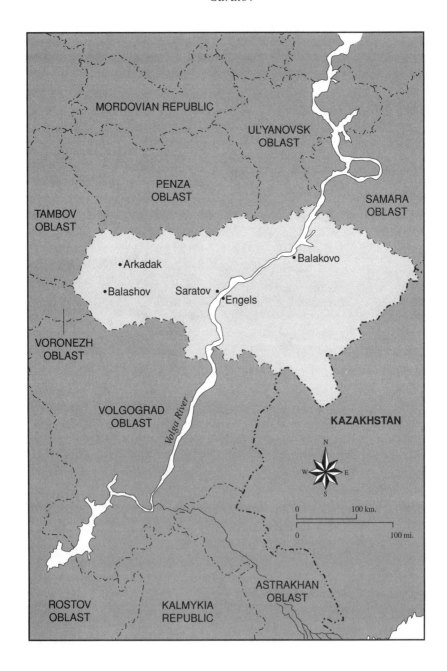

CHAPTER FIFTEEN

Political Ambition, Elite Competition, and Electoral Success in Saratov Oblast

Regina Smyth

THE BALLOT of December 12 presented Saratov's voters with puzzling choices among seemingly endless alternatives. It is perhaps surprising that most regional parties and candidates offered little information to simplify voters' decisions. Only the regional organizations of the Communist Party of the Russian Federation (KPRF) and Liberal Democratic Party of Russia (LDPR) made party-based appeals and worked to expand ties to the electorate. In response, voters narrowly confirmed their past pattern of supporting conservative representatives.

This chapter focuses on why other parties evidenced a persistent lack of leadership in the electoral arena and why they remained isolated from the voters whose support they needed to gain political power. In a series of political races in which single-member district candidates won by margins of less than 1 percent of the popular vote, a conservative outcome was not inevitable. Sound political choices on the part of individual aspirants—in particular, a reluctance to invest in party building or, indeed, to associate with their party—led to anomalous outcomes in single-member districts and a disastrous outcome for reform parties in the party-list race. Conservatives prevailed in regional elections because they were better politicians who responded effectively to the incentives embedded in the electoral law and political environment at the time of elections.

463

In Saratov, both the regional KPRF and the LDPR capitalized on their ability to mobilize existing organizations that had established ties to the regional electorate. These organizations enabled them to solve the collective-actions problems inherent in party building. In addition, these parties were able to exploit existing cleavages to expand their appeal beyond their organizational base. In contrast, reformers failed to use available resources to formulate a strategy to overcome these advantages. Although some reformers built regional party organizations, the organizations were not used to connect to the electorate, nor did they solve the problem of interparty rivalry among elites. It is ironic to note that the availability of resources to reform parties precluded effective cooperation toward the collective goal of reform. The specter of political ambition undermined the opportunity for reform and moderate leaders to unite and overcome the legacy of the past. Election outcomes are shown in appendix 15A-1.

From Societal Cleavages to Mobilized Support: Organizing Saratov's Voters

Saratov city, founded in 1590, sits on the Volga River in the center of the region. It is typical of many oblast centers in that it consists of a historical city center surrounded by enormous industrial complexes. It is also typical in size; Saratov's population had grown to just around one million in 1993. Across the river from the center sprawls the oblast's second city, Engels. Around these two cities radiates the Russian steppe, with collective farms infrequently dotted with small towns and villages. Against this backdrop, electoral contestants in 1993 confronted the problem of how to construct successful teams of elites, activists, and voters given significant uncertainty about the future of the regional economic base and consequent uncertainty about voters' interests. An examination of their efforts illustrates the central problem that stymied many attempts (the KPRF and LDPR being notable exceptions) to win political power: a failure to form organizational or programmatic connections to the electorate.

The region's heterogeneous representation in the national Congress of People's Deputies and in the oblast soviet elected in 1990 demonstrates the diversity of elite interests. The extent of conflict appeared in the regional soviet's reaction to the presidential order to disband in the fall of 1993. The local legislature voted narrowly to sanction Boris Yeltsin's dissolution of the Congress of People's Deputies and to ignore his order to disband the regional soviet. In response, the reformers resigned, mandating new elections.

Such elite-level conflict is mirrored in mass opinion data. Survey data collected by the editors of this volume show an electorate divided into thirds. One-third voiced positive affect toward Russia's Choice and one-third voiced negative affect. The remainder were either uncertain or did not know the party. The same pattern is reflected in assessments of LDPR and KPRF. Voters showed notable uncertainty across a wide range of issues. For instance, 30 percent of respondents were not sure how their economic situation would change over the next year; 69 percent were unsure about the implications of reform in the next five years. Such uncertainty about parties and issues was reflected in expressed candidate and party preference. When surveyed, more than 50 percent of the respondents who intended to vote had not decided which vote they would cast. Given this flux in mass opinion, political entrepreneurs, both candidates and party leaders, had the opportunity to reinforce or reshape existing social cleavages to win support in their bids for office.

Many of the potential cleavages noted in other chapters of this book also existed in Saratov. The most prevalent of these divisions, between urban and rural areas and agricultural and industrial production, constituted a significant legacy of the Soviet period. Both the formal party structures and informal governance of the region institutionalized political competition over the allocation of resources between elites in each group. This competition continued throughout the early transition. Further, ethnic policy during the Stalin period exacerbated social tensions. In Saratov, conflict emerged between the Volga German minority and ethnic Russians.

Yet with the exception of the KPRF and LDPR, regional politicians either did not organize around these cleavages or were unsuccessful in their efforts. For example, despite past evidence of support for antireform candidates in rural areas and precipitous drops in agricultural production during the Yeltsin tenure, the urban-rural split was not reflected in party development. Most notably, the Agrarian party did not have an organization in the expansive rural areas of the region. KPRF efforts remained concentrated in the oblast capital. In fact, Russia's Choice was the only reform party to organize in these districts, but even it concentrated its efforts exclusively on the largest city in each of the rural districts: Balakovo to the east and Balashov to the west. Only the LDPR, Russia's Choice, and Yabloko supported single-member district candidates in these districts.

Industrial cleavages were similarly underexploited. Workers clustered in the industrial regions of the city were not well organized before elections and did not organize for political action to influence elections. In the oblast capital, military industrial plants, the backbone of Saratov's industrial economy, were particularly hard hit by the cutbacks in military spending. By 1993, economic reform had forced partial plant closings and cutbacks in regional schools, medical facilities, day care centers, and other service organizations. In spite of economic hardship, workers did not have independent political organizations. The large union structure of the Soviet period remained intact, although it was renamed The Professional Union of Workers and Free Labor. Funded by failing enterprises, the union drew its membership both from workers and management and its main function remained settling labor disputes on the shop floor. The union had a split personality. Although union leaders affiliated with Democratic Russia, the members remained divided.[1] The failure of the leaders to collect enough signatures to register as candidates indicates the lack of popular support for and lack of structure in the union organization.

In contrast to workers, the organized city pensioners were actively courted by the KPRF. These groups already had active organizations based on Soviet-period structures within the large enterprises. Prior to elections, these organizations held frequent meetings for members to air complaints and to demand resources from local government, often organizing letter-writing campaigns or visits to city officials. During the campaign period, factory-based pensioners' groups invited candidates to speak and to take part in question and answer periods. These were some of the very few well-attended candidate meetings during the campaign period. In an interview, Anatolii Gordeyev argued that veterans' and pensioners' organizations retained considerable membership overlap with the KPRF and provided a core of activists and voters for the party during the campaign period.[2]

Despite Saratov's ethnic homogeneity (reported in chapter 1 of this volume), ethnic conflict provided a basis of mobilization, but only for nationalist parties and candidates. By far the most salient regional issue for nationalist parties emerged in 1991, when Yeltsin decreed the formation of a new homeland in Engels as compensation for losses incurred when the ethnic Germans were deported early in World War II. In spite of the small number of Germans and the lack of any reference to the restoration of property in the decree, popular reaction was very strong. Local residents organized protests, blockaded roads and bridges, hung posters and leaflets, and distributed anonymous letters warning of a rebirth of fascism in order to garner support against the homeland movement in a regional referendum.[3] The referendum split local political forces.[4] The oblast administration supported the antihomeland movement, and reform leaders backed the proposed autonomous republic, confirming local suspicions that they placed Moscow's interests over regional interests. The conflict provided an opportunity for an outsider, Nikolai Lysenko, to enter the political arena and build a personal base of support among the anti-German nationalists and organize the National Republican Party of Russia (NRPR).[5] Most important, the nationalist movement spawned organizations that linked elite leaders to an interested public primed to pay close attention to nationalist issues. Lysenko's success demonstrated how the homeland issue could join political entrepreneurs, activists, and voters.

In contrast to the KPRF and LDPR, the reform parties had no organized voter base or institutional base. Although a small branch of Democratic Russia was formed in response to 1990 parliamentary elections, the reform movement stalled until 1991 when new organizations emerged in reaction to local officials who supported the coup plotters. Even turbulent national politics during the 1991 and 1993 coups did not provoke mass demonstrations as they had in other oblast capitals. From 1990 through 1993, the Democratic Party of Russia (DPR), the Republican party, the Social Democratic party, and Civic Union also functioned in Saratov, although none had a large popular following or influence in local government. The regional organization of Democratic Russia, the base of Russia's Choice in 1993, was rooted in the local Association of Entrepreneurs and Leaseholders. In addition, several candidates affiliated with the four democratic parties that organized regionally listed previous party affiliations in their public information, including Free Russia, The Party of Economic Freedom, and the Christian Democrats. The most active of these organizations, the DPR, fragmented in early 1993 in the wake of a split between its national leaders.[6]

District lines reinforced these cleavages, diluting support for the reform parties. The district boundaries of 1993 were drawn to separate urban and rural regions, giving voice to different interests. The oblast center was divided into two districts and the central regions, which had formerly been represented by radical deputies joined with Engels, a hotbed of conservative nationalist sentiment, to form one district. The industrial regions of the oblast center, whose representatives to the 1990 Congress of People's Deputies were mostly conservative, made up a second district. A third, predominantly rural, district around the small city of Balashov also incorporated areas of strong nationalist sentiment. A final district was formed to the east of the oblast capital. It included one city, Balakovo, together with a huge area of collective farms and small villages.

The Party-List Race: Building Ties to the Electorate

Once in the polling booth, Saratov's voters did support conservative parties, but the vote was not dominated by the KPRF. Surprising most local activists, the LDPR won a decisive victory in the party-list race, garnering 26.6 percent of voter support. The KPRF was second with 15.3 percent, and Russia's Choice, Yabloko, and Party of Russian Unity and Accord (PRES) together received barely more than 26 percent of the vote. Although it would be convenient to rely on a structural or socioeconomic explanation for the failure of the reform movement, and, in particular, for the poor showing of Russia's Choice, such an explanation is not very satisfying. As Yitzhak Brudny points out, a structural explanation does not provide much leverage in St. Petersburg, where strong support for reform parties was evidenced across the socioeconomic spectrum. This section argues that the results in the party-list race can be explained best by the political behavior of local leaders rather than the socioeconomic base of regional voters.

These results show the value of party organization. On average, parties lacking representation in the oblast did 18 percent worse than their national totals. Conversely, parties with regional organizations did considerably better than the national average with one glaring exception: Russia's Choice.

Simply having a regional organization did not guarantee electoral success. Rather, success in the list race depended on the incentives facing party leaders and candidates and on how they responded to these incentives. As Joseph Schlesinger wrote, "As rational individuals, office seekers will put forth only as much effort [in creating party organizations] as they believe is essential to realizing their own ambitions. They will only join in creating, shaping and maintaining political organizations best suited to their purpose."[7] Schlesinger's observation resonates with the Russian experience in 1993. Only the KPRF and LDPR members saw the development of a mass political party as necessary for election and only these national party leaders ensured that success in single-member districts would be tied to the success of the party. Among reformers, a number of regional elites used centrally generated party organizations to pursue individual electoral aspirations. Further, many reform candidates with access to personal resources avoided parties altogether, opting to run in the single-member districts or for the Council of Federation as independents. Both dynamics undermined efforts to build collective party identities.

These dynamics were magnified by incentives embedded in the electoral law. As Timothy Colton points out in the introduction to this volume, several provisions of law made it possible for candidates to avoid party affiliation. The mixed system and split-ballot structure ensured that candidates who wished to avoid party membership could do so. Voters were not constrained to vote for the same party in the list and single-member district races. In addition, the nomination procedure did little to dissuade independent candidates, because signatures could be easily collected without a party organization. These factors ensured that local list candidates had little chance of obtaining a seat in parliament and therefore little incentive to invest in party building. The law required the formation of a national (Moscow-based) list and allowed for a regional list that would be printed on the ballot. National parties developed a two-tiered system whereby seats would be awarded first to the central party nominees (often quite a long list) and then to local parties. Local party delegations were to be allocated seats according to the success of the party in that region and the likelihood of regional candidates making the cut was extremely small. Finally, candidates could run on both the party list (regional or central) and in the single-member districts. If a party's candidate was elected in a single-member district, the next candidate on the list could be awarded the seat.

Potential candidates reacted astutely to the incentives in the law. They quickly realized that the costs of party formation outweighed the benefits they would accrue—particularly in the short run. The calculation was clear: parties are an indirect means of obtaining political resources and, ultimately, votes. The primary resource that parties offer candidates in established democracies is a well-understood party label that acts as a signal for the electorate. In times of transition, the value of a party label is extremely uncertain: voters do not know what parties stand for and leaders and candidates do not know if the party will be discredited or defunct by the next election. As a result, candidates without political experience, monetary support, or organizational alternatives, particularly those previously excluded from political life, were left to build the satellite parties radiating from Moscow in the region. For these candidates, the institutional incentives were not to build party identification in the electorate (which would help their party in the list race), but rather to use party resources to create support for their own candidacies in single-member districts.

Saratov's Reform Movement: Intense Conflict, Weak Parties

As the previous section makes clear, individual responses to the national election law undermined efforts to link regional reform party organizations and the region's voters. Among candidates without access to political resources, the import of national parties from Moscow evoked intense competition. New alliances based on the desire of local leaders to form footholds in the political arena emerged in the registration period and divided existing coalitions.

These patterns were particularly acute among reform parties. One observer reported intense rivalry for control of the Russia's Choice bloc because candidates expected the central party to command large monetary resources and the support of the Yeltsin-appointed administrative apparatus throughout the oblast.[8] Those who were excluded from positions in the government party joined other groups, notably Yabloko and PRES. These three groups splintered the elite strata of the democratic movement in Saratov, undermining what political expertise had existed prior to the election period. Moreover, competition within these organizations diminished their ability to persuade voters to support them. Even parties with financial and organizational resources were paralyzed by internal friction. Like external competition, internal conflict was a disease of the reform parties and it was most obvious in the Russia's Choice organization.

The lack of attention to the collective enterprise within the Russia's Choice camp was the result of internal party politics. The early struggle for control of the party was won by Valerii Davydov who commandeered the Russia's Choice organization in support of his run for the Federation Council. The resources Davydov acquired with the Russia's Choice label were significant. The office manager at campaign headquarters confirmed that local officials were in constant contact with Moscow and received both monetary and material resources from the central party organization. Several times during the campaign, central party officials visited local headquarters and even campaigned for Davydov and other candidates. This effort was unparalleled among the other parties.

The availability of central resources transformed Russia's Choice into a Western-style campaign organization. The party's staff occupied a large suite of offices with a number of telephones and computers. The offices housed a paid full-time crew of approximately thirty staffers. This enabled the organization to create a hierarchy of specialized positions such as media coordinator, regional coordinator, and campaign director for each of the three races. No other party organization had the staff to assign workers to individual tasks. The party also sponsored several polls run by local scholars. Along with full-time staff, Russia's Choice had the largest number of students on their payroll performing every task from collecting signatures to agitating at bus stops in the final weekend of the campaign.

Russia's Choice also had branches in each of the single-member districts. In Balashov, the party had an office and telephone line and a staff of four people. This operation was in daily contact with the oblast party headquarters in Saratov city and with the one-person operations in the small towns and villages throughout their district.[9] The Balashov committee also ran its own partisan newspaper. In Arkadak, a small town to the northeast of Balashov, a committee of three activists collected signatures, distributed campaign materials, and organized campaign meetings for Davydov and Vladimir Isayev.[10] On the other side of the oblast, in Balakovo, the Russia's Choice organization was led by their local candidate, the vice chair of the city soviet, Aleksandr N. Sergeyenkov. Here the party evidenced crafty recruiting in light of past electoral support of Sergeyenkov, a popular local leader, and previous representative to the Congress of People's Deputies. However, the party's resources did little to foster identification in the electorate, because Sergeyenkov ran as an independent and concentrated his efforts on securing his own victory.

Access to monetary resources enabled Russia's Choice to use the media as a campaign tool. The Russia's Choice candidates were the first to hang campaign posters throughout the city—albeit ten days before the elections. Their posters were the only ones printed in color and the only posters not printed in Saratov oblast. In addition, the local party purchased extensive television time and newspaper ad space. Television time was apportioned between the candidates, with the bulk of it going to Davydov himself. In addition, the party sponsored concerts of nationally noted artists as well as local street musicians who delivered campaign slogans between sets in the town square.

If nothing else, the experience of Russia's Choice in Saratov demonstrates that organizational structure and material resources are not sufficient to win Russian elections. Despite access to seemingly unlimited funding and political expertise, Russia's Choice won only 12 percent of the vote in the oblast—significantly less than its national average. The party officially ran candidates in three of the four districts in the oblast, but in fact sponsored candidates in all four districts. It also nominated three candidates to the party list.[11] However, no effort was expended promoting the national list or even publicizing the local nominees who were on the list. The party's poor showing in the list race is therefore no surprise.

Other democratic parties evidenced the organizational dilemmas of Russia's Choice without the financial resources. Of all the reform parties, Yabloko, which started from 0 percent support at the beginning of the campaign and received almost 9 percent of the vote a month later, was the most successful. The bloc's issue-oriented campaign separated it from other local parties.[12] Unlike Russia's Choice, Yabloko devoted its sparse resources to promoting the party and its message and trying to educate voters about the merits of both the national and local party platforms. Yabloko's regional stance reflected its base, a tenuous alliance of members of the oblast's Social Democratic and Republican parties. The governing board included representatives of both partners and met regularly to discuss strategy. The board determined the nominees to the party list, selected single-member district candidates in proportion to Social Democratic and Republican party members, and approved the local party platform.[13] However, despite this seeming commitment to organization, there were considerable tensions between party leaders and candidates over party priorities during the campaign.[14] Like Russia's Choice, party leaders lacked the mechanisms necessary to impose party discipline on their candidates.

PRES was also an alliance of local party activists drawn from the Social Democrats and the regionally based Party of Economic Radicals. The regional list included three candidates, all of whom ran in single-member districts.[15] PRES managed to secure more than 5 percent of the vote in the oblast, but little of this success can be attributed to local campaign efforts. The party lacked both material and human resources to mount a wide-ranging local campaign. In the end, PRES was the only party that withdrew all its single-member district candidates in order to aid the cause of other reformers.

The snap elections hindered the organization of other parties. Several parties were not represented in the region, including the Constructive Ecological Movement of Russia (KEDR), the Russian Movement for Democratic Reform (RDDR), and the Agrarians. The Civic Union organization was even more haphazard and personalized than either PRES or Yabloko, despite the claim that the party had support in local industry.[16] The local origins of the party were in Aleksandr Rutskoi's People's Party of Free Russia, which was banned from participating in the elections after Rutskoi's arrest following the coup. Because of this narrow base and the imprisonment of Rutskoi, the local Civic Union organization was totally unprepared for electoral competition. Their staff was very small—only two full-time workers—and they were very poorly equipped. In addition, the party received minimal assistance from the central Civic Union party organization.

Likewise, despite its relative historical strength in Saratov, Nikolai Travkin's DPR lacked the political resources to mount a campaign. The rupture between central party leaders was mirrored in the fissures in local party organizations in Saratov. Despite this setback, the local party did field three list candidates, including the oblast party chair. DPR's campaign was solely based on press releases and the accumulation of endorsements from local political organizations.[17] Again a preexisting base served a party well, as DPR got almost as many votes as PRES in the final balloting and more than its national average.

Although they nominated a single local candidate to the national list, the Women of Russia organization did not play any role in the campaign. Unlike other party organizations they did not have offices in the city. They did not distribute leaflets or hang posters and their local media time was used to rebroadcast speeches by central leaders. These broadcasts focused heavily on social issues, particularly education and health care. Several opponents argued that the local efforts of Women of Russia were engineered by the KPRF in the region in order to provide an alternative for dissatisfied voters reluctant to vote for the Communists. Whether these rumors were true or the basic appeal was effective, the national party won almost 10 percent of the vote in the region—just 2 percent less than Russia's Choice.

Success of the KPRF and LDPR: Good Strategies, Strong Parties

How did the LDPR and KPRF manage to escape the divisions that plagued the democratic parties? The answer lies in some very smart decisions taken at the center that altered the incentives for regional candidates as well as the availability of a wider range of strategic options during the campaign period. While other regional parties were actively recruiting disparate candidates for open districts, the KPRF and LDPR had competition for nominations and carefully screened nominees to ensure compliance with central party strategy. They did not try to field candidates in every district if suitable candidates were not available. They did not form regional lists that would dilute the message of the center.

In terms of campaign strategies, the crucial difference between these parties and their counterparts was their existing party structures at the time elections were announced. Both parties had critical human resources, a core of activists that served as the backbone of their organizations, and an attentive group of voters. The primary task of the local campaign was to make sure that these people voted. Moreover, the local organizations of the LDPR and KPRF were much less visible throughout the campaign period, leading the democrats to dismiss them as a threat. They did not obtain local media coverage nor did they generate mass media campaigns designed to increase name recognition. Instead, both parties worked through existing organizations to activate rather than convince those constituencies.

The KPRF had the most loyal electorate entering the campaign. After the demise of the Communist Party of the Soviet Union (CPSU), the local Communist party had been reconstituted around its natural constituency, the veterans' and pensioners' organizations in the large enterprises.[18] These groups formed the basis of the local party's active but low-profile campaign. Local strategy was clear: ensure that supporters would turn out to vote on December 12. Party leaders were aware of the antiparty sentiment that existed even among Saratov's conservative voters and were careful not to stimulate it. For example, when party activists asked questions or challenged opposition candidates in public forums, they did so under the name of The Club of Voters, a loose coalition of KPRF activists. Party representatives rarely appeared in public. In addition, candidates in the single-member districts did not flaunt their party affiliation except in party-organized rallies and talks.

In a similar way, the regional Communists did not engage in mass propaganda. The local party mirrored the strategy of the central party, observing the central party's ban on television advertising. They did not offer a local platform nor did they comment on the national leadership. Campaign activity was carried out through the pensioners and veterans' clubs in large enterprises, thereby making the party an exclusively urban phenomena. Unlike the democratic parties the Communists did not rely on paid students to campaign. There were no large posters or placards, no megaphones or concerts. The Communists' public displays were primitive handbills and one-page photocopied posters distributed and hung by party activists.

The LDPR drew on the support of a number of small nationalist groups that had sprung up in response to the Volga-German conflict and the influx of refugees into the oblast. It was the only party in the list race that located its organization outside of the oblast center. Like Lysenko's NRPR, the LDPR had its headquarters in Engels, the heart of the anti-German movement. A full-time staff of two coordinated the loose alliance of small groups, providing a solid organizational base. The centerpiece of the alliance was a local paper, *Saratovskii Patriot,* that claimed to be independent of any particular organization but was rumored to be funded by the LDPR. However minimal, the organization proved effective enough to mobilize the core nationalist voters: activists and sympathizers enlisted during the Volga-German struggle.

The success of the LDPR in the party race in Saratov should not have come as a great surprise. Past political representatives from the region had affiliated with the nationalist blocs in the former Russian Congress and in the local soviets. The support for Vladimir Zhirinovskii in the 1991 presidential election was quite high in the small cites and rural regions surrounding Balashov as well as in Engels. This base of popular support gave the LDPR a target audience in the oblast. The message of the party activated the nationalist sentiment that had been formed during the anti-German campaign and had been propagated by other nationalist groups.

Explaining Outcomes: The Importance of Strategy

The strategies employed by local party leaders and their ability to carry out those strategies provide a cogent explanation of the regional outcome in the party-list race. Saratov's democratic and centrist parties concentrated their efforts and resources on broad-based appeals focused on their national leaders. Given the short lead time prior to elections, this strategy was ineffective. Most reform and centrist parties did not have the staff, money, access to experienced politicians, or time to implement a consensus-building campaign and, as the case of Russia's Choice demonstrates, wealth and organization does not always produce electoral success.

In contrast to reformers, the local KPRF ran a campaign aimed at mobilizing the core of voters that remained loyal to the party after the 1991 coup. Voter's meetings were conducted on a small scale and leaders relied on activists to promote turnout at the meetings. Unlike the democratic and reform parties, voter meetings were well attended and the Communists were able to get their message out. In the party-list race, the mobilization strategy did secure the support of the faithful but it did not broaden the party's appeal within the electorate. The LDPR successfully combined these two strategies in Saratov—and won both in a single-member district and in the party-list race. The *Saratovskii Patriot* and activist meetings provided an effective outreach to the party's core support of voters in small regional parties. In addition, the aggressive organization of the independent nationalist candidate, N. N. Lysenko, created a pool of voters that were loyal to the LDPR in the list race, because Lysenko's own party did not make it on to the ballot.

The impact of the political factors was asymmetric and, it is ironic to note, worked against the government party as well as other reform parties. Unlike St. Petersburg, Moscow, or even Sverdlovsk where reform movements had strong leadership and were well developed, Saratov's democratic movement was small and fragmented. These organizations tended to be extremely top heavy with few activists and even fewer ties to the electorate. In contrast, the conservative parties used established local organizations to mobilize core constituencies. Local political networks were activated to ensure that voters understood the complicated ballot, were registered correctly, and would make it to the polls. The resources of national party organizations were used to broaden the appeal of the party to right-leaning voters rather than ambitious candidates in the single-member districts.

The development of the LDPR and KPRF continued in the postelection period as the reform parties remained mired in conflict. The trends in vote totals over three additional elections—regional elections in 1994, parliamentary elections in 1995, and presidential elections in 1996—supports the proposition that the KPRF has been most effective in building ties to voters. Vote totals for the KPRF rose in every election in Saratov, from 15.3 percent in 1993 to almost 50 percent support for Gennadii Zyuganov in the second round of the presidential election in 1996. Although comparing elections across different constituencies is problematic because the political dynamics are so different, it is significant that the KPRF has been able to meet the challenge of organizing to influence disparate constituencies in local and all-Federation districts. Although total support for LDPR has declined, regional vote totals still outpace national levels in an oblast in which its organizational base is extremely strong.

A significant indication of development of the KPRF is embodied in the fate of Oleg Mironov, a Communist candidate defeated in the single-member district in 1993. Mironov was elected in the same district in 1995, defeating thirteen candidates, including a representative of the LDPR. In this case, the party organization recognized Mironov as an asset and guaranteed him a viable shot in the next election by seating him in parliament on the party list. Through this type of careerism, the party is able to develop mechanisms ensuring party discipline. The LDPR fosters the same type of career development in its structure of regional and subregional offices that employ a number of activists.

The reform parties do not offer similar career structures, nor is there stability in party cadres. In fact, between 1993 and 1996 there were several key defections from reform party organizations. In 1995, Valery Davydov, discredited by his loss in 1993, ran for office in the rural district in Balashov sponsored by Forward Russia. Aleksandr Zhavoronskii, a former member of the governing board of Russia's Choice, was elected to the oblast duma as a representative of Yabloko. In 1996, Vladimir Sanatin, the former chair of the Yabloko organization, ran on the Beer Lover's party ticket. Thus, much of the party activity within the reform parties still entails elite rivalry and maneuvering to capture resources rather than reaching out to the voters. Despite the claims of elites that the reform parties had learned a lesson in the wake of their defeat in 1993, it appears that personal ambitions and institutional incentives have combined to hinder cooperation in pursuit of collective goals.

Individual Candidates to the State Duma: Resources and Strategies

Winners and losers in the single-member district races did not mirror the results in the party contest. Unlike the list race, single-member district elections were heavily dominated by local forces. Part of the reason for this disparity is obvious: party-list races were directed at a national constituency and the single-member district races could be tailored to local interests. District-level races provide the opportunity for campaign managers and candidates to capitalize on local organizations, interest groups, and issue publics. Candidates could win the election based on personal ties, patronage or service networks, regional parties, or concentrated social groups. As a result, individual candidates were not held hostage to the national parties' messages or resources.

For candidates, the structure of the electoral law decoupled the decision to run for office from the decision to affiliate with a party. By running in a single-member district race, candidates could avoid the costs of party formation and the burden of a party label if they felt that either factor would hurt their chances of winning. The split ballot also gave the advantage to local elites with the ability to garner personal votes. In addition, the provision for straight plurality rule in single-member districts established an inverse relationship between the number of candidates entered in a race and the number of votes necessary to win. With the entry of every new candidate, there was an incentive for additional candidates to enter because the number of voters needed to win decreased. As a result, district races typically had several contestants, further advantaging candidates with a personal following. Finally, the lack of a residency requirement allowed candidates to shop for "winnable" districts given their electoral resources.[19]

The decision to join a party divided the candidates into three groups. Because party membership was essentially a decision based on access to electoral resources, the decision to join was correlated with the candidate's choice of electoral strategies. One group of successful candidates combined personal followings with control of well-established, independent, regional political organizations. These candidates used their organizational base to mobilize rather than expand their constituencies beyond their personal followings. In fact, several candidates who were affiliated with parties ran as independents because of uncertainty about the value of the party label and its effect on voter support. Most prominent in this category was the Communist candidate in the Saratov district, Gordeyev.

A second type of candidate relied on party affiliation to broaden his or her core base of support. A notable example was the LDPR candidate in the rural Balashov district, Andrei M. Dorovskikh, who had local prominence in the urban areas of his district but needed the backing of the LDPR resources to gain votes from rural regions. He won by 1 percent of the vote.

A third type of candidate ran on both the list and in the single-member districts. These tended to be candidates who were members of the "imported" reform parties and blocs. Lacking personal resources, experience, or a voter base, these candidates relied on the scarce collective resources of the parties to build support. The primary strategy of these candidates was similar to their parties' strategies: to increase name recognition without getting bogged down in substance. The candidates nominated by Yabloko and PRES are good examples of this type.

Independent candidates, those who did not have either official or de facto party membership, fell into two categories. The first were candidates with access to material resources that they thought would allow them to build coalitions without party ties. The second were candidates who had no resources and no chance of winning in this round of elections.[20] Both types focused on increasing name recognition as a basic strategy and tended to look forward to increasing their fortunes for future elections.

As this discussion indicates, the difference between the party-list race and dual- and single-member district races was that candidates in the latter had better knowledge of their constituents, were well known, and could rely on their reputations and past political action to ensure some basis of support. Each of the four races in Saratov demonstrates the superiority of a mobilization strategy and the power of a solid loyal following within the electorate over other political resources such as money, organization, staff, and equipment. In addition, the individual races show how the effectiveness of local candidates was influenced by the factors listed previously.

The Race for the Heart of Saratov

Nine candidates contested the race in the oblast capital—although at least two of the Democrats officially withdrew in the final days of the election. By December 10, Yevgenii V. Motornyi claimed the support of all three organized reform parties: Russia's Choice, PRES, and Yabloko.[21] Principally sponsored by Russia's Choice, Motornyi had access to resources through the party and through his own personal wealth. However, he ran a modest campaign directed solely at familiarizing voters with his name. Motornyi refused to talk about issues. He did not hang posters or distribute flyers. His advertisements in the paper consisted of cartoon drawings of himself or photos with his young daughter.[22] His television time was used to rebroadcast rock concerts. Rather than showcasing local notables to enhance the appeal of the party, the notables were relying on party loyalty and reputation to win the election for them.

The most prominent independent candidate, Mikhail Y. Zaitsev, spent vast sums of money on television and newspaper advertising.[23] In an extended interview, Zaitsev indicated that he had conscientiously adapted American campaign tactics and built an American-style campaign organization.[24] His ads in both the print media and on television focused on personal attributes rather than a substantive campaign message. They depicted him playing chess with his father, fishing, working with his children, and cooking for his family. He published his platform only once during the campaign, a document fraught with generalities. Zaitsev managed to come in third in the field.

The surprise winner in the district was the candidate of the Communist party, Gordeyev. In contrast to Zaitsev, Gordeyev appeared on television only once, ostensibly to correct the impression that voters had received from the local press that he was 54 years old.[25] In fact, Gordeyev was a thirty-nine-year-old entrepreneur whose business card listed him as a bank director and general manager of Germiz, one of the largest enterprises in the city. Despite these credentials and access to resources, Gordeyev ran a deceptively humble campaign, spending only the money allotted from the central election commission, hiding his personal wealth, and listing his profession as "economist" on campaign documents. His political image was also deceptive. His posters were handwritten without a photo or color printing. Gordeyev operated his campaign through well-attended voters meetings organized by veterans and pensioners clubs within the large enterprises The mobilization strategy was successful, and Gordeyev won the nine-way race with 19.7 percent of the vote to Motornyi's 15.7 percent.

The Engels District

The Saratov race underscores the importance of existing political organizations that delivered votes for independent candidates. Competition in the Engels district, the other urban district, shows the same result. The overwhelming winner was the ultranationalist Lysenko who entered the race with considerable monetary resources, an organized electoral base, and a party organization behind him. He used all these resources to their best advantage, winning with a remarkable 23.5 percent in an eight-way race. Lysenko conducted an extensive media campaign and produced very polished campaign literature. In addition, Lysenko maintained a high profile during the campaign period, standing on the street with his family shaking hands, attending rallies, and creating scandals that got national press attention.[26] The popularity of the NRPR prior to elections made Lysenko a clear front-runner. Despite this position, other candidates did not take him seriously until it was too late.

Four days before the election, the reform parties' polls showed that Lysenko had a substantial lead over all his opponents. In an attempt to thwart Lysenko's victory, the democrats, led by Yabloko, called a meeting of all of the candidates in the district except for Lysenko. Party leaders tried to convince contestants to drop out of the race, leaving a single candidate and invalidating the race. Several candidates did not cooperate. Mironov believed that regardless of the poll data, he would be the beneficiary of conservative sentiment in the district. The independent candidate Aleksandr N. Malayev refused because his own data did not corroborate reformers' polls. As a result, all the candidates remained registered.[27] The polls were vindicated.

The Rural Districts

The campaigns in the rural districts were also marked by last minute attempts at tactical maneuvering. In the final days of the campaign in Balakovo, the LDPR candidate appeared to lead the chair of the Balakovo city soviet and Russia's Choice candidate, A. N. Sergeyenkov. On the eve of the election, the Yabloko candidate, Yelena A. Sergun, dropped out of the race and urged her supporters to vote for Sergeyenkov. However, Sergun's name remained on the ballot and she received almost 14 percent of the vote. Despite this, Sergeyenkov won, eking out victory by .1 percent. The crucial difference for the outcome in Balakovo was Sergeyenkov's strong personal following based on his work in the city soviet. He won because he dominated the voting in the city, whereas his opponents split the support of the rural areas.

In the second rural district, Balashov, Dorovskikh provided one of the LDPR's five victories in single-mandate district races. A lawyer and local activist, he had a strong base in the urban portions of the district because of his challenge to corrupt local officials in the oblast administration. In addition, Dorovskikh presented himself as part of the LDPR team widening his appeal in the rural regions of the district. The race was won in one precinct in the city of Krasnoarmeisk, which had been at the center of the Volga-German conflict. Thus, Dorovskikh's campaign, which activated local issues, played a critical role in the outcome.

The expected winner in Balashov, Konstantin N. Kondrat'ev, a long-time instructor in the agricultural institute and television personality, relied exclusively on an extensive network of former students to campaign and vote for him on the basis of personal loyalty. Kondrat'ev won a large number of precincts in the district. In contrast, Isayev, a nationally known democrat and government official, was confident that his national reputation and personal ties to the district in which he was born would get him elected. He made only one campaign sweep through the district.

In summary, the races in the single-member districts again underscore the importance of preexisting structures, organized constituencies, and the ability of candidates to mobilize these constituencies around local issues.

Candidates lacked the time, experience, organization, and money to familiarize voters with their personal history or platforms. Successful candidates were able to exploit their preexisting local networks or were savvy enough to join a party and run in a district in which their party label was advantageous. In contrast to the party-list race, the factors that shaped election outcomes were overwhelmingly local in nature. These races highlight the weakness of the LDPR in district-level competition. Except for Balashov, the LDPR was unable to attract quality candidates to run on the platform, and as Lysenko's success demonstrates, nationalist support is not homogeneously behind the LDPR.[28]

These races also show the problems inherent in drawing conclusions based on only one election. All of the single-member districts in Saratov were decided by very small margins. Different outcomes could be produced by small changes in the level of turnout or in the entry of an additional candidate in the race. These possibilities were realized in the parliamentary elections held in December 1995, in which all four of Saratov's incumbents were unseated. None of the four was able to use his office to provide goods and services to secure sufficient electoral support for reelection. KPRF candidates soundly defeated incumbents in Balakovo, Balashov, and Engels districts. However, the KPRF's incumbent, Gordeyev, was roundly trounced by Boris V. Gromov, a popular general and leader of the nationalist movement, My Fatherland.

The Federation Council: Local Machines in Action

All four of the candidates in the race for the Federation Council relied heavily on personal votes based in patronage networks. This race most closely approximates machine-style politics of early 1900s urban America. The focus of the race was on the delivery of services, jobs, and federal subsidies. The successful candidates, Andrei Belykh and Dmitri Ayatskov, won by acting in accordance with their political reputations and using the campaign period to activate voter loyalties built up over their years in political office.[29]

Of the four candidates, three were longtime colleagues and members of the local governance structure. Belykh, Yurii Kitov, and Dmitri Ayatskov all had been employed at the largest chicken processing plant in the oblast prior to entering city and oblast administration. At the time of elections, Belykh was the governor of the oblast, Kitov the mayor of Saratov, and Ayatskov his vice mayor. The fourth candidate, Davydov, was a former chair of a city raispolkom, the founder and head of the Democratic Russia movement in the oblast, and the chair of Russia's Choice.

Past political activity and current position of the candidates heavily influenced the race for the Federation Council.[30] As early as November 26, a poll of registered voters indicated voter preferences that mirrored the percentage of support that candidates received on election day.[31] Voter support was clearly linked to delivery of services. In a blatant display of patronage power, Belykh and Kitov used their administrative positions to deliver governmental decrees that increased social spending during the campaign period. These funds were targeted at key groups in the population—such as the university community. Voters were well informed about the activities of their governor and mayor, because their positions afforded each control of newspapers. The newspaper of the oblast administration printed numerous articles on both the personal life and political platform of Belykh. The newspaper of the city administration not only supported Kitov but also carried articles against Davydov and Ayatskov. Kitov distributed free copies of these papers at electoral meetings.[32]

It is not surprising that Belykh, the stereotype of a colorless Soviet bureaucrat, was effective at translating his office into consistent support across the oblast. His control over budgetary allocation gave him strong ties with the industrial managers and agricultural leaders in the region. In addition, several opponents alleged that Belykh threatened to fire regional administrators who were not willing to campaign aggressively for him.[33] At the very least, Belykh used his office and staff as his main source of campaign support. He did not make extensive campaign trips or television appearances, instead relying on his staff to alert and activate his constituency. Belykh's past political activity was as gray as his campaign style. As a member of the 1990 Congress of People's Deputies (CPD), Belykh was not affiliated with any party, and his voting record put him in the middle-right of the deputies' corps. The cornerstone of his campaign was increased protection for pensioners and the preservation of other social programs. He was endorsed by Civic Union and the Officer's Union. In addition, despite his appointment to the presidential apparatus by Yeltsin, Belykh claimed a respect and sympathy for the new Communist party that endorsed his candidacy. In his public appearances, he made a point of discussing his long tenure in the party and the various positions he had held.

Kitov's flamboyant campaign style and charismatic appeal make him the antithesis of the sterile Belykh. Yet, despite this appeal, the mayor was not able to turn his office into a successful platform for oblast-wide office. He presided over a city whose infrastructure was crumbling: the papers were full of complaints about housing, public transport, medical services, and road conditions. Given the severity of the problems, it was not surprising that Kitov did not even carry the city. In addition, Kitov's past political activity did not serve him well. As a member of the Congress of People's Deputies, Kitov had been a member of the Agrarian Union but voted consistently for reform and listed his second party affiliation as Democratic Russia. Yet, as the mayor of the city, his natural constituency was the urban worker population. To reconcile these factors, Kitov attempted to form a local electoral bloc, "Center," using the resources of his office. He claimed the support of ten large enterprises, as well as the trade union, and a number of societal organizations, but this was mostly bluster.[34] "Center" may have had the support of some local economic leaders and personal friends of Kitov, but it had no voter base.

Ayatskov, an extremely ambitious politician, presented a professional and competent demeanor without appearing dull. As vice mayor, his access to resources were less obvious than either Kitov or Belykh but he also did not carry the burden of public expectation. Ayatskov effectively used his position to cultivate support in important groups in the electorate that extended beyond city boundaries. Most notably, he had personally ensured improved housing for the region's military officers and the return and preservation of the Orthodox cathedral in the center of Saratov city.[35] In addition, Ayatskov used his personal resources to widen his appeal. Like Zaitsev, he was a member of the Group of 13 and therefore had access to unlimited monetary resources. He used this money to build a staff, to publicize his campaign, and to win endorsements—thus ensuring independence from Kitov. His "team" included political leaders from Yabloko and the Democratic Party of Russia. The vice mayor was also endorsed by PRES and the Democratic Party of Russia and he campaigned with members of Russia's Choice.[36] In addition, anonymous campaign materials carried stories of Ayatskov's connection to the Union of Muslims, a national organization based in Saratov.

Much of Davydov's campaign strategy was summarized earlier. Of all the candidates, this representative of the party of power was the most like an old-time machine politician. However, Davydov's heavy reliance on media and agitation, supplemented by a fairly extensive schedule of voter meetings, demonstrates that he did not have the core constituency available to the other candidates in the race. Although he clearly recognized the power of patronage and used it build his own foundation in Democratic Russia, Davydov did not have the type of personal network to win an oblast-wide race. Nor did his affiliation with Russia's Choice bring him enough support to win in a four-way oblast-wide race.

As was true elsewhere, these candidates were more successful at mobilizing strongly entrenched pockets of popular support than they were in expanding their appeal. This was a race won on past action and entrenched coalitions, not contemporary campaigning. Of all of the races, the race for Federation Council hinged on critical local factors: the quality of the candidates and their existing ties to social groups.

The weakness in the regional party system, translated into a weakness in the oblast duma, raises the possibility of the creation of a regional machine based in the hierarchic structure of the presidential administration. It is possible that the most important result of the 1993 elections was the rise of Dmitri Ayatskov in the race for the Federation Council. The campaign period revealed Ayatskov to be a masterful tactician and popular candidate. In interviews with the author in June 1995, members of the oblast duma claimed that there was an intense power struggle underway between Ayatskov and Belykh for control of the presidential apparatus. In spring 1996, Belykh was dismissed by Yeltsin because of his lack of support for the government party in 1995 parliamentary elections and replaced by Ayatskov.

Ayatskov has steadily built on the patronage network evidenced in his campaign and has been able to command dominance in local press and television coverage. The decline in economic conditions, persistence of a large public service sector, postponement of gubernatorial elections, and the lack of cooperation among regional elites in opposition to Ayatskov create the conditions for the consolidation of a patronage-based political machine that could easily dominate politics in Saratov.

Conclusion

The news for democratic consolidation in Saratov is not all bad. Although there was considerable speculation about systematic fraud in the 1993 election, in subsequent elections turnout has been raised, the number of spoiled ballots and votes "against all" have decreased, and the claims of outright fraud have diminished. Interparty competition seems to be growing increasingly open. However, intraparty politics on the regional level remain as obscure and closed to voter influence as they did in 1993. The regional perspective shows the national party system in the Russian Federation to be extremely underdeveloped.

The politics of Saratov's elections provide important clues about the relationship between repeated elections and democratic institutionalization. These clues are not so much evident in the winners and losers but in the inability of most elites, other than the KPRF and LDPR, to cooperate in an effort to form parties that link the voters and elected officials. Aldrich argues that for parties to "make democracy workable" they must be able to solve three critical problems inherent in democratic systems.[37] Parties must be able to channel the ambitions of office-seekers; link voters and leaders; and build and sustain majorities necessary for collective decisionmaking in government. The view from Saratov shows that national parties have not yet developed to solve these problems. Whether they are able to overcome the obstacles embedded in the electoral system and constitutional structure will be shown in time. In the meanwhile, analysts should take care not to make judgments based solely on the view from Moscow, where political competition may appear to be more structured, obscuring disarray at the regional level and the critical importance of local factors.

Appendix 15-1. *Electoral Outcomes in Saratov Oblast*

Candidate	Partisan affiliation[a]	Employment	Percent of vote received
Balakovo District, 155			
Sergeyenkov	Independent (Russia's Choice)	Assistant chair, city soviet	19.8
Yul'yankin	Independent (KPRF)	Assistant raion administrator	19.7
Bogdanov	Independent (LDPR)	Director of Industrialists, Volsk	17.8
Uglev	Independent (Russia's Choice)	Academic researcher	9.0
Sergun	Yabloko	Assistant director, firm (alternative)	Withdrew (13.9)
Balashov District, 156			
Dorovskikh	LDPR	Lawyer	30.4
Kondrat'ev	Yabloko	Instructor, Saratov Agricultural Institute	29.0
Isayev (Russia's Choice)	Independent	Government, vice minister	21.5
Saratov District, 157			
Gordeyev	Independent	Director, Germiz	19.7
Motornyi	Russia's Choice	President of private company	15.7
Zaitsev	Independent	Chairman of the board of directors, Germiz	13.9
Fedotov	Civic Union	Director, joint stock company, Valzhonka	11.0
Nikitin	Yabloko	Lawyer	5.7
Kail'	Independent	Director, Saratov energy plant	4.7
Kamshilov	Independent	Chair, privatization fund of Saratov	3.0
Gubkin	Independent (NPSR)	Retired	2.5
Portnov	PRES	Director, Saratov Development Fund	Withdrew
Engels District, 158			
Lysenko	NRPR	Journalist	23.5
Mironov	Independent (KPRF)	Professor	16.8
Malkov	Independent	Assistant raion administrator	10.9
Chernyshev	Independent	Instructor	7.6
Yastrebov	Yabloko	Student, Saratov Technological Institute	7.4
Malayev	Independent	Professor, Saratov Law Institute	7.1
Markov	Russia's Choice	Assistant chair, Engels Privatization Fund	6.5
Veshnev	PRES	Instructor	4.0
Federation Council			
Belikh	Independent	Governor, Saratov oblast	30.8
Ayatskov	Independent	Vice mayor, Saratov city	29.6
Kitov	Independent	Mayor, Saratov city	27.0
Davydov	Russia's Choice	Director, private enterprise	23.7

Source: Unpublished data received by the author from regional officials in 1995.

a. In cases in which the candidate ran as an independent but was openly supported by a party, the party is identified in parentheses.

Notes

1. Interview with Aleksandr Zhavoronskii and Victor Raikel', December 8, 1993.

2. Interview with A. N. Gordeyev, December 11, 1993.

3. "Saratov Residents on Establishment of German Republic," *Izvestiya*, April 20, 1992, p. 2. Reprinted in *FBIS-USR-92-051*, May 1, 1992, p. 54.

4. The issue was subject to mass referendum in the oblast in 1992 and failed. The Engels soviet voted to reject the formation of the homeland and appealed to the Russian Congress of People's Deputies not to ratify the republic without considering the referendum results. The Congress complied.

5. A journalist from St. Petersburg, Lysenko wrote for the nationalist newspapers *Nash Sovremennik* and *Molodaya Gvardia*. The NRPR organized in thirty-six other regions in Russia but failed to collect enough signatures to appear on the ballot. The Saratov Homeland Union allied with the NRPR, resulting in the nomination of its chair to run on the unsuccessful party list. Other nationalist organizations in Saratov were the Association of Patriotic Strength, the Patriotic Movement of the 11th of February, and the National Salvation Front.

6. Interviews with Aleksandr Kuz'min, vice chair of the Balashov organization, December 6, 1993, and Vladimir Fedotov, chair of Civic Union, December 9, 1993.

7. Joseph A. Schlesinger, *Political Parties and the Winning of Office* (University of Michigan Press, 1991), p. 33.

8. Interview with Yurii Chernyshev, a Yabloko activist, December 2, 1993.

9. Smaller branches did not receive monetary or material support from the oblast organization. In the case of Balashov, the local patron was a city official appointed through the presidential network. Interview with Kuz'min, December 6, 1993.

10. Interview with Yelena Dublenko, December 5, 1993.

11. The Russia's Choice list included Vladimir Yuzhakov, the director of Privolzhki Cadre Center (formally the Higher Party School), and the two candidates from Saratov and Engels districts, Yevgenii Motornyi, a private entrepreneur, and Victor Markov, a law professor.

12. On December 11, Yabloko published an open letter warning voters that they were following the road to extremism. They attacked Lysenko and likened him to Hitler. *Saratov*, no. 219 (December 11, 1993), p. 1. Twelve candidates from six parties signed a letter condemning Lysenko. *Saratovskiye Vesti*, no. 249 (December 8, 1993), p. 1.

13. The list included Vladimir Sanatin, chair of the organization; Denis Yastrebov, economics graduate student at the Polytechnic Institute; and Konstantin Kondrat'ev, researcher at the Agricultural Institute.

14. The bloc nominated the leader of the Social Democratic party, Nikitin, to run in Saratov and then withdrew its nomination because of Nikitin's dissension from the party program. Sergun compromised her party membership by appearing

on television with Davydov urging voters to support Russia's Choice and its candidates. This was not the bloc's policy.

15. These were V. Portnov, the director of the City Privatization Committee, who ran in the Saratov city district; and V. P. Veshnev, a professor of physics, who ran in the Engels district. The third candidate was L. N. Karagod, who ran in the Balakovo district.

16. Civic Union fielded two list candidates: Fedotov and Nikolai Vladimirov, the former chair of the city soviet.

17. The DPR campaign consisted of press releases distributed by the party's press center claiming more than 7,000 signatures and indicating that the local party members were numbers 36, 107, and 118 on the DPR list. *Saratovskiye Vesti*, no. 230 (November 16, 1993), p. 1.

18. Gordeyev argued that although the party was "not what it once was," these two branches remained a source of loyal political activists who worked on behalf of the Communist candidates. Interview, December 11, 1993.

19. Lysenko blatantly shopped for a secure district. *Saratovskiye Vesti*, no. 247 (December 4, 1993), p. 2. Reform parties were not effective at recruiting local celebrities. Kondrat'ev was the only candidate actively recruited by reformers. Interview, November 29, 1993.

20. Most candidates realized that their chances of victory were very small. For Kail' the election provided opportunity and state-sponsored funds to garner a political reputation and experience for future local elections. Interview, December 2, 1993. Fedotov believed his candidacy would draw support from Russia's Choice. Interview, November 30, 1993.

21. "Interview with the Candidate: I Believe That the New Parliament Will Be Better than the Old," *Saratovskiye Vesti*, no. 251–52 (December 10, 1993), p. 1.

22. One such cartoon depicted Motornyi on a rocket with the slogan, "There is a motor in Motornyi." The slogan on the picture of his daughter was, "Vote for my Dad; he's a good guy."

23. Interview with Zaitsev, December 3, 1993. Zaitsev was a member of the Group of 13 and the Fund in Support of the Russian President, political organizations of wealthy businesspeople formed to promote candidates in the elections. Other candidates supported by the fund, Aleksandr Malayev in Engels and Aleksei Yl'yankin in Balakovo, were also unsuccessful.

24. Zaitsev used a paid full-time staff of ten including a driver, a personal pollster (a local sociology professor), and technical media consultants. The staff occupied a spacious suite in the city center equipped with computers, telephones, television, and videotape machines. Interview with Zaitsev, December 3, 1993.

25. Gordeyev was the only candidate who complained of unfair treatment by the press. Friday before the election the newspaper *Saratov* ran a letter to the editor that accused him of price gouging on a deal to sell potatoes in 1987. *Saratov*, no. 219 (December 11, 1993), p. 3.

26. On Sunday, December 5, Lysenko claimed that the Kazakh mafia attempted to assassinate him. Within three hours, his campaign committee had distributed printed materials publicizing the attempt, and an article detailing the attack appeared the following day in the Moscow-based *Molodaya gvardia*. The article was

reprinted in the local press. "They Can Beat Me, but They Can Never Beat the Idea of a Great Russia," *Saratovskiye Vesti,* no. 251–52 (December 9, 1993), p. 3.

27. The report of this meeting is based on interviews with members of PRES, Yabloko, and Russia's Choice on Friday, December 10, 1993.

28. Divergent interests are evident in the nationalist's behavior in parliament. Lysenko joined the alternative nationalist party, Russian Path, and had a voting score of -21. In contrast, Dorovskikh earned a score of -79. A. Sobyanin, Report on the Votes of Deputies in the State Duma, March 1994.

29. Two additional candidates attempted to register. According to V. Kaby-shev, the chair of the Saratov District Election Commission, Rashkin secured the required number of signatures in support of his candidacy, but part of these were rejected because they were not listed correctly on the signature forms. "Only For-eigners Are Able to Observe Our Elections," *Saratov,* no. 211 (December 1, 1993), p. 1. Rashkin himself argued that he had been disqualified on political grounds. "Time Was Very Short," *Avtorskoye pravo,* no. 38 (November 26, 1993), p. 3. Fel-low Communist Gordeyev (interview, December 10) said that his own entry into the race in Saratov forced Rashkin to move to the all-oblast district at the last mo-ment, impeding Rashkin's ability to collect sufficient signatures. As noted previ-ously, Zhavoronskii also failed to secure enough signatures to register.

30. Candidate platforms were similar, and all four supported the passage of the constitution. See *Saratov,* no. 240–41 (November 27, 1993), p. 1.

31. "The Four Go from the Start," *Saratovskiye Vesti,* no. 239 (November 26, 1993), p. 2.

32. Yabloko and PRES joined together to castigate Kitov for this and other transgressions, including the use of city vehicles for campaign purposes and his treatment of Ayatskov. *Saratov,* no. 210 (November 30, 1993), p. 1.

33. Pavlov, the activist from PRES, claimed to have called Belykh to confront him on this issue on behalf of the democratic candidates. The governor assured Pavlov that he was not using his position to win the race, but in the period follow-ing the election several local administrators were removed from their posts. Interview, December 9, 1993.

34. See the letter from A. Belyaeva, in *Saratov,* no. 210 (November 30, 1993), p. 1.

35. Ayatskov was endorsed by disparate groups: the Youth Union of the DPR, Yabloko, PRES, Archbishop Pimen of the Russian Orthodox Church, and the Offi-cers Union. The archbishop died just five days before the election. On December 11 the candidates of Russia's Choice placed an ad in *Saratov* honoring the arch-bishop and his work on behalf of the restoration of churches in the oblast. *Saratov,* no. 219 (December 11, 1993), p. 1. Before his death, Pimen himself placed an ad thanking Ayatskov for his assistance in solving various problems for the church. *Saratovskiye vesti,* no. 247 (December 4, 1993), p. 1.

36. In interviews, party activists revealed that Ayatskov secured these endorse-ments with large donations to each party. The PRES endorsement was published with a scathing critique of Kitov's failures to implement the reform program in the city. *Saratovskiye Vesti,* no. 244 (December 2, 1993), p. 1.

37. John H. Aldrich, *Why Parties? The Origins and Transformation of Political Parties in America* (University of Chicago Press, 1995).

CHAPTER SIXTEEN

Kursk

A Preserve of Communism

Neil J. Melvin

SITUATED IN the heart of the rural Black Earth zone, Kursk oblast has long been considered one of the most conservative regions in Russia. Under Soviet rule Kursk served as a bastion of support for the regime, while during the perestroika years the oblast offered little sustenance to supporters of the democratic movement and only weak encouragement for Gorbachevite reformist Communists. After 1991 socioeconomic change in the region generated by Moscow's reformist policies and the shock waves caused by the collapse of the USSR fostered increasing hostility to the Russian government.

Given Kursk's history of reactionary conservatism and a range of social and economic factors, including the dislocation of the transition period, which favored antireform political forces in the oblast, the results of the December 1993 elections—the absolute rejection of the new constitution, the triumph of Vladimir Zhirinovskii and the Communist Party of the Russian Federation (KPRF) on the list vote, and clear victories for three conservative Communists and the local governor in the territorial contests—were, perhaps, not surprising.[1] As with much of the rest of rural central Russia, Kursk oblast seemed to have fulfilled its traditional role as a bulwark for backward-looking conservatism. A closer examination of the elections in Kursk, however, suggests that behind the apparently straightforward electoral outcome lay a more complicated story: an election of missed opportunities for more moderate local political forces.[2]

Kursk

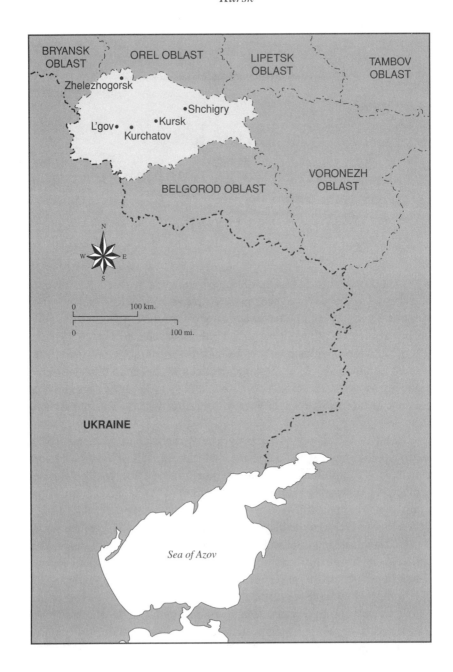

Although geographically and politically on the periphery of the country, Kursk was not isolated from the broader processes of economic, social, and political transformation affecting the rest of Russia in the immediate post-independence period. By late in 1993, the processes of change in Kursk had fostered the emergence of new political groupings and provided them with the opportunity to mount a serious challenge to the domination in the oblast of a highly conservative political elite. As the outcome of the election indicates, this opportunity was not exploited by local reformist and centrist groups. In the case of Kursk, what needs to be explained is not why the Communists and Zhirinovskii were successful in the region—the socioeconomic structure of the oblast's population and their conservative political culture clearly favored socialist-nationalist groups—but why their victory was so comprehensive.

A detailed analysis of the election suggests that the inability of moderate political forces in the region to prevent an overwhelming victory by reactionary groups was the outcome of four principal factors: local elite configuration, the structure of the electoral process, the failure of centrist forces in Moscow to establish a credible political alternative to the reformist or nationalist-socialist groups, and the tactical choices made by individual local candidates. In combination, these factors ensured that there was little united or effective opposition to the organization of the Communists or Zhirinovskii's nationalist message.

Later in this chapter I will examine in detail the sources of victory for the extreme conservatives. In the first section, I will outline the structural factors (socioeconomic and political-cultural) that provided the foundations for the Communist-nationalist success. In the second section, I will analyze the role of new political elites in undermining the former Communist domination of the region before the December elections. In the third section, I will consider the election campaign, focusing on the process of coalition formation, the policy platforms of individual candidates, and the tactics employed in the election. I conclude the chapter with two sections that examine the failure of centrist candidates and draw some brief conclusions about the importance of the elections for the subsequent political development of the oblast.

Socioeconomic and Historical Background to the Election

Even in the most favorable of economic and political conditions, Kursk was unlikely to offer reformist and centrist groups a high level of support.

The most significant factor in favor of the Communists-nationalists in the region was the demographic and socioeconomic structure of the local population. By December 1993, the formidable structural obstacle that faced reformist and centrist candidates had been accentuated by the political and economic turmoil of the early independence years, which had struck the region particularly hard. Together, these factors served to reinforce the traditionally conservative political culture of the region.

According to the last Soviet census, by 1989 the population of Kursk oblast had reached 1,339,414.[3] The majority of the urban population was concentrated in the city of Kursk (population 424,239), the main industrial center in the region and the focus for cultural activity in the area. Other towns had significantly smaller populations, including Zheleznogorsk (85,192), Kurchatov (41,085), L'gov (25,643), and Shchigry (21,187). At the end of the 1980s, the rural population of the oblast stood at 566,264.[4] The balance between urban and rural populations in Kursk region gave the oblast one of the lower levels of urbanization in the Russian Federation.[5]

In many rural areas more than 25 percent of the population was sixty years of age or older; this compares to a figure of less than 15 percent in most urban areas. In Kursk, the conservatism characteristic of rural communities in general was enhanced by an age structure heavily skewed to the upper-age cohort—in other words, those who had been most heavily socialized into Soviet beliefs. With much of rural life still governed by collectivist practices and the patronage networks of the highly conservative farm management, the villages were always going to be a major challenge to reformist and centrist candidates.

In the early 1990s the age structure of the rural population, the tradition of close communities rooted in serfdom, along with the continuing strength of Communist structures in the villages meant that Boris Yeltsin's socioeconomic policies found little support in the countryside. Indeed, by 1993 there was evidence that the traditional conservatism of the rural areas of the oblast had become the basis of a renewed defensive collectivism in the face of the deteriorating economic situation in the countryside, notably the government's failure to pay for agricultural produce.[6]

Although the region's towns faced difficult economic conditions, Kursk's rural population was experiencing disproportionate and severe hardship as a result of the economic crisis. In the years before the December elections, villagers endured disadvantageous terms of trade, a widening price gap between agricultural and industrial goods, and a deterioration in rural wages relative to the urban areas. As a result, inflation had inflicted far more damage in the countryside than the towns. Material problems were compounded by a strong sense among the rural population that government policy toward the countryside marked an abandonment of the Soviet official commitment to overcoming differences between urban and rural areas.[7]

Moscow's attempts to foster significant change in the rural economy and society had largely failed. Although there were 2,030 registered private farmers in Kursk by the autumn of 1993, agriculture in the region remained primarily a collective activity. In Russia as a whole, farm reorganization had been associated with a high number of farms retaining their status as collective labor organizations. In July 1993, only 5 percent of European Russia's private farmers were located in the Central Black Earth region, compared with 24 percent in the North Caucasus or 14 percent in the Volga region.[8] This resistance to private farming reflected both the traditionally greater collectivism in these areas and an underlying competition over land between new and existing economic elites—a fight for the good soil.[9]

In the context of the general economic crisis, the economic interdependence of towns and villages in the oblast—the agroindustrial complex—had locked the local economy into a spiral of mutually reinforcing decline. Most of the more than 90 industrial enterprises in Kursk and the majority of factories in the other urban areas of the oblast at the time were closely linked to the agricultural sector. Falling agricultural production and raised costs had pushed the reprocessing industry into acute crisis, and poverty in the villages meant that demand for new agricultural machinery largely dried up in 1993. Although registered unemployment in the oblast—a predominately urban phenomenon—stood at only 3,600, there was considerable hidden unemployment in the villages and most local observers expected an acceleration in unemployment from September onward as several factories were planning large-scale layoffs.[10]

With traditional sources of employment and wealth in the district in decline, by the autumn of 1993 new economic activity had yet to make a significant impact on the local economy. There were only 200 "entrepreneurs" registered in Kursk in September 1993. Limited though new economic activity was, it had been instrumental in fostering a redefinition of interests among the former managerial elite and had created a new, influential economic elite based on trade and services. New types of external economic actors, in the form of Moscow-based investment funds and banks, had also begun to penetrate the area.[11] The central concern of all of these groups, and the key to their future success, lay in influencing the process of privatization to their advantage and then establishing local political protection for their gains.[12]

Although there was little in the way of ethnic tension in the oblast, the collapse of the USSR had fostered a nationalist mood in the region.[13] With the establishment of an independent Russia and Ukraine at the end of 1991, Kursk acquired the status of a border region. In practical terms this meant an immediate increase in social and economic pressure on the oblast. Cross-border economic links were severed overnight and large numbers of Ukrainian citizens converged on the region in search of Russian rubles through trade, work, or criminal activity.[14] Russian disengagement from its former imperial entanglements also led to the resettlement in the oblast of Russian soldiers from Central Europe and migrants and refugees from the "Near Abroad."[15] At the same time, the creation of a sovereign Ukraine was viewed by many as dividing historic Russian lands and the single Russian people.[16] Difficulties related to the new border were seen as a direct consequence of Yeltsin's support for the demise of the Soviet Union.

Although regional hostility to the Russian government's reformist agenda was directly attributable to the socioeconomic dislocation of the transition period, it also stemmed from a traditionally conservative political culture rooted in the collective rural communities of the oblast. Under tsarist rule, Kursk had one of the most oppressive forms of serfdom in the empire and was a center for the activities of the antisemitic Black Hundreds movement.

During the Soviet era, the region had particularly important links to the Communist party hierarchy, with both Nikita Khrushchev and Leonid Brezhnev closely connected with the area.[17] In the late 1980s and early 1990s, conservative local sons such as Ivan Polozkov, the first leader of the Russian Communist party, and Aleksandr Rutskoi, former vice president of Russia, played central roles in national politics. The prominence of local figures among the Soviet elite helped to foster a strong association between the region and the communist order, a relationship that was undergirded by Kursk's part in World War II.

In the summer of 1943, Kursk was at the center of one of the major battles on the Eastern Front and afterward was included in the list of the fifteen most devastated cities in the Russian Federation. The role of Kursk in the Great Patriotic War (World War II) became a central component of the region's identity, a fact reflected in a network of museums devoted to the battle of Kursk and in the centrality accorded to veterans organizations and the military in the life of the oblast. A close dovetailing of the history of the Communist party and celebration of Kursk's role in the war was fundamental to the mythology that sustained Soviet rule in the region.

The strong tradition of conservatism in Kursk ensured that during the perestroika years deputies from the region took little part in the activity of reformist political blocs such as the Interregional Group in the USSR Supreme Soviet,[18] gravitating instead to the factions of the conservative camp.[19] The region did, however, vote for Yeltsin in the 1991 presidential election.[20] After independence, voters in the oblast returned to their old ways, electing highly conservative deputies and also voting against President Yeltsin on the key questions in the April 1993 referendum.[21]

Despite the region's conservatism, in the latter years of perestroika Kursk did produce an indigenous opposition to communist rule. In 1989, a fledgling democratic movement appeared in the oblast based around an environmental organization *(Rodnik)*. In late 1990, activists in this movement served as the core for the creation of a local branch of Democratic Party of Russia (DPR). In the early 1990s, this small nucleus of opposition played a crucial role in fragmenting the region's once monolithic political elite.

Political Change and New Elites in Kursk Oblast

Although the political culture of the region, its social structure, and the economic difficulties of the transition favored highly conservative candidates, as a result of the process of political transformation emanating from Moscow during the late perestroika era and accelerating with Russian independence, after 1991 the power and cohesion of the local Communist elite had been severely weakened. At the same time, the former dominance of the Communists was challenged by the emergence of a local democratic movement and the administration as significant local political forces.

In the year immediately following the 1991 coup, there was little visible change in the oblast. During this period the reformist forces remained small. Despite the abolition of the Communist party, the former political elite continued to control the oblast. There were, however, two important personnel changes at the highest levels of the Kursk political system that were later to prove fundamental to the ability of the socialist movement to determine the political life of the region.

In the aftermath of the August 1991 putsch, as in many other regions, Yeltsin appointed a new head of the local administration, Vasilii Shuteyev, and established the position of representative of the president in Kursk oblast, a post filled by Aleksandr Kureninov. Initially, the reformist movement, led by Kureninov and Shuteyev, worked together to circumscribe the power of the local Communists. By the beginning of 1993, however, the informal alliance between the reformists and the administration had fractured. The democratic movement began to lose cohesion as Kureninov and the leadership of the DPR grew increasingly antagonistic toward each other. In contrast, Shuteev had transformed the administration into the most powerful organization in local affairs.

The Socialist Bloc

Although the ban on the Communist party following the 1991 putsch presented a problem for the organization of Communist forces in the area, the dominance of Communist deputies in the oblast and raion-level soviets provided a natural base to which the residual Communist party could gravitate. However, although control over the soviets and the presence of Communist sympathizers in powerful positions throughout the oblast meant that the precoup political network that had controlled the area remained largely in place, this was not the Communist party of old.

The ideology of the Soviet system was largely in tatters and was defended with conviction by only a few hard-liners who formed small parties with little influence. At the same time, the ban on the Communist party had broken up the main institutions of Communist rule in the oblast—the party cells and committees in each workplace and public organization. Following the coup, the real strength of the Communists lay not in any formal organization or belief system but in the network of relationships that had made up local government and management in the oblast, a network composed almost entirely of former apparatchiki, those who owed their position to a career in, or allegiance with, the Communist party. This was especially the case in the rural areas.

Initially, this network provided a powerful basis for controlling political developments in the oblast. Its utility was demonstrated in April 1993 when opposition to President Yeltsin's referendum proposals was organized through this network. In addition, the head of the oblast soviet, Vladimir Likhachev, relied on this network to mobilize support for his successful campaign in April 1993 to win the parliamentary seat vacated by Aleksandr Rutskoi.[22]

Personal relationships were, however, a poor substitute for the discipline of the former Communist party, and new economic and political interests placed the cohesion of the former Communist elite under strain. The candidacy of a number of leading figures from the socialist bloc who ran against Likhachev in the April election demonstrated that the Communist movement was now far from monolithic. Leading figures in the socialist bloc in the oblast were ready to unite against Yeltsin and the policies of the Russian government, but when it came to distributing power in the region, political cohesion quickly broke down. In such a situation, different interests within the socialist network were prepared to promote their own candidates and individuals were ready to pursue their careers at the expense of unity.[23]

The Reformist Bloc

From the early part of 1993, changing economic conditions in the oblast, the loss of a clearly defined "enemy," and the political difficulties of the democrats in Moscow began to fragment the reformist movement in Kursk. Central to this process of disintegration was Aleksandr Kureninov. The choice of Kureninov as Yeltsin's representative following the coup had been a surprising one. He had previously worked as head of the ideological section in the Kursk KGB. Kureninov's strong public opposition to the 1991 putsch, however, persuaded the oblast leadership of the Democratic Party of Russia (DPR) that he was committed to change, and they nominated him to become the local presidential representative. In fact, the appointment of Kureninov provided the catalyst for a division in the local movement between the former leadership of the Kursk democrats who supported an agenda based primarily on radical political reform and also local supporters of the Moscow-inspired drive for further rapid economic change.

From its inception, the DPR in the oblast had been a loose coalition of activists and representatives from political parties united on the basis of their opposition to Soviet domination. Although vocal in its opposition to the 1991 coup, the Kursk branch of the DPR was a very weak organization. Of the 130 deputies in the city soviet, only nine identified with the DPR, whereas in the oblast soviet only three to five of the 200 deputies could be considered loyal to the movement. By the beginning of 1993, the loose ties that bound together the disparate forces that made up the DPR in the oblast were beginning to unravel.

In March 1993 a clear split emerged between Kureninov and the political radicals of the DPR over how the campaign for the April referendum should be conducted. Following this initial split and the poor support shown for Yeltsin in the oblast during the referendum, the tension between the different strands of the reformist movement became more pronounced. In response to the call by the national leadership of the DPR to create local organizations to unite reformist elements for future elections, a division again appeared in the movement with the radicals and Kureninov establishing parallel and competing organizations. Whereas the radicals demanded sweeping democratization in the region, Kureninov's organization sought to engage the support of new economic interests in the oblast, particularly those connected with privatization, by stressing the need for further economic reform.[24]

The struggle for the soul of the opposition movement finally came to a head on September 2, when the radical core of the DPR wrote to Yeltsin accusing Kureninov of conducting a campaign to slow the democratic process in the oblast and requesting his immediate removal.[25] The appeal to Moscow signaled the disintegration of the reformist bloc in the oblast. As a result, two delegates were sent from Kursk to the founding congress of Russia's Choice in October; Kureninov and a delegate from the radical wing of the DPR.

The Administration

Although officially neutral, following the 1991 coup the administration and particularly Shuteyev, its new head, came to play a central role in political developments in the oblast. Before his appointment, Shuteyev had been a leading industrial manager in Kursk. Although certainly an important economic figure in the oblast, he was not part of the inner circle of political power. His rapid elevation to head the administration introduced an element of uncertainty into the local political system. Coming from outside the narrow ruling political elite, he owed his promotion to Yeltsin rather than to local political patrons, and his network of contacts was rooted in the nomenklatura of enterprise managers rather than the old Communist party elite.

Shuteyev emerged as a cautious reformer rather than a radical. Nevertheless, his backing for initiatives from Moscow was crucial to the reform process in the oblast. Under his leadership, the administration was gradually decoupled from Communist domination. As a result, the administration was able to provide the bureaucratic means to enforce presidential decrees that circumscribed the activities of the local Communists and forced them to operate within the law, especially in regard to elections.

With Shuteyev's support, fundamental economic reforms were implemented that were also to have important political consequences. The central role played by the administration in privatization drew important economic actors, notably the enterprise managers, away from the socialist network and closer to the technocrats in the administration. In addition, it was as a consequence of the economic reforms promoted by the administration that the cohesion of the two leading local political movements—the reformists and the socialists—came under severe pressure.[26]

New Political Institutions in the Oblast

A wide range of political organizations was officially registered in the oblast on the eve of the election, but very few of them performed any significant functions. At best, official political organizations could mobilize only a handful of activists. The single largest group of public organizations was oriented toward the reformist movement; however, these were also the weakest political organizations in the area.[27] A number of formal organizations had also been established by different figures and groupings within the socialist bloc.[28] Although informal contacts continued to be the glue that held this bloc together, these organizations provided an important link between the leadership and the rank-and-file activists. Zhirinovskii's Liberal Democratic Party of Russia (LDPR) and the DPR were also registered in the oblast, but each commanded only a few local activists.

As well as dedicated political organizations, a number of economic associations with a political significance had been created in the area. Under pressure from the difficult economic environment and the challenge of privatization, in early September 1993 the Kursk oblast Union of Entrepreneurs was established to lobby on behalf of business.[29] Despite its claim to represent a wide range of interests, this organization was in fact based on the old directors corpus and operated as a pressure group for enterprises tied to the agroindustrial complex. It had very good links to the administration through Shuteev, himself a former industrialist.

In 1991 a branch of the Organization of Peasants and Farmers of Russia (AKKOR), an agrarian reform movement led by the proreformist Vladimir Tikhonov, was established in Kursk. The organization worked actively to develop private farming in the oblast and to assist the private farmers who were already registered in the area.

The September–October "Events"

President Yeltsin's September 1993 decree suspending the activity of the soviets had two important effects on the political situation in the oblast immediately before the elections. First, the presidential decree dissolving the soviet structure and the subsequent storming of the White House in Moscow served to intensify hostility to Yeltsin and the Russian government among the local population. Second, the eventual suspension of the activity of the local soviets and the concentration of power in the hands of the Kursk administration further weakened the cohesion of the socialist political elite in the oblast.

In a series of emergency sessions of the oblast soviet in late September, local deputies made clear their opposition to Yeltsin's actions and they refused to support the formation of electoral committees or the dissolution of the soviets.[30] The opposition to Yeltsin's actions displayed by the Kursk soviet was characteristic of local soviets throughout Russia but hostility to the president's actions was intensified in the region by the powerful local following for Aleksandr Rutskoi, one of the leaders of the October putsch, a native of Kursk and until April 1993 a deputy from the region.

The activity of the Kursk soviet was vociferously resisted by local democratic activists and Kureninov, the presidential representative in the oblast. The September–October crisis revealed, however, that it was the administration, rather than the democratic movement, that constituted the principal challenge to the local Communist elite.[31] Although Shuteyev expressed his dislike for the confrontation in Moscow, by late September he had also made clear his obedience to the president and opposition to any illegal actions, thereby neutralizing the local soviet.[32]

Following the assault on the White House in Moscow, the local soviets quickly abandoned their resistance. By October 11 the administration had closed most of the raion soviets.[33] The oblast soviet lingered until the end of the month in the hope that it could influence the composition of the electoral commissions, but by the end of October, political power in the oblast had passed almost completely into the hands of the administration.[34]

On the eve of the electoral campaign, the political situation in the oblast was, therefore, in considerable flux. The socialist movement enjoyed a number of significant advantages, most notably a strongly conservative electorate reflecting the local demographic and social structure, the political culture of the region, the socioeconomic crisis in the area, and disenchantment with the collapse of the USSR. The September to October events in Moscow had also been poorly received in the oblast. The socialists did not, however, enjoy an unassailable position.

From the late 1980s the Communist organization had been under almost continuous pressure. In the latter years of the Gorbachev era, the established networks of political patronage in Kursk were weakened by the replacement of the local Communist grandees with a new generation of leaders. The ban on the Communist party following the 1991 putsch and the dissolution of the soviet structure in 1993 had destroyed the institutional base of the Communists in the oblast, and the emergence of Russian nationalist, agrarian, and a number of separate Communist parties threatened to fracture further the antireform political constituency. As a result of these changes, by October 1993 the Communists in the oblast no longer functioned as a single, cohesive group, and they were particularly weakly organized in the city of Kursk.

The once dominant position of the socialists in the oblast was also threatened by the presence of a considerable number of voters, particularly in the city of Kursk, who were opposed to the Communists. If the socialist movement was to be challenged, these voters would have to be welded into a single electoral bloc.

Mobilizing the anticommunist voters would, however, be difficult, for like the socialists, the reformist movement, too, faced severe problems. By November 1993, the foremost local reformist figures were involved in an internecine struggle and lacked a credible popular leader, resources, or a disciplined local movement capable of conducting the electoral campaign. Indeed, the oblast did not have a single formal political organization that could serve as the main means to mobilize significant numbers of activists or voters.

The unknown quantity in the local political equation was the position of Shuteyev. The administration constituted the only local organization that could significantly challenge the power of the socialist movement, especially in the countryside. Shuteyev's support had been essential for economic reform in the area, and his actions were crucial in containing the local soviet during the September–October crisis. The administration, however, had been neutral in a narrowly party political sense. Determining the role of the administration soon emerged as the central struggle of the campaign.

The Election

Despite the significant advantages enjoyed by conservative forces in the oblast on the eve of the elections, the broad set of political and socioeconomic changes introduced during the perestroika period and in the early years of independence had created new political opportunities in Kursk. The decisions of political actors, as much as the deeper structural factors, were therefore to play an important role in shaping the outcome of the elections. The fluidity that characterized political life in the oblast in late 1993 ensured that this electoral contest was to have a critical influence on the future political trajectory of Kursk.

Electoral Topography

Given the significance of the urban vote for the prospects of reformist and centrist candidates, the structure of electoral districts in the oblast was likely to have an important influence on the outcome of the elections. For the December elections, the electoral boundaries established for previous elections in the region were redrawn. The oblast as a whole was to serve as the basis for the election of two deputies to the Federation Council (District 46), whereas the region was split into two single-seat districts (Districts 98 and 99) for the election of the Duma deputies.

Federation Council electoral District 46 had an overall ratio of registered urban to rural voters of 0.83 to 1 (451,879 in the five main urban centers/544,506 in small rural towns or villages).[35] Winning in this district would be extremely difficult for the reformists, but moderate conservatives appeared to have good prospects.

In Duma electoral District 98 (505,173 registered voters), the chances for non-Communist candidates were particularly strong. The ratio of registered urban to rural voters was two to one. Based on the April referendum, the political geography of the district was divided along three axis: the three Kursk city raions were generally proreform; the two northeastern rural raions were moderate; and the other seven rural areas and the town of Shchigry (only 32 percent voted for Yeltsin in April) were highly conservative. If the Communists were to be beaten, the moderate Kursk electorate would have to be mobilized and support in key rural raions ensured.

Finally, in Duma electoral District 99 (491,212 registered voters) the ratio of urban to rural voters was 0.31 to 1. In April 1993, five rural raions in the south had voted for the president, eight had emerged as moderate, and six as conservative. Seventy-five percent of the electorate in Kurchatov (30,015 voters) had voted for Yeltsin in April, but in the highly conservative towns of Zheleznogorsk (66,187 voters) and L'gov (19,196 voters) the figures were only 40 percent and 38 percent, respectively. Victory for a non-Communist candidate could only be achieved here by winning in the villages.

The Campaign

Before the election, direct opposition to the Communist political machine had been largely confined to the reformist movement. However, throughout November and December, a new political force emerged in the oblast: representatives of new economic interests. Initially, the leaders of this grouping forged an alliance with key sections of the reformist movement and, at the same time, sought to build links with Shuteev. In response, the Communists tried to limit the influence of the administration and prevent the establishment of any form of coalition involving Shuteev.

Stage 1: The Formation of Electoral Blocs and the Nomination of Candidates

As in many parts of Russia, the signature campaign in the oblast was an extremely complicated process. The need to collect signatures simultaneously for national parties and to nominate local candidates for national party lists and for local territorial districts served to highlight the weak links between regional and national political institutions. In particular, the campaign demonstrated the poor organization of local parties and the low level of party allegiance. Overall, the signature and nomination campaign was characterized by considerable confusion and a convoluted process of political maneuvering by prospective candidates and political organizations.

The Socialist Bloc

The signature and nomination campaign caused considerable tension within the ranks of the socialist bloc. At the beginning of the campaign, there was no KPRF slate of candidates; instead there was a variety of individuals who pursued their own nomination independently.[36] The former head of the oblast soviet, Vladimir Likhachev, was nominated by the Agrarian Union, which then organized the collection of signatures for him, primarily from rural centers.[37] Three leading members of the socialist bloc, Nikolai Kononov, president of Kursk Agricultural Institute, Aleksandr Mikhailov, former president of Shchigry soviet of People's Deputies, and

Nikolai Ivanov, deputy director of Kursk Labor Center, collected signatures as part of the Socialist Workers' party national list.[38] Ultimately, this list failed and only Mikhailov collected sufficient signatures to run in a territorial district.

At the Second National Congress of the Agrarian party held in Moscow, Vitalii Gukov, a leading member of the Kursk socialist bloc, opted for a position on the party's national list. Gukov was already president of the local Agrarian party and also of the Kursk Agrarian Union. He was joined on the Agrarian party national list by Valentina Luneva, president of Fatezh Raikom of Trade Union of Workers in the Agroindustrial Complex. Luneva also became a candidate for the rural L'gov territorial district.[39]

The Reformist Bloc

In the course of this first phase of the election campaign the disintegration of the local reformist movement was completed with its fragmentation into three main groupings.

RUSSIA'S CHOICE.   Having attended the founding congress of Russia's Choice in Moscow, on October 2 Kureninov sought to establish a regional branch of Russia's Choice in Kursk.[40] At the founding congress of the local movement, the split in the reformist forces was clearly apparent. Most of the radical leaders of the DPR were absent, replaced by entrepreneurs, local intelligentsia, and members of the administration.[41] During the meeting, the lack of unity within the reformist bloc was noted, but it was thought that a united list of candidates could be agreed on at a later date.[42] A slate of candidates drawn largely from the intelligentsia was agreed on.[43] However, by the end of the month this list had been replaced by one based on the local leadership of Russia's Choice.[44]

DEMOCRATIC RADICALS.   At this early stage of the election campaign, the remnants of the DPR in the oblast were still active. A meeting of the oblast and city sections of the Association of Voters, an organization established in opposition to Kureninov, was called on October 23 to discuss the formation of a list of candidates.[45] At the meeting it was agreed to collect signatures for two candidates for the Federation Council.[46]

REFORMIST–NEW MONEY.   As it became apparent that the reformist bloc was disintegrating, many of the leading figures in the local Russia's Choice organization left the movement and joined a new political coalition based on the moderate reformist Russian Movement for Democratic Reform (RDDR) and a number of local entrepreneurs. The potential success of this new alliance lay in the prospect of combining the organizational resources of the RDDR with the financial resources of the new business interests. The main characteristic of the grouping was a strong emphasis on professionalism and economic issues.[47]

At the heart of this new political coalition was a group of young entrepreneurs whose money came from trade. Following Yeltsin's decree calling for early elections, this group decided to establish a committee to represent its interests at political meetings, to support independent candidates, and to work "for the consolidation of democratic forces." The leadership of the committee was dissatisfied with the Kursk Union of Entrepreneurs and its exclusive focus on industrial production.[48] As the two reformist groups in the oblast fragmented, the RDDR became the organizational vehicle for their political ambitions.[49]

Headed by a former ally of Kureninov, E. N. Alekseyev, the RDDR offered prospective candidates both the services of local activists to collect signatures and the chance to appear on the national party list. Three former members of Russia's Choice were put forward for the RDDR party list: V. N. Sayenko, president of Oblast Property Foundation in the administration; the entrepreneur Larisa A. Samotes, and the academic Aleksandr A. Grachev. Samotes and the academic Nikolai Pridvorov, both of whom had previously been active in Russia's Choice, were nominated to run in the two territorial districts. Leonid Usenkov, the leader of the businesspeople, was put forward as a candidate for the Federation Council.[50] Strong overtures were also made to Shuteyev, who would have become their second candidate for the Federation Council. At this stage, this group appeared to be a potentially powerful rival to the socialist bloc.

The Governor

Shuteyev was one of the first candidates to register, and he was endorsed by the Association of Entrepreneurs. The governor used the administration to collect quickly the required number of signatures.

Independent Candidates

The remaining candidates collected signatures through their own local organizations and usually from a specialized constituency. Fedor N. Ryzhkov, the rector of Kursk Polytechnic, for example, collected the majority of his signatures from students in the institute.[51] Although organizationally weak, the LDPR collected sufficient signatures locally for two candidates, the oblast coordinator of the party, Artor A. Chubur and Yurii M. Ruda, a member of the Central Committee of the Party, who was also nominated for the national party list.[52]

Stage Two: Election Campaigning

Although many of the alliances established during the first stage of the campaign were subsequently to disintegrate, the signature and nomination campaign established the broad parameters for the subsequent political contest (see figure 16-1).

The Socialist Bloc

The Communists came away from the first stage of the campaign with the most coherent grouping. The bloc represented an alliance between the leading members of the socialist network in the oblast and was composed of two main groupings of candidates.

"OFFICAL" COMMUNISTS. The inner core of the socialist bloc consisted of four "official" Communist party candidates. This slate was formed from the most powerful Communists in the oblast. Before the signature campaign there had been, at best, weak coordination between the figures in this group (signaled by the fact that several candidates joined party lists other than that of the Communist Party of the Russian Federation). The alliance came into existence only in the final days of the signature campaign, and candidates within the coalition often failed to act as a unified group during the election campaign.

Initially, the official Communists consisted of just three candidates. Likhachev and I. P. Vorob'ev were to challenge for the Federation Council, and Mikhailov was to run for the Duma in Kursk district. A deal had been struck with the Agrarian party whereby the Communists would not run in the predominately rural district of L'gov, leaving the way open for the Agrarian candidate Luneva. Links between the Communists and the Agrarian party were close and maintained through a number of organizations with overlapping leadership. Likhachev was originally nominated by the Agrarian Union, headed by Gukov, the leader of the Agrarian party in the

Figure 16-1. *Candidates and Alliances following the Signature Campaign*

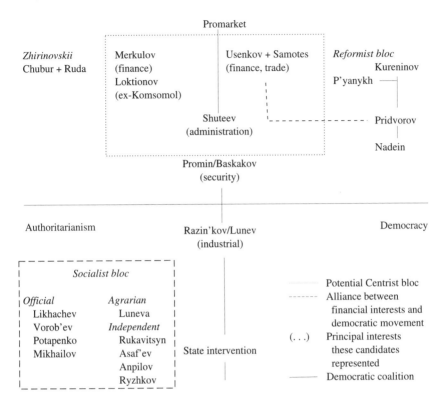

oblast. Gukov was also copresident with Aleksandr N. Anpilov of the Movement for People's Power and Reform for the People. As the campaign progressed, however, Aleksandr Potapenko, who had initially campaigned independently from the three main Communists, joined the inner core of Communist candidates, and the Agrarian candidate was marginalized.

The strongest candidate among the official Communists was Vladimir Likhachev, a former kolkhoz president, who had become head of the oblast soviet following the August 1991 coup. In his campaign, Likhachev focused on the need to strengthen production and to provide much greater support for the needs of the villages. In his speeches he spoke out against the constitution and attacked Yegor Gaidar. Likhachev was also against the sale of land. Although never presented as forming a ticket, contacts between Likhachev and the other leading Communist candidate for the Federation Council, Vorob'ev, were close. During the campaign Vorob'ev made very few open public appearances and focused mainly on closed meetings in factories and farms arranged through the Communist network.

Aleksandr Mikhailov was the most politically orthodox of the official Communist candidates. He made few public appearances, but when he did he spoke against "the constitution of the dictator." Mikhailov's former position as head of the raion soviet in Shchigry gave him an important presence in the countryside, and neocommunist organizations such as People's Power and Reform for the People provided the organizational infrastructure for his campaign in the city. As president of the oblast Executive Committee of the Communist Party of the Russian Federation (KPRF), he also had close contacts with the national movement, which was why he also appeared on the Communist party list.

"INDEPENDENT" COMMUNISTS.   The second part of the socialist bloc consisted of four "independent" candidates—Anatolii P. Rukavitsyn, Ryzhkov, Vsevolod I. Asaf'ev, and Anpilov—who were attached to the Communist network but were only secondary or peripheral figures in it, and the Agrarians. The presence of some of these candidates in the campaign caused acute friction within the bloc because although the independent Communists campaigned against the constitution and the Russian government alongside the official Communists, they stood against the inner core of Communist candidates in the territorial contests. The motivations for standing for election among this group were mixed. Some simply felt that as important local figures they were also entitled to a place in Parliament—Rukavitsyn was a former second secretary disgraced following a driving-while-intoxicated accident—and others such as Anpilov were pursuing more long-term careerist goals.

Toward the end of the campaign, the relationship between independent and official Communists grew tense, particularly when a split occurred between the official Communists and the Agrarian party. The main reason for the rift between the Communists and the Agrarians was the candidacy of Aleksandr Potapenko in the rural L'gov territorial district. In a television interview early in the campaign, Potapenko admitted to being a member of the Communist Party of the Russian Federation but claimed he had split from it and was running as an independent against the instructions of the party. It later became apparent, however, that Potapenko was still in close contact with leading Communists in the oblast—indeed he remained a member of the obkom of the party—and was running as a covert Communist candidate. As the alliance between the leading Communists and the

Agrarian party broke down, a number of the independent Communists drifted away from the official Communists and toward the Agrarian party. Anpilov, in particular, became an unofficial candidate for the Agrarians against Mikhailov in District 98 (Kursk).[53]

Although Luneva was the sole candidate of the Agrarian party for a territorial district, her campaign was dominated by Vitalii Gukov, the powerful leader of the local branch of the Agrarian party. The Agrarian party program was designed to appeal to the rural dwellers, but the party, ironically, lacked an effective base in the countryside. It was the Communist elite that had inherited the organizational structure of the Soviet Communist party in each rural district rather than the Agrarians. The control of the countryside exercised by the leading Communists was the main reason the Agrarian party did unexpectedly poorly in the villages of the region.

The Reformist Bloc

The reformists emerged from the signature campaign in a far more disorganized form than the Communists. The DPR failed to get any of its candidates nominated and was politically sidelined for the rest of the election. The local branch of Russia's Choice became the personal political vehicle of the presidential representative, Kureninov, and was shorn of the support of all the main reformist leaders and parties in the oblast. Indeed, considerable efforts were made by reformist candidates to get Kureninov to withdraw his candidacy. The only local organization to provide serious support for his campaign was the regional branch of the Organization of Peasants and Farmers of Russia (AKKOR). Using the private farmers in the oblast as a gateway to the wider rural population, AKKOR organized meetings for Kureninov in the villages and the AKKOR director, Petr Pereversil, traveled with Kureninov in rural areas.

At electoral meetings, Kureninov tied himself firmly to the Russia's Choice banner. He spoke in support of further privatization and the extension of private farming *(fermirizatsii)* and came out strongly in favor of the constitution. He also described private property as the "foundation of the state."[54] Kureninov often faced intense hostility, especially over the new constitution and the shelling of the White House. His general passivity and total lack of charisma did little to help the cause of Russia's Choice. During the campaign he was dogged by rumors that a large new house being built for him had been a gift from the leadership of the oblast soviet.

The most active reformist candidate was Sergei P'yanykh, the deputy head of the Antimonopoly Committee. In 1990 he became one of the handful of DPR deputies in the oblast soviet. During the August 1991 coup, while working in the Ministry of the Interior, he is reputed to have drawn a pistol on a general supporting the plotters. Before the election, he had been a member of the Republican party, but in November he decided to join Yabloko.[55] He was extremely promarket and campaigned on the protection of citizens' rights.

Petr Nadein was one of the more successful reformist candidates, largely because he could employ the infrastructure of the administration to support his campaign. A former cultural worker in the Communist party, his position as president of the administration's Committee for Culture and Art meant that he could rely on cultural workers employed in the administration—in libraries, schools, and museums—to arrange meetings in many areas. He was the only candidate to get his program published in raion papers.[56]

Nikolai Pridvorov, the remaining reformist candidate, was largely marginalized during the campaign as the initial alliance between the RDDR and the new business interests broke up. Reflecting his background in the study of law, Pridvorov campaigned in support of the constitution, stressing the need for good laws in the new Parliament and competent professionals to enact such laws.[57]

Evolving Centrism

The disintegration of the reformist movement in Kursk and the unpopularity of reformist—particularly radical reformist parties—in the oblast fostered the emergence of a loose grouping of centrist candidates toward the latter stages of the election campaign. The move to form an alliance was led by Leonid Usenkov, the twenty-eight-year-old director of the sugar trading group Linkor, the fifth largest private organization in the oblast. During the signature campaign, Usenkov had emerged as the spokesperson for new business interests in the region and allied himself with the moderate reformists of the RDDR.[58]

The main focus of Usenkov's program was on economic issues. He called for measures to stimulate production and to reduce taxes and price differentials between rural and urban products. Reflecting the international trading base of his company—Linkor had offices in Kiev—he also called for the restoration of economic links between the former republics of the

USSR, particularly with Ukraine and Belarus. Usenkov was very supportive of the constitution as a means of keeping Russia united and providing
the basic legal framework for private sector business activity.[59]

Although members of the RDDR worked for Usenkov until election day,
as it became clear that being associated with a reformist group, particularly
a Moscow-based organization, could be a liability in Kursk, Usenkov severed his connection to the party. In the last days of the election, Usenkov
tried to change the direction of his campaign. He adopted a more centrist
position, focusing on moderate economic reform and toning down his initial commitment to radical political change. Usenkov also sought to foster
an alliance with Gennadii Merkulov, an independent centrist candidate.

The young president of the Moscow-based Aviation-Marine Check Investment Fund, Merkulov was in many ways similar to Usenkov. Although
not linked to any party, he was initially on the national list of the Association of Independent Professionals. When this organization failed to secure
sufficient signatures to run as a party list, he decided to seek nomination in
his home town instead. Merkulov organized one of the most successful
campaigns of the election. He kept clear of any party label and rather than
outlining specific policies, he sought to build an image of independence
and competence backed by two main conservative constituencies: the military and the church.

There were 10,000 serving military personnel in the oblast who together
with their families and the large number of veterans constituted a sizeable
voting bloc. Merkulov's wife was the daughter of a local general and his investment company specialized in financial services for the military. Both of
these factors gave him unchallenged access to the armed forces. Merkulov's rating was also greatly enhanced by endorsement from the church.[60]
His electoral agent was a priest, Father Nikodim Yevmolaty,[61] and he also
received support from other powerful church leaders.[62]

Another successful campaign was run by Sergei P. Loktionov, the head
of youth organizations in Kursk. Loktionov's campaign was built almost
entirely on the infrastructure of the ex-Komsomol. He was nominated for
the national list of the Future of Russia–New Names party and was funded
by Kursk Bank, which was run by the former head of the local Komsomol.
He also used the youth organizations in the city and oblast to organize
events to promote his candidacy. The core of Loktionov's campaign was
directed at the youth in the area, although he also cultivated other important
constituencies. Trained as a surgeon, Loktionov also sought to build support on the basis of the large number of medical personnel in the oblast and

from the cultural intelligentsia. He also campaigned hard in the rural areas. He stressed the need to give significant financial support to agriculture and made a great deal of his conversion to Christianity. He expressed great sympathy for monarchism and was critical of government tax policy on new entrepreneurs.[63]

The Administration

If the centrist candidates were to be successful, much depended on forging an alliance with the governor, with whom they shared many common interests.[64] Shuteyev had potentially the strongest political machine in the oblast in the form of the administration. The infrastructure of the administration, especially the more than 1,000 personnel employed in its agriculture sections, provided Shuteyev with a powerful organization to break the stranglehold on the villages held by the Communists. During the campaign Shuteyev continued to support privatization and an extension of private farming in the oblast and made a great deal of his technocratic credentials as a professional manager and administrator.[65]

Like other representatives of the administration, for Shuteyev the single most important issue in the election was the constitution. Shuteyev believed that without a constitution the country would be ungovernable.[66] Passing the constitution would not only ensure a stable environment within which the administration could operate but it would also enshrine the right to private property, thereby protecting the gains of privatization. A week before the election Shuteyev announced that he was abandoning his personal campaign to work full-time to get the constitution passed. Despite the overtures of the centrist candidates, Shuteyev remained independent from any of the other blocs or candidates.

Marginal Candidates

Although the Civic Union ran two candidates in the oblast, its campaign was lackluster. Aleksei Lunev, a former deputy in the Russian Parliament, was inactive, and as a Civic Union candidate in a rural area he had no obvious constituency. Yurii T. Razin'kov was better placed, being a member of the Kursk Union of Industrialists, which also supported his candidacy. He was in close contact with Civic Union in Moscow and received campaign materials from the national organization. As leader of the factory trade union, he could also use ten to twelve union workers to canvass for him, had access to the union paper and the thirty-three branches of his union across the oblast. Razin'kov was, however, handicapped by the fact that the interests of factory directors were far more powerfully represented in the campaign by Shuteyev, whereas small and new businesses looked to the RDDR–Usenkov alliance or the independent Merkulov as their candidates.

The two Zhirinovskii candidates operated on the margins of the political contest and it was only in the last week of the campaign that they became a serious force in Kursk itself. Neither candidate developed an identity separate from Zhirinovskii and all their efforts were focused on promoting their leader. Chubur, one of the local candidates, used his twenty-minute television appearance simply to state that Russia should become a great power, needed a new hymn, flag, and coat of arms, and concluded his broadcast with fifteen minutes of photographic stills of Zhirinovskii.

The security interests in the oblast were represented by two candidates: Anatolii Pronin, a major-general in a Moscow division of the KGB, and Anatolii Baskakov, deputy head of the Criminal Investigation Division of the Kursk branch of the Ministry of Internal Affairs. Pronin relied on his brother, who was head of the Kursk division of the Ministry of Internal Affairs, to organize his campaign.[67] Conducting a campaign by proxy did little, however, to endear Pronin to local voters. Baskakov, on the other hand, was far more successful. Being part of the 1980s team from the USSR Procuracy that had exposed corruption in Uzbekistan, he had strong popular political credentials. Baskakov's perceived independence, coupled with a program that stressed law and order, was antishock therapy but proprivate property and for a reduction in taxes on profit, gave him a popular platform in the oblast. He used the militia, including the local police paper, as the organizational infrastructure for his campaign.[68]

Campaign Tactics

The differing political resources available to candidates produced two main approaches to the electoral campaign. The single most powerful political resource available during the campaign was access to existing organizational networks. The informal links that had been established by leading members of the former Communist party proved to be a particularly important political force in the oblast. This network was led by experienced leaders with access to key resources and spanned the rural-urban divide in a way that no other political organization did. The administration, too, offered Shuteev a powerful organizational base that gave him the opportunity to campaign in the villages.

Candidates with access to either the socialist network or the administration could target their campaign. Election workers could be mobilized, meetings arranged, and opponents could be shut out. With such assets, there was no need to conduct a high profile campaign, and candidates in these networks did not hold mass meetings or rallies. For the existing political elite, it was an election fought in the shadows, lobbying through their local network of contacts and on the phone.

The particular challenge for candidates without a developed organization structure was to break into the conservative citadel of the countryside. Because the policies of individual candidates were often similar, party labels had little impact, and new local organizations were weak, a great deal came to depend on the character of the individual candidate. Many of the opposition candidates, especially the younger ones, adopted a campaign approach that focused more on personality and style rather than substance. They also employed the previously unknown political weapons of humor and sarcasm. The key new factor in the election that went some way to help offset the imbalance in organizational resources was money.

In December 1993, for the first time in the oblast, the media was no longer a political resource under the monopoly control of the Communists. Money permitted candidates access to newspaper, television, and radio coverage and became one of the most effective ways to reach the electorate, especially the rural population. Although some of the urban population had subscriptions to national papers (the numbers of such publications penetrating the countryside was probably small), it was the local papers that played the most important role.[69] The official paper in the oblast, *Kurskaya pravda,* adopted an essentially passive position, providing information rather than analysis or opinion. With most of the raion papers controlled by those within the socialist political network, a great deal depended on independent papers produced in Kursk.[70]

The independent press in the city consisted of three papers: *Gorodskiye izvestiya, Molodaya gvardiya,* and *Khoroshiye novosti.* The latter was devoted to sensationalism and advertising and steered clear of politics.[71] Both of the other papers gave extensive coverage to candidates who sought to challenge the socialist bloc. These papers, especially *Gorodskiye izvestiya,* published a series of interviews with such candidates, printed the economic program of Russia's Choice, and also launched attacks against Communist candidates.[72] Because of the difficulty of penetrating the rural areas with print, television became the most powerful campaign tool available to candidates. Beginning November 22, each candidate was entitled to 20 minutes of free time on television. The head of local television ensured a militant neutrality in this regard. Candidates were also allowed to purchase advertising.[73]

The young independent candidates made the best use of the media. Merkulov ran a high-profile campaign. He gave as many interviews as possible,[74] and spent considerable amounts of money on political advertising.[75] Loktionov and Usenkov used similar tactics. On December 6, a poster war began in Kursk. Merkulov used large color posters printed in Moscow, a move considered to be a humiliation for Likhachev and Shuteyev who could only afford smaller black and white ones. Previously, those who occupied the leading positions in the oblast had also controlled all resources. Merkulov's campaign showed that the link between political power and economic might was changing. In the last week of the campaign, all three of the young candidates bought large amounts of time on television as a means of getting access to the rural districts.

Explaining Electoral Outcomes

The results of the election confirmed Kursk's standing as one of the most conservative of Russia's oblasts and underlined the political direction of the region first revealed in the April 1993 referendum. Indeed, the vote against the constitution in December 1993 (57 percent against) was almost identical to that against the president in April 1993 (58 percent against). The poor level of support for Russia's Choice (10.64 percent) even in urban areas and strong backing for the conservative parties (LDPR, 33.48 percent; Communists, 20.03 percent; Agrarians, 11.46 percent) also suggests that opinion in the oblast was extremely hostile to the government's socio-economic policies.

The strong conservatism of the region was further emphasized in the single-mandate contests.[76] Three of the four candidates from the inner core of the socialist bloc were triumphant. In contrast, the reformists were comprehensively defeated in all aspects of the election and their organizations disintegrated. None of the main reformist candidates managed to make it into the top three places for any of the contests, and the leader of Russia's Choice in the oblast—the presidential representative Kureninov—was pushed into a humiliating last place in the campaign for the Federation Council.

The overwhelming victory of Communist and nationalist forces in all aspects of the election owed much to the range of structural factors outlined in the first section of this chapter. The numerical superiority of rural residents and the gulf in political attitudes that divided rural and urban areas in the oblast was the single most important factor explaining the outcome of the elections in Kursk. All of the electoral contests were split along broadly urban-rural lines, with the overall results confirming the division of the oblast into the city of Kursk and the liberal town of Kurchatov, on the one hand, and a number of highly conservative towns and the countryside on the other. It was control of the latter areas that ensured success for the Communists. Not only were the rural inhabitants significantly more conservative than their urban neighbors but they had far higher rates of mobilization than the urban population. In District 98 the urban turnout was 53 percent and the rural turnout 66 percent, whereas in District 99 the comparative figures were 55 percent and 73 percent.[77]

Although the urban-rural divide worked to the general advantage of the Communist candidates, it also became the source for internal friction within the socialist bloc. Somewhat ironically, during the election the vanguard party of the urban working classes found that it had its political foundations sunk deepest in the villages, with most of its leadership having made their careers in agriculture. Faced by a challenge from the Agrarians in their main constituency,[78] the Communists were forced to campaign on issues that appealed specifically to the rural population, including attempts to placate the local church.[79]

As a result, the Communists often found themselves proposing measures that ran counter to the interests of the urban population (e.g., higher prices for agricultural produce). Forging a blend of policies that could straddle both rural and urban constituencies became increasingly difficult. In part, this problem lay at the heart of the difference between the primarily urban-based "independent" Communist candidates, who campaigned in the factories and among the workers in the towns, and the largely rural-based "official" Communists. The divide that opened between different Communist groups and the Agrarians highlighted the fact that even the strongest political alliances were having difficulty addressing the new pressures emerging in the oblast.

Although the success of the Communists and the defeat of the reformist candidates was always the most likely electoral outcome given the range of factors fostering conservatism in the oblast, the overwhelming success of the Communists came as a surprise to many in the region. The Communist victory was built on a range of interwoven factors. These included control of a powerful political network, the continuing loyalty of large parts of the local population to Communist candidates, and the recent experience of economic and social hardship. The firm control over the villages exercised by the four candidates of the inner core of socialist network also ensured that the Communist vote was not too divided between official and independent candidates. However, close analysis of the results suggests that the strength of the Communist victory was also contingent on the failure of their opponents to establish a coherent opposition.

Despite the power of the socialist movement in the oblast, particularly its inner core of candidates, centrist candidates enjoyed a number of important advantages. The centrist candidates (Shuteyev, Usenkov, Merkulov, and Loktionov), unlike the local reformists, had command over significant political resources, notably the organization of the administration and the financial might of the new money candidates. There was, in fact, also a sizable non-Communist electorate in the region. Voters in this constituency were not, however, ready to vote for the reformists in significant numbers. Instead, they indicated a strong preference for a progressive conservative agenda.

Merkulov and Loktionov developed an electoral program that skillfully fused a conservative domestic political agenda (support for the Church, the military, and even monarchy), reformist economic policies (accelerated privatization and lower taxes on entrepreneurs), and an assertive foreign policy in defense of Russia's external, particularly economic, interests. This mixture of policies had a broad appeal in the oblast, and toward the end of the campaign, Usenkov adopted a similar approach to the campaign. Shuteyev's policy agenda was close to the position of the centrist candidates (see figure 16-1).

The support for the centrist position was clearly displayed in the election results, particularly in urban areas.[80] Shuteyev achieved an important success, being elected to the Federation Council close behind Likhachev, the leading figure in the local socialist movement. With the backing of the administration, Shuteyev scored important successes in the countryside, winning in nine of the twenty-eight rural raions of District 46 and coming second in most of the remainder. Candidates representing new economic interests also mounted a strong challenge to the hegemony of the Communist political elite, particularly in the urban areas. In the Federation Council contest, Usenkov won all three raions in the city of Kursk, with Shuteyev second in two, and Usenkov also took Kurchatov, again with Shuteyev second.

In Duma District 98, non-Communist candidates polled particularly well. Merkulov took all of Kursk, and Loktionov was second in the city with the Communist Mikhailov third and the reformist P'yanykh in fourth place. Without the backing of the administration to penetrate the countryside, the centrist candidates faced severe problems with their campaigns in the villages. In heavily rural Duma District 99, the Communist victory was comprehensive. Potapenko piled up votes in the urban areas of L'gov and Zheleznogorsk and also scored well in the villages, coming first in nine of the nineteen rural districts. The Agrarian party candidate and an independent Communist were second and third, respectively.

Given the similar policy position occupied by the centrist candidates and the benefits that would have accrued if they had worked together, why did they fail to develop an alliance? Four main factors explain the lack of cooperation among the centrist candidates: the configuration of political elites derived from the perestroika period, the interaction of four simultaneous electoral contests, the absence of a credible centrist political organization at the national level, and the personal ambition of the centrist candidates.

During the latter years of the Gorbachev period and the early years of independence, opposition to Communist political supremacy in the region had been conducted by reformist candidates and organizations. When the economic reforms initiated by Moscow reformers produced a new business elite anxious to protect its gains, the representatives of new money naturally gravitated to the organizations that directly opposed the Communists, the local reformist movement. During the campaign, however, it soon became apparent that being linked to reformist organizations was highly damaging politically—especially in the rural areas. By the time that the new business interests broke with moderate reformists, the damage to their images had been done.

The tactical error of the new money–reformist alliance was accentuated by the structure of the electoral process. Although designed to foster the creation in Kursk of new political institutions, primarily parties, holding four parallel electoral contests created a diverse set of incentives for local candidates. On the one hand, the elections served to consolidate the local Communist organization and to maximize the party-list vote for the Communist and Liberal Democratic parties, and on the other, it fostered the disintegration of reformist-centrist organizations, which in turn functioned to minimize the party-list vote for such organizations.

At the start of the election, the Communists succeeded in making the Russian government's record the central issue in the election. Specifically local issues played no part in the campaign. Local anger caused by Yeltsin's decision to use force against the Russian Supreme Soviet also provided the Kursk Communists with considerable political ammunition. Shifting the agenda of local political debate entirely onto national issues ensured that the structure of the electoral process worked to the advantage of the local Communists. Both independent and official Communist candidates could unite against the constitution, the reformist parties, and the Russian government and, in this way, offset tensions in the socialist bloc caused by rivalry over the territorial contests. Communist candidates were keen to present themselves as an extension of the national Communist party and its campaign against the Russian government because this reinforced their local position as leading representatives of resentment about the socioeconomic situation. The national campaign of the KPRF and campaigns of the Kursk Communists, therefore, served to reinforce each other.

In contrast, for the centrist and particularly the reformist candidates, being linked to the national campaign of their respective parties proved to be a major liability. Some of the candidates received material from the central campaign in the form of posters and leaflets (materials from the RDDR, Russia's Choice, the DPR, Civic Union, Yabloko, Future of Russia–New Names were observed in the region) but this was little compensation for the negative image of the national movements in Kursk.

Hostility to the national reformist parties served to accelerate further the collapse of the reformist movement in the region with most reformist candidates abandoning their affiliation to a national party and running as independents. Under the pressure of popular local hostility to reformist organizations, the alliance between the moderate RDDR and entrepreneurs disintegrated. With Moscow-based reformist parties highly unpopular, local reformist candidates and their allies had little incentive to campaign for national parties, indeed, such campaigning directly harmed their prospects in the local contests.

With the parliamentary election divided into separate contests for the Duma and Federation Council, there was also little reason for candidates campaigning for the alternative chambers to cooperate. Shuteyev, whose support for other candidates would have given them the organizational backing they required, had little interest in assisting candidates running for the Duma. Shuteyev's involvement in the Federation Council contest and his strong interest in having the new constitution passed ensured that the governor was focused only on elections that directly affected his narrow interests. An alliance with the main centrist candidates, even the independent ones, was viewed as tactically risky and threatened Shuteyev's support from the industrial lobby.

With the four simultaneous contests discouraging the creation of political alliances among centrist candidates at a local level, the only way to foster some level of integration would have been to create a national political movement that could create an incentive structure to encourage centrist candidates to cooperate. However, as Daniel Treisman notes in chapter 5 of this volume, the centrist parties never constituted a viable political force in the election. Lacking credible national parties to integrate the campaigns of local centrist candidates and, in particular, to draw the governor into coalitions with other local candidates, opposition to the Communists was highly fragmented.

Fragmentation was further accentuated by the personal ambition of the centrist candidates. In Duma District 98 the combined vote of Merkulov and Loktionov would have ensured victory over the orthodox Communist Mikhailov without having to improve their performance in the rural areas. Despite repeated calls for a single candidate, neither Loktionov nor Merkulov would withdraw. Mikhailov was, therefore, able to triumph when the centrist vote was split.

Conclusion

Following the December elections, a Kursk paper concluded that "Kursk oblast remains a preserve of Communism."[81] The comprehensive victory for the Communists and nationalists was not, however, inevitable, despite the strength of local antireformist sentiments. The December elections were conducted at a time of unprecedented flux in the region. Rapid political and economic change had denuded former political alliances and fostered a complex and subtle reorientation in the nature of politics in the area. The elections marked the first comprehensive attempt to weld new and existing local interests into coherent electoral blocs in response to the changes of the previous five years.

The most significant change in the contours of the Kursk political landscape thrown up by these subterranean changes was the disunity within the former Communist elite and the appearance of important counter elites. The emergence of new elites had also been accompanied by the development of new sources of political power in the region. Although established organizations remained the single most important political resource, money had emerged as a powerful new factor, particularly when coupled with the media. As a result, new candidates could challenge the monopoly of information and publicity previously held by the established political elite. Together, these circumstances had created a situation in which for the first time Communist power in the region faced a serious challenge.

Before the December elections, the organizational structure of the Soviet Communist party had been destroyed, as had the institution of the local soviet. Moreover, the political power formerly wielded by the Communists in the oblast was increasingly concentrated in the hands of the administration. By late autumn of 1993 the local socialist movement was divided, with many of its leading figures involved in an internal struggle for power. The great success of the local Communists in the elections was their ability to reanimate the network of personal contacts at the heart of the Soviet-era system of rule and to turn this network into a coherent political movement. The structure of the elections greatly assisted this development by providing the Communists with a set of incentives to work together.

In contrast, the opponents of the Communists faced a range of hurdles that discouraged cooperation. Opposition to the Communists in the oblast was initially based on the reformist movement. Given the political traditions, social structure, and experience of the transition in the oblast, the reformist candidates and their liberal economic and political agenda were, however, never likely to achieve significant success in Kursk. The autumn electoral campaign led to the complete collapse of the reformist movement in the oblast, and in the December elections, the Kursk electorate comprehensively rejected the reformist candidates. With the reformists pushed to the margins of local politics, the central battle in the region became a struggle to establish the dominant form of conservatism.

A number of candidates in the election shared a progressive conservative agenda that reflected a set of common political and economic interests. This agenda would have been enhanced considerably in the region by cooperation between the centrist candidates. There was also significant support for reformist conservatism. Shuteyev's success in the election demonstrated that a moderate conservatism could command significant support, whereas with better coordination a centrist candidate could have captured the predominately urban Duma District 98. If the independent centrist candidates had forged an alliance with Shuteyev to create a reformist conservative bloc backed by the power of the administration in the countryside, the party-list voting in the oblast would have been considerably less favorable to the Communists.

A centrist coalition was not forthcoming. Whereas the relationship between the four elements of the electoral contest served to bring the national and local campaigns of the Communist movement together, it worked to splinter centrist and reformist groups. Lacking credible local centrist political organizations and with individual candidates unprepared to stand down to maximize the anticommunist vote, centrist candidates ended up campaigning separately and often in opposition to each other.

The most significant aspects of the December elections in Kursk were, therefore, the inability of new elites to break the previous stranglehold of the Communists in the oblast, the failure of reformist conservatism, and the triumph of the reactionary conservatism of the rural Communists. This outcome was the product of factors particular to the local electoral struggle that in combination with developments at the national level ensured that the choices of Kursk's electorate were arranged to the advantage of the candidates associated with the socialist bloc, reinforcing their considerable structural advantages in the oblast.

As a founding political event, the December elections had a fundamental impact on the subsequent trajectory of local politics.[82] In particular, the elections greatly accelerated the process of elite political consolidation in the oblast. The major beneficiaries of this process were the Communists who used the election campaign to reestablish their organization in the region after a time of considerable turmoil. The pluralistic elite that had existed in the oblast during the early years of independence was subsequently replaced by a far more homogenous structure. Although the governor continued to challenge the hegemony of the Communist political machine, following the December elections Kursk emerged as a reborn Communist stronghold.[83]

Notes

1. Summaries of the Kursk results for the party lists and the constitution are shown in tables 1-7 and 1-8 in this volume.

2. The application of models of electoral behavior derived from established democracies to the December election is fraught with problems, notably because many of the social, economic, and political relationships that inform these approaches were largely absent in Russia in 1993. For example, the notion that party identification is primarily the product of group membership and socialization conducted in the family can, at best, offer only a partial explanation of voting behavior in a society without a recent history of partisanship and with very weak group identities. Nor, given the unstructured and fluid nature of Russian society, is it easy to identify the defined sets of interest that underlie rational models of voting. Never-

theless, the broad approaches developed to explain voting in other democracies can offer considerable insight into voter behavior in 1993. This study finds that it is the sociological approach, coupled with a weak form of the party identification model, a historical analysis of political tradition in the region, and consideration of the economic environment that provide the best indications of voting intentions, if employed with caution. See Seymour Martin Lipset and Stein Rokkan, eds., *Party Systems and Voter Alignments: Cross-National Perspectives* (New York: Free Press, 1967); Richard G. Niemi and Herbert F. Weisberg, eds., *Classics in Voting Behavior* (Washington, D.C.: CQ Press, 1993); and Edward R. Tufte, *Political Control of the Economy* (Princeton University Press, 1978). In Kursk, it was the numerical dominance of rural voters in the electorate—especially those in the upper-age cohort, a population that had historically been socialized into a conservative value system and identification with the Soviet system, in particular the Communist party, and the poor economic situation—that explained the large vote for the Communists and nationalists. However, these approaches alone are insufficient to account for electoral outcomes in Kursk. The responsiveness of the local political system, or rather lack of it, to key sections of the electorate was also crucial to the electoral outcome. The structure of the electoral process, the configuration of local elites, the relationship between local and national political organizations, the media, and the tactics of individual candidates all played a vital role in accentuating the victory of highly conservative political forces.

3. Gosudarstvennyi Komitet SSSR po Statisktike, *Vsesoyuznaya perepis' naseleniya 1989g.* (Moscow: Vestnik Statistiki, 1990), p. 62.

4. Ibid., pp. 454–57.

5. See table 1-5, this volume.

6. For the specific rural problems of Kursk see "Golodnyi kormilets: Katastroficheskoe polozhenie v agrarnom sektore Kurskoi oblasti," *Sovetskaya Rossiya,* May 6, 1993, p. 2. Also Justin Burke, "Rural Conservatism Holds Back Reforms in Russian Agriculture," *Christian Science Monitor, World Edition,* July 9, 1993.

7. Stephen K. Wegren, "Rural Reform in Russia," *RFE/RL Research Bulletin,* vol. 2, no. 43 (October 19, 1993), pp. 43–53.

8. Wegren, "Rural Reform in Russia," p. 48.

9. President Yeltsin's October decree to promote the privatization of agricultural land prompted an extremely hostile reaction from many members of the former local Communist elite. See "*O regulirovanii zemel'nykh otnoshenii i razvitii agranoi reformy v Rossii*" (October 17, 1993).

10. *Molodaya gvardiya,* September 11, 1993, p. 2.

11. *Khoroshiye novosti,* November 8–14, 1993, p. 2.

12. By the autumn of 1993, 64 enterprises had already been sold and a further 275 were being prepared for privatization in early 1994. One-fifth of the population had invested its privatization vouchers in share auctions for local enterprises. *Molodaya gvardiya,* July 31, 1993, p. 2.

13. The ethnic composition of the region in 1989 was: Russian, 96.9 percent; Ukrainian, 1.7 percent; and Belarusian, 0.3 percent.

14. Negotiations had taken place to create an economic cooperation zone to link the five eastern areas of Ukraine with the five oblasts of the Central Black Earth

zone. "Heads of Russian and Ukrainian Border Provinces Pledge to Cooperate and Not to Do Damage to One Another," *Izvestiya,* July 1, 1993, p. 4. Translated by Irina Demchenko, in *Current Digest of the Soviet Press,* vol. 45, no. 26 (1993), pp. 20–21.

15. *Kurskaya pravda,* October 19, 1993, p. 1.

16. The region's population is the product of a long process of ethnic, primarily slavic, intermixing. In the rural areas Russian language continues to be heavily laced with Ukrainian and occasionally Belorussian words and phrases. Thus, although the vast majority of the population identify themselves as Russian, such identification is based on a particular local understanding of ethnicity. For many in the oblast, Ukrainians, Russians, and Belorussians were seen as three branches of a single Russian people (*Russkii* or *Rossiisskii narod*). Ethnicity was subtly interwoven with a regional identity.

17. Khrushchev was born in the village of Kalinovka near Kursk. Brezhnev came to the oblast at age fifteen and spent his early working life as a land surveyor in the district.

18. V. A. Kolosov, N. V. Petrov, and L. V. Smirniagin, eds., *Vesna 89: Geografiya i anatomiya parlamentskikh vyborov* (Moscow: Progress, 1990), pp. 159–207.

19. On the Sobyanin rating of the eight deputies from Kursk oblast, five were identified as right of center, two as moderate conservatives, and four as extreme conservatives.

20. In the 1991 Russian presidential election, the city of Kursk was among those that gave Yeltsin his largest vote (75 percent), and even the rural areas offered him significant support (65 percent). "Breakdown of Success," Interfax, Moscow, June 13, 1991, FBIS-SOV-91-115 (June 14, 1991), p. 48.

21. Question 1 ("Do you have confidence in the president?")—only 42.89 percent voted "for," with 57.11 percent "against." Question 2 ("Do you support the socioeconomic program of the president and the government?")—"for," 39.56 percent, and "against," 60.44 percent. Question 3 ("Do you consider it necessary to hold urgent presidential elections?")—"for," 61.80 percent, and "against," 38.20 percent. Question 4 ("Do you consider it necessary to conduct urgent elections for the People's Deputies of the Russian Federation?")—"for," 56.55 percent, and "against," 43.45 percent.

22. Despite the presence of a well-known and highly conservative candidate from outside the oblast, Viktor Alksnis, Likhachev triumphed. Alksnis carried the urban areas, but Likhachev controlled the countryside. The opposition forces, the democratic candidate V. I. Yakovlev and entrepreneur N. S. Maltsev, were completely squeezed out of the race.

23. The other leading conservative candidates to run in the by-election were Vitalii Gukov and Aleksandr Mikhailov.

24. The first leader of the organization, Sergei P'yanykh, worked in the Anti-Monopoly Committee of the administration. Other leading figures included E. N. Alekseyev, the deputy leader of the Kursk soviet, a firm supporter of privatization in the city with close links to the administration; Liudmila Samotes, the leader of the Union for Workers in Small and Medium-Size Businesses; and a number of lo-

cal entrepreneurs. Several of the members of the committee were drawn from the Property Foundation (*Fond Imushchestva*) of the administration, which was responsible for managing privatization.

25. Interview with Valerii Yakovlev, one of the leaders of the radical wing of the local reformist movement, Kursk, December 10, 1993.

26. Accompanying the breakup of existing political organizations was a growing opposition to government policies and a loss of support for Yeltsin. In a comparative study of the political temperature of the Russian regions, Kursk was identified as among a small group of areas where opposition to the president and his program were growing. A. Sobyanin, E. Gel'man, and O. Kayunov, "Politicheskii klimat v Rossii v 1991–1993 gg.," *Mirovaya ekonomika i mezhdunarodnye otnosheniya*, vol. 9 (1993), pp. 20–32.

27. There were six registered reformist organizations: the Republican party; the Social Democratic party; the People's party; Kursk Foundation for the Support of Democracy and Reform; the Kursk Oblast/Regional Center of the Russian Movement for Democratic Reform (RDDR); and the electoral association.

28. The Agrarian Union, formed by the collective farm chairs; the Communist Party of the Russian Federation, led by Aleksandr Mikhailov and claiming 7,000 members in the oblast; the Agrarian party, led by Vitalii Gukov and claiming 500 members in the oblast; and the Movement for People's Power and Reform for the People, led by Vitalii Gukov and Aleksandr Anpilov and based on the former trade unions.

29. *Gorodskiye izvestiya,* September 18, 1993, p. 3.

30. *Kurskaya pravda,* September 24, 1993, p. 1; and *Gorodskiye izvestiya*, October 2, 1993, p. 1.

31. *Molodaya gvardiya*, September 25, 1993, pp. 1–2. *Gorodskiye izvestiya,* October 7, 1993, p. 1. Declarations of support for Yeltsin published in the local press were signed by Russia's Choice, the Social Democratic party, the Republican party, the People's party, the RDDR, the Association of Humanism and Charity, the presidium of the oblast committee of the Union for Workers of Small and Medium Businesses, and the Fund for Economic Reform, and a number of new firms. The local church also adopted a position in opposition to the radicalism of the soviet. *Molodaya gvardiya,* October 5, 1993, p. 1.

32. *Kurskaya pravda*, October 2, 1993, pp. 1–2; *Gorodskiye izvestiya,* October 2, 1993, p. 2; and *Molodaya gvardiya,* October 6, 1993, p. 1.

33. *Kurskaya pravda*, October 13, 1993, p. 1.

34. *Kurskaya pravda,* October 9, 1993, p. 1; October 16, 1993, p. 1; and November 2, 1993, p. 1.

35. Although the Soviet census identifies the population of Kursk oblast as 57.6 percent urban and 42.4 percent rural, in this chapter only those living in the five largest urban settlements are considered *urban* voters. There was little to distinguish the small towns from surrounding villages, and voters in small urban areas voted as part of the rural bloc.

36. At this stage, the KPRF did not exist as a defined and cohesive political organization in the oblast. Links with the national party were maintained through Mikhailov, but the remaining leaders of the socialist bloc had yet to commit them-

selves to the KPRF. Only in the latter stages of the signature campaign was a link between the national party and the inner core of the Communist candidates established making them "official" Communist party candidates.

37. *Kurskaya pravda,* October 20, 1993, p. 1; and *Gorodskie izvestiya,* November 20, 1993, p. 1.

38. *Gorodskiye izvestiya,* October 16, 1993, p. 1.

39. *Gorodskiye izvestiya,* October 21, 1993, p. 1.

40. *Gorodskiye izvestiya,* October 5, 1993, p. 1; and *Molodaya gvardiya,* October 2, 1993, p. 1.

41. *Molodaya gvardiya,* December 5, 1993, p. 2.

42. *Kurskaya pravda,* October 22, 1993, p. 1.

43. *Kurskaya pravda,* October 15, 1993, p. 1.

44. Kureninov; Liudmila Samotes, president of the oblast Committee of Trades Union of Workers in Medium and Small Businesses; Yurii Donchenko, director of the private enterprise VED; A. I. Khoroshil'tsev, head of the Kursk branch of the Orlov Higher School of the Ministry of the Interior; P. I. Pereversil, president of the oblast Association of Peasant and Farmer Enterprises; and Pyotr Nadein, president of the Committee for Culture and Art of the oblast administration. *Kurskaya pravda,* October 29, 1993, p. 1.

45. *Kurskaya pravda,* October 22, 1993, p. 1.

46. *Kurskaya pravda,* November 2, 1993, p. 1.

47. *Kurskaya pravda,* November 12, 1993, p. 1.

48. *Molodaya gvardiya,* October 26, 1993, p. 2.

49. *Molodaya gvardiya,* October 19, 1993, p. 1.

50. *Kurskaya pravda,* October 26, 1993, p. 1.

51. *Gorodskiye izvestiya,* October 30, 1993, p. 1.

52. The signature campaign was considerably complicated by the fact that some candidates were simultaneously nominated at two levels: for territorial electoral districts and for national party lists. Overall, eighteen individuals connected with the region ran as candidates on nine party lists. Nine of these candidates were simultaneously candidates in Kursk territorial districts. The largest bloc from Kursk was five candidates for the list of the Russian Movement for Democratic Reform. Three deputies from Kursk (one each from the Communist party, the Agrarian party, and the LDPR) were eventually elected on party lists. Candidates from Kursk did not figure highly on any party list. The highest placed candidate was N. Goncharov, who was fortieth on the Communist party list.

53. Anpilov was publicly endorsed by Gukov, the head of the Agrarian party in the oblast, during Anpilov's televised political broadcast.

54. *Molodaya gvardiya,* December 8, 1993, pp. 1–2.

55. *Molodaya gvardiya,* December 4, 1993, p. 5. P'yanykh associated himself very closely with Yabloko, and this interview was accompanied by a half page devoted to the Yabloko program.

56. *Golos raiona: Gazeta Korenevskogo raiona,* November 30, 1993, p. 2; and *Znamya Oktyabrya: Gazeta Glushkovskogo raiona,* November 26, 1993, p. 1.

57. *Gorodskiye izvestiya,* December 9, 1993, pp. 1, 3.

58. *Gorodskiye izvestiya,* December 9, 1993, p. 3.

59. Interview with Leonid Usenkov, December 1, 1993.

60. In the late perestroika period, the local Church became a significant political force in the district. In 1990, when Aleksandr Rutskoi decided to run for election to the Congress of People's Deputies in Kursk, a local priest, Father Nikodim Yevmolaty, emerged as his strongest competitor. Yitzhak Brudny, "Ruslan Khasbulatov, Aleksandr Rutskoi, and Intra-Elite Conflict in Post-Communist Russia, 1991–94," in *Patterns in Post-Soviet Leadership*, edited by Timothy J. Colton and Robert C. Tucker (Boulder, Colo.: Westview Press, 1995), pp. 75–101. Since then the Church has continued to be an important political actor, and during the December election many of the leading candidates, including the Communists, sought its endorsement.

61. *Gorodskiye izvestiya*, November 27, 1993, p. 1.

62. *Molodaya gvardiya*, December 4, 1993, pp. 2, 8.

63. *Molodaya gvardiya*, December 8, 1993, pp. 2, 3.

64. The agenda advocated by Shuteyev and the centrist candidates was often remarkably similar and rested on a strong commitment to law and order (particularly passing the new constitution as a means to establish a legal framework), further economic reform, legal protection for private property, and a range of broadly conservative social and political policies.

65. *Gorodskiye izvestiya*, December 11, 1993, p. 2.

66. *Kurskaya pravda*, December 4, 1993, p. 1.

67. His brother had some reformist leanings and opposed Rutskoi during the October confrontation in Moscow. *Molodaya gvardiya*, October 6, 1993, p. 1.

68. *Vestnik militsii*, no. 11 (December 1993), pp. 1–2.

69. Central papers were rarely to be found in the kiosks of Kursk: *Tsentral'naya Rossiya*, a reformist regional paper, was, however, available in the city.

70. In general, the raion papers did not publish disinformation about the elections; rather they produced selective accounts or no information at all, and most published the text of the constitution.

71. Reflecting the fact that the founder of the paper was a former Komsomol functionary, Yurii Vorotnikov, in the final stages of the election campaign the paper chose to endorse Sergei Loktionov. *Khoroshiye novosti*, November 27, 1993, p. 1, and December 4, 1993, p. 1.

72. *Molodaya gvardiya*, November 27, 1993, p. 2; *Gorodskie izvestiya*, November 25, 1993, p. 1; and the series of interviews in *Gorodskie izvestiya*, December 7, 1993. *Gorodskiye izvestiya*, November 30, 1993, p. 2. On December 8, *Molodaya gvardiya* published a political assassination of Asaf'ev and Rukavitsyn, and on December 7, the eve of the election, *Gorodskiye izvestiya* published photographs of large houses allegedly belonging to leading Communists, including Likhachev, and built with public funds.

73. Political advertisements for each candidate could not be shown more than four times a day and for no more than thirty minutes in total. They cost 3,000 to 10,000 rubles for one minute on the radio and 12,000 to 40,000 for one minute on television. *Molodaya gvardiya*, November 16, 1993, p. 1.

74. *Molodaya gvardiya*, December 7, 1993, p. 3.

75. In an interview with the author, Merkulov claimed to have spent 30 million to 40 million rubles on the campaign (December 10, 1993).

76. The full list of candidates in the Kursk region territorial contests, their positions, political affiliations, and votes received are set out here: *Federation Council District 46 (Kurskii)*: Likhachev, V. N., former president Kursk oblast soviet, Official Communist, 48.8 percent; Shuteyev, V. I., Head of Kursk oblast administration, Independent, 45.4 percent; Vorob'ev, I. P., head of Kursk section of the Moscow Railway, Official Communist, 28.1 percent; Usenkov, L. N., general director of agency Linkor, Independent/RDDR, 24.9 percent; Kureninov, A. A., representative of the Russian president, Russia's Choice, 13.9 percent. Note percentages do not add up to 100 percent because each voter was required to vote for two candidates. Also, all percentages are calculated as proportion of valid votes cast minus votes "against all." There were 77,218 votes against all candidates. *Duma District 98 (Kurskii)*: Mikhailov, A. N., former president Shchigry raion soviet, Official Communist/KPRF, 24.2 percent; Merkulov, G. N., president Aviation-Marine Investment Fund, Independent, 13.6 percent; Loktionov, S. P., president City Youth Foundation, Independent/Future of Russia–New Names, 12.7 percent; Ryzhkov, F. N., rector Kursk Polytechnic, Independent Communist, 10.5 percent; P'yanykh, S. P., deputy head Kursk State Committee for Anti-Monopoly Policy, Yabloko, 9.1 percent; Ruda, Yu. M., manager of enterprise Svetlyachok, LDPR, 8.0 percent; Pronin, A. N., section head, Kursk MVD (Ministry of Internal Affairs), Independent, 7.1 percent; Pridvorov, N. A., law lecturer Kursk Polytechnic, RDDR, 5.7 percent; Anpilov, A. N., former president of Lenin raion soviet, Independent Communist, 3.9 percent; Asaf'ev, V. I., academic secretary International Academy of Information, Moscow, Independent Communist, 3.2 percent; Razin'kov. Yu., president of trade union at Kurskagromash, Civic Union, 2.1 percent. Against all were 32,307. *Duma District 99 (L'govskii)*: Potapenko, A. F., head of the Wagon Depot of the Moscow Railway in L'gov, Official Communist, 23.8 percent; Luneva, V. G., president of raikom of the Trade Union of Agro-industrial Workers, Agrarian, 19.3 percent; Rukavitsyn, A. P., director of the AO Kurskglavsnab, Independent Communist, 14.2 percent; Baskakov, A. V., deputy head of investigation section of the Kursk MVD, Independent, 13.7 percent; Chubur, A. A., worker at Kurchatov Center for Youth Tourism, LDPR, 10.6 percent; Nadein, P. I., president of Committee for Culture and Art of Kursk administration, Independent/Reformist (Russia's Choice), 9.2 percent; Samotes, L. A., president of oblast Trades Union of Workers in Medium and Small Businesses, RDDR, 5.1 percent; Lunev, A. E., unemployed, Civic Union, 4.2 percent. Against all were 41,961.

77. Each electoral contest involved different numbers of spoiled ballot papers. General figures for voter turnout were therefore calculated on the basis of the data for the Federation Council contest.

78. In what theoretically should have been its natural constituency, the Agrarian party did extremely poorly. Although the weak performance of Agrarian candidates in the territorial contests owed a great deal to Communist domination of the rural areas through their organizational network, the strong support for the LDPR and the Communists on the party-list vote suggests that villagers were not persuaded by the policies or leadership of the Agrarians. On the list vote the LDPR

was first in twenty-seven of the area's twenty-eight rural raions and second in one, while the Communist party was first in the remaining raion and second in twenty-one districts. The Agrarians managed only second in six rural raions and were third in the rest.

79. Viktor Chemodurov, "Kommunisty vzletayut k vysotam vlasti s 'zapasnykh aerodromov,'" *Rossiiskiye vesti,* October 28, 1993, p. 2.

80. The constitution passed in the city (for 55 percent) and in Kurchatov (for 63 percent) and in three of the twenty rural raions.

81. *Molodaya gvardiya,* December 18, 1993, p. 1.

82. Lipset and Rokkan have argued that the party systems of the 1960s in Western Europe reflected the cleavage structures of the 1920s. Such continuity came from the capacity of political organizations once established to retain their hold on sections of the electorate. The emergence of Kursk and other oblasts of the Black Earth zone as strongholds for the antireform movement suggests that a freezing of political allegiance similar to that which occurred in other democracies in early phases of their development may be under way in certain parts of the Russian Federation.

83. In subsequent elections Kursk oblast was consistently one of the most conservative regions in Russia. In the December 1995 Duma elections, the KPRF polled 28.29 percent in the party-list contest and both incumbent Communist deputies won (District 96, A. N. Mikhailov, 35.22 percent; and District 97, A. F. Potapenko, 39.81 percent). There were no candidates affiliated with national centrist or reformist organizations. Reflecting the local popularity of Rutskoi, his movement Great Power (*Derzhava*) out-polled the KPRF on the list vote gaining 30.69 percent, and the candidates who came second to the Communists both ran as representatives of Great Power (District 96, S. P. Loktionov, a former centrist candidate, 23.52 percent; and District 97, V. M. Mikhal'chev, 15.87 percent). In the 1996 presidential elections Gennadii Zyuganov polled 52.1 percent in the first round and 58.62 percent in the second. By comparison, Yeltsin managed 24.5 percent and 36.53 percent, respectively.

Kemerovo

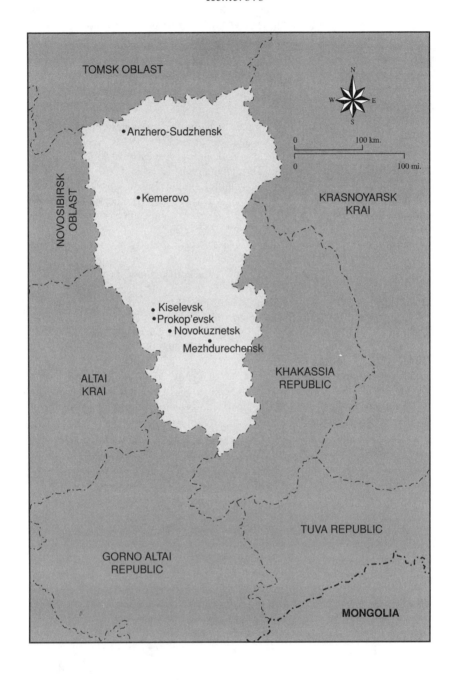

CHAPTER SEVENTEEN

The Kuzbass
Liberals, Populists, and Labor

Stephen Crowley

WITH THE virtual absence of campaigning by political parties in Kemerovo oblast, a region far from European Russia, the election raises questions of the ability of Moscow-based political parties to influence election outcomes in more far-flung regions. In addition, the region's identity is wrapped up in heavy industry, particularly coal mining. Because coal miners are the most independent and political militant segment of Russian labor, the election raises questions about labor and electoral politics during a painful economic transformation. Also, despite the importance of heavy industry and coal mining, both industrialists and miners fared poorly in the election, in contrast to the success of those who will be called here *authoritarian populists* (most notably Aman Tuleyev). In fact, although the miners' movement gave the region a reputation for being proreform and supportive of Boris Yeltsin, Vladimir Zhirinovskii won convincingly, and five out of six local candidates were elected on platforms sharply opposed to Yeltsin's policies. This chapter will explain why party campaigns played such a minimal role; why in an industrial region both managers and labor candidates were unsuccessful; and why authoritarian populists won so convincingly.

I would like to acknowledge the following for their gracious help during the research of this paper: Pyotr Bizyukov, Leonid Gordon, Olga Khomenko, Viktor Komarovskii, Leonid Lopatin, as well as those who gave of their time to be interviewed.

The Kuzbass

Kemerovo oblast, popularly known as the Kuzbass (for the Kuznetskii coal basin), is located in western Siberia, roughly equidistant to the eastern and western borders of Russia. It was first written into the map of the Russian federation in 1925, and soon thereafter its coal reserves became strategically important to Joseph Stalin's industrialization drive. The Kuzbass is Russia's largest coal basin, and 20 percent of the region's population is directly employed in the coal industry. The region is highly industrialized: although the region represents only 2 percent of the Russian population (in an area roughly the size of Hungary), it produces almost 40 percent of Russia's coal, as well as 14 percent of its steel.[1] The region has chemical and other industries in addition to coal and metallurgy.

Within the region, the population centers are fairly diverse. The city of Kemerovo, the administrative center, is the least industrial, with little coal mining, some chemical plants and manufacturing, and universities and a relatively high number of professionals; Novokuznetsk, at 600,000 the same size as Kemerovo, is highly industrial, with coal mining and steel making–two of the city's four metallurgical plants employ more than 30,000 workers each; towns such as Prokop'evsk and Mezhdurechensk as well as smaller settlements are almost exclusively devoted to coal mining.

The Kuzbass became prominent on the political map of the Soviet Union in July 1989, when Mezhdurechensk miners set off a strike wave that spread first throughout the Kuzbass, and then throughout the Soviet Union. The strike received much attention as the largest workers' collective action in Soviet history; Mikhail Gorbachev would argue subsequently that the strike marked the beginning of the end of the USSR.[2] The miners remained engaged in the political life of the Soviet Union and post-Soviet Russia by forming independent worker organizations aimed explicitly at improving the miners economic position through the political sphere.

The precedent of the miners' strike also activated other social groups in the region. Within weeks of the miners' first strike, an environmental movement sprang up, protesting the rather abysmal ecological conditions of the region. Although that movement soon waned as other concerns rose on the agenda, radical reformers also became emboldened by the miners' example and allied with the movement to push for political and social change. Far from Moscow, the region soon became one of the most politicized in Russia, as first the miners, then radical reformers, and finally political reactionaries joined regional and national political battles.

One of the most interesting questions about the Kuzbass concerns the miners. Although their participation in political life was unexpected, the direction of their political demands was even more so. After their first strike, when they called for such basic necessities as soap, the miners soon transformed their demands, and in less than two years had allied themselves with Yeltsin and liberal reformers against Gorbachev. Moreover, they called for the removal of the Communist party from its position of hegemony and for a sovereign Russia—in effect, for the dismantling of the Soviet Union—and despite working in the Soviet Union's most heavily subsidized industry, they pushed for the rapid introduction of the market.

A full explanation for this dramatic transformation would require a separate chapter,[3] but a brief argument can be made as follows. Even while coal miners were calling for an end to communist rule, they continued to use the ideological concepts they had inherited from the Soviet era. Though calling for the market, miners had in mind a very different concept from that of radical reformers: as producers of material goods, they argued that they deserved a just wage regardless of the market value of their product. Because in their eyes they were not receiving a just wage, they were being exploited by the nomenklatura. The miners of the Kuzbass continued to use these class concepts from the Soviet milieu, which above all focused conflict on the question of distribution: "Who is getting rich from our labor?"

This distributional conflict was particularly acute in the Kuzbass. Living conditions and social infrastructure were horrid there, as many miners and their families lived through the Siberian winters in barracks, and the availability of basic consumer goods was quite low even by Soviet standards. In fact, miners were joined by others in the region in arguing that they were but a colony of Moscow—giving up raw materials at low prices fixed by the center and receiving a small amount of finished goods in return.

As the Soviet state proved unable to fulfill the promises it made to the miners after their first strike, Yeltsin began to promise the miners greater control over their resources, including the transfer of the Kuzbass coal reserves from Soviet to Russian jurisdiction. Throughout 1991, the last year of the Soviet Union, the Kuzbass coal miners remained firmly allied with Yeltsin and liberal reformers: among other activities, the miners actively gathered signatures for Yeltsin's presidential nomination and ran his regional campaign.

Yet by the presidential election in 1991, the political battle in the Kuzbass had been joined. Tuleyev, a former railway switchman who had risen to the chair of the regional soviet, ran against Yeltsin for the presidency.[4] Although at the beginning of his campaign, Tuleyev spoke in favor of privatization and Yeltsin's economic program, toward the end he denounced it as an "antipeople policy" that would destroy the standard of living for the average Russian. The coal miners' movement labeled Tuleyev the "stalking horse of the CPSU," and miners harassed him at campaign stops. Yet in the end Tuleyev won 45 percent of the presidential vote in the Kuzbass, as opposed to Yeltsin's 40 percent; it was the only region Yeltsin lost.[5]

The coal miners, together with the region's liberal reformers, remained allies of Yeltsin and bitter opponents of Tuleyev. During the failed putsch of August 1991, the Kuzbass was one of the few places outside of Moscow and Leningrad to mobilize against the coup, when some forty-one mines shut down.[6] Tuleyev, on the other hand, traveled to Moscow, met with the coup leaders, and reported back to his constituents in the Kuzbass that he greatly sympathized with many of the goals of the coup leaders but found their method of usurping power unconstitutional.[7]

For their political loyalty, Yeltsin appointed leaders of the miners' movement to positions of authority in the Kuzbass: strike leaders Mikhail Kislyuk and Anatolii Malykhin were named governor (or head of the regional administration) and the president's personal representative for the region.[8] Moreover, and despite the market rhetoric embraced by both Yeltsin and miner-leaders, the miners were further rewarded with greater subsidies to the coal industry: when Yeltsin liberalized prices in January 1992, he tripled miners' wages despite a declared tight monetary policy.[9] During the campaign for the referendum in April 1993, miner-activists backed Yeltsin, who traveled to the region to shore up his support. He made promises of material assistance for the miners, including wage hikes, an action that Tuleyev labeled as bribery.

Such warm relations with Yeltsin and support for his program were not universal in the Kuzbass. In particular, the liberalization of prices had important political repercussions for the Kuzbass as elsewhere in Russia. The higher wages the miners gained created a local inflationary spiral on top of the already high inflation rate.[10] The miners' gains led to a backlash, first from pensioners and others directly dependent on the state budget and later from other industrial workers in the region. This resentment was successfully exploited by Tuleyev and his allies, who helped drive a wedge between the miners' movement and other segments of the population. Later, as wages went unpaid and even miners' living standards stagnated and began to collapse, Tuleyev's opposition to Yeltsin's economic policies helped drive the wedge between rank-and-file miners and leaders of the miners' movement.

Tuleyev's popularity stems in no small part from his efforts to defend the interests of the region in the struggles with the Russian "center" in Moscow. As the miners had done in their battle with the Soviet Union, Tuleyev and other Siberian leaders demanded the "decolonization" of the region. Tuleyev denounced the institution of presidential representatives in the regions as "unnecessary and even harmful," and stated that Yeltsin's economic policy meant that the regions were "getting fleeced" by Moscow. He called for the economic independence of the Kuzbass, and to further its autonomy he demanded it be granted the status of a republic.[11]

With his sharp opposition to Yeltsin's program during a period of tremendous economic hardship, Tuleyev's popularity grew immensely, and the standing of miner-leaders and Yeltsin's appointees declined by a similar amount. When Kuzbass residents were asked in 1992 if there was anyone in the Congress of People's Deputies who represented their own personal interests, 41 percent said Tuleyev, and only 2 percent chose Kislyuk.[12] Given his position as an unpopular and unelected official, Kislyuk, the former leader of the miners and Yeltsin's hand-picked governor, reached a compromise with Tuleyev, a move that was quickly denounced as betrayal by liberal political leaders in the Kuzbass.[13]

The reconciliation did not survive Yeltsin's disbanding the Russian parliament in October of 1993. Kislyuk initially took the position that both the president and the parliament had overstepped the law and that both should compromise. Representatives of thirteen parties and movements in the Kuzbass announced their agreement with the constitutional changes decreed by the Russian president, which they saw as necessary to prevent disaster. Kislyuk later instructed the deputies of the Kemerovo regional soviet to disband.

Tuleyev, for his part, proposed that the Siberian agreement interregional association immediately stop paying taxes and delivering coal, oil, gas, and electricity, prevent federal elections from taking place, and declare the area a "Siberian Republic." His proposal was rejected, and Tuleyev eventually complied with the orders to disband the regional soviet, though he made clear he viewed Yeltsin's actions as unconstitutional.[14] Thus the Kuzbass was sharply divided and highly politicized on the eve of the December election.

Party-List Campaign

Although the region was politicized, national political parties were almost invisible during the election campaign. With some significant exceptions, parties made their presence known in the Kuzbass almost exclusively through television. Geographically, the Kuzbass is far from Moscow, making it difficult for national parties to penetrate. With limited resources and time, especially in an abbreviated campaign period, there is more return on spending campaign resources in European Russia in terms of population, the costs and time involved in travel and in transporting campaign literature. Further, despite a politically active population, national parties had not put down deep roots.

But more important than the physical distance and the limitations of the parties was the psychological distance Kuzbass residents perceived between themselves and Moscow. For example, whereas leaders of the miners' movement and Tuleyev were bitter ideological opponents, both had exploited the rhetoric of the Kuzbass as a colony of Moscow, used for its cheap resources and then forgotten. Moreover, although national political battles were extremely important for the politically active, for the average Kuzbass resident the struggles in Moscow were little more than an abstraction. In the main, the big questions for the Kuzbass were not the ones of national politics but the question of relations between the region and the center and national policies that directly affected the daily life of the region: tax policy, coal prices, rail tariffs (which determined the profitability of materials exported from the region), and so on.

For these reasons, the campaign centered not around which political party might carry the region but on which local candidates were going to represent the Kuzbass and its interests in Moscow. Russia's Choice, however, with its significant resources, was the one party able to reach from Moscow to western Siberia. It had offices filled with campaign literature, which it succeeded in spreading around the urban centers. It bought the most advertising space by far in the regional press. It also dominated local television, and in this it may have been helped by the fact that the head of the Kuzbass television and radio company was himself a candidate for the Federation Council on the Russia's Choice ticket.[15]

Russia's Choice also benefited from a core of committed activists in the region. The bloc was the only one that successfully nominated candidates for each local election (four single-member districts and the Federation Council); in fact, these were virtually the only local candidates that identified themselves as being affiliated with any political party at all. Further, although they had successfully gathered enough signatures to have themselves nominated, most of the Russia's Choice candidates conceded that they had little to no chance of getting elected and their purpose was to use their campaign to agitate for Russia's Choice, the constitution, and the policies of Yeltsin and Yegor Gaidar.[16]

The bloc's backers included a prominent industrialist who helped bankroll the local campaign and appeared with the candidates on local television spots. Russia's Choice was also supported by at least some of the leaders of the miners' movement, though not without controversy, as we shall see. In fact, one of the best campaign opportunities for Russia's Choice involved the threat of a miners' strike over wages that went unpaid for months. Rather transparently, the miners took advantage of the government's vulnerability in a campaign period in order to extract concessions. This was a game played by both sides, however: Gaidar made well-publicized trips to both Vorkuta (a mining region in the Far North) and the Kuzbass, formally as government minister and negotiator, but clearly as candidate proving his ability to take action and reduce social tensions. The trips received national media attention, and Gaidar appeared prominently on local television, where he backed the proposed constitution and his Russia's Choice party. His picture with local Russia's Choice candidates soon appeared in campaign literature and print advertisements. (Despite Gaidar's visit, not only did local Russia's Choice candidates lose, but the party's share of the party-list vote was almost 2 percent below its national average.)

As stated, miner-activists were split on support for Russia's Choice; though they generally backed reformers, there was little consensus on whom to back within the democratic camp. The more radically reformist workers' committees supported Gaidar's team, while the Independent Miners' Union (NPG) backed Anatolii Sobchak's Russian Movement for Democratic Reform (RDDR).[17] As Vyacheslav Sharipov, the chair of the Kuzbass NPG explained, RDDR was concerned with workers' issues, such as jobs, and was in favor of a "social partnership"—the corporatist structure of labor agreements that some trade unions in Russia have proposed. Moreover, the miners were not the only labor representatives on the list, as the independent seamen's union and the Confederation of Free Labor were also represented. Further, the list called itself a *movement* rather than a *party*, and it was one of the few lists in the democratic camp that contained no members of the current government—an important point, Sharipov argued. More simply, the independent trade unions (such as the NPG) were looking for some group to ally with, and the leaders of RDDR were likewise looking for allies.[18] This last point seems particularly salient: as Aleksandr Sergeyev, chair of NPG Russia, confided to a journalist, the independent unions were told that they could ally with RDDR during the election campaign, and then once in parliament could leave to vote as they wished.[19]

This divergence within the Kuzbass miners' movement—with one group supporting Sobchak's list, the other much closer to Russia's Choice—led to a local scandal during the campaign. When Gaidar announced his visit to prevent the strike, Sharipov, in the name of the NPG and the Workers' Committee Council, threatened to withhold votes from party lists that included government officials if the government did not agree to concessions. Although this was a seemingly rational bargaining tactic, Sharipov had a clear conflict of interest, because he was one of the top candidates on the RDDR party list. More important, members of the Workers' Committee considered that such a statement was extremely dangerous, in that it could play into the hands of their opponents—the Communists. They issued sharp statements in the local press and television denouncing Sharipov's position and claiming that the miners' organizations had agreed to no such position.[20]

Although RDDR also had the backing of some local liberal activists, support among both liberal reformers and miner-activists was clearly divided. Ironically, the bloc's position in relation to other reformist forces was further blurred by a visit by Sobchak, the bloc's leading candidate. When Sobchak campaigned in Kemerovo, his speeches focused almost exclusively on support for Yeltsin's proposed constitution, and he made very little effort to distinguish the position of his party from current economic and political policy. In the end, despite an auspicious beginning as an alliance between reformers and miners in the region, RDDR won only 6.5 percent of the vote in the Kuzbass, just slightly more than 2 percent above its national average.

Other party lists were almost invisible. Despite the importance of regional issues, Sergei Shakhrai's Party of Russian Unity and Accord was virtually nonexistent. With a minimal rural population, the Agrarian party enjoyed little base from which to organize, but the Communist party was also largely absent. This was despite the fact that Tuleyev was mentioned as a potential future presidential candidate for the Communists. What remained of the local apparatus was in the hands of Tuleyev, and he chose to focus his resources on local races, ensuring the election of himself and his allies to parliament. Throughout the campaign, Tuleyev, the region's dominant political figure, distanced himself from any party or bloc, with little hint of the prominent role he would later play in the Communist Party of the Russian Federation (KPRF).

Moreover, the party that did carry the Kuzbass, Vladimir Zhirinovskii's Liberal Democratic Party of Russia (LDPR), had almost no organization in the region. LDPR gained close to 30 percent of the vote, 6 percent above its national average. The local campaign involved a small group of activists distributing crudely printed handbills. Without question, Zhirinovskii's success in the Kuzbass was almost exclusively the result of television.

In short, the evidence for political party formation, an essential component of representative democracy, was very weak at best in the Kuzbass. As concerns the party-list segment of the election, local party organizations and campaigning (as opposed to television) had a limited impact. This was not the case with elections to the single-member districts and the Federation Council. Here individual figures and regional connections, rather than political parties with platforms and organizations, were important. National political issues, to the extent they were important, became real in the Kuzbass in battles between local candidates for parliament.

The Players

Although almost all candidates ran independently of political parties, the contenders for single-member districts and the Federation Council fell into four broad categories, considerably more amorphous than the party blocs. As elsewhere in Russia at the end of 1993, the Kuzbass was politically divided into two camps, described by their opponents as *Communists* and *so-called democrats*.[21] In the heavily industrialized Kuzbass two other groups were discernible as well: industrial managers and labor, in particular the organized miners. Candidates from all the groups spoke of both the need for reform and "social guarantees" for the population during the painful transition. Nevertheless, candidates of the opposing camps spoke bitterly of their rivals and predicted disastrous results should they be elected.

The Liberals

The political actors in the "democratic" camp, almost universally intellectuals, clearly wanted to establish liberal democracy in Russia—that is, democracy and capitalism. At the same time they earned the nickname of "so-called democrats" given to them by their opponents, in that they were clearly willing to use coercion to silence the opposition. For the democrat-intellectuals in the Kuzbass, this led to a sharp contradiction. On the one hand, this group of political actors often described how the miners' strike of 1989 awakened their political consciousness. Gennadii Mityakin, Federation Council candidate on the Russia's Choice ticket, related his impression on first seeing miners occupying the city square: "It was the most magnificent event in my life, simply colossal. It was the first time in my life that I saw my own people [narod]."[22]

On the other hand, many of these liberal intellectuals were faced with the realization that their economic program was increasingly unpopular in the region. Some explained this fact by referring to the "lumpen consciousness" of the population, and consequently of the need for an "intermediate period" of strong presidential rule before Western-style democracy could be implemented.[23] Hence these "democrats" supported the administrative shutting down of newspapers they did not agree with, as well as the closure of the regional parliament—the most popular political institution in the region. The power of the democrats rested not in the local parliament but in the governor, who was not elected and very unpopular, yet was the most powerful figure in the region.[24] Thus the "democrats" held power in the Kuzbass thanks to presidential appointment, and the region's most popular figure by far was their political opponent Aman Tuleyev. Given the dismal state of the economy and the fact that their government was in power, the democrats were clearly in a difficult position before the election.

The Populists

What the liberals referred to as "Communists" might more accurately be referred to as authoritarian populists. On the one hand, their positions were not unreasonable. They argued, for instance, that the local government should be elected rather than appointed by the president. They argued further that given the enormous poverty many people were experiencing, reformers had lost touch with the travails of the average citizen.

On the other hand, as with the liberals, there was no shortage of hypocrisy in their statements. One got a strong sense that their version of populism implied the use of a strong hand, if not outright fascism.[25] In fact, if

Zhirinovskii did not exist, he would not have to be invented because others were already waiting to take his place. One such person is Tuleyev.

Tuleyev, as chair of the regional soviet, enjoyed approval ratings of between 70 to 80 percent.[26] He was an opponent of Yeltsin long before it was popular: he not only ran against Yeltsin for the Russian presidency in 1991, but as a Russian People's Deputy he allied himself with forces opposed to Yeltsin.[27] Even as a candidate for the Federation Council, after supporters of the parliament had suffered a bloody defeat, Tuleyev was unrepentant: he proudly wore his People's Deputy pin and campaigned openly against Yeltsin's actions in September and October, which he compared to Hitler's putsch. He continued to support the idea of a Siberian republic (or guberniya) as a solution to the problems of the Kuzbass.

Tuleyev radiates charismatic appeal. As I waited for an evening meeting (after his typical day of campaigning before enterprise labor collectives), Tuleyev swept open the door and strode boldly into the room, while his underlings scurried around him like mice. Once settled in for an interview, lipstick was visible on his collar. Whether speaking to a single person or to a television audience, Tuleyev is a captivating speaker: he beats his chest and pulls his hair for emphasis, and he addresses his listeners in a direct language usually suited to intimates talking around a kitchen table. Tuleyev claims to be studying for an advanced degree in psychology in order to better relate to the people.[28]

Yet Tuleyev's popularity is only partly attributable to charisma. Part Soviet regional boss and part pork-barrel politician, Tuleyev is able to deliver for his constituency. During times of crisis, he flies to Moscow, works the hallways and offices, and returns with something tangible for the Kuzbass, which is popularly referred to as "Tuleyev's money." As chair of the region's parliament, he directed his goodwill toward his natural constituency—those most vulnerable to market forces, such as pensioners and others directly dependent on the state budget.[29] Several informants reported that at the end of regular parliamentary sessions, such as the one in which he pushed through a motion to let pensioners ride public transportation for free, people lined up to kiss his hands.

Tuleyev's economic platform was fairly straightforward. In good populist form, Tuleyev called for both a sharp cut in taxes and a significant increase in social spending. He argued that the country's main problem was the decline in production, that the Chinese model offered a way out of Russia's morass, and that his main difference with his opponents was his call for a return to regulated prices. He openly supported the defenders of the

Russian White House, though for their backing of the constitution rather than their military action. "The elections are taking place under the conditions of dictatorship," he said, adding prophetically, "If the elections aren't rigged, those who urge a correction to the course of reform will win 60 percent of the vote."[30]

It is far from clear that Tuleyev's popularity in the Kuzbass could translate into political success in Russia as a whole, but it is nonetheless important to contrast Tuleyev's success with that of a politician such as Zhirinovskii. In particular, Tuleyev's brand of populism is not based on Russian nationalism, nor could it be, given that he is part Tatar and part Kazakh.[31] In general, nationalism (either in terms of relations with non-Russian minorities or in terms of Russia's lost standing in world politics) rarely surfaced as an issue during the campaign in the Kuzbass. The success of Tuleyev and Zhirinovskii in the Kuzbass had little to do with nationalism and much to do with a general dissatisfaction with the status quo.

Among those themes that were raised successfully in the Kuzbass campaign was the sense of chaos and anarchy *(bezvlast'e)*. With bitter irony the region's citizens pointed to the city of Prokop'evsk as a symbol of disorder. Prokop'evsk is a mining town that literally sits on top of the richest coal reserves in Russia, yet the city's boilers fail to provide sufficient heat during the Siberian winter, so that people wear their coats and hats in school and in their homes. Related to this sense of chaos was the concern with crime. But crime had additional meaning to people in the Kuzbass beyond the fear of personal safety and the security of property. This additional meaning had to do with economic crime, the sense that others, usually members of the mafia, were taking advantage of a chaotic situation to enrich themselves.[32]

Most important—and hardly surprising given the prevailing conditions—the campaign's biggest issue was the economy. Politicians and citizens alike spoke at length about declining living standards, the number of citizens living below the poverty level, inflation, and the threat of impending unemployment. Workers at state enterprises were most concerned with their pay being detained for months at a time, which not only made life difficult in itself but, given the rate of inflation, greatly discounted their wages in real terms once it was finally paid out. (Miners in the region threatened to strike and stopped work at a few mines over this issue in the month leading to the election.)

Given these concerns, one would expect in this industrial region that two social groups in particular—industrial managers and labor—would have a significant impact on the campaign. We will examine each in turn.

Industrialists

In the Kuzbass the political center—such as it was—was occupied by the region's industrialists. Although relatively few ran as candidates,[33] industrialists also played a role behind the scenes as backers of different candidates. Given their economic resources and their power base, and the fact that industrialist candidates were occupying a position in the political spectrum that should appeal to most voters, one would expect for them to do quite well.

Yet the region's industrialists were not politically united. Candidates across the political spectrum received backing from industrialists, virtually the only social actors with sufficient resources to make significant contributions to the various campaigns. Klimov, the director of the successful chemical firm of Tokem, provided backing for the region's Russia's Choice candidates.[34] Other industrialists backed Tuleyev.[35] Still others, such as the administration of the Kuznetsk Metallurgical Complex, backed competing candidates, apparently to have "their person" in parliament no matter what the outcome.

Several industrialists ran as candidates themselves, usually on a platform that placed them near the political center. One such candidate was Aleksandr Botalov, who as the director of the coal association "Kuzbassugol'" appeared to have strong resources. Moreover, he appeared to be particularly well positioned, in that his two opponents were women, both running on platforms that stressed women's issues and rights and who seemed destined to split their potential votes.

In this coal region Botalov was not the only coal "general" (as bosses in the coal fields are known) to become directly involved in the campaign. Another was Yurii Malyshev, Russia's biggest coal boss. Malyshev headed Rosugol', the state company that superseded the old coal ministry; in typical post-Soviet fashion, Rosugol' operated as part state ministry, distributing subsidies from Moscow throughout the coal fields, and part private corporation, seeking diamond and gold concessions and other profit-making enterprises unrelated to the coal industry. Owing to the structure of property rights in the Russian coal industry, Malyshev had the authority to hire and fire mine directors, presumably giving him tremendous influence over them. Though Malyshev denied this, it was widely held that he collected signatures to place himself on the ballot through the personnel departments of various mines: secretaries were said to simply copy names and passport numbers off the books.

The race for the Duma seat in the district comprising Novokuznetsk, a major industrial city, pitted two candidates with a strong backing from industry. The first was Anatolii Tkachenko, the hand-picked candidate of the local branch of the Russian Union of Entrepreneurs and Industrialists, a group composed of both new entrepreneurs and directors of the city's giant steel and other factories.[36] Young and looking very much the part of a modern businessperson, Tkachenko ran a small, successful firm supplying producer goods to some of the area's large industrial enterprises. Tkachenko's politics placed him in an intermediate position in the political spectrum, both among local and national politicians. For example, Tkachenko pointed to Western Europe as an economic model, rather than America or China, by arguing for a state role in a market economy and a strong welfare state. He also campaigned on the need to create new workplaces to absorb the future unemployed.

Despite being the candidate of the industrialists' union, Tkachenko faced a candidate with even more resources. Viktor Medikov was the only candidate in the region to run explicitly as a professional politician: he had been a member of the USSR Supreme Soviet. His campaign literature spoke of his experience in doing those activities so familiar to members of the U.S. Congress: constituent service and correspondence.[37] More important, however, was the backing of one of the region's industrial giants—the Kuznetsk Metallurgical Complex. The local industrialist's union (and the director of the Kuznetsk plant was a member of the union) did not appear to put a large amount of resources into ensuring that their candidate, Tkachenko, won.[38] This was not the case with the Kuznetsk plant.

Labor

Although industrialists were placing themselves at the political center and claiming to speak for those employed in industry, what of labor? Where did it fit in this political schema, and how did it influence the campaign and the election outcome? Again, this is not a theoretical question for the heavily industrialized Kuzbass. Moreover, the region's coal miners not only have significant numbers, but, unlike most workers in Russia, they have independent organizations and present a real social force in the region. Further still, the miners have been heavily involved in politics: the miners were active in several prior campaigns, from the elections to the regional and Russian parliaments in 1990, where they sent a number of miners and like-minded supporters into office, to the presidential campaign of 1991.

Certainly the most rational electoral strategy would be one appealing to the bulk of the voters—the working class. Moreover, a rational electoral strategy would appear to be a centrist one—supporting some form of social democracy, trade union rights, economic reform with guarantees for labor—in short a program that provides for labor's participation in the reform process. This was in fact what most miner-leaders described as their political and social goals. But when discussion turned to concrete political action, the language was not subtle but rather Manichean—two years after the failed coup and the end of the Soviet Union, in an independent Russia holding democratic elections while undergoing both large-scale privatization and dramatic economic decline, it was still a question of "us" versus "them." For these labor leaders, brought to power on the strength of the miners' strikes, "they" were the "Communists" and "we" were the "democrats."

There was little consensus on whom to back within the democratic camp. As noted, the leaders of the NPG allied with RDDR. Aleksandr Sergeyev, chair of NPG Russia, appeared on several national television commercials for RDDR and was high on its party list, but also ran (as an independent candidate) in his home district of Prokop'evsk. Although he ran a prolabor campaign in a heavily mining district, he campaigned in the district for only one week, and the campaign consisted largely of his one free television slot and a visit to a few mines. Despite being the national leader of the independent miners' union, he was not well known in his district because he had risen to prominence in Moscow, and his colleagues wrote off his chances well before the election.[39]

As NPG leaders were supporting RDDR, members of the Kuzbass Council of Workers' Committees, the other regional miners' organization, found themselves much closer to Yeltsin, Gaidar, and Russia's Choice. Aleksandr Aslanidi, former council member and executive director of *Nasha gazeta,* a newspaper founded by the miners' movement, ran as an independent candidate for the Federation Council but campaigned on a platform of support for Yeltsin's constitution, the West as a political and economic model for Russia, and for continuation of the current reform policies.[40] His campaign was considered to be so close to that of Russia's Choice that a meeting of democratic candidates for the Federation Council was held in the hopes of persuading some of the lesser-known candidates to withdraw. The meeting was held in the Council of Workers' Committees offices and chaired by the Council head Vyacheslav Golikov. Golikov argued that Aslanidi had the best chance out of the democratic candidates, and urged Mityakin, the Russia's Choice candidate, to withdraw. Mityakin conceded that he had very little chance to win, but considered his campaign important as a means of getting his message out and as a foundation for future campaigns. He continued his campaign.[41]

This divergence within the Kuzbass miners' movement—with one group supporting Sobchak's list, the other much closer to Russia's Choice—led to the local scandal over the threat to not vote for government candidates. This inability to agree on distancing themselves from the government, even as a bargaining tactic, illustrates the difficult position in which the Kuzbass miners found themselves on the eve of the parliamentary election. The miners' movement had originally allied itself with Yeltsin in the hopes of improving the material position of miners. Yet although miners had been rewarded for their position by continued subsidies and wage hikes, since then delays in getting their wages, unpaid vacations, threats of mine closures—not to mention the overall economic hardship in Russia—meant that dissatisfaction among rank-and-file miners was very near the boiling point.[42] Given these conditions, backing the status quo was certainly not a winning electoral strategy. But before examining strategies that were successful, we must first turn to the election outcomes themselves.

Explaining Outcomes

Candidates supported by liberals and miner-leaders lost every election in the Kuzbass, with one important exception. Industrialists also fared poorly, except for those allied with Tuleyev. Tuleyev and his allies won five out of the six seats at stake in the Kuzbass. Tuleyev himself easily came in first of the eight candidates for the upper house, with an overwhelming 80 percent of the vote (see table 17-1). Moreover, his coattails were long: his protégé Sergei Burkov won the Duma seat from the city of Kemerovo, and his ally Medikov won the seat from Novokuznetsk. A third seat was won by Galina Parshentseva, the deputy chief of the Anzhero-Sudzhensk Department of Social Defense, and the last seat was one by Nina Volkova, head of the state retail store system in Prokopevsk. Volkova included among her ideological allies Travkin's Democratic Party of Russia, the Civic Union, and Zhirinovskii.[43]

Table 17-1. *Winning Candidates for the State Duma and Federation Council*

District	Candidate	Party	Percent of vote
Andzhero-Sudzhensk, 89	Parshentseva	Independent	54.3
Kemerovo, 90	Burkov	Independent	22.8
Novokuznetsk, 91	Medikov	Independent	50.8
Prokopevsk, 92	Volkova	Independent	38.3
Federation Council	Tuleyev	Independent	80.2
Federation Council	Aslanidi	Independent	20.6

Source: Central Electoral Commission of the Russian Federation, January 5, 1994.

Two competing explanations might account for the success of particular candidates in the Russian election. One would focus on the resources that candidates bring to the electoral process, such as financial backing and political connections. The second would explain candidates' success by the ideological appeal of their platforms. Although these explanations are ultimately complementary, I will argue that the position a candidate claimed along the political spectrum was more important than the candidate's resources.

The candidates with the strongest resources were those allied with industrialists or those who were industrialists themselves. If resources alone were to explain election outcomes in this case, one would expect industrial candidates to have been most successful. One resource that any candidate allied with industrialists had was access to enterprise labor collectives. This provided a virtually cost-free forum for the candidate before a captive (if not captivated) audience.[44] Although plant workers may have found such speeches little more than an annoyance, such campaign stops were certainly important during a very short campaign period in which name recognition was crucial. After television and radio advertising, this was certainly the most important campaign technique.

Yet not all candidates had equal access to meetings before enterprise labor collectives: one needed the blessing, if not the outright endorsement, of plant management. This meant those allied with industrialists, or those who stood a good chance of getting into office, were given access to enterprise labor collectives. In the Kuzbass Tuleyev, Medikov, Tkachenko, and Malyshev campaigned almost daily in various enterprises.[45] Plant newspapers, often widely subscribed to if for no other reason than they provided the cheapest source for television listings, were also a forum to which candidates could have access. Although these newspapers rarely backed only one candidate, articles discussing candidates and their platforms most often featured those candidates closely allied with industrialists.[46]

Given such resources, and the fact that the industrialist candidates often occupied a middle position in the political spectrum, one would expect for them to do quite well. Yet this was not the case. We have already mentioned one potential explanation for their lack of success—that the region's industrialists themselves were not united. Yet this lack of a united front by the industrialists is not sufficient to explain the failure at the polls of particular candidates.

One such candidate was Yurii Malyshev. Going into the election Malyshev appeared to be holding all the cards. As head of Rosugol', Malyshev was responsible for the distribution of coal subsidies throughout Russia, a point of no small importance for the Kuzbass. Malyshev won the endorsement from Governor Kislyuk, and it was widely assumed that he had the backing of the region's coal generals.[47] Malyshev ran frequent ads on television, campaigned heavily in the region, and his movements received much attention from the media. At his various campaign stops, Malyshev claimed credit for social infrastructure that had been built with coal subsidies: he helped dedicate a new tram line in Prokopevsk, supervised the repair of the water supply in Kiselevsk, and promised he would build a new children's hospital in Novokuznetsk.[48]

Yet such campaign tactics may have backfired, as people in the region began to derisively refer to Malyshev as the "good uncle," a paternalistic figure promising to take care of all those under his wing. Indeed, despite all his resources, Malyshev did not win, failing to overcome the fact that he was perceived as a member of the nomenklatura.[49] This was a problem that other industrialist candidates faced, in that their very strength was also a weakness: in many people's eyes they were still bosses who continued to lord over people's lives as in the past.

Malyshev was not the only industrial manager to suffer this fate. Aleksandr Botalov, director of the coal association Kuzbassugol' appeared particularly well positioned to win. Although there were only three women candidates out of a total of twenty-six running for different seats in the Kuzbass, two were successful—the maximum number possible, because the third ran in the same district as one of the other women. Botalov was the only other candidate in this district, where both women ran on similar platforms supporting women's rights and what might be considered traditional women's issues, such as social protection of the population, better health care, and services for children. During the campaign it looked almost certain that these two women would split their potential vote, and would in a sense defeat each other, especially because they were up against the male director of a large coal association. Yet Galina Parshintseva, deputy head of the local Department of Social Defense, won. Although in the absence of exit polling there is no evidence on why people in the Kuzbass voted as they did, one can hypothesize that the advocacy by all three female candidates for social protection resounded with most of the voters.[50]

Another winning candidate, Viktor Medikov, enjoyed significant backing from one industrial giant. The Kuznetsk Metallurgical Complex put a significant amount of resources behind him: it financed the campaign, paid two plant managers to work on the campaign full-time, donated all the literature that was printed at the plant, and provided automobiles and drivers for the campaign staff.[51] Yet Medikov's relationship with the steel giant was not straightforward: as a member of the Supreme Soviet, he had spoken strongly about the horrific environmental conditions of Novokuznetsk, and he pinned much of the blame directly at the door of the Kuznetsk plant.[52] Yet when the Soviet Congress disbanded, Medikov accepted a job as the plant's deputy director. The plant had a clear interest in cultivating such a political relationship: built in the first years of Stalin's industrialization drive, Kuznetsk was desperately in need of funds for reconstruction. Because the plant was not expected to make a profit anytime soon, this money was not likely to be provided by foreign capital, leaving open only the political channel of funding from Moscow.

For his part, Medikov the professional politician changed from supporter of the environment to defender of the region's largest polluter; he also transformed his politics from a member of the interregional group in the Soviet parliament and an early defender of the miners' movement to a close political ally of Tuleyev.[53] Medikov campaigned heavily with the popular Tuleyev, and his campaign aides argued over whether their platforms were "identical" or merely "very similar." Indeed it is impossible to determine which factor was more important, Medikov's industrial backing or his alliance with Tuleyev.

The overwhelming victory by those called Communists by their opponents (they did not identify themselves as such) stands in contrast to the winner of the second seat in the upper house, Aleksandr Aslanidi, erstwhile leader of the miners' movement. Aslanidi's campaign included the defense of Yeltsin, his reforms and his constitution, and upholding the West as an economic and political model for Russia.[54] Yet Aslanidi clearly did not win from the strength of his platform or an effective campaign. In fact, his campaign was disorganized: at the outset, Aslanidi conceded that he had virtually no idea about how to run his campaign, and entire days were wasted in the logistics of speaking before a single audience of 200 or, in one case, 50 voters.[55]

But Aslanidi's difficulties extended beyond lack of experience. When presenting his platform in front of his natural constituency—coal miners—Aslanidi's message was not well received, to say the least. At one such presentation, he described a trip to Austria, which he claimed opened his eyes to the much greater living standards in the West. After pushing Yeltsin's proposed constitution, he spoke of the need for further market reform (and even defended Gaidar) in front of miners who had not been paid in months.

Aslanidi's speech was cut short several times by angry remarks and questions—among which were pronouncements that politicians cannot be trusted, that the miners were tired of being lied to, and that anyone who traveled abroad was suspect as well. These miners also made clear their dissatisfaction with a reform that not only failed to give visible results but had created tremendous hardship and promised more. Yet Aslanidi, one of the chief leaders of a miners' movement that had helped bring an end to the Soviet Union, now stood before his potential constituents as a defender of the status quo.[56]

Aslanidi's success resulted not from strong support from miners or from his platform, but rather from the newspaper he helped run. *Nasha gazeta,* established in December 1989, in the wake of the first miners' strikes, was one of the very first legal independent newspapers in the Soviet Union. It became the biggest paper in the Kuzbass, though the reasons for its success are partly controversial: its opponents claim the former paper of the regional party committee, *Kuzbass,* was forced to survive under harsh conditions, pointing to the ten days that it was closed in September 1993. These same people claim that *Nasha gazeta* has received favorable credits and other concessions from Yeltsin's government. Yet probably the major reason for its being the most widely read paper in the Kuzbass is that the paper provided free subscriptions to the region's pensioners. Although a questionable move in economic terms, this was nothing less than a brainstorm, because rather than being a profit-making venture, *Nasha gazeta* is quite openly a political paper; it has no pretensions to objectivity. Its content could best be compared with such U.S. opinion weeklies as the *Nation* or *National Review.*

The newspaper literally ran Aslanidi's campaign from start to finish: with Aslanidi himself as executive editor, the paper financed the campaign through loans, published page-long articles that were little more than campaign ads, while the editor-in-chief acted as his campaign manager and the paper's journalists were his campaign workers.[57]

As for the media in general, the free time allotted to candidates on television and radio seemed to be handled fairly, even though the chair of the Kuzbass television and radio company, Mityakin, was himself a candidate for the Federation Council.[58] The fact that the television station was under the control of the liberals came through in the region's nightly television news program "Pulse," which was openly supportive of certain policies and candidates.

One example illustrates the bias in the news program, as well as the ideological bind in which the miners found themselves. A delegation of Vorkuta miners arrived in the Kuzbass to seek support for their strike, which was aimed not only in gaining back wages but in putting pressure on the government for a comprehensive program for the coal industry. Like the Kuzbass's Sharipov, they argued that the miners should threaten to withhold votes from government candidates during the election campaign unless the government agreed to their demands. At a press conference one of the Vorkuta miners suggested supporting someone besides Gaidar, some "third people" between the Communists and the free marketers. His statement was cut short by the chief correspondent from Kuzbass television, who shouted, "What 'third people'!? Name names; I want to hear names," before going on to suggest that the only possible alternative were those imprisoned after the defense of the White House. The correspondent, also the program's nightly newscaster, displayed his interjection repeatedly on local television, without bothering to show the Vorkuta miner's response to his question.[59]

Was there a third choice, real or potential, for the voters of the Kuzbass, above all the region's industrial workers, who had led one of the strongest anticommunist movements in the history of the Soviet Union and yet were clearly threatened by the liberal's economic reform program? Why were the region's labor leaders unable to propose an alternative to the neocommunist populists and the liberal free marketers? Why were labor leaders of Russia's most heavily subsidized industry allied with the radical reformers?

The miners had been rewarded by Yeltsin, through greatly increased subsidies and other means. Moreover, in some sense the miners had come to power—Kislyuk, the region's governor, was appointed from the ranks of the miners' movement by Yeltsin, as was Malykhin, the president's personal representative for the Kuzbass. But this argument is insufficient. Overwhelming evidence had been accumulating that the policy of the pre-election government was leading directly to mine closures, and this process might occur quickly, especially if the government party won. Rumors were circulating of a World Bank proposal calling for the rapid closure of many Russian coal mines, and even government officials were hinting that if they won the election, they would have to face down labor, especially its most organized sector—the coal miners.[60]

Rather, there were other, broader factors at work—in particular the ideological legacy of the Soviet experience. As they had during their struggle to end Communist party hegemony, the Kuzbass miners clung to a univariate world view—it was still a struggle of "us" against "them," or communism versus democracy. They were thus using an old political map to plot strategy in an increasingly complex world.

The complexities included the fact that their erstwhile allies in the anti-Communist struggle—the liberals—were now carrying out policies that threatened the miners' very livelihood. Indeed, workers faced a class predicament—the threat of unemployment, plant closures, and deindustrialization in general. Although individual workers have different exit options, owing to differences in age and skill, the future of entire industrial communities are at stake, giving workers strong common interests.

The Kuzbass miners implicitly used class concepts from the Soviet era, even when they were fighting against Communism. In pushing for the market, they used a labor theory of value, through which they argued they were being exploited by the nomenklatura even while being heavily subsidized. They continue to use such concepts today, arguing that the old nomenklatura have become new entrepreneurs. In this way the coal miners understood their social situation in class terms, but were without an ideological framework to organize these notions, because the language of class was the language of the enemy.[61]

Moreover, the communist experience had discredited the notion of "socialism" in any sense of the term. Even when faced with a challenge as a class, and while using class concepts to comprehend their situation, the Soviet experience has taken the idea of socialism, or even social democracy, off the political agenda. This has left workers not only without an alternative *to* capitalism, but even without an alternative *within* capitalism. With workers thus immunized against class-based appeals, workers and their dissatisfactions are available for the appeals of authoritarian populism and nationalism.[62]

Further still, the experience of the Communist party has meant that parties are associated by workers as something alien to them, as a vehicle for intellectuals and others to steer the lower classes in one direction or another. The discredited concept of political parties was perceived by virtually all candidates running in the Kuzbass: other than those running on party lists, only candidates from Russia's Choice decided to identify themselves as members of a political party. All other candidates ran as independents (including Tuleyev, a future leading candidate of the KPRF). The result was no vision of an alternative for workers, and no institutional channel to express their grievances in the political realm.

The stark political choices that workers and others in the Kuzbass faced during the election led to significant cynicism about democracy. The most popular political expression leading up to the election was clearly "We don't believe in anyone." As one miner yelled at Aslanidi during a campaign stop, "We can elect people, but we'll always be suppressed from above." Without genuine representation for labor, workers are available for the appeals of nationalists and others claiming to defend their rights. In the absence of a party genuinely allied with workers, miner-leaders supported the liberals while their rank and file voted for Tuleyev and Zhirinovskii. But these votes were cast cynically, as workers were not deceived, and in the process the concept of democracy was devalued.

Although the miner-leaders remained committed to liberalism in some form, there is no doubt that opinion in the region shifted dramatically from the earlier days of the miners' movement. Although Yeltsin fared less well in the 1991 presidential election in Kemerovo relative to his success elsewhere, this was clearly the result of the native son Tuleyev rather than strong anti-Yeltsin sentiment. Survey data from the region do show a shift since the beginning of 1992 (and economic liberalization) from support for liberals and worker committee activists to support for Tuleyev and the regional parliament he headed.[63] The most stunning transformation, however, is between the deputies elected from the region in 1990 and those elected in 1993. The change is clear and dramatic—whereas the Kuzbass sent radical reformers and moderates to parliament in 1990, they sent conservative delegates to the Duma in 1993. The Sobyanin score for Kemerovo deputies in 1990 was 44, second only to Moscow and St. Petersburg in the ten regions studied in this volume; the score for 1993 to 1995 was -35, which was lower only in Kursk and Bashkortostan in the same ten regions.[64]

Moreover, Tuleyev's successes have extended beyond the 1993 election. In April 1994, Tuleyev and his supporters won two-thirds of the seats to the

Kemerovo regional parliament, and Tuleyev was unanimously elected the parliament's chair.[65] In the 1995 parliamentary elections, Tuleyev joined the Communists (KPRF), receiving the third position on the national party list, his charisma balancing the decidedly uncharismatic Zyuganov. With Tuleyev's popularity in the Kuzbass, the KPRF won a stunning 48 percent of the region's votes in December 1995, second only to North Ossetiya out of Russia's 89 regions.[66] (After the election, Tuleyev declined a Duma seat, preferring to remain in the Kuzbass.) Tuleyev even ran for president in 1996, but as a "reserve" candidate to Zyuganov, and his name was often mentioned as a potential prime minister had Zyuganov gained the presidency.[67]

Conclusion

Several points are worth emphasizing in conclusion. First, in the Kuzbass political party structures and national party campaigns were quite weak. Although in a sudden and abbreviated campaign period, this was to be expected—and was found in other regions as well—the virtual absence of campaigning by party blocs was particularly pronounced in the Kuzbass. This is all the more curious in that the Kuzbass has been a highly politicized region for several years and has had an impact on Russian politics disproportionate to the size of its population.

The weakness of party campaigning in the Kuzbass can be explained by its Siberian location and the consequent perception of being far from Moscow. In contrast to the national party campaigns, regional politics and regional politicians were paramount concerns during the election period. National political issues were important, but it was on the regional level that such issues were played out and became meaningful for residents of the Kuzbass. This reflected Tuleyev's success in setting the regional political agenda: he adroitly appropriated the discourse the miners and liberal reformers used in their earlier battle with the Soviet "center" to attack the Russian "center" (supported now by the same liberals and miner-leaders). As before, he argued, Moscow was exploiting the Kuzbass much like a colony, and the Kuzbass needed a strong alternative leadership to defend its rights and interests.

Further, candidates representing industry fared poorly in this industrial region. The failure of industrialists and self-styled centrists was evident throughout Russia; but in the Kuzbass there were especially striking cases of industrial candidates losing despite holding enormous resources. Their campaigns, especially that of Malyshev, head of Rosugol', stressed their ability to take care of the region in paternalist fashion. This approach appears to have backfired. Their paternalism was derided, in part because it was all-encompassing: by electing captains of industry to positions of political power, political and economic power would once again be concentrated in the hands of the few. This, at least, was how Kuzbass residents explained their position.

Finally, the election campaign in the Kuzbass witnessed the failure of labor to craft class-based appeals to workers. Miner-activists remained allied across class lines with liberal intellectuals, despite overwhelming evidence of what that liberalism portends for coal mining as a way of life. Workers outside of coal mining remained unorganized and were hardly represented at all. Yet workers were clearly angry and disillusioned both by communism and their first taste of the market. Because organized labor did not appeal to their interests, workers were left available to the appeals of others.

Indeed, class-based appeals were important, and both Tuleyev (and his allies) and Zhirinovskii employed them successfully, if in different ways. Yet they appealed not to labor per se but to the losers of the reform process, a substantial group in a country in which living standards had dropped considerably. Both Zhirinovskii and Tuleyev were populists in their promises of quick solutions to seemingly intractable problems and in their very style: both spoke to the public not as intellectuals but as intimates sitting around the kitchen table. Yet beyond being populists, both represented an authoritarian strain of populism—the deal they offered was one of tangible rewards in return for support and quiescence. This is a familiar refrain for citizens of former communist societies.

It is not too surprising that many Russian citizens find such appeals attractive, but it is a turnaround for the Kuzbass miners. This was the sort of boss the miners rebelled against when they had the opportunity to do so, suggesting they would prefer an alternative to paternalistic protection and domination. Yet in the current political climate miners and other workers were offered no such alternative and could craft none of their own. Given abysmal economic conditions, it is little wonder that when forced to chose between a liberalism promising more of the same and authoritarian-style populism, miners and other workers chose the latter.[68] In the absence of survey data, one can only present hypotheses about why miners would make such a dramatic switch from Yeltsin to Zhirinovskii and Tuleyev. One hypothesis would be that although miners everywhere are given to radicalism, the direction their radicalism takes is undetermined. Somewhat more pessimistically, the coal miners might simply be the avant-garde of Russian politics—they were one of the first social groups to support perestroika, but when they became dissatisfied, they turned against Gorbachev and became one of the first groups to support Yeltsin. Now that Yeltsin has failed to deliver, they appear ready to turn elsewhere, perhaps anywhere.

Notes

1. Eighty-seven percent of the population are urban dwellers. AVISTA database, available at Duke University Library.
2. Mikhail Gorbachev, *Zhizn' i Reformy* (Moscow: Novosti, 1995), 2 volumes.
3. See Stephen Crowley, *Hot Coal, Cold Steel: Russian and Ukrainian Workers from the End of the Soviet Union to the Post-Communist Transformations* (University of Michigan Press, 1997).
4. In getting nominated to run for the presidency, he collected more than 300,000 signatures, mostly from industrial enterprises. "Tuleyev on Presidential Election Platform: Moscow." *Selskaya Zhizn*, May 28, 1991, in FBIS-SOV-91-106, June 3, 1991, pp. 83–85.
5. Tuleyev came in fourth in the overall voting, with 6.8 percent of the votes cast, just behind Zhirinovskii's 7.8 percent. TASS, "Soobshcheniye: Tsentral'noi izbiratelnoi komissii po vyboram Prezidenta RSFSR," *Pravda*, June 20, 1991, p. 1. Miners' districts were said by political observers in the region to have gone for Yeltsin and not Tuleyev in 1991. Interview, Leonid Lopatin, November 29, 1993.
6. Although Clarke and Fairbrother see this as a modest turnout and evidence of the miners' conditional support for "liberal reformers," this appears to be a case of seeing the glass as half empty. Simon Clarke and Peter Fairbrother, "After the Coup: The Workers' Movement in the Transition to a Market Economy," in Simon Clarke and others, *What about the Workers: Workers and the Transition to Capitalism in Russia* (London: Verso, 1993). That the miners' protests were taken seriously is reflected in coal minister Shchadov's suggestion to the coup leaders of imposing martial law on the Kuzbass.
7. The text of Tuleyev's statements can be found in Leonid N. Lopatin, compiler, *Rabocheye Dvizheniye Kuzbassa* (Kemerovo: Kemerovo Izdatel'stvo, 1993).
8. Kislyuk was a manager in an open-faced mining concern who joined the miners during their 1989 strike and became the chief architect of the miners' demands for economic independence. Malykhin was a gruff but quick-witted miner who came to national prominence during the second all-Union strike of 1991.
9. The concessions were made after strikes broke out. Subsidies to the coal industry absorbed 20 percent of the revenues of the Russian state by May 1993. "Fedorov Proposes New Measures to Stabilize Ruble," *Izvestiya*, May 8, 1993, cited in *RFE/RL Daily Report*, May 11, 1993. Efforts to place the industry on the market

without subsidies quickly failed and would have led to the closure of many coal mines in Russia.

10. Prices in coal regions were sometimes 50 percent more than in surrounding regions. Simon Clarke and Peter Fairbrother, "After the Coup: The Workers' Movement in the Transition to a Market Economy," in Clarke and others, *What about the Workers*, pp. 186–87.

11. "Kak nam obustroit Sibir," *Rossiiskaya gazeta*, April 2, 1992, p. 2; April 11, 1992, pp. 3–6; James Hughes, "Regionalism in Russia: The Rise and Fall of Siberian Agreement," *Europe-Asia Studies*, vol. 46, no. 7 (1994), 1133–61.

12. *Rossiiskaya gazeta*, December 18, 1992, pp. 3–4.

13. Ibid., June 2, 1993, p. 1.

14. This was consistent with his view of the August coup.

15. The candidate was Gennadii Mityakhin, who claimed to be very careful not to abuse his office and appeared on television only in a general advertisement for all the regional Russia's Choice candidates. Still, there was a rather clear conflict of interest.

16. Almost all Russia's Choice candidates in the Kuzbass conceded that their chances of winning were minimal, despite what appeared to be a well-funded organization. They were also one of the few groups of political actors to speak in terms of laying the groundwork for future campaigns.

17. It should be noted that the workers' committees had atrophied from their once strong position as head of the strike movement, and their strength now came more from allies in the regional administration than from rank-and-file support.

18. Interview, Vyacheslav Sharipov, November 23, 1993. Even within the NPG there was a lack of unity on which candidates to support. In Novokuznetsk, the local NPG leader, Aleksandr Smirnov, campaigned as the agent of Yurii Pyl, a candidate for the Federation Council and a prosecutor running on a proreform and anticrime platform. Smirnov supported him because he was a "professional" who would do something about the crime problem. The fact that Tuleyev was almost ensured one of the region's two Federation Council seats, meaning that Pyl was up against Aslanidi, the miners' candidate, did not seem to bother Smirnov. Interview, December 12, 1993.

19. Victoria Pope, *U.S. News and World Report* correspondent, personal communication. Indeed, Sharipov's arguments in favor of RDDR sounded rather like ex post facto attempts to distinguish it from the pack of like-minded party lists. On the whole the bloc had a hard time distinguishing itself from other liberal opponents. On this point see chapter 4, this volume.

20. According to Golikov, "Such a statement against one part of the democratic wing during an election campaign is extremely destructive. . . . We have more serious opponents with whom we must fight." *Nasha gazeta*, November 25, 1993, p. 1.

21. Nearly all political actors in the Kuzbass described the political space in such stark terms.

22. He continued, "I said to myself, 'Here are the real people [Vot on narod].'" Interview, Gennadii Mityakin, November 26, 1993. Many other political actors and candidates dated their political awakening to the first miners' strike, and often spoke of what they did "after the strike." Nikolai Chizh, another Federation Coun-

cil candidate, aligned with Russia's Choice, discussed during a campaign forum how the strike had "opened his eyes," after which he became involved in environmental issues and was elected deputy for ecology on the city executive committee. He is currently deputy head of the regional administration for the city of Novokuznetsk.

23. Vladimir Lebedev, a candidate on the RDDR party list, made this point most strongly, though in his political views he was moderate relative to other liberals. Interview, November 25, 1993. One candidate, Bella Denisenko, a former people's deputy in the Russian parliament and the acknowledged leader of Russia's Choice in the Kuzbass, had risen to political prominence by allying with the miners' movement, but candidly expressed a readiness to jettison her former partners, because they were not willing to swallow the bitter pill of further shock therapy and mine closures. Interview, December 9, 1993.

24. According to a survey done in November 1992 by the Kuzbass Center for the Study of Public Opinion at Kemerovo State University, the regional soviet received a positive rating of 26, whereas the Congress of People's Deputies, the Supreme Soviet, and the president all received negative ratings. Mikhail Kislyuk, the head of the regional administration, received a rating of -44.

25. To the extent that antisemitic sentiments are related to fascism in Russia and elsewhere, an extreme form was presented by Vladislav Streligov, the former deputy chair of the Kuzbass soviet and a close ally of Tuleyev, at the end of an extended conversation on Kuzbass politics. Dropping his guard, he conveyed his view of the world as one controlled by a conspiracy of Jewish bankers. Interview, December 8, 1993. Antisemitic statements, if not in this extreme form, were not the sole property of this political wing, however. Mityakin, the Russia's Choice candidate for the Federation chamber, explained his quite strained relationship with Governor Kislyuk by referring to the latter's ambitious nature, a product of his being a Jew. (Kislyuk, for his part, referred to himself as Orthodox when a visitor inquired about a Roman Catholic Madonna statue in his office.)

26. Data provided by the Kuzbass Center for the Study of Public Opinion at Kemerovo State University.

27. A good statement of Tuleyev's political philosophy, and that of the Fatherland Faction he represented, is contained in his speech to the Congress as published in *Rossiiskaya gazeta*, April 11, 1992, pp. 3–6.

28. Interview, November 29, 1993.

29. Tuleyev's opponents explain his political success by referring to the large number of pensioners in the region, an explanation that has become part of local folklore. In fact, according to the AVISTA database, Kemerovo oblast does not have a greater percentage of pension-age citizens than Russia as a whole. It may have more people on pensions because of the low pension age for underground miners, who can retire at twenty-five years of service regardless of age. This explanation would not bode well for Tuleyev's opponents who like to believe that Tuleyev's politics still do not resonate in the miners' milieu.

30. Interview, November 29, 1993.

31. Though the Georgian Stalin successfully employed Russian nationalism, Tuleyev's physical features clearly mark him as an ethnic "other." In fact he

claimed that his opponents had tried to use his ethnicity against him, in distributing a photograph of him with the Chechen Ruslan Khazbulatov, over the caption: "Two Russians for Russia?" Although Tuleyev is addressed in public as Aman Gumirovich, his official name as it appeared on the ballot is Aman-Gel'dy Moldagasyevich.

32. The mafia has become quite an amorphous concept that can include anyone from gang members to entrepreneurs operating within the law. One candidate, Yurii Bubentsov, argued that he was considerably handicapped because he was listed on the ballot as the director of a "commercial structure," which had negative connotations related to the mafia, rather than an enterprise involved in production.

33. Many argued that unlike the Congress of People's Deputies, the new Duma would require full-time politicians, and most industrialists did not want to lose their current positions.

34. For example, Mityakin says Klimov, the director of Tokem, paid for the signatures that Mityakin gathered, one-quarter of which were collected at Klimov's plant.

35. Although he declined to name them, Tuleyev said industrialists in Moscow had paid for his television advertisements, of which there were quite a few.

36. Tkachenko also enjoyed the backing of the local trade union Unity, though on closer inspection this union turned out to be another union of entrepreneurs, which used the stronger legal provisions available to trade unions when registering with the authorities. Interview, December 7, 1993.

37. According to his campaign literature, as a member of the Soviet parliament, Medikov had "thirteen receptions for citizens with personal problems in Novokuznetsk alone," and he received 500 appeals from citizens, 350 letters, as well as 100 telegrams during parliamentary sessions. "Professionals with Common Sense Should Be in Parliament," campaign brochure printed by the Kemerovo Council of Labor and War Veterans, undated.

38. Another problem was that the union appeared to be a rather loose grouping. It would meet and discuss common interests and coordinate activities, no doubt including how to influence Moscow for concessions to the region. However the group contained contradictory as well as common interests, such as between small entrepreneurs with more interest in the acceleration of reform and state plant directors interested in a more controlled pace of reform. Win or lose, Tkachenko was not particularly concerned. He would continue with his business Sibmetallurgmont, and once the December election was over he planned to leave Siberia for a vacation in Miami.

39. In fact when the miner-candidate for the Federation Council, Aleksandr Aslanidi, campaigned in Prokopevsk, he appeared with Sergeyev's opponent, Valerii Biryukov of Russia's Choice. Sergeyev was chastised by regional NPG leaders for showing up even for just the last week of the campaign, because negotiations between the union and the government were taking place in Moscow.

40. As Aslanidi explained during his campaign, "namely the market and democracy allow people to live better and more free than we lived under 'developed socialism.' There, in market conditions, people who work—I've seen them myself—are unfettered, smiling, free. There are unemployed—yes, there are serious

problems, and society there sympathizes and takes care of these problems. But what is important is something else: there every person who is not working *dreams* of becoming a working person—there's a powerful stimulus for progress!" *Nasha gazeta*, November, 23, 1993 (original emphasis), p. 3.

41. Author's transcript. The other candidate at the meeting was Yurii Pyl, a prosecutor running on an anticrime platform.

42. This was probably true for workers throughout Russia. *Izvestiya* argued before the election that a social explosion was possible at any moment in any region. November 26, 1993, p. 1. On the tension in the mining regions, see also *Izvestiya*, November 24, p. 1, and November 30, 1993, p. 1.

43. "But not Russia's Choice," she continued. "They created all the problems." Interview on Kuzbass television, November 30, 1993.

44. The setting allowed candidates to focus on economic questions, particularly the future of the workplace in an uncertain environment—the very strength of industrialist politicians. Candidates who campaigned in public places at forums that relied on advanced publicity and voluntary attendance ran the risk of appearing before small audiences. At one such candidate's forum, at a local "House of Culture" in a mining borough of Novokuznetsk, fifty people at most—mainly pensioners—turned out for a "political show" that included musicians, dancers, and comedians. Nevertheless, the candidates Aslanidi and Bubentsov, both self-described democrats, spent most of the day at this one event.

45. One of Medikov's campaign workers claimed that they had visited every enterprise in Novokuznetsk, and most of the enterprises and mines within their district. Tkachenko's daily schedule included between three and five enterprise speeches, which were often lengthy. Aslanidi, who was not allied with industrialists, campaigned before labor collectives in mines where he had connections through the miners' movement. One can only assume that directors saw this granting of access as an exchange in the event the candidate was successful, allowing future access for the director to a member of parliament.

46. Thus the papers for the Kuznetsk Metallurgical Complex and the West Siberian Metallurgical Complex, the two industrial giants of Novokuznetsk with more than 30,000 employees each, typically featured articles on Tuleyev, Medikov, Tkachenko, and Malyshev, and much less frequently on Aslanidi or others candidates of the "democratic" camp. According to one employee at Kuznetsk, her department head announced to the employees one day, "I recommend you vote for Tuleyev," and it was assumed that this request came from somewhere higher up.

47. Malyshev argued during the campaign that the Kuzbass deserved "special status," and he mentioned no apparent contradiction in his representing the Kuzbass in the Federation Council, while representing the interests of miners in other regions through Russugol'.

48. Malyshev claimed of such actions: "In this way we will lower the tense atmosphere in the mining regions." Interview on the television news program "Novosti," December 1, 1993.

49. This was particularly a problem for Malyshev, because he was based in Moscow.

50. At a meeting at the Dzherzhinskii mine in Prokopevsk between the miners and Aslanidi and Valerii Biryukov, the local Russia's Choice candidate, several miners verbally attacked Aslanidi for his positions before they were cut off by a woman who accompanied the candidates. The woman happened to be an attorney and Russia's Choice supporter who was married to the mine's NPG chair. When she stood up and rebuked the miners for not supporting the reform candidates, she was obviously a much more eloquent spokesperson for these views than either the Russia's Choice candidate or the future "senator" from the Kuzbass, suggesting that other potentially successful women candidates are available.

51. As one of the full-time campaign aides from the Kuznetsk plant explained, it was only right that the plant should have "its" person in parliament: "We built this city, the housing, the transportation, even the circus, all the social infrastructure." Interview, Vitalii Korolev, December 8, 1993.

52. According to figures provided by the Novokuznetsk regional museum, the average life span in the city for men is 6.7 years less than the Russian average, and infant mortality was the highest there in all of Russia. Metallurgical plants are some of the worst polluters in the former Soviet Union.

53. On Medikov's support for the miners' strikes, see the transcript of his speech before the Supreme Soviet in Viktor Kostyukovskii, *Kuzbass: Zharkoye Leto 89-ogo* (Moscow: Sovremennik, 1990), pp. 79–83. Medikov's opponents called his reversals "political prostitution."

54. Aslanidi's campaign slogan, "For the old and weak — continue socialism; for the young and strong — give the chance to earn and live as they deserve," was an attempt to meld his support for the market with his understanding that pensioners were crucial to the election outcome.

55. During an argument among campaign leaders at the *Nasha gazeta* offices, Aslanidi's campaign managers picked up a book to illustrate the difficult constraints they faced. The book was a campaign manual translated from English and distributed by the National Democratic Institute based in Washington. The campaign manager noted that much of the text discussed the operation of telephone banks, an unhelpful suggestion in a land of few phones. The book also suggested beginning a campaign well before the typical six-month campaign period; the Russian campaign was little more than a month long.

56. Aslanidi's appearance as a candidate before miners' collectives strongly contrasts with his performance at a meeting of Kuzbass miners' representatives two years earlier (I also attended) that voted to end a two-month strike aimed at gaining Russia sovereignty. Aslanidi has since become more soft-spoken and reflective in a workers' environment that often chooses dynamic and even gruff leaders.

57. Journalists from the paper attended Aslanidi's campaign functions as agents of the candidate, introducing him with a rousing speech before sitting down to report on the event as a correspondent for the paper. *Nasha gazeta* journalists also ran press conferences for the candidate, sitting on the other end of the microphones from their colleagues at other papers.

58. On the other hand, his political opponents claimed that some candidates were given free television time that directly competed with soap operas and other

popular programs, whereas candidates of the democratic camp were given more favorable times. Interview, Vladislav Streligov, December 8, 1993.

59. Author's transcript.

60. For example, the *RFE/RL Daily Report* cites an AFP story that argued, "In private . . . members of the Russian government are saying that, in the new year, the Yeltsin leadership will have to follow the example of Thatcherite Britain and face down a challenge from organized labor. They say that the only industries in which independent unions are strong enough to mount a sustained strike are coal-mining and defense production and that the government could defeat a strike in either. This is because coal stocks are high following the general fall in production. . . ." Elizabeth Teague, "Gaidar Warns Insolvent Firms," *RFE/RL Daily Report,* November 15, 1993, pp. 1–2. Such plans were evidently put aside when the government parties were defeated in the polls.

61. David Ost, "Labor, Class, and Democracy: Shaping Political Antagonisms in Post-Communist Society," in *Markets, States, and Democracy: The Political Economy of Post-Communist Transformation,* edited by Beverly Crawford (Boulder, Colo.: Westview Press, 1995).

62. Beverly Crawford suggests the metaphor of workers' being allergic to class based appeals; I have here changed it to workers' being immunized by the experience of communism. Crawford, "Markets, States, and Democracy: A Framework for Analysis of the Political Economy of Post-Communist Transformation," in *Markets, States, and Democracy.*

63. By November 1992, Golikov, the strongly pro-Yeltsin worker committee chair, proved to be very unpopular among Kuzbass residents: 61 percent disapproved of him, and only 7 percent approved. As noted earlier, former miner-leader and current governor Kislyuk received an overall rating of -44. Data provided by the Kuzbass Center for the Study of Public Opinion.

64. See tables 1-6 and 1-8, this volume, as well as Colton's discussion of the limitations and usefulness of the Sobyanin scores in chapter 1. The 1990 scores were for the First Congress.

65. However, there was an unprecedented low turnout in the local elections of one-third of eligible voters. *Rossiiskaya gazeta,* April 5, 1994, p. 2.

66. Robert Orttung and Scott Parrish, "Duma Votes Reflect North-South Divide," *Transition,* vol. 2, no. 4 (February 23, 1996), pp. 12–14.

67. Although the Communist success would appear to indicate renewed support for their working-class ideology, workers in the Kuzbass and elsewhere were offered little alternative. For the December 1995 election, Sergeyev, the national leader of the miners' NPG, joined the "left-center" but still pro-Yeltsin Rybkin bloc; the trade union federation FNPR (Federatsiya Nezavisamykh Profsoyvzov Rossii) reached across class lines to industrialists to form the so-called Union of Labor. Both blocs were trounced at the polls. Moreover, even the Communist party choose not to direct its appeals to the working class; the party's presidential candidate, Zyuganov, dropped the notion of class from his rhetoric almost entirely, replacing it with the struggle for the nation as a whole. Boris Kagarlitsky, "Russian Trade Unions and the 1995 Elections," *Labour Focus on Eastern Europe* no. 52

(Autumn 1995), pp. 64–69; Veljko Vujacic, "Gennadiy Zyuganov and the 'Third Road,'" *Post-Soviet Affairs*, vol. 12, no. 2 (April–June 1996), pp. 118–54.

68. According to one postelection survey Zhirinovskii was supported above all by blue-collar workers in state-owned industrial enterprises, earning average or above-average wages. (The survey was conducted by VTsIOM.) "Who Voted for LDPR," *Izvestiya,* December 30, 1993, p. 4. Since the election, fascist organizations have been finding the workers' milieu fertile ground for organizing. See Aleksandr Burtin, "Fascists Who Speak the Truth," *Novaya yezhednevnaya gazeta,* September 9, 1994, reprinted in *Current Digest of the Post-Soviet Press,* vol. 46, no. 37 (1994), pp. 8–9.

Primor'e

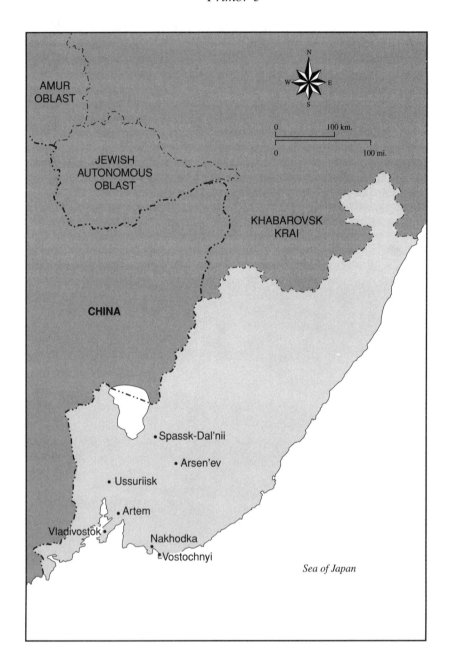

CHAPTER EIGHTEEN

Primor'e

Local Politics and a Coalition for Reform

Katherine G. Burns

ALL POLITICS is local. This saying has particular significance for the 1993 elections in Primorskii krai. While a Moscow executive engineered a founding election, in Primor'e executive power focused on local power consolidation. The implicit tension between these two goals—one central and one local—largely dictated electoral results in the region.

Localization[1]—the process by which local issues take precedence over national ones—had two important consequences for the elections in Primor'e. First, it found expression in strong local executive power and shaped the governor's goals in his bid for a seat on the Federation Council. Second, it gave rise to a loosely formed opposition group, which, in the context of the elections, crystallized into a "reform coalition" under the leadership of a strong single-mandate candidate. Reform coalition candidates won two of the three single-mandate seats in the State Duma and one seat in the Federation Council. The lines between the two camps were far from clear and gen-

I would like to thank Timothy Colton and Jerry Hough for their invaluable assistance in conducting this study and their insightful comments on written drafts. Special thanks to Joel Ostrow, Jane Prokop, and Alexandra Vacroux for their assistance in establishing research contacts in Vladivostok, and to Yitzhak Brudny and Margot Light for their support and comments. I would especially like to acknowledge David Woodruff, whose detailed knowledge of the region, insightful explanations, and helpful comments have immeasurably contributed to this study. All errors are, of course, my own responsibility.

erally varied from issue to issue. Under these circumstances, interest grouping and political parties fell prey to factional struggle, which weakened their internal cohesion as well as their political determination.

The chapter is divided into three sections. The first begins with a brief discussion of the local context that facilitated the rise of Primor'e's particular brand of localization. The second examines the ways in which localization drove the race for the Federation Council and the referendum on the constitution. The third explores the limits of localization and the formation of the reform coalition in the races for the State Duma. The chapter thereby evaluates the strength and durability of the forces driving electoral outcome in Primor'e and draws conclusions about the prospects for democratic consolidation in Russia.

The Historical Context: Localization Takes Root

Nine thousand three hundred kilometers and seven time zones east of Moscow, it is perhaps hardly surprising that politics in Primorskii krai has been largely isolated from the bustle of the national capital. Physical distances aside, the krai's proximity to Asia—poised on the northern borders of North Korea and the People's Republic of China, and a mere hour's flight off the coast of Japan—has raised psychological barriers between Moscow and Vladivostok. Of Asia, yet not Asian, Primor'e is at once divided from the Russian heartland and from its Asian neighbors.

Cold War barriers compounded Primor'e's sense of isolation. Home to the Soviet Union's formidable Pacific Fleet, Vladivostok was a closed city until 1992. An opening to Asia in the post–Cold War era, although it raised hopes of economic prosperity, did little to mitigate the krai's sense of isolation. The new era brought an influx of Asian businesses to the region, but increased interaction with Asian neighbors raised fears of a new "yellow peril." Old memories die hard in Russia's Far East, and Asian incursions have been a feature of the region's political geography for centuries. Until the middle of the nineteenth century, Chinese trappers and traders flourished in Haishenwei, today's Vladivostok, and by 1877, "four of every five civilians in Vladivostok were Chinese or Korean."[2] A 1991 agreement between Moscow and Beijing ceded 15 square kilometers of Primor'e border area to China, further inflaming local fears and raising suspicions that Moscow did not have the region's best interests in mind. The new influx of Asian traders stirred old memories, and, in the context of the elections, provided fertile ground for nationalist appeals.

Weakened ties to Moscow have further compounded fears of a perceived Asian "threat." In the post-Soviet era, the krai has perhaps felt more isolated from European Russia than ever before. Rising rail tariffs and air fares make travel to the Western regions of Russia a virtual impossibility for most krai residents and have severely curtailed the exchange of goods on the Trans-Siberian Railroad. Perhaps the most obvious indication of central neglect has been an end to the generous subsidies and government orders that were the life-blood of the local economy in the Soviet era. Much of the krai's economic structure traditionally focused on the extractive industries: coal, timber, and nonferrous metallurgy. Exploited during the Soviet era for these raw materials, the krai was heavily dependent on the center for investment and technological inputs. When central subsidies began to dry up in the early 1990s, Primor'e's economy suffered accordingly. Overall production in Primor'e fell 20.6 percent between 1990 and 1993.[3] The krai's military-industrial complex is in a sad state of decay. In 1990 Primor'e's nineteen military-industrial enterprises accounted for 20.9 percent of industrial employment; by 1993, all were in sore need of investment and several were on the brink of bankruptcy.[4]

An initial flurry of trading activity in 1992 raised hopes that interaction with Asia would alleviate the krai's growing economic crisis. However, with nonpayments endemic and local infrastructure hopelessly underdeveloped, Asian businesses limited their activity to export of raw materials, often demanding payment in advance, or even resorting to barter. By 1993, misplaced hopes that the opening of Vladivostok would bring increased prosperity contributed to the krai's growing sense of isolation. Total turnover in Primor'e's three main ports—Vladivostok, Vostochnyi, and Nakhodka—actually fell in 1993, as did levels of foreign trade activity in the krai's enterprises.[5]

Local support for the federal government's reform policies waned with the fortunes of the local economy. In both the June 1991 presidential elections and the April 1993 referendum, Primor'e's support for President Yeltsin was substantially higher than that of Russia as a whole.[6] Similarly, the Sobyanin rating for the Primor'e delegation at the First Party Congress in 1990 was a liberal 35. The rating for the 1993 delegation, however, fell to -4.[7]

By December 1993, with hopes for economic revitalization dashed, growing xenophobic fear of Asian encroachment, and increasing isolation from Moscow, political activity in the krai focused almost entirely on a local strongman—the governor, Yevgenii Nazdratenko.[8] Vowing to protect the krai from Asian incursions and to wrest subsidies from Moscow for the region's ailing enterprises, Nazdratenko came to power in March 1993, at the head of a union of enterprise directors. President of Vostok, a mining corporation in the north of the krai, and a former deputy of the Russian Federation, Nazdratenko combined locally grounded managerial know-how with political experience. The new governor promised solutions to the krai's woes. If Moscow was unwilling or unable to solve local problems, Nazdratenko would. Thus, local issues found representation in strong local executive power.

The governor's power base was the Primorskii Manufacturer's Shareholding Corporation—PAKT—that represented thirty-six of the region's most powerful enterprises, employing 9 percent of the regional workforce.[9] PAKT sought to consolidate economic power in the krai by ensuring that privatizing PAKT enterprises remained securely in the hands of local directors. To this end, PAKT directors acquired controlling packets of shares in the region's largest enterprises and set out on a quest for political as well as economic domination of the krai. Nazdratenko was the expression of that political will. As governor, he granted interest-free loans to PAKT enterprises, financed by the regional budget, and appointed PAKT leaders to key positions in the local government.

The governor's economic and political drive for power had important consequences for the December 1993 elections. Nazdratenko's efforts effectively established the local arena as the legitimate locus of political activity. The fact that local political figures, from all points of the political spectrum, accepted this localization of the political space bears testimony to the fertile ground on which the governor's message fell. Local "democrats" are a case in point. With strong and politically astute local leaders and a history of local party organization unrivaled in the krai, radical and moderate reformers might have been expected to focus their political energies on the national contests in December 1993. Instead, they chose to concentrate their energies on issues of purely local importance.

As the first Russian legislature was elected, political interest in Primor'e focused on a fierce struggle between the offices of the Vladivostok city mayor and the krai governor. Elected in the summer of 1993, Viktor Cherepkov did not fit the krai administration's plans for local power consolidation. Formerly an officer in the Pacific Fleet, Cherepkov had neither the credentials nor the experience of the PAKT bosses. His main claim to fame was his electoral mandate, of which he took full advantage in his caustic criticism of krai administration power politics. For this he won the enmity of the local governor and the hearts of the democratic opposition. Excluded from the PAKT power machine, and alarmed at the governor's escalating power, local democrats were Nazdratenko's natural opponents. Cherepkov became the focal point of their political activity. Even Yeltsin's special representative to Primor'e, Valery Butov, threw himself into the fray in support of Cherepkov. In the immediate run-up to the December elections, therefore, the krai administration waged a spirited campaign aimed at discrediting the city mayor and removing him from office. Active democratic involvement in local struggles lent local issues a degree of legitimacy not enjoyed by the national races. By focusing on the local political space, democratic forces ultimately legitimized a system that could only favor the local governor—the very localization that propelled Nazdratenko to power and that the governor was shaping into a formidable local machine.

The notion that a strong local executive was the only answer to the krai's woes gained further ground during the bloody events of October 1993. The spectacle of a national legislature literally under fire from the executive further discredited Moscow as a source of support, undermined local faith in the democratic process, and rallied local forces behind the governor. Capitalizing on heightened local disillusion with Moscow and taking his cue from the center, Nazdratenko further solidified his grip on power by supporting the disbanding of both krai and city soviets. Executive power ruled in Primor'e. No local legislature operated in Primorskii krai until January 1995.

Localization—based on historical isolation, compounded by economic hardship, and ultimately celebrated in local political institutions—determined the contours of political space during the December elections. In the electoral context, localization played three important roles: first, it circumscribed the goals of important political actors, restricting them to the local arena; second, it defined the political and economic resources available to candidates; third, it shaped candidate messages to the electorate. Localization was particularly important in the race for the Federation Council, which featured the governor's race. It also had important consequences for the races to the State Duma.

Localization in Action: Federation Council and the Constitution

In a political arena fixated on local issues, it should come as no surprise that the main focus of the elections was the local governor. In a sense, his was not a campaign for the national legislature at all. For the governor, this was purely a local affair. Electoral mandate would boost the legitimacy of Nazdratenko's drive to consolidate local power. Indeed, campaigning for the Federation Council was more a trial run for prospective gubernatorial elections—Nazdratenko's ultimate goal—than a sortie into the national political arena.[10] As governor and PAKT protégé, Nazdratenko's political resources went unrivaled in the krai. Strong-man campaign tactics conveyed a message focused almost exclusively on extolling his image of strong effective leadership (a man "able to get things done"). Nazdratenko won a handsome 72.9 percent of the vote partly on the basis of his reputation, but, more important, because of his ability to marshal the forces of enterprise managers and workers, the press, and his own administration to his cause.[11] In effect, Nazdratenko maintained a powerful grip on the key channels to power in the krai (see table 18-1).

The governor's campaign mustered support in three ways. First, the governor mobilized industrial managers to gather signatures from workers for candidate registration. According to several different sources, Nazdratenko's policy consisted of handing out signature lists to managers of PAKT enterprises with instructions to have workers fill them out. Workers reluctant to sign were threatened with the loss of their jobs. PAKT managers also campaigned at their enterprises urging workers to vote for the governor.

Second, the governor used administrative power to employ a carrot-and-stick policy that elicited support through special concessions or use of force. When Nazdratenko disbanded both the krai and city soviets, he delegated the majority of their responsibilities to himself and his team. He was thus able to unilaterally institute policies that would increase his popularity, such as his policy of providing benzene to pensioners at reduced rates. In a city such as Vladivostok, which has a population of approximately 100,000 pensioners, this policy was highly effective. The krai administration granted special favors to workers such as giving workers a half day off the Friday before the December 12 elections to allow them to vote early. Perks aside, the krai administration was able to rally support through forceful measures. Perhaps the most dramatic exhibition of Nazdratenko's tactics and capabilities came less than a week before the election. On a day's notice, Nazdratenko summoned all city and district heads to a meeting in Vladivostok, ostensibly to promote the constitution. Twenty-eight administration heads attended. In a mass meeting, which dragged on for hours and which was highly reminiscent of the "bad old times," official after official rose to express support for the krai administration and demand the removal

Table 18-1. *Primorskii Krai Voting Results*

District	Winner	Partisan affiliation	Percent of vote
State Duma			
51	Glubakovskii	Yabloko	29.8
52	Ustinov	Independent	39.3
53	Nesterenko	Independent	27.4
Federation Council			
25	Nazdratenko	Independent	72.9
25	Gayer	Independent	42.5

Source: Unpublished results provided by Primorskii krai electoral commission. Results reported as percentage of valid votes, not counting against all votes.

of Yeltsin's representative, a strong supporter of the mayor's office.[12] The officials threatened a general strike if their demands were not met.

Third, the krai administration enjoyed privileged access to the local media, and wielded sufficient power to silence critical voices. Throughout the election campaign, laudatory accounts of the administration's past and current achievements dominated the local news. Moreover, Vladimir Shkrabov, the editor-in-chief of *Krasnoye znamya,* a popular krai newspaper with 65,500 subscribers, was a founding member of PAKT. In this newspaper, at least, no articles critical of the administration appeared.

Over the course of the campaign, most critical voices in the local press found themselves either shut down or else under heavy fire. Perhaps the most extreme case was that of the Primorskii Commercial Television Company—PKTV—the most critical televised news media in Vladivostok. PKTV's program frequently featured interviews with Cherepkov and other members of the anti-Nazdratenko coalition. However, PKTV was unable to broadcast during the entire election campaign, and Cherepkov did not make even a single televised appearance during this period. Despite PKTV's high ratings with viewers—an independent poll showed that 92.93 percent of viewers watched PKTV on a regular basis, higher than for any other television company in Vladivostok—the krai administration closed the company down in the early autumn, claiming that PKTV's material was "low quality" and accusing the station of broadcasting pornographic material. PKTV's closure coincided with the disbandment of the city soviet, one of PKTV's original founders, and the mayor's office took over its administration. Cherepkov lost no time in taking his appeal to the Moscow Ministry of the Press, and the station was reopened. PKTV's success was short-lived. Shortly after reopening, the krai administration again closed it down, citing an order from the Moscow Ministry of Communications, which banned commercial enterprises from operating in official buildings. PKTV did not reopen.[13]

PKTV was not the only member of the media to come under fire from the krai administration. With two weeks to go before the election, *Utro Rossii*, formerly the newspaper of the krai soviet and stubbornly critical of the governor and his team, was threatened with eviction from its premises. The pretext was the newspaper's lack of official sponsorship, due to the soviet's disbanding, and its consequent loss of the right to housing in a local administration building. Through pleas and deals, *Utro Rossii* was able to gain the time necessary to cover the election campaign before the eviction. The timing of the administration's move to evict the newspaper suggests a calculated move on the part of the administration to silence a critical voice.[14]

A more dramatic incident involved the case of Vladivostok Television's Mikhail Voznesenskii, whose national television reports in October showed clips of Nazdratenko with Rutskoi. After this incident, the krai administration hounded Voznesenskii, and on November 15 his office at the television station was the scene of gun fire. Voznesenskii escaped unscathed, but sources in Vladivostok suggested that the krai administration was responsible for the shooting.[15]

With his stranglehold on local power channels complete, Nazdratenko set about establishing his image of efficient local leadership. This he accomplished in two ways. First, he skillfully manipulated the local political struggle to his own advantage. Portraying himself as a man under fire from incompetent political adversaries, who had no real interest in the fate of the krai, Nazdratenko shifted the blame for local problems to the offices of the mayor. Not only was the mayor incapable of performing his duties (clearing roads in the winter, ensuring ambulance service, and so on), so the governor claimed, but the constant petty bickering issuing from the mayor's office was obstructing the governor's efforts to right the local economy. To an electorate beset by economic hardship and fed up with official incompetence, establishing a credible scapegoat was a highly effective tactic. Second, Nazdratenko ran a skillful campaign designed to appeal to the widest possible range of voters. In the case of the worker vote, for example, Nazdratenko's campaign sought to defuse potential worker-manager conflict by hitting on issues of concern to both workers and managers, such as the need for government subsidies for electrical power and for transportation along the trans-Siberian railroad. The campaign centered on issues that affected every inhabitant of the krai: resolution of the energy crisis, lower internal quotas for maritime products in an effort to put fish in the stores of Vladivostok rather than Moscow, and cheap bread.[16] The policy of quota and tax retention, in particular, clearly won Nazdratenko support from such non-PAKT industrial giants as Dal'moreprodukt, the huge privatizing enterprise that held a monopoly on marine products in Primor'e. In effect, Nazdratenko's platform accurately addressed the concerns of the voters, and the governor's reputation for efficiency bolstered voters' faith in his ability to fulfill his campaign promises.

In sum, while the governor's campaign propelled him to national office, its goals were essentially local. His strategies and campaign message were formulated accordingly. It is an interesting fact that throughout the campaign, while other candidates published advertisements and campaign platforms, not a single paper published a comprehensive campaign platform for the governor, nor did his picture appear in the press with a platform attached. Rather, articles on Nazdratenko featured his exploits as governor or his role as hero or villain (depending on the political orientation of the paper) in the local power struggle. In choosing to focus on local issues, and deliberately underemphasizing the national nature of the institution to which he aspired, Nazdratenko's campaign called into question the very legitimacy of the new national institutions.

If there was one national campaign that the governor openly endorsed, it was the referendum on the constitution. The krai administration ran an active campaign on behalf of the constitution. Interviews and round tables featuring krai administration officials appeared on local television, and the head of the krai electoral commission gave a laudatory "information session" on the constitution. There can be no question, however, that the local governor viewed passage of the constitution as an essential component of his drive for local power consolidation. Indeed, his job depended on it. Two weeks before the election, Anatolii Chubais summoned all Far Eastern governors to Blagoveshchensk for a meeting on the constitution. According to participants, Chubais told local administration heads that failure to pass the constitution in their region would cost them their jobs. Needless to say, the campaign for the constitution heated up after that. In Primor'e, local leaders fell into line, and even representatives of political parties that did not endorse the constitution dared not oppose the newest administration directive.[17] The constitution passed in Primorskii krai with 51.75 percent participation and 71.45 percent of participants voting favorably, well above the national average of 58.43 percent.

If Nazdratenko was effective at promoting his own candidacy, the same cannot be said of his colleagues. Two Nazdratenko allies participated in the race for the Federation Council. Despite their close links to the governor, their campaigns lacked the spark and vigor of the governor's race, and both faired poorly at the polls. With the vast administrative forces at his command, why did the governor fail to promote like-minded candidates? Ironically, the governor's own campaign goals and strategies were largely to blame. Nazdratenko's campaign promoted strong regional leadership—his own—and spun a web of centralized local control around himself. In view of the governor's goal—legitimizing local rule by achieving electoral mandate—promoting strong colleagues with claims to his own power base could lead to factions within his camp and give rise to rival power centers.[18] Nazdratenko thus wasted little time on his colleagues' campaigns.

Yevdokiya Gayer won the second seat on the Federation Council. A former USSR People's Deputy, prominent member of the Interregional Group of Deputies, and deputy head of the State Committee on the Social and Economic Development of the North, Gayer was most renowned for her vocal support of Andrei Sakharov in the Congress of People's Deputies. For this she earned the reputation of a supporter of the underdog, ready and able to come to the assistance of minorities and victims of unfair policies and unscrupulous politicians. Her campaign focused almost exclusively on promoting her image of a kind, honest, and capable person who would bring a touch of compassion and humanitarianism to the cut-throat and power-hungry world of politics. With few resources, Gayer ran a modest campaign largely limited to the Vladivostok area. She could not raise the funding to pay for time on the air, had difficulty arranging meetings with workers at PAKT enterprises, and did not even have a car to travel around the krai. No ally of Nazdratenko, Gayer was unofficially endorsed by Russia's Choice and used an office in the city government building for her campaign headquarters. Nonetheless, Gayer, like Nazdratenko, took the position that local conflict should be resolved in the interests of getting down to business. Indeed, Gayer successfully combined two key elements of Nazdratenko's own strategy—proven leadership ability and official distaste for local squabbles—to propel her to victory in the Federation Council. That these two factors—the only ones common to the rival, yet ultimately successful campaigns—were key to electoral victory was evident as the votes came in: an informal exit poll I conducted in Vladivostok indicated that nearly 40 percent of respondents voted for *both* Gayer *and* Nazdratenko.

In sum, the rules of the game in the Federation Council race were set by the local governor. The governor structured local political space to favor one campaign only—his own. If other players were to be successful, they had to play by his rules. That an opposition candidate won the second seat in the race reflects her ability to harness key elements of the governor's platform to her own star.

The Limits of Localization: State Duma

The particular brand of localism at work in Primorskii krai had peculiar repercussions for the race for the State Duma. The krai administration made no serious effort to ally itself with any political party. Taking its queue from Moscow, the local executive remained largely aloof from partisan politics. In single-mandate races, the krai administration expended little energy for the campaigns of its allies[19]—this despite the considerable resources at its disposal. As a result, no administration-backed candidate won in the districts. With krai administration attention directed elsewhere, candidates from radical and moderate reform parties successfully moved in to secure victory in two of the three single-mandate districts.

Party Races: Weak Local Parties

Except for unusually high levels of support for the Women of Russia (and correspondingly low support for socialists), party voting patterns in Primor'e did not differ substantially from national trends. Parties in Primor'e were distinguished by their weak local structures. Most parties had no local organization to speak of, and those with the best organization were weakened by their involvement in local political struggles.

As across Russia, Vladimir Zhirinovskii's Liberal Democratic Party of Russia (LDPR) carried the day in Primorskii krai with 23.3 percent of the local vote. The krai's support for moderate reformers was slightly higher than the national average, and support for radical reform was slightly lower. Analysis of party voting by raion shows that the LDPR did best in rural areas and in industrial centers remote from the krai capital. The highest votes for the LDPR were in the northern reaches of Arsen'ev okrug and in heavily industrial and mining regions of the southern Ussuriisk okrug. Voting for the Women's party tended to correlate with voting for the LDPR: in regions in which the LDPR came first, Women of Russia came second. In the krai capital, however, Russia's Choice actually beat the LDPR, with Yabloko and Women of Russia close behind.

Ironically, these voting results represent a radical departure from the political legacies of Primor'e's three electoral districts. Arsen'ev was traditionally the most democratically inclined okrug. The Sobyanin rating for Arsen'ev deputies in 1990 (First Party Congress), for example, was a radical 82.2.[20] By December 1993, Arsen'ev was the most conservative okrug in Primor'e. Vladivostok, on the other hand, had the most conservative 1992 (Sixth Party Congress) rating of the three okrugs: -3. In December 1993, Vladivostok returned the strongest reform endorsement of the three okrugs. These figures suggest that the suffering inflicted on Arsen'ev's large extractive and military-industrial complex enterprises contributed to a substantial conservative swing in the year preceding the elections. Although Vladivostok also suffered, conditions in the krai capital were considerably better than in rural areas, and Vladivostok's comparatively educated population produced a stronger democratic endorsement.

Voter dissatisfaction with the elections was evident in the high number of votes cast against all parties. This trend was particularly evident in areas dominated by military-industrial complex enterprises. In one such raion, dominated by an atomic submarine factory, nearly 15 percent of the vote was cast against all parties. In general, voter dissatisfaction in Primor'e was higher than in Russia as a whole: 7.1 percent of Primor'e voters voted against all parties, while the national average was only 4.2 percent.

The most unusual aspect of Primor'e voting was strong local support for Women of Russia, nearly twice as high as the national average: 8.1 percent of Russian voters but 15.3 percent of voters in Primor'e. This was primarily the result of effective local leadership—Svetlana Orlova, running number 17 on the party list, was an energetic and business-oriented woman and the general director of her own "charitable women's organization," called "Anna." Clearly prosperous, her company ran its own newspaper, with a respectable tirage, as well as a restaurant, and maintained good relations with the krai administration.[21] Although Orlova did not campaign extensively in the media, she did appear on television twice in the week preceding the elections. One of Women of Russia's strongest assets in Primor'e was its noninvolvement (at least officially) in the local political struggle. Perhaps the best expression of this, in the words of one voter in Arsen'ev, was the popularly expressed sentiment: "At least they haven't done anything to us yet!"

If Women of Russia was blessed with strong local leadership, most parties in Primor'e were weak and unorganized. In large part this was due to the brevity of the campaign, but also to weak links between central and local party organizations. As a result, coordination between local party organizations and party-endorsed single-mandate candidates was poor. The strongest local parties, namely the radical reformers, became embroiled in local political struggles and consequently suffered from internal fracturing.

Local party structures in Primor'e suffered from weak links to their central organizations. Parties that sported important local leaders—those who won high slots on the party list—made even less effort to organize locally than parties without powerful local candidates. The LDPR and the Democratic Party of Russia (DPR) both had highly placed Primor'e candidates on their lists and candidates from these parties went to the Duma. The LDPR ran two candidates on the party lists, Yevgenii Bol'shakov, who was placed number 40 on the list and made it to the Duma, and Nikolai Zolotov, number 137 on the list, and also a candidate in the Vladivostok single-mandate district. The LDPR had no local party organization and the local campaign was virtually nonexistent. However, the central LDPR organization maintained a strong vertical connection with its local candidates. Decisions regarding party-list candidates were taken in Moscow, and the two party-list candidates did not coordinate their campaign efforts. Rather, the local campaign was centrally controlled: Zhirinovskii flew Zolotov to Moscow for instruction and consultation. Zolotov did appear in the press and on television in his capacity as a single-mandate candidate and did promote the LDPR platform, but Bol'shakov did not even appear once.

The DPR case was similar. The head of the local DPR organization, Yurii Yakovlev, ran number 13 on the party list, and consequently made little effort to coordinate the local campaign. With good Moscow contacts and a party list that was not divided along regional lines, Yakovlev was not obliged to do much to secure his seat. Consequently, the DPR campaign was extremely disorganized. Apparently, Yakovlev failed to realize that candidates chosen by the party for single-mandate districts also had to run on the party lists. The local organization therefore selected its three strongest candidates to run in single-mandate districts, while less well-known candidates were slotted to run on the party list. It was not until they arrived in Moscow to submit their candidates that the local DPR representatives realized their mistake. By then it was too late. In Arsen'ev, two DPR candidates ran against each other in the single-mandate race. Although the weaker candidate requested to withdraw, he was unable to do so. He had handed all his campaign money from the krai electoral commission over to the DPR party head (and was unable to retrieve it), and was therefore financially unable to withdraw his candidacy. Only one DPR candidate, Valerii

Nesterenko, was successful, and he chose to collect signatures and run as an independent. The fact that an unofficial DPR candidate won in the okrug that returned the lowest DPR vote in the krai suggests that Yakovlev's failure to effectively coordinate the local party organization contributed significantly to the DPR's poor showing in Primor'e.

In sharp contrast to those parties with highly placed local candidates on their lists, parties without any local candidates made concerted efforts to devise their own local campaign strategies. The Communist Party of the Russian Federation (KPRF), for example, had a well-organized and wide-reaching local organization, particularly in Arsen'ev. The KPRF was the only party that had observers at all the *uchastki* in Vladivostok. A comparison with Primor'e's 1991 voting behavior shows that the Communists had lost ground heavily in the krai. While 25.1 percent of Primor'e voted Communist in 1991, the figure fell to 11.3 percent (combined figure for the KPRF and the Agrarians) in the December 1993 elections. This shift is clearly related to the KPRF strategy of backing nominally independent candidates in single-mandate districts. According to the local party secretary, the Communist party backed candidates in both Arsen'ev and Ussuriisk, collecting signatures and distributing campaign literature. The Communist candidate in Ussuriisk, Mikhail Beseden, came in third out of five candidates, but the Arsen'ev candidate, Azat Yusupov, lost by only 0.1 percent or 351 votes. Although the KPRF performed poorly in 1993, local organization in Primor'e served the party well in 1995 when they won 18.4 percent of the local vote.

Weak local party structures meant that few parties managed to coordinate effectively with their candidates in single-mandate districts. Parties that broke their lists down regionally, however, fared somewhat better in this respect than those that maintained unified party lists. Election rules stipulated that single-mandate ballots would not list party affiliation, however, where party lists were broken down regionally, local leaders, all of whom also ran in single-mandate districts, were listed on the party-list ballot. For this reason, the names of candidates from parties that broke their lists down on regional lines appeared twice on the ballot—once on the party-list ballot and once on the single-mandate ballot. Such was the case of the successful Yabloko candidate from Vladivostok, Mikhail Glubokovskii, whose name appeared both on the party ballot and on the single-mandate ballot. Because of this rule, voters in Vladivostok could identify the Yabloko candidate's party affiliation in the single-mandate voting, despite the fact that party affiliation was not listed on the single-mandate ballot itself. Conversely, the LDPR list was not broken down regionally, which meant that LDPR voters did not have the opportunity to identify their candidate in the single-mandate race. The LDPR candidate in Vladivostok came second in the single-mandate race and claimed that LDPR voters had complained they were not able to identify their candidate in the single-mandate race. The fact that particularly high numbers of voters voted against all single-mandate candidates in precisely those raions in which the LDPR did exceptionally well also suggests that dissatisfied LDPR voters were not able to identify their candidates in the single-mandate races. This may explain in part why high levels of support for the LDPR in party-list voting did not translate into support for LDPR single-mandate candidates.[22]

The strongest local parties fell prey to infighting. Such was the case of the radical reformers. To begin with, reform parties at the center did not co-ordinate among themselves. This resulted in considerable local confusion. Sergei Novoselov, for example, a Primor'e member of the Republican party, found himself running on two lists (Russia's Choice and PRES), and withdrew in confusion. Similarly, a member of PRES found himself on two lists and had to withdraw. Poor coordination among central party organizations was compounded by poor links between central and local party organizations. The local Russia's Choice organization received no financial assistance from the center, precious little information, and virtually no direction.

Such difficulties aside, Russia's Choice was severely fractured in Primor'e. This was primarily due to its overinvolvement in local politics. Indeed, the krai administration's push to limit the legitimate forum of political debate to the locality, and, most important, opposition acceptance of this policy, meant that radical reformers in Primor'e focused their energies more on the krai administration than on the election process per se. As a result, the most prominent members of Russia's Choice did not even run on the ballot, strategizing instead to run for the local legislature. Anatolii Zabolotnikov and Il'ya Grinchenko, both prominent members of the Social Democratic party, chose this route.[23] Others, such as Sergei Solov'ev, the head of the disbanded city council, were so disillusioned that they withdrew from politics completely.

Engagement in the local struggle severely fractured the local Russia's Choice organization. Debate centered on whether or not to ally with the krai administration. Reformers were the biggest threat to the administration because of their relatively long history and comparative organization. The Social Democratic party traced its origins back to 1985, when Grinchenko opened the Democratic Club. The club became the center of gravity for all manner of individuals discontent with Communist party rule and the headquarters of Democratic Russia. It opened affiliated organizations in Arsen'ev and Ussuriisk. By 1990, important members of the club were active in krai politics. Grinchenko was on the krai soviet, as were other important Social Democrats.

Trouble began when the Social Democrats discovered they were in the minority. Frustrated with their inability to push through their programs in the krai soviet, Grinchenko and Zabolotnikov decided to strategically ally themselves with the krai administration. Believing that a new governor (and a new soviet) would better serve their political purposes, they supported Nazdratenko's appointment as governor in March 1993. In the summer 1993 race for mayor, Zabolotnikov, at the behest of the krai administration, ran against an ultimately victorious Cherepkov, and in October, Grinchenko supported the disbandment of the krai soviet. Both took jobs in Nazdratenko's administration. Grinchenko's policies and affiliation with the krai administration were not without consequences at the Democratic Club. As the elections approached, members broke off to join Civic Union, DPR, and PRES. While a loyal core of Social Democrats remained, the group had fractured.

With election campaigns underway, the head of the local Republican party, Igor Alekseyev, decided to bring his party into the Russia's Choice camp. Not all Republicans agreed: Vladimir Nikiforov, a Republican and member of the city soviet, denounced the Social Democrat–Nazdratenko alliance and took a job in Cherepkov's administration; Nikiforov decided instead to work for Glubokovskii's campaign. Similarly, David Brodyanskii, another well-known Republican, broke openly with Alekseyev and went to work for Gayer and for Igor Ustinov, an independent candidate in the Ussuriisk single-mandate district. However, important Republicans such as Vitalii Sovasteyev were selected to run on the Russia's Choice party list, along with Vladimir Ksenzuk, a Social Democrat and old friend of Grinchenko's.

Thus, as the election campaign got underway, radical reformers at the local level were initially stronger than those in Moscow. Although at the central level Social Democrats supported Russia's Choice and Republicans supported Yabloko, in Primor'e, both parties supported Russia's Choice. Unfortunately, the alliance was short-lived. Disagreement between local Social Democrats and Republicans broke out over the alliance with Nazdratenko. Uneasiness, partly a result of central party neglect, formed the basis of the rationale behind those Social Democrats who supported an alliance with the Nazdratenko team. As one member said, "After all, he's in power, so why shouldn't we be?" The Republicans disagreed, stating that the policy of alliance with Nazdratenko would compromise the goals of the Russia's Choice platform. Rather, they advocated opposition to the krai administration, whose economic policies, they felt, did not foster market reform. Conflicts between Republicans and Social Democrats heated up when Grinchenko proposed that Russia's Choice endorse Nazdratenko's candidacy to the Federation Council. Even for those Republicans allied with the Social Democrats, this was too much. In a heated discussion, Republicans opposed the endorsement and Nazdratenko was voted down.

Russia's Choice in Primor'e ultimately won a respectable 14.1 percent of the vote. The local organization contributed to this modest success in two ways. First, the bloc agreed to endorse powerful independent candidates in single-mandate districts. Thus, Russia's Choice endorsed Gayer in the race for the Federation Council and Igor Ustinov, the successful candidate in the Ussuriisk okrug. Second, the bloc registered at least one success in its campaign to rid the krai of Nazdratenko and his allies. The bloc's efforts effectively neutralized one administration candidate running in the Vladivostok single-mandate okrug. The candidate in question was Mikhail Savchenko, head of *Vladdorblagoustroistvo,* the organization responsible for municipal activities. Russia's Choice leaders published a letter in the local press blaming Savchenko for ineffectual policies that led to the organization going bankrupt. In the process, the authors claimed, Savchenko and his team reaped financial windfalls. The accusation was particularly serious not only because it suggested that Savchenko was corrupt but also because it provided evidence that disruptions in the "preparations for winter" were not solely a result of the mayor's bad offices. Savchenko provided no defense.[24]

Limited victories in the local struggle aside, the most successful campaign tactic employed by Russia's Choice was its affiliation (albeit belated) with strong single-mandate candidates. As with other local party organizations in Primor'e, radical reformers were weak and unorganized. The bloc fell apart after the elections, and in the 1993 to 1995 period, reform power in Primor'e became, if possible, even weaker.

Single-Mandate Races: Building a Coalition for Reform

If local reform parties were weak, local reform candidates were strong. Reformers won seats in two of the three electoral districts in Primor'e.

Credit for this success largely went to Igor Ustinov, a powerful independent candidate in the Ussuriisk okrug. Ustinov won the endorsement of Russia's Choice and spearheaded a broadbased reform coalition that propelled a Yabloko candidate to victory in the Vladivostok okrug. Only in Arsen'ev did the reform coalition fail to win a seat. Two forces drove the elections in the single-mandate districts: the weak campaigns of the krai administration candidates and the strong showing of the reform coalition.

LIMITED LOCALIZATION: WEAK KRAI ADMINISTRATION CAM-PAIGNS. The krai administration had the tools to win the single-mandate races, but it failed to use them effectively. Nonetheless, the administration did make some effort to direct voting to the State Duma. One way to do this was through the local electoral commissions. In single-mandate districts, the administration used its influence over local electoral commissions to limit the field of candidates by weeding out those most obviously opposed to the governor. Igor Lebedinets, Nazdratenko's vice governor, was in charge of the krai electoral commission and packed it with the administration's people. The commission became a tool in the hands of the administration. In Vladivostok, for example, the commission used its power to block young entrepreneur Vladimir Krupin from registering. A talented banker and head of the region's most successful commercial bank, Krupin posed a serious threat to entrenched local interests. Although he submitted the requisite number of signatures on time, the electoral commission ruled 400 of them unacceptable.[25]

In the northern Arsen'ev district, electoral commission interference was particularly blatant. Here the electoral commission foiled an attempt by a Russia's Choice candidate to register: Vitalii Sovasteyev submitted the appropriate documents but the commission refused to accept them because they were in facsimile form. Sovasteyev requested the originals from Moscow, but although they arrived in Vladivostok in time, they "got lost" in the bureaucratic maze of the krai administration. He was unable to register. In other cases, however, the Arsen'ev electoral commission bent the rules by granting deadline extensions for submission of signatures to favored single-mandate district candidates. The deadline was set at midnight Moscow time or 7 A.M. Vladivostok time, but the krai commission unilaterally decided to accept signatures only until midnight Vladivostok time. In Arsen'ev, however, the commission granted selected deadline extensions. The head of the Arsen'ev commission allowed DPR candidate Valerii Nesterenko to submit his signatures at 7 A.M. Moreover, the commission took particular pains to ensure that Nesterenko registered successfully. Nesterenko's signature lists were not in order when he submitted them. He had not signed them all himself, as demanded by regulation. A debate ensued in the Arsen'ev electoral commission, and the head of the electoral commission placed a personal call to Moscow to get approval for accepting the forms. She reportedly called Nesterenko at home and told him, "It is imperative that you participate in this race."

There is some evidence to suggest that the krai administration used more forceful measures to convince candidates to withdraw. Such, reportedly, was the case with Svetlana Goryacheva, deputy public prosecutor of the city of Vladivostok, former People's Deputy of the Russian Federation, and well-known and outspoken member of the Communist party. Goryacheva collected signatures and registered to run in the Ussuriisk okrug. Her candidacy was widely regarded as exceptionally strong. Although she initiated an energetic campaign, she inexplicably withdrew on November 24, claiming bad health and shock from her experience defending the White House in October. Sources in Vladivostok, however, held that Nazdratenko pressured her to withdraw.[26]

Besides circumscribing the field of candidates, the electoral commission failed to ensure fair and equal access to the media. Several parties complained that the commission did not announce a November 15 deadline to apply for free airtime. As a result, some parties were forced to forfeit their right to free media access. Grievances on media coverage were also the responsibility of the electoral commission. Although the electoral commission did designate a Committee on the Press and Information responsible for hearing grievances, it failed to inform candidates of their rights. If candidates did hear about the committee, the fact that it was chaired by Vladimir Shkrabov, founding member of PAKT and powerful Nazdratenko ally, was sufficient deterrent to complaints.

Another way in which the administration attempted to get involved in the race for the State Duma was by seeking alliance with local party structures. In particular, Nazdratenko sought endorsement from Russia's Choice. The question of whether or not to endorse the local governor caused great consternation and strife within the Primor'e Russia's Choice bloc and tore at the fabric of an already fragile alliance. Whether or not this was a premeditated strategy on the part of the krai administration is an open question, but in any case, the candidacy was ultimately not accepted, and

Russia's Choice remained allied with the mayor's office against Nazdratenko. Subsequently, the governor stressed his independence from political parties and did not seek further endorsement from other groups.

Despite the arsenal of resources at the disposal of the krai administration, no administration-backed candidate won in the single-mandate districts, and administration meddling in Russia's Choice failed to seriously undermine the reform vote or prevent two reformers from gaining seats in district voting. There were at least three reasons why the governor's efficiency in successfully running his own race and the race for the constitution did not translate into electoral victory in the races for the lower house. First, Nazdratenko's administration was still very much in the process of consolidating its grip on power in the krai. Nazdratenko had held office for less than nine months when the elections took place. His administration lacked experience in the electoral arena. Second, the administration was more concerned with local issues, which it felt would more effectively ensure consolidation of the governor's power. Third, and most important, it was not in the administration's interest to support strong candidates with legitimate claims to the governor's own power base. In short, the governor was not willing to share his power. The brevity of the campaign, and the fact that the administration was consumed with more immediate matters, meant that the administration did not have the time to form solid relationships with powerful and politically reliable allies.

As a result, the administration made strategic mistakes in the State Duma race. The most obvious of these was the fact that in every single-mandate district, the governor's team ran at least two candidates. In Vladivostok, two candidates received assistance from the krai administration in gathering signatures, gaining access to channels for distributing campaign literature, and paying for television appearances. Mikhail Savchenko was hand-picked by Nazdratenko in a meeting in early November, at which krai administration officials developed a strategy for running their own candidates in all three okrugs. A second krai administration candidate, Aleksei Ryndovskii, the mayor of Artem, announced his candidacy after Savchenko had already been selected. Both did quite poorly. Ryndovskii came in third place and Savchenko came in last. The pattern was repeated in Ussuriisk, where Mikhail Lusnikov, a lawyer employed by the city administration and Aleksandr Kostenko, the director of a PAKT enterprise, split the vote. In Arsen'ev, two administration-backed candidates were supported by different PAKT enterprises, suggesting that differences of opinion within PAKT itself contributed to a poorly coordinated administration policy in this district. In the city of Spassk-Dal'nii, Vladimir Shapnevskii was supported by PAKT lumber enterprise Spassklesmash, while the city of Arsen'ev itself supported Azat Yusupov, director of PAKT military aviation plant "Progress." Again, the two split the vote.

STRONG LEADERSHIP FOR REFORM: THE RACE IN USSURIISK.   The race in the Ussuriisk single-mandate district was dominated by independent candidate Igor Ustinov. Ustinov won 39.3 percent of the vote in a field of five candidates, more votes than any other single-mandate candidate in the krai.[27] Voter dissatisfaction in this electoral district ran high, with 18.12 percent of voters casting ballots against all candidates in the single-mandate race. Only Ustinov received more than this. An effective leader, Ustinov eventually allied himself with Russia's Choice and spearheaded a reform coalition that pulled in candidates from other single-mandate districts.

Ustinov's success is largely a testimony to political skill. He was by far the most savvy and politically astute of the single-mandate candidates, not only in Ussuriisk but throughout the krai. A People's Deputy of the Russian Federation since 1990, director of the Nakhodka port and, since 1992, chair of the Nakhodka Free Economic Zone (FEZ), Ustinov was politically experienced and had a firm grasp of market economics. He clearly ran the most professional campaign in Primor'e. His campaign was based on three main principles: effective social welfare programs, support for small- and medium-sized business, and unencumbered territorial development. Although his program did not call outright for a Primorskii free economic zone, it clearly implied that FEZ privileges would entail the kind of investment and prosperity enjoyed in Nakhodka: "(My program) is directed at building up Primorskii krai. The only way I see here, is the creation of free economic territories, like ours . . . it is important that the problems of the region be decided not in Moscow, but in the localities. These principles lie at the basis of the bill we have prepared: 'On the Status of Primorskii krai.'"[28] Much of Ustinov's appeal derived from his success in obtaining official status and extensive funding for the Nakhodka FEZ. Although the zone did not begin functioning until the summer of 1992, at the time of the election approximately 300 firms using foreign capital had registered, and money was pouring into the area. Ustinov himself secured a loan of 20 billion rubles for the zone, and much of the money had gone to developing local infrastructure, as well as supporting new businesses. In short, Ustinov proposed a plan of action, backed up with a track record that proved he was capable of implementation.

Ustinov's campaign effectively transmitted his message to the voters. He hired three professional campaign managers from Moscow who coordinated his entire campaign effort. His local campaign managers were hand picked and dedicated. Colorful and imaginative posters went up all over the okrug, an "Ustinov" van covered in posters carried him to the meetings at schools and factories, which he ceaselessly attended, and he advertised widely and gave interviews in all the major newspapers.

Ustinov's campaign efforts extended beyond the immediate single-mandate district. In fact, Ustinov's political acumen, as well as the obvious wealth of his campaign, drew his less financially successful allies to him. Russia's Choice candidates on the party list requested to campaign with him. He campaigned with Gayer in Ussuriisk and Nakhodka and allied himself with Russia's Choice. Ultimately, Ustinov's leadership spearheaded a coalition of reform candidates that reached across single-mandate borders to candidates in the Vladivostok and Arsen'ev districts. The fact that Ustinov avoided conflict with the krai administration, at least over the course of the campaign, bears further testimony to his political skill. Much of this was due to his history of cooperative efforts with Nazdratenko when the two worked together as People's Deputies. More than this, however, Ustinov's platform steered clear of conflict with the governor's office. The important bill, "On the Status of Primorskii krai," to which he referred often in his campaign, illustrates this point. This was a krai administration document that called for enhanced local autonomy in economic planning, retention of profits and tax returns in the krai, and an effective end to Moscow's economic control of the area.[29] Thus, Ustinov ran a professional campaign and led a coalition of reform candidates while successfully side-stepping the krai administration.

BUILDING A COALITION FOR REFORM: THE RACE IN VLADIVOSTOK. Mikhail Glubokovskii won the Vladivostok race handsomely with slightly more than 29.8 percent of the vote in a field of six candidates.[30] However, 22.75 percent of the Vladivostok vote was cast against all candidates. Only Glubokovskii received more than this. Glubokovskii succeeded due to the support he received from the broad-based reform coalition centered on Ustinov. As a result of this support, the local Russia's Choice organization ultimately endorsed Glubokovskii. Several aspects of Glubokovskii's campaign contributed to his inclusion in the coalition. First, Glubokovskii was himself an impressive and articulate candidate; second, the Russia's Choice candidate in Vladivostok was compromised by ties to the krai administration; third, Republicans both inside and out-side the local Russia's Choice bloc supported Glubokovskii. Ultimately, however, the most decisive element in Glubokovskii's success was support from the popular Ussuriisk candidate, Ustinov.

Both Glubokovskii (Yabloko number 127) and Vladimir Ksenzuk (Rus-sia's Choice number 68) were chosen from party lists and therefore did not gather signatures in Vladivostok. Both ran in a fairly hospitable environ-ment: an overwhelmingly urban okrug, Vladivostok voted more strongly than the krai as a whole for the president and his economic policies in the April referendum.[31] Polls taken before the election indicated that Ksenzuk led by a wide margin. A poll conducted in early November rated Ksenzuk in the lead, with 23.5 percent (of those who said they would participate) fa-voring his candidacy, and only 5.1 percent favoring Glubokovskii. Another poll, taken fewer than three weeks before the election, showed Ksenzuk maintaining his wide margin. In the election itself, Ksenzuk's vote fell to 12.9 percent, while Glubokovskii's soared to 29.8 percent. Furthermore, the Vladivostok vote for Yabloko (11.45 percent) was considerably lower than for Russia's Choice, which won first place in Vladivostok party-list voting with 17.3 percent of the vote.

Glubokovskii's initial low ratings meant that other candidates failed to recognize him as a serious challenge. This was in part because of Glubok-ovskii's political inexperience. While other candidates were making names for themselves on the local political scene, Glubokovskii spent 1990 finish-ing up his doctoral dissertation on the "Biological Evolution of Salmon." He limited political activity to involvement, between 1990 and 1992, with a group called "The Long-Term Ecological Program for Primorskii Krai." Political inexperience notwithstanding, Glubokovskii's articulate, intellec-tual demeanor served him well in the public eye. Moreover, he successfully formulated a campaign platform that appealed to a wide range of voters. While supporting reform in principle, he condemned the government's pol-icy of "shock without therapy." He branded other parties (although taking care not to explicitly refer to Russia's Choice) as too "extremist," and blamed such extremism for the bloodshed at the White House in October.

The Glubokovskii–Russia's Choice alliance was largely a result of Rus-sia's Choice involvement with the krai administration, which sorely com-promised Ksenzuk's candidacy. Ksenzuk's biography identified him as a native of Vladivostok, a former deputy in the krai soviet and the general di-rector of the Joint Stock Company "Ellik," a company that worked on intro-ducing credit cards to Primor'e. On paper, he appeared to represent the interests of Vladivostok's new businesses. In reality, however, his firm maintained close ties to "Kommersant," a PAKT enterprise run by Anatolii Pavlov, Nazdratenko's deputy. Ksenzuk's PAKT affiliation was well known in the krai and raised serious questions about the legitimacy of his association with Russia's Choice.

Republicans within the local Russia's Choice bloc were particularly skeptical of Ksenzuk, and indeed of Social Democratic alignment with the krai administration in general. As the campaign progressed, Republicans within the Russia's Choice bloc became increasingly unwilling to support the Ksenzuk candidacy. Republican solidarity proved stronger than Russia's Choice bloc loyalty, and it was Republicans—not Social Democrats—who worked for Gayer, Ustinov, and Glubokovskii. Unlike Ksenzuk, Glubokovskii was free of krai administration involvement and was clearly situated in the mayor's camp: his office was in the city administration building and his campaign manager, Vladimir Nikiforov, a Republican, worked both for Glubokovskii and Cherepkov. When Gayer set up headquarters in the city administration, Glubokovskii's campaign became associated with this popular candidate to the Federation Council.

Glubakovskii's real windfall came when Ustinov extended his support, political and financial, to the Yabloko candidate's campaign. With only a week to go before the elections, Republican members of the Russia's Choice bloc withdrew their support for Ksenzuk and endorsed Glubokovskii. Sympathy for Glubokovskii reached a climax when Ustinov organized and financed a roundtable discussion on local television. Glubakovskii was included, but Ksenzuk was not. Other important participants included Gayer and Eduard Gurchenkov, the reform candidate in Arsen'ev. In one swoop Glubokovskii was thus publicly identified with Russia's Choice, as well as with Ustinov and Gayer, both powerful, and ultimately successful, candidates. Glubokovskii's subsequent dramatic rise in the polls was clearly a result of this open endorsement from the reform coalition.

SQUEEZING PAST THE POST: THE RACE IN ARSEN'EV.   The reform candidate in Arsen'ev was not successful. Eduard Gurchenkov came in third in a field of five candidates with only 21.3 percent of the vote.[32] The failure of the reform candidate in Arsen'ev was partly due to his own poorly conceived campaign strategy, but also to the reform coalition's inability to extend its power beyond Ussuriisk and Vladivostok, to Arsen'ev. Independent candidate Valerii Nesterenko won the Arsen'ev race with 27.4 percent of the vote, narrowly beating his nearest competitor, Azat Yusupov, by a mere 0.1 percent of the vote.[33] Nesterenko's success was a function of weak planning on the part of the krai administration, which ran its candidates against each other in this race.

Gurchenkov's platform did little to ingratiate him with the voters. The platform stressed the complete withdrawal of government from the economic sphere and failed to address the concerns of a predominantly industrial electorate. Gurchenkov's failure was largely a function of poor coordination with the reform coalition. Russia's Choice did attempt to register two candidates in the Arsen'ev race, but failed on both counts. Well into the election campaign, the bloc belatedly decided to endorse Gurchenkov. By then it was too late. Moreover, Gurchenkov was not wholly receptive to Russia's Choice advances. Preferring to maintain his distance, Gurchenkov believed that association with Russia's Choice would hurt his chances of success in Arsen'ev.[34] He expressed strong reservations about the Vladivostok Social Democrats, preferring instead to rely on those Social Democrats he knew from the Arsen'ev branch of the Democrats Club. He opposed the local DPR and refused to join the local PRES. He was, however, sympathetic to Yabloko and to RDDR. Gurchenkov worked well with Republicans and established an important alliance with Gayer, appearing with her on television and participating in joint meetings. Whatever his misgivings about the Social Democrats, the Arsen'ev Democrats Club recommended that Russia's Choice extend unofficial endorsement to Gurchenkov, and he was subsequently included in the roundtable discussion sponsored by Ustinov. These efforts, however, proved insufficient to propel Gurchenkov to victory.

Independent Nesterenko won the race. The director of the Hanskii Nature Reserve, Nesterenko was a fairly well-known figure in the Arsen'ev okrug. His campaign platform focused on moderate economic reform and ecological issues, on which he was an authority. Clearly a man of considerable independent initiative, Nesterenko tapped a wide network of friends and coworkers, in a last-ditch effort to collect the requisite number of signatures to run in the single-mandate race.[35] He successfully gathered the bulk of signatures on his own, with a small number of signatures supplied through the local DPR organization. Nesterenko's campaign relied on his own initiative. Over the course of the campaign he barely slept, driving ceaselessly from meeting to meeting (he had his own car) and distributing much of his campaign literature himself. Attempts to elicit support from both the krai administration and the local Russia's Choice organization were unsuccessful.

Nesterenko's success was clearly a function of poor krai-administration coordination in the Arsen'ev single-mandate district. Two competing PAKT candidates ran against each other in Arsen'ev. To complicate matters further, Nesterenko himself won campaign backing from Spassk Cement, the huge PAKT cement-producing enterprise that dominated the Spassk economy. In effect, three PAKT-supported candidates ran in Arsen'ev okrug. This suggests that competing interests within PAKT itself were largely responsible for the outcome of the race in this district.

In sum, although the reform coalition was successful in propelling its candidates to victory in the Ussuriisk and Vladivostok single-mandate races, it could not secure victory in Arsen'ev. Here, poor coordination within the reform camp coupled with Gurchenkov's poorly conceived campaign platform and coy response to reform-camp advances sealed the fate of the reform effort. Instead, an independent candidate squeezed past the post in split voting between krai–administration backed candidates.

Conclusion

In the wake of post-Soviet Russia's first general election, fears of a national polity dominated by the hugely successful ultra-rightist Liberal Democratic party were mitigated by the fact that in single-mandate districts, reform candidates carried the day. Across Russia, radical reformers won more seats in the State Duma than any other party, due to their strong showing in the districts. These results suggest that, at least at the level of individual candidates, support for reform in Russia was very much alive in December 1993.

This chapter's analysis suggests otherwise. Despite the strong showing for reform candidates in single-mandate districts, and even reform victory in one Federation Council race, support for reform remained weak in Primor'e. Reformers were weak on three counts. First, local party structures were severely fractured. This was in large part due to weak coordination between central and local party organizations, but also to the fact that local reform parties, and radical reform in particular, fixated on a local struggle with the krai administration. As a result, internal strife and competition rocked the reform camp. Indeed, although the Republican–Social Democrat alliance held, in principle, for the duration of the campaign, it collapsed immediately afterward. By the time of the 1995 elections to the State Duma, it was difficult to find two local reformers in the same party.

Second, the reform coalition that successfully propelled two single-mandate candidates to victory in 1993 was primarily dependent on the leadership of one independent candidate: Ustinov. The fact that he ran as an independent underscores the weakness of the reform parties. Unable to form a coalition themselves, they turned instead to an established independent candidate. In any case, coalitions based primarily on the efforts of one individual are unlikely to endure. Less than a year after his election to the State Duma, Ustinov attempted to register for Primor'e gubernatorial elections. The election was called off, but Ustinov's foray into the local political arena cost him his career. Nazdratenko waged a highly effective campaign to discredit the competition. By the time of the 1995 State Duma elections, Ustinov was a spent political force. He did not run in a single-mandate race. Instead, his place in the Ussuriisk single-mandate district was won by Svetlana Goryacheva, a powerful local leader, also running second on the KPRF party list. In general, it would seem, the 1993 reform coalition in Primor'e was based more on leadership than on reform. Ustinov's leadership won him the 1993 race and was the driving force behind the reform coalition. By 1995, new leaders rose to take his place. The fact that the 1993 leader was a reformer and the 1995 leader a Communist seemed of little consequence to the voters.

Third, much of reform candidates' success in 1993 was predicated on the relative noninvolvement of the krai administration in the race for the State Duma. There can be little question that serious krai administration involvement in this race would have cost reformers their seats. By the time of the 1995 elections, the krai administration had consolidated its power locally and turned its attention to the national races. Powerful Nazdratenko supporters won two seats in the State Duma; the third went to Goryacheva in Ussuriisk. Following the example of Ustinov, the popular 1993 Yabloko candidate from Vladivostok did not even register for the single-mandate race, though he did retain his seat by virtue of his position on the party list. In the 1995 Federation Council, Gayer was replaced by Nazdratenko supporter Vladimir Vedernikov. Gayer did not participate in the 1995 races.

The nominal losers in the 1993 races were Nazdratenko and his allies, along with the economic basis of their support—the Primorskii Manufacturer's Shareholding Corporation. Although Nazdratenko won his seat on the Federation Council, no ally of his ran successfully, and several of his opponents won seats in the State Duma. Understood within the context of localization, however, Nazdratenko has been a great success. Yeltsin representative Valerii Butov and Vladivostok city mayor Viktor Cherepkov, both Nazdratenko opponents, lost their jobs within a few months of the December 1993 elections. Both were replaced by ardent Nazdratenko supporters. In December 1995, Nazdratenko successfully held gubernatorial elections in which he won a stunning 69.6 percent of the vote, with more than 62 percent of the electorate participating.[36] Importantly, Nazdratenko has also been able to deliver respectable local support for President Yeltsin. In the 1996 presidential elections, Primor'e voted 29.6 percent for the president in the first round of the elections and 52.3 percent in the second round.[37]

The period between the 1993 and 1995 elections to the State Duma did see the development of substantial local party structures in Primorskii krai. The potential proliferation of power sources associated with the development of local parties would seem to hold out some hope for the unencumbered expression of independent opinion characteristic of democracy. Indeed, with the rise of viable party organizations, executive power in Primor'e reached out to form important alliances with local parties. Unfortunately, these did not extend to the reform camp. Between 1993 and 1995, Nazdratenko formed a solid alliance with the local branches of the LDPR and Women of Russia. In 1995, Svetlana Orlova, the successful 1993 leader of the Primor'e Women of Russia won in a single-mandate race. The strong local showing for the LDPR in 1995, approximately twice the national average, bears witness to the fruits of this alliance. Following the 1993 elections, Nazdratenko came into increasing conflict with Moscow over an escalating local energy crisis and the demarcation of the Sino-Russian border in krai territory.

What do the 1993 elections in Primor'e say about the prospects for democratic consolidation in Russia? Certainly the elections bore the markings of democracy—intense local debate and the successful election of competing candidates to national office. However, in the periphery, the elections provided a springboard for local power consolidation. In this way, national elections served to foster the development of a powerful local executive, harboring small affection for national democratic institutions and increasingly in conflict with the center.[38] Few things could be worse for democracy.

Notes

1. The trend toward localization in Russian politics is discussed in reference to the April 25, 1993, referendum by Wendy Slater, "No Victors in the Russian Referendum," *RFE/RL Research Report*, vol. 2, no. 21 (May 21, 1993), p. 17.

2. John J. Stephan, *The Russian Far East: A History* (Stanford University Press, 1994), p. 84. Chinese traders in modern-day Vladivostok continue to refer to the city as Haishenwei, and even in 1993 many of the smaller border towns in the krai bore their original Chinese names. This failure to Russify border areas helped bring historical fear of "yellow peril" into the immediate present.

3. The national figure for the same period is 35 percent. Some Primor'e industries fared particularly poorly. Production in the chemical and petrochemical industries, for example, dropped nearly 60 percent, and cement production fell by 71.8 percent. *Primorskii Krai v 1993 gody: statisticheskii yezhegodnik* (Primorskii krai in 1993: a statistical yearbook) (Goskomstat Rossii Primorskii krayevoi komitet gosudarstvennoi statistiki, Vladivostok), pp. 99–101. Figures for Russia from *Rossiiskii Statisticheskii Ezhegodnik* (Russian Statistical Yearbook) (Moscow: Gosudarstvennii Komitet Rossiiskoi Federatsii po Statistike, 1995), p. 311.

4. Figures from *Dal'nii Vostok Rossii Ekonomicheskii Yezhegodnik 1992* (Economic Yearbook of the Russian Far East, 1992) (Khabarovsk: Economic Research Institute), cited in *Russian Far East Update,* vol. 3, no. 4 (April 1993), p. 8.

5. Direct trade fell by 4 percent in 1993. *Ekonomicheskii Yezhegodnik: Sotsial'no-ekonomicheskoe razvitie Primorskogo kraya* (Statistical Yearbook: The economic development of Primorskii krai) (Vladivostok: Mezhdunarodnyi institut kon"yuktury i prognozirovaniya, 1994), p. 23.

6. In June 1991, 64 percent of Primor'e voters voted for Yeltsin. The average for Russia was 59.7 percent. In the April 1993 referendum, 65.9 percent of Primor'e respondents answered "yes" to the question: "Do you trust the president of the Russian Federation?" The national average was 59.9 percent.

7. Average rating for the Primor'e delegation for the 1993–95 period. Michael McFaul and Nikolai Petrov, *Politicheskii al'manakh Rossii* (Political Almanac of Russia) (Moscow: Carnegie Endowment for International Peace, 1995), p. 299.

8. Peter Kirkow's characterization of Nazdratenko as a regional "warlord" conforms with the analysis in this chapter. Peter Kirkow, "Regional Warlordism in Russia: The Case of Primorskii *Krai,*" in *Europe-Asia Studies*, vol. 47, no. 6 (September 1995), pp. 923–47.

9. Alexandra Vacroux, "Privatization in the Regions: Primorskiy Kray," in *Russia: Creating Private Enterprises and Efficient Markets* (Washington, D.C.: The World Bank, The Private Sector Development Department, 1994), p. 41, cited in Kirkow, "Regional Warlordism in Russia," p. 927.

10. After several failed attempts to hold gubernatorial elections, Nazdratenko successfully won local electoral mandate in December 1995, when Primor'e was one of only five subjects of the Federation permitted to hold gubernatorial elections

simultaneously with elections to the Federal Assembly. He won close to 70 percent of the vote. The governor had hoped to further boost his own position by holding gubernatorial elections before elections to the local legislature, but opposition from the national Russia's Choice organization foiled earlier attempts. The fact that Nazdratenko considered his campaign for the 1993 Federation Council a stepping stone in his drive for gubernatorial elections was confirmed by Igor Lebedinets, vice governor (in 1993) and Nazdratenko's chief advisor. Interview with Lebedinets, December 4, 1995.

11. In accordance with voting reports from the Central Electoral Commission, all votes for candidates are reported as a percentage of valid votes, not counting the vote against all candidates.

12. Yeltsin representative Valerii Butov retained his position only a few weeks past the elections. He was fired in January 1994 and replaced by Nazdratenko crony Vladimir Ignatenko.

13. This description is based on *Utro Rossii* articles on October 7 and December 11, 1993, p. 1; *Vladivostok*, December 11, 1993, p. 11; and an interview with Cherepkov, December 8, 1993.

14. This view was expressed in *Utro Rossii*, November 27, 1993, p. 2, and in an interview with the newspaper's editor-in-chief, Yurii Mokeyev, November 28, 1993.

15. The shooting received national attention when it was reported in *Izvestiya*, December 1, 1993, p. 5. Voznesenskii himself believed the krai administration was responsible, claiming he had been threatened. Interview with Voznesenskii, April 19, 1995.

16. Bread cost nearly twice as much in Vladivostok as in Moscow.

17. The local Democratic Party of Russia (DPR) candidates, for example, openly supported the constitution, and even Azat Yusupov (unofficially yet openly endorsed by the Communist party) called on voters to "acquaint themselves with the document" and "make their own choices." The national organizations of both the DPR and KPRF officially opposed the constitution.

18. Nazdratenko's fears were well founded. In December 1995 Anatolii Vasyanovich (1993 candidate for the Federation Council) initiated a campaign for governor. With election ballots already drawn up, however, he withdrew his candidacy under extreme pressure from Nazdratenko and apparently in fear for his life. His was the only candidacy seriously capable of challenging Nazdratenko. Interview with Vasyanovich advisor, December 12, 1995.

19. This is in sharp contrast to other regions, such as Nizhnii Novgorod, in which the governor ran a vigorous and largely successful campaign on behalf of his supporters.

20. These figures are calculated from delegate ratings under the old okrug system. Because the territorial lines do not correspond exactly, delegates whose electoral units fell between two "new" okrugs were counted twice—once in each of the new okrugs.

21. In 1993 Orlova was a strong Nazdratenko supporter (interview with Orlova, December 8, 1993), and by 1995 the governor officially supported her successful

campaign in a single-mandate district. Interview with Nazdratenko, December 15, 1995.

22. Interview with Nikolai Zolotov, LDPR single-mandate candidate, December 17, 1993. Zolotov won 15.2 percent of the vote.

23. Although in 1993 both planned to run for the local legislature, neither actually ran. A new krai legislature began work in January 1995, but it was dominated by administrative heads of cities and districts, positions held by appointment of the local governor.

24. After the elections, Savchenko was promoted to vice governor and put in charge of energy issues. In August 1996 President Yeltsin ordered his removal from office, charging him with responsibility for the krai's crippling energy crisis.

25. Signatures require an accompanying identification number (generally a passport number), and the signatures in question were accompanied by student numbers. The electoral commission ruled this unacceptable. By the spring of 1995 Krupin's bank was in serious trouble. Under pressure from the krai administration, the bank made excessive loans to the local energy giant, Dal'energo. Dal'energo could not pay its debts, and the bank turned to the administration for help. The krai administration refused to get involved until Krupin resigned.

26. Although Goryacheva was not officially on the KPRF party list, her candidacy was sponsored by the local party organization, which assisted her in the signature gathering campaign. Interview with Goryacheva, December 20, 1995,

27. He won 32.2 percent of the vote if the vote against all candidates is taken into account.

28. This quote is taken from an interview with Ustinov in *Utro Rossii*, December 8, 1993, p. 2.

29. I. Grinchenko, *O statuse Primorskogo kraya*, Primorskii krai administration document, 1993. The fact that this document was prepared by Grinchenko, the krai leader of the Social Democrats, demonstrates the strategic connection tying Ustinov, Nazdratenko, and Grinchenko together in an unlikely alliance.

30. He won 23 percent of the vote if the vote against all candidates is taken into account.

31. In response to the first question, "Do you trust the President?" 71 percent of Vladivostok voters answered "yes." The result for the krai as a whole was 64.25 percent. In response to the second question, "Do you endorse the socioeconomic policy of the president and the government since 1992?" 64 percent of Vladivostok voters answered "yes," while the total for the krai was 56.81 percent. In response to the third question, "Do you think it is necessary to hold presidential elections?" the results in Vladivostok were 30 percent against elections, and for the krai, 27.59 percent. In response to the fourth question, "Do you think it is necessary to hold parliamentary elections?" the Vladivostok results were 40 percent for elections, and in the krai as a whole, 38.42 percent. Results reported in *Vladivostok*, April 27 and April 28, 1993.

32. He won 17.3 percent of the vote if the vote against all candidates is taken into account.

33. The reform camp could claim some responsibility for Yusupov's failure in this race. In districts where he was well known, Gurchenkov out-performed Yusu-

pov. Indeed, Gurchenkov significantly out-performed Yusupov in six of twenty-one raions in the Arsen'ev okrug.

34. According to Gurchenkov, association with Russia's Choice elicited negative reactions from Arsen'ev voters. Interview with Gurchenkov, December 12, 1993, Vladivostok.

35. Nesterenko was one of the DPR candidates originally selected to run in the single-mandate district race.

36. Unpublished voting results provided by the Primorskii krai electoral commission, December 1995.

37. The figures for Russia were 35 percent in the first round and 53.8 percent in the second. Figures on Primor'e voting reported in the *Vladivostok News*, no. 121 (June 21, 1996) and no. 122 (July 11, 1996) at http://vlad.tribnet.com/archive/iss122/news.htp and http://vlad.tribnet.com/archive/iss122/news.htp

38. At the time of this writing, Nazdratenko was under intense criticism from Moscow for his handling of a severe energy crisis in Primor'e. The krai administration planned to hold a local referendum on September 22, 1996, on confidence in the governor. In an article in *Zavtra*, a hard-line opposition newspaper, Nazdratenko denounced the Gaidar government, former foreign minister Kozyrov, and former Primor'e governor Vladimir Kuznetsov for caving in to foreign demands on the demarcation of the Sino-Russian border. *Zavtra*, no. 35 (August 28, 1996), pp. 1, 3.

CHAPTER NINETEEN

Bashkortostan

The Logic of Ethnic Machine Politics and Democratic Consolidation

Henry E. Hale

DOES ETHNIC diversity undermine democratization? This question quickly rose to the top of scholarly agendas as the USSR crumbled, seemingly ushering in an age of nationally charged violence. Observers began to speculate even about mighty Russia, wondering whether its twenty ethnically defined republics would rend the fledgling federation asunder. Chechnya was ready to lead the charge, plunging into a war of independence with Moscow. Tatarstan has at times seemed ready to follow, boycotting federal votes and ignoring central law. But the majority of Russia's republics, including Bashkortostan, have remained oddly tranquil. Although eager to declare "sovereignty" and claim greater autonomy, these republics have consistently conducted federal elections, and ethnic tensions there have remained low. How can we explain such differences in the success of democratic institutions in Russia's constituent republics?

This chapter considers the case of Bashkortostan's 1993 election to Russia's Federal Assembly. Indeed, the results of this election were dramatic and puzzling, and not only in ethnic terms. Ethnicity appeared to play a remarkably insignificant role in the federal campaigns. Yet while ethnic Bashkirs make up less than a quarter of the population, they won five of eight territorial seats in the new parliament as a whole. Indeed, the republic sent a delegation to Moscow that was decidedly proautonomy, and a heated

599

Bashkortostan

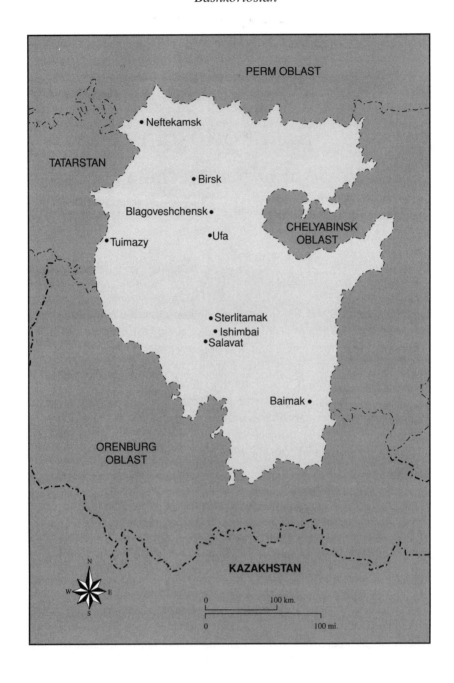

race for the republic's presidency essentially overshadowed the federal campaign, with the incumbent prosovereignty leader soundly defeating a scrappy pro-Moscow opponent. Adding an additional twist to the results in this predominantly urban republic, Agrarians won four of six territorial seats in the State Duma and ran away with the party-list vote. The explanation, I argue, lies largely in the ethnic structure of the republic. Unlike Tatars in Tatarstan, the Bashkirs' status as a small minority in their own republic forces Bashkir leaders not to politicize ethnicity and instead encourages them to seek electoral victory by mobilizing the enormous power of the state, particularly in rural communities.

Ethnic Structure and Politics

Many theorists have argued that ethnic division and democracy do not go well together, and some contend that democratization actually exacerbates nationality tensions.[1] Others reply that policymakers can democratize and craft institutions in ways that moderate ethnic claims.[2] Although undoubtedly many factors influence the success of democratic institutions in multiethnic societies, this chapter argues that ethnic composition and the structure of state power are extremely important. If one assumes that representatives of a given ethnic group are in charge in a given democratizing republic, that leadership will have strong incentive to pursue radical separatist claims only when that group represents a majority or near-majority of its voting population. As Pauline Jones Luong demonstrates in chapter 20, this volume, this is the case in Tatarstan.

If the group in question makes up only a small minority of the population, the leadership has incentive to pursue a delicate balancing strategy in order to gain a majority vote, a policy one might venture to call *subtle civic sovereignization*. First, the minority policymakers will buttress their own group's leadership position in the republic. Second, they will promote the spread of their own culture and language to the greatest extent possible without arousing the ire of other groups. Third, they will tend to favor autonomy for their republic in order to reinforce these policies; but they cannot take things so far as actually to secede. Fourth, and most important, such leaders will make great efforts to neutralize ethnicity as a meaningful aspect of these issues. Thus although they may pursue republican "sovereignty," they will tend to define the community that is to be made sovereign in civic rather than ethnic terms, and they will pursue alliances with key members of other groups as part of this effort to defuse ethnic politics. Such a strategy is more likely to be successful when the state controlled by members of the minority group is quite strong, as is indeed the case in Bashkortostan. In such an instance, one can expect state power to be extremely important in both federal and local elections at the same time that ethnicity plays a relatively small role in campaigns and voting.

The chapter's analysis of the 1993 election in Bashkortostan traces the impact of the two main factors just discussed (ethnicity and state power), and weighs them against the impact of four broadly defined variables that have been discussed previously in this volume. The hypotheses they generate include the following:

—Candidate strategies: those candidates and parties will tend to do well that have the best campaigns (well funded, highly organized, aggressive, and media prominent) or the greatest name recognition. Candidates with party affiliations or endorsements will do better than those without them, all other things being equal.

—Social interests: the distribution of votes for candidates and parties will tend to reflect the distribution of sectoral, class, or geographic interests in society.

—Rules of the game: the Duma's single-mandate districts will promote more radical candidacies or candidacies based on segments of society with a solid plurality of support since there are no runoff elections.

—Historical legacy: voters in Bashkortostan will vote for candidates espousing slower economic reform and political autonomy from Moscow as they have consistently done in the past.

The Context: Demographic, Historical, and Political

Bashkortostan, nestled along the southwest slopes of the Ural mountains, is an interesting case for an electoral study because of its unusual ethnic mix as well as its economic importance to the Russian Federation. Ethnically, Russians compose only 39 percent of the population according to the 1989 census. But the Bashkirs, who give their name to the republic, are a mere 22 percent. The remainder consists mostly of Tatars, who eclipse Bashkirs in their "own" republic with 28 percent of the population. Although each of the three groups has a significant presence in each part of the republic, Bashkirs predominate in the mountainous southeast, Tatars in the gentle hills of the northwest, and Russians in the industrial cities of the central region. Bashkirs are predominantly rural, with only 42 percent living in cities or towns. In contrast, 83 percent of Russians and 58 percent of Tatars live in urban areas. Ethnic boundaries are rarely clear-cut, however, as is illustrated by the fact that 20 percent of self-proclaimed Bashkirs in 1989 reported their native language to be Tatar.[3]

As can be seen in table 1-5, Bashkortostan is somewhat less urbanized (63.8 percent) than the Russian Federation as a whole (74 percent). It is an industrial powerhouse with two vital sectors: the military-industrial complex and the oil industry. Not only does the republic pump its own oil, the local media likes to boast, but its refineries and oil-chemical plants process 51 percent of the oil treated in the Russian Federation.[4] Out of a population of more than 4 million, however, some 900,000 are pensioners.[5]

Two issues have dominated Bashkortostan politics since Soviet President Mikhail Gorbachev first pulled back the restrictions on free speech and gave local governments some real autonomy: economic reform and "sovereignty." In economics, the republic leadership under Supreme Soviet President Murtaza Rakhimov has tended to favor a gradual transition to a market economy in which the state supports collective farms and key industries while they adjust. Popular opinion has traditionally backed Rakhimov in this conservatism, as is reflected strongly in earlier votes and polls. In 1991, Bashkortostan gave reformist Boris Yeltsin a slight majority in Russia's first presidential election, but this 50.1 percent was significantly below the Russian average of 59.7 percent. In the April 1993 Russian referendum, only 40.7 percent voted confidence in Yeltsin, compared to 59.9 percent in the Russian Federation as a whole (see table 1-6). Survey data conducted in the republic in 1993 as part of this volume's research project support these assessments. Only 7 percent were for rapid marketization, whereas 40 percent opted for a gradual approach and 24 percent opposed it altogether. Although only 12 percent said private farms should be banned or severely restricted, a plurality said they should be allowed to "coexist" with but not systematically replace state and collective farms. Rural areas have tended to be more conservative. In one late 1993 poll conducted by the Bashkir Agricultural University, only 15 percent supported any kind of private land ownership.[6]

The bigger issue, however, has been the republic's drive for sovereignty. Although Bashkir nationalists have gone so far as to argue that secession would make Bashkortostan a "second Kuwait," republic leader Rakhimov's policy has been more subtle. Basically, the idea is not to try to secede

but to use the implicit threat of secession to win concrete economic and political concessions from Moscow. Thus when Russia's regions signed the
Federation Treaty on March 31, 1992, Bashkortostan won a special appendix to the treaty that recognized Bashkortostan's claim to own the land and
natural resources on its territory, among other things. Bashkortostan did not
pay any taxes to the Russian Federation in 1992 but began to pay them
again in 1993 as the two sides made progress in negotiating a bilateral
treaty to define their relationship.[7]

The sovereignty drive has proven quite popular, and its leaders are justified in claiming it has multinational support. In April 1993, 76 percent of
those voting in the republic agreed that "The Republic of Bashkortostan in
the interests of her peoples should have economic independence *(samos-
toyatel'nost')* and treaty-based relations with the Russian Federation on the
basis of the Federation Treaty and the appendix to it from the Republic of
Bashkortostan." Nevertheless, this project's surveys in late 1993 showed
that 30 percent of the republic's population disapproved of the general principle of republic sovereignty declarations in Russia, and 20 percent approved and 25 percent were indifferent.

If the Bashkirs cannot themselves make up an anti-Moscow majority,
some observers have speculated that they will naturally tend to join with the
Tatars in a "Turkic Alliance" to oppose the Russians and Russia. Indeed,
Tatars and Bashkirs are very close ethnically; their languages are both
Turkic and mutually intelligible and they are both traditionally Muslim.
The survey data do hint that the building blocks for such an alliance are in
place at the level of mass opinion. Asked whether they considered their
"motherland" to be the former USSR, Russia, or the republic in which they
live, a striking 65 percent of Tatars answered "the republic," just under the
figure of 74 percent for Bashkirs. The vast majority of Russians, however,
declared their motherland to be Russia or even the former USSR. Tatars
were also fairly close to Bashkirs in their support for declarations of sovereignty and the right to secede generally, diverging from Russian opinion.

These figures, however, are better understood not as reflecting the common ethnic aspirations of two brotherly Turkic peoples but as an indicator
of Rakhimov's success in defining the idea of "Bashkortostan" in essentially civic terms. Indeed, once one begins to invest "sovereignty" issues
with ethnic content, the Turkic Alliance comes crashing down. Asked
whether everyone in a Russian Federation republic should be fluent in the
titular language of that republic, Bashkirs with an opinion split nearly
evenly on the issue, a fact that by itself indicates that Bashkir support for
sovereignty is not entirely ethnically driven. Tatars, on the other hand, op-

posed the proposition by a ratio of nearly 3:1. Thus formal organizations claiming to represent Bashkirs and Tatars have shown little propensity to cooperate. Indeed, it is generally these cultural issues that divide them, with Tatars fearing "Bashkirization."

Further testimonial to Rakhimov's success in building a broad, multiethnic base of support is the fact that nearly one-third of the republic's Russians appear to be at least passive supporters of the republic's sovereignty. It is surprising to note that in the survey, 29 percent of the Russian population both declared Bashkortostan to be their motherland and stated that they were indifferent to or supportive of sovereignty for Russia's republics in general. The fact that so many Russians (as well as Tatars and Bashkirs) declared they were indifferent to sovereignty (not supportive of it) suggests Rakhimov may be pushing the limits of what he can achieve before provoking the other groups, although the 1993 referendum results suggest he can win their votes when needed.

The 1993 Elections in Bashkortostan

The Russian federal election was not the only one to take place in December 1993. In a race that far overshadowed campaigns for parliamentary seats, two local political titans were battling to become the first president of the Republic of Bashkortostan. This struggle laid bare one of the republic's most serious political cleavages, pitting unionist against sovereignty-seeker. The political forces it unleashed had a major impact on who won Bashkortostan's seats in the federal parliament. Both presidential candidates were among six people competing for two Federation Council seats, and the latter were often seen as a sort of bonus that the new president's team would win. In the end, Supreme Soviet President Murtaza Rakhimov won the presidency, and, together with his loyal prime minister, Anatolii Kopsov, became one of Bashkortostan's delegates to the Federation Council. They owed their victories mostly to a carefully cultivated good reputation based on popular economic policies, a strong political grip on rural regions, and a mighty effort led by state-run media to blacken the name of their key opponent.

The Bashkir Presidency and the Federation Council

Bashkortostan's announcement of a presidential election was both unexpected and long awaited. In 1991, in the heat of the sovereignty drive, many republics created their own presidencies, and Bashkortostan began to follow suit, slating the election for December 15, 1991. After several candidates stepped forth, Supreme Soviet president Rakhimov suddenly postponed the vote, arguing that there was no need for a presidency at that time. The postponement lasted until just after the 1993 October rebellion, when Yeltsin's emboldened administration hinted it might appoint a distinct executive branch of power in Bashkortostan if the republic did not create one itself. The panic-stricken leadership then scurried to hold a presidential election on the same day as the federal election, December 12, 1993.[8]

Opponents argued Yeltsin's implied threat was just a convenient excuse for Rakhimov to call elections in a hurry, making it highly unlikely that a challenger could organize a winning campaign in the short time available (about a month). Whatever the leadership's real motives, it proceeded to set up a series of very strict presidential nomination requirements. Perhaps most controversial was the rule whereby the president of Bashkortostan must be able to speak the Bashkir language, which according to the 1989 census ruled out 83 percent of the population. Further, in order to be officially registered, a candidate had to collect 100,000 signatures, the same amount entire parties were expected to collect in the whole of Russia in the federal election.

One scrappy opponent, however, managed to clear all the nomination hurdles: Rafis Kadyrov, the then thirty-eight-year-old president of one of the Russian Federation's first large private banks, Bank Vostok. Born in a small village and having worked as a doctor before 1989, he founded his bank using a good-faith loan from a local mullah as start-up capital. Soon thereafter, he won election to the republic's legislature, where he was a noted critic of the incumbent leadership.[9] At the time of the election, Bank Vostok had more than forty branches throughout Bashkortostan, providing him a large pool from which to draw devoted corps of volunteers. Further, nearly 25 percent of the republic's population had invested their privatization vouchers in Kadyrov's holding company, Vostok.[10] He also enjoyed the support of Bank Vostok's own newspaper, the feisty three-and-a-half-year-old weekly *Ekonomika i My,* which boasted it had the highest circulation of any paper in Bashkortostan, nearly 300,000.[11] In the end, Kadyrov managed to collect 111,820 signatures in his run for the presidency, enough to get him into the race but far behind Rakhimov's 422,892.[12]

As might be expected, issues of economic reform and sovereignty dominated the presidential–Federation Council campaign. Although the speeches of the two presidential candidates really differed little on issues of marketization, they clashed mightily over Rakhimov's sovereignty policy. Rakhimov admitted the republic's economy was in bad shape but argued that his sovereignty policy was bringing in revenues that directly enabled Bashkortostan to be better off than other parts of the Russian Federation and allowed it actively to invest in social programs. On this platform, Rakhimov won support from many key republic organizations, including local trade unions, the Union of Journalists, the Agrarian party, the Agrarian Union, and the Communist party.[13] Despite the fact that his opponent was a prominent entrepreneur, in his bid for the presidency Rakhimov also secured the support of the head of the republic Council of Entrepreneurs, Nikolai Shvetsov, a competitor in the Federation Council race.[14] It is surprising that the leader of the anti-Moscow sovereignty drive even managed to secure backing from some of the republic's key ethnic Russian leaders, including Shvetsov. More striking, Rakhimov was favored by Aleksandr Arinin, the head of the most prominent ethnic Russian organization, *Rus',* which had led the opposition to Bashkortostan's sovereignty movement.[15] This is particularly surprising given that Kadyrov campaigned explicitly on a pro-Moscow, antisovereignty platform.

Kadyrov lambasted Rakhimov's record, homing in on the sovereignty drive. "The main task of the president of Bashkortostan will be the quick normalization of relations with Russia and the Russian government," he declared.[16] Rakhimov's sovereignty drive, he claimed, had brought the republic to the brink of economic disaster by alienating it from Russia, jeopardizing subsidies and defense orders.[17] With these views, Kadyrov picked up support from some important political groups but got nowhere near the kind of backing from big power brokers that Rakhimov enjoyed. Kadyrov received the blessings of the local branch of Nikolai Travkin's Democratic Party of Russia, Bashkortostan's branch of the Tatar Social Center, Vladimir Zhirinovskii's Liberal Democratic party, and the local branch of the Party of Constitutional Democrats.[18]

It is important to note that the presidential race also reflected a battle between Moscow and the capital Ufa for control over Bashkortostan, a phenomenon that showed up clearly in patterns of media coverage. Rakhimov embodied republican authority, evidently not discouraging underlings from using the power at their disposal to extol his virtues and to give Kadyrov's reputation a frothy mud bath. Official television news broadcasts and newspapers were grossly biased against Kadyrov and in favor of Rakhimov. The head of the main republic television company said it was normal for a television station to support a candidate it liked, and that it nevertheless gave equal time for candidates to appear personally and present their views directly to the people.[19] The republic's central election commission agreed.[20]

Kadyrov, for his part, evidently enjoyed the blessings of Russia's central authorities, support that seemed to manifest itself mostly in well-timed favorable reports in central state-run and independent media. Kadyrov's main line of attack on Rakhimov, for instance, was a scandal based on privileged loans that the republic's leadership gave itself, a story picked up and carried widely by the Moscow-based press.[21] In one particularly telling episode, just days after local media ran stories suggesting Kadyrov's Bank Vostok was financially unsound, the Russian television channel's news program *Vesti* aired a Kadyrov press conference. As the narrator lauded him for creating one of Russia's strongest banks despite being based so far from Moscow, viewers heard Kadyrov talk about his successes, so great that his bank was now going international.[22]

According to the final vote tally, Rakhimov won the presidency overwhelmingly with 69.2 percent of the valid ballots cast, compared to Kadyrov's 30.7 percent. Kadyrov did not win in a single rural county and won majorities in only four small cities. Rakhimov absolutely dominated the rural vote, winning more than three quarters of it. Kadyrov supporters speculated that local administration officials, appointed by Rakhimov, had an easy time persuading collective farm chairs and farmers that they might suffer a cut in state support if they did not deliver the vote to the leadership. Although Kadyrov's paper and organizational backing were critical to the success he did enjoy, they could not penetrate rural areas and could not compete with state-run media, especially television, even in the cities. Ultimately, the negative campaign against Kadyrov seemed effective in stunting any growth in his support. People also appeared generally to believe Bashkortostan was better off than surrounding regions of Russia.

Broadening our perspective to include the Federation Council race, four other candidates competed, and nearly all were political heavyweights in the republic: Prime Minister Anatolii Kopsov, former prime minister Murat Mirgazyamov, president of the republic Council of Entrepreneurs Nikolai Shvetsov, and professor-entrepreneur Vil' Gareyev. Along with Rakhimov, Prime Minister Kopsov won the other Federation Council seat, campaigning basically on one ticket with Rakhimov (see table 19-1). Kopsov, ex-director of the huge oil concern Bashkirenergo, appeared with Rakhimov on most of his whistle-stop tours of the republic, and enjoyed nearly all of the same advantages. The other three candidates were never really in the race, lacking the political backing and media attention that the presiden-

Table 19-1. *Federation Council Election Results, 1993*

Candidate	Affiliation	Percent of vote
Rakhimov	Independent	62.6
Kopsov	Independent	53.0

tial hopefuls received. Entrepreneur Shvetsov, whose advisor claimed he headed a large political network with cells in every Bashkortostan city, may have possessed the organizational and financial resources to take on the victors in the cities; but he, like Kadyrov, failed to penetrate the village.[23]

It is clear that state power was absolutely critical in this vote. The winners were the two top republican officials, and the fact that they scored such a crushing victory in rural areas suggests their positions did play an important role in influencing local administrations and collective farm directors, who are in a strong position to manipulate flows of information and get out the vote. The Rakhimov-Kopsov team's views also coincide well with those of a popular majority as expressed in the opinion polls and referenda discussed previously. This was likely an important factor in their victory, although most of their competitors' positions were not very different, except on sovereignty. Further, they were indeed endorsed by more political parties and blocs than their opponents. No candidate, however, publicly affiliated himself with a party or bloc in this race. Geographic loyalty to Bashkortostan may also have been a factor, as republican residents generally voted for the candidates (Rakhimov-Kopsov) that most vigorously promised to represent their particular interests as opposed to all-Russian ones. Socioeconomic interests may also have been important: both winners made their careers in the oil industry, which is not surprising in this big oil republic. If socioeconomic interests are key, however, it is odd that the winners' strongest support came not from the city but from the village. Further, defense industry representative Gareyev did poorly and no Agrarian joined the race. It is also important to note the success of local media attacks on Kadyrov, suggesting campaigns were important, at least negative ones conducted on official news media.

Ethnicity, on the other hand, appears to have been a minor factor in the election. Bashkir Rakhimov got 62.6 percent of the vote, yet only 22 percent of the population is Bashkir. Russians Kopsov and Shvetsov got 53.0 and 12.3 percent respectively, yet Russians make up 39 percent of the population. The only Tatar, Mirgazyamov, received just 12.4 percent, but the republic is 28 percent Tatar. Further, ethnic themes played little role in the winning team's campaign, although it did reflect moderate Bashkir interests. Instead, one finds two sets of motley political alliances. After failing in his own bid to get on the presidential ballot, the leading Tatar activist Karim Yaushev backed the pro-Moscow but ethnically Bashkir Kadyrov, who received 30.7 percent of the vote, whereas the most prominent Russian activist (Arinin) supported Rakhimov, as did the Russian Shvetsov. All this suggests Rakhimov's strategy was to downplay ethnicity, coopting key Russian leaders and touting his Russian prime minister so as to take wind from the sails of his largest and potentially most contentious constituent group. Thus ethnicity appears to have been important mostly insofar as Rakhimov had to work to defuse it as an issue.

The Unionwide Party Race

If ultranationalist Vladimir Zhirinovskii's Liberal Democratic party was the big story in the party race in Russia as a whole, the Agrarian party carried the day in Bashkortostan. Its 25.0 percent of the vote eclipsed its nearest rival, the Communist party, which managed 15.2 percent. Sergei Shakhrai's Party of Russian Unity and Accord (PRES) did the best among the reformist electoral blocs with 12.9 percent, edging out Zhirinovskii's loyal list, which received 12.6 percent. The most radical reformist bloc, Russia's Choice, received a paltry 8.6 percent, just behind the centrist Women of Russia bloc's 9.3 percent. None of the remaining blocs cleared 5 percent.

These results pose many puzzles to the observer. Why, for example, did the Agrarian party more than triple its unionwide average in a region that is 65 percent urban? Why was Zhirinovskii's party so far below its national average? Why did PRES emerge as the strongest reformist party in the republic? This study begins by analyzing each bloc's performance in the republic, moves on to consider why voting results differed from the Russian norm, and then looks at broad patterns of liberal-conservative support.

The Agrarians' success reflects a variety of factors, including sectoral voting, state power, and party organization. As its name would lead us to expect, the Agrarian party won most of its support in the countryside, suggesting people did vote according to sectoral economic interest. A regional analysis shows that it received up to a third of the vote in Bashkortostan's most rural districts. It is important to note that turnout in mainly rural counties approached 80 percent, much higher than in the capital Ufa where turnout was under 50 percent and in other cities where the figure was under 60 percent.[24] This, of course, magnified the results for parties with rural support. The party's conservative stance on agricultural issues also fits well with peasant attitudes described previously.

The Agrarians were not limited to rural support, however, winning outright in every district except the most urban one. They even won in a district that included a large part of the capital Ufa where 82 percent of the population is urban. Here the leader of the Agrarian party's republic organization also won a single-mandate seat in the Duma with a strong showing even in the city. Nevertheless, the Agrarians also won the party race in the Sterlitamak district, which is 75 percent urban, without fielding a candidate there.

Other factors also worked in favor of the Agrarian party. It is significant to note that it was one of only two parties to enjoy the clear blessings of the republican leadership. Not only did Rakhimov control appointments to key village posts, but his administration had invested great resources in agriculture that surely gave his preferences significant weight in the countryside. This might also explain the odd results of this project's preelection survey, in which only 3 percent of the republic population said they would vote for the Agrarians, whereas as many as 10 percent had already decided to vote for PRES. Although this might indicate problems in the survey's rural sample, it might also testify to the effectiveness of state pressure when applied decisively in rural areas.

The Agrarians were also relatively well organized, with a full-time apparat of six members as well as supporters in rural locales. The bloc was one of the most active in the republic, nominating two candidates and making endorsements in four of the six Bashkortostan districts, actively supporting them in the localities.[25] Its local leader was telegenic and important enough to be placed in the number four spot on the federal party list. One can also observe a slight correlation between Agrarian support and non-Russian areas, but this probably reflects the fact that most Russians are city dwellers. Nevertheless, it may have helped Agrarians that their local leader was a Tatar, and the survey suggests Agrarian support was slightly higher among Tatars than other groups. One top Agrarian leader said the Muslim love of the land fit well with his party's ideals.

The Communist party finished second in the Bashkortostan party race, receiving 15.2 percent of the vote. It was surprising that their worst two performances occurred where one might expect a workers' party to perform best—in the two most urban districts of the republic, which included the capital, Ufa. The figures in these regions are not too far off their republic averages, but they may reflect that most of their support was coming from middle-sized towns. This would be buttressed by the fact that they polled slightly lower in the most rural district. Overall, though, they finished second in every district except Kalininskii District 4, the most urban, where they came in fourth. The survey suggests that the Communists were not receiving the ethnic Russian protest vote that they cultivated in 1995, as Russians in 1993 tended to be *more* opposed to the Communists than were Tatars and Bashkirs. Communists clearly had high name recognition, although much of this was negative. Nevertheless, as nearly everywhere in the former Soviet Union, the Communists could find a hard core of volunteers and support amongst the population that must have helped in a situation in which few other parties had any local infrastructure. The party did not take advantage of this as they might have, however. The local organization only grudgingly participated in the campaign, declaring the new parliament illegitimate and the vote "the most undemocratic election in essence in the whole period of the existence of Russia." They only fielded one serious candidate for the single-mandate races, and he pulled out before being registered.[26]

Shakhrai's PRES was another success story in Bashkortostan, outpacing all of its reformist rivals and placing third in the republic's overall tally with 12.9 percent of the vote, nearly double its federal average. Given that it was created only in the run-up to the election, how can its local fortunes be explained? One answer is that PRES was uniquely active in Bashkortostan. Not only was it the only bloc observed to run advertisements on local television, but it was the only bloc to nominate candidates in as many as three out of the six republic districts. It was also one of only four blocs to put candidates on a regional list from Bashkortostan. Shakhrai himself was also one of only two party leaders to include Ufa on a campaign stop, where he got major coverage in the local media. Not all PRES-nominated candidates in single-member districts may have boosted the bloc, however. Two of them, Gazim Shafikov and Najib Valitov, were relatively inactive in the campaign, Shafikov because of illness and Valitov because of philosophy. The other nominee, Aleksandr Arinin, may well explain why PRES received its largest share in Kalininskii District 4. Arinin, as will be discussed later in the chapter, led the most prominent Russian cultural organization in the republic, well known for criticizing the republic's sovereignty drive. He also was a tremendously energetic campaigner and used his organization's newspaper to his advantage. Whether or not he solicited it, Shakhrai also received the endorsement of a wide range of other local notables, including entrepreneurial leader Nikolai Shvetsov and Yurii Utkin, the mayor of Ishimbai and a leading Duma candidate. Thus at the time this book's survey was conducted, PRES was far ahead of all other parties in the polls, with 10 percent of the population declaring their support for it.

Two other factors stand out that may have played important roles in the PRES success. For one thing, PRES was the only party to put federalism at the heart of its platform, and it was widely perceived to be the party of regional autonomy. This could have been expected to play well in a republic in which 76 percent of the population voted for economic independence and treaty-based relations with Russia. Perhaps for this reason, PRES clearly enjoyed the support of the republic's powerful leaders. Thus when Shakhrai visited Ufa, positive images of him sitting shoulder-to-shoulder with Supreme Soviet President Rakhimov filled local media. Such treatment was not accorded the only other bloc leader to visit the republic, Civic Union's Arkadii Vol'skii.

With such backing, one might wonder why PRES did not do better still, especially given its perceived stance on the republic's hot-button issue, sovereignty. Initially, as with most new parties, its local infrastructure was weak and it had low name recognition. Further, its choice of candidates was bound to send very confusing messages to voters. For example, it nominated two well-known candidates widely seen to hold opposite views on the party's core issue of federalism: a key leader of the Russian movement against Bashkir "ethnocracy," Arinin, and Bashkir cultural rights activist and writer Shafikov. Further, the centrist economics of list candidate Al'bert Khusainov[27] also differed from the explicit Reaganomics of Valitov. There is also the irony of Shakhrai himself, aligning with the sovereignty-seeking Bashkir leadership while being associated with the Yeltsin regime that was pushing what republics saw as a strongly center-oriented constitution. It is of course possible that vagueness was an advantage, that people saw in PRES what they wanted to see. It is also possible that diversity was part of Shakhrai's strategy to prove one could build "unity and accord" in Bashkortostan. Whatever the answer, this raised serious questions about what a vote for PRES meant in Bashkortostan—in the southern regions of Baimak, it may have meant a vote for Shafikov and Bashkir ethnic autonomy, while in Ufa it may have meant a vote for the elimination of ethnicity-based federal structures and more direct ties between cities and the central government. This problem is magnified by the fact that in most cases, the candidates were better known than the party.

Before the election, most observers would have been astounded to learn Vladimir Zhirinovskii's Liberal Democratic party would win more than 12 percent of the vote in Bashkortostan. They would have been flabbergasted to hear this was less than half of what he received throughout Russia. One can largely explain his relatively weak showing in the republic if one assumes few Bashkirs and Tatars would vote for the Russian ultranationalist. If one considers that only about 40 percent of the republic's population is Russian, and if we infer that his supporters consisted primarily of Russian voters, his 12.6 percent makes up slightly more than a quarter of the local Russian vote. This would mean he actually did slightly better than his 25 percent federal average among the Bashkortostan Russians, suggesting Russians there were somewhat more restive, unhappy with the Bashkir leadership. It probably also reflects the fact that Zhirinovskii did get some non-Russian support, however, as revealed in the survey. The LDPR did have a local organization, but it was not very visible and nominated no candidates for single-mandate seats in the republic.

Considering the political views prevalent in Bashkortostan in recent years, it should come as no surprise that reformist parties fared poorly, with the exception of PRES. Although political ideology could explain their failure, one might also blame the parties themselves for essentially abandoning the region. The most radical party, Yegor Gaidar's Russia's Choice, received 8.6 percent of the vote, scarcely more than half its federal average. It made virtually no effort to campaign locally; no major candidate visited the republic and the bloc nominated no candidates from Bashkortostan. One lone candidate in Tuimazynskii District 7 put support for Russia's Choice at the center of his campaign, but the bloc did not nominate him. Russia's Choice also had no visible local infrastructure, and evidently suffered the effects of republican leader Rakhimov's opposition. This is in marked contrast to PRES, which campaigned actively and managed to garner half again as many votes. The survey also suggests that Russia's Choice, by ignoring Bashkortostan, sacrificed an early base of support because it then occupied second place in the polling, behind only PRES, with 5 percent support. Grigorii Yavlinskii's bloc Yabloko and Anatolii Sobchak's Movement for Russian Reforms fared even worse, receiving 3.9 and 2.5 percent of the vote, respectively. Although Yavlinskii nominated one candidate in Sterlitamak District 6, these blocs also had very weak infrastructures in the region and made little visible effort to campaign locally. No major candidate of theirs visited Bashkortostan to campaign. Basically, the radical and moderate reformers appear to have written Bashkortostan off before the race began.

Although it was a surprise that centrist blocs fared so poorly in this traditionally centrist, industrial republic, their failure corresponded to their collapse across the whole of Russia, as described elsewhere in this volume. Of the centrist groups, only Women of Russia did respectably well, receiving 9.3 percent of the vote. It may have been helped by the fact that not a single woman was a candidate for a single-mandate Duma district in Bashkortostan.

When we step back and see how these voting patterns relate to those of Russia as a whole (table 1-4), we get some interesting insights into which factors are most important. Initially, we note that both the Agrarians and PRES did significantly better in Bashkortostan than their federal averages, whereas the LDPR, Russia's Choice, and Yabloko all fared much worse. All other parties and blocs did not vary more than 3 percent from their federal figures.

How can these patterns be explained? One notes that the only two parties above their federal averages were those two that the republic's leadership most evidently supported: the Agrarian party and PRES. This strongly suggests state power was an important electoral force. From this perspective, the Rakhimov administration effectively gave local voters a choice between two parties, one moderately reformist and one conservative. Given this choice, as would be expected in a conservative region, the conservatives got two-thirds of the vote. It is also possible, however, that people simply liked these parties for the same reasons they also liked the local leadership. As we have seen, these two parties were also the most active locally. Civic Union was the only other bloc to nominate more than one candidate in the single-mandate districts, but it had other problems, as is described in Daniel Treisman's chapter. The other deviations are easier to explain. As argued previously, Zhirinovskii's relatively poor showing can be accounted for by the presence of many non-Russians. The performances of Russia's Choice and Yabloko likely reflect the region's traditional conservatism and their low local presence.

If we try to paint the picture in even broader strokes, one sees that Bashkortostan gave 52 percent of its votes to socialists and nationalists, which is about 9 percent more than the country as a whole. Reformists, with 28 percent in the republic, fared worse than their federal average by about 8 percentage points. In part, this reflects what we knew before: Bashkortostan is a relatively conservative republic. This result is striking, however, because conservative forces as a whole did well despite a poor performance by Zhirinovskii's party. This suggests the Agrarians may have picked up much of the "protest vote" that went to the LDPR in other regions. If non-Russian conservatives were also fed up with the Communists, the Agrarian party remained the only protest vehicle, the lone conservative party untainted by previous rule and by ethnic chauvinism.

Single-Mandate Duma Races: Ethnicity, State Power, and the Village

In 1993 Bashkortostan sent a much more conservative and much more Bashkir delegation to Moscow than it had in 1990.[28] According to one ranking of legislative voting records, the 1990 group fell almost exactly in the center of the conservative-liberal spectrum on average (table 1-6), whereas the 1993 team has pursued a decidedly conservative agenda. In 1990 Tatars came out big winners, securing eleven of twenty-seven seats while Bashkirs and Russians scored six apiece. But in 1993 Tatars won but a single seat, as did Russians, and Bashkirs took four. How can we explain such shifts? This section first seeks to explain each 1993 race in isolation (see table 19-1) then the conclusion steps back to explain broader patterns that are evident. Because of space considerations, I consider the most complex races in the most depth, briefly summarizing the others (see table 19-2).

Baimakskii District 2: Economics before Ethnicity

The mountainous south is the Bashkir core of Bashkortostan, so if Bashkir ethnicity is important anywhere, it should be important there. Baimakskii District 2 is the most Bashkir of districts, with 43 percent of the population Bashkir, 38 percent Russian, 11 percent Tatar, and 55 percent living in urban areas. In 1990 this region sent a centrist delegation to the Congress, and in 1993 its deputy tended to vote conservative. A superficial look at overall results suggests ethnicity lost out dramatically in a head-to-head contest with agrarian economic interests, but a deeper analysis reveals a somewhat different story.

It is no surprise the only two writers running for parliament ran in Baimakskii District 2. Gazim Shafikov, in particular, preached ethnic cultural revival.[29] Yet in what would seem the most fertile soil in the republic, Bashkir ethnic appeals failed to bear fruit as Shafikov collected a disappointing 11.7 percent of the vote, well behind two agrarians. Both state farm chair Akhmetgalei Galiyev and district agroindustrial trade union president Nikolai Pavlov won endorsements from the Agrarian party and campaigned on agrarian issues. Galiyev ultimately won the vote with 33.1 percent, edging out Pavlov with 29.3 percent. The other writer, Azat Ab-

Table 19-2. *State Duma Election Results, 1993*

District #	Candidate	Affiliation	Percent of vote
Baimakskii, 2	Galiyev	Independent	33.1
Birskii, 3	Mirsayev	Independent	44.7
Kalininskii, 4	Arinin	PRES	38.4
Kirovskii, 5	Asayev	Agrarian party	29.8
Sterlitamakskii, 6	Utkin	Independent	51.1
Tuimazynskii, 7	Sayetgaliyev	Independent	43.5

dullin, won 20.7 percent and entrepreneur Rim Niyazgulov finished last with 5.3 percent of the vote.

Looking only at the surface, the big story in Baimak is that ethnic interests were impotent in the face of economic sectoral interests. People preferred agrarians to cultural activists. When one examines county-by-county (raion) results, however, a striking pattern emerges: the most heavily Bashkir areas voted strongly for the Bashkir agrarian, Galiyev, and the most heavily Russian areas turned out in force for the Slavic agrarian, Pavlov. This outcome can mean one of two things. One possibility is that voters cast their ballots first and foremost for economic reasons, and only secondarily for ethnic ones. It could also mean that Bashkir voters primarily looked to vote for a candidate of their own ethnicity but preferred a Bashkir who talked about economics to one who talked about culture. Thus although Bashkir ethnic activism alone may not be a winning strategy, Bashkir voters in this region do appear to have factored ethnicity into their electoral calculus.

Others factors may also have played a role, however. Geographic loyalty may partly explain poor showings by Shafikov and Abdullin, because both had long lived in big cities far away from the district (Ufa and Moscow, respectively). Further, the Agrarian party endorsement again coincides with very strong candidate performance. The only other party with district representation was PRES, which nominated Shafikov. He was likely better known than his party, however, and his vote totals were about even with those of PRES in the district and the republic in general, suggesting the party had little impact. Campaigns also may have mattered: not only were Shafikov and Abdullin from outside the district, but they were reportedly ill during parts of the race, giving the local Agrarians a campaigning advantage. The writers' name recognition alone appears not to have been enough. State power played little role, and majoritarian electoral rules would not likely have produced a different winner. Overall, agrarian interests, ethnicity, the Agrarian party, and campaigns combine for a strong explanation of Galiyev's victory.

Birskii District 3: State Power in the Village

In 1990, the tranquil farms of Birskii District 3 sent the republic's most conservative delegation to the Supreme Soviet. In 1993, the conservative tradition continued, with new deputy Ramil' Mirsayev voting regularly with hard-liners in the State Duma. These results are fairly easily explained: Mirsayev was a strongly state-backed agrarian in the most rural republic district.

Covering the northern reaches of Bashkortostan, Birskii District 3 contains seventeen rural raions and four cities of between 20,000 to 35,000 people. The only big urban center is Neftekamsk, a city of 122,000. Despite the fact that 62 percent of the population lives in rural areas, however, only one candidate came from the countryside in 1993. The district also features a fairly well-balanced mix of ethnic groups; only about 20 percent of the people are Russians, whereas approximately 25 percent are Bashkirs and about 30 percent are Tatars.

State power was decisive in this race. The winner was forty-three-year-old Ramil' Mirsayev, an ethnic Bashkir who was for nearly ten years the deputy minister of agriculture and produce of Bashkortostan in charge of construction. Publicly endorsing the program of the Agrarian party as well as the republic's sovereignty drive, he stressed his ministry's record of improving village infrastructure by laying gas pipelines and paving roads.[30] This clearly won him the loyalty of many a village leader, and he was able to capitalize on this support, far outpacing his nearest rival with 44.7 percent of the vote. Political parties seemed less important. Although the Agrarian party endorsed Mirsayev, it also endorsed a collective farm chair (Boris Tsypyshev) who received a mere 11.0 percent of the vote. The only candidate actually nominated by an electoral bloc was Civic Union's Yurii Sharipov, the head of one of the republic's most successfully converted defense concerns. With 9.8 percent of the vote, however, he fared much better than his bloc, suggesting the latter in no way helped him. Campaigns did seem weakly important; Mirsayev's campaign was well organized, apparently rivaled only by those of Civic Union's Sharipov and entrepreneur Robert Akhiyarov. Although the dynamic Akhiyarov's well-financed campaign may have helped him finish second with 13.7 percent, Sharipov's own reputation apparently damaged his candidacy: he was widely known as the candidate who had promised to "telephonize" every house in Ufa if elected to the USSR Supreme Soviet in 1989, a promise that went sadly unfulfilled.

Socioeconomic factors appear not to have been decisive in this district. Although Mirsayev's success hinged on his credible claim to represent agrarian interests, state power explains why voters chose him over farm chair Tsypyshev. Ethnic appeals also appeared insignificant; Tatars make up a district plurality yet not one was nominated to run. It remains a mystery, however, why five of seven candidates were Bashkir when Bashkirs make up only a quarter of the population. Further, the only Russian candidate (Tsypyshev) received far fewer votes than there are Russian voters in the region. Geographic interests also mattered little, as Mirsayev won from distant Ufa. A majoritarian electoral system would not likely have changed this outcome.

Kalininskii District 4: Russian Backlash Victorious

Of the single-mandate Duma districts, Kalininskii District 4 is the most urban and the most Russian. Russians, Tatars, and Bashkirs make up 53, 28, and 11 percent of the population, respectively. The district contains the eastern half of Ufa (formerly the separate city of Chernikovsk), the nearby city of Blagoveshchensk, and two rural counties. It is 93 percent urban. Only one rural county has a non-Russian (Tatar) majority, and Ufa and Blagoveshchensk all have Russian majorities. In 1990, this district's voters sent a radical reformist delegation to the Congress. With this profile, it is not surprising the winning candidate was an ethnic Russian from a reformist party, PRES. But it is surprising that this candidate won on a strong antisovereignty platform in a republic in which the sovereignty drive was quite popular and in a district in which Russians just barely made up a majority. It is also interesting that a low-paid professor managed to beat out two entrepreneurs with well-financed campaigns, as well as an ethnic Russian oil man.

The thirty-seven-year-old Aleksandr Arinin was in all likelihood the best known of the four candidates. Although he had worked for two years in the regional committee of the Communist party and headed the subdepartment of History of the Fatherland and Culture at a local university, he was best known as leader of the Russian cultural center *Rus'*. According to one of his newspaper campaign articles:

> He boldly stepped into the fiercest whirlpool of social life. Driven by the participants of the "parade of sovereignties," Russia was carrying itself with closed eyes, risking breaking apart into tiny pieces. And someone had to say that we cannot permit the striving to overcome overcentralization to turn into local egoism, that we cannot permit sins committed by the leadership of the CPSU to be laid on the head of the Russian people. Here in the republic this was said in the most decisive tone by Aleksandr Arinin. And he not only said, but did much in order to create a counterweight to separatist forces.[31]

Arinin joined Shakhrai's PRES out of a personal regard for Shakhrai and because it was the only party to put a federal philosophy at the heart of its platform.[32] Arinin clearly fit the PRES bill in economics, tending to support promarket reforms while avoiding what he saw as the radicalism of Russia's Choice.[33] Perhaps learning from his failed run for the republican legislature in 1990, Arinin was an extremely energetic and effective campaigner, averaging five meetings with voters per day, sometimes making as many as ten.[34] He also used *Otechestvo,* the newspaper put out by his Russian cultural center, mailing it out free to voters in the run-up to the election. It is surprising that he even secured an alliance of sorts with the republic leadership despite his well-known opposition to its sovereignty drive. This came about, some opponents said, after a negotiating session between Arinin and Prime Minister Kopsov, Rakhimov's Russian deputy.

Arinin faced three formidable opponents, including two well-funded and well-organized entrepreneurs (Dayanov and Nuridzhanov) and a local legislator from the oil complex (Rezyapov). The state actors so important in the Federation Council and party races did not play much of a role in Arinin's victory. Arinin's alliance with Rakhimov appears to have been more of a truce than a merger, because the former's support for the latter was largely passive. Although two candidates were bloc-nominated, political parties also appear to have been unimportant. Arinin's party affiliation with PRES may have helped him, but PRES had little organizational support in Ufa and he himself was better known than the party. Judging by PRES's relatively strong showing in the district, one can conclude that Arinin helped PRES more than the other way around. Entrepreneur Rashit Dayanov's affiliation with Civic Union may actually have hurt him, given the wide disparity in the vote percentages garnered by him and by his unpopular bloc. Name recognition was undoubtedly important, as Arinin was identified with the antisovereignty movement that had a strong core following in the Russian city. Campaigning also clearly mattered, although Arinin's energetic grassroots activity appears to have been much more effective than Nuridzhanov's television barrage, although this may be because the former had a preexisting constituency to which he could signal.

Indeed, turning to social interests, the ethnic factor that was a nonissue in the Federation Council race seems to have been decisive. Arinin was best known for stands on ethnic issues, as reflected in his campaign. Economic interests seem to have had little impact; Arinin was a professor and stressed broad economic themes rather than particular interests. The final piece of the puzzle, however, is the rules of the game. The plurality electoral system allowed Arinin to win with 38.4 percent of the vote, drawing on ethnic symbolism that may not have garnered him a majority. Although his reformist economic views did not stand out greatly from those of his opponents, his play to Russian cultural anxiety was a winning strategy.

Kirovskii District 5: Agrarian Wins the City

Kirovskii District 5 contains the other half of the republic's capital city, but with an important demographic twist: attached to it are five largely rural counties. Although only 18 percent of the district population is rural, this proved decisive as a lone Agrarian party candidate beat out six city-folk in this race, garnering a plurality. Despite the fact that the district is predominantly Russian, a Tatar won the seat, a fact not surprising given that the core rural areas are also largely Tatar. Thus a very conservative Tatar agrarian won 29.8 percent of the vote in a highly urban and highly Russian district, which sent a moderate centrist delegation to the Supreme Soviet in 1990.

Republic Agrarian party leader Rais Asayev owes his victory primarily to three factors: the rules of the game, agrarian interests, and his own activity. Asayev is the picture-perfect agrarian, a lifelong farm worker who made his way up to become chair of the locally famous collective farm Luch. He accordingly won landslide victories in each rural county. Given the plurality electoral rules, his rural votes alone would have been enough to defeat his six urban rivals, although he also performed respectably in the capital. Even if he and his farm were not well known enough to ensure a rural victory, he had the apparat of his Agrarian party at his disposal. Because he was also the number four candidate on the Agrarian party's federal candidate list, he enjoyed extra exposure as the bloc's local representative. The only other candidate to be nominated by a bloc was political science professor Sergei Lavrentiyev. Although he was the district's most creative campaigner, his bloc (Future of Russia–New Names) proved to be ineffective and he ended up with only 8.4 percent of the vote. Lavrentiyev's efforts show that campaigns in and of themselves did not make a huge impact, especially because Asayev had no highly organized personal campaign team other than his party and purchased no television ad time.[35] Nevertheless, the candidate with the most aggressive media blitz, lawyer-entrepreneur Pavel Dmitriyev, did manage to win the urban vote, garnering a total of 19.5 percent. Ethnic interests appear to have played little role and no candidate made ethnicity the centerpiece of his campaign in this district. No candidate enjoyed the clear backing of central republic authorities, making state power unimportant in this race.

Sterlitamakskii District 6: Power and Oil

Sterlitamakskii District 6 contains Bashkortostan's biggest and most polluted oil-chemical industrial cities next to Ufa: Sterlitamak, Salavat, and Ishimbai. It also contains six rural counties, but they make up only a quarter of the population. Although a small rural component was the key to victory for a lone agrarian in Kirovskii District 5, no candidate from the village came forth in this district. This was not because of a shortage of pretenders; ten individuals successfully put their names on the ballot, although one withdrew before the race got under way. All but one candidate hailed from Sterlitamak or distant Ufa, undermining any regional support base they might have claimed. In the end, however, it probably mattered little that the winner was the only candidate from the city of Ishimbai. More important was that this person, Yurii Utkin, was the powerful and popular mayor of that city and that he had the strong public backing of the republic's electoral juggernaut, Supreme Soviet President Rakhimov. He likely also benefited from a highly visible campaign, his background as an honored oil worker, and economically conservative and prosovereignty views that fit those of his constituents. Ethnicity looks to have played little role, as a Bashkir won 51.1 percent of the vote in a district that is 43 percent Russian, 25 percent Tatar, and only 18 percent Bashkir. Thus the district that chose a reformist and largely Russian group in 1990 elected a Bashkir siding with the Duma's most conservative forces in 1993.

Tuimazynskii District 7: A Bashkir Agrarian Wins a Tatar District

The race in Tuimazynskii District 7 followed a familiar pattern: an agrarian won in a district with an urban majority. The district's population is 53 percent urban, containing three medium-sized cities of nearly 100,000 people, one town, and twelve largely rural counties. Located in the western part of the republic that borders Tatarstan, it is the most Tatar of districts; 44 percent of its residents are ethnically Tatar, 28 percent are Russian, and only 18 percent are Bashkir. The winner was ethnically Bashkir Zifkat Sayetgaliyev, the director of the Bashkir Scientific Research Project-Making-Technological Institute of Animal Husbandry and Feed Production. Formerly the head of the collective farm Ulyanova, he was first secretary of a county Communist party organization before taking his job at the institute. Endorsed but not nominated by the Agrarian party, he basically campaigned on its platform, calling Yeltsin's reform path a big mistake. He favored Rakhimov's sovereignty policy. He beat a former USSR minister who was actually nominated by the Agrarians but who campaigned from Moscow and did not even show up for the televised debate. The other candidates were an oil man, two of presidential candidate Kadyrov's bankers, and a lone radical reformist who toed Russia's Choice's line but did not enjoy its nomination (and won a paltry 11.3 percent of the vote). No candidate had clear state backing. In the end, Sayetgaliyev won with 43.5 percent of the vote, far outpacing his nearest rival, replacing the district's old conservative parliamentary delegation with an even more conservative figure.

The Constitution Rejected

As elsewhere in Russia, President Boris Yeltsin's draft constitution met fierce debate in Bashkortostan, but with a republic twist. Although Moscow opponents attacked the power that would fall into the hands of the president, Bashkortostan proponents of "sovereignty" primarily argued the constitution was attempting to roll back republics' hard-won autonomy. Because the republic leadership sympathized with such opposition, local state-run media strongly criticized the draft. In Bashkortostan, therefore, one found a real, even-handed exchange of ideas on the constitution; central Russian television overwhelmingly argued for the constitution, and local television campaigned against. In the end, well over the necessary 50 percent of registered voters participated in the referendum in the republic, but of these only 42.0 percent approved the document.

The constitution's few proponents in the republic argued it was the best hope Russia had to escape its economic and political crisis. Most of all, they stressed that it provided a real guarantee of human rights and freedoms, such as the right to private property, for the first time in Russia's history.[36] The fact that it gave Russia a strong president was good, they argued, because "in today's conditions a president without sweeping powers is not really needed."[37] Others argued that although the constitution might not be perfect, Russia cannot survive without one; thus Russians must vote for this one and amend it later.[38] Some rather powerful local politicians supported the document, including presidential contender Kadyrov and Union of Entrepreneurs leader Shvetsov.

Most opponents, led by the republic Supreme Soviet itself, focused their attack on the position the draft assigned republics.[39] As opposed to earlier presidential and parliamentary draft constitutions, this one omitted the word *sovereign* when referring to republics, dropped the Federation Treaty from the text, subordinated the latter to the constitution, and made republics equal in rights to regions.[40] This, wrote two prominent republican jurists, "logically completes the transformation of federative Russia into a unitary, totalitarian Russia."[41] Opponents also attacked what they called excessive presidential power in the draft, whereby, among other things, the president has the power to declare a state of emergency, appoints key government officials, and can dissolve the parliament merely by nominating an unacceptable prime ministerial candidate three times.[42] Others still disagreed with the approval process, which did not give people enough time to consider the document and which could have meant that 25 percent of the population determined how the remaining 75 percent lived.[43] A few even criticized the part on human rights, saying it really only defended the rights of "speculators" and "robbers."[44] Many suggested it was naive to believe it would be easy to amend the document later.

The constitution vote tended to push Bashkirs and Tatars together and to split the Russians. At the elite level, local Tatar and Bashkir groups so vehemently opposed the draft that some representatives of both sides issued a joint resolution condemning it and calling for the creation of a confederation between Bashkortostan and neighboring Tatarstan, something the Bashkirs had earlier opposed (although the Bashkirs quickly rejected this).[45] Breaking down the vote shows that only a handful of counties voted for the document when there was not a large Russian population there, suggesting that Bashkirs and Tatars tended to oppose the document.[46] Russians, however, appear to have been ambivalent, because there are several instances in which mainly Russian counties voted against the document. This is in agreement with this book's survey, which shows that Bashkirs and Tatars overwhelmingly disapproved of the draft, and Russians were for it by a margin of 2:1. The most striking pattern, however, is that officially recognized "cities" supported the document, with Ufa nearly 2:1 for it, whereas 71 percent of the largely rural counties voted against.

Overall, therefore, local state power and regional interests won out over central state power and federation-wide interests. Republic leaders' opposition to the document could explain why it fared so poorly in the highly dependent village. The local leadership evidently also prompted republican media to be critical of the draft; but this was somewhat counterbalanced by support from unionist banker Kadyrov and his newspaper as well as the central Russian media.

Winners and Losers: Broadening Our View

Winners most obviously include the individual candidates ending up with the most votes. But they also include the broad interests and policies reflected in the team of politicians that headed to Moscow. In this vein, we can say that winners include representatives of state power, agrarians, ethnic Bashkirs, sovereignty, the oil industry, and conservative economic policies. Losers include private business, Moscow, ethnic Russians, ethnic Tatars, and reformist economic views. One might think even more broadly, questioning whether democracy itself was victorious in Russia in 1993. How democratic was the election? Did it reflect or promote the kinds of coherent political institutions necessary for stable democracy?

Explaining Individual Winners and Losers

Looking at each race in isolation, results are often overdetermined. In most cases, many factors may have decided who won, with state power, campaign tactics, and agrarian interests frequently entering the picture. Looking at all Bashkortostan races at once, however, patterns emerge that enable us to home in on the most important causes, producing a layered explanation.

State power was the most important factor: in every race in which a candidate either occupied a top state post or enjoyed strong backing from the republican leadership, that candidate won. This was true even of the party-list race, where the two parties with the most evident leadership blessings were the only two to perform significantly better than their federal averages. The local leadership's power derived from four main sources, as touched on earlier with regard to specific cases. First, it controlled appointments to key local leadership posts, who in turn had the power to influence (probably indirectly) underlings in favor of a particular campaign. This was most likely important in the more isolated and dependent countryside, where high voter turnout magnified successes, as will be discussed. Second, the state controlled most important local media, a factor more weighty in the presidential and party-list races than the territorial Duma contests. Third, it had great financial resources at its disposal. Fourth, the views of its leadership were on the whole compatible with public opinion as expressed in surveys and earlier votes, although this may reflect local media influence. In any case, view compatibility alone cannot explain why a state-backed candidate defeats a non-state-backed candidate with similar views.

In the races in which there was no state-backed candidate, a certain constellation of other factors tended to produce a winner. This combination was (1) a coherent, previously self-conscious, and sizable base of support grounded on a particular social interest; (2) a well-organized campaign (often including party support) that signaled strongly to this constituency; and (3) rules of the game that allowed a candidate to win with a plurality of the vote. Only two groups followed this pattern, but with dramatic results: the Agrarians and ethnic Russians.

The Agrarians' sweep of the republic's election was dramatic; they captured four of six territorial seats and received by far the greatest percentage of the party-list vote. In every race in which an Agrarian ran, an Agrarian won. In two Duma races and the party-list race, state power also backed agrarians, a fact that is critical to understanding their success. Indeed, in the one case in which a state-backed Agrarian challenged one without that support, Birskii District 3, the state-backed candidate won. But even in the other cases, rural voters turned out in droves behind their candidates, giving them strong pluralities even in highly urban districts.

What is it about the Agrarians that gave them such power while blocs campaigning on other economic interests (such as the industrialists) failed to mobilize much support? For one thing, the Agrarians were particularly well organized at the republic level. They had the services of the Agrarian party's full-time staff, the Agrarian Union, and agroindustrial trade union cadres, each of which had close contact with farm chairs and were able to mount effective campaigns.[47]

The campaign was critical, but it appears critical only insofar as it sent a signal to a previously self-conscious, relatively coherent base of support: farmers. One can find many reasons to think rural voters in Bashkortostan would be a more coherent, yet more easily manipulable, voting force. Rural areas in Russia are often known for their relative lack of information sources. They frequently do not have access to the same television channels as do cities, and their kiosks carry fewer newspapers and journals. This means village residents have a greater tendency to depend on the same sources of information. Their lives are also somewhat more likely than urbanites' to revolve entirely around the same activities, because social organizations are fewer and occupational diversity less. Rural communities are also arguably easier to mobilize electorally than urban ones. For example, farm chairs are often in a position to manipulate what little information comes into the village. Further, because it is easy to determine how a particular collective farm voted, leaders can threaten to deny it key resources if its votes do not come out right. One might also dare to cite rural traditions of deference, the odd peasant uprising notwithstanding. As implied by Mancur Olson's logic, it is also generally easier to mobilize small, compact communities for collective action than large, dispersed ones, a factor that helps explain high rural voter turnout.[48]

Only one other group appears to have followed this general constituency-signaling pattern of electoral success, albeit in a much more limited way: ethnic Russians. Although Arinin was the only candidate in the territorial Duma races to make ethnic Russian symbolism an obvious part of his campaign, it was effective for him. The keys to his success were a vigorous grassroots campaign effort and significant name recognition; but these were primarily important insofar as they sent strong signals to a relatively coherent preexisting constituency: restive Russians. Arinin's newspaper, *Otechestvo*, the title of which translates as "Fatherland," enjoyed wide circulation and had regularly presented the ethnic Russian cause in the republic. Many Russians favored the Bashkortostan sovereignty drive, but many did not and this created a resentment that evidence suggests began to boil over among Russians in the year leading up to the election. Arguably, Zhirinovskii's strong showing reflected just this trend. The final element in his victory, of course, was the plurality rule. He ran on issues with a limited electoral appeal, but all he needed was a quarter of the vote. Other ethnic groups do not seem to have been conducive to this pattern of mobilization, although this is not completely clear. Overall, it appears that Rakhimov and the ethnically Russian prime minister Kopsov struck an informal deal with Arinin whereby Rakhimov would tolerate Arinin's ethnic signaling to win a seat in the Duma so long as he did not mobilize the Russian community against Rakhimov and Kopsov in the presidential and Federation Council races.

Together, state power and the constituency-signaling pattern of campaigning can explain the outcome in every Bashkortostan race except one. In Baimakskii District 2, voters had two Agrarians to choose from, neither strongly state-backed. The result, as described previously, depended on ethnicity. Bashkirs voted for the Bashkir Agrarian; Slavs voted for the Slavic Agrarian. To complete the explanation, therefore, we add ethnicity as a secondary factor.

The explanation complete, one can step back and consider the critical role of campaigning in Bashkortostan. Campaigns were not very effective in creating new constituencies, but appeared to be decisive in signaling to preexisting ones. Indeed, many losing candidates had very creative, well-organized, and well-financed campaigns, including such entrepreneurs as Kadyrov, Nuridzhanov, Akhiyarov, and Shvetsov, as well as lawyer-entrepreneur Dmitriyev and political scientist Lavrentiyev. These candidates made mostly broad policy appeals as opposed to those aimed at particular social interests, and this rarely produced a victory in the single-mandate districts. Given informational chaos and a lack of time to sort it all out, people simply looked for candidates who were saying familiar things and who could present themselves as credible defenders of an interest they already identified with. Thus a candidate bearing the stamp of the Agrarian party or Agrarian Union, as well as perhaps that of the farm chair or republic leader, tended to stand out. Similarly, Arinin's prior reputation as a staunch defender of Russian interests was critical in such a situation. Money and television time mattered little if it did not aim at a particular electoral group.

Winners and Losers in the Broader Sense

Which interests came out ahead in the 1993 election in Bashkortostan? The state itself clearly did, as top officials won the republic presidency, both Federation Council seats, and two territorial Duma seats, and their preferences also prevailed in the party-list and constitutional votes. Particularist republic interests were also victorious, as candidates supporting the sovereignty drive won most races. Bashkirs also did well, capturing five of eight territorial mandates. Agrarians won all five races they contested, and the new republic delegation was overwhelmingly conservative. Finally, oil interests also seem to have come out well, as the winners of the presidential and Federation Council races, as well as one Duma race, were all former oil men.

Losers most dramatically included private enterprise; at least one entrepreneur contested each local race but not one of them won a seat. Perhaps related to this is the fact that the few reformist candidates also lost decisively, the one exception being PRES's Arinin. Moscow also lost out, as local voters rejected the draft constitution and elected strong proponents of the republic's sovereignty drive, with the major exception again being Arinin. Ethnic Russians captured fewer seats (two of eight) than their share of the population would have predicted (39 percent). Tatars won only a single seat despite making up 28 percent of the population, marking a significant departure from 1990 when Tatars won eleven of twenty-seven congressional mandates.

Our layered explanation cannot fully account for such broad patterns of results. We must ask why the state itself might push conservative views and sovereignty, for example. One answer might be that this is simply what state leaders happen to have wanted. But it seems too unlikely that coercion or coincidence in today's Russia could make so many candidates agree on sovereignty and economic conservatism. Indeed, it was hard to tell the substance of many candidate platforms apart, especially based on the information appearing in the press. The pattern seems to reflect long-standing public opinion in the region or historical legacy. Indeed, the people of this republic have consistently supported the sovereignty drive and opposed Yeltsin's radical reforms. Although this broad opinion trend cannot explain why any one of the many candidates espousing similar views won a particular race, it can explain why the winning candidates almost all ended up in agreement.

None of these explanations, however, account for why Bashkirs enjoyed such success at the expense of Tatars and Russians. With the major exception of the presidential race, I encountered no complaints that any candidates were experiencing barriers to participation based on ethnicity. State power may have had an indirect impact, however; if most state appointees were Bashkirs, state officials running for office would be more likely both to win and to be Bashkir. Although both state-backed Duma victors were indeed Bashkirs, there are many other races to be explained. One possibility is that the result was pure chance. A more likely explanation would note the fact that most Bashkirs are rural and that Bashkirs make up a plurality (35 percent) of the republic's rural population, according to 1989 census data.[49] To the extent that Agrarians are expected to do well, one might also expect Bashkirs to be strongly represented. A further explanation would be that Bashkirs feel a particularly strong sense of efficacy in the republic, resulting from the facts that the republic is named after them, that their leader is himself Bashkir, and that the perestroika-era national revival movement would have reinforced such feelings. It also might reflect a view that Bashkirs *should* be the representatives of Bashkortostan, because other groups are collectively represented elsewhere. But survey data show that Bashkirs were actually more likely *not* to be interested in the federal election than were other groups, although this could simply reflect complacency in knowing that their interests would be well represented. Most likely, therefore, Bashkirs scored such stunning successes because they occupied many top republic posts, had a sense of political efficacy that other groups lacked, and were a plurality in critically important rural areas on which the state focused electoral pressure. This is consistent with the argument about "subtle civic sovereignization" posited earlier, whereby Bashkir policymakers could be expected to consolidate their group's leadership position in the republic, but quietly, in ways that do not involve overt ethnic discrimination.

The Consolidation of Democracy

Was "democracy" a winner in Bashkortostan? We must consider first of all whether the election was actually democratic. If one takes *democracy* to refer simply to the degree of competition and participation in political life,[50] then the federal elections in Bashkortostan would seem to have been quite democratic. Candidates who could organize a core team of supporters were generally able to put their names on the ballot and campaign. The candidates reflected a wide range of social interests, and voter turnout was reasonably high in the republic. The presidential race, however, did not allow for much competition, because many qualified contenders could not meet very severe nomination requirements, including language restrictions.

If one takes a more demanding definition of *democracy,* considering fairness and the means at the disposal of different candidates to win votes, one might draw a more negative conclusion. State officials had a tremendous advantage in state-run media, which should ideally be neutral because they are financed by the population as a whole. State officials also evidently had great influence over local officials in a good position to deliver the vote (especially in rural areas). The absence of spending limits also created an advantage for those with greater resources, although this does not appear to have helped entrepreneurs much. On the whole, however, candidates had the opportunity to raise money, voice their positions, and take their message to the grassroots. Although many of the races could certainly have been more fair, they were not far out of line with what would normally be expected in a young democracy.

Did this election reflect or help build the kind of institutions that would provide for a stable democracy in the future, most critically political parties? Parties serve numerous important functions in a democracy, such as simplifying the choices voters face, grooming leaders, and structuring debate. For democracy to be consolidated, its parties will need to be well-structured and institutionalized, fairly coherent in ideology, and clearly differentiated from other parties. Did the 1993 election in Bashkortostan reflect these features? The answer is: only partially.

First, federal parties had strikingly weak presences in Bashkortostan. They nominated only nine of thirty-eight district-based Duma candidates, and only two of these managed to win. Further, in one of these cases the candidate (Arinin) helped the party more than the party helped the candidate, and only the Agrarian party appeared to be a significant asset to its candidates. Leading republican politicians such as Rakhimov and Kadyrov seemed to believe that they, as representatives of all the people, should be above parties. In addition, apart from the activity of nominees, local campaigning on the part of federal blocs was nearly invisible.

Second, local blocs and candidate alliances had little connection to federal blocs. Initially, there were ethnic organizations such as the Tatar Social Center, *Rus',* and the Bashkir People's Party. Although Tatar organizations sometimes had links to Tatarstan, the Bashkir ones tended to be purely local. *Rus'* was also based locally, but its leader (Arinin) ran with PRES. Kadyrov's network of energetic supporters was also primarily local; he apparently enjoyed close relations with the Democratic Party of Russia, but he had refused to join it. The party of power—in other words, state officials—had also steered clear of party affiliation. Shvetsov's network of entrepreneurs and scholars was also independent. Despite disparate views on key issues such as sovereignty, Rakhimov, Arinin, and Shvetsov did end up on the same side in key races. All claimed or demonstrated links to Sergei Shakhrai and his PRES, however, a factor that may have kept these odd bedfellows together. On the whole, there was little integration between federal and local political organizations. If one moves beyond parties to the realm of political alliances, pragmatism and personal connections would seem to have been more important than ideology. Thus antisovereignty Russian organizations such as *Rus'* failed to endorse Kadyrov's bid for the presidency and relatively prosovereignty Tatars supported it, even though sovereignty was the main issue of contention.

Third, most party lines were fairly coherent as they stretched to the local level, at least to the extent there was a local party to have a line. The Agrarian party was one of the most active local parties, and it consistently nominated and endorsed economically conservative Agrarians. Civic Union, Russia's Future–New Names, and Yabloko also nominated candidates consistent with the party's platform. PRES, however, was a different story. It nominated both sovereignty-seekers and unionists, economic centrists and free marketeers, a fact that foreshadowed the party's virtual collapse in the run-up to the 1995 Duma elections.

This analysis suggests several conclusions about the state of democratization in Bashkortostan in 1993. The federal election was reasonably democratic for a young democracy. With a few prominent exceptions, electoral blocs were coherent ideologically and their local representatives were in line with their federal counterparts. On the other hand, federal parties and blocs were nearly nonexistent in Bashkortostan and had very few links to the most prominent republican political organizations. Further, the race for the republic presidency was far from being perfectly free and fair. With the benefit of hindsight, it is clear that the 1993 election in Bashkortostan represented a failed attempt to engineer a "founding election." It merely represented the latest in a series of opportunities for the republic to demonstrate its economic conservatism and did not provide a lasting institutional framework for this self-expression. Instead, local power struggles dominated the scene, and only the Bashkir republic leadership demonstrated any staying power.

Conclusion

The 1993 election in Bashkortostan illustrates that the ethnic composition and power of the state can powerfully affect the success of democratization efforts. The politicking we find in Bashkortostan strongly resembles that which we would expect to find where representatives of a small minority group occupy the top posts of a strong state apparatus. The Bashkir leader has pursued sovereignty for his republic, but has defined it essentially in civic rather than ethnic terms and has sought to cooperate with the Russian federation. At the same time, he has sought to reinforce his own group's grip on power, but in subtle ways that would not provoke other groups into active opposition. He has thus sought to depoliticize ethnicity in Bashkortostan, creating alliances with key members of other ethnic groups in order to maintain power.

Bashkir ethnic activism alone did indeed prove to be a losing strategy, and the local leadership did not attempt it. In the one district in which it was clearly tried, the very most Bashkir of districts, the strategy failed; although having decided to vote for an Agrarian, voters chose a Bashkir Agrarian over a Slavic one. Nor was there evidence that Rakhimov's team pursued a "Turkic Alliance" against the Russian Federation and Russians. The leader of the Tatar Social Center bitterly opposed Rakhimov. But Tatar voters tended to support Rakhimov and his sovereignty policy anyway, as well as to oppose the draft constitution, suggesting that Rakhimov did not need to woo Tatars' self-proclaimed representatives. If anything, the Bashkir elites were more interested in courting the Russians. The leader of the region's most prominent Russian rights organization (Arinin) favored the Bashkir leader of the sovereignty drive in his presidential bid, as did the Russian Shvetsov. Further, both Bashkir and Russian activists were united on PRES's party list, and Rakhimov's own number two man was a Russian (Kopsov). Thus even most counties with a Russian majority chose Rakhimov for the presidency and were split on the constitution. Ethnicity was likely important in Zhirinovskii's vote, however, with the non-Russian population sharply reducing his party's vote totals in the republic. This did not appear to translate into ethnic voting in other races, however. The one possible exception is Arinin's victory in Kalininskii District 5, but the effects of his campaign were successfully localized (the result of a Rakhimov-Kopsov-Arinin arrangement) and did not affect the struggle for power over the republic as a whole.

Thus although many theorists have warned of the dangers of democratization in multiethnic societies, the 1993 election in Bashkortostan adds weight to the argument that institutions matter, that ethnicity is more likely to be defused as a political weapon during democratization when no one group makes up a voting majority, and when the group in charge controls a state strong enough to forge cross-group alliances yet not so strong as to impose its will. Since 1993 Bashkortostan has continued in its ethnic moderation. Although Rakhimov replaced his ethnic Russian prime minister with a

Bashkir in 1994 after a corruption scandal, he also signed a new bilateral treaty with Moscow reinforcing his ties to the federation.

Notes

1. Dankwart A. Rustow, "Transitions to Democracy: Toward a Dynamic Model," *Comparative Politics*, vol. 2, no. 3 (April 1970), pp. 337–63; Rupert Emerson, *From Empire to Nation: The Rise of Self-Assertion of Asian and African Peoples* (Harvard University Press, 1960); Timothy M. Frye, "Ethnicity, Sovereignty and Transitions from Non-Democratic Rule," *Journal of International Affairs*, vol. 45, no. 2 (Winter 1992), pp. 599–623.

2. Donald J. Horowitz, "Comparing Democratic Systems," in Larry Diamond and Marc F. Plattner. eds., *The Global Resurgence of Democracy* (Johns Hopkins University Press, 1993), pp.127–33; Donald J. Horowitz, *A Democratic South Africa? Constitutional Engineering in a Divided Society* (University of California Press, 1991); Arend Lijphart, "Constitutional Choices for New Democracies," in Diamond and Plattner, *Global Resurgence of Democracy*, pp. 146–58; Juan J. Linz and Alfred Stepan, "Political Identities and Electoral Sequences: Spain, the Soviet Union, and Yugoslavia," *Daedalus*, vol. 121, no. 2 (Spring 1992), pp. 123–60.

3. Strengthening Democratic Institutions Project (SDI), Report on Ethnic Conflict in the Russian Federation and Transcaucasia (Harvard University, John F. Kennedy School of Government, 1993), p. 10.

4. Television company Bashkortostan, program "Nedel'ya," December 4, 1993.

5. Rafis Kadyrov, *Ekonomika i My*, no. 50 (December 4–7, 1993), p. 4.

6. Anvar Akhmadeyev, *Izvestiya Bashkortostana*, November 26, 1993, p. 2.

7. Tax data are from Mark Nagel of Harvard's Government Department and Law School.

8. *Delovoi Ural*, no. 45, November 17–23, 1993, 1.

9. *Sovetskaya Bashkiriya*, December 8, 1993, p. 1.

10. *Sel'skaya zhizn'*, reprinted in *Ekonomika i My*, no. 51, December 8–10, 1993, p. 13.

11. Interview with Aleksandra Bryantseva, *Ekonomika i My* editor, December 12, 1993.

12. Bashkortostan Central Election Commission, *Sovetskaya Bashkiriya*, November 27, 1993, p. 1.

13. *Izvestiya Bashkortostana*, November 19, 1993, p. 2; *Sovetskaya Bashkiriya*, November 30, 1993, p. 1; *Sovetskaya Bashkiriya*, November 26, 1993, p. 1; *Izvestiya Bashkortostana*, December 4, 1993, p. 1.

14. *Vechernyaya Ufa*, November 24, 1993, p. 2.

15. Interview with Aleksandr Arinin, November 30, 1993.

16. *Vechernyaya Ufa*, December 8, 1993, p. 2.

17. *Ekonomika i My*, no. 50, December 4–7, 1993, p. 2; *Vechernyaya Ufa*, December 8, 1993, p. 2.

18. *Vechernyaya Ufa*, November 30, 1993, p. 1; *Ekonomika i My*, no. 48 (November 20–26, 1993), p. 5; *Ekonomika i My*, no. 51, December 8–10, 1993, p. 6.

19. Interview with Fanil' Kudakayev, president of the Teleradio company Bashkortostan, December 16, 1993.

20. *Sovetskaya Bashkiriya*, December 7, 1993, p. 1.

21. For example, *Izvestiya*, *Rossiiskaya gazeta*, and *Trud*, according to *Izvestiya Bashkortostana*, December 8, 1993, p. 1.

22. "Vesti," Russian Federation Television, channel 2, November 25, 1993. The attacks on Kadyrov and his bank were printed in *Vechernaya Ufa*, November 18, 1993, p. 1, and were also carried on local television programs. Kadyrov began the controversy by attacking two Bashkortostan banks in interviews on Russian Television and Moscow-based radio.

23. Interview with Igor' Rabinovich, political advisor to Nikolai Shvetsov, December 4, 1993.

24. Measured for the constitution and presidential votes, which is in all likelihood roughly similar.

25. *Sovetskaya Bashkiriya*, November 30, 1993, p. 1.

26. *Izvestiya Bashkortostana*, December 4, 1993, p. 1.

27. *Sovetskaya Bashkiriya*, December 10, 1993, p. 2.

28. The lack of available data made it difficult to calculate the ethnic composition of Bashkortostan's six election districts. Figures are therefore estimates based on population figures by raion from the Russian Federation's Goskomstat and reports from the republican Statistical Administration, 1993, and ethnic distribution figures by raion from the 1989 census. Unfortunately, the ethnic distribution of Ufa is not broken down into its component raions and some raions and cities have changed categories or borders between those years, making possible only rough calculations.

29. Interview with Gazim Shafikov, November 26, 1993; Round table number two for bloc candidates, Bashkortostan TV.

30. For example, see *Sovetskaya Bashkiriya*, December 7, 1993, p. 2.

31. *Sovetskaya Bashkiriya*, December 8, 1993, p. 2.

32. *Otechestvo*, no. 37, December 8, 1993, p. 1.

33. Interview with Aleksandr Arinin, November 30, 1993.

34. Interviews with Arinin and other observers who knew Arinin, including political scientist Sergei Lavrentiyev, December 15, 1993.

35. Interview with Rais Asayev, December 3, 1993.

36. R. Tropinin. "Ya progolosuyu za konstitutsiyu," *Otechestvo*, no. 37, December 8, 1993, p. 2.

37. Pyotr Tryaskin, *Sovetskaya Bashkiriya*, December 8, 1993, p. 3.

38. V. Pakutin, *Vechernyaya Ufa*, December 9, 1993, p. 2.

39. *Sovetskaya Bashkiriya*, November 30, 1993, p. 1.

40. *Nezavisimaya gazeta*, November 4, 1993, p. 1, and November 5, 1993, p. 1.

41. Zufar Yenikeyev and Mikhail Bugera, *Vechernyaya Ufa*, December 8, 1993, p. 2.

42. Rafik Gibadatov, *Izvestiya Bashkortostana*, December 10, 1993, p. 3.

43. Rais Tuzmukhametov, *Izvestiya Bashkortostana*, December 2, 1993, p. 2.

44. *Sovetskaya Bashkiriya*, December 10, 1993, p. 3.

45. *Izvestiya Bashkortostana*, November 25, 1993, p. 1.

46. A point made in the untitled anonymous report "12 Dekabrya v Bashkorto-stanye" obtained in 1994.

47. *Izvestiya Bashkortostana*, November 30, 1993, p. 1

48. Mancur Olson, *The Logic of Collective Action: Public Goods and the Theory of Groups* (Harvard University Press, 1965), pp. 22–36.

49. Goskomstat RSFSR, *Natsional'nyy Sostav Naseleniya RSFSR* (Moscow: Respublikanskiy informatsionno-izdatel'skiy tsentr, 1990) p. 133.

50. In other words, Robert Dahl's "polyarchy." Robert A. Dahl, *Polyarchy: Participation and Opposition* (Yale University Press, 1971).

CHAPTER TWENTY

Tatarstan

Elite Bargaining and Ethnic Separatism

Pauline Jones Luong

THE DECEMBER 1993 electoral experience in Tatarstan both sets this ethnic republic apart from the other regions discussed in this volume and places it center stage. Tatarstan presents the only case in this volume in which the election to the Federal Assembly effectively failed to take place—that is, the national parliamentary election in the Tatar Republic was invalidated by insufficient voter turnout, just over 13 percent and well below the required 25 percent.[1] At the same time, Tatarstan is perhaps the most dramatic illustration of the gap between the intentions of the Moscow elite in engineering a founding election in December 1993 and the actual outcomes that this election produced. In other words, the December 1993 election was not only about consolidating democracy in Russia but also fundamentally concerned the future integrity of the Russian Federation itself. President Boris Yeltsin's own emphasis on garnering support for the constitution rather than on the new parliament preceding the election is a clear indicator that, as much as Yeltsin and the Moscow elite wanted to solidify their own roles in a democratic Russia, they wanted at least as much, if not more, to solidify the Russian Federation. Instead, the December 1993 election in Tatarstan invoked existing separatist tendencies among the re-

I wish to thank all of those individuals in Tatarstan who were interviewed or provided information for their assistance with this chapter. None of these individuals, however, are accountable for the analysis presented.

Tatarstan

public's ethnic Tatars and hence gave the republic's leaders a crucial bargaining chip with which to challenge Moscow's definition of federalism.

The uniqueness of Tatarstan's electoral outcome can be explained, in short, by the failure of elites at both the national (or federal) and regional level to bargain and reach a consensus on the nature of Tatarstan's relationship with the Russian Federation. The lack of elite consensus regarding such a fundamental issue enabled Tatarstan's president, Mintimer Shaimiyev, to exploit the increasing tensions between Tatar separatists and Russian profederation forces within the republic. In following this strategy, his intent was clearly not to cause ethnic civil war in his republic but to use the election to illustrate the strength of nationalist sentiment in Tatarstan to increase his leverage vis-à-vis Moscow and force Yeltsin to the bargaining table. Although elite consensus at the federal level was achieved in February 1994 when Yeltsin and Shaymiyev signed a mutually acceptable agreement, the repeat elections held in March 1994 clearly indicate that there remained a lack of elite consensus within Tatarstan itself on its status vis-à-vis Russia. As a result, ethnic divisions continue to shape politics in this republic, and hence impede Tatarstan's further democratization.

Explaining the Outcome: Failure of Elites to Bargain and National Disunity

As the recent wealth of literature on democratic consolidation emphasizes, a crucial component of democratic consolidation in any state undergoing democratic transition is elite bargaining and consensus.[2] In short, this means that all relevant actors in the political process must negotiate and ultimately agree on a set of rules that will guide the development of democratic institutions, most important of which are those rules that govern elections.[3]

Similarly, theories of federalism have long emphasized the centrality of the bargaining process "between prospective national leaders and officials of constituent governments" to reaching a mutually satisfactory and hence lasting federal arrangement.[4] Whatever the impetus behind federal arrangements, their initial foundation depends on establishing a contract (often in the form of a constitution) between potential members of the proposed federalist structure.[5] Their fate, moreover, also rests on the nature of this bargain; that is, if and when the initial agreement is invalidated or considered to be no longer useful by one or more party (perhaps by changes in geography, economic conditions, foreign relations, etc.) the propensity for federalism to continue is minimal.[6] Therefore, above all else, for two or more territorial bodies to establish and maintain a federal system, the political situation must be conducive to ongoing bargaining. First of all, as William H. Riker explains, because striking a bargain is the essence of a federal arrangement, then "all parties [must be] willing to make them."[7] This undoubtedly necessitates a recognition on both sides of the mutually beneficial outcome from negotiating a viable federal contract.[8] Second, the two sides must have the authority and confidence to strike a bargain. In other words, both parties are aware that unless the outcome of their negotiations (in other words, the federal arrangement) receives support from their respective constituencies, they will incur serious domestic difficulties later. Thus, where nationalist aspirations exist that object to federalism, successful bargaining is especially difficult to achieve.

Elite consensus is a particularly crucial component of successful democratization in multiethnic states. Dankwart A. Rustow, for example, argues that the primary necessity in a new democracy is national unity. Although this does not require a societal consensus on all social, political, and economic questions, it does mean that "the vast majority of citizens in a democracy-to-be must have no doubt or mental reservations as to which political community they belong."[9] Nor does this necessarily demand a homogeneous population, though such subconsciously accepted national identity is less likely to be present and more difficult to achieve in communities that are strongly divided along ethnic lines. In short, the political struggle that accompanies the transition to democracy has to take place between individuals or groups within an established nation rather than over the definition of the nation itself. Likewise, unless the nation is defined to the satisfaction of all citizens, the rules governing the emergent democracy cannot be agreed on and maintained because groups with competing visions of "the nation" will be reluctant to establish a unitary political system under which each receives equal representation.

In order to fully appreciate the underlying causes of failed bargaining and national disunity, however, it is also necessary to understand the institutional structure within which it failed to take place. In other words, elite negotiations do not take place in a vacuum but within the larger social, economic, and political context. Regarding the case at hand, the failure of bargaining between Moscow and Tatarstan's elites and among elites within Tatarstan itself is not a wholly recent phenomenon but should instead be understood as part of the Soviet institutional legacy and its influence on the development of post-Soviet politics.

Prelude to the December 1993 Election: Soviet Legacies and Post-Soviet Politics

Tatarstan's unique demographic, economic, and political profile leading up to the December 1993 elections promotes three key characteristics in post-Soviet Tatarstan, each of which is crucial for understanding the electoral outcome. First, the Tatar Republic's demographic composition and economic potential inherited from Soviet administrative-territorial divisions makes ethnic separatism both a salient issue and viable option in the post-Soviet period. Second, Tatar elites have consistently attempted, and failed, to alter the status of their titular republic as an autonomous republic of Russia within the Soviet Union; hence the question of Tatarstan's appropriate political status remains unresolved within the Russian Federation. Third, since the fall of the USSR, national elections and referendums held in Tatarstan have served as symbols of this republic's struggle to redefine its relationship with Moscow and, as a result, have polarized ethnic divisions in the republic into profederation and separatist forces.

The Salience of Ethnic Separatism as an Issue and Option

What is today known as the Tatar Republic was established as the Tatar Autonomous Soviet Socialist Republic (ASSR) on May 27, 1920, by a joint decree of the Central Executive Committees of the Party and of the Soviet of People's Commissars. Its official boundaries geographically excluded nearly 75 percent of Volga Tatars from membership in the new republic, thus squelching the voiced aspirations of Tatar nationalists who had actively participated in the Bolshevik Revolution for a pan-Turkic state encompassing the larger area of the Middle Volga region.[10] As a result, Tatars have never enjoyed more than a slight numerical advantage over other ethnic groups in their own titular autonomous republic, particularly Russians. Since 1926, for example, Tatars have constituted between 44 and 49 percent of the republic's total population, whereas Russians have made up between 42 and 43 percent.[11] Even today, despite a fairly constant rise in birthrates, Tatars still make up only 48.5 percent of the republic's total population; the remainder is made up of Russians (43.3 percent), Chuvash

(3.7 percent), Ukrainians (0.9 percent), and 103 other minor ethnic groups.[12]

One only needs to look to neighboring Bashkortostan to understand the effect of this demographic situation. Whereas the fact that no one group comes close to constituting a majority has encouraged cooperation and coalition-building among ethnic groups in the Bashkir Republic, the near-even split between Tatars and Russians in the republic has historically fueled ethnic competition. This became clear during the "loosening" of restrictions on public speech and the media under Gorbachev, when both Russians and Tatars began to articulate their long-standing grievances in the late-1980s. The former claimed, for example, that Tatars dominated the nomenklatura and generally received a disproportionate share of available jobs and social services,[13] while the latter complained that their national republic was forcibly Russified.[14]

Following the break-up of the Soviet Union, demographic divisions translated directly into political ones—that is, ethnic Tatars and Russians became increasingly divided on the question of Tatarstan's status with regard to the Russian Federation. In fact, the first unofficial sociopolitical organizations formed in 1988, the People's Front of Kazan and the Tatar Social Center were (and remain) divided precisely along these lines; the former is profederation and primarily composed of Russians, while the latter is a proseparatist group with virtually exclusive Tatar membership.[15] Other groups that have formed since then are continuing this trend.

Tatarstan's role in the Soviet economy has also served to fuel ethnic separatism. First, it is a source of internal animosity. Tatars have historically resented the fact that the most valuable natural resource (oil) and finished industrial products of their titular republic are used according to Moscow's discretion. Moreover, their ability to exploit their own economic potential is greatly constrained by structural realities. For example, the then Soviet and now Russian government control the oil pipelines that run through the republic, making it possible for Moscow to prevent Tatarstan from exporting its own oil and securing the refined-oil products it needs from neighboring Bashkortostan. Thus, the question of how much oil the republic must produce is still decided outside the republic. Even the industrial sector cannot survive on its own, because the republic's manufacturing plants depend on raw materials from other parts of the Russian Federation.

At the same time, Tatarstan's economic assets provide it with the potential to prosper outside of the Russian Federation. Although both its volume of oil production has declined since 1975 (from 104.6 million metric tons in

1975 to 30.2 in 1992) and its share of total Russian Federation oil output dropped to 7.67 percent in 1993, Tatarstan retains many unexploited oil reserves and is still the second largest oil producer in the former USSR (after Tyumen' oblast in West Siberia).[16] Nor is oil the largest or only potentially profitable sector of the republic's economy; machine building and metal working, such as truck manufacturing in Naberezhniye Chelny and industrial-equipment production in Kazan, make up the bulk of the republic's total output (39.8 percent as of 1985) and employ more than 50 percent of its workforce.[17] The chemical industry, with its main plants in Kazan and Nizhnekamsk, also constitutes a significant portion (13.2 percent) of Tatarstan's total output.[18] Today, Tatarstan is one of the twenty-five most industrialized areas of the Russian Federation, and one of the few administrative divisions in which industrial growth actually increased in 1993.[19]

The Unresolved Question of Tatarstan's Political-Administrative Status

In large part to remedy their political and economic situation under Soviet rule, the leaders of Tatarstan have on several occasions sought to change their republic's administrative and hence political status from an autonomous republic to a Union republic, in which they would enjoy the full benefits of *korenizatsiya* (nativization) and a greater degree of control over the local economy. Their first attempt dates back to the formation of the Soviet Union in 1922 when the Tatars asserted their right as the fifth largest ethnic group in the USSR to enjoy the same status and hence privileges of a Union republic. They made a second attempt at changing their status from an autonomous to a Union republic when the Soviet Union drafted a new constitution in 1936.[20] A third, but by no means final, attempt to become a Union republic in 1989 was made during the debate at the Nationalities Plenum.[21] None of these attempts succeeded in formally redefining the republic's relationship with the center.

Even after the Soviet Union began to disintegrate in mid-1991, Russia and Tatarstan were still unable to reach a mutually acceptable agreement on the terms of their relationship. In May 1991 Tatarstan's leaders agreed to sign the Union Treaty only in the capacity of a full member of the USSR, a demand that then chair of the Supreme Soviet Mintimer Shaimiyev believed was consistent with the republic's own declaration of sovereignty in August 1990.[22] Russia disregarded Tatarstan's demand for equal membership in the Commonwealth of Independent States (CIS) and, while seeking its own sovereignty, attempted to set severe and arbitrary limits on Tatarstan's.[23] Immediately before the December 1993 parliamentary elections, a possible opportunity for agreement was presented by the Russian Federation treaty. Yet both sides refused to make the necessary concessions to strike a bargain. Rather, they remained obstinate such that no consensus could be reached; Kazan demanded nothing less than an asymmetrical federation in which the republics have greater autonomy and a higher status than the other territorial units, while Moscow insisted on treating each of its constituent parts as equals.

The Role of Elections and Referendums in the Post-Soviet Period

Tatarstan's political elite has effectively used national elections and referendums held since the fall of the USSR as key symbols of their dissatisfaction with their republic's current status within the Russian Federation and weapons in their efforts to renegotiate the republic's status. In short, President Shaimiyev has manipulated both the conduction of these elections and their outcomes to magnify the strength of Tatar nationalists' drive for complete succession as a means of increasing Tatarstan's bargaining leverage with Moscow. Perspectives on Tatarstan's independence are actually better represented on a continuum; between Russian groups who support Moscow's predominance in the republic's affairs and Tatar groups who demand complete secession, there are those who advocate autonomy in varying degrees. Yet the overwhelming effect has been the polarization of sociopolitical forces in the republic into profederation versus separatist, which are essentially divided along ethnic lines.

This is perhaps best illustrated by the June 1991 election for Russia's president. Just two weeks after the Tatarstan government agreed to take part in this election, the republic's Supreme Soviet announced that Tatarstan would not officially hold elections, but it recognized "the right of citizens of Tatarstan to vote in the elections for the head of Russia on their own."[24] Such a radical change in the decision of the leadership was interpreted as an endorsement for the Tatar nationalists' position to boycott this election on the grounds that it would mean holding "elections in Tatarstan for President of the former mother country," and of their demand for full independence from the Russian Federation.[25] Soon after, the various Tatar social and political organizations, with the Tatar Social Center as their organizational leader, began launching an intense struggle for Tatarstan's complete withdrawal from Russia. Large, public rallies, serving both as an arena for articulating nationalist ambitions and promoting ethnic fears, became a recurring phenomenon.[26] At one such rally, Tatar national groups made it clear that those who voted for the Russian Federation president (namely, Russians) were not only anti-Tatarstan, but anti-Tatar.[27] Meanwhile, the number of primarily Russian organizations espousing support for the territorial integrity of Russia increased rapidly in mid- to late 1991 and began responding to their Tatar counterparts with similar tactics.[28] One of their primary aims was to display popular support for the election specifically and the Russian Federation more broadly.[29] It is not surprising that Russians made up the vast majority of those who chose to participate in the 1991 Russian presidential elections.[30]

It is hardly a coincidence that the Tatarstan government decided to hold presidential elections for the republic during the same month and year (June 1991) in which the elections for president of the Russian Federation were taking place, even though they were not officially participating in the latter.[31] In fact, the expressed purpose of this was to redirect the focus of Tatarstan's population and politicians toward internal (i.e., the republic's) rather than external (i.e., Russia's) affairs. More important, this political move was designed to take Tatarstan's declaration of sovereignty to its logical conclusion—that is, the creation of a head of state—and thus foil Moscow's intention to elect a president of the Russian Federation as a sign of the country's unity under a single, democratically elected leader.[32]

The political elite followed a similar strategy with the March 21, 1992, referendum on Tatarstan's sovereignty and the April 25, 1993, Russian Federation referendum. First of all, the referendums were implicitly and explicitly presented as a demonstration of support within the republic for Tatarstan's sovereignty and the integrity of the Russian Federation, respectively.[33] Regarding the March 1992 referendum, answering anything but "yes" to Tatarstan's sovereignty was also portrayed as an act against both Tatarstan and the Tatar people.[34] Moreover, the voting patterns seemed to confirm this ethnic split across the population of Tatarstan on the issue of sovereignty, with the vast majority of Tatars endorsing the referendum while most of the Russian population either failed to participate or contested the results.[35] Individual and group endorsements of the April 1993 referendum were not so much based on a pro-Yeltsin stance as they were on a pro-Russian reaction. For Russians, the negative outcome was a warning sign that nationalist support was much stronger than they had realized, or at least that the Tatarstan government wanted it to appear that way.[36] The Tatar nationalists' campaign against the April 1993 Russian Federation referendum similarly provoked counterdemonstrations by profederation groups. Thus, during the 1993 wave of rallies, some of their spokespersons warned that Tatarstan's independence—that is, a "Tatar Tatarstan"—would only mean greater discrimination against and hardship for the Russian population.[37]

Second, the March 1992 and April 1993 referendums were at the center of the continuing power struggle between Moscow and Kazan. Despite statements to the contrary from Tatarstan's leaders, Moscow interpreted the March 1992 referendum as a blatant attempt at secession.[38] Given the complex and ambiguous wording of the referendum's only question, this interpretation was not unfounded.[39] In fact, it seemed to coincide well with Tatarstan's desire for an elevated status within the Russian Federation, because the threat of secession (whether real or perceived) gave Tatarstan more potential bargaining leverage. The referendum that took place in April of the following year can similarly be viewed as a direct appeal from Moscow to supporters of the federation within Tatarstan, particularly the Russian population, to reverse the republic's trend toward secession before it was too late.[40] Tatarstan's response, therefore, was to discredit Yeltsin by publicly blaming its decision not to participate in the referendum on Russian leaders' unwillingness to sign a separate treaty with the republic.[41]

Election 1993: Ethnic Separatism and Elite Discord

The December 1993 election can best be understood as the culmination of the previously discussed trends in post-Soviet Tatarstan. Separatism had become a contentious issue along ethnic lines within Tatarstan; those who supported the continuation of current relations with Russia were largely Russians, while those who preferred greater autonomy from Russia were almost uniformly Tatars. In fact, according to data from the national election survey, preceding the December election Tatars were three times more likely than Russians to consider Tatarstan their homeland and to completely endorse the right of self-determination and succession for republics within the Russian Federation.[42]

By the end of 1993, there was still no consensus on Tatarstan's political status with regard to the Russian Federation, either among elites at the national level or at the republican level. Tatarstan's leadership continued to press for a bilateral treaty that Moscow was not prepared to sign. Finally, and most important, President Shaimiyev once again viewed a national election as an opportunity to exaggerate the strength of Tatar separatist forces in order to induce an agreement with Moscow on Tatarstan's own terms. Thus, with the "assistance" of the Tatar nationalist groups' skillful campaign against the election and the lackluster campaigns of inexperienced candidates to the State Duma, he successfully transformed the December 1993 parliamentary election into a referendum on Tatarstan's independence from Russia.

In short, the December 1993 election was yet another episode in the symbolic war between Kazan and Moscow over their relationship. From Moscow's standpoint, electing representatives to the State Duma presented the opportunity to form stronger political links between the Russian Federation and Tatarstan. In fact, this intention is reflected in the electoral rules that Moscow designed; specifically, the emphasis on electoral associations (i.e., political parties, blocs, and movements) being national, not regional, and the fact that the 50 percent required to validate the referendum is based on the entire population rather than calculated by region.[43] At the same time, however, Moscow did not make a concerted effort to persuade Tatarstan to officially participate in the elections and referendum or even include the issue of federalism in the draft of the Russian constitution, a point that was made repeatedly by Tatarstan officials.[44] The view of the election from Kazan placed equal, if not greater, significance on its role in solidifying the federation. Thus, the Tatarstan government's decision *not* to officially endorse the elections was intended as a clear sign to Moscow that it would continue to deny *any* formal political ties with the Russian Federation until its demands were met for a separate, bilateral treaty.

Moreover, the government of Tatarstan explicitly portrayed the election to the republic's population as an invasion of Tatarstan's sovereignty and a direct violation of its constitution. In fact, official statements and articles published regularly in the central press regarding the December elections focused on condemning the draft of the Russian Federation's constitution. For example, Indus Tagirov, chief advisor to the president on Republican Nationality Affairs, warned that the elections to the State Duma and constitutional referendum presented a direct threat to Tatarstan's sovereignty (as well as to other parts of the Russian Federation) because they were designed to ensure President Yeltsin's, and hence Moscow's, dictatorship.[45] The chair of the republic's Supreme Soviet also made strong statements against the Russian constitution when asked about the upcoming elections.[46] Although the Tatarstan parliament did not make an official statement of any kind in relation to the elections themselves, at the behest of Shaymiyev himself, it formally condemned the Russian constitution following proceedings with strong nationalistic overtones.[47]

Although the government of Tatarstan officially adopted a position of neutrality toward the election—that is, it did not either officially endorse or oppose the December 1993 election, ostensibly leaving the question of whether or not to vote up to the citizens of Tatarstan—it nonetheless had a great deal of influence on both the conduction of the election and the outcome. First of all, by nature of his esteemed position and broad popularity, Shaimiyev had a significant impact on peoples' attitudes toward the election. Nor was he hesitant to express his opinion. For example, asked at a press conference organized for reporters on November 4 whether or not he would participate in the upcoming elections and referendum, Shaymiyev responded that he would "not vote [on December 12] and [hoped] that the majority of the people of Tatarstan also [would] not vote."[48] In addition, he had publicly declared earlier that "no *genuine* citizen of Tatarstan would participate in a referendum that denied the sovereignty of his republic."[49]

Indeed, candidates, leaders of sociopolitical organizations, newspaper editors, and eligible voters alike agreed that Shaimiyev's statements alone would have the single greatest negative impact on voter turnout, particularly among the Tatar population that elected him.[50] In sum, they argued that by making his own opinion widely known, Shaimiyev expressed to potential voters an official disapproval of the elections and the referendum, which would either provide some direction for those who were confused, validate the convictions of those who, for whatever reason, were opposed to the elections, or simply frighten those who supported the election into not voting. This is entirely consistent with patterns of voting behavior since the fall of the Soviet Union; turnout was very high, particularly in rural areas in which Tatars constitute a majority of the population, when the government of Tatarstan officially endorsed elections and referendums (for example, the election of Tatarstan's president in 1991 and the referendum on Tatarstan's sovereignty in 1992) and much lower when the government took a neutral stance (for example, the all-Russian referendum in April 1993 and the December 1993 election; see figure 20-1).

Second, the Tatarstan government used its *official* neutrality to *unofficially* aid the antielection campaign of the Tatar nationalists. Although these groups clearly would have preferred Shaimiyev to boycott the election, they were satisfied that their demands had, for all intents and purposes, received his endorsement. Thus, at the very least, the decision *not* to

Figure 20-1. *Voting Turnout in Tatarstan, 1991–93*

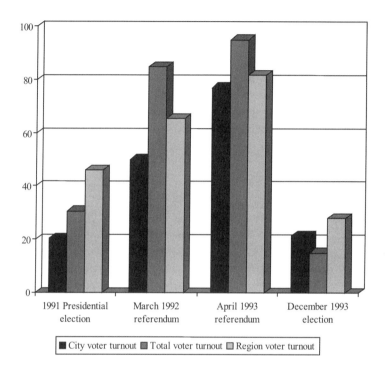

Source: Goskomstat, Kazan, Tatarstan.

formally participate in the December 1993 election fueled their antielection stance.[51] At the most, it gave them complete freedom from governmental interference in the conduction of their antielection campaign activities and increased access to state resources. The Tatar nationalists were therefore able to orchestrate an immediate and steadfast campaign against the election that arguably played the most significant role in defining the very legitimacy of holding the election as the real issue at stake in December.

Tatar nationalist organizations made their opposition known to the government and the public at large almost immediately after Yeltsin's showdown with the Russian Parliament began in September.[52] In fact, several such groups, including the Tatar Social Center, Ittifak, Suverenitet, the youth organization Azatlik (Freedom), and nineteen others were the first to formally boycott the elections, and even organized a special committee to plan and coordinate their antielection campaign.[53] Each of these groups agreed to pursue its most effective method of mobilizing popular support for boycotting the elections. Suverenitet, for example, continued to publish and distribute its own newspapers, which contained appeals to citizens of Tatarstan not to take part in the elections of "neighboring Russia" and articles condemning Yeltsin and the Russian constitution.[54] As its contribution, Iittifak organized public meetings in its main strongholds—the cities and the surrounding rural areas of Naberezhniye Chelny, Nizhnekamsk, and Al' metevsk—"in order to spread [its] message that these [were] the elections of a uncivilized foreign government."[55] Azatlik mobilized antielection sentiment among Tatar youth, particularly in the cities.

Despite some internal differences, all groups opposing the election consistently made the same two arguments against them. The first of these claimed that participation in the elections was immoral because Yeltsin had illegally launched an assault on the Russian Parliament in order to produce elections that would endorse his undesirable economic reforms. The second argument was that merely holding the election and referendum directly violated Tatarstan's declaration of sovereignty, made in August 1990, and its recently adopted constitution.[56] Among Tatar nationalist organizations, the latter argument was clearly the strongest and most passionate of the two.[57] In fact, these particular groups often portrayed casting one's vote as an act of treason against the independent state of Tatarstan, either implicitly or explicitly, in their flyers and newspapers. Some flyers were as tame as, "NO to elections of a neighboring country in the Sovereign State of Tatarstan! Yes to welcoming the Independent State of Tatarstan!" Others reproduced the warning on the front page of Suverenitet's October issue: "Not one real patriot of Independent Tatarstan will go to the elections for the State Duma of the neighboring Russian Federation! Participation in the elections of neighboring Russia is treason against the state interests of our paternal Tatarstan!"[58]

Each of the two arguments was deliberately directed at a particular audience.[59] The first appealed to many Russians and nonnationalists in general who were appalled by the October events in Moscow. In fact, this was the primary objection voiced by the Tatarstan branch of the Communist party, which joined the Tatar nationalists in boycotting the election.[60] The second was aimed largely at the Tatar population. Given that the voter turnout in the Tatar-dominated countryside was essentially nonexistent, the latter argument seems also to have been the most effective.[61] Moreover, survey data for Tatarstan reveal that nationality had the strongest correlation with intention to vote: 51 percent of Tatar respondents versus 29 percent of Russian respondents did *not* intend to vote in the December 1993 election. Similarly, it was found that 50 percent of those respondents with Tatar spouses versus 35 percent of those respondents with Russian spouses did *not* intend to participate in the upcoming election.[62] Most important, the sum effect of these arguments was to effectively define the primary campaign issue as *whether* to vote rather than *for whom* to vote—not for Tatars or Russians per se but for the bulk of Tatarstan's population.

Throughout the December 1993 election, the Tatar nationalists' did not experience any kind of government interference. During the campaign, Tatar nationalist groups essentially had free reign over the countryside. For example, despite numerous complaints of their actively preventing individuals from seeking nomination for office in the region of Zakamiya, Tatar nationalist organizations were allowed to continue their activities. These tactics were in fact quite successful, because the fewest number of registered candidates were in the okrugs that encompassed the Zakamiya region—Naberezhniye Chelny (one), Nizhnekamskii (two), and Al'metevskii (two). These okrugs also experienced the lowest voter turnout in the republic (see table 20-1). Moreover, Tatar nationalist groups actually received greater access to state-owned resources, such as the media. For example, supporters of the antielection campaign were frequently allowed to make statements against the elections on public television stations free of charge. Beyond the campaign itself, Tatar nationalist groups were able to keep voting precincts throughout the countryside from opening on election day with the help of local representatives of the electoral commission and otherwise encourage rural residents not to cast their votes with the assistance of local state leaders.[63]

Third, the Tatarstan government exploited its position of "neutrality" to encumber the campaigning efforts of the candidates running for the State Duma. As mentioned previously, throughout the actual campaign and even before it began, those groups espousing antielection rhetoric and distributing nationalist propaganda were not subjected to the same electoral rules as the candidates, which undoubtedly helped their cause. Meanwhile, candidates to the State Duma were subjected to strict supervision and unreasonable regulatory measures. In short, the government's official "nonparticipation" meant that it could manipulate electoral rules for its own benefit; that is, by enforcing those that were in its best interest and ignoring those that were not. Such behavior can be identified beginning with the nomination process. In early November, for example, Shaimiyev protested the collec-

Table 20-1. *1993 Election Outcome By Okrug (District)*

Okrug	Voter turnout (percent)	Candidate receiving majority	Political affiliation
Al'metevskii	6.5	Shtanin	RiZ[a]/Russia's Choice
Moskovskii	16.7	V.A. Belyayev	Soglasiye/RiZ
Naberezhniye Chelny[b]	n.a.	N/A	N/A
Nizhnekamskii	12	V.D. Kobyakov	RiZ
Privolzhskii	21.2	V.V. Mikhailov	RiZ/Russia's Choice

Source: *Izvestiya Tatarstana* and *Respublika Tatarstan*, December 14, 1993, p. 1.

a. Blok Ravnopraviye i Zakonnost', a Kazan-based voting block that supports Tatarstan's continued membership in the Russian Federation and equal treatment of ethnic groups within Tatarstan.

b. There were no candidates registered in this okrug, where *Ittifak* is extremely influential.

tion of signatures by "former Russian people's deputies" who sought nomination for candidacy in Tatarstan on the grounds that regulatory bodies in the Russian Federation had not yet authorized them to do so.[64] Likewise, when Kamil Yabatovich Shaidarov offered free beer in order to attract supporters for his candidacy in Kazan, he was immediately asked to stop by the Tatarstan authorities who claimed that he had violated campaign regulations.[65] Another interesting example concerns one of the three potential candidates for the Soviet federatsii, Aleksandr Lozovoi, who was actually a government official.[66] Although he had succeeded in gathering the necessary number of signatures for candidacy, he failed to turn them into the local electoral commission on the required day, and thus prevented elections to the upper house of Russia's new parliament from taking place in Tatarstan as a result of an insufficient number of candidates.[67]

In addition, candidates were denied the financial and institutional support that they were entitled to under the Russian Federation's official electoral rules. The majority of candidates, for example, experienced serious funding difficulties in large part because the local electoral commission, under direction from the Tatarstan government, refused to give them the 2,000 rubles they were supposed to receive for campaigning.[68] Moreover, according to both well- and poorly funded candidates, campaign financing itself was not regulated at all by government officials to ensure that candidates complied with official directives from Moscow.[69] Thus, many blamed the vast differences between candidates' financial resources on the fact that sources and amounts of funding went completely unscrutinized. Candidates also complained that state institutions did not appropriately "cooperate with [their] campaigning needs" as instructed.[70] In fact, Vladimir Aleksandrovich Belyayev, candidate for the State Duma in Moskovskii okrug, complained to me during an interview that he was "warned" repeatedly not to use his administrative office at the Kazan Aviation Institute for any "campaign activity."[71]

Perhaps most damaging, candidates were also not granted free and equal access to the media as required by the Russian Federation's Statute on Information Guarantees of the Election Campaign and Edict of the President . . . on Information Guarantees for Participants in the 1993 Election Campaign. It is not surprising that the Tatarstan government essentially controlled all forms of media in the republic during the election. Thus, in addition to violating the media's right to be free from "unlawful interference" by continuing censorship in some form, it violated (or simply allowed the violation of) several of the candidates' rights delineated in this statute and edict. Television and radio companies, for example, were not obliged by the state or republic Electoral Commission to "establish and publicly declare . . . the amounts of the fee for the allocation of broadcasting time."[72] Nor was any broadcasting time or newspaper space "afforded candidates . . . free of charge," with the exception of the aforementioned televised debates. None of the candidates—with the exception of Kurnosov who hired an advertising agency to conduct his campaign—was given access to price lists for advertising on television, radio, and in newspapers. Moreover, the candidates as a whole were not aware of any offers for free broadcasting time or newspaper space—despite the *Izvestiya Tatarstana* editor's insistence, for example, that his paper offered all candidates an opportunity to print their platforms free of charge.[73]

Furthermore, there was also no demand made on agents of the mass media to offer candidates an equal opportunity to present their views or campaign platforms. Editors of television, radio stations, and newspapers alike were thus empowered to turn away certain candidates and give others an advantage.[74] The profederation paper *Kazanskiye vedomosti,* for example, refused to print campaign ads for Kamil Yabatovich Shaidarov because he was viewed as an antifederation candidate.[75] The Tatar-language press denied access to any candidate because of his or her stance on the elections in particular and the Russian Federation in general. Thus, although it is true in theory that if a candidate had money he or she could buy time on television or space in newspaper, even sufficient campaign funds did not guarantee access to the media.[76]

It is important to note, however, that independent of direct government interference in the election, the candidates campaigns were simply ineffective. First of all, the above-described situation was compounded by the candidates' "too little too late" approach to campaigning in general. For example, three days prior to the elections, candidates had published little more than their platforms in local newspapers, did not actively hand out campaign flyers on the street, in workplaces, or even at the university and institute campuses, scarcely used television campaign commercials, and had still not posted a significant amount of their signs or placards around the city. In short, less than a week before December 12, it was not at all clear to the average person on the street that an election was imminent. The survey data substantiates this observation: Controlling for national origin and place of residence, more than half of all respondents experienced no pre-election agitation in the workplace and more than 80 percent of all respondents saw no campaign posters at all during the preelection campaign.[77] The voters as a whole thus lacked knowledge of the individual candidates and their platforms. This was clear not only from surveys of students at Kazan State University and several interviews with average citizens, but also from discussions with members of the business and academic community. The vast majority was not aware of the candidates running for office in their particular okrug, let alone their platforms. Many did not even know in which okrug they were supposed to vote.[78] Nor did the majority of candidates publish literature in Tatar or somehow make an attempt to gain the attention of the Tatar population, particularly in the countryside.[79]

As mentioned before, the candidates were effectively prevented from defining the voting issues of the election campaign. Thus, they faced a situation in which they were competing, not against the positions of other candidates on specific campaign issues but against the position of socio-political groups that opposed the elections themselves. Yet, the candidates seemed to realize much too late that *the* campaign issue—whether or not to vote—had already been determined by the Tatar nationalists. In fact, the first public mention that a citizen should vote (no matter for whom he or she voted) to express support for the election itself, for example, was not until the televised debates between candidates in Moskovskii and Privolszhkii okrugs, just a few days before the election.[80] Rather, candidates' campaign strategies consistently focused on more or less concrete problems facing society, such as economic reform and social security. Although most of the candidates did list support for the integrity of the Russian Federation as part of their platforms, this was not presented as a reason to vote in the elections but to vote for a particular candidate. Yet, because all candidates were assumed to be profederation, this was not an effective method of increasing voter turnout. Candidates might have campaigned for the constitutional referendum in order to encourage a greater number at the polls, yet not one followed this strategy.[81] Another interesting point is that all the candidates with whom I spoke seemed convinced that the elections in their respective okrug would "take place" (that is, have the necessary 25 percent turnout). The only deviation from this norm is Valerii Viktorovich Kurnosov, who did express the need to give people a reason to vote. He saw this more as a matter of increasing their trust in politicians and politics, however, rather than raising perceptions of the election's legitimacy.[82]

The candidates had several logistical strikes against them: first, the rush of the elections gave them a limited amount of time to plot campaign strategies and canvass support; second, the freezing temperatures at that time of the year made handing out campaign flyers or holding rallies unappealing and volunteers for pasting-up placards hard to find; and third, most faced a scarcity of campaign funds. At the same time, however, they were able to collect a sufficient number of signatures for registration; had no trouble finding volunteers to post flyers in the last few days before the elections; and at least two candidates with no monetary problems to speak of, Kurnosov and Rashit Garifziyanovich Akhunov, launched similarly uninspiring campaigns. Kurnosov was endorsed and financed by a Kazan-based import-export firm and Akhunov is a notorious tycoon who lives and conducts business in Moscow. Although both of these men had very nicely printed campaign posters, they were not publicly displayed until a couple of days before the election. Moreover, Kurnosov's main poster featured only his picture and name. Akhunov also paid for a well-done commercial, but it was only on television for two or three days and was only aired on a privately owned channel that requires a special antenna, thus being available to only a small portion of the population. This is not to say that money was not important, because it was undoubtedly necessary to print flyers and recruit staff, but that it was not the decisive factor in the candidates' poorly constructed campaigns.

In sum, it seems that the Tatarstan's government "neutrality" did not prevent it from exercising a great deal of influence. Rather, Kazan had as much or more control over the December 1993 electoral campaign and outcome as Moscow. Responsibility for this lies at least in part with the Central Electoral Commission (CEC) for the Russian Federation for not adequately regulating Tatarstan's local electoral commission. Yet, it is arguable that Tatarstan's "neutrality" also enabled the local electoral commission to go unregulated—that is, if Tatarstan had officially participated in the elections, the government would have exercised more control over the republic's electoral commission. Instead, Tatarstan officials ignored accusations

of inappropriate conduct by electoral commission chairpersons, who enjoyed much greater control over the activity of commission personnel than
in any previous election or referendum. Electoral commission chairpersons
were given complete autonomy with regard to the conduction of the election. In one polling place, for example, electoral commission members
complained that their chair, an ethnic Tatar, insisted on keeping ballots for
the candidates and the referendum separate so that voters would not automatically fill out both. In another, committee members were told by their
chair that their future employment depended on a low turnout: "The lower
the turnout, the better for all of us." Moreover, the Tatarstan government
did nothing at all to use either the media to inform voters or electoral commission personnel to motivate voter turnout, as it had in previous years.[83]
For its part, Moscow's only real presence in Tatarstan during the December
election and referendum was the televised debates between electoral associations and an occasional television appearance by Yeltsin himself. It is
not clear, however, whether Moscow was simply ill-prepared to exercise
electoral control in Tatarstan or whether the Russian Federation leadership
forfeited its control to Tatarstan's government for fear of retaliation, as it
had experienced after the April 1992 referendum.[84]

Election 1994: The Effects of Elite Bargaining and Consensus

Both the conduction of the electoral campaign and the outcome of the repeat election to the Russian Federal Assembly held in Tatarstan in March
1994 illuminate further the key factors influencing the 1993 election. In
particular, they make clear the direct link between the absence of a federal
agreement between Kazan and Moscow and the failure of the 1993 election
to take place and the ability of Tatarstan's government to manipulate ethnic
divisions within the republic for its own ends.

In short, the results of the 1993 election provided the leaders of both the
Russian Federation and Tatarstan with a strong incentive to strike a federal
bargain in the very near future. Moscow was acutely aware that a lower-
than-required voter turnout undermined its attempt to cement political ties
with the republic while increasing Tatarstan's bargaining power. The fact
that the elections were invalidated had the potential to invigorate the republic's demands to become an independent nation-state with popular approval. Shaimiyev, too, was undoubtedly aware of Tatarstan's enhanced
bargaining power as one of three administrative territories within the Rus-

sian Federation in which the 1993 election was invalidated by insufficient turnout and one of the few in which the constitution was defeated.[85] Yet, at the same time, he felt a certain sense of urgency to cement Tatarstan's position within the Russian Federation in light of the Tatar nationalists' renewed drive for complete secession and Vladimir Zhirinovskii's apparent widespread popularity.

Thus, when Shaimiyev made it clear to Moscow immediately following the December 1993 election that Tatarstan's full participation in the repeat elections scheduled for March 13, 1994, would be impossible unless an agreement was reached between the two governments, Moscow was ready and willing to come to the bargaining table. Thus, Yeltsin and Shaimiyev resumed their negotiations in early January and signed a bilateral treaty in February 1994—just before the scheduled repeat election—from which both Moscow and Kazan were positioned to gain politically. For Moscow, the February treaty clarifies the relationship between the federal and republican governments of Russia and Tatarstan, respectively, in a way that the Russian Federation Constitution does not while maintaining a balance of power very close to what it prefers. In fact, the only key differences between this new agreement and the constitution is that the former grants Tatarstan the right to determine questions related to citizenship and military service within its own borders; the issue of Tatarstan's sovereignty is noticeably absent from the text.[86] Yet it also sets an important precedent for Tatarstan's elevated or asymmetrical status in the Russian Federation and the use of bilateral agreements as a means of settling disputes between the two governments. This alone not only provided a means for Shaimiyev to augment his own power and influence but, as the presumed architect of this agreement, to secure his position within the republic as well.

More important, the signing of a bilateral treaty in February not only secured official sanctioning of the 1994 repeat election in Tatarstan, it also essentially guaranteed that the election would actually take place (that there would be sufficient turnout to validate the election). In contrast to the December 1993 election, Shaimiyev and the Tatarstan government had a dual incentive to ensure that the repeat election was validated by sufficient turnout, if not fully endorsed by an overwhelming rate of popular participation. First of all, the election represented an important symbol of the bilateral treaty itself and, as a consequence, Tatarstan's new status within the Russian Federation. As in the past few years since the break-up of the USSR, the election served as a symbol of the Tatar Republic's struggle to redefine its relationship with the Russian Federation. This time, however, it represented the consolidation of Tatarstan's continued membership in the Russian Federation—albeit on an elevated level. Insufficient turnout, then, would have had the effect of a referendum against the recent bilateral agreement, just as the December 1993 elections had symbolized Tatarstan's strong rejection of a relationship with the Russian Federation without special recognition or privileges.

Second, a valid election in March was a means of consolidating Shaimiyev's own power (as well as enhancing his popularity) both within and outside of Tatarstan. On the one hand, he would automatically win the support of largely Russian social and political organizations that since independence have consistently demanded not only Tatarstan's continued membership in the Russian Federation but also the holding of "free and fair" (or at least more "democratic") elections in which to participate. It is not surprising that Russian members of these locally based organizations made up the majority of candidates to the State Duma.[87] On the other, Shaimiyev himself had an opportunity to be elected as one of Tatarstan's two representatives in the Federation Council. Indeed, that this was his intention from the beginning is indicated by the fact that he announced his candidacy even before the treaty had been signed and he officially acknowledged that the repeat election would be held in March.[88] Once Shaimiyev decided to become a candidate to the upper house of Russia's new parliament, he also committed himself personally to ensuring that there would be sufficient turnout to validate the election. Simply put, invalid elections would call into question his popularity at home as well as jeopardize his future as a prominent decisionmaker in Moscow.

Right from the start, the March 1994 election looked quite different from the election held just three months earlier. Long before election day, Shaimiyev expressed official support for the election and emphasized the need for all "loyal citizens" of Tatarstan to participate.[89] Through the local electoral commission and media, he actively mobilized the eligible voting population to go to the polls. In fact, this time local electoral commission chairs were allegedly warned of severe consequences if turnout was insufficient, and newspaper editors and radio station managers were made aware that any "negative publicity" regarding the election would be considered a personal attack against the president himself and Tatarstan.[90]

Moreover, full government support of and participation in the March 1994 election also meant the "withdrawal" or absence of "covert" government support for the nationalists' campaign to boycott the election and, instead, the endorsement of its own candidates. Although Russian and Tatarstan elites had reached a consensus on the definition of their political relationship by this time, ethnopolitical divisions continued to be salient within the republic itself and hence Shaimiyev continued to manipulate these divisions. Thus, once again, Tatar nationalists immediately voiced their opposition to holding the repeat election, and later, fully rejected the terms of the bilateral treaty signed in February.[91] Yet, in direct contrast to the December 1993 election, they were not allowed to make any public antielection statements, were deliberately denied access to the media and other key resources, and were prevented from campaigning in the countryside where they enjoy their largest support.[92] The withdrawal of official "support" for the Tatar nationalists was exacerbated by the fact that only they had no outside allies in their opposition to the election; the Communist party decided not only to endorse the March 1994 election but to run several candidates.[93]

Not only did the Tatarstan government's active participation in the election damage the Tatar nationalists' antielection campaign, it also helped the nomenklatura candidates defeat those candidates less favorable to the current regime. Many candidates affiliated with RiZ (Ravnopraviye i Zakonnost'), for example, accused the government of interfering in the election to ensure the victory of candidates representing the Unity and Progress party over their own electoral bloc. This interference entailed not merely some form of campaign assistance, such as additional finances or media access, but direct tampering with voting procedures, ballots, and the tabulation of votes.[94]

In sum, both sufficient voter turnout and the victory of candidates to the Federal Assembly most preferred by the current regime were ensured in 1994, as opposed to 1993. As a result, in 1994 overall voter turnout more than quadrupled from that of December 1993, only one RiZ candidate to the State Duma received a majority of the popular vote in 1994, compared to four in 1993, and both Shaimiyev and Farid Mukhametshin, the chair of Tatarstan's Supreme Soviet, were elected to the Federation Council by an overwhelming majority (see table 20-2 for details).

Conclusion

Both the December 1993 and March 1994 election in Tatarstan illuminate that Moscow cannot successfully engineer a founding election to either consolidate democracy or solidify the Russian Federation without securing the full support of the regions. This requires elite bargaining and

Table 20-2. *1994 Election Outcome by Okrug (District)*

Okrug	Winning candidate	Affiliation	Percent of vote
Al'metevskii	Yegorov	Unity and Progress	73.9
Moskovskii	Morozov	Unity and Progress	46.8
Naberezhniye Chelny	Altykhov	Communist party	40.9
Nizhnekamskii	Bagautdinov	Communist party	69.1
Privolzhskii	Mikhailov[a]	RiZ/Russia's Choice	23.9
Federation Council	Shaimiyev	Unity and Progress	91.2
Federation Council	Mukhametshin	Unity and Progress	71.1

Source: "Ravnopraviye i Zakonnost," Bulletin' ib RiZ, no. 2, March 1994, p. 1.

consensus—between center and regional elites as well as among regional elites regarding the definition of both federation and democracy. In short, Moscow's failure to understand the need to bargain or negotiate with Tatarstan's leaders *before* the December 1993 election led to a different outcome than it had originally intended. Instead of either consolidating democracy or solidifying Russia's territorial integrity, this election invoked existing separatist tendencies among the Tatarstan's ethnic Tatars and hence gave the republic's leaders a crucial bargaining chip with which to challenge Moscow's definition of federalism.

With the signing of a bilateral treaty between Moscow and Kazan, the question of Tatarstan's status is more or less resolved between central and regional elites. This alone made possible the successful outcome, for elites in both Moscow and Kazan, of the March 1994 election. Yet, the issue of ethnic separatism remains unresolved within the republic itself. Groups continue to be polarized into proseparatist and profederation factions, which are divided essentially along ethnic lines. In short, there is no consensus among elites within Tatarstan on the proper relationship between their republic and the Russian Federation. As a result, the democratic consolidation process is hindered not only in the Tatar Republic but in the Russian Federation as a whole.

Notes

1. According to Article 39 of the "Regulations on the Elections of Deputies to the State Duma in 1993" issued in President Boris Yeltsin's decree on October 1 1993, a minimum of 25 percent of registered voters must participate in the elections for the results to be validated. Elections to the Federation Council were not held at all because only two of the three required candidates registered by the stipulated deadline.

2. See, for example, Samuel P. Huntington, *The Third Wave: Democratization in the Late Twentieth Century* (University of Oklahoma Press, 1991); Guillermo O'Donnell and Philippe C. Schmitter, *Transitions from Authoritarian Rule: Tentative Conclusions about Uncertain Democracies* (Johns Hopkins University Press, 1986); and Adam Przeworski, *Democracy and the Market: Political and Economic Reforms in Eastern Europe and Latin America* (Cambridge University Press, 1991).

3. In particular, see O'Donnell and Schmitter, *Transitions from Authoritarian Rule*, pp. 59–61.

4. William M. Riker, *Federalism: Origin, Operation, Significance* (Little, Brown, 1964), p. 11. See also Carl J. Friedrich, *Trends of Federalism in Theory and Practice* (New York: Frederick A. Praeger, 1968).

5. Riker, *Federalism*, pp. 11–12.

6. See, for example, Ursula K. Hicks, *Federalism: Failure and Success, A Comparative Study*, pt. 3, pp. 171–96.

7. Riker, *Federalism*, p. 12.

8. Riker argues that the mutual benefit derived from federal arrangements is always based on military defense and expansion. Yet, although this may be part of the potential gains considered by prospective federal partners, in recent decades other benefits such as political stability, economic growth, cultural unification, and ethnic peace have been at least if not more important than this.

9. Dankwart A. Rustow, "Transitions to Democracy: Toward a Dynamic Model," *Comparative Politics*, vol. 2, no. 3 (April 1970), pp. 350–51.

10. Azade-Ayse Rorlich, *The Volga Tatars: A Profile in National Resilience* (Stanford, Calif.: Hoover Institution Press, 1986), pp. 133, 138.

11. Ibid., pp. 138, 172.

12. M. R. Mustafin and R. G. Khuzeyev, *Vse o Tatarstane: ekonomiko-geograficheskii spravochnik* (Kazan: Tatarskoye Knizhnoye Izdatel'stvo, 1992), pp. 13–15, 21–22.

13. Interview with Vladimir Aleksandrovich Belyayev, founder and president of the multinational movement Soglasiye (Concord), professor of Sociology and Political Science at the Kazan Aviation Institute, and candidate for the State Duma in Moskovskii Okrug, on December 7, 1993.

14. That this has been their chief complaint since the beginning of perestroika is clear in the agendas of the major Tatar nationalist group that emerged during this period: the Tatar Social Center. Organizations that formed later—for example, Suverenitet (Sovereignty) and Ittifak (Unity)—also view their primary task as restoring the Tatar culture.

15. Uli Schamiloglu, "The Tatar Social Center and Current Tatar Concerns," *Radio Liberty Report on the USSR*, vol. 1, no. 51 (December 22, 1989), pp. 11–15. The People's Front of Kazan and many profederation groups that emerged after its formation do have some Tatar members. There are also a few Bashkir and Chechen members of the Tatar Social Center and other proseparatist groups.

16. See Matthew J. Sagers, "The Energy Industries in the Former USSR: A Mid-Year Survey: Oil," *Post-Soviet Geography*, vol. 34, no. 6 (June 1993), pp. 361, 344; Leslie Dienes, "Prospects for Russian Oil in the 1990s: Reserves and

Costs," *Post-Soviet Geography*, vol. 34, no. 2 (February 1993), p. 103; and Charles E. McLure Jr., "The Sharing of Taxes on Natural Resources and the Future of the Russian Federation," in Christine I. Wallich, ed., *Russia and the Challenge of Fiscal Federalism* (Washington, D.C.: World Bank, 1994), p. 190.

17. Matthew J. Sagers, "Regional Industrial Structures and Economic Prospects in the Former USSR," *Post-Soviet Geography*, vol. 33, no. 8 (October 1992), p. 498, 506, 510.

18. Sagers, "Regional Industrial Structures," p. 506.

19. *Razvitiye ekonomicheskikh reform v regionakh Rossiiskoi Federatsii* (Moscow: Goskomstat, 1993), p. 132.

20. For a detailed account of this, see Rorlich, *The Volga Tatars*, chapters 10 and 11.

21. See "On The Basis of Leninist Principles, to a New Quality of Relations between Nationalities—Debate at the Plenary Session of the CPSU Central Committee," *Pravda*, September 21, 1989, pp. 1–7.

22. N. Morozov, "Tatarstan's Position," *Pravda*, May 18, 1991, p. 2, as translated by *Current Digest of the Soviet Press* (hereafter *CDSP*), vol. 43, no. 20 (June 19, 1991), p. 26; Aleksandr Bogomolov, "Tatar President on Sovereignty," July 18, 1991, p. 8, in Foreign Broadcast Information Service Report (hereafter FBIS)-USSR-91-026, August 27, 1991.

23. Gyuzel Faizullina, "Tatar Patriots Recall Ivan the Terrible," *Kommersant*, no. 22 (June 26, 1991), p. 12, in *CDSP,* vol. 43, no. 21 (June 26, 1991), p. 24; Bogomolov, "Tatar President on Sovereignty."

24. Viktor Radziyevskii, "Good-Bye Russia," *Moscow News*, no. 26 (June 30–July 7, 1991), p. 5; and *CDSP*, vol. 43, no. 21 (1991), p. 24.

25. Radziyevskii, "Good-Bye Russia," *Moscow News*, no. 26 (June 30–July 7, 1991), p. 5; Yevgenii Skukin, "Ordinary Ittifak Fascism," *Rossiiskaya gazeta* (November 28, 1991), p. 3; *CDSP*, 43, no. 47 (December 1991), p. 5; *CDSP*, vol. 43, no. 21 (June 26, 1991), p. 24, emphasis added; and personal interview with Fauziya Bairamova, chair of the national independence party Ittifak (Alliance), in the Kazan Supreme Soviet building on November 26, 1993.

26. "Tatarstan—Freedom Square Seethes," *Pravda*, October 17, 1991, p. 1, as translated by *CDSP,* vol. 18, no. 42 (November 20, 1991), p. 29.

27. According to members of the Tatar Social Center, flyers to this effect were mostly posted and distributed in areas densely populated by Tatars. (Refer to Discussions with The Tatar Social Center representatives at the election polling places on December 12, 1993.) In addition, Bairamova promoted this view during antielection "meetings" held in Naberezhniye Chelny and Nizhnekamsk. (Refer to Interview with Bairamova.) Moreover, Tatar national groups openly questioned the loyalty of the Supreme Soviet deputies and then chair Mintimer Shaimiyev before they decided not to "officially" hold elections.

28. This includes the movements *Grazhdane Rossiiskoi Federatsii* (Citizens of the Russian Federation), *Dvizheniye Demokraticheskikh Reform Tatarstana* (Tatarstan Movement for Democratic Reform), and *Russkoye Dvizheniye* (Russian Movement), among others.

29. Discussion with Albert Gatin, coordinator of the People's Front of Kazan, during the Supreme Soviet session on November 25, 1993. The several photographs of these rallies that he showed me, in addition to his own description, indicate that they were comparably large and boisterous to those of the Tatar nationalists.

30. According to election data published by Central Electoral Commission and compiled by political analyst Dmitrii Toropov, more than 80 percent of the voters came from Russian-dominated areas of Tatarstan. See *CDSP,* vol. 43, no. 47 (December 25, 1991), p. 4. (This is not to say that Russians who voted in June 1991 were anti-Tatar but that they were perceived to be.) Conversely, Tatars are in effect responsible for electing the current president, Mintimer Shaimiyev, because few Russians actually participated in Tatarstan's presidential elections, which, not coincidentally, was also held in June 1991.

31. Faizullina, "Tatar Patriots Recall Ivan the Terrible"; Radziyevskii, "Good-Bye Russia."

32. Rafael Khakimov, advisor to the president of Tatarstan, as much as admitted this in his article, "Na Konstitutsionnom soveshchanii voprosy ne mogut reshat'sya mekhanizm bol'shinstvam tak schitayut, po krainei mere, nekotoriye sub'ekti federatsii," *Nezavisimaya gazeta,* June 24, 1993, pp. 1–2.

33. As in the case of the 1991 Russian presidential election, the latter referendum did not even officially take place in the republic, though the Supreme Soviet "[ensured] the right of citizens to participate." Tatar national groups launched a similar campaign against holding this referendum. "Tatarstan to Protect Right to Participate in RF Referendum," *Federatsiya,* no. 38, April 6, 1993, p. 1, as translated in FBIS-*Central Eurasia,* April 30, 1993, p. 51.

34. See, for example, "Vse na referendum," *Suverenitet,* vol. 10, no. 5 (March 1992), p. 1. This is one of the newspapers published by the sociopolitical organization Suverenitet.

35. In areas heavily populated by Tatars both turnout and "yes" votes are in the 90th percentile, whereas these are much lower for the Russian-dominated cities. See election data published by the Central Electoral Commission and compiled by Dmitri Toropov, as well as Ye. Ukhov, "Tatarstan Referendum 'Demonstrates Balance of Forces,'" *Trud,* March 21, 1992, p. 1, as translated in FBIS-*Central Eurasia,* April 2, 1992, p. 33, and Ann Sheehy, "Tatarstan Asserts Its Sovereignty," *RFE/RL Research Report,* vol. 1, no. 14, April 3, 1992, p. 4.

36. Only 22.5 percent of Tatarstan's eligible voters participated in the referendum, thus invalidating its results. (Refer to "Referendum v respublike ne sostoyalsya," *Sovetskaya tatariya,* no. 81, April 27, 1993, p. 1.) Many Russians who did vote in favor of Yeltsin commented to me that they did not believe their votes were actually counted by the republic's electoral commission headquarters.

37. Russian People's Deputy Vladimir Morokin, "Don't Call People on to the War Path," *Rossiiskaya gazeta,* February 7, 1992, as translated by *CDSP,* vol. 44, no. 5, March 4, 1992, p. 17; and discussion with Albert Gatin.

38. Inna Muravyova, "Test of Responsibility," *Rossiiskaya gazeta,* March 6, 1992, pp. 1–2, as translated in *CDSP,* vol. 44, no. 5 (March 4, 1992), p. 17; Valery

Zorkin, "A Threat to Statehood and Human Rights," *Rossiiskaya gazeta*, March 19, 1992, p. 1, as translated by *CDSP*, vol. 44, no. 8 (March 25, 1992), pp. 6–7; *CDSP*, vol. 44, no. 11 (April 15, 1992), pp. 21–22.

39. The exact wording of the referendum question was, "Do you agree that the republic of Tatarstan is a sovereign state, a subject of international law, building its relations with the Russian Federation and other republics and states on the basis of treaties between equal partners." (Refer to Sheehy, "Tatarstan Asserts Its Sovereignty.") For Moscow's specific objections to the wording, see "Resolution by Russian Supreme Soviet on Referendum Wording," *Rossiiskaya gazeta*, March 21, 1992, p. 1, as translated by FBIS-*Central Eurasia*, April 3, 1992, pp. 92–93.

40. *CDSP,* Interview with Mintimer Shaimiyev, *Tatarstan*, vol. 45, no. 14 (May 5, 1993), pp. 11–12.

41. Farid Mukhametshin, chair of the Supreme Soviet of the Republic of Tatarstan, stated in an interview with *Nezavisimaya gazeta*, "Despite Tatarstan's tremendous desire to sign a treaty with the Russian Federation this year on the mutual delegation of power, we did not succeed in doing so. And this wasn't our fault but that of the Russian side. . . .If a treaty between Russia and Tatarstan is not signed, I am afraid that our republic will not take part in the April all-Russia referendum." From Radik Batyrshin, "Kazan and Ufa Are against the Referendum in April—Cheboksary Is in Favor," *Nezavisimaya gazeta*, December 31, 1991, p. 3, as translated by *CDSP,* vol. 44, no. 52 (1992), pp. 20–21.

42. National election Tatarstan Survey, 1993.

43. For example, Yeltsin's "Regulations on the Elections of Deputies to the State Duma in 1993" required "electoral associations" (including groups, parties, and coalitions) to gather no more than 15 percent of their signatures for registration from the same region.

44. XVII Sessii Verkhovnogo Soveta Respubliki Tatarstan, "Ofitsial'noye soobshcheniye," *Izvestiya Tatarstana*, no. 231–32, November 26, 1993, p. 1. President Shaimiyev, "Tselostnost' Rossii zavisit ne tol'ko ot Moskvy." *Kazanskiye vedomosti*, no. 243, November 25, 1993, p. 5. "Golosovat' s zakrytymi glazami ne khochetsya," *Kazanskiye vedomosti*, no. 244, November 26, 1993, p. 1.

45. Indus Tagirov, "The Situation Has Changed, But the Problems Remain," *Respublika Tatarstan*, no. 232 (November 18, 1993), pp. 2–3. Tagirov is also the president of the World Congress of Tatars, a counterorganization to the Tatar Public Center that was organized under the aegis of the Tatarstan government and in effect acts as the "official" voice on Tatar affairs.

46. Vladimir Shervchuka's interview with Farid Mukhametshin, "Vse osnovano na balanse vetvey vlasti," *Izvestiya Tatarstana*, no. 229 (November 23, 1993), p. 1.

47. XVII Sessii Verkhovnogo Soveta Respubliki Tatarstan, "Ofitsial'noye soobshcheniye," *Izvestiya Tatarstana*, no. 231–32, November 26, 1993, p. 1. I personally witnessed the Supreme Soviet's discussion of this condemnation on November 25, 1993, during which members known or suspected to express views in favor of the Russian constitution were shouted down and physically prevented from speaking.

48. *Respublika Tatarstana*, November 5, 1993, p. 1; and *Izvestiya Tatarstana*, November 5, 1993, p. 1.

49. *Izvestiya Tatarstana*, October 29, 1993, p. 1 (emphasis added).

50. This opinion was consistent throughout my interviews with candidates Kamil Yabatovich Shaidarov (November 29, 1993), Ivan Grachev (November 30, 1993), Rashit Akhmetov (December 6, 1993), Valerii Viktorovich Kurnosov, and Vladimir Aleksandrovich Belyayev (December 7, 1993); with the leaders of Suverenitet (November 22, 1993) and The Tatar Social Center (December 12, 1993); with the editors of *Respublika Tatarstan* (November 25, 1993) and *Idel-Ural* (November 26, 1993); and with Russian and Tatar students at Kazan State University (December 2 and December 3, 1993) as well as Tatar factory workers (November 29, 1993).

51. Interviews with Bairamova and Makhmutov.

52. See, for example, the October 1993 issues of the Tatar-language newspapers *Millat* (Nation), and *Idel-Ural*. (The latter newspaper was given the same name as the autonomous Muslim state created in Kazan in 1918, but later abolished by the Bolsheviks.)

53. Rashit Akhmetov, *Politicheskaya situatsiya v Tatarstane nakanune vyborov* ("The Political Situation in Tatarstan on the Eve of the Elections"), personal daily log for November 1, 1993.

54. See the whole issue of *Suverenitet*, no. 11 and no.12 (October 1993); *Nezavisimost'* (Independence), no. 9 (September–October, 1993).

55. Interview with Bairamova.

56. According to Tatar nationalists, chapter 5 (titled "Republic of Tatarstan—Sovereign Government") of Tatarstan's constitution secures the republic's existence as a sovereign state and thus forbids any outside interference in its internal affairs from foreign governments without its explicit consent. Supporters of the Russian Federation, however, point to article 19 of the constitution's third chapter (titled "Citizenship in the Republic of Tatarstan—Equality of Citizens"), which entitles citizens of Tatarstan to dual citizenship in the Russian Federation. (Refer to *Konstitutsiya Respubliki Tatarstana*, Kazan, 1993, pp. 34, 38–39).

57. In every discussion that I had with leaders and members of Suverenitet, Ittifak, and the Tatar Social Center, this was the first argument that was mentioned and the one about which people became most excited. One member of Suverenitet even presented me with a collection of his poems that he had dedicated to this topic.

58. Quote in text is in headline in *Suverenitet,* vol. 33, no. 12 (October 1993), p. 1.

59. Informal discussion with members of the Tatar Social Center and Azatlik at a voting precinct in Sovetskii raion (Kazan) on election day.

60. Interview with Aleksandr Ivanovich Salii, first secretary of the Communist Party of the Republic of Tatarstan (CPRT), at the Supreme Soviet session on November 24, 1993.

61. Refer to the electoral results printed in either *Izvestiya Tatarstana* or *Respublika Tatarstana* on December 14, 1993, p. 1.

62. V. Nugmanov and others, "Vybory pozadi. Sdelan li vybor?" *Respublika Tatarstana,* no. 250, December 14, 1993, p. 1; Igor' Il'in, "Vybory v Tatarstana ne sostoyalis', Yest' nad chem podomat!" *Izvestiya Tatarstana,* no. 245, December 14, 1993, p. 1.

63. Interviews with various leaders of Tatar nationalist groups, including Makhmutov (Suverenitet) and Bairamova (Ittifak), RiZ members, and candidates to the State Duma. See also INTERFAX, "Poll Assesses Voting Intentions in Tatarstan," Moscow: INTERFAX, November 27, 1993, reprinted by FBIS-*Central Eurasia,* December 1, 1993, p. 55.

64. "Tatarstan Cautions Former Deputies on New Candidacy," Moscow Programma Radio Odin Network, November 1, 1993, translated in FBIS-*Central Eurasia,* November 1, 1993, p. 41.

65. Interview with Kamil Yabatovich Shaidarov on Monday, November 29, 1993.

66. At the time, Aleksandr Lozovoi was the chair of the Supreme Soviet and viewed by some as an "official candidate." From interview with Rashit Akhmetov, candidate for State Duma in Moskovskii okrug, on December 6, 1993.

67. Interview on Tuesday, November 30, 1993, with Ivan Grachev, who collected the necessary amount of signatures to register as a candidate for the Federation Council. For elections to occur, however, at least three candidates had to be registered. Under the circumstances, Grachev decided instead to run as Tatarstan's candidate on the National List for Yabloko.

68. Both Rashit Akhmetov and Vladimir Belyaev complained about this during interviews I conducted. The basis for their grievances was confirmed by a phone conversation with Lyubov' Akimovna Guseva, head of Tatarstan's electoral commission for the December elections.

69. In fact, it was Kurnosov and Shaidarov, both of whom have ample financing from business connections, who first mentioned this to me. See chapter 6 of Yeltsin's "Regulations on the Elections of Deputies to the State Duma in 1993," *Polozheniye o vyborakh deputatov gosudarstvennoy dumy v 1993 godu* (Moscow: Izvestiya, 1993) for campaign financing regulations.

70. See chapter 5 of Yeltsin's "Regulations on the Elections of Deputies to the State Duma in 1993."

71. Interview on December 7, 1993.

72. "Polozheniye ob informatsionnikh garantiyakh predvybornoi agitatsii." *Rossiiskaya gazeta,* no. 204 (November 2, 1993), p. 4.

73. Interviews with *Respublika Tatarstana* editor and Lyubov' Ageyeva, editor-in-chief of *Kazanskiye vedomosti.*

74. Ibid.

75. Shaidarov revealed this to me during an interview. He is considered antifederation because he is a leading member of Milli Majlis. Nonetheless, he supports the continuance of Tatarstan's political relationship with the Russian Federation but wants the republic to have complete economic and cultural autonomy.

76. Interviews with candidates.

77. National election survey for Tatarstan, 1993.

78. I interviewed and surveyed forty university students with a variety of majors on December 2 to 3, 1993. In addition to those already mentioned, I conducted interviews with Anvar Rashidovich Kasimov, senior researcher at the Institute of Mathematics and Mechanics at Kazan State University and former political activist (November 28, 1993), a factory worker (name withheld), and business entrepreneur Dmitrii Viktorovich Masyagin (November 29, 1993), the Nesmelov family, in which each member of the family is employed in some level of academia (November 30, 1993), and Yurii Lukyanov, vice director of a large bakery in Kazan (December 3, 1993), to name a few.

79. One candidate in Privolzhskii okrug, Belyayev, did print one piece of his campaign literature in Tatar and even passed it out in the rural areas of his voting district. He won a majority of the votes cast.

80. I attended the taping of these debates, which was held on December 4 and 5 at Kazan State University; they were not broadcast until December 9 and 10.

81. This conclusion is based on interviews with two of the four candidates in Moskovskii Okrug, four of the seven candidates in Privolskii Okrug, and a perusal of all eleven candidates' campaign literature.

82. Interview with Kurnosov on December 7, 1993.

83. Interviews with electoral commission personnel on December 12, 1993. See also "Professionals . . . ne trebuyut," *Vechernyaya Kazan*, no. 143 (November 29, 1993), p. 1.

84. "Appeal by President B. N. Yeltsin to the Supreme Soviet of the Republic of Tatarstan," *Rossiiskaya gazeta,* March 20, 1992, p. 1, as translated in *CDSP*, vol. 44, no. 11 (April 15, 1992), p. 22; and "Tatarstan Referendum Backs Sovereignty," a compilation of six articles, *CDSP*, vol. 44, no. 12 (April 22, 1992), pp. 6–8.

85. The other two federal administrative territories in which the 1993 election was invalidated by insufficient turnout were Chechnya and Chelyabinsk.

86. See *Dogovor Rossiiskoi Federatsii i Respubliki Tatarstan o razgranichenii predmetov vedeniya i vzaimnom delegirovanii polnomochii. Mezhdu organami gosudarstvennoi vlasti Rossiyskoi Federatski i organami gosudarstvennoi vlasti Respubliki Tatartan.* (Agreement of the Russian Federation and the Republic of Tatarstan "On the delimitation of spheres of authority and the mutual delegation of power.") Special thanks to Bruce Allen of the Conflict Management Group in Cambridge, Massachusetts, for providing me with a copy of this document.

87. "Ravnopraviye i zakonnost'," *Byulleten' ib Riz,* no. 2 (March 1994), p. 1.

88. Sergei Fedatov, "Shaymiyev to Run for Federal Parliament: Kazan Agrees to Nominate Its Candidates for Parliamentary Election," *Kommersant-Daily,* January 29, 1994, as translated in FBIS-*Central Eurasia,* January 31, 1994, p. 39.

89. See, for example, "S dumoi o Dume," *Vechernyaya Kazan*, no. 32, March 1, 1994, p. 1; and Boris Bronshteyn, "Chernoye, beloye v period ramazana: pered vyborami v Tatarstane," *Izvestiya,* March 10, 1994, p. 4.

90. Follow-up telephone interviews with members of the electoral commission and major newspaper editors in Kazan, March 1994.

91. See, for example, Dmitrii Lukashov, "Milli Majlis trebuyet otstavki prezidenta Tatarii, Kurultay protiv vyborov v federal'noye sobraniye Rossii," *Segodnya,* February 23, 1994, p. 3; and Amir Makhmud, "Bol'shiye problemy

inostrannoi Rossii svyazani s nezavisimost'yu gosudarstva Tatarstan," *Suverenitet*, no. 3 (February 1994) and no. 4 (March 1994).

92. Dmitry Lukashov, "Vybory v Tatarii sostoyalis' no natsionalisty namerery' vse nachat' snachala,'" *Segodnya*, March 17, 1994, p. 3; and follow-up telephone interview with Amir Gubayevich, Suverenitet's chair.

93. Bronshteyn, "Chernoye, beloye v period ramazana."

94. *Izvestiya Tatarstana*, March 19, 1994, p. 1; and follow-up telephone interviews with two candidates from RiZ in March 1994.

CHAPTER TWENTY-ONE

The Failure of Party Formation and the Future of Russian Democracy

Jerry F. Hough

THE ELECTION of 1993 is now a distant memory. The shock of the victory of Vladimir Zhirinovskii's Liberal Democratic Party of Russia in the party-list election and the defeat of Yegor Gaidar's Russia's Choice are now seen in perspective. Despite the fears of many, Zhirinovskii was not a candidate whose 8 percent support in the 1991 Russian presidential election and 22.9 percent support in the 1993 Duma election foreshadowed a Hitler-like breakthrough if economic conditions did not improve. The defeat of Yegor Gaidar proved to be much more a repudiation of him as a person and his specific policy than a repudiation of the prodemocratic, promarket revolution.

Nevertheless, the 1993 election remains a highly important one for an understanding of Russia and the process of democratization. The recent literature on democratization has focused on events in Latin America and southern Europe in the 1970s and early 1980s. Yet democracy was first introduced in Latin America, southern Europe, and eastern Europe in the nineteenth and early twentieth centuries and frequently failed before finally—we hope—being established on firm grounds in the 1980s. Hence, as Alfred Stepan has argued, the recent literature does not actually analyze democratization but redemocratization.[1]

669

Moreover, the recent literature deals almost exclusively with Catholic countries—and at a time when a Polish pope was strongly supporting democracy in order to liberate Poland and was pressuring the Church in Latin America and southern Europe to give wholehearted support to the consolidation of democracy. Accommodating negotiation among the elite to achieve democracy is much easier when all members of the elite are members of a centralized church that had been doubtful about democracy in the past, but whose leader is now determined to promote it.[2]

Scholars in the past inevitably had to examine countries at earlier stages of democratization, and they had a very different view of the process. Few were inclined to explain the establishment of parliamentary supremacy in England in 1688 or the creation of the Continental Congress in America in 1774, the National Assembly in France in 1789, the Duma in Russia in 1906, and the Diet in Japan in 1945 simply in terms of consensual elite negotiation. Frequently the military has not been an equal, let alone subordinate, participant at the negotiating table, even in Turkey today, let alone Algeria.

The current Russian case is especially valuable for political scientists precisely because we are witnessing democratization at the very early stages when competitive elections are being introduced—a rare opportunity in the late twentieth century outside Africa.[3] The 1993 election was actually the third that had been held in Russia since 1989, but it was the first since the Bolshevik Revolution in which parties were introduced, and thus it marked a key stage on the path to full democracy.

Founding Elections and the Stage of Democratization

The literature on the redemocratization of Latin America and southern Europe gives great importance to "the founding election" in those areas in the 1970s and the 1980s. It describes the elite negotiation that preceded these elections in a way that has little resemblance to what happened in Russia. Some might think that Russia is unique, perhaps because it is not "Western." Such a conclusion would be profoundly misguided or, at least, very premature. The phrase "founding election" was developed to describe countries undergoing redemocratization instead of democratization; if we look at true founding elections at the early stage of democratization, we find them much more similar to Russian elections.

From a broader perspective, democratization is a long process. Some 175 years passed between the Glorious Revolution in England and the introduction of universal suffrage and between the French Revolution and the establishment of the Fifth Republic. Universal white male suffrage was introduced in the United States fifty years after the American revolution, female suffrage ninety years later, and universal Black suffrage another forty-five years later. Southern Europe and the developed countries of Latin America began democratization more than a century ago, and it is hoped that this time the process is far enough under way that democracy may be institutionalized. But even now we should recall Guillermo O'Donnell's words in 1992 about the "weak and incomplete democracies" of Argentina, Brazil, Chile, and Uruguay and his warning that "the paths that lead from a democratic government to a democratic regime are uncertain and complex and the possibilities of authoritarian regression are numerous."[4]

The redemocratization in Latin America and southern Europe did, in fact, reflect a fairly broad consensus within the elite of their respective countries. So long as there is fairly broad agreement among the elite, the problem, in the words of Giuseppe Di Palma, is "to craft democracies."[5] Because the elite at late stages of democratization have had experience both with democracy and dictatorship in the past, the negotiations may be fairly tranquil. To the extent that each is represented in the party system that arises, the party system may have some stability.

The early stage of democratization frequently does not have such a character. The transformation of the British parliament into the country's dominant political institution came after decades of turmoil and even civil war. The Glorious Revolution of 1688 was followed by profound levels of suspicion and distrust among the political elite. "Hogarth," Bernard Bailyn wrote, "not Gainsborough was [England's] true depicter." He quotes with approval from J. R. Jones.[6]

[There were] absurd tales of large Papist armies, mysterious movements by night, secret papers scattered in the highways, of projected invasions from France and even from Spain. The wildest rumors swept the nation. Fires were confidently attributed to Papist incendiaries unless clear proof existed to the contrary. A flood of pamphlets, many written by informers, stimulated fears . . . [in] the fevered imagination of the time.

According to Bailyn, conspiratorial thinking was not limited to the masses, but affected the prime minister, the king, the opposition, and the educated population in the American colonies.[7] The leader of one of the parties, Alexander Hamilton, and the number two official in the other, James Madison, had coauthored *The Federalist Papers* only five years earlier. Yet the two parties soon were accusing each other of virtual treason: "The Republicans claimed that the [Jay] Treaty put us completely in the hands of Great Britain, that it was a betrayal of our Revolution; the Federalists claimed that opposition to the Treaty came only from those who were the tools of France."[8]

The top historian of the democratization of England believed the Reform Act of 1832 was produced by the July Revolution of 1830 in France, as a result of which "popular spirit became so inflamed that the issue lay plainly between solid reform and revolution."[9] Democratization in France, Spain, and Italy occurred in its first decades over the objections of the Church, and the legitimacy of democratic institutions was not really recognized in these countries by the Church and the elites allied with it until after World War II.

The problems are particularly great when the definition of community has not been solved. In his classic article on transitions to democracy, Dankwart Rustow emphasized that democracy could fairly easily handle social and economic issues, but that issues of community were much harder. Rustow quoted with favor a statement by Ivor Jennings: "The people cannot decide until somebody decides who are the people."[10] Arend Lijphart has explored the special kinds of "consociational democracy" that can work in such countries, but Lebanon is a constant reminder that these arrangements can be fragile.[11]

Sometimes, as in Colombia, parties that arise in the early stages of democratization can play a key role for decades, but this is unusual.[12] Even after mass parties were formed in America in the 1830s (see chapter 2), the Whigs lasted for only twenty years, and not a single American president from 1841 to 1860 was even renominated by his party, let alone reelected.

In the broadest terms the party systems of the United States and Britain can be seen as being more stable over time than the actual parties, but this is by no means always the case. Brazil is extreme in the variety of party systems it has had since 1830, but it is far more typical than Colombia or the United States:[13]

Brazil has had seven distinct party systems: (1) there were two parties during most of the Empire (1830s to 1889); (2) the one-party arrangements of the different states during the Old Republic (1890s to 1930); (3) an embryonic multiparty polity (1930 to 1937); (4) a multiparty (1946 to 1964); (5) two parties in a hegemonic party system under military rule (1966 to 1979); (6) a transition period that began with the promise of allowing multiple parties to compete still under an authoritarian regime, but later resulted in maintaining bipartism in most states (1979 to 1984); (7) a move to multipartism in the waning months of military rule (1984 to 1985); and a return to a multiparty democracy (1985 to the present).

Not only have party systems often been unstable over a long period, but the parties themselves can behave in "inappropriate" ways. Three of the most important countries of the postwar period—West Germany, Japan, and Italy—were dominated for decades by a single party. Their left-wing parties did not move sufficiently to the center nor did the large umbrella parties splinter enough to lose their dominance. No doubt, the fact that all three were defeated powers in the war played a part; the occupying western powers had a major impact on their party formation as well as their constitution making, and the local elites probably found it useful to unite to present a common front to the victorious powers. Nevertheless, even Great Britain has retained a significant third-party system throughout this century that "should" have disappeared. Tony Blair and the Labour Party won what was termed a stunning landslide—and deservedly so—but we should not forget that the Labour Party received only 43.1 percent of the vote and that eleven parties won seats in the Parliament.

In short, even when we look at advanced democracies, we find many countries that do not follow the usual rules. We must be careful in generalizing about the Russian election of 1993 and the early stages of party formation. The party-less period of the Articles of Confederation lasted not only through the Revolutionary War but more than seven years after its conclusion—a total of thirteen years. Thirteen years after 1991 will bring us to 2004. We should be as cautious in concluding that we have seen an institutionalizing Russian political system as analysts of America should have been in 1783 and 1784.

The Peculiarities of Russian Parties

Nevertheless, although no one in 1989 and 1990 expected party formation in the Soviet Union to be simple, even pessimists were surprised by the utter chaos of the party systems of 1993 and 1995. Of course, it can be argued, as Joel Ostrow does, that the 1993 election did not feature real parties. Except for the Communist party, this is quite reasonable if we accept Joseph LaPalombara and Myron Weiner's definition of a party. The first of their four criteria for a party was "continuity in organization—that is, an organization whose expected life span is not dependent on the life span of current leaders," and the second was "manifest and presumably permanent organization at the local level, with regularized communications and other relationships between local and national units."[14]

Only history will reveal the life span of the parties that ran in 1993, but only the Communist Party of the Russian Federation seems likely to qualify as a party by this definition, and its leaders may well change its name to persuade the voters that it is truly social-democratic. Our participant-observers in the regions all paint the same picture of little connection between the single-member races and the party-list elections. They asserted that the single-member races were determined by highly idiosyncratic local and personal factors. Only the Communists seemed to have a permanent organization at the local level, but Evelyn Davidheiser testifies to a lack of central direction, financing, or even interest in the local contests among the national Communist party.

The other parties were worse. Russia's Choice was a coalition of Democratic Russia activists from the late 1980s and younger men from Yeltsin's executive branch. The latter, as Michael McFaul and Judith Kullberg describe accurately, were extremely cavalier toward the former. The Russia's Choice national list was relatively short, and the rest of the seats were to be distributed to those regions in which Russia's Choice received the most votes. Thus a candidate's position on the regional list was crucial, and the democratic activists often were put in the second or third spot.

The reason for this is not always clear. Perhaps it simply reflects the general preference given by Russia's Choice to market values over democratic ones. Gaidar in his memoir noted that Gennadii Burbulis, Arkadii Murashov, and Aleksei Golovkov (whom he calls his own right-hand man in 1992) never had good relations with the leaders of Democratic Russia, but it was Burbulis who headed the preelection staff of Russia's Choice and Golovkov who was its responsible secretary.[15]

Perhaps the phenomenon noted by Regina Smyth in Saratov is more general: the money and resources at the disposal of Russia's Choice provided powerful incentives for unscrupulous candidates to try to appropriate it for their own uses and the democratic activists may not have been sufficiently entrepreneurial to prevail in this battle. Whatever the cause, one of the strengths of this volume—and one of the most important components from a foreign policy perspective—is its documentation of the variety of the ways that a Russia's Choice party financed by the West failed to function properly at the local level and that that aspect of technical assistance to promote democracy failed.

The lack of a tie between central party leaders and the localities is, as has been seen, not unusual in comparative perspective. The same is true of many of the shortcomings of the national parties. The habitual personalistic description of parties mentioned by Joel Ostrow—the party of Gaidar, the party of Shakhrai, the party of Zhirinovskii, the party of Zyuganov, and, in fact, the inclusion of Grigorii Yavlinskii's name in the party name Yabloko—is a typical phenomenon in democratization of developing nations.[16] Some of the minor parties were quixotic attempts to have influence or efforts to seek publicity that underlie the continual rise of insignificant parties in all countries.

But the way many of the major parties were formed and operated still seem extraordinarily peculiar in light of the various generalizations in the comparative literature, and a seasoned scholar might suspect that the young scholars writing the chapters about these parties made some major, naive mistakes of analysis. The authors accurately described what took place, however improbable the events might seem.

Even for personalistic parties, the Russian parties seemed based on little "elite negotiation" in any meaningful definition of the term. To be sure, any significant party is formed through negotiation among members of the elite, but the phrase, to have meaning, implies negotiations among elite groups of some solidity who have an economic, organizational, institutional, or political base. It is striking how little of this was involved in the negotiations for party formation in 1993 or 1995, except within the executive. Although concrete data are still lacking, the hypothesis that best fits the data about 1993 is that the president and his top political advisers encouraged the formation of a series of parties with a base in the government or the president's entourage in order to maximize the president's power.

The non-Communist party that seemed most institutionalized was the so-called government party, Russia's Choice. McFaul is accurate in describing many of the strange tactical mistakes made in the campaign by Russia's Choice, but its fundamental strategic decisions are even stranger. When the leaders of Russia's Choice thought they could obtain 40 percent of the vote in a multiparty race, they were seeking the scale of support received by the American Republican party, the British Conservative party, or the German Christian Democratic party for decades. Yet they made no effort to form the kind of coalitions or make the type of compromises associated with such broad-based parties. Russia's Choice directed its main attack on the industrialists who traditionally are key parts of the base of big conservative parties, and it denounced the type of social issue—even nationalism—that a Republican party always uses to broaden its electoral base.

Indeed, although Russia's Choice called itself a *presidential party,* its leaders made no effort to adopt a program that the president would have supported. Yeltsin's electoral behavior in his struggle with Mikhail Gorbachev in 1990, in the 1991 presidential campaign, in the April 1993 referendum, and in the 1996 presidential campaign was identical: adopt a totally populist program and promise subsidies and benefits to every group.

Russia's Choice, by contrast, decided that its best election strategy was to initiate shock therapy two months before the election, promise even greater suffering after the election, and then in the weeks before the election not pay many workers, peasants, and even soldiers the wages they had already earned. This party also repeatedly ran a slick television commercial whose accurate message was that the party primarily represented the new rich. Yeltsin must have been horrified—or amused—by the electoral strategy, and he cannot have been involved unless he decided that the party's only role was to get Western support for the destruction of the Congress and subsequent Western financial assistance.

In December, the executive committee of Russia's Choice did decide to reach beyond its nominees and support a number of independents and nominees of other parties. It endorsed ninety-nine people who had been nominated by Russia's Choice, seventy-one independents, and eighteen nominees of other parties, but it decided to endorse no one in thirty-one districts. The endorsement of other candidates by Russia's Choice was successful in eight of eleven districts in Moscow and St. Petersburg but in only seventeen of seventy-eight districts in the rest of the country.[17]

It is instructive to look at the Sobyanin rating scores for the deputies in the 1993 to 1995 Duma and compare them with the Russia's Choice endorsements before the election. The victorious candidates nominated by Russia's Choice had an average score of 75.1 (on a scale of +100 to −100), and, if we exclude one clear-cut tactical endorsement of a conservative to defeat a once-radical local governor,[18] then the victorious other candidates endorsed by Russia's Choice had an average score of 64.3. Fewer than 8 percent of other deputies had a score more radical than the endorsees of Russia's Choice.

But if we look at the thirty districts in which Russia's Choice endorsed no one, we find that eleven had deputies with Sobyanin scores placing them among the half of the deputies with the most radical scores and five among the top 30 percent of deputies. If we look at the sixty-four districts in which Russia's Choice supported another candidate but lost, twenty-five of the winners had a score that placed them among the half of the deputies with the most radical score, but only five of these were in the top quarter of the most radical. Even when Russia's Choice was reaching out in December to broaden its coalition, it clearly was endorsing only the most radical of candidates and avoiding more moderate reformers. We can only guess how many more of the latter would have been elected if Russia's Choice had followed a more embracing strategy either early or late in the campaign.

The leaders of Russia's Choice were so confident of victory that they scheduled a live nationwide television victory party titled "To Meet the New Political Year." As two sociologists noted, the preliminary results "turned out to be so shocking that the most authoritative sociologists who appeared on the program . . . literally lost the gift of speech before the microphones."[19] In retrospect, the wonder is not that Russia's Choice received only 15.5 percent of the vote but that it received so many. The 3.9 percent the party received in 1995 seems more appropriate in 1993 as well, and its large vote in 1993 is, most of all, a testimony to the power of television.

Even after the election the leaders and chief supporters of Russia's Choice could not understand what had happened. How could a majority of the population have voted for Yeltsin's economic reform in April 1993 and not for Russia's Choice in December, they asked? Before the election, Sobyanin and his team had analyzed prospects for radical victory on the assumption that Yeltsin won the referendum with his radical program, not his populism, and that the referendum showed "the distance between the positions of the citizens and the deputies, which has been increasing from year to year."[20] His charges of fraud, reported by Timothy Colton earlier, were largely based on the unspoken assumption that the population *must* have voted for Russia's Choice, as predicted. Thus, fraud in vote counting was the only explanation for the reported outcome. It was the classic misjudgment of revolutionary Jacobins about the nature of public opinion.

Other major parties seem just as peculiar. Daniel Treisman, for example, describes a party (Party of Unity and Accord; PRES) that proclaimed it was for power for the regions and republics but that was headed by the leading centralizer in the Yeltsin entourage, Sergei Shakhrai, and by Gaidar's alter ego in the first Yeltsin government, deputy premier Aleksandr Shokhin. It was tacitly supported by Premier Viktor Chernomyrdin. As Ellen Mickiewicz reports, "Sergei Shakhrai's [ads] were unusual for their clear appeal to nationalistic values not much remarked upon in a Western press fixated on Zhirinovskii's use of this card."[21] Kullberg notes the surprisingly strong "Moscow flavor" of a politician who supposedly was appealing to the regions.

Shakhrai's "regional" PRES party actually was a fraud, or, at best, a forerunner of Chernomyrdin's more accurately labeled "government party" of 1995. After the election Shakhrai returned to his old positions of abolition of the republics and the strengthening of the central government. He was one of the architects of the war in Chechnya. The "regions" he wanted to strengthen were the regional chiefs appointed by Moscow, and some of his strongest support came in republics he wanted to abolish because he had used his position to cut some deal with an authoritarian republican president.[22]

Treisman talks about another reform opposition party, Yabloko, whose leader refused to hold press conferences or to campaign on the grounds that "the more rarely we appeared, the less the electorate would get sick of us," as his campaign manager put it. Yavlinskii campaigned for more gradual economic reform but was one of the authors of the 500-Day-Plan, which was far more radical than anything Gaidar was introducing or proposing.[23] The party claimed it was seeking to be a party representing mass desires for gradual reform, but its party list both in 1993 and 1995 was composed entirely of young academics, overwhelmingly from Moscow institutes. A careful content analysis of the platforms of the 1993 parties by Sarah Oates found that Yabloko's platform was marginally more pro-market than Russia's Choice, as was PRES's platform.[24]

The Yavlinskii-Boldyrev-Lukin bloc is often treated as the major democratic hope, but the twenty deputies on its list included only three men who served as Russian Congress deputies and no person with significant administrative experience outside the foreign policy sphere. Almost all twenty were scholars or former scholars—almost always economists. The same was true of its district candidates, and it was not surprising that only seven of eighty-six Yabloko candidates were elected.

Another party, the Russian Movement for Democratic Reform, did not want power but hoped to serve as a democratic opposition to whomever did, and its leader did not take it seriously enough to garner more than 8.7 percent of votes in St. Petersburg, where he was mayor. Its leaders were shocked to receive less than 5 percent of the vote.

A centrist party, Civic Union, claimed to speak for both industrialists and workers, but it ignored trade union leaders. It also ignored worker interests. Its major real program was nomenklatura privatization essentially based on the informal expropriation of the shares of ownership in the enterprise that had allegedly been given "the collective"—that is, largely the workers. Not surprisingly, the workers did not support it.

Davidheiser describes an oppositional Agrarian party that put the six top agricultural officials of the government in its top slots—the very officials who were responsible for not paying the peasants for their 1993 crop and were overseeing an agricultural policy of exploiting the countryside to subsidize the major cities. These included in the number 3 spot on the list Aleksandr Zaveryukha, Chernomyrdin's hand-picked deputy premier for agriculture who came from his own home region of Orenburg. The party had its office in the government building of the Committee (Ministry) of the Food Industry. The Agrarian party really *was* a government party, and it did so poorly because the peasants understood this.

Even Women of Russia was peculiar. It originally was described as a conservative party, an offshoot of the Communists. Then it was judged a centrist party on the basis of its voting in the Duma. But, as time passed, the presence of Yeltsin's chief adviser on women, a subordinate of his in Sverdlovsk, in the number 3 spot on the ticket, seemed increasingly important.

The Parties That Did Not Bark

But if the parties that did emerge in 1993 seem strange, the truly strange aspect of the election were the parties that did *not* emerge. This book has naturally focused on the election that was held in 1993, and in traditional fashion Colton examines the correlates of support for the parties that were on the ballot. The character of Russian public opinion on issues emerges less clearly. There has been a tendency in the West to accept the bipolarized view of Russian opinion propagated by those on the Russian right who want to say the choice has been limited to "reform" or Communism. Yet, in fact, Russian opinion on economic reform, national issues, and democracy has tended to correspond to the classic bell-shaped curve.

In one sense, the Russian revolution of 1991 has been overwhelmingly successful. Although many in the French elite, for example, did not really accept the legitimacy of the French Revolution for many decades, few Rus-

sians want to return the old order. A strong majority wants to restore a federation with the old Soviet republics; only a small minority favor "radical
economic reform," and fewer still define that as would Gaidar or an American; a substantial number, including many who call themselves democrats,
would not object to a military dictatorship of the "proper" type. But few under the age of 60 want the reestablishment of the old system, and a large
majority want marketization and democratization, however they define
them. Zhirinovskii favored gradual market reform. Even the Communist
leadership desperately wanted to take a more social democratic position but
felt constrained by the unattractiveness of the Communist name to all but
the older hard-liners.

The nature of Russian opinion on issues at the time of the 1993 election
has been reported in earlier work,[25] but two of the simplest questions in our
survey make the point most graphically. The questions were also asked at
the time of the 1995 Duma and 1996 presidential election, and the answers
from all three time points are presented to document the relative stability of
opinion.[26] All responses are shown in percent.

What Do You Think about the Transition to a Market Economy in Russia?

	1993	1995	1996
1. Should be rapid	13.6	6.5	6.6
2. Should be gradual	43.6	44.7	52.7
3. Against a market economy	17.9	22.5	16.7
4. Hard to say	23.9	25.8	23.7
5. No answer	1.0	0.5	0.3

Is the West Following the Goal of Weakening Russia with Its Economic Advice?

	1993	1995	1996
1. I am sure of it	28.0	35.4	33.3
2. Probably yes	24.1	23.6	26.1
3. Probably not	14.3	13.6	14.2
4. I am sure not	11.1	6.9	7.2
5. Hard to say	21.9	20.1	19.0

As is often emphasized, the young on the whole have a different set of
attitudes than the old, but the following data on those from twenty-four to
thirty-two years old, including data from a 1997 survey specifically of this
age group, demonstrate that the differences should not be exaggerated.[27]

Twenty-Four- to Thirty-Two-Year-Olds: What Do You Think about the Transition
to a Market Economy in Russia?

	1993	1995	1996	1997	1997[a]
1. Should be rapid	18.6	9.2	9.8	10.5	12.2
2. Should be gradual	51.3	55.3	62.4	55.6	60.7
3. Against market economy	10.7	11.8	7.8	11.5	7.1
4. Hard to say	18.1	23.0	19.3	21.7	19.4
5. No answer	1.3	0.8	0.7	0.7	0.5

a. Seventeen-year-olds.

Twenty-Four- to Thirty-Two-Year-Olds: Is the West Following the Goal of Weakening Russia with Its Economic Advice?

	1993	1995	1996	1997	1997[a]
1. I am sure of it	15.1	22.7	22.4	23.5	19.9
2. Probably yes	27.5	25.7	27.1	34.2	37.8
3. Probably not	18.6	21.1	19.7	17.7	15.6
4. I am sure not	16.6	11.3	10.4	6.9	7.5
5. Hard to say	21.7	18.8	20.2	17.5	18.8
6. No answer	0.6	0.4	0.2	0.3	0.3

a. Seventeen-year-olds.

The views revealed in the question about the speed of reform reappeared
in responses to questions about privatization, the sale of land, price controls, foreign investment, and so forth. The support either of those wanting
a total market solution or a return to the past marginally declined over time.
Only on the question of the privatization of large enterprises was there a
major decline in support,[28] but the steady rise in the suspicion about the intentions of the West testify to the emotion behind the feelings.

Our survey showed that a majority of the population in 1993 did not have
an opinion about the Chinese model of economic reform—still another sign
of the truncated nature of the debate in Russia—but 32 percent had a favorable opinion compared to 12 percent unfavorable. The proportion of people
with a college education who had no opinion fell to a still high 44 percent
and the unfavorable opinion rose to 18 percent, but 38 percent were favorable. But although most knew little about China, a strong majority did, in
fact, want large elements of the reform in China: privatization of trade and
small business but much greater caution about major industry, strict controls on the sale of land, foreign investment but under tight controls, high
tariffs against imports, price controls, and social welfare measures.

In the realm of nationality policy, 69 percent thought the break-up of the Soviet Union had done more harm than good (41.8 percent said simply it was harmful), but only 20 percent thought it did more good than harm. Only 56 percent of ethnic Russians called Russia their Motherland *(Rodina),* and the others said it was the USSR or their region.

Eighty-three percent wanted a stronger Commonwealth of Independent States in 1993, and 93 percent thought Russia had an obligation to defend Russians in other republics. In 1995, a new question revealed that only 6 percent thought Ukraine should be an independent country with customs controls and 26 percent an independent country with open borders.

In 1996, the normative evaluation of the breakup of the USSR was identical, and the proportion of ethnic Russians who called Russia their Motherland had fallen to 47 percent. In the 1997 survey of twenty-four- to thirty-two-year-olds in 1997, 57 percent called the breakup of the Soviet Union more harmful and 27 percent said it produced more good, but only 43 percent of ethnic Russians saw Russia as their Motherland.

When Russians were asked in 1995 whether they would support a leader who would reestablish the USSR or one who would develop Russia, only 30 percent answered the USSR, 47 percent Russia, and 23 percent did not know. The same pattern of answers emerged on Chechnya: only a third favored granting the republic its independence, but there was no desire for a war on the issue. The Russians as a whole very much wanted greater integration with the non-Russian republics, but not by force, and they gave no evidence of wanting the kind of restoration of empire proposed by Zhirinovskii. In general, they understood that a strong Moscow center repressing the republics would also repress Russian regions.

In short, Russian public opinion emerged from our 1993 survey (as well as later ones) as very "normal," very moderate, very centrist from an American point of view. As to be expected, Russians were quite negative toward policies that had failed and the politicians who produced them. They quite reasonably believed that American advice was so harmful that it must be intended to weaken Russia, even if ideological dogmatism was the actual explanation. But they also rejected the Soviet past. They naturally wanted the strong government protections always found in the democracies of developing nations, but at a minimum they wanted something like the mixed economies of Sweden and America.

The most striking feature of the 1993 election was that out of thirteen parties in 1993—or even forty-three in 1995—no party offered the Russian population the "normal" centrist program it wanted. Everyone talked about "gradualism" and "social defense," but no one other than the Communists indicated that they might be serious left-center reformists, and the Communist message was not consistent. Treisman was correct in saying that parties such as Yabloko, PRES, and Russian Movement for Democratic Reform (RDDR) were centrist in their general language, but the population was correct in believing that their leadership and their lack of serious programs meant that they were essentially like Russia's Choice: parties of unrealistic intellectuals who would carry out a similar economic policy. Yavlinskii was the author of the 500-Day Plan, Shakhrai and Shokhin were two of the four radical deputy premiers of the first Yeltsin-Burbulis-Gaidar government, and Anatolii Sobchak and Gavriil Popov of RDDR were members of the Interregional Group in the USSR Congress and the founders of Leningrad and Moscow democracy.

The politicians leading the parties in the Duma election were not, however, the only politicians in Russia. A second striking result that emerges from most of the articles on the elections in the oblasts and republics is the rise of political bosses and political machines in the regions. National parties were not able to build coalitions, but local leaders often were. As a result, the great majority of them were able to win election to the Federation Council, and often with large majorities.

In almost all the regions, the political machine is controlled by the executive—the head of administration in the oblasts and the presidents in the republics. Robert Moser's description of Transformation of the Urals in Sverdlovsk oblast and Nigel Gould-Davies' of Fond Vybor in Nizhnii Novgorod oblast are basically those of local machines. But Kullberg is right to emphasize Luzhkov's role as "a major supplier of property" as a key base to his "political machine," and the point has general applicability. In Kursk, the strongest machine was controlled by the chair of the former regional soviet—that is, the regional legislature—but with the heads of administration coming to be replaced by elected governors, the Kursk pattern is likely to remain an exception. Indeed, Aleksandr Rutskoi won as governor in Kursk in 1997.

In practice, Yeltsin tended to be fairly responsive to local political forces in appointing heads of administration. Leonid Brezhnev was willing to tolerate relatively liberal obkom secretaries such as Gorbachev, Eduard Shevardnadze, and Yeltsin along with conservative ones so long as they were loyal to him. Yeltsin has behaved in much the same fashion. He removed those who challenged him directly and those who supported his Moscow enemies, but he was content to support relatively radical former college instructors in Sobchak in St. Petersburg and Boris Nemtsov in Nizhnii Novgorod, a relatively apolitical plant manager in Kursk, a more nationalist and politicized industrialist in Primorskii territory, a nonnationalist populist in Kemerovo, a professional city politician-administrator in Moscow, and so forth. In regions not covered in this book, a real nationalist was head of administration in Krasnodar, and experienced Communist party officials who emphasized food subsidies occupied these posts in Orel and Ul'ianovsk.

The successful Republican leaders were also adept in building coalitions. In Bashkortostan, as Henry Hale reports, only 22 percent of the population are Bashkirs, but the leader of the Supreme Soviet, Murtaza Rakhimov, was able, without creating unrest, to impose a requirement that the president must be able to speak the Bashkir language. The base of his power was naturally the rural machine, both because more Bashkirs live in the countryside and because he appointed the county (raion) and city chief administrators. However, Rakhimov also created an alliance with the head of the ethnic Russians in Ufa, Aleksandr Arinin, even supporting Arinin's centralizing candidate, Sergei Shakhrai.[29]

The American Progressive Movement and its successors were scornful of the corrupt political bosses, but the great sociologist Robert Merton was far closer to the truth when he emphasized the positive functions they served.[30] The Nazdratenko's, the Luzhkov's, the Rossel's, the Nemtsov's are serving the function of the city bosses of America of a century ago. They are not, of course, trying to protect and mobilize immigrants, but the functional equivalent are the workers of the large industrial enterprises and the peasants of the collective and state farms who need protection just as much as did the American immigrants. Because the central social welfare issue involves the question of food subsidization, they cannot be city officials but "state governors" who can distribute money and resources to the farms as well as to the urban dwellers. They are, many of them, corrupt and authoritarian; they may try to solidify their support with control of the media and perhaps even a little creative vote-counting.

But if these bosses can build strong local parties or machines, they did not participate in the formation of strong national parties in 1993 or 1995. None of them ran for president in 1996. This was what the parties of 1993 and 1995 were lacking. Forty-year-old professors who entered politics four years prior and who had no significant administrative experience simply were not credible leaders of a country. Sergei Baburin, a moderate nationalist who was a law school professor and is now deputy chair of the Duma was no more credible than Gaidar, Shakhrai, or Yavlinskii—or Ruslan Khasbulatov, chairman of the Russian Congress, who had a similar background. Even aside from his bizarre views, Zhirinovskii is not a credible candidate for president. Indeed, people such as Gaidar, Shokhin, and Yavlinskii might well become chair of the Council of Economic Advisers in the United States, but they certainly would not be thought to have the experience to be Secretary of Treasury.

Academics were not the only inexperienced politicians. Aleksandr Rutskoi was an air force colonel in 1990. Ivan Rybkin was the chair of Communists of Russia in the Congress of People's Deputies and a member of the Agrarian party in 1993 before being elected chair of the State Duma in 1994. He moved energetically to a right-centrist position and tried to form a centrist party. But for five years previously Rybkin had been a forty-three-year-old district committee first secretary in the city of Volgograd.[31]

Indeed, one of Zyuganov's major problems in winning support was that in more than twenty years of party work, he was never party first-secretary of a county, city, or state or chair of the executive committee of a soviet. He served as head of the propaganda department (the deputy of the ideological secretary) in Orel for ten years when Yegor Stroyev, now the governor of Orel and chair of the Federation Council, was the agricultural secretary in the province, a rank above. In 1985 Stroyev became Orel obkom first secretary and a member of the Central Committee in 1986, and Zyuganov received a minor job in the Central Committee apparatus. In 1989, Stroyev became Central Committee secretary for agriculture and Zyuganov deputy head of the ideological department. Even if one believes that Zyuganov is sincere in proclaiming moderate views, one can still wonder if he has the political experience and administrative capability to rule effectively.

An Agrarian party—or even the Communist party—that was led by Stroyev and called for a Chinese-like agricultural reform based on leasing of land, market prices for products, and promotion of rural and small-town industry would have been taken seriously by the electorate. The same is true of Moscow mayor Yurii Luzhkov or Nazdratenko of Primorskii krai heading a party with the posture of a nationalistic American Republican party. Even Nemtsov, perhaps the least impressive of the major bosses, would have been more credible than Yavlinskii in charge of Yabloko. Analogous figures would have been leading figures in the Democratic or Republican party, and their absence seriously weakened the Russian parties.

What Went Wrong?

The overall picture that emerges from this study is encouraging about Russian public opinion in the first half of the 1990s but discouraging about the political institutions that arose to mobilize and represent this opinion. Nevertheless, as discussed early in this chapter, we should never forget that almost thirteen years passed between the onset of the American Revolution and the inauguration of George Washington. From the perspective of the late twentieth century, the period of the Articles of Confederation is but a twinkle of time. Times of transition are excruciatingly long if you must live through them, but blissfully short once the historian can show the conclusion to which they "inevitably" led.

So it will probably be with the current Russian transition. From one perspective, the Communist Party of Russia has had remarkable success. It received 12.4 percent of the vote in 1993, 22 percent in 1995, and 40 percent for Zyuganov (the leader) in 1996 (if those who voted "against all" are excluded). If Communists win the next election, and if they preserve the democratic system, the opposition will coalesce in self-defense. Even without such a victory, it is possible that when the banks and the industrialists finally become interested in industrial development, they will support a candidate such as Luzhkov in building a broad-based nationalist party. If so, Russia may quickly move to an institutionalized party system, and historians will marvel at how quickly and smoothly it all occurred. Lebed might follow a coup d'etat by creating a presidential party. Or if the Communists fail and the party system does not consolidate for whatever reason, if postcommunist Russian history comes to resemble Brazil's, historians will explore why Russia was structurally like Brazil rather than other countries where stable party systems formed.

We are thus writing in the midst of a transition with an uncertain outcome, and we do not know whether we are in the middle of a rapid or slow period of party formation in historical perspective. It is as if we were in the 1780s talking about the political consequences of the American Revolution and analyzing the politics of the Continental Congress in detail, or as if we were talking about the system spawned by the French Revolution in 1793, four years after the revolution and six years before Napoleon took power.

Nevertheless, regardless of the time frame involved, there were major shortcomings in the early stages of institution formation in postcommunist Russia, and we can at least make some generalizations about this stage of political development and draw some implications. Some of the reasons have already been discussed in partial terms, but a number of problems have general theoretical and policy interest and deserve emphasis.

1. Endemic Early Problems of Party Formation

Russia is not the first country to experience difficulties in party formation. The United States did not have serious national protoparties until the mid-1790s, nearly twenty years after the revolution, and its real mass parties were created only sixty years after the revolution. In Africa, the same scholars who thirty years ago stated that "political parties are the most crucial political structures shaping the new African polities," now hardly include the word party in their index and write about "personal politics" in which "politicians [are] operating largely without the aid of effective institutions and in a manner that discredits the institutions that exist."[32] "Politics in most Black African states do not conform to an institutionalized system. They are not an activity in which individuals and organizations engage publicly to win the right to govern or to influence a government's policies within an overall and legitimate framework of agreed-upon rules."[33]

There are two sets of endemic problems. One is ideological suspicion of parties. Even the most widely cited scholar on political parties today, Giovanni Sartori, discusses the Downs model and the tendency of parties to maximize votes by going to the center as "an explanation of how democracies inevitably deteriorate and end up performing as meanly as they do."[34] Most contemporary scholars take Schumpeter's entrepreneurial definition of parties for granted, and Sartori is extreme in this respect,[35] but the first democratizing generations almost always have a strong sense that parties subvert national unity and interfere with the rational discussion of how to achieve the common good. Richard Hofstadter's classic study of party formation in the United States emphasized that early Anglo-American political thought featured "the root idea . . . that parties are evil."[36] Alexis de Tocqueville in the 1830s likewise wrote that "parties are an evil inherent in free governments."[37]

In addition, those raised within a truly authoritarian state, especially one based on the divine right of kings, have little conception of the peculiar combination embodied in the leader of a constitutional democracy. Such a ruler must put together a coalition representing the majority, but work within the framework of limits protecting minorities from the majority. When people raised within a highly authoritarian regime think of democracy, they normally retain their old concept of the king, modifying only their view of how he should come to power. In the words of Gordon Wood, classical Whig thought of the eighteenth century, which infused much "progressive" thinking, saw "republican magistrates [as] no more 'representative' of the people than monarchs. . . . Both hereditary and elected rulers were considered clothed with a special authority and 'exalted from among the people, to bear rule.'"[38]

The second endemic problem of early party formation is structural. A graduate of an American college today who wants to go into politics must work within a well-defined system of institutions, rules, and incentives. At some later point in life, a few may succeed in modifying the rules of the game, but at the beginning they must follow them if they are to succeed.

By contrast, there are no firm organizations at the early stage of democratization within which ambitious young politicians may try to work their way. Few rules exist to restrain them, and the incentive system leads them to "maximize profit," either in terms of seeking to get quickly to the top or of using politics for maximum financial gain. Small wonder that the first parties tend to be highly personalistic and ephemeral. Africa has been already mentioned, but it is scarcely unique. Latin America began to democratize in the nineteenth century, but Sartori still could write in 1976, "The literature on Latin American parties incessantly speaks of factionalism, *personalism*, and the like."[39]

The United States was no different. The American Federalists and the Jeffersonian Republicans barely outlasted the period in which their founders, Hamilton, Jefferson, and Madison, played a leading role. The Whigs in retrospect look like the creature of Henry Clay and Daniel Webster, and a series of former presidents in this period left their parties to see if their personal charisma could form the base of a new party.[40] Abraham Lincoln gained the presidency with no major administrative experience in Illinois and two year's experience in Washington in the House of Representatives. The lack of institutionalized parties was a major reason the country had a terrible civil war.

Schumpeter's definition of politicians as entrepreneurs seeking to maximize votes and get elected implies that they should respond quickly to the logic of an electoral system and take whatever rational decisions are necessary for victory. In fact, Schumpeter insisted on four preconditions for a successful democracy that actually imply a very constrained framework in which the rational struggle for votes must take place. There must be (in a later phrase) a political culture featuring "democratic self-control" and "a large measure of tolerance for differences of opinion." In addition, "the effective range of political decisions should not be extended too far."

To a surprising extent, the Russian public has shown strong political tolerance both in public opinion polls and practice, and it has been astonishingly patient in the face of severe economic difficulties. This, no doubt, is confirmation of a key tenet in modernization theory: an educated population is a prerequisite for a stable, well-functioning democracy, and Russia has an extraordinarily well-educated population. In 1994, 65.6 percent of the Russian population 15 years of age or older had a high school diploma or better, 93 percent of those between the ages of 25 and 34.[41]

But Schumpeter went beyond factors associated with societal "political culture" to posit preconditions that Russia was a long way from achieving in 1993. The third of Schumpeter's preconditions was "the services of a well-trained bureaucracy of good standing and tradition, endowed with a strong sense of duty and a no less strong *esprit de corps.*" The first of his preconditions was high-quality politicians: "Experience seems to suggest that the only effective guarantee is in the existence of a social stratum, itself a product of a severely selective process, that takes to politics as a matter of course."[42]

Schumpeter understood that being a successful politician, like being a successful corporation president, requires a learning experience, a stable institutional framework in which to learn the rules of the game, and an administrative structure that creates the confidence that it is worthwhile to think seriously about policy because policies will be carried out.

2. The Peculiarities of Russian Democratization

Whatever the path of Russian democratization in the future, it has been atypical in the past. If democratization is seen as a 175-year process, then democratization in Russia should, no doubt, be seen beginning with the zemstvos in the 1870s. Because the growth of an educated, urbanized, and occupationally differentiated population with a participant political culture is a key element in democracy, the emphasis placed on such development during the Communist period made it a real part of the democratization process. The Communist regime also constantly emphasized the legitimacy of concepts such as democracy and the importance of political participation.

Even from such a perspective, Russia is only two-thirds through its democratization process, but it has also reached the present point in an extremely unusual manner. Most countries begin the process of democratization with the creation of informal restraints on their leaders that serve to protect "life, liberty, and property" and with the establishment of semidemocratic legislatures. Most countries become quasi-constitutional or liberal before they become democratic. As their population becomes more educated and urbanized, they tend, although with interruptions, to be granted the right of greater participation in politics.

The Communist leaders, by contrast, explicitly denied the legitimacy and possibility of limited government. Communist ideology went beyond the normal feeling of illegitimacy of parties at the early stages of democratization in its emphasis on the unity of the interests of the working class and then the people as a whole. Communist leaders insisted that the "representative of the working class" had the duty to represent its interests in the historically defined manner and that this duty justified the most rigorous repression of opposition. The distinctive feature of the Communist dictatorship—the feature that the word *totalitarian* should have connoted rather than terror—was its lack of normal constitutional restraints and its unusual restrictions on individual freedom.

Marx and Lenin also provided democrats of the future with little guidance. They denied that government played a useful, let alone a necessary, role in the capitalist economy, and Lenin saw no value in competitive political elections and parliamentarianism. Their view of the utopian future was fully within the tradition of anarchism. There was to be planning, but the state was to wither away. Western democracy, they made clear, was "a state" and hence was also to wither away Decisions were to be made by some general will, however that was to be ascertained. Westerners treated the utopianism of Marx and Lenin as empty propaganda and were, no doubt, right on one level. However, students were being indoctrinated in the utopianism, and people such as Gorbachev and Shevardnadze—and even Yeltsin in a way—were strongly affected by it.

Hence neither Russia's "political class" nor "the attentive public" learned anything about the character of semifree electoral competition, the nature of limited government and a free press, or the normal give-and-take between executive and legislature during the usual authoritarian period. Whatever the grave shortcomings of the Russian elections and the weakness of the Duma, they are creating a political class with new political skills. A series of mistakes, major as well as minor, were and will be inevitable before Schumpeter's "social stratum . . . that takes to politics as a matter of course" is created.

In this sense Yeltsin is the typical right-wing authoritarian leader who often emerges in the early stages of constitutional democracy in the world, and the Duma has powers similar to many legislatures at this stage. But the successful among such regimes feature the economic growth of predemocratic Korea or of Indonesia over recent decades. If Yeltsin continues to have the economic record that Mobutu had in Zaire, it is not clear how long the military or the population will tolerate the current line of development.

3. Peculiarities of the Russian Legislative Tradition

The scholarly literature emphasizes the strong tendency for early political parties to emerge out of the legislature. Conceivably in long-term perspective, Russia too will have such an appearance. Zyuganov has ended the old practice of having a Communist party apparatus independent of the Duma, and his party has really risen as a legislative party rather than from the old Communist party.[43] Power to the People (Nikolai Ryzhkov's party) was formed externally to the legislature but acquired an important deputy core only after the election. If the banks decide to form a serious party in alliance with the industrialists, they are likely to choose politicians from the legislature as the leaders of the party.

There have, however, been major obstacles to such a development—first of all, the newness of the legislature and several peculiar features of it. Whatever the nature of party-like groups in the British Parliament prior to 1832, British politicians had seen the Parliament as the main arena for political action and had gravitated toward it. When changes in the electoral rules in 1832 created a need to have mass parties, leading politicians in Parliament were the natural individuals to take on the task. The Russian legislative leaders had often been in politics for only a few years, and they had little feel for legislative life, let alone for political parties. They have had little opportunity to form a political class.

In addition, as discussed in chapter 2, the Russian legislature elected in 1990 was organized in a peculiar manner. The legislative organ, the Supreme Soviet, had little power, and it was dominated by its top leaders and the committee chairs, not by its faction leaders. The factions were much stronger within the Congress, but they were dealing with fundamental constitutional questions on a more sporadic basis.

The Communist party was the country's dominant political institution, and party theory suggests it should have played a major organizational role

in the legislative. However, neither Gorbachev and his people, Ivan Polozkov and the Russian Communist party, nor the Communists of Russia faction in the Russian Congress ever seem to have assimilated the concept of a
parliamentary party. On the democratic side, the first quasi parties—the
Interregional Group within the USSR Congress and Democratic Russia
within the Russian Congress—really were revolutionary organizations
rather than normal legislative parties. Indeed, both soon began campaigning for the liquidation of the Congress in which they were formed.

Finally, the rules both within the Russian Congress and the Duma produced incentives for a fragmentation of parties rather than the consolidation implied by the election rules. With each faction being granted one seat
on the reconciliation commissions of the Congress or on the Duma Council,
deputies had the incentive to form as many factions as permitted. It was
eventually decided that new factions had to contain thirty-five members to
be officially recognized. A fair number of radicals were elected as independents in the districts in Duma election, but instead of joining Russia's
Choice, they formed a new faction, the Union of December 12, that seemed
almost identical in its political views.[44]

4. Peculiarities Produced by the September 1993
Dissolution of the Congress

Authors throughout this book have emphasized the importance of
Yeltsin's sudden and surprise call for an election only two and a half
months after the dissolution of the Congress. A lack of time gave political
actors little time to think and organize.

In addition, however, the form of the resistance to the dissolution and the
bloody confrontation with which it ended also had potential impacts that
are hard to judge. But they may have been enormous. The banning of a
number of nationalist parties and the imprisonment of several key leaders
led to a reduction in the number of parties on the ballot, or at least the absence of some key parties. This had consequences other than intended. The
absence of nationalist parties that received less than 5 percent of the vote
probably increased the representation of conservative parties in the Duma
rather than decreased it. The only small parties to lose representation and to
have their votes distributed across the political spectrum to parties with 5
percent were right-wing and center parties.

The most interesting potential impact of the dissolution of the Congress
came from the removal of several major centrist leaders of the opposition to

Yeltsin from the contest. Vice President Aleksandr Rutskoi and Supreme Soviet Chair Ruslan Khasbulatov rightly called the Yeltsin dissolution of the Congress unconstitutional, and they correctly said that because of an explicit clause in the constitution, Yeltsin's action automatically removed him from office and elevated the vice president to the presidency. Rutskoi, in fact, "assumed" the presidency. This would have been a brilliant and even constitutional strategy if Rutskoi, by then an Air Force general, had been supported by the military in a showdown with Yeltsin, but it seemed far less brilliant when military support was not forthcoming and Rutskoi and Khasbulatov found themselves in prison.

But imagine that Khasbulatov and Rutskoi had vehemently protested the dissolution of the Congress, called Yeltsin a dictator, but agreed to participate in the election as leaders of centrist parties defending democracy. In July 1991, Rutskoi had allied with seven of the most prominent supporters of perestroika, including Yakovlev and Shevardnadze, in a manifesto supporting an Association of Democrats.[45] He had the most plausible and even courageous record of criticism of Gaidar from November 1991 onward. Gaidar's team, he said at the time, consisted of "little boys in pink trousers, red shirts, and yellow shoes."[46] He could say that he had been right about their competence.

Rutskoi had been put in charge of farm policy, but without the power to institute one. In an interview with me in March 1993, he said that the threat to Russia no longer came from the West but from the fundamentalism of the Middle East to the South, from South Asia, or from the Far East (for example, China). When asked if he were not afraid that exploratory efforts by Westerners offering investment would not be used for industrial and military espionage, Rutskoi answered, "Treat us as you did Germany and Japan after World War II." It is easy to see how Rutskoi could have packaged his positions into a very attractive political program for a proagricultural and moderately nationalistic—but not anti-Western—party.

Khasbulatov for his part had been elected first deputy chair of the Russian Supreme Soviet in 1990 precisely because he was a Moscow-based Chechen who was a radical economist supporting Yeltsin. He was seen as Yeltsin's man, but also a representative of the non-Russian republics and their interests in the government. If he had formed a regional party promising to defend the rights both of republics and oblasts in a federal system, if he had damned Yeltsin's constitution for its utterly cavalier exclusion of the Federal Treaty Yeltsin had signed with the republics, he surely would have cleared the 5 percent limit. But, of course, if Yeltsin had known his constitution would be effectively criticized on these grounds, he almost surely would have had to present a constitution that was less centralizing in character.

The entry of Rutskoi and Khasbulatov centrist parties into the 1993 election would have changed its dynamics radically. It is most unlikely that PRES and the Agrarian party could have cleared the 5 percent minimum, and other party alliances might have been formed before the election. Indeed, Yeltsin himself might have been forced to form a presidential party as the only way to turn the election into a referendum on his dissolution of the Congress.

5. The Lack of Societal Institutions

No concept has become more fashionable in the discussion of the transition to democracy in Communist societies than *civil society*. None has been more confused, misleading, and harmful. In general, civil society usually refers to the existence of groups and institutions that mediate between society and the state and that are independent of the state, but it can also include free individuals. However, it was used by Tocqueville and Marx—and, no doubt, other intellectuals of the time—to mean civilized society, a society with laws, what Max Weber called a rational-technical society.[47]

Irrespective of its vagueness, or perhaps because of it, the concept of *civil society* has come to be used widely in the contemporary West, but with different meanings. A French scholar retains its nineteenth-century meaning: "a vast ensemble of constantly changing groups and individuals whose only common ground is their exclusion from the state."[48] Americans focus more on groups, but themselves come from many different and conflicting intellectual traditions: the post-Hitler concern with the ability of authoritarian rulers to mobilize people in an atomized society; the classic American pluralist literature on the importance of interest groups and parties to represent and aggregate public opinion and serve as transmission belts of opinion to the black box of the state; the New Left insistence on participatory democracy because of elite dominance of interest groups and political parties.

The assumptions and values underlying these intellectual traditions are wildly different. Those who talked of atomization and mass society could be quite pessimistic about modern society. In 1946 (but not a decade later) Talcott Parsons could talk of the impersonality of modern industrial society and its propensity to charismatic rulers and leaders.[49] Hannah Arendt and William Kornhauser did not see inevitability, but were deeply concerned about the isolation in mass society:[50] "The chief characteristic of the mass man is not brutality and backwardness, but his isolation and lack of normal social relationships. . . . Total loyalty—the psychological basis for total domination . . . can be expected only from the completely isolated human being . . . without any social ties to family, friends, comrades, or even mere acquaintances."

The American pluralists, by contrast, almost always saw Americans enmeshed in a rich group structure at the local level and represented by a myriad of interest groups in higher politics. Yet they too were part of the generation for whom the victory of Hitler was a dominant event of their youth, and they too were not unhappy to see low levels of mass participation and to see groups represented by persons integrated into the elite.

V. O. Key is commonly considered the top political scientist of the mid-twentieth century. He saw interest group representatives as members of a common "leadership echelon," and he argued that "to a considerable degree the work of the spokesmen of private groups, both large and small, proceeds without extensive involvement of either the membership or a wider public." Key even surmised that "the pluralistic interactions among leadership echelons may occur, and may be tolerable, precisely because leadership clusters can command only a relatively small following among the masses."[51]

The Baby Boom generation, by contrast, came of age during the Civil Rights movement of the 1960s and the Vietnam War. They understood that E. E. Schattschneider was right when he stated that "the flaw in the pluralist heaven is that the heavenly chorus sings with a strong upper-class accent,"[52] and a white male one at that time. They knew that "the best and the brightest" had plunged the country into war. Mass demonstrations were helping to bring rights to Blacks and build resistance to the war. All this led the generation of the 1960s to look at mass participation with the warmest of eyes, and their concepts of participatory democracy were quite different from their parents' pluralistic democracy.

But whatever the desirable political arrangements in modern industrial (really postindustrial or postmaterialist) countries, and this was what people really were debating, those born in 1910 inevitably had a much clearer understanding of European countries at an earlier stage of democratization and industrialization than those born in the 1940s. The college textbooks of the older generation described the very difficult process of democratization and very imperfect democracy of Europe and America of the nineteenth century, let alone of the 1930s.[53] The textbooks of the postwar generation, by contrast, glorified the supposedly seamless democratic tradition of the West.

It is the most profound mistake to forget the real experience of democratization in the West. Universal suffrage and meaningful electoral control over the executive is little more than a century old in Europe. Civil society in the sense of small group activism, all the more so that associated with issues such as environmentalism, was not the base of the creation of modern democracy in the nineteenth century. Maurice Duverger emphasized that the bases of mass democracy were provided by large societal institutions—churches, trade unions, business and agrarian interest groups, and urban political machines. They became part of the coalition on which broad-based political parties were formed, and they became the mobilizing and fund-giving institutions that permitted the broad-based parties to function. "There must be a fairly large number of cases of political parties created by groups of intellectuals," Duverger said. "It is, however, very rare for such a party to enlist sufficient popular support for it to be successful in countries with universal suffrage."[54]

Soviet society too had large institutions that represented the interests of different sectors and societal groups, if imperfectly.[55] When these institutions were destroyed in the revolution of 1991, nothing arose to replace them. Western foundations and governments tried to promote democratization through the encouragement of the formation of small groups of intellectuals, not major societal institutions. Russia's Choice and other "reform" parties were discouraged from trying to form broad-based parties in which business groups, agrarian groups, trade unions, and ethnic groups were included in the coalition because all these were "conservative" and might want the kind of government welfare state that Americans take for granted. (It is paradoxical—and a sign of the myopic Western conception of Russian democracy—that this kind of political pressure in the United States is called "liberal," not "conservative.")

As a consequence, the West encouraged the formation of an atomized society, mobilizable by an authoritarian tsar in precisely the ways that Kornhauser and Arendt analyzed. By working to create terror about the Communists in a society with characteristics that Kornhauser and Arendt described, Yeltsin was able to ensure that people would cling either to the one solid societal institution—the Communist party—or to the tsar.

6. The Role of the Media

Many have commented on the importance of central control of television in Russian democracy, particularly in elections in which Boris Yeltsin has been directly involved—the April 1993 referendum and the 1996 presidential election. Three articles in this book deal with the media in the 1993 election. They demonstrate that generalizations about the role of the media are difficult in the best of circumstances, and they are peculiarly difficult in Russian elections in which Yeltsin is not a participant.

For example, Colton found that the best educated and best informed were, not surprisingly, those who paid the most attention to the media, both print and television. They tended to be the strongest supporters of Russia's Choice. But does this show that the media had an impact on them or that those with a natural propensity to vote for Russia's Choice were the better educated who gave special attention to the media because they found any pro-Russia's Choice bias congenial? It is not easy to sort out cause and effect.

To what extent were the media biased in any case? This question is not a simple one either. Laura Helvey in chapter 7 reported studies showing that Russia's Choice received nine hours of coverage on Ostankino and Russian television. Ellen Mickiewicz and Andrei Richter reported that the total Channel 1 coverage during the campaign gave Russia's Choice ninety-one minutes, the Communists four minutes, and the Liberal Democrats two minutes; whereas Channel 2's coverage of the three parties was forty-three minutes, six minutes, and four minutes, respectively.[56] Obviously even the counting of coverage is not simple, and the nature of content is even more difficult to judge.

The degree of the bias for Russia's Choice in the media coverage is not, however, the crucial question about the impact of the media. Whatever else the election showed, it demonstrated that the media did not produce an outpouring of mass support for Russia's Choice.

Helvey points us in the right direction when she begins her chapter with a discussion of agenda setting. In the West, the institutional framework is stable, and agenda setting refers to policy questions. In the Russian context, the crucial question is what is kept off the agenda or out of the news. That the higher mortality rates since 1990 have resulted in some two million excess deaths is discussed in some of the opposition press, but is given little attention on television.[57] The success of the Chinese economic reform is, to say the least, not a subject of frequent news coverage.

In the 1993 Duma election and the 1996 presidential election, the crucial question was whether centrist candidates and parties could gain name recognition. There is no question about the one-sided coverage in the 1993 April referendum or the strong pro-Yeltsin tilt in the 1996 presidential election.[58] In the latter, the issue was not simply the coverage of Yeltsin and Zyuganov but the virtual news blackout of the credible centrist candidates until it became certain that Yeltsin would be one of the candidates in the runoff—and then only some favorable coverage of General Lebed to draw anti-Yeltsin voters away from Zyuganov.

The key issue in the 1993 election as well was the failure of really centrist political parties to form and gain public support. A population that had come to think in very centrist terms on a wide range of policy issues had not learned to think of parties and politicians in the same way. As Steven Crowley put it, the public still looked at politics in a Manichean manner. Coal miners tend to be a special breed, but Yitzhak Brudny found much the same thing at the base of the lack of "pocketbook voting" in St. Petersburg, as did Kullberg in Moscow.

It is from this perspective that we must explore the role of television and the non-Communist national media. They made no effort to analyze Western parties as coalitional, moderate entities to be emulated, and they did nothing to build up centrist candidates. (The contrast with the American media's treatment of presidential candidates is striking in this respect.) Instead they supported Yeltsin's definition of the political space as involving a struggle between reform and conservatism. They played a key role in labeling centrists as conservatives and defining the moderate Congress and its leaders as hard-line and undemocratic.

The same issue is at the center of the debate about Zhirinovskii's voters. If the election was essentially structured in a free manner, then Zhirinovskii's vote was a frightening indication of a strong fascist danger in Russia and the possibility of a Zhirinovskii victory in a presidential election in the future. Some in the West expressed precisely such alarm at the time.[59] Many sociologists whose polls missed the rise of Zhirinovskii claimed afterward that he had gained his vote in the last few days of the campaign. Yet 11 percent of the decided voters in our national sample who were interviewed in November expressed a preference for Zhirinovskii at that time, 18 percent of those interviewed from December 1 to December 4, and 19.5 percent of those interviewed from December 5 to December 9.[60] If the Zhirinovskii vote was not a last-minute whim, the situation seemed particularly worrisome.

But the situation was very different if the Zhirinovskii vote were simply a response to an artificial political space largely created by the media. With the leading "centrist" parties really being radical in their economic program, with a real centrist party not having formed, with Zyuganov largely unknown and having little real opportunity to persuade voters that he would not return the country to the Brezhnev past, Zhirinovskii, as Davidheiser argues, became the only credible non-Communist opposition, especially for the ill-informed for whom Zhirinovskii was defined by television ads as the real alternative to Gaidar. From this perspective, Zhirinovskii was not simply a random protest vote, but the natural one in the situation as it had been structured. In retrospect, it is clear that Davidheiser's interpretation was correct, and it is supported in the data analysis of the Zhirinovskii voter by the two editors.[61]

7. The Interests of the King

Like the ghost in *Macbeth,* Yeltsin's presence hangs over this chapter, this book, and the election itself, not really present but always present. It was he and his men who created the election, who shaped its rules, who controlled campaign finances and the television media, who sanctioned the formation of a series of parties from the right-wing PRES to the centrist Women of Russia to the left-wing Agrarians that were really government parties. It was Yeltsin's definition of the issues—reform versus communism—that defined the character of the campaign and reinforced Manicheanism in the electorate.

Clearly the strongly centralized Communist party that merged with the Soviet state had left a strong feeling against political parties in Russia. But when ideology runs strongly in conflict with politicians' self-interest, it tends to be modified. Jefferson and Madison learned to overcome their aversion to parties when it became important to them to organize a legislative party in 1793. Washington retained his deep aversion to party activity in substantial part because it corresponded to his interests as president at the time.

So it was with Yeltsin. The election of the Russian Congress of People's Deputies in 1990, unlike that of the USSR Congress of People's Deputies in 1989, had been quite democratic,[62] and the Congress itself had a potential two-party system in Democratic Russia and Communists of Russia. The Russian political system was structured along the lines of the French, and it was based on the assumption that the president, premier, and the legislature would have the kind of cohabiting relationship that François Mitterrand had with the National Assembly. Once the Communist system was overthrown and the economic program introduced by Gaidar in November 1991 failed to produce the promised results, the country and a majority of Congress deputies turned against the Gaidar team in the government, although not the president. The logic of the system dictated that the parties realign more along economic lines and that the president cohabit with the majority as Mitterrand had done in France.

But Yeltsin also understood the relationship of his power to a strong party system. After his election as president, Yeltsin strove mightily and successfully to break down the emerging party system and to maintain the Manichean imagery of the election of 1990. But the two "party" system that Yeltsin emphasized was based on a single criterion for distinguishing between deputies: were they for or against the augmentation of presidential power? Those who were in favor of dictatorial rule by the president were called democrats or reformers and those who were opposed were called Communists. Yeltsin probably supported the radical reform path because its proponents knew they could not obtain majority support and needed an authoritarian president and must support him.

Pro-Yeltsin analysts shifted their putative "party identification" of the deputies as deputies changed their attitude toward Yeltsin and the constitutional change he was promoting.[63] When the majority of the Congress swung into opposition to the president, Yeltsin's people even denied the democratic character of the 1990 election, despite the evidence to the contrary and despite the fact that the Congress had originally elected Yeltsin chair and even gave him the two-thirds vote necessary to create an elected presidency. When Yeltsin dissolved the Congress of People's Deputies in September 1993 and called a snap election that gave parties only a month to form and collect signatures on petitions and less than a month to campaign, he obviously intended to ensure that the logic of the electoral law not have a real chance to work.

The electoral chaos described in this book, much of it created deliberately by the "king" trying to maximize his power, may be quite typical of the early stages of democratization. An excellent analogy to the role of Yeltsin in Russia is found in the role of the king in eighteenth-century Britain. Lewis Namier, as we saw, insisted that the political parties of that time were not like modern parties. Parliament in mid-century was dominated by "the Government party," which "owed its large majority in the House of Commons to the patronage of the Crown." Through the use of appointments, grants, and rewards, the king ensured the loyalty of enough members of parliament to maintain his effective control, and he was greatly aided by the distortions in the electoral system embodied in the phrase "rotten boroughs." Indeed, even the opposition was essentially compelled to rally around the heir-apparent who became their patron.[64]

An earlier student of British politics, Moishe Ostrogorski, described the corruption involved in the crassest of terms:[65]

> In the beginning . . . the post [of patronage secretary] was created for the corruption of members in the criminal sense of the word. Ministers bought their majority by payment of actual cash; they had a window in the House itself where members came to be paid for their votes after the division. The First Lord of the Treasury, having too much to do, created, in 1714, the office of political secretary to the Treasury to aid him in these financial operations.

Ostrogorski saw parties themselves as part of the problem, but Namier took the opposite perspective: "It is not Parliament as such, but the system of firmly organized parties under single leadership, which precludes an active, personal participation of the King in Government."[66] The expansion of the suffrage in 1832 and the organization of mass parties, not by coincidence, was associated with the end of the real power of the monarchy.

American Responses

This book has focused on the 1993 election and the events leading up to it inside Russia. Russia, however, does not exist in a vacuum. In the wake of the cold war, many have concluded that the United States can afford to concentrate on such tasks as support of democracy, economic reform, and nation building. Russia has been a centerpiece of this effort in the 1990s.

The Russian political system was modeled in substantial part on the French, with a premier responsible to both the president and the legislature. When Viktor Chernomyrdin was named premier in December 1992, he announced an industrial policy that the majority of the legislature approved. However, Boris Yeltsin appointed Boris Fedorov as the new deputy premier for economics and finance. Fedorov was a monetarist economist who had been Russian representative at the World Bank in Washington and who strongly supported the policy advocated by Yegor Gaidar and the International Monetary Fund. The United States and the IMF strongly supported

Fedorov and his policy. By insisting on a shock therapy that was supported by only a small minority of the Russian population, the administration guaranteed a conflict between Yeltsin and legislators who were responsive to public opinion.

Yeltsin had a choice: either to have a confrontation with the Congress or to "cohabit" with the Congress and basically accept its economic policy, as French presidents generally have done. Yeltsin wanted to dissolve the Congress or otherwise render it impotent, and he sought the support of the United States for this action. On March 12 the Clinton administration asserted that the West would not object "if Yeltsin suspends an antidemocratic parliament," and the *New York Times* emphasized the importance of the statement by calling it a "strong signal." The next day President Clinton called Yeltsin an "honest democrat, small 'd,' [who is] passionately committed to reform."[67]

When Yeltsin's effort to take powers from the Congress failed in March, the two sides agreed on a referendum on April 25 in which the key question was whether the voter supported Yeltsin's economic and social policy. Yeltsin became extremely populist in his promises and spoke of a change in policy. He appointed Oleg Lobov, who had been a leading opponent of Gaidar's policy in September 1991, as minister of the economy and first deputy premier.

During the summer of 1993 Lobov and Fedorov engaged in a fierce struggle over the fundamental direction of economic policy, and Chernomyrdin came to support Fedorov. On August 29, Lobov presented a memorandum to Yeltsin on his plan, and the next day Yeltsin wrote on the memorandum. "In principle I support the proposals. Please submit a draft edict within ten days."[68] A working group was set up to work out the final version, and the business newspaper *Kommersant* reported that Fedorov was supported in the cabinet only by the IMF and the remnants of the Gaidar team.[69]

Yet, precisely at this time, "sources close to the president" were leaking the information to *Izvestiya* that Yeltsin was inclined to take radical steps against the Congress. Larry Summers, Undersecretary of the Treasury, flew to Moscow for meetings on September 14 and 15. Both the IMF and the World Bank were delaying loans (of $1.5 billion and $600 million, respectively), the *New York Times* reported, "as a carrot to push Moscow to get its economic house in order."[70] On September 16, Lobov was replaced as first deputy premier by Yegor Gaidar, and the Lobov plan disappeared.[71] Its author became executive secretary of the Security Council—a very low-profile post until a crisis erupted over Chechnya a year later. On the eve of the Summers visit, President Clinton, when asked whether the United States should be talking with Vice President Rutskoi as well as Yeltsin, answered, "I don't think we should be hedging our bets." As *New York Times* columnist William Safire put it, "The Russian leader—assured that no Clinton bet on him would be hedged—made his move."[72]

Obviously one's evaluation about American support for Yeltsin and for Fedorov's economic program depends on a series of judgments. These include the optimal path of economic reform, the likelihood that radical economic reform will produce an explosive political reaction, and the desirable or necessary relation of marketization and democracy in early and middle stages of capitalist development. Whole books can be written on each of these issues, and this is not the place for a discussion of them.

There is, however, one aspect of the problem on which this book does shed light and that does deserve mention—the campaign strategy of Russia's Choice and the character of American support for that party. Gaidar's election program included an immediate fourfold increase in bread prices, a promise of a tenfold increase in rents, and a sharp reduction in subsidies to industry. When Gaidar came to power in September, the government attempted to limit money supply and bring inflation under control by delaying payment to many workers and even soldiers of the salaries they had earned and to peasants for crops they had delivered.

It is not surprising that President Yeltsin refused to identify with such a program, for it went contrary to every principle on which he campaigned in the 1991 and 1996 presidential elections and the 1993 referendum. He probably thought that it was the price that had to be paid for American support and that the composition of the Duma would not matter greatly so long as his constitution was ratified and the Duma had little power.

What is surprising is that Americans would support such a program. Very few practical American politicians would dream of any analogous steps on the eve of an American campaign, and President Clinton has been one of the most successful in seeking to ascertain public opinion, to move to the center of the political spectrum, and to build a broad coalition. It is very difficult to believe that those like the president who understood American democratic politics, those who understood Russian politics, and those who understood economic transitions were brought together in an effective way in designing a program for supporting Russian democracy in the wake of the dissolution of the Congress. One fears that the fundamental question of whether American security interests are best served by the model of economic reform the United States has strongly supported has been decided in similar manner.

A series of the details described in the various chapters of this book about the technical assistance given to Russia's Choice create the same impression. These include the slick Russia's Choice television advertisements that assumed a prosperous middle class, "the endless supply of campaign paraphernalia" observed by Moser in the party's Yekaterinburg office, the how-to-win-a-campaign booklet emphasizing the importance of phone banks seen by Stephen Crowley in telephone-scarce Kemerovo, the concentration of attention that Smyth observed among Saratov politicians in acquiring funds Russia's Choice sent into the region rather than on the winning of votes.

The problem goes much further. If American political science has any basic bias that is too universal and too deeply imbedded, it centers on the virtues of a broad-based two-party system. It was assumed that Russia's Choice could obtain 35 to 40 percent of the vote and acquire a majority together with satellite reform parties. It was to be in American terms a "Republican" party or in British terms a Conservative party. Yet everyone knows that big business is a crucial component of such parties and that big business wants protectionism in the stage before it is competitive on the world market. Everyone knows that such parties must adopt some kind of social issues (at least mild nationalism and traditional values such as a pro-life policy today) and that the small town and countryside are a natural part of their base. Russia's Choice, however, denounced big business as the nomenklatura, rejected any nationalism or traditional values, and (unlike China) followed an economic reform that exploited the small town and countryside. Americans praised this policy—pushed for such a policy— and then seemed surprised that it garnered only 15 percent of the vote.

Similarly, the American tradition has emphasized checks-and-balances between the executive and the legislature, fear of the tyranny of the majority, the importance of federalism and local elections, the primacy of pragmatism over dogmatism, and the movement of political leaders toward the center. The economy for over a half century has featured strong governmental regulation and a welfare state and once was correctly called "a mixed economy." The Keynesian prescription for depression and recession is taken for granted across the political spectrum.[73] Except in President George Bush's superb speech in Kiev in August 1991, however, no one spoke for the fundamentals of the American political tradition.[74]

The problems with the American involvement in Russian democratization were, no doubt, exacerbated by the total lack of political experience of

Russian democrats. Five years previously, the great majority in 1993 had been college professors and institute scholars in a dictatorship with an unusually closed political system. In other countries the politicians with whom we are dealing much more experienced and self-confident in dismissing advice that they consider naive in local conditions.

The odds are reasonably good that political developments in Russia will not lead to a national security disaster for the United States. The Russian elite has such a keen memory of repression that there are probably limits on the degree of centralization it will accept. The Russians are so eager to rejoin the West, for both cultural and defense reasons, that they will probably forgive many Western mistakes. Control over nuclear weapons will probably be maintained. Someone like Aleksandr Lebed or Yurii Luzhkov will probably establish a regime like that of South Korea or Thailand instead of like that of Napoleon Bonaparte, or the Communists may become like the Polish and Hungarian Communists and win as a moderate social democratic party. However, the outcome is still totally unclear. As the game of Russian roulette reminds us, we should weigh the high odds of winning, but also the character of the consequences if we lose.

But in any case the issues go far beyond Russia. Whatever happens in Russia, the twenty-first century will be the century when Asia and Africa pass through the stages of development seen in Europe between 1850 and 1950. It is fully possible they will fall into many of the same mistakes, and the West needs to be politically sophisticated in the advice and support it gives. Even in 1998, economic demands are being made on Indonesia with little indication that possible long-term political consequences at a time of political transition are being fully weighed.

The first lesson that the West needs to relearn is the complexity of the democratization process in the West. The cold war ideological struggle with the Soviet Union led the West to prettify its own history. Americans need to reflect not only on European but also on American history, not only on the fifty years between the evolution of mass parties but also on the fact that full democratization for white males was quickly followed by the massive nativist know-nothing movement and Civil War. The democratization process in Europe was even more protracted and fraught with danger for the international community.

The experience of England of George II and III, the America of Thomas Jefferson and Boss Tweed, the Germany of Otto von Bismarck and Adolf Hitler, let alone the France of Napoleon Bonaparte and Napoleon III or the Russia of Pyotr Stolypin and Vladimir Ilyich Lenin reminds us not only of the problematic character of the process of democratization, but of the variety of the imperfections. We must understand that the choice is not simply between military or totalitarian dictatorship and the ideals of advanced Western democracy, but that there are many intermediate choices.

If the West is really serious about promoting democratization around the world, it must develop theories of democratization that include all stages of the democratization process. Our advice cannot be limited to that which is appropriate only for an advanced democratic system with well-established parties. We must distinguish between less benign and more benign imperfections. Tocqueville was right to fear that democracy was destabilizing America in the 1830s, and the city bosses of the post–Civil War period made a positive contribution to American political and economic development. Some authoritarian regimes in Latin America featured death squads, while authoritarianism in Taiwan, Singapore, or Mexico seems like that of Western Europe in the nineteenth century, with positive as well as negative sides. Economists have developed prescriptive models that, accurate or not, have an impact, and political scientists must become more serious in their theoretical analysis of the process of democratization as well.

Notes

1. Alfred Stepan, "Paths toward Redemocratization: Theoretical and Comparative Considerations," in Guillermo O'Donnell, Philippe C. Schmitter, and Laurence Whitehead, eds., *Transitions from Authoritarian Rule: Comparative Perspectives* (Johns Hopkins University Press, 1986), pp. 64–84.

2. Although the Catholic Church often was antidemocratic in Latin America and southern Europe, it was a strong supporter of democracy and tolerance in the United States. Indeed, in the late 1890s the American church so angered the Vatican on these matters that the Pope officially condemned "Americanism." Thomas T. McAvoy, *The Americanist Heresy in Roman Catholicism, 1895–1900* (University of Notre Dame Press, 1963).

3. To be sure, when the chair of the Duma elected in 1993 titled his book on the Russian legislature, *The State Duma: The Fifth Attempt*, he reminded us that Russia actually had competitive elections between 1907 and 1917. However, these elections were so long ago that they had little impact on the 1980s and 1990s. I. P. Rybkin, *Gosudarstvennaya Duma: piataya popytka: Ocherk noverishei istorii predstavel'noi vlasti v Rossii* (Moscow: Mezhdunarodny Gumanitarnyi Fond Znanie, 1994).

4. Guillermo O'Donnell, "Transitions, Continuities, and Paradoxes," in Scott Mainwaring, Guillermo O'Donnell, and J. Samuel Valenzuela, eds., *Issues in*

Democratic Consolidation: The New South American Democracies in Comparative Perspective (University of Notre Dame Press, 1992), pp. 17–19.

5. Giuseppe Di Palma, *To Craft Democracies: An Essay on Democratic Transitions* (University of California Press, 1990).

6. Bernard Bailyn, *The Origins of American Politics* (Alfred A. Knopf, 1968), pp. 15, 33–34; J. R. Jones, *The First Whigs: The Politics of the Exclusion Crisis, 1678–1683* (London, 1961), pp. 20–22, 34, and 38.

7. The best description of the relation of religion and mass conspiracy thinking in the colonies is found in Carl Bridenbaugh, *Mitre and Spectre: Transatlantic Faiths, Ideas, Personalities, and Politics, 1689–1775* (New York: Oxford University Press, 1962), pp. 55–56, 233, and 258.

8. Joseph Charles, *The Origins of the American Party System: Three Essays* (Williamsburg, Va.: The Institute of Early American History, 1956), pp. 123–24.

9. Charles Seymour and Donald Paige Frary, *How the World Votes: The Story of Democratic Development in Elections*, vol. 1 (Springfield, Mass.: C. A. Nichols Company, 1918), pp. 115–16. This is a two-volume study of how electoral systems had evolved throughout the world in the decades and even centuries before 1918, and it provides a good deal of information on party evolution as well. It is an indispensable source for anyone studying the subject.

10. Dankwart A. Rustow, "Transitions to Democracy: Toward a Dynamic Model," *Comparative Politics*, vol. 2, no. 3 (April 1970), p. 351; Ivor Jennings, *The Approach to Self-Government* (Cambridge University Press, 1956), p. 56.

11. Arend Lijphart, *Democracy in Plural Societies: A Comparative Exploration* (Yale University Press, 1977).

12. One of the two major parties that arose in 1840s in Colombia always won a majority until 1990. Ronald P. Archer, "Party Strength and Weakness in Colombia's Besieged Democracy," in Scott Mainwaring and Timothy R. Scully, eds., *Building Democratic Institutions: Party Systems in Latin America* (Stanford University Press, 1995), p. 164.

13. Scott Mainwaring, "Brazil: Weak Parties, Feckless Democracy," in Mainwaring and Scully, *Building Democratic Institutions*, p. 355.

14. Joseph LaPalombara and Myron Weiner, eds., "The Origin and Development of Political Parties," in Joseph LaPalombara and Myron Weiner, *Political Parties and Political Development* (Princeton University Press, 1966), p. 6

15. Yegor Gaidar, *Dni porazhenii i pobed* (Moscow: Vagrius, 1996), pp. 284, 305, and 308.

16. After the 1995 election, a writer in the newspaper of the Agrarian party referred to the "Zhirinovtsii" instead of the Liberal Democrats, and he explained the defeat of the Agrarian party by its need for "Personalities." *Sel'skaya zhizn'*, January 16, 1996, p. 2.

17. "Kandidaty Vybora Rossii," *Argumenty i fakty*, no. 49 (1993), p. 9.

18. The governor of Sakhalin had been a leading radical, hailed by the Moscow reformers, but he had turned against them. They supported a conservative independent who had a -38 score against him.

19. A. Oslon and E. Petrenko, *Parlamentskie vybory 12 dekabrya 1993 goda: sotsiologiya elektoral'nogo povedeniya* (Moscow: Fond "Obshchestvennoye mnenye," 1994), p. 4.

20. A. Sobyanin, E. Gel'man, and O. Kaiunov, "Politicheskii klimat v Rossii v 1991–1993gg," *Mirovaya ekonomika i mezhdunarodnye otnosheniya*, no. 9 (1993), p. 25.

21. Ellen Mickiewicz, *Changing Channels: Television and the Struggle for Power in Russia* (Oxford: Oxford University Press, 1997), p. 162.

22. A good English-language analysis of the vote in the republics is found in Robert Moser, "The Impact of the Electoral System on Post-Communist Party Development: The Case of the 1993 Russian Parliamentary Elections," *Electoral Studies*, no. 4 (1995). For republic-by-republic descriptions of the 1993 election, as well as a long analysis of the republican data collected in this study, see Mikhail Guboglo, *Razvivaiushchiisiya elektorat Rossii. Etnopoliticheskii rakurs* (Moscow: Institute etnologii i antropologii RAN, 1996), 3 vols.

23. For Gaidar's justified contempt for the 500-Day-Plan, see his *Dni porazhenii i pobed*, pp. 64–68. The difference between Yavlinskii and Gaidar (and his team) is that Yavlinskii in 1990 and 1991 quite reasonably combined his extreme monetarism with support for the then existing integrated economy covering all republics and therefore supported Gorbachev and his Union Treaty. Gaidar and his team supported Yeltsin and his desire for an independent Russia. Yeltsin never forgave Yavlinskii for his support of Gorbachev, and Yavlinskii never forgave Gaidar and his friends for the success and often riches that came with betting on a winner.

24. Sarah Oates, "Russian Party Platforms: Charting Issues in the 1993 and 1995 Duma Campaigns" (paper presented to the conference on "Party Politics in Post-Communist Russia" at the University of Glascow, May 23–25, 1997), p. 20.

25. An early article that explored opinion on issues from the unweighted 35,000 oblast data was Jerry F. Hough, "The Russian Election of 1993: Public Attitudes toward Economic Reform and Democratization," *Post-Soviet Affairs,* vol. 10, no. 1, (January–March 1994), pp. 1–37. Data from the 1993 national sample and a later 1995 election study were reported in Jerry F. Hough, Evelyn Davidheiser, and Susan Goodrich Lehmann, *The 1996 Russian Presidential Election* (Washington, D.C.: Brookings, 1996).

26. The 1995 and 1996 preelection surveys cited were all national samples conducted by the same team in Russia as the 1993 study, and they all included 3,800 respondents from essentially the same 100 raions in 69 regions of Russia as the 1993 study. The 1995 study was sponsored by the Brookings Institution, with the principal investigators being Evelyn Davidheiser, Susan Goodrich Lehmann, and Jerry Hough, and funding provided by the National Science Foundation. The 1996 data are from a June preelection study, with the same principal investigators, but with funding from the MacArthur Foundation. (The postelection study, not cited, was financed by the National Science Foundation.) Answers on a range of other questions are reported in Jerry F. Hough and Susan Goodrich Lehmann, "The Mystery of Opponents of Economic Reform among the Yeltsin Voters," in Stephen White, Mathew Wyman, and Sarah Oates, eds., *Elections and Voters in Postcommunist Russia* (London: Edward Elgar, 1998), pp. 184–221.

27. The 1997 data are from a Brookings-sponsored study of youth values in March 1997. The principal investigators were Susan Goodrich Lehmann and Jerry Hough, and the funding came from the MacArthur Foundation and the National Council for Soviet and East European Research. The 1993, 1995, 1996 data on twenty-four- to thirty-two-year-olds come from the 650-odd respondents in the respective national sample, and the 1997 data are from the 2,769 respondents in the national sample who were twenty-four to thirty-two years old and the 1,068 who were seventeen.

28. The percentage who completely or on the whole supported such privatization fell from 37.9 percent in 1993 to 20.2 percent in 1995 and 22.6 percent in 1996, with an additional fifth of the respondents undecided. Such support among twenty-four- to thirty-year-olds fell from 51.2 percent in 1993 to 32.0 percent in 1996.

29. Although Shakhrai spoke about power to the regions, he advocated independent taxing powers at all levels, including the cities, and hence he was especially popular with Russians in republican cities who wanted independence from republican officials, who rested more on the rural non-Russians of the republics. Rakhimov also, no doubt, was looking for a candidate to distract votes away from Gaidar's Russia's Choice.

30. Robert K. Merton, *Social Theory and Social Structure,* rev. ed. (Glencoe, Ill.: Free Press, 1957), pp. 70–81. For a series of excerpts arguing the pros and cons of the question, see Bruce M. Stave and Sondra Astor Stave, eds., *Urban Bosses, Machines, and Progressive Reformers,* 2d ed. (Malabar, Fla.: Robert E. Krieger, 1984), pp. 3–142.

31. In 1990, Rybkin became second secretary of the Volgograd regional committee (obkom), but that was after the obkom lost all power.

32. James S. Coleman and Carl G. Rosberg Jr., *Political Parties and National Integration in Tropical Africa* (University of California Press, 1964), p. v. David E. Apter and Carl G. Rosberg, *Political Development and the New Realism in Sub-Saharan Africa* (University Press of Virginia, 1994) has two references to political parties and party systems in its index. See p. 337. Robert H. Jackson and Carl G. Rosberg, *Personal Rule in Black Africa: Prince, Autocrat, Prophet, Tyrant* (University of California Press, 1982), pp. ix–x and 1.

33. Ibid.

34. Giovanni Sartori, *Parties and Party Systems: A Framework for Analysis,* vol. 1 (Cambridge: Cambridge University Press, 1976), p. 324.

35. Schumpeter explicitly criticized definitions with a policy component, but defined a party simply as "a group whose members propose to act in concert in the competitive struggle for political power." Joseph A. Schumpeter, *Capitalism, Socialism, and Democracy* (New York: Harper and Brothers, 1942), p. 283.

36. Richard Hofstadter, *The Idea of a Party System: The Rise of Legitimate Opposition in the United States, 1780–1840* (University of California Press, 1970), p. 9. The first two chapters deal with this theme.

37. Alexis de Tocqueville, *Democracy in America*, translated by George Lawrence (Harper and Row, 1966), p. 174.

38. Gordon S. Wood, *The Creation of the American Republic, 1776–1787* (University of North Carolina Press, 1969), pp. 134–35.

39. Sartori, *Parties and Party Systems*, p. 82.

40. Martin Van Buren with the Free Soil party in 1848 and Millard Fillmore with the American party in 1856.

41. *Obrazovanie naseleniya Rossii (po dannym mikroperepisi naseleniya 1994 g.)* (Moscow: Goskomstat Rossii, 1995), p. 7.

42. Schumpeter, *Capitalism, Socialism, and Democracy*, pp. 290–95.

43. As Davidheiser noted in chapter 6, only two of the eighteen members of the 1990 Politburo of the Russian Communist party were included on the party list of the Communist party in the 1993 election, and one was Zyuganov himself.

44. Remington and Smith, "The Early Legislative Process in the Russian Federal Assembly."

45. *Nezavisimaya gazeta*, July 2, 1991, p. 1.

46. Radio Rossii, December 1, 1991, in Foreign Broadcast Information Service, *Daily Report: Soviet Union*, December 2, 1991, p. 4.

47. Karl Marx and Frederick Engels, ed. and with introduction by C. J. Arthur, *The German Ideology, Part One* (New York: International Publishers, 1970), p. 57, and C. J. Arthur's introduction on pp. 5–6.

48. Patrick Chabal, *Power in Africa: An Essay in Political Interpretation* (New York: St. Martin's Press, 1991), p. 83. Chabal says he follows J. Bayart in his approach to the subject.

49. Max Weber, *The Theory of Social and Economic Organization*, translated by A. M. Henderson and Talcott Parsons; edited with an introduction by Talcott Parsons (New York: Oxford University Press, 1947), p. 71.

50. Hannah Arendt, *The Origins of Totalitarianism* (Harcourt, Brace, 1951), p. 310 and 316. See also William Kornhauser, *The Politics of Mass Society* (Glencoe, Ill.: Free Press, 1959), pp. 212–22.

51. V. O. Key Jr., *Public Opinion and American Democracy* (Alfred A. Knopf, 1961), p. 530.

52. E. E. Schattschneider, *The Semisovereign People: A Realist's View of Democracy in America* (Holt, Rinehart, and Winston, 1960), pp. 34–35.

53. One of the major intellectual figures of the 1920s and 1930s, Harold Laski, remarked in 1933 that "the thesis is universally admitted that the legislatures of the modern state are in an unsatisfactory condition." Harold J. Laski, *Democracy in Crisis* (University of North Carolina Press, 1933), p. 77.

54. Maurice Duverger, *Political Parties: Their Organization and Activity in the Modern State*, 3d ed., translated by Barbara and Robert North, with a foreword by D. W. Brogan (London: Methuen, 1969), p. xxxi.

55. See the discussion of "institutional pluralism" in Jerry F. Hough, *The Soviet Union and Social Science Theory* (Harvard University Press, 1977), pp. 10–12, 22–25, and 43–46, and Jerry F. Hough, "Pluralism, Corporatism, and the Soviet Union," in Susan Gross Solomon, ed., *Pluralism in the Soviet Union: Essays in Honour of H. Gordon Skilling* (New York: St. Martin's Press, 1982), pp. 52–53.

56. Ellen Mickiewicz and Andrei Richter, "Television, Campaigning, and Elections in the Soviet Union and Post-Soviet Russia," in David L. Swanson and Paolo Mancini, eds., *Politics, Media, and Modern Democracy* (Westport, Conn.: Praeger, 1996), p. 120.

57. Hough, Davidheiser, and Lehmann, *The 1996 Russian Presidential Election*, pp. 93–94.

58. See Mickiewicz, *Changing Channels*, pp. 135–46 and 167–89.

59. See Michael McFaul, *Understanding Russia's 1993 Parliamentary Election: Implications for U.S. Foreign Policy* (Stanford, Calif.: The Hoover Institution, 1994), pp. 1–2 and 27–28.

60. In the thirty-five regional polls of 1,000 respondents each, 14 percent of those interviewed in November who expressed a preference named Zhirinovskii.

61. In addition to Colton's chapter, see Hough, "The Russian Election of 1993."

62. This is documented in detail in Jerry F. Hough, *Democratization and Revolution in the USSR, 1985–1991* (Brookings, 1997), chap. 9.

63. The well-known roll-call indexes created by Aleksandr Sobyanin, a scholar working with the Yeltsin forces, defined "reform" and "conservative" solely in terms of support for Yeltsin, and they show the changing support for the president in the Congress. See, for example, Alexander Sobyanin, "Political Cleavages among the Russian Deputies," in Thomas F. Remington, ed., *Parliaments in Transition: The New Legislative Politics in the Former USSR and Eastern Europe* (Boulder, Colo.: Westview Press, 1994), pp. 181–216.

64. Lewis B. Namier, *England in the Age of the American Revolution* (London: Macmillan, 1930), pp. 61–65.

65. Ostrogorski, *Democracy and the Organization of Political Parties,* vol. 1, p. 71.

66. Namier, *England in the Age of the American Revolution*, p. 54.

67. John Lloyd, "Yeltsin's Rivals Set to Derail Reforms," *Financial Times*, March 10, 1993, London edition, p. 22; Elaine Sciolino, "U.S. Backs Yeltsin but Fears he Might Oust Legislature," *New York Times*, March 12, 1993, p. A6; Elaine Scicolino, "U.S. to Back Yeltsin if He Suspends Congress," *New York Times*, March 13, 1993, p. A4; Richard L. Berke, "Clinton Defends Backing Yeltsin as Elected Chief," *New York Times*, March 14, 1993, p. A1.

68. *Rossiiskaya gazeta*, September 18, 1993, p. 1.

69. "Yeltsin Sets Up Constitutional Working Group," ITAR-TASS, September 9, 1993, in FBIS-*Central Eurasia*, Daily Report-93-174, September 10, 1993, p. 20; *Kommersant-Daily*, September 10, 1993, p. 2.

70. Steven Greenhouse, "I.M.F. Delays $1.5 billion Loan to Russia Because Reform Is Stalled," *New York Times*, September 20, 1993, p. A3.

71. Gaidar had been offered the job before the sixteenth, but his memoirs are not clear on the day. He accepted on the sixteenth. Gaidar, *Dni porazhenii i pobed*, pp. 272–74.

72. William Safire, "Yeltsin Planned His Coup," *New York Times*, September 23, 1993, p. A27.

73. Many speak of a rejection of Keynes, but, in fact, the struggle for a balanced budget at a time of economic prosperity is a demand for a return to Keynesianism. Indeed, Keynes advocated a surplus during prosperity.

74. Francis X. Cline, "Bush, in Ukraine, Walks Fine Line on Sovereignty," *New York Times*, August 2, 1991, pp. A1, A8. Ukrainian nationalists found the speech too cautious, and, with an election coming, American liberals were glad to denounce it as "the chicken Kiev" speech. Now that the needs of partisanship have passed, the speech needs to be reexamined and its themes reused.

CONTRIBUTORS

Yitzhak M. Brudny, *Hebrew University of Jerusalem*

Katherine G. Burns, *Ph.D. candidate, Massachusetts Institute of Technology*

Timothy J. Colton, *Harvard University*

Stephen Crowley, *Oberlin College*

Evelyn Davidheiser, *University of Minnesota*

Nigel Gould-Davies, *Hertford College, Oxford University*

Henry E. Hale, *Harvard University*

Laura Roselle Helvey, *Elon College*

Jerry F. Hough, *Duke University*

Judith Kullberg, *University of Michigan*

Pauline Jones Luong, *Yale University*

Michael McFaul, *Stanford University*

Neil J. Melvin, *University of Leeds*

Robert G. Moser, *University of Texas at Austin*

Joel M. Ostrow, *Loyola University*

Regina Smyth, *Pennsylvania State University*

Daniel Treisman, *University of California at Los Angeles*

INDEX

Abdullin, Azat, 616–17

Academy of Sciences Voters' Club, 326

Adams, John Quincy, 41

Advertising, campaign: cost of, 219, 246, 447; expenditure levels, 223, 225; and media partisanship, 322; regulations, 15, 218–19, 245–46. *See also* Free time rules; Television campaigning; *individual candidates and parties*

African political parties, 687

"Against all" option: as campaign strategy, 445–46; electoral rule, 10; Moscow districts, 336; national, 63–66, 124; Nizhnii Novgorod, 449–50; Primorskii krai, 578, 581, 587, 588; Saratov oblast, 485; St. Petersburg district elections, 62, 377, 380; Sverdlovsk oblast, 399, 424

Age/vote correlations, 84, 87, 90–91, 97, 368, 370

Agrarian party: advertising strategies, 199–200, 225; campaign financing, 199; campaign strategies, 81, 169, 187–88, 191, 196, 203, 206; candidate endorsements, 56; candidate profiles, 55, 191, 192–95;

coalition building skills, 205; constitutional referendum, 303–04, 305–06; election results, 177; financing, 198, 200; formation of, 185; government members, 183, 185–86, 194, 197, 679; Kursk campaign, 505–06, 508–09, 510–11, 517, 518, 520; Kuzbass campaign, 540; leadership, 106, 107; media coverage, 252; Moscow campaign, 311; *1995* Duma election, 57; organizational structure, 106, 161, 178, 195; policy programs, 182, 186–87, 190–91; public awareness, 48, 196; Saratov campaign, 465, 472; signature campaign, 17, 161; St. Petersburg campaign, 358, 363, 366, 371; Sverdlovsk campaign, 398, 403, 405, 406–07, 412, 414, 415, 418–19, 420; voter support patterns, 29, 87, 90–91, 97, 102, 203–04, 420. *See also* Agrarian party in Bashkortostan

Agrarian party in Bashkortostan: campaign organization, 626–27, 632; election results, 29, 601, 628, 629; Federation Council election, 609; party-list election, 610–11,

715

ذ